AF775731

Environmental Issues and Sustainable Development

Edited by Suriyanarayanan Sarvajayakesavalu and Pisit Chareonsudjai

Published in London, United Kingdom

IntechOpen

Supporting open minds since 2005

Environmental Issues and Sustainable Development
http://dx.doi.org/10.5772/intechopen.87467
Edited by Suriyanarayanan Sarvajayakesavalu and Pisit Chareonsudjai

Contributors
Monika Sogani, Zainab Syed, Kumar Sonu, Aman Dongre, Gopesh Sharma, Concepción Paz, Eduardo Suárez, Jesús Vence, Adrián Cabarcos, Teki Surayya, Kizito Kwena, George Njomo Karuku, Fredrick Ayuke, Anthony Esilaba, Kazutoshi Fujihira, Rikiatu Husseini, Stephen B. Kendie, Patrick Agbesinyale, Ruby E. Jalgaonwala, Msafiri Yusuph Mkonda, Tao Ma, Nairong Tan, Xiaolei Wang, Fanfan Zhang, Hui Fang, Michael Fratantuono, Sarah House, Sam Weisman, Hassan M. Heshmati, Ardhendu Sekhar Giri, Gary Yohe, Shakeel Mahmood, Carmen Teodosiu, Irina Morosanu, Daniela Fighir, Carmen Paduraru, Lavinia Tofan, Kanagamani Krishnasamy, Geethamani P., Narmatha M., bouzid gassoumi, Fatma Ezzahra Ben Mohamed, Houcine Ghalla, Rafik Ben Chaabane, Yıldırım İsmail Tosun, R. Sasmitha, Muhammed Iqshanullah, R. Arunachalam, Chinta Srinivas, Michael Thomas Aide, Christine Aide, Indi Braden

© The Editor(s) and the Author(s) 2021
The rights of the editor(s) and the author(s) have been asserted in accordance with the Copyright, Designs and Patents Act 1988. All rights to the book as a whole are reserved by INTECHOPEN LIMITED. The book as a whole (compilation) cannot be reproduced, distributed or used for commercial or non-commercial purposes without INTECHOPEN LIMITED's written permission. Enquiries concerning the use of the book should be directed to INTECHOPEN LIMITED rights and permissions department (permissions@intechopen.com).
Violations are liable to prosecution under the governing Copyright Law.

CC BY

Individual chapters of this publication are distributed under the terms of the Creative Commons Attribution 3.0 Unported License which permits commercial use, distribution and reproduction of the individual chapters, provided the original author(s) and source publication are appropriately acknowledged. If so indicated, certain images may not be included under the Creative Commons license. In such cases users will need to obtain permission from the license holder to reproduce the material. More details and guidelines concerning content reuse and adaptation can be found at http://www.intechopen.com/copyright-policy.html.

Notice
Statements and opinions expressed in the chapters are these of the individual contributors and not necessarily those of the editors or publisher. No responsibility is accepted for the accuracy of information contained in the published chapters. The publisher assumes no responsibility for any damage or injury to persons or property arising out of the use of any materials, instructions, methods or ideas contained in the book.

First published in London, United Kingdom, 2021 by IntechOpen
IntechOpen is the global imprint of INTECHOPEN LIMITED, registered in England and Wales, registration number: 11086078, 5 Princes Gate Court, London, SW7 2QJ, United Kingdom
Printed in Croatia

British Library Cataloguing-in-Publication Data
A catalogue record for this book is available from the British Library

Additional hard and PDF copies can be obtained from orders@intechopen.com

Environmental Issues and Sustainable Development
Edited by Suriyanarayanan Sarvajayakesavalu and Pisit Chareonsudjai
p. cm.
Print ISBN 978-1-83880-916-4
Online ISBN 978-1-83880-917-1
eBook (PDF) ISBN 978-1-83880-928-7

For EU product safety concerns:
IN TECH d.o.o., Prolaz Marije Krucifikse Kozulić 3, 51000 Rijeka, Croatia, info@intechopen.com or visit our website at intechopen.com.

We are IntechOpen, the world's leading publisher of Open Access books

Built by scientists, for scientists

5,300+
Open access books available

130,000+
International authors and editors

155M+
Downloads

156
Countries delivered to

Our authors are among the
Top 1%
most cited scientists

12.2%
Contributors from top 500 universities

BOOK CITATION INDEX
CLARIVATE ANALYTICS
INDEXED

WEB OF SCIENCE™

Selection of our books indexed in the Book Citation Index
in Web of Science™ Core Collection (BKCI)

Interested in publishing with us?
Contact book.department@intechopen.com

Numbers displayed above are based on latest data collected.
For more information visit www.intechopen.com

Meet the editors

Prof. Dr. Suriyanarayanan Sarvajayakesavalu, MSc, MPhil, Ph.D., is Deputy Director Research of Vinayaka Mission's Research Foundation (VMRF) - Deemed to be University. Prior to this position, Dr. Suriyanarayanan served as a post-doctoral fellow at the University of Turin, Italy, and a project coordinator, faculty, and head (I/c) at the Department of Water and Health, JSS Academy of Higher Education and Research (formerly Jagadguru Sri Shivarathreeshwara University), Mysuru, India. He also served as a science officer for SCOPE, Beijing, Research Center for Eco-Environmental Sciences (RCEES), Chinese Academy of Sciences, from April 2015 to March 2017. He also serves as a Nodal Officer for SCOPE India activities under the JSS Academy of Higher Education and Research. He has research experience in the areas of environmental monitoring, radiation ecology, and environmental microbiology. He is a recipient of the Young Scientist research grant award from the Science and Research Board (SERB), Department of Science and Technology, Government of India. He also secured the prestigious visiting scientist fellowship from the Chinese Academy of Sciences in 2016–2017.

Pisit Chareonsudjai, MSc, MPhil, Ph.D., currently works at the Department of Environmental Science, Khon Kaen University, Thailand, where he oversees the master's degree program in Intellectual Property and Innovation Management. His administrative experience includes serving as the assistant to the president of research affairs, associate dean for research and academic services, department head, director of graduate programs, initiator of the northeast science park, director of the intellectual property management office, and director of the university royal initiative project office. His areas of expertise are soil microbial ecology, bacterial biofilm, soil heavy metal pollution, and intellectual property and innovation management.

Contents

Preface

This book provides an overview of current environmental issues and sustainable solutions. Nowadays, both developed and developing countries are paying much attention to environmental management practices. This book is a resource for students, researchers, and decision-makers in the field of environmental management. It consists of twenty-three chapters, each focusing on a certain environmental issue. The chapters are developed across five themes: natural resources, waste management, climate change, sustainability, and pollution management.

Section 1 – "Natural Resources"

Chapter 1 presents a case study on developing the capabilities needed to adapt to freshwater shortages and enhance prospects for human security in Panchkahl Municipality, Kathmandu, Nepal. Data from the study suggest the need for further system transformation to promote adaptation.

Chapter 2 addresses microfinance practices and value-added, non-wood forest products for a sustainable environment, using a state in India as an example. This study reveals opportunities for using natural resources sustainably and encourages forest dwellers to become micro-entrepreneurs.

Chapter 3 addresses the consequences of different processes in the grassland ecosystem in the shola forest and grassland mosaic of the Nilgiri Biosphere Reserve (NBR), South India.

Chapter 4 describes the effects of climatic variability on harmful algal blooms, providing systematic knowledge to manage and mitigate their impacts.

Chapter 5 addresses the need to improve models for effective communication and to answer policy-relevant questions. Study findings reveal that there is a need to improve communication between decision-makers and the public to advance knowledge and understanding of results at the appropriate decision-making hub and the associated community.

Chapter 6 discusses the rights and responsibilities of forest fringe communities in Ghana and Collaborative Forest Management (CFM) in the northern region. It explores the levels of awareness of communities of these rights and responsibilities.

Section 2 – "Waste Management"

Chapter 7 elaborates on microbial fuel cell technology and its application for dairy wastewater treatment. It provides useful insight for integrating this technology with existing conventional wastewater treatment methods to achieve the degradation of various dairy pollutants, including emerging micropollutants.

Chapter 8 is a study of municipal solid waste generation in Dir City, District Dir Upper Khyber Pakhtunkhwa (KP), Pakistan. The study finds that the spatial distribution of waste generation varies across the city. For example, a high rate of generation was found in the Rehankot and Shaow areas, whereas low generation rates were found in fringe areas.

Chapter 9 provides a review of RS waste management strategies, highlighting applications for removing contaminants from wastewater in single and multi-component systems, and in static or continuous operation modes.

Chapter 10 discusses hazardous wastes and their management.

Chapter 11 reviews the structure and dynamics of organic soils and explains their creation, evolution, and ultimate fate. It focuses on degraded peatland net primary productivity because of potential forthcoming differences attributed to rainfall, temperature, vegetation, hydrology, and permafrost disappearance.

Section 3 – "Climate Change"

Chapter 12 addresses multiple deleterious consequences of climate change. It talks about the causes of climate change and its effect on the planet, environment, plants, animals, and humans. It also discusses climate change adaptation and preventive strategies.

Chapter 13 is a review distinguishing the levels of vulnerability and resilience between the people who live in high potential zones and low potential zones in Tanzania. Study findings suggest that farmers with weak adaptive capacity should be carefully and immediately attended to, otherwise their livelihood options can destroy the environment further.

Chapter 14 is a study assessing the potential impact of climate change under a range of scenarios on intercrops of maize and improved pigeon pea varieties developed and released in Kenya.

Section 4 – "Sustainability"

Chapter 15 discusses how the spatial carrying capacity of cities, river basins, and regional transformation adapt to environmental changes, as well as the direction of carrying capacity improvement.

Chapter 16 discusses non-timber forest products and the associated economic activities. It also relates habitat management aspects along with commercial invasion, which have become detrimental to the environment.

Chapter 17 describes the methodology for designing sustainable structures with examples of control systems for promoting sustainable structure design and the process of producing and revising sustainable structure design guidelines.

Section 5 – "Pollution Management"

Chapter 18 is an experimental study describing the encapsulation of the polluting gases NO_3, NO_2, CO_2, and N_2 by the calix[4]arene molecule. Study results clearly explain the charge distribution reactivity.

Chapter 19 describes the development of solid pellet technology for molten salt in heat transport processing. The apatite phosphate, molten salt in slime-salt bath mixes was investigated under microwave radiation heating, resulting in insoluble sorbent fines dissolved in a porous basket. Study findings are helpful for advanced fuel energy storage with favorable economic potential and intrinsic properties.

Chapter 20 provides a detailed and comprehensive account of the numerical approaches proposed to analyze the fouling phenomenon that occurs inside exhaust gas systems. It examines in detail the main characteristics of each numerical model as well as their main strengths and weaknesses and simulation capabilities.

Chapter 21 reviews how advanced oxidation processes (AOPs) help in removing pharmaceutically active compounds (PhACs) in which hydroxyl radicals (HO) act as common oxidants to improve the biodegradability of further treatments. The chapter concludes that treatment with AOPs increases efficiency when compared to the efficiency of an individual process.

Finally, Chapter 22 describes the human health consequences of endocrine-disrupting chemicals (EDCs). It provides information on routes of exposure, metabolism, and mechanisms of action of EDCs. It also discusses the main consequences of EDCs, including obesity, diabetes, reproductive disorders, and cancer. The chapter ends with a discussion of preventive strategies to minimize exposure to EDCs.

Overall, this book enhances understanding of various environmental issues, changes, and sustainable solutions. The information contained herein will help to improve the skills of environmental scientists and decision-makers. It also contributes to the exchange of best practices for developing and implementing methods for environmental management.

Suriyanarayanan Sarvajayakesavalu
Professor,
Vinayaka Missions Kirupanandavariyar Arts and Science College,
Vinayaka Missions Research Foundation Deemed to be University,
Salem, India

SCOPE – India (*Scientific Committee of Problems of the Environment*),
JSS Academy of Higher Education and Research (JSSAHER),
Mysuru, Karnataka, India

Pisit Chareonsudjai, Ph.D.
Faculty of Science,
Department of Environmental Science,
Director of Ph.D. and Master Programmes in Environmental Science,
Director of Master Programme in Intellectual Property
and Innovation Management Graduate School,
Khon Kaen University,
Khon Kaen, Thailand

Section 1

Natural Resources

Chapter 1

Collaboration to Counter Fresh Water Scarcity and Promote Human Security

Michael Fratantuono, Sarah House and Sam Weisman

Abstract

In the autumn of 2017, two professors and 13 undergraduate students from Dickinson College (Carlisle, Pennsylvania, US) engaged in 3 weeks of field research in Nepal. The students were assigned to one of four teams. Each was assisted by a pair of graduate students affiliated with Tribhuvan University (Kathmandu, Nepal). Each team conducted numerous semi-structured interviews in one of four wards of the Panchkahl Municipality of Kavrepalanchok District. When they returned to the US, each student team generated a 50-page report that summarized their findings. To frame the findings of those reports, the authors of this chapter constructed a basic yet original systems model. Their analysis suggests: (1) the importance of collaboration among system participants as the key to developing the capabilities needed to adapt to fresh water shortages and enhance prospects for human security and (2) the need for further system transformation to further promote adaptation.

Keywords: climate change, fresh water, human security, collaboration, subcommunities, adaptation, systems analysis

1. Introduction

In autumn of 2017, two faculty and 13 undergraduate students from Dickinson College—located in Carlisle, Pennsylvania, US—traveled to Panchkahl Municipality of Kavrepalanchok District, Nepal, to engage in 3 weeks of field research. Fieldwork consisted of numerous interviews conducted in four different wards of Panchkahl. When they returned to the US, each team completed a 50-page research paper that focused upon the ability of the respective community members to handle risks to their human security stemming from shortages of fresh water resources. In spring of 2018, the authors studied the four reports to distill high-level themes. As well, they constructed a basic yet original systems model to frame the relationships emerging in the reports.

Via that inductive process, this chapter offers the following thesis. Although the availability of fresh water was scarce and access to fresh water was constrained: (1) a successful collaboration among the community members and nongovernmental organizations had enhanced the capabilities relevant to adaptability and resilience, and thus, human security; and (2) future progress was contingent on the additional empowerment of women as well as the ability of the government to become a more trusted collaboration partner.

IntechOpen

2. Program design

The students and faculty who conducted the field research were participants in a semester long Dickinson Global Mosaic Program [1], "Climate Change and Human Security in Nepal [2]." The program was 2 years in the making. As part of the building process, the Dickinson professor who initiated the program traveled to Nepal on two occasions and established a relationship with the Institute for Crisis Management Studies (ICMS), a master's program affiliated with Kathmandu-based Tribhuvan University. The director of the ICMS designated a project coordinator for the initiative.

The professor and the project coordinator negotiated the activities, locations, and logistics. The Coordinator suggested four wards as the research sites: Hokse, Kharelthok, Koshidekha, and Sathighar Bhagawati. The wards, located to the east of Kathmandu, were part of Panchkhal Municipality of Kavrepalanchok District, located in Province 3 of Nepal. As well, the Coordinator agreed to recruit ICMS graduate students who would provide general assistance to the Dickinson students and serve as guides and translators during the field-research.

Fourteen students enrolled in the program. It consisted of three phases. Phase one included 9 weeks of study in Carlisle that incorporated three courses each taught by a different professor[1] plus one team-taught qualitative research methods course.[2] Furthermore, in phase one, the students were assigned to one of four teams.

Phase two consisted of 3 weeks of field research in Nepal that lasted from late October to mid-November. The advantage of the four-course structure was that there were no scheduling issues when faculty and students traveled to Nepal.[3]

During phase three, which lasted for 4 weeks, each team generated a 50-page research report that summarized their findings. Those four written reports provided the qualitative data for this chapter.

3. Important concepts incorporated in the on-campus courses

3.1 Human security

The United Nations Development Programme [3] offered the first generally accepted description of the term human security. Many alternatives have since been proposed. One schema, designed with Nepal in mind, illustrates interconnections among ecosystems and climate security; water and energy security; food and health security; environmental security; and nuclear and biological security ([4], p. 3).

3.2 Resilience

Many definitions have also been proposed for resilience. Nevertheless, a description offered by Twigg [5] is helpful. Community resilience includes the capacities to: "anticipate, minimize and absorb potential stresses or destructive forces through adaptation or resistance"; "manage or maintain certain basic functions and structures during disastrous events"; and "recover or 'bounce back' after an event ([5], pp. 8-9)." A caveat he offers ([5], p. 10) is relevant to this chapter.

---

[1] "Global Environmental Change and Human Security"; "Climate Risks and Resilience in Nepal"; "Collaboration as a Vehicle for Creating Value."

[2] "Climate Change and Human Security in Nepal."

[3] Due to personal reasons, Professor Fratantuono and one student were unable to travel to Nepal.

Individuals can be members of several communities at the same time, linked to each by different factors such as location, occupation, economic status, gender, religion or recreational interests. Communities are dynamic: people may join together for common goals and separate again once these have been achieved.

3.3 Collaboration

In recent decades, the environments confronting citizens and professionals in all domestic and global settings have exhibited rapid change and increasing complexity [6]. Those developments have made collaboration among organizations an increasingly relevant way to achieve objectives beyond the reach of any single entity. For example, Goal 17 of *Sustainable Development Goals* [7] views multi-stakeholder partnerships as an "important vehicle" for making progress toward "the achievement of the sustainable development goals in all countries, particularly developing countries."

3.4 Approaches to adaptation

In 2010, Nepal's Ministry of Environment released the *National Adaptation Programme of Action (NAPA) to Climate Change* [8]. The report reflected the results of a 2-year, multi-stakeholder effort. After the Dickinson Mosaic Program had concluded, a Ministry of Forests and Environment report [9] also pointed to the need for collaboration. At the outset, the latter described the NAPA as an ongoing process that "will leave no one behind"; included numerous functionally based working groups; and recognized the need for engagement by multiple types of stakeholders ranging from local to national levels.

3.5 Basic system concepts

Meadows [10] explains that a human system has three essential components: elements; interconnections; and a purpose. Elements may be either physical items or intangible items. Interconnections are the relationships that hold the elements together: for human systems, they include customs, rules, or laws. The purpose of the system reflects intended outcomes. Since systems can be nested within systems, purposes can be nested inside other purposes.

She also explains that systems have three important attributes: self-organization, hierarchy, and resilience. Self-organization is the "capacity of a system to make its own structure more complex" ([10], p. 79). Hierarchy is the arrangement of systems and subsystems that tends to arise when self-organizing systems engage in the "process of creating new structures and increasing complexity" ([10], p. 82). In a manner consistent with Twigg [5], Meadows says resilience arises from the rich structure of many feedback loops that can work in different ways to restore a system even after a large disturbance. Resilient systems can be dynamic in nature and evolve over time.

3.6 Qualitative research methods

A few weeks into the semester, the three Dickinson professors assigned the students to one of four research teams. The teams were asked to develop questions for three different types of semi-structured interviews. Each type was intended for one of three different groups of interviewees: individual household members; key informants; and focus group participants. The teams shared proposed interview questions with the professors, took their comments, and engaged in fine-tuning.

Thank you for taking the time to talk with us today. We are a group of students from Dickinson College in the United States and we are working with the Institute for Crisis Management Studies of Tribhuvan University in Kathmandu to learn about your community and the challenges it faces. The goal of the interview is to understand how weather and climate-related events and other hazards have affected your community and how resilient you and the community are in anticipating and adapting to these events and disasters.. .. Participation in the conversation is totally voluntary.. .. May we have your permission to audio and video record the conversation?

To what hazards is the community currently exposed?

Prompt: Disasters (large storms, landslides, earthquakes, floods, and disease)

Prompt: Weather or climate related (heat, drought, erosion, and rainfall)

Please write answers on the cards. Let us place the cards on the table and discuss the results.

Of the weather and climate-related hazards you noted, which have gotten more frequent or intense?

Over what time period: 5, 10, or 15 years?

How have the hazards you described affected the community?

Prompts: Food availability/production, water, health, livelihoods, and income.

What areas of the community are most at risk to the hazards?

What members of the community are the most affected/impacted?

Prompts: Women/men, poor/wealthy, and caste/ethnicity

Why do you think this is?

What actions has the community taken to reduce the impacts of the hazards?

Have the actions you described improved the situation and/or reduced risks?

How does the community work together to cope or respond to changing conditions?

Where does the community get information to improve the situation?

If something happens (weather event, disaster, etc.), where does the community turn for help?

Do you seek assistance (financial, resources, and training) from groups outside the community?

Has it been helpful? Do you think the community has a clear understanding of actions that can reduce risks associated with hazards?

What more do you think should happen to address the hazards and to meet the community needs?

Table 1.
Example of a focus group survey instrument: Subset of comments, permission requests, and questions.

When ready, each team forwarded their work to the ICMS graduate students, who provided further comments to the students and translated the survey instruments. All four teams used the "Toolkit for Measuring Community Disaster Resilience" [11] and Twigg [5] as their points of reference for designing their surveys. To illustrate, **Table 1** provides a condensed version of the focus group survey instrument created by one of the four teams.

4. Context for the field research in Nepal

4.1 Geography and climate

The geography of Kavrepalanchok District, and Nepal more generally, includes five major zones. From the lowest elevation to the highest, they are the Terai, Siwalik, Middle Hills, High Hills, and the Mountains including the Himalayas.

The two major agricultural regions that served as the focus of the Nepal Mosaic were the Terai and the Siwalik. The Terai has a warm, subtropical climate, and land that can be irrigated to grow rice and vegetables. The Terai generates most of Nepal's' agricultural output [12].

At the time of the research, teams learned that farmers of the Siwalik primarily planted maize and millet as their major subsistence crops on terraces dug into the hillsides. Rainfall was a major source of water in the zone, but the land did not retain much of the water that resulted from rainfall. Springs, streams, and natural aquifers were other important water sources that were supplemented by man-made water-channeling infrastructure and water-storage ponds and facilities. Land in the

Siwalik was subject to landslides. Far more devastating, in April of 2015, an earthquake of magnitude 7.8 on the Richter scale, centered in Gorkha, a district near Kathmandu, killed 9000 people and resulted in billions of rupees in damage. In the wards of Panchkhal located in the Siwalik, the earthquake destroyed buildings and homes, and disrupted aquifers and water-infrastructure.

Due to the elevation differences, each zone had its own microclimate. Nonetheless, all models forecasted increases in temperatures at the country level in coming decades that ranged from 2° to 6° Celsius, increases more pronounced than those at the global level. Projections for rainfall trends were even more varied than those of climate change, yielding results that ranged from a 30 percent decrease to a 100 percent increase by 2100, when compared to the 1970–1999 average. Moreover, climate change could destabilize the monsoon season, leading rainfall to increase and become more intense during a shorter season [13].

Those factors led Nepal's Ministry of Population and the Environment ([14], p. 1) to say:

Nepal is one of the most vulnerable countries to climate change, water-induced disasters and hydro-meteorological extreme events such as droughts, storms, floods, inundation, landslides, debris flow, soil erosion, and avalanches.

4.2 Demography and economy

Nepal's population tripled between 1960 and 2010. As of 2017, it totaled approximately 30 million people and was expected to continue to grow into the future, though at a slower rate. Nepal was characterized as a Least Developed Country by the United Nations. Roughly one in four people lived below the international poverty level of US$ 1.25 per day. Agriculture accounted for nearly one-third of Nepal's GDP; thus, the onset of climate change had contributed to the struggles of the people ([15], p. 17). Furthermore, Nepal had inadequate infrastructure and was not a destination for foreign direct investment, factors that together suggested a shortage of the technological and financial resources needed to adapt to climate change.

4.3 Political context and governance structures

Nepal broke into a civil war in 1996, fueled by sharp disparities in living standards between rural and urban populations and by discrimination against social classes, women, and indigenous ethnic groups. A peace agreement was signed between insurgents and authorities in 2006. An Interim Constitution agreed in 2007 ended the 240-year-long Hindu Monarchy. In the ensuing decade, nine different coalition governments were formed. In September of 2015, the current Constitution of Nepal replaced the 2007 Interim constitution.

In the decade following post-war reunification, government reform was slow in coming. For example, the first local elections in 20 years in the wards of Panchkahl took place in the summer of 2017 [16], only a few months before the Dickinson research trip. At the outset, local governments were headed by unelected bureaucrats or community leaders, leading to increases in corruption [17]. During that era, building capacity for local governance was clearly not a priority. To fill the void, community groups emerged and worked alongside nongovernmental organizations to help promote collaboration and resilience in the face of challenges.

As of 2017, the governance structure of Nepal consisted of seven provinces, which collectively comprised 77 districts. In turn, each district was made up of municipalities, each municipality of wards, and each ward of various villages or clusters of people who did not have their own formal governance structures.

5. On-the-ground research in Nepal

Once in Nepal, the Dickinson student teams were partnered with a pair of graduate students—one male and one female for each team—who served as guides, and as language and cultural translators. In the field, each of the four teams conducted interviews in accordance with the semi-structured interviews they had previously created. Each team managed to conduct about 20 household interviews, six or so expert interviews, and two focus group interviews. (In each case, teams asked for participants' permission to record the interview.) Given the outmigration in some wards by single young men and by husbands in search of more stable income for their families, women were more highly represented than men in the interviews.

While in the field, students took turns each day asking primary and follow up questions and taking notes. Each evening, the teams reviewed what they had heard, and revised and upgraded their notes. When the teams returned to campus, they spent the final 4 weeks of the semester further refining their data and revisiting course materials and other sources as they completed their respective 50-page team-written research reports.

6. A model of community resilience and human security

In spring of 2018, Ms. House and Mr. Weisman, students who had both participated in the program, enrolled in a special co-research course with Professor Fratantuono. Together, all three carefully reread and discussed the 50-page papers submitted by each student team at end of 2017. As they did so, Professor Fratantuono took the lead in shaping a systems-model that synthesized concepts from the program and themes that emerged as all three authors interpreted the reports. As the model evolved, it served as a framework for describing data. First versions of this chapter were written in spring of 2018. Since that time, Professor Fratantuono has revised the model and the chapter.

The model incorporates ideas and imagery suggested by Meadows. She illustrates systems using stocks, flows, flow valves, and feedback loops. She explains that systems may display sub-optimal or problematic behavior. If so, she proposes 12 leverage points to promote system alteration ([10], pp. 145-165). Although Meadows does not make the distinction, the three authors say that the 12 alterations may be of two types: system modification or system transformation. Modification entails adjusting, repairing, rearranging, or embellishing components of an existing sub-system or system. Transformation entails either changing the membership, rules, purpose, or even the conceptualization of an existing system; or incorporating a new sub-system into an existing hierarchy. The model—a diagrammatic representation [18]—is presented in **Figure 1**. **Figure 2** is the Legend for the symbols in **Figure 1**.

Recalling Twigg [5], the upper left corner of **Figure 1** identifies four relevant types of community members: households and proprietors, organized community groups, nongovernmental organizations, and local government officials.

The model includes three tiers. The left-most stock of the upper tier represents tangible resources (people and economic resources) and intangible resources (trust, legitimacy, intercultural competency, and goal-related knowledge) available to community members. The second stock represents capabilities (organizational and operational) relevant to a community's efforts to adapt to challenges, and hence relevant to the community's resilience in the face of fresh water shortages Twigg [5].

The upper tier also includes two flow valves. Flow valves control the volume and rate at which information, water, money or other factors flow from stock-to-stock.

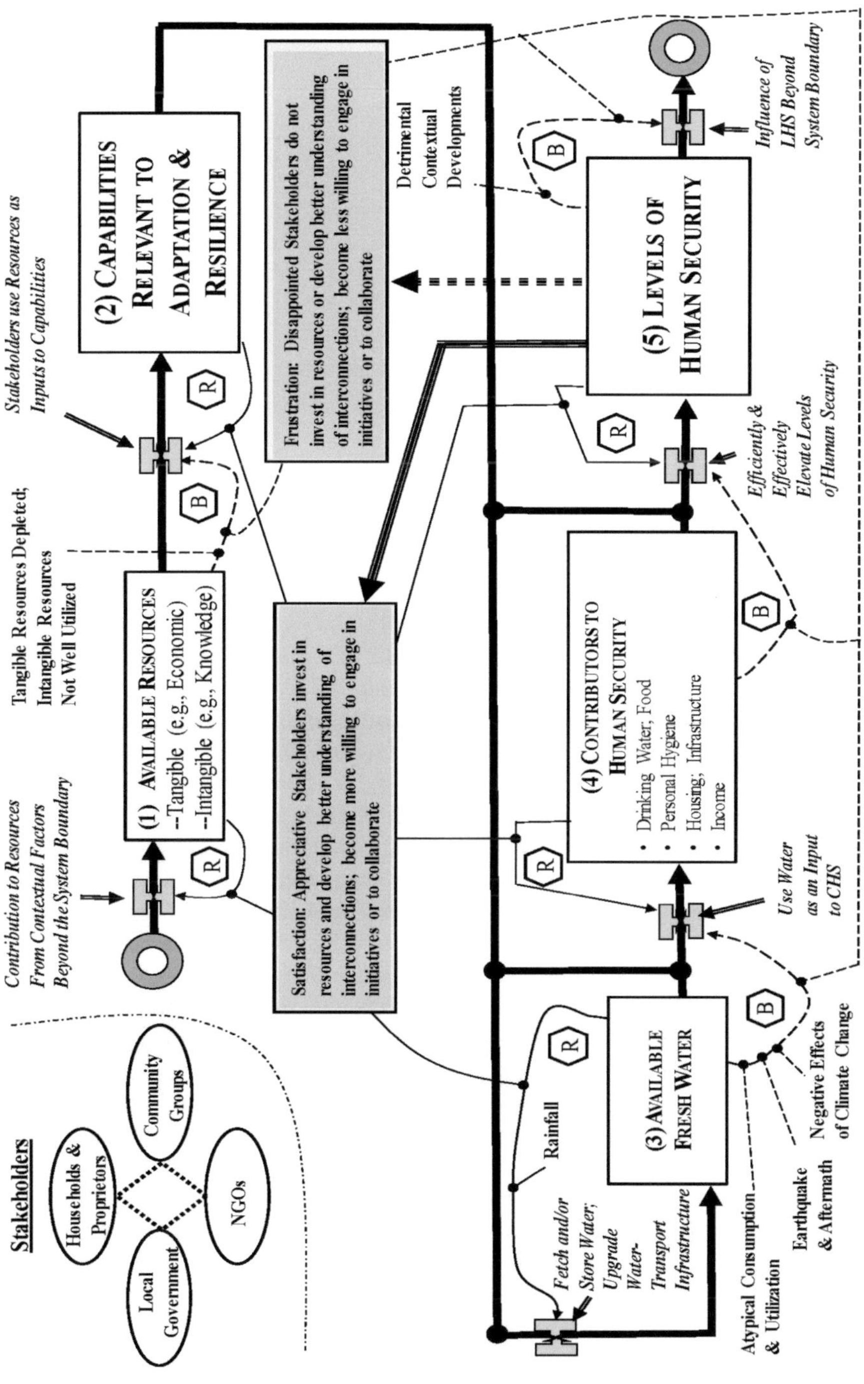

Figure 1.
Model of elements and interconnections that promote human security.

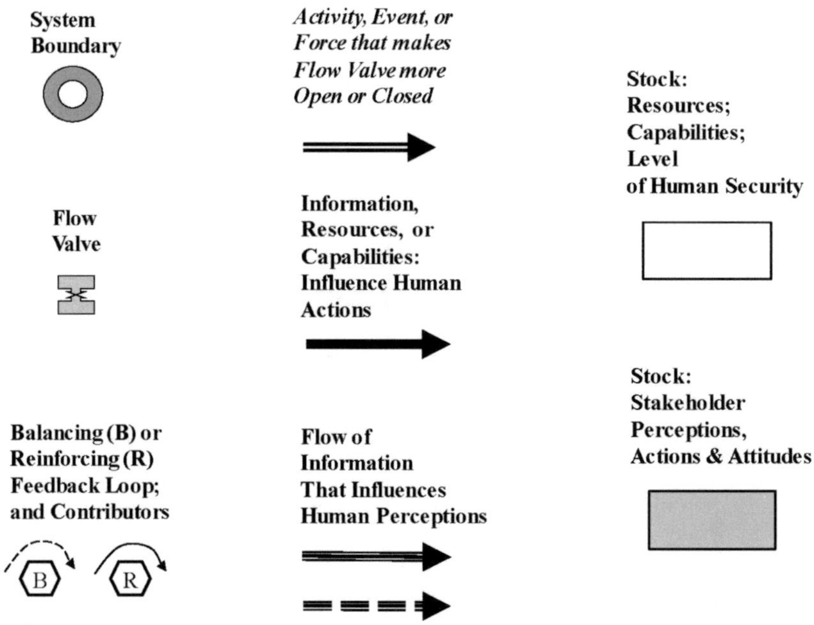

Figure 2.
*Legend for **Figure 1.***

Valves are adjusted by either natural forces or human actions. The left-most valve indicates that developments beyond the system boundary contribute to resources available to a community. The second indicates that members will use the stocks of available resources as inputs to capabilities ([19], pp. 103-105).

The bottom tier of the model includes three more stocks and four more flow valves. The first three valves suggest the ability of members to leverage one or more of the capabilities included in stock 2 as they engage in actions that, respectively, influence flows into one of the three stocks. The fourth, right-most valve indicates that the level of human security attained in a community may have implications for developments beyond the system boundary. Of note, stock 2 and stock 5, labeled in larger font, are the most important to the specification of the model: contingent on human actions, Capabilities enabling Adaptation and Resilience in the face of fresh water scarcity contribute to rising Levels of Human Security.

Balancing and reinforcing feedback loops are present throughout the model. The loops influence the degree to which human actions open or close a flow valve. In this model, while balancing loops amplify actions that deplete a stock's magnitude, reinforcing loops amplify actions that restore or elevate a magnitude. In the top and bottom tiers, the model includes loops between one stock and one flow valve.

For example, in the bottom tier, the flow valve that precedes the stock of available water represents actions by community members—for example, fetch water—to make fresh water available for use. A reinforcing loop indicates the ability of rainfall—perhaps enhanced by new storage methods—to restore or amplify the stock. In turn, the valve that follows the stock represents actions that that draw down the water stock. The associated balancing feedback loop (illustrated with a dashed arrow) indicates that both the use of water, plus other contributing factors such as a hotter climate, will draw down the magnitude of the stock.

The middle tier includes two lightly shaded stocks: satisfaction or frustration experienced by community members resulting from the outcome of previous efforts to enhance human security. As suggested by the various rays, respectively, emanating from those two stocks, satisfaction will enhance the influence of reinforcing loops throughout the model, and frustration the influence of balancing loops.

7. Insights via a system lens

7.1 Unequal vulnerability to scarcity of fresh water

The students did encounter subcommunities that had different vulnerabilities to shortages of fresh water.

7.1.1 Spatial disparities

In Koshidekha ward, located in the Terai, members explained that many people had to travel long distances to collect water from a holding pond, or from the Sun Koshi River. In Hokse ward, while some farmers worked the land of the Siwalik, others worked the land of the Terai. A subset of the latter group, those working the valley floor and growing crops near a stream, had reliable access to water for field irrigation, resulting in larger crop yields and higher incomes than those realized by farmers working the nearby hills, who had to carry water to their crops.

In both wards, location-related factors created disparities in the vulnerability of some people: those who resided the farthest from sources had to work much harder at water fetching and storage (stock 3 and the associated inflow valve). Furthermore, at that point in time, there were no capabilities (stock 2) that could be leveraged in the short-term to overcome those location-related challenges.

7.1.2 Disabled children

In Kharelthok ward, located in the Siwalik, the research team interviewed a teacher at a school for disabled children. She explained that her students had historically been socially ostracized by other ward members and thus disadvantaged. As well, the level of human security of the children (stock 5) was fragile, since their capacity for adaptation was quite limited (stock 2) and they required more fresh water resources than other community members to perform activities that supported contributors to human security (stock 3 and stock 4 and associated flow valves). To illustrate, their education involved training in self-care skills such and using the toilet, and they needed to bathe and have their clothes washed more often than did other same-age children. Essentially, the training was intended to help them leverage the capabilities relevant to the three sets of inflow valves in the lower tier of **Figure 1**.

Given efforts by the school to raise awareness, community members had begun to recognize the children's basic rights, to respect their participation in the community, and to recognize they needed support in times of need. Enhanced recognition and ensuing social validation elevated the children's human security (stock 5).

7.1.3 Women

In Nepali society, husbands and fathers often dominated a household. In community meetings, the voice of men could override the opinions of women; or worse, women were sometimes discouraged by men from using newly formed skills. Those dispositions made it difficult for women to advocate their interests and to express their insights with other ward members about ways that water might be more effectively and efficiently utilized (inflow valve to stock 5). Those factors essentially acted as constraints on the influence of reinforcing feedback loops on the intangible stocks of knowledge and on capabilities relevant to adaptation and resilience (stock 1 and stock 2), and as well increased frustration (shaded stock) among women.

Furthermore, women were disproportionately impacted by the shortage of fresh water. They bore the responsibility for making difficult daily decisions about priorities and tradeoffs in order to conserve scarce water for their families (flow from stock 3 to stock 4).

More dramatic, fresh water shortages and existing social mores had implications for a woman's health (stock 4 and stock 5). For example, the strenuous chore of collecting and carrying water (inflow valve to stock 3) could lead a woman to suffer a prolapsed uterus.

As well, women who attempted to maintain hygiene during menstruation were challenged by a lack of fresh water (stock 4). Even more troubling, the leader of a women's group located in Hokse explained that the general water shortage had led farmers to turn to various chemically based products such as pesticides to boost productivity; thus, when rains did occur, chemical residuals included in water runoff resulted in health threats when women used the supposed fresh water for personal care (stock 5).

Furthermore, women of the Kharelthok and Sathighar Bhagawati wards said other challenges arose when a woman was pregnant. That is, since some men prioritized water use for agriculture (inflow valve to stock 3), a lack of fresh water for properly preparing food could reduce a woman's intake of important sources of nutrition, thereby threatening the health of both the woman and her unborn child (stock 5).

7.2 General frustration with government initiatives

Frustrations were often associated with Government Initiatives. As a first illustration, in Sathighar Bhagawati, in the wake of the earthquake, one person said that a local NGO had to pressure the government to bring relief. Another said that when providing relief, the government did not deliver all the funds it had promised and that the funds had been unequally shared (stocks 1 and 2 and associated inflow valve to stock 2). As a result, community stakeholders were unsure whether they should wait for the remaining promised funds and projects or should themselves take the first steps. The uncertainty hindered progress toward improving community resilience (balancing feedback loops influencing stock 2).

One farmer took issue with the arms-length relationship the ward office had with community members. Although receptive to immediate needs, the office had little interest in prevention and rarely visited locales to get a first-hand understanding of a reported problem. That disposition squeezed information flows and detracted from the government's ability to provide in a timely fashion appropriate resources to enhance capabilities and strengthen resilience. As well, those factors increased frustration and thus the detrimental effects of the balancing feedback loops associated with stock 1 and stock 2.

A technician working at an agricultural cooperative said that the government had not provided enough support after the earthquake. That perception eroded trust in government and caused both decreased political engagement and lower voter turnout in subsequent elections.

Perhaps most provocative, a person in Kharelthok explained that the 2015 earthquake had damaged homes and other infrastructure throughout the ward. Water (stock 3) was needed to do construction; but water was also in short supply for other uses. The government announced an initiative to build a road that ran upward from the valley, through the village of Manesau, and then further upward to the village of Manegau. To help finance the project (stock 1), the ward office collected NPR 15,000 (US$ 134) from each Manegau household. Nonetheless, construction stalled, leading villagers to claim that ward officials had misused the funds. A budget released by the ward office included reimbursement; but that did not quell the anger of villagers. In protest, they cut off supply from a water tap running downhill to Manesau. Experiencing an extreme shortage of fresh water, the downhill community chopped down trees to further impede access to Manegau. At the time of the research, local leaders were holding hearings to resolve the conflict; but the team could not stay on site long enough to hear the outcome.

7.3 Successful collaborative efforts

In contrast to the previous set of examples, the following set illustrates that successful collaborative efforts generated satisfaction among stakeholders.

7.3.1 Women's self-help groups

Across the four wards, the research teams met women who had been motivated to form self-help groups in which they had autonomy and that enabled them to provide inclusive, informal support to one another and other villagers. Despite challenges, including a shortage of financial resources (stock 1), the women's groups had earned trust and legitimacy both within the community, and with external organizations.

Some women's groups tried to help poor and uneducated women by reaching out to them via pamphlets posted on community information boards about their activities. They initiated training programs to improve various skills, including IT and computer courses and unemployment training (stock 2); and supported sewing shops that employed women (stock 4). As well, one team found that the group they interviewed collected funds and provided loans in times of hardship (stock 1), a model based on historic self-help councils.

Women had sometimes benefitted from external assistance. For example, the Red Cross had provided training in rudimentary medical matters to members of one group, who then passed their knowledge on to other villagers (stock 1). Through hard work, those women had become authorities on healthcare and livelihood training (stock 4) in their respective villages.

Collectively, those initiatives suggested capabilities associated with two thematic arenas of resilience suggested by Twigg [5]: knowledge and education (stock 1); and risk management and vulnerability reduction (stock 2).

7.3.2 Agricultural cooperative

In Hokse, the team interviewed the Vice President (VP) of an agriculture-focused cooperative that was active among several villages of the ward. The organization was the product of a merger between two previously existing but independently operating cooperatives. The first had provided seeds, tools and water pumps to farmers at subsidized rates; the second had concentrated on helping manage villagers' savings. When founded in 2012, the cooperative had 30 members. By 2017, membership had expanded to roughly 800 people. Cooperative members had to be Nepali citizens and residents of a ward within the municipality. Membership fees ranged from $3 to $25; but nonmembers could make contributions.

Although staff at the local cooperative level reported to the district cooperative association, they did not get much technical support from the district—that general support came from regional and national organizations. Nonetheless, the local cooperative did receive loans of up to four million rupees (approximately $62,500 in 2017) from the district office at a low rate of interest. Those resources enabled the co-op to extend loans of up to $1000 that could help farmers harvest crops or purchase livestock and land (stock 1). The VP noted that loans were typically repaid in full and on time; but sometimes, a bad harvest would force farmers to delay their payments until the following year.

The VP explained that if more funds were to become available, then the cooperative could extend loans to help rebuild homes that had been impacted by the 2015 Gorkha earthquake and were still in a state of disrepair. Furthermore, women could apply for loans at a reduced rate of interest that enabled them to explore entrepreneurship.

The VP also offered insights on a few other matters. The expansion of the cooperative had prompted new methods for two-way communication among community members and the cooperative, including a Facebook page, phone calls, and notice boards; an insurance program for local crops and cattle; and training to farmers to introduce organic farming methods (inflow valve to stock 4).

7.3.3 Navjyoti

Navjyoti is affiliated with the Sisters of Charity of Nazareth, an international congregation. They became active in Nepal in 1988. They focused on the poor and on women via educational initiatives. Community members appreciated their efforts (shaded Stock of satisfaction).

A worker for the organization explained that prior to the earthquake of 2015, among other activities, they had provided skills training for women (stock 1 and inflow valve to stock 2) and had channeled funds to women's-groups for farming or economic development (stock 3). Following the disaster, Navjyoti expanded outreach to the broader Koshidekha community.

At the time of interviews by the research team, several households shared water from a single tap that ran for only part of the day at very low pressure. In response, Navjyoti planned to support the Sun Koshi River Project, an effort to expand the number of pumps that could force-feed water to communities. When completed, the additional pumps would give community members greater access to fresh water (stock 3) that would be used to enhance the Contributors to Human Security (stock 4).

However, the Project would require substantial monetary resources. Although Navjyoti was willing to cover 60 percent of the cost, they hoped to receive contributions from households to cover the remaining 40 percent. Since many households could not afford the fee, Navjyoti was also ready to recruit volunteers to contribute their time and labor in lieu of money.

7.3.4 The red cross

In Kharelthok, the Red Cross maintained an active presence. It had helped establish a committee of community members that met each month to identify problems and develop proposed solutions to the Red Cross workers. Ward members explained that the Red Cross had provided different types of assistance, ranging from hearing aids for the elderly to funds for a disabled young woman so she could start a business and support herself (stock 4).

Community members also noted, however, that Red Cross efforts were sometimes off-target. To illustrate, while some farmers explained the organization had shared seeds (stock 1) with the community that were no longer useful in the dryer climate, others noted that although it had subsidized animal husbandry (stock 2), cattle and goats required a disproportionate amount of water.

8. Final comments

8.1 The key to human security: access to fresh water

In retrospect, in the four wards visited, the stock of fresh water was being drawn down both by typical activities and as well by the influences of climate change, the residual effects of the Gorkha earthquake on water infrastructure, and the atypical need to use water for construction projects to repair earthquake-related damage. Access to fresh water, often determined by locational factors, was a key determinant of human security.

8.2 Capabilities relevant to adaptability and resilience

The capabilities required to enhance access to available stocks of fresh water and to more effectively utilize stocks were significant contributors to the level of human security in each of the four wards. In turn, the presence or magnitude of such capabilities was contingent on the degree to which stakeholders had engaged in collaborative efforts. Successful collaborations contributed to positive feedback loops and additional collaboration: success bred success. In contrast, government shortcomings as a collaborator indicated that the bureaus had further work to do in order to be trusted partners.

8.3 System modification: provision of additional resources

System modification had taken place in the wards visited by the teams. Two sets of initiatives had increased information flows. First, the agricultural cooperative used numerous communication strategies to learn about community members' needs, address those needs, and inform the community about services. Second, the Red Cross and Navjyoti had provided education and training dedicated to enhancing the knowledge of various community members, thereby allowing communities to navigate tough circumstances.

Looking ahead, members of various wards identified access to additional financial resources as their most immediate need as a first step toward gaining access to fresh water and thereby enhancing human security. An illustration was associated with the efforts by the agricultural cooperative. Even more striking were the funds sought by Navjyoti to help finance the Sun Koshi River Project, dedicated to installation of numerous water pumps to provide fresh water to communities in the Terai.

8.4 System transformation: initial progress, but more to do

Meadows [10] says that while "the rules of a system define its scope, boundaries, and degrees of freedom," ([10], p. 158) self-organization in human systems reflects the ability to "create whole new structures and behaviors" ([10], p. 159). The authors regard alterations of those types as transformations.

A striking development in the four wards had been the emergence of citizens groups (women's groups; agricultural cooperative) and international nongovernmental organizations (Navjyoti; Red Cross) as system stakeholders. Those changes took place in the space left open by immature local government. As a qualification, however, although international NGOs had successfully encouraged communities to generate their own responses and at the same time provided resources to make those responses successful, initiatives that were off target prevented the community from self-organizing and ultimately decreased its ability to respond to its own problems. Nonetheless, and more important, interviews suggested that in most cases, those stakeholders who engaged in collaboration in different subcommunities were the most reliable and effective target for new stocks of tangible and intangible resources.

Alterations associated with rules and self-organization had begun to spill over to goals. That is, efforts by IGOs to cooperate with members of villages and wards had for the most part strengthened the capabilities relevant to adaptation and resilience and ultimately to human security. Nevertheless, although increased self-organization had challenged traditional power structures and created new hierarchies, self-organization had also led to conflict as was the case for the protesters who cut off the water flow between Manegau and Manesau. Such instances tended to reduce the levels of trust community members assigned to collaboration partners. At the same time, governments at the ward level—and in some cases even the district level—had not yet earned legitimacy in the eyes of most community members. Essentially, to move on from those types of outcomes and enhance community resilience, there was a need for more learning-by-doing among community members as well as for further maturation and engagement of local government as a system stakeholder.

While communities had made progress in their efforts to promote human security, there were of course avenues for additional progress associated with system transformation. In the wards visited, there was some early evidence of changing paradigms. The most poignant illustration surfaced in the interview with the woman who headed the school for the disabled. She noted that a greater number of community members had come to recognize the fundamental right of their disabled compatriots to dignity and full status.

Furthermore, in the wards visited, there was also some evidence about the rising status and autonomy of women. As a counterpoint, however, there was also evidence that long-held existing paradigms had prevented women from being able to make important decisions regarding water use, elevated threats to their health, reduced their voice in community forums, and constrained their opportunities to develop independent sources of income. The latter set of circumstances suggested that deep-seated cultural dispositions would not be transformed in a short period of time.

Author details

Michael Fratantuono[1]*, Sarah House[2] and Sam Weisman[3]

1 Department of International Business and Management, Department of International Studies, Dickinson College, Carlisle, Pennsylvania, USA

2 Dickinson College Class of 2020 (volunteer), AmeriCorps, USA

3 Dickinson Class of 2018 (Program Coordinator), The Kaizen Company, Kingdom of Jordan

*Address all correspondence to: fratantu@dickinson.edu

IntechOpen

© 2020 The Author(s). Licensee IntechOpen. This chapter is distributed under the terms of the Creative Commons Attribution License (http://creativecommons.org/licenses/by/3.0), which permits unrestricted use, distribution, and reproduction in any medium, provided the original work is properly cited.

References

[1] Dickinson College Global Mosaic Program. Available from: https://www.dickinson.edu/homepage/603/mosaics

[2] Dickinson College. Nepal Global Mosaic. Available from: http://blogs.dickinson.edu/nepalmosaic/

[3] United Nations Development Programme. Human Development Report. New York, NY: Oxford University Press; 1994

[4] Upreti BR, Bhattarai R, Wagle S, editors. Human Security in Nepal: Concepts, Issues and Challenges. Kathmandu: Nepal Institute for Policy Studies and NCCR; 2013. p. 3

[5] Twigg J. Characteristics of a Disaster-Resilient Community: A Guidance Note, Version 2. Aon Benfield UCL Hazard Research Centre Website. 2009. Available from: https://www.researchgate.net/publication/305615592_Characteristics_of_a_disaster-resilient_community_a_guidance_note_version_2/link/5a1fe492aca272cbfbc33eb8/download

[6] United States National Intelligence Council. Global Trends 2035: Paradox of Progress. DC: Washington; 2017. Available from: https://www.dni.gov/files/documents/nic/GT-Full-Report.pdf

[7] United Nations Development Programme. Sustainable Development Goals. 2015. Available from: http://www.undp.org/content/dam/undp/library/corporate/brochure/SDGs_Booklet_Web_En.pdf

[8] Government of Nepal Ministry of Environment (MoE). National Adaptation Programme of Action (NAPA) to Climate Change. Kathmandu, Nepal; 2010. Available from: www.moenv.gov.np

[9] Government of Nepal Ministry of Forests and Environment (MoFE). Nepal's National Adaptation Plan (NAP) Process: Reflecting on lessons learned and the way forward; 2018

[10] Meadows DH. Thinking in Systems: A Primer. White River Junction, VT: Chelsea Green Publishing; 2008

[11] GOAL. Toolkit for Measuring Community Disaster Resilience. 2014. Available from: https://www.goalglobal.org/images/5101_HN_OP_006_11_Resilience_Toolkit_English_B02.pdf

[12] Gartaula HN, Niehof A, Visser L. Shifting perceptions of food security and land in the context of labour out-migration in rural Nepal. Food Security. 2012;*4*(2):181-194

[13] Government of Nepal Ministry of Science, Technology and Environment. Economic Impact Assessment of Climate Change in Key Sectors in Nepal. Kathmandu, Nepal; 2013. Available from: www.moste.gov.np

[14] Government of Nepal Ministry of Population and the Environment. Nationally Determined Contributions. Kathmandu; October 2016. Available from: https://www4.unfccc.int/sites/ndcstaging/PublishedDocuments/Nepal%20First/Nepal%20First%20NDC.pdf

[15] Selvaraju R. Managing climate risks and adapting to climate change in the agriculture sector in Nepal. In: Environment and natural resources management series. Climate, Energy and Tenure Division (NRC), Food and Agriculture Organization of the United Nations (FAO); 2014

[16] International Foundation for Electoral Systems (IFES). Elections in Nepal 2017 local elections: Frequently asked questions. In: Asia-Pacific IFES. Arlington, VA, USA; 2017. pp. 1-8

[17] Bhusal T. Democracy without Elections: 15 Years of Local Democratic Deficit in Nepal. South Asia: London School of Economics; 2016

[18] Sheridan TB. Modelling Human-System Interaction: Philosophical and Methodological Considerations. Hoboken, N.J: John Wiley and Sons; 2016

[19] Coulter M. Strategic Management in Action. 5th ed. Upper Saddle River, NJ: Pearson; 2010

Chapter 2

Microfinance Practices and NWFPs Value Additions for Sustainable Environment: w.r.t. Andhra Pradesh, India

Teki Surayya

Abstract

A Forest Living Community (FLCs) family in the study area, on an average, required Indian National Rupee (INR) 37533 (US $ 75 approximately) for their survival. Out of this 36.4% amount is sourced from agriculture activities, 20% from NWFPs sale, 23.6%, agriculture labour activities, and about 20% amount is coming from Mahatma Gandhi National Rural Employment Guarantee Act (MGNREGA) works activities. When FLCs require microfinance for NWFPs value additions and other needs, they can access it from Self-Help Groups (SHGs), moneylender, relatives and friends, banks and governments. FLCs required microfinance for subsistence, health, education, marriage, and pilgrimage purposes. Microfinance plays a key role in Non-Wood Forest Products (NWFPs) value addition, adopting Eco-Friendly Technology (EFTs), and cost - benefits of such NWFPs value addition to FLCs. The amount of income coming from NWFPs harvest and sale can be increased by way promoting NWFPs value additions using Eco-friendly Technology (EFT).

Keywords: NWFPs, microfinance, environment, forest, value additions

1. Introduction and statement of the problem

Forest living communities (FLCs) essentially depend on forests for meeting their basic needs of food, cloth, shelter and other essentials. FLCs get direct income through Non-Wood Forest Products (NWFPs) harvest and trade sale. Commonly the FLCs sell their NWFPs harvest without value addition, which results in less income, if FLCs make value addition to the harvested NWFPs their income can be increased by 400%. To undertake NWFPs value addition the FLCs require microfinance assistance and eco-friendly technologies. If they are provided with microfinance to meet their basic needs and procuring eco-friendly technologies, the FLCs can undertake NWFPs value addition for increasing their income level. Therefore the main purpose of this study is appreciates prevalent microfinance practices, NWFPS value additions and EFTs that are available to the FLCs to enhance their income level and reduce drudgery of FLCs that gradually lead to arrest environmental degradation [1–3] and up keep of natural resources.

2. Mainstream microfinance institutions

In India major sources of microfinance are (a) organized sector (banks, government agencies [4] etc.) and (b) un-organized sector (money lender, traders relatives, friends etc.) The former is regulated by government bodies like Reserve Bank of India (RBI), banking regulation act etc., and the later has no formal regulatory bodies. Microfinance falls under the primary sector and they are supposed to meet specific pre-decided targets.

3. The SHG-bank linkage phenomenon

3.1 Model-I: bank – SHG - members

In this SHGs are formed by group members themselves, after surviving for six months the SHG can link itself with a bank close to the group members and deposit their entire saved amount into the bank account. The bank sanctions credit/loan to the SHG four times to the groups saved and deposited amount e.g. the SHG saved INR 1000 and deposited into bank savings account, the bank sanctions an amount INR 4000 as credit, thus total amount INR 5000 is available to the SHG for onward lending to the group members.

3.2 Model-II: bank - facilitator agency - SHG - members

The second groups are formed by NGOs (in most of the cases) or by government agencies. The groups are nurtured and trained by these agencies. Government or other community-based organizations to take the lead in forming the SHGs, and then provide savings and credit facilities by the banks. Even after the linkage with banks, these facilitating agencies continue interacting with the groups. Most linkage experiences begin with this model with Non-Government Organizations (NGOs) playing a major role. This model has also been popular and more acceptable to banks, as some of the difficult functions of social dynamics are externalized.

3.3 Model - III: bank – NGO - MFI (micro-finance institute) - SHG - members

Due to various reasons, banks in some areas are not in a position to even finance SHGs promoted and nurtured by other agencies. In such cases, the NGOs promoted and nurtured the groups and also act as financial intermediaries. First, they promote the groups, nurture and train them and then approach banks for bulk loans for on-lending to the SHGs. The banks lend to these intermediaries for onward financing to the groups or their members.

Study area selection:

Rationale of selecting, Atmakuru (Atmakur) /Kurnool, Pembi (Nirmal) /Adilabad, Polavaram (Eluru) /West Godavari in Andra Pradesh these forest divisions are bestowed with NWFPs abundantly.

4. Methods of NWFPS value additions

When the researcher undertook research study survey in the select geographical area, the investigator observed and noted the below outlined NWFPs value addition systems. These value addition systems can be categorized into two [5] different value additions system: i) Manual system, adding value to NWFPs conventionally by FLCs e.g. stitching leaf plates with bamboo nails and ii) technology supported system, doing value NWFPs with the help of EFTs e.g. stitching leaf plate with the help of sewing machine.

Grading: dividing all harvest (collected NWFPs) into various type considering the harvest color, weight, size, appearance, etc. This grading will help the harvester to seek enhanced price for different grades.

Washing: collected NWFPs can be washed with water or can wiped with cloth in case of NWFPs, such as, gums, up rooted herbs, bulbs etc., can benefit NWFPs harvester.

Sizing: Harvested medicinal herbs necessitate cutting herbs into different sizes of the harvested herb. This sizing value can be undertaken harvester that benefits them in sourcing better price and increased market.

Aeration: after harvesting NWFPs its life (longevity) period can be enhanced especially in case of Mahua (*Madhuca latifolia*) Kullu (*Sterculia urens*), Gooseberry/ Aonla (*Emblica officinalis)* this value addition enhances the [6] bargaining power of the harvester and enable him/her to earn more price, which eventually lead to increase income level and better quality of life to the forest dwellers who harvests NWFPs.

Steaming: NWFP like Gooseberry/Aonla (*Emblica officinalis)* needs to be deseeded, to deseed the harvested Gooseberry fruits can be steamed, after steaming the fruits will become soft to deseed safely and pulp of Gooseberry can be dried in the sun light seeds can be traded separately. This will have dual benefit of increased price separate trade for pulp and seeds.

Warehouse: NWFPs are natural resources, [7] they will come in appropriate season, yet consumption of NWFPs will be done every day. NWFP like Mahua flowers will come in summer season for a couple of months, if the harvester sells it as soon as it is harvested, he or she gets below normal price as everybody may sell the harvested stocks which results increased supply that results in weak bargain power of seller. Alternately the harvest can be stored in warehouse for a couple of months or more which will enable the seller to get better and increased price.

Breaking: NWFPs like Mahua seeds, Sal seeds, and sal seeds, Achar (Buchanania lanzan) seeds are having upper hard husks that can be broken with sticks to get inner required grains that give the harvester a better price.

Fastening: *Bauhinia vahlii* (leaf/*eistar aaku*) are harvested [8]) from large barker which are used as material for making for meals plates, cups etc. which are bio-degradable and eco-friendly. The forest [8] dweller harvest these green leave and sell in loose without value addition. But these loose leaves drying for a couple of days three to four leaves can be fastened with the help of bamboo stick small nails or can be stitched with the help of sewing machine and further with the help of the compressor an edge can be made to make like dining steel plate which give five to six time more price than if sold in as raw leaves.

Crushing: NWFPs like soap nuts [9], Emblica officinalis, *Terminalia chebula*. and *Terminalia chebula* Retz are hard nuts. These nuts can be crushed with grinding machine or manual crushing implements that will give enhanced prices to the harvester, further the crushed powder can be packed and sold in the local market or distant market.

Baking: NWFPs like sal seeds have wings like parts, to make it tradable the wings like part is to be dissected from the seed this can be done by way of baking the seeds in the fire with the fuel wood, which can fetch better price to the forest dweller/harvester.

Microfinance: while conducting the research study survey it was learned that, forest dwelling communities sell their NWFPs as soon as they harvested for want of money at low price to fulfill daily needs. If these forest dwellers are provided [1–3] with access to small amount of money (microfinance) to obtain their daily needs, they can store and add value to the harvested NWFPs that will give them more price and arrests distress sale of NWFP.

5. Microfinance practices and NWFPS value additions

This part of the paper outlines microfinance requirements, sources and prevailing other microfinance practices and also FLCs livelihood sources and their augmentation.

As exhibited in **Table 1** Mean household size in the selected forest range places is 4.4 (three to six members) which is in sync with emerging nucleus family system and it is partly to secure Government welfare scheme benefits including ration card, MGNREGA work card etc. To secure survival and daily needs of forest dwellers, they do various income generating activities such as NWFP harvest and trade, artisan labour, public project wages, and sundry other items As exhibited **Table 1**, the forest dwellers are taking up, non-destructive eco-friendly based techniques that facilitate NWFPs value additions, enhanced earnings and better quality of life. In the long run all these contributes for reducing poverty amongst forest dwellers and decreased environmental degradation and increased green forest cover.

From above **Table 2** this can be inferred that mean amount of money needed for forest dwellers in all places of the study for procuring food for all times a day meals and for other daily needs, shopping goods is INR 37533. Out of this INR 13665 is provided by agriculture and allied sources, next INR 8677 is materializing from trading of NWFPs. The remaining amount has been sourced from other activities as shown in the **Table 2**.

Microfinance activities profile of researched places: the researcher has made an attempt to profile microfinance activities that were prevalent in the research study places.

Table 3 exhibits access of microfinance to forest dwellers, it could be observed that Atmakur range, SHG is having access to 51% of microfinance requirements, next comes indigenous banker who extends financial assistance up to 25%,, remaining is purveyed other sources as shown in the **Table 3**. Similarly other ranges accessibility to various microfinance requirements are shown in the above **Table 3**.

As shown in the **Table 4**, it is observed that the primarily forest dwellers require for family members healthcare that has share of 26%, next is for food that has share of 21.8%, and remaining is for other activities as shown in the **Table 4**.

The investigator had group meetings with the forest dwellers and collected the views that revealed that the forest dwellers are yet to aware fully the benefits of NWFPs value addition, emerging innovative and eco-friendly technologies. Hence,

Forest range & (Division) / District	Amount of financial resources required for household survival *	Household size (No. of persons)
Atmakuru (Atmakur) / Kurnool	36500	4.33
Pembi (Nirmal) / Adilabad	38600	4.54
Polavaram (Eluru) / West Godavari	37500	4.25
Mean	37533	4.37

Sources: Estimated based on field survey 2014.
**Threshold financial sources need to facilitate subsistence and other survival for forest dwellers in terms of money and money equivalents.*

Table 1.
Amount of money required for survival of the forest dwellers.

Name of the range and (division) / District	Income from NWFP		Income from agricultural sources (including subsistence)		Income from MGNREGA		Agriculture labour and other source		Total INR
	INR	%	INR	%	INR	%	INR	%	
Atmakuru (Atmakur) / Kurnool	7154	19.6	13797	37.8	7811	21.4	7738	21.2	36500
Pembi (Nirmal) / Adilabad	7801	19.7	13587	35.2	6832	17.7	10380	27.4	38600
Polavaram (Eluru) West Godavari	7800	20.8	13612	36.3	8175	21.8	7913	21.1	37500
Mean	7585	20.0	13665	36.4	7606	20.3	8677	23.6	37533

Source: field survey 2014.

Table 2.
Different sources of survival to the forest dwellers.

Name of the range	Atmakuru (Atmakur) / Kurnool		Pembi (Nirmal) / Adilabad		Polavaram (Eluru) / West Godavari		Total	
Source of Micro Credit	**Score***	**% of score**	**Score***	**% of score**	**Score***	**% of score**	**Score***	**%**
Moneylender	17	25.0	21	30.9	16	23.9	54	27.8
Banks/ Government	06	9.0	08	10.3	07	10.4	12	6.2
SHG	35	51.0	27	42.6	29	43.3	91	46.9
Relatives and friends/others	10	15.0	12	16.2	15	22.4	37	19.1
Total	68	100	68	100	67	100	194	100

Source: field survey 2013–2014. Score- Individual responses for a particular source for meeting microfinance requirement including multi responses.*

Table 3.
Forest dweller access to microfinance in the researched places.

the concerned Government and NGOs should be initiate necessary interventions to create awareness and facilitate NWFPs value additions and also provide market linkages to the value added NWFPs.

Figure 1 an integrated network that is envisaged and as shown in the **Figure 1**, all stakeholders should collaborate, cooperate and coordinate to achieve the integrated objective. Providing livelihoods to forest dwellers is a comprehensive issue and strong integration and involvement of all systems (lateral integration, forward/ market linkages) and stakeholders including forest dwellers Public Policy makers, Government, NGOs/Civil societies. Enhancing livelihoods and ensuring welfare to the poor forest dwellers is a Global concern in general and India in particular. This is a challenge and to be addressed together, fastening all stakeholders' involvement in the evolution and execution of the envisaged policy. As shown in **Figure 1**, integrated linkages to all these entities must be promoted as strategic measure to secure

Name of the range	Atmakuru (Atmakur)Kurnool		Pembi (Nirmal) Adilabad		Polavaram (Eluru) / West Godavari		Mean value of study area
Purpose	**Score**	**% of Score**	**Score**	**% of Score**	**Score**	**% of Score**	
Subsistence	18	21.7	21	22.3	17	21.3	21.8
Health	22	26.7	26	27.7	19	23.8	26.0
Education	09	10.8	05	5.3	04	5.0	7.0
Pilgrim	10	12.0	13	13.8	12	15.0	13.6
Marriage	15	18.0	19	20.2	17	21.3	19.8
Others	9	10.8	10	11.7	11	13.6	12.0

Source: field survey 2013–2014.

Table 4.
Forest dwellers microfinance required for various activities.

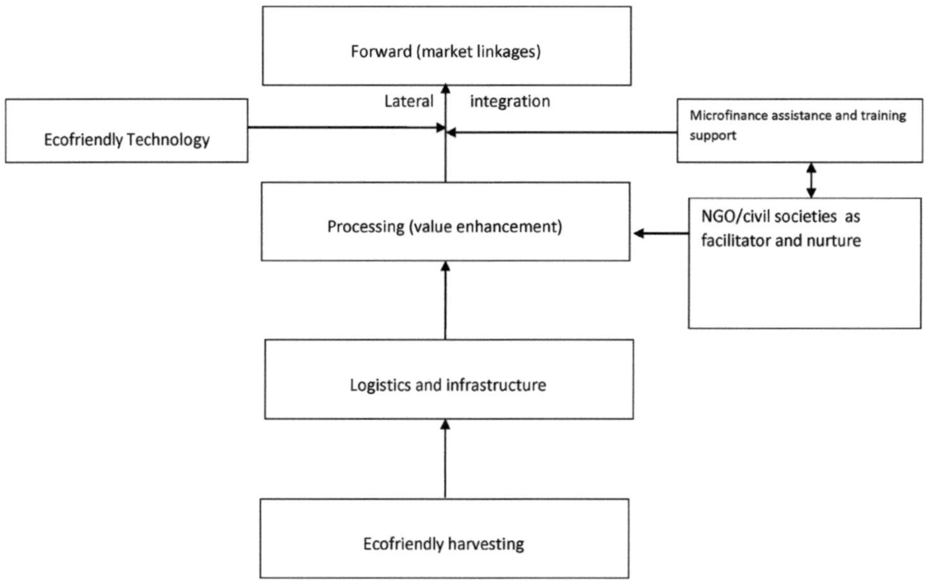

Figure 1.
Networking of NWFP processing, microfinance, EFT, logistics and infrastructure [10].

the intended goal of providing subsistence requirements. Eco-friendly NWFPs value additions [11] necessitates eco-friendly technologies which will rendered numerous benefits including reducing environmental degradation, deforestation yet, enhanced income to the forest dwellers. Technological and Scientific research institutions may shoulder the responsibility for promoting conventional [12] NWFPs value addition techniques.

6. Conclusions and suggestions

Average amount of money required for FLCs in the study area for procuring food items to 3 square meals a day and for other daily needs, cloths etc., is INR 37533. Out of this INR 13665 is provided by agriculture and allied activities, next

INR 8677 is materializing from trading of NWFPs. The quantum of money that can be earned by way of trading NWFPs may be enhanced through appropriate value additions with the help of eco-friendly technologies, which will have multiple benefits including enhanced self-employment, raised income yet reducing environmental degradation and increased forest cover, better flora and fauna health.

It was observed about 47% of microfinance assistance is provided by Self-Help Groups, yet indigenous banker is providing about 28% of total requirements of the forest dwellers. It is deduced that self-help groups will act as purveyors of microfinance requirements of the forest dwellers.

It is observed that the primarily forest dwellers require for family members healthcare that has share of 26%, next is for food that has share of about 22%. Group meetings with the forest dwellers revealed that the forest dwellers are yet to aware fully the benefits of NWFPs value addition, emerging innovative and eco-friendly technologies. For example if AONLA (*Emblica officinalis)* sold in raw form as tender fruit they may get say INR 50 Kilogram (Kg.) if they make value addition in form boling the AONLA fruits remove the seed and dry the pulp in the sunlight now the price of the dried AONLA pulp can be sold @ INR 200 after making provision for process loss and overhead. Hence, the concerned Government and NGOs should - initiate necessary interventions to create awareness and facilitate NWFPs value additions and also provide market linkages to the value added NWFPs.

Dedicated linkages tagging all concern parties to be evolved to facilitate increased income level of forest dwellers. These integrated linkages with all concern entities must be promoted as strategic measure to secure the intended goal of providing subsistence requirements. Eco-friendly NWFPs value additions necessitates eco-friendly technologies which will rendered numerous benefits including reducing environmental degradation, deforestation yet, enhanced income to the forest dwellers. Technological and Scientific research institutions may shoulder the responsibility for promoting conventional NWFPs value addition techniques.

Effective development plans to facilitate increased earnings and better quality life to the forest dwellers must incorporate measures for better threshold logistics which can link forest dwellers value added NWFPs reach the distant market to get remunerative earnings. Yet there should provision for microfinance that encourages the forest dwellers to become micro-entrepreneurs. Involvement of voluntary organization to support NWFPs value addition, imparting training, and helping forest dwellers to market their value added NWFPs.

Author details

Teki Surayya
Department of Commerce and Management Studies, Adikavi Nannaya University, Rajahmundry, Andhra Pradesh, India

*Address all correspondence to: tekisunny@gmail.com

IntechOpen

© 2021 The Author(s). Licensee IntechOpen. This chapter is distributed under the terms of the Creative Commons Attribution License (http://creativecommons.org/licenses/by/3.0), which permits unrestricted use, distribution, and reproduction in any medium, provided the original work is properly cited. cc BY

References

[1] Pethiya B P and Teki Surayya, "Role of Micro Finance in Marketing of NTFP's and improving the living standard of rural poor". IIFM, News Letter, vol. III, No. 02, June, 2000a

[2] Pethiya, B.P. and Surayya, Teki. 2000b. Financing the Environment. Indian Journal Of Forestry, Vol. 23(2): 168-173, 2000, Dehradun, India.

[3] Pethiya, B.P. and Surayya, Teki. 2000, Role of micro finance in marketing NWFP and improving the living standard of rural poor, IIFM, News letter, Vol. III, No. 2, June 2000c pp. 8-9.

[4] NABARD's SHG-Bank Progress, cited on 20th October 2007, on line available from URL http://www.nabard.org/pdf/highlights%200607.pdf

[5] Pethiya B P and Teki S, "Emerging Microfinance Practices: with special reference to Forest Dwelling community in Andhra Pradesh and Madhya Pradesh states". Journal of Paradigm, volume VIII, No. 1 January–June, 2004, MIT, Ghaziabad, pp 81-97

[6] Prasad Ram, P.C. Kotwal and Manish Mishra. 2002. Impact of harvesting of Emblica officinalis (Aonla) on its natural regeneration in central Indian forests. Journal of sustainable forestry. Vol. 14, no. 4, 2002.

[7] Prasad Ram. 2001. Documentation of published and unpublished literature on non-timber forest products in India. OT report and MRM dissertation on NTFPs from 1989-1999 at IIFM, Bhopal.

[8] Teki Surayya, (2000) "Dependence of Forest Dwellers on Fuel- wood and Non-wood products for their survival and pertinent Marketing Issues" Proceedings of International Workshop on Agro-Forestry and Forest Products, November, 2000, NEHU, Aizwal, Mizoram, India.

[9] Teki Surayya "A study on dependence of forest dwellers upon fuel wood and non-wood forest products for survival and pertinent marketing issues: a case study of North Andhra Coastal Districts", funded by IIFM Bhopal (1999-00)

[10] Pethiya B Pand Teki Surayya "Assessing the Impact of Micro-Finance as a tool for adoption of appropriate technology and conserving the environment", Fund by IIFM, Bhopal, (2003)

[11] Mishra, Manish, Taki Surayya and R. P. Mishra. 2001. Observation on the phenology and fruit yield of Achar (Buchanania lanzan) tree in the tropical forest of Orissa state. Paper submitted in the Symposium on: The Art and Practice of Conservation Planting under the topic "Tropical Tree Seed Research" Taiwan.

[12] Teki Surayya, Manish M, R. Mishra "Marketing of selected NTFPs (Non-Timber Forest Products): A case study of Koraput, Malkangiri and Rayagada Districts, Orrissa State" the Journal of Non-Timber Forest Products, Vol. 10 (3/4): 186-194, 2003, Dehradun

Chapter 3

Ecosystem Changes in Shola Forest-Grassland Mosaic of the Nilgiri Biosphere Reserve (NBR)

R. Sasmitha, A. Muhammad Iqshanullah and R. Arunachalam

Abstract

The Shola grasslands are tropical montane forests found in the high altitudes of Western Ghats separated by rolling grasslands. These unique ecosystems act as the home for many of the floral and faunal endemic species and also serve as the water reservoir for the Nilgiri Biosphere Reserve. The grassland let the rainwater to flow through the sholas into the stream and provide water to the region throughout the year. The region once covered with tropical montane forest and grassland was transformed into a land of plantation over the centuries. As the grasslands are easy to clear off, tea estates, coffee estates and timber plantations were established by the British and later by the Indian forest department to satisfy the various need of the growing economy. Majority of this region are being replaced by the invasive tree species and agricultural plantations. This led to the loss of major proportion of the shola forest and grassland. Many developmental works have been carried out in the region and these developmental activities results in the gradual disappearance of the ecosystem. These ecosystem need to be conserved and hence, identifying the knowledge gap and application of current state of knowledge is necessary.

Keywords: biodiversity, endangered species, environmental changes, montane forest, shola-grassland

1. Introduction

The shola forest-grassland is the tropical montane forest found in the upper reaches of India's Western Ghats. This mosaic ecosystem is native only to the southern Western Ghats and found in the high altitude mountains of Kerala, Tamil Nadu and Karnataka. This is a unique system where the vast grassland is interspersed with the forest. The forest is made up of evergreen native trees which are dwarf in nature and the hill slopes are covered with native grass species. The vegetation is double layered storey with closed canopy. These ecosystems have high water retention capacity, absorb rains and retain them within their soil. The grassland let the rainwater to flow through the sholas into the stream. The streambed and decaying litter of forest holds the water and release it slowly released to form small streams and these streams joined to form large streams and then rivers throughout the year. Thus it acts as the water reservoir of the region of the Nilgiri Biosphere Reserve. This shola-grassland is the origin to many of the rivers in Tamil Nadu and Kerala region.

2. Shola-grassland ecosystem

Tropical montane evergreen forests, locally called as sholas (borrowed from the Tamil word "Sholai") naturally coexist with grasslands at an elevation range of 1400–2700 km [1]. The shola-grassland ecosystem mosaic consists of rolling grasslands with shola fragments limited to sheltered folds and valleys in the mountains alienated from the grasslands with a sharp edge. As, sholas commonly have constant cloud cover they can be classified as lower montane cloud forest or upper montane cloud forest depending on elevation [2].

Widespread transformations of shola forest-grasslands into plantations and agricultural lands are increasing and these are the common global phenomenon affecting Africa, southern Asia, Europe, Australia, North America and South America [3–9]. The mega diverse countries like India sheltering about 200,000 of all known species are threatened largely by clearing of vegetation [10–12]. This biodiversity in India, is mostly concerted in the Western Ghats which is a 1600 km long mountain range classified as a biodiversity hotspot with a high degree of species endemism and also with many worldwide threatened species having a very restricted distribution [13–17]. Shola forests-grassland mosaics of the Nilgiri hills are characterized by high level of endemism due to the unique climatic conditions. They are rich in flora and fauna with many of them are endemic to the region.

3. Flora

Sholas contain vegetation species of both tropical and temperate affinities [10] and many of them are endemic to the region. Phytogeographical analysis of shola genera reveals that genus found on the periphery of shola fragments and as isolated trees on grasslands are typically temperate (Rubus, Daphiphyllum and Eurya) or sub-tropical (Rhododendron, Berberis, Mahonia are Himalayan) in origin. On the other hand, species found within shola fragments are IndoMalayan or Indian in origin [18, 19]. Dominant overstory species in the shola include members of Lauraceae, Rubiaceae, Symplocaceae, Myrtaceae, Myrsinaceae and Oleaceae while dicotyledonous understory species are dominated by Asteraceae, Fabaceae, Acanthaceae, [20, 21]. Monocot species in the understory are dominated by members of Poaceae, Orchidaceae and Cyperaceae [21]. Species were found to be significantly influenced by soil moisture (overstory and understory) and soil nitrogen (understory only) alongside the edge-interior gradients in shola fragments [16].

4. Fauna

The shola-grassland ecosystem mosaics are home to many threatened faunal species due to their unique climate, evergreen nature and high altitude. They act as the home for many faunal species of conservation concern including the tiger (*Panthera tigris tigris*), dhole (*Cuon alpinus*), gaur (*Bos gaurus gaurus*) Nilgiri langur (*Trachypithecus johnii*) and Nilgiri marten (*Martes gwatkinsii*). The Nilgiri tahr (*Niligiritragus hylocrius*) which is endemic to the ecosystem-mosaic has been studied thoroughly over the years [11, 14, 20, 22–25]. Through habitat preferences, faunal species also have been observed to reflect the shola-grassland ecosystem mosaic pattern. Despite a lack of resource-driven interspecific competition, small mammal communities in the Nilgiris showed a high degree of preference for either shola or grassland. On the other hand, these patterns were masked in exotic plantations [26]. Invasive species in the shola-grassland ecosystem mosaic also observed with strong habitat selection patterns and show a strong preference for shola cover.

5. Diminishing shola forest-grassland ecosystem: causes

The shola grasslands act as the water harvesting and water storage structures and they store large quantities of water from the mountains. These ecosystems are home to many floral and faunal species and they are rich in biodiversity. As the grasslands are depleting, flora and fauna which are endemic to the region are under severe threat. Many of the perennial rivers of Tamil Nadu and Kerala are originating from this forest-grassland mosaic. With the depletion of these unique ecosystems, the water streams are drying up and impacted the region.

The shola-grassland ecosystem is one of the most diverse but threatened landscape of the Western Ghats. These ecosystems are very sensitive to climate and climate changes have greater influence on this forest-grassland. These unique ecosystems are being degraded by many natural and anthropogenic pressures. Since the mid-nineteenth century, land use changes fragmented the Nilgiri shola forest grassland. Land management of the Nilgiri Hills is considerably changed by British company and crown governments [27] and beginning in 1837, tea and eucalyptus plantations were established and expanded them. During World War II, wattle, eucalyptus and pine plantations were promoted at the expense of highly diverse and resource-rich grasslands and shola forests by the colonial state. Grasslands and sholas were gradually cleared to provide plantation lands and wood [27–29]. Planting of timber-yielding exotic tress mainly Black wattle (*Acacia mearnsii*) and eucalyptus has been a cause of distress in these landscapes. As the grasslands are easy to clear off, tea estates, coffee estates and timber plantations were established by the British and later by the Indian forest department to satisfy the various need of the growing economy. This resulted in the loss of major proportion of the shola forest and grassland. Many developmental works have been carried out in the region and these developmental activities results in the gradual loss of the ecosystem. Between 1973 and 2014 Shola grasslands area had seen a 66.7% decline. A study carried out in the region revealed that the plant diversity and quality of the natural environment were very much affected in the highland region. Exotic weeds, conversion of native forest into timber plantations, encroachment of forest areas by midlands and lowlands, grazing of natural forest areas by domestic animals, poaching by encroachers, human population growth, ecotourism and pilgrimage, industrial effluent affected areas, pollution and contamination, forest fires and illicit felling were the reasons pointed out as the changing trend of biodiversity [30].

In the shola grasslands of state Kerala, the recent demographic changes have increased dependence on firewood, at the same time, the introduction of new crops like lemongrass and higher livestock stocking rates have put further pressure on these systems [31]. In Nilgiri also the grasslands are extremely threatened, as they are widely afforested with exotic tree plantations, mainly for energy needs [32]. According to various studies, eucalyptus-afforested grasslands in the Nilgiri suffered from significant hydrological impacts, such as reduced water yield and stream flow, and reduced seasonal runoff volume [33–36]. These disequilibria have relentlessly affected native sholas and grasslands through increased incidence of fire and expansion of invasive species [37, 38].

A documentation study carried out in the region reveled that factors responsible for the diminishing shola forest grassland ecosystem include extensive land conversion such as conversion into agricultural plots, commercial plantations, developmental activities, plantation of exotic trees and burning practices, annual fires.

As the grasslands are easy to clear off, tea estates, coffee estates and timber plantations were established by the British and later by the Indian forest department to satisfy the various need of the growing economy. Exotic trees such as eucalyptus, wattle, cinchona and pine and shrubs like *Lantana camara, Parthenium, Scotch broom* and *Gorse* are fast growing in nature and hence they easily compete with native plant species and grasslands by invading the forest-grassland ecosystem [39]. The indigenous mixed forests in the Nilgiris district were replaced by commercial and industrial crops which affect the ecological balance of the region [40]. Except in protected areas, conversion of land into commercial plantations, agricultural lands and construction activities such as hydrological dams has resulted in extensive deforestation. The latest Draft Forest Policy of the central government promotes these plantations, even though the State Forest Department has stopped promoting them and there has a ban on them officially since 1996 [1].

The statistical data on the climate variability and future projections for shola forest of the Nilgiris revealed that rainfall pattern was likely to reduce during southwest monsoon and increase towards northeast monsoon and the extreme rainfall events could further results in higher flooding. The overall temperature expected to increase more in 2050 and 2070 due to manmade pressures and some intolerant endemic species could get loss due to increasing greenhouse gas emission and fires would result in the loss of endemic habitat of shola forests. The climate change also expected to shift and alter fruiting and flowering pattern of the endemic species [41]. There had been decrease in dense forest cover (32 km^2), open forest (2.38 km^2), scrub class (1–24 km^2), grass land (11.54 km^2), dense tree cover (4.93 km^2), plantation crops (5.73 km^2) and meager level of water bodies, increase in rocky surface (16.60 km^2), estates (26 km^2) and also expansion of urban areas (14.47 km^2). The results also showed that the montane grasslands and shola forests of the Nilgiris has been destroyed by widespread tea plantations and commercial plantations, easy vehicle access and the extensive monoculture [32]. Projected climate change would likely to multiply the invasion intensity of alien species. Also the montane grasslands and shola forests of the Nilgiris has been destroyed by widespread tea plantations and commercial plantations, easy vehicle access and the extensive monoculture [39]. The area once covered with native forests was transferred into land of plantation over centuries. This led to the loss of major proportion of the ecosystem. Many developmental works also have been carried out in the area. The region is being affected by various kinds of encroachment. This resulted in loss of endemic species of birds and animals by affecting their food reserve, gradual disappearance of wild edible fruits and other plant species and the native forest is reducing in a faster manner which also results in man-animal conflicts thus ultimately affects the biodiversity of the region. A documentation study carried out in the region revealed that the area is facing soil related issues such as loss of soil fertility, loss of soil beneficial microbial activity, subsoil compactness, incidence of frequent soil erosion and unsuitability of the soil to produce profitable crop. The study also stated indiscriminate use of fertilizers and pesticides, soil transportation, repeated application of chemical inputs beyond recommended level, use of heavy farm machineries, cultivation of exotics, loss of local natural vegetation, faulty land resettlement, loss of natural wind breaks, mono-cropping and loss of healthy soil biological process have contributed high damage to the natural soil ecosystem of the region [42].

6. Conclusion

The shola grasslands are tropical montane forests found in the high altitudes of Western Ghats separated by rolling grasslands. The shola-grassland ecosystem has undergone severe habitat loss mainly due to exotic tree plantations, widespread commercial plantations, extensive monoculture, harvesting of shola species and cattle grazing. The ecosystem is likely to undergo extinctions in plant and animal species due to loss of habitat. Further, climate change is also expected to modify the equilibrium between the forest and grassland. Shola is a very sensitive type of vegetation. As it is sensitive to climate, once it vanishes from its original habitat, it is very difficult to make it reappear. Identifying the knowledge gap and application of current state of knowledge is necessary for responding to these issues. There is an urgent need to map the extent of loss of grasslands, exotic plantations and spread of invasive species in each forest division.

Conflict of interest

The authors declare no conflict of interest.

Author details

R. Sasmitha[1*], A. Muhammad Iqshanullah[2] and R. Arunachalam[1]

1 Agricultural College and Research Institute, Tamil Nadu Agricultural University, Tiruvannamalai, India

2 STAC, Tamil Nadu Agricultural University, Tirunelveli, India

*Address all correspondence to: sasmitharaghu@gmail.com

IntechOpen

© 2020 The Author(s). Licensee IntechOpen. This chapter is distributed under the terms of the Creative Commons Attribution License (http://creativecommons.org/licenses/by/3.0), which permits unrestricted use, distribution, and reproduction in any medium, provided the original work is properly cited.

References

[1] Cordero RL, Suma M, Krishnan S, Bauch CT, Anand M. Elements of indigenous socio-ecological knowledge show resilience despite ecosystem changes in the forest-grassland mosaics of the Nilgiri Hills, India. Palgrave Communications. 2018 Aug 21;4(1):1-9.

[2] Bruijnzeel LA, Hamilton LS. Decision time for cloud forests. IHP Humid Tropics Programme Series, No. 13, UNESCO, Paris, 2000.

[3] Baldi G, Paruelo JM. Land-use and land cover dynamics in South American temperate grasslands. Ecology and Society. 2008 Dec 1;13(2).

[4] Bredenkamp GJ, Spada F, Kazmierczak E. On the origin of northern and southern hemisphere grasslands. Plant Ecology. 2002 Dec 1;163(2):209-29.

[5] Fensham RJ, Fairfax RJ. A land management history for central Queensland, Australia as determined from land-holder questionnaire and aerial photography. Journal of Environmental Management. 2003 Aug 1;68(4):409-20.

[6] Hoekstra JM, Boucher TM, Ricketts TH, Roberts C. Confronting a biome crisis: global disparities of habitat loss and protection. Ecology letters. 2005 Jan;8(1):23-9.

[7] Neke KS, Du Plessis MA. The threat of transformation: quantifying the vulnerability of grasslands in South Africa. Conservation Biology. 2004 Apr;18(2):466-77.

[8] Vega E, Baldi G, Jobbágy EG, Paruelo J. Land use change patterns in the Río de la Plata grasslands: the influence of phytogeographic and political boundaries. Agriculture, ecosystems & environment. 2009 Dec 1;134(3-4):287-292.

[9] Zhao S, Peng C, Jiang H, Tian D, Lei X, Zhou X. Land use change in Asia and the ecological consequences. Ecological Research. 2006 Nov 1;21(6):890-896.

[10] Bunyan M, Bardhan S, Jose S. The shola (tropical montane forest)-grassland ecosystem mosaic of peninsular India: a review. American Journal of Plant Sciences. 2012 Nov 27;3(11):1632.

[11] Daniels RR. The Nilgiri Biosphere Reserve and its role in conserving India's biodiversity. Current Science. 1993 May 25;64(10):706-8.

[12] Mohandass D, Davidar P. Floristic structure and diversity of a tropical montane evergreen forest (shola) of the Nilgiri Mountains, southern India. Tropical Ecology. 2009 Dec 1;50(2):219-229.

[13] Bond WJ, Parr CL. Beyond the forest edge: ecology, diversity and conservation of the grassy biomes. Biological conservation. 2010 Oct 1;143(10):2395-2404.

[14] Das A, Krishnaswamy J, Bawa KS, Kiran MC, Srinivas V, Kumar NS, Karanth KU. Prioritisation of conservation areas in the Western Ghats, India. Biological Conservation. 2006 Nov 1;133(1):16-31.

[15] Gimaret-Carpentier C, Dray S, Pascal JP. Broad-scale biodiversity pattern of the endemic tree flora of the Western Ghats (India) using canonical correlation analysis of herbarium records. Ecography. 2003 Aug;26(4):429-44.

[16] Jose S, Sreepathy A, Kumar BM, Venugopal VK. Structural, floristic and edaphic attributes of the grassland-shola forests of Eravikulam in peninsular India. Forest Ecology and Management. 1994 Jun 1;65(2-3):279-91.

[17] Myers N, Mittermeier RA, Mittermeier CG, Da Fonseca GA, Kent J. Biodiversity hotspots for conservation priorities. Nature. 2000 Feb;403(6772):853-858.

[18] Nair KK, Menon AR. Endemic arborescent flora of the sholas of Kerala and its population and regeneration status. Shola Forests of Kerala: Environment and Biodiversity. Kerala Forest Research Institute, Peechi. 2001:209-36.

[19] Suresh HS, Sukumar R. Phytogeographical affinities of flora of Nilgiri Biosphere Reserve. RHEEDEA-KERALA-. 1999;9(1):1-21.

[20] Davidar ER. A note on the status of the Nilgiri Tahr in the grass hills in the Anamalais. Journal of the Bombay Natural History Society. 1971;68(2):347-54.

[21] Swarupanandan K, Sasidharan N, Chacko KC, Basha SC. Floristic and ecological studies on the Sholas of Idukki District. Shola Forests of Kerala: Environment and Biodiversity. 2001:259-86.

[22] Daniels RJ. The Nilgiri Tahr: an endemic South Indian Mountain goat. Macmillan India; 2006.

[23] Mishra C, Johnsingh AJ. Population and conservation status of the Nilgiri tahr *Hemitragus hylocrius* in Anamalai Hills, South India. Biological Conservation. 1998 Nov 1;86(2):199-206.

[24] Rice CG. Habitat, population dynamics, and conservation of the Nilgiri tahr, *Hemitragus hylocrius*. Biological Conservation. 1988 Jan 1;44(3):137-56. DOI: 10.1016/0006-3207(88)90099-7

[25] Rice CG. *The behavior and ecology of Nilgiri tahr (Hemitragus hylocrius Ogilby, 1838)* (Doctoral dissertation, Texas A&M University. Libraries).

[26] Shanker K. The role of competition and habitat in structuring small mammal communities in a tropical montane ecosystem in southern India. Journal of Zoology. 2001 Jan;253(1):15-24. DOI: 10.1017/S0952836901000024

[27] Krishnan S. Landscape, Labor, and Label: The Second World War, Pastoralist Amelioration, and Pastoral Conservation in the Nilgiris, South India (1929-1945). International Labor and Working Class History. 2015 Apr 1;87:92.

[28] Cederlöf G, Sutton D. The Aboriginal Toda. On Indigeneity, Exclusivism and Privileged Access to Land in the Nilgiri Hills, South India. Indigeneity in India. 2005:160-86.

[29] Sivaramakrishnan K. Modern forests: Statemaking and environmental change in colonial eastern India. Stanford University Press; 1999.

[30] Rajasekaran, R. Participation in Tamil Nadu Afforestation Project – A Beneficiary Analysis. [Thesis]. Tamil Nadu Agricultural University; 2013.

[31] Chandrashekara UM, Muraleedharan PK, Sibichan V. Anthropogenic pressure on structure and composition of a shola forest in Kerala, India. Journal of Mountain Science. 2006 Mar 1;3(1):58-70.

[32] Thirumalai P, Anand PH, Murugesan J. Changing land use pattern in Nilgiris Hill environment using geospatial technology. International Journal of Recent Scientific Research. 2015;6(4):3679-83.

[33] Samra JS, Sikka AK, Sharda VN. Hydrological implications of planting bluegum in natural shola and grassland watersheds of southern India. InSustaining the Global Farm. Selected papers from 10th International Soil Conservation Organization meeting held at Purdue University 2001;338-343).

[34] Samraj P, Sharda VN, Chinnamani S, Lakshmanan V, Haldorai B. Hydrological behaviour of the Nilgiri sub-watersheds as affected by bluegum plantations, Part I. The annual water balance. Journal of Hydrology. 1988 Nov 30;103(3-4):335-45.

[35] Sharda VN, Samraj P, Chinnamani S, Lakshmanan V. Hydrological behaviour of the Nilgiri sub-watersheds as affected by bluegum plantations, part II. Monthly water balances at different rainfall and runoff probabilities. Journal of Hydrology. 1988 Nov 30;103(3-4):347-355.

[36] Sikka AK, Samra JS, Sharda VN, Samraj P, Lakshmanan V. Low flow and high flow responses to converting natural grassland into bluegum (*Eucalyptus globulus*) in Nilgiris watersheds of South India. Journal of hydrology. 2003 Jan 10;270(1-2):12-26.

[37] Kodandapani N, Cochrane MA, Sukumar R. Conservation threat of increasing fire frequencies in the Western Ghats, India. Conservation Biology. 2004 Dec;18(6):1553-61.

[38] Srinivasan MP. The ecology of disturbances and global change in the montane grasslands of the Nilgiris, South India. University of Kentucky: Louisville, USA; 2011.

[39] Sasmitha R. A Diagnostic Study on the Environmental Issues and Developing Sustainable Ecological Strategies in the Hilly Tribal Ecosystem [Thesis]. Tamil Nadu Agricultural University; 2019

[40] Sathyanarayanan CR, Chandra N. The Lost Landscapes and Livelihood: A Case Study of the Alu Kurumba of Nilgiris, Tamil Nadu. Journal of the Anthropological Survey of India. 2013;62(2):821-50.

[41] Fathima, Tabassum Ishrath, R.K. Somashekar, and J. Mohammed Ahmed. Projecting Climate Variability in the Purview of Future Climate Projections for Shola Forest of Nilgiris, Westernghat in South India. International Journal of Advanced Research. 2019;7(1):876-883. DOI: 10.21474/IJAR01/8396.

[42] Sasmitha R, Arunachalam R, MuhammadIqshanullahA.Documentation of Soil Related Environmental Issues and It's Contributing Factors: A Study among the Hilly Tribes of the Nilgiri District. Madras Agricultural Journal. 2019 Jun 2;106.

Chapter 4

Considering Harmful Algal Blooms

Ruby E. Jalgaonwala

Abstract

Problematic harmful algal bloom is wide and tenacious, upsetting estuaries, coasts, and freshwaters system throughout the ecosphere, alongside disturbing human health, social life as well as national economy. Particular environmental factors supports growth of algal blooms, temperature always is significant when speaking about water-ecosystem. Disparity in temperature also found to affect the interaction of physical, chemical and biological parameters so it is equally imperative to consider effects of climate change, as change in climatic conditions supports unwanted growth of algae. Also inconsistency in climate equally contributes to the apparent increases of HAB, therefore effects of climate change needs to be totally comprehended along with development of the risk assessments and effective management of HABs. Increased HAB activities have a direct negative effect on ecosystems and they can frequently have a direct commercial impact on aquaculture, depending on the type of HAB. Causing economic impact also, as there is still insufficient evidence to resolve this problem. Therefore this chapter considers the effects of past, present and future climatic variability on HABs along with impacts of toxins release by them, on marine organism as well as human beings correspondingly, mitigation of HAB with help of suitable biological agents recognized.

Keywords: algal blooms, toxins, mitigate, climate change

1. Introduction

Ecosystems on earth plays an important role in regulating climate and as well as a fundamental life-giving resource for human kind. Aquatic ecosystems are majority supported by photosynthetic organisms that fix carbon and produce oxygen, comprise the base of food web. Though, under sure circumstances, the abundance of various taxa reaches level that cause harm to humans and other organisms. These proliferations habitually are referred to as 'harmful algal blooms' (HABs), that includes a variety of species and consequences that humans perceive as adverse. HABs occur in all aquatic environments such as freshwater, brackish and marine and at all latitudes. We know in the nature algae are a normal part of the aquatic ecosystem, forming the actual base of the aquatic food web as they are large and very diverse group of organisms, the majorities are microscopic in size, except some macroscopic algae. Mainly the microscopic algae are most often as single cells, other than some can form chains and colonies. For the most part micro algae live in the water, whereas others live in or near to the sediment or attached on to some of surfaces for some time also for entire life cycle. Many of macro algae are also known as seaweeds they can be multicellular and complex. Algal blooms also acts as natural important component for many aquatic systems, generally spring blooms are triggered by some seasonal warming, increased availability of light and nutrient and

IntechOpen

also water column stratification. These blooms are significant part for energy and material transport through the food web, as well plays an important role in the vertical flux of material out of the surface waters therefore these blooms are known to be prominent considering with those acknowledged as "harmful." These algae can form harmful algal blooms, when they assemble and grow in massive amounts damaging the ecosystem, or if the algal community shifts to species that makes some toxin compounds disrupting the normal food web and also harmful to human beings [1]. Problem of harmful algal bloom is wide and persistent, affecting numerous estuaries, coasts, and freshwaters system throughout the world, along with disturbing ecosystems, human health, social life style as well as dilemma for economy systems.

2. Algal blooms

HABs consist of organisms which are able to deplete oxygen levels in water systems; it also kills life in same water system and lasts for several days to months [2]. They are considered harmful as producing massive biomass and toxins. Huge amount of cell biomass produced by them hinders the light penetration resulting into decreased density of submerged aquatic vegetation [3]. Decaying, these algal blooms increases oxygen consumption leading to mortality of aquatic life in that area [4]. The effects of the blooms have been identified in numerous ways, even in the marine ecosystem were aquatic life gets exposed to toxins by ingestion. Therefore biological control of HABs is seen to be an economically and environment-friendly resolution [5]. In addition some biotic organisms were isolated and used to eradicate HABs, for example secretion of *Cyanobacteriolytic* substances by bacteria [6]. Characteristic species-specific interaction by some virus [7], the bursting of host cells, and the virus lytic cycle [8]. Viral degradation has the benefit of the species-specific attack. Golden algae have also been found as a mitigator of microcystis cells as well as toxin degraders. (**Figure 1**) shows spreading of algal blooms in different climatic conditions [9].

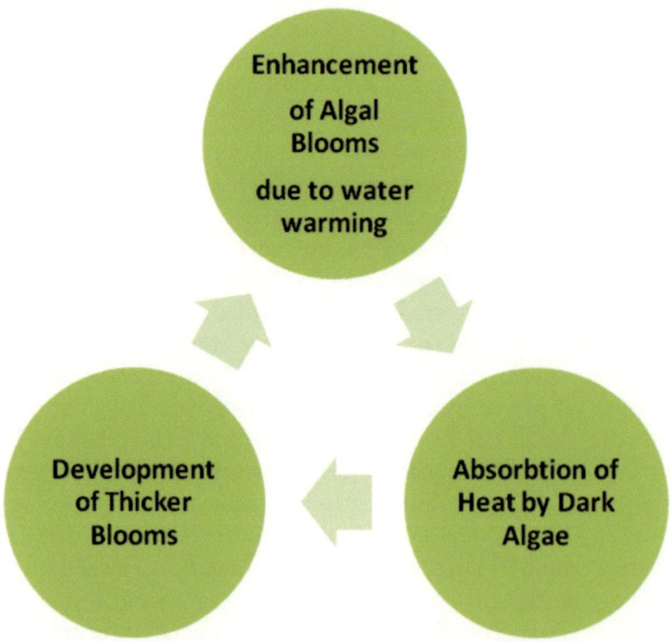

Figure 1.
Pervasiveness of different conditions enhancing HABs.

Some environmental factors found to supports growth of algal blooms. The temperature always is important when bearing in mind about water-ecosystem [10]. Increase in heat could significantly expand Chlorophyll-*a* concentration, signifying that warmer conditions could develop a dominant population of Cyanobacteria [11]. Reports suggest that variation in temperature also affects the interaction of physical, chemical, and biological parameters in shallow lakes. Were for Cyanobacteria, these factors emulate fluctuating physiological changes such as nutrient uptake capacity, N-fixation, as well as optimum temperature. Effect of temperature was also noticed with *Microcystis aeruginosa* biomass production [12]. It is important to note that freshwater HABs caused by Cyanobacterial blooms appear to be the most noticeable examples of warming induced intensification indicating that the temperatures yielding maximal growth rates for many Cyanobacterial HABs [13, 14].

Evident shows that there is an increase and spreading of phytoplankton bloom globally in the sea and also nutrient loading is dependent on biomass composition. As such autotrophic growth can result only from the increased photosynthesis and primary production must be an outcome of improved nutrient levels. All through addition of nutrients, variation in the amount of nutrient be practical, encouraging struggle for resources among various community and species. As near to coast food fortification is caused due to riverine input in connection with dissimilar discharges, resultant of new nutrient input eliciting some new algal blooms. Breathing space and geographical location generally influences nutrient availability, acting as significant aspect in defining their eutrophication values. As known geographical factors including latitude, elevation, and longitude possibly affects the openness of nutrients to algal growth. Were elevation is amazingly associated with strength of light and also human interference. Availability of nutrition also found to be elevated in some of the lakes at high elevation [15]. Accordingly the all-inclusive occurring of marine phytoplankton blooms can be linked to improved primary production rates. It is important to note that global wave of phytoplankton was firstly reported on Dino-flagellate *Gyrodinium aureolum* in some European waters, which was beforehand present in some other north-east coast of the U.S. Similarly, many species spread globally and was responsible for shellfish poisoning global wave of HABs [16]. Lake Taihu was also reported for annual Cyanobacteria occurrence [17]. Considering research from last some decades, capabilities for management of HABs have grown with scientific advances working independently. New technological developments have altered the way to monitored and managed HABs [18–20]. Problems related to HAB are serious and worse in many parts of the world, however thinking, working capabilities and existing knowledge can help to curtail impacts to protect marine resources community health.

3. Control agents related to HABs

Studies have been carried out to find a better way of controlling HABs. Different biotic factors have been identified to mitigate the option of HABs. Where use of different bacteria was done to tone down HABs in coastal and freshwater community [21].

4. Toxins

The most toxic algal strain is *M. aeruginosa,* which constantly produces microcystins, acts harmful to aquatic organisms as well as to humans. Were microcystins have been reported as tumor-promoting [22]. Some bacteria mainly acts antagonistic towards Cyanobacteria and are predatory bacteria, some other acts as toxin-degrading. Were Predatory helps to make an environmentally pleasant solution to available HABs. Also number of prey–predator and the mechanism of Cyanobacterial lysis, were some effectual biological control approach [23]. Few of Cyanobacteria mitigated using the secretion of *Cyanobacteriolytic* substances by some *Bacillus* Sp. typically *Bacillus cereus* and [24], *S. neyagawaensis* [25], *Streptomyces* [26], *Pseudomonas fluorescens* species [27]. *Pedobacter* Sp. secretes some mucus-like secretion as self-defense against *M. aeruginosa*. *Raoultella* Sp. removes *M. aeruginosa* by dissolving microbial metabolites and humic acid [28]. *Agrobacterium vitis* use Quorum sensing to lyse *M. aerugenosa* [29]. *Sandaracinobactor sibiricus, Methylobacterium zatmanii* and *Rhizobium* Sp. use lytic mechanism to remove *M. aeruginosa* [30]. Some *Bacillus* Sp. use cell-to-cell contact mechanism and production of an extracellular product to remove *Aphanizomenon flos-aquae* [31] and *M. aeruginosa* [32, 33]. Several reports suggested that algal viruses often existed at stable numbers, even when their hosts were absent [34]. With claim of that summer and spring season showing the eminent decay of cultivated viruses succeeding to four-seasons of analysis [35]. The regular seasonal study also noticed that the stumpy decay of algal virus during the wintry weather that permitted for the survival of about 126 continues days under the ice-cover in the freezing freshwater pond [36]. These agents show high specificity and high efficiency, but it gain limited attention due to high cost, as also requires upscaled level experiment confirmation [37].

5. Fish species used to mitigate HABs

Fish species for all time used an option for bloom removal as number of fishes can ingest and digest the toxin itself. Therefore Bio-manipulation is a promising tool to control HABs for the lake-ecosystem [38]. High toxin production during bloom conditions [39] the massive fish kill was also reported, as its challenging for fishes to survive in oxygen-poor conditions, which suggest result another option to remove HABs [40].

6. Zooplanktons used to mitigate HABs

Several natural grazing environments are having selective herbivores like *Cyclopoid, Copepods*, and *Calanoid*, affecting Cyanobacterial growth by lowering Cyanobacterial densities [41]. Zooplankton show eco-friendly, contamination-free, and low-cost exclusion, but not beneficial at low oxygen conditions. Furthermore it was found that *Daphnia longispina* can ingest many Cyanobacteria [42]. For example grazing is one of the fore most mitigation options for zooplankton, *Daphnia ambigua, Eudiaptomus gracilis* shows graze on *M. aeruginosa* [41]. Besides *Cyclopoid copepods* graze on *Anabaena, Microcystis,* and *Planktothrix* species [41].

7. Fungi used to mitigate HABs

Studies, show that fungi have algicidal activity, and some findings also showed that fungi could produce antibiotics to lyse HABs [43]. Some fungal species, attack directly for lysis of Cyanobacteria or algal species [43]. *Trichaptum abietinum, Lophariaspadicea, Irpexlacteus, Trametes hirsute, Trametes versicolor* and *Bjerkandera adusta* was used to remove *Microcystis* and *Oocystisborgei* [43]. Uses of bio-flocculation method were algae, itself used as a control agent (**Figure 2**) [44]. Flocculating micro

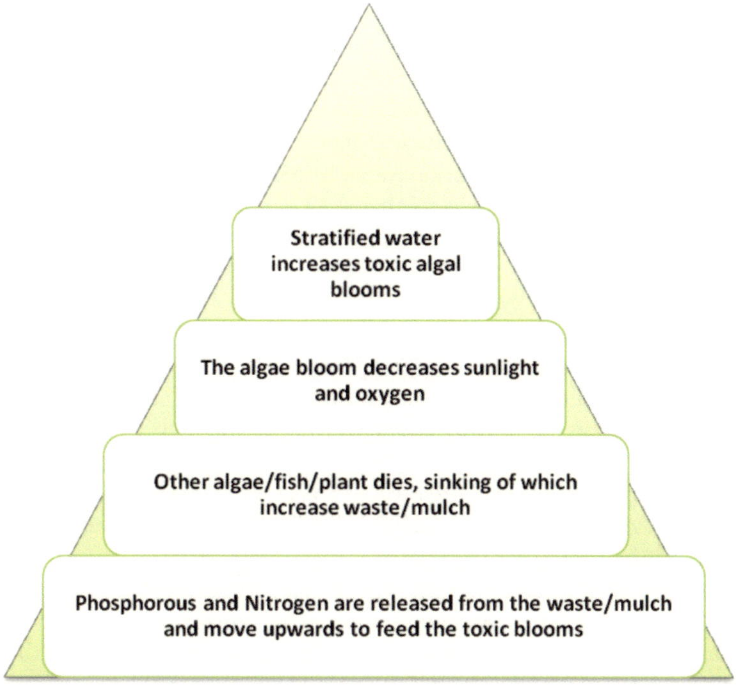

Figure 2.
Interface events of environment and microorganism with HABs.

alga could be used to concentrate non-flocculating alga of attention. The main advantage of this method is that it does not require any flocculating agent [44]. *Ankistrodesmus falcatus, Scenedesmus obliquus* flocculate *Chlorella vulgaris,* and *Tetraselmis suecica* flocculates *Neochloris oleoabundans* [44]. A species of golden alga (*Poterioochromonas* Sp. strain ZX1), is identified as a feeding agent for toxic *M. aeruginosa* and also does not affected by cyanotoxin.

When working with HAB it becomes equally important to consider effects of climate change, as change in climatic conditions supports unwanted growth of algae. At many instance record shows that HABs intensify as water have warmed closer to temperatures that yield maximal growth [18, 45, 46]. It becomes essential to notice that in marine systems, warming has been concerned with intensifying multiple HABs in a number of mid and higher latitude regions [45–47]. On the other hand, these regions with increasing frequencies and intensities of HABs due to progressive warming may be balanced by region that warms beyond of the optimal range for other HABs [47]. Considering together, all such circumstances hypothesis avowed by several case studies explains that HABs may be migrating pole-ward with progressive warming [46–48]. Such migration of HABs to new ecosystems, conversely may create significant risk to aquatic ecosystems, humans and other animals living near them. Because of which indigenous species, experiences selective pressures and thus suffer the most population declines [49, 50].

8. Intention for formation HABs

There is no conclusive report available for the causes of HABs, unfortunately, the causes of HABs are uncertain to date. Though, some of the factor which are thought accountable for causing HABs are briefly described here. An attempt made in **Figure 2** to show interface between some environmental events and microorganism with HABs.

Coastal contamination from a variety of source including household and industrialized effluents is most imperative factors in the growth of HABs. The majority times eutrophication by nutrient enrichment outcomes as blooms of algal growth, from which several are toxic to humans and as well as marine organisms. Contemporary research suggests that eutrophication and climate change are two most important processes that help for proliferation and expansion of Cyanobacterial blooms [51]. It is also important to know that nutrient enrichment can modify the species framework of ecological system [52]. Also inhabitant biota gets displace as the surroundings becomes enriched with nitrates and phosphates [53]. As the coastal eutrophication and improved offshore nutrient concentration taking place offshore due to vertical integration have been linked with the expansion of large biomass, eventually foremost to harmful impacts on ecosystems, human health and fisheries resources. At the same time if eutrophication increases nitrogen and phosphorus inputs, the ratio of these nutrients to silicates becomes very high. This favors non-diatom species including several harmful species. Additionally, it is believed that high concentration of phosphorus, and a low total nitrogen to total phosphorus (TN:TP) TN: TP ratio, are favorable for the production of Cyanobacteria blooms. Recent studies, represents that Cyanobacteria usually dominates in lakes with low TN/TP ratio and are rare in lakes with high TN:TP ratios [54, 55]. Cyanobacteria dominate in lakes where TN:TP mass ratio is below 29:1.

Nutrients consequent from anthropogenic activities have resulted in the increase in HAB account also at some places, unusual heavy rains have resulted in blooms of *L. polyedrum* owing to nutrient rich runoff into the coastal waters. Blooms of Dinoflagellate *Pfiesteria* are found in estuaries of middle and southern Atlantic coasts. The main factors controlling cycles of Dinoflagellates, includes water salinity, pH, nutrients and temperature to one side from these, studies in North California have illustrated that they thrive well near sources of organic phosphates released from sewage treatment plants [56, 57], talk about some Coastal and Continental Shelf Zone (CCSZ) and also Open Oceanic Zone (OOZ) of the Indian segment, were algal blooms can develop only when the calculated rate of biomass increase exceeds the rate of loss generally the grazing and sedimentation rates. As once a bloom develops, it persist for a long epoch under low growth if the rate of loss is small. Still the interactive effects of future eutrophication and changed climate on harmful algal blooms are versatile, and according to current knowledge such processes are likely to enhance the magnitude and frequency of these events. Temperature rise and precipitation associated with climate change falls into broad ranges, also qualms exist in their upshot stratification as North Sea flushing species like *Dinoflagellates* and *Raphidophytes* increase considerably. Some species of *D. acuminata, P. minimum, F. japonica and C. antique* are observed in this region frequently, representing an increase in HAB [58]. Discrepancy in temperature affects circulation patterns, and causes variation in the physical structure of water column that supports occurrence of HABs [59].

9. HAB and impacts

It is very important to consider harmful Cyanobacterial blooms (cHABs) as they are have noteworthy socioeconomic and environmental outlay, by having impact on water quality, drinking water, agriculture, fisheries, tourism, food web pliability, habitats, along with anoxia and fish kills [60]. Also high biomass accumulation and degradation of algal blooms possibly leads to depletion of dissolved oxygen, light attenuation and clogging of fish gills, resulting in fish kills and thousands of other marine life, as direct degradation of the ecosystem [61]. The most critical impacts of algal blooms are on human being health, toxins, produce HABs cause acute and chronic health effects in mammals including humans. For example toxins produced during harmful algal blooms are some of the natural toxic substances directly killing fish/shellfish and other marine life also accumulating in fish and sea food leading to human poisoning after ingestion of contaminated sea food [62]. Sometimes toxins produced during algal blooms may not found toxic to fish and other marine existence. On the other hand, they accumulate in fish and mollusks and move up the food chain and showing shocking impact on humans. Therefore aquatic toxin diseases are categorized into two types as. Shellfish carry toxins that facilitate to paralytic, neurotoxic, diarrheic and amnesic shellfish poisoning. Next type of poisoning is through mollusks tend that occurs during algal blooms. Fish takes toxin that escort to ciguatera and tetrodotoxin poisoning. Poisoning of fish is found more localized and also associated with parts of specific reefs and fishes. Sometimes bloom occurrence of species of Dinoflagellate *Pfiesteria* in estuaries of some middle and Southern Atlantic coast hint that anthropogenic stress on marine environment has caused fish kills and related health hazards in humans also [56]. Species of *Pfiesteria* are also known to cause lesions in fishes. Additionally, we humans can be exposed to toxins that are directly released into water and air. This occur as expected, cell disruption caused through human activities including water treatment. As known such phenomenon frequently occurs in the Gulf of Mexico where residents and beach goers are exposed to toxins through seas spray. Toxins can then be inhaled and lodged in the nose and throat and can down into the lungs. General symptoms associated with this are irritation in respiratory system and frequent coughing.

10. Oceans upwelling

Ascending motions caused due to oceanic circulation is well-known as 'Upwelling', which bring into being some affects to the environmental conditions, beside increases the nutrient content in euphotic zone thus increasing the productivity of the province. Noteworthy findings [63] suggested various factors inducing upwelling off the south west coast of India [64], also have worked to come across the occurrence of the upwelling route along the Dakshina Kannada Coast of India and description shows that upwelling was found to occur from month of March to October along the coast this could be one of the factor for occurrence HABs along the southwest coast of India.

11. Unhealthy coral reefs

Unhealthy coral reefs play a very imperative role in the formation of blooms, as healthy coral reefs are free of external algal growth [65]. Unhealthy conditions/death of corals is generally for the reason that pollution of oil or depositions of sediments leading to encrustations of corals by calcareous materials and algae, plus may in turn lead to the death of zooplanktons and some higher fishes in the food web. Also endolithic algal bloom can cause disease named White Syndrome (WS), entailing of distinct lines between healthy and strong corals and dead ones. Such endolithic algae, including *Ostreobium* Spp. penetrate the coral tissues of tabular *Acropora* Spp., in turn affecting the corals with micro-lessions, which makes them susceptible to infiltration by many pathogens. Some example includes *Gambierdiscus toxicus*, a benthic Dinoflagellate finds way on the dead corals, releasing ciguatoxin which is responsible for causing Ciguatera Fish Poisoning (CFP) [65]. Thus if contaminations affects water quality and coral reefs are affected than *G.toxicus* is likely to bloom, causing widespread release of ciguatoxin. The loads for food, water and fuel continue to increasing to support this ever increase human population. These changes in climate and nutrients are contributing to eutrophication and expanding global footprint of harmful algal blooms (HABs) worldwide. It is now clearly known that the global expansion of HABs is continuing, with increasing abundance, frequency, and geographic extent of HABs, with new species being documented in some new areas [48].

12. Influences of climate change

Inconsistency in climate equally contributes to the apparent increases of HAB, therefore effects of climate change needs to be seriously understood alongside with development of the risk assessments and effective management of HABs. This chapter considers the effects of past, present and future climatic variability on HABs. The one thing we are sure regarding climate is that it is changing and for all time. With complex nature of climate, temperature is only one of many factors to be considered. Each biological life has a temperature window within which it can survive. The direct upshot of global warming with elevated water temperature may affect seasonal composition of the phytoplankton, including changes in seasonal succession, and the position of biogeographic boundaries. There is still insufficient evidence to resolve this problem.

There has been a considerable boost in phytoplankton biomass over the last decades in definite regions of the North-East Atlantic and North Sea, particularly more in the winter months. Also in the North Sea a significant increase in phytoplankton biomass has been found in both intensely anthropogenically-impacted coastal waters and the comparatively less-affected open North Sea. Considerably decreasing trends in nutrient concentrations suggest that these changes are not being driven by nutrient enrichment. The increase in biomass appears to be associated to warmer temperatures and evidence that the waters are also becoming less turbid, thus allowing the normally light-limited coastal phytoplankton to more effectively utilize lower concentrations of nutrients [66]. A study of entity phytoplankton groups has shown increased temperatures were associated with an earlier timing of the highest abundance of some Dinoflagellate species. In disparity, the diatom species examined have not shown such a shift [67]. Coastal time series of HAB phytoplankton are much shorter in extent. Most began in the 1990s various HAB species are flagellates, life forms that are favored by augmented temperatures though direct influences on cellular processes and circuitously through increased stability of the water column. An increase in sea surface temperatures may facilitate the range expansion of HAB species [48].

Eventually elevated and extreme bursts of precipitation be able to increase the amount of runoff from the land and number of floods also. This may enhancing stratification in estuaries and sea lochs favoring the growth of Dinoflagellates. Some humic material during these events may increase the absorption of available nutrients which may promote growth of phytoplankton [48]. It is well-known that changes in temperature, pH, light, nutrient supply and water movement affects algal bloom dynamics as well as their toxicity. Climate change show predictable impact on these variables to differing extents in dissimilar regions [48, 68]. Also a lower pH has the potential to influence the speciation of

Predator/Killer	Habitat	Mode of action	Major host	Reference
Rhizobium sp.	Ambazari Lake, Nagpur India	Lysis	*Microcystis aeruginosa*	[30]
Halobacillus sp.		Bioflocculation	*Microcystis aeruginosa*	[33]
Pedobacter sp. (MaI11–5)	Lake and water treatment plant	Mucous-like secretion from cyanobacteria for self-defense	*Microcystis aeruginosa*	[5]
Myoviridae	Shallow lowland dam reservoir in Central Poland	Species specific interaction	*M. aeruginosa*	[7]
Cyclopoid copepods	Lake Ringsjon southern Sweden	Grazing	*Anabaena, Microcystis*and Planktothrix species	[41]
Trichaptum abietinum	The soil of bamboo forests (Hangzhou, China)	Direct attack	*Microcystis aeruginosa, Microcystis flosaquae Oocystisborgei*	[43]
Lophariaspadicea	The soil of bamboo forests (Hangzhou, China)	Direct attack	*Microcystis aeruginosa*	[43]
Ankistrodesmus falcatus	Freshwater	Bio-flocculation	*Chlorella vulgaris*	[44]
Scenedesmu sobliquus	Freshwater	Bio-flocculation	*Chlorella vulgaris*	[44]

Table 1.
Removal of harmful algal blooms by means of some microorganisms.

nutrients for example nitrogen, phosphate and silica which accounts important for phytoplankton growth [69]. Increased HAB events have a direct detrimental effect on ecosystems and they can often have a direct commercial impact on aquaculture, depending on the type of HAB. Causing economic impact which will be severe as in rural areas impacts to the aquaculture industry will have a disproportionate impact on the economy of the local area. Considering all known aspects about HABs some attempts were made for removal of harmful algal blooms with help of microorganisms as shown briefly in **Table 1**.

13. Manifestation of climate change and HABs

Climate change is negatively impacting health and leading to harmful transformation in aquatic ecosystems [70, 71]. Rising temperatures leading to acidification and oxygenation which alters basal metabolic functioning and species distributions along with the timing of essential biological activities [72, 73]. Due to acidification physiological stress found to increase among sensitive marine species along with growth inhibition of calcifying organisms. As ocean deoxygenation alters the distribution and survival of aquatic organisms [74, 75]. This further alters structure and functioning of marine and freshwater ecosystems. Temperatures rise have predictable impact on the occurrence and concentration of marine diseases, habitat loss, including ocean deoxygenation inviting various environmental contaminants [76, 77]. As increased level of carbon dioxide in atmosphere has generated decreased value of pH in surface waters, offshore, coastal and upwelling marine regions, including freshwater environments [78, 79]. Decreased pH shifts the carbonate system to decrease bicarbonate concentrations and increases dissolved CO_2, thereby increasing carbon availability for photosynthesis [80]. Now such process downgrades the value of metabolically costly carbon-concentrating-mechanisms so that many species of phytoplankton evolved change that may alter the competitive balance among the species [81]. Climate change is now shifting the occurrence and distribution of marine species of various organisms around the world. Therefore frequency and impact of algal blooms have considerably increased around the world in recent decades [82]. Human modifications of the environment such as port construction, release of contaminated water, enriching nutrient by recreation, tourism, fishery, aquaculture, impacts harmful algal contributions [83]. As the reason HABs are now migrating to new ecosystems, therefore considerable risk to aquatic ecosystems and the humans is also found to increase. There is no doubt that oceans are getting warm because of accumulation of CO_2 in the atmosphere through various activities [78]. Elevated CO_2 offers the potential to rebalance the distribution of primary producers that rely upon inorganic carbon for performing photosynthesis [84]. Hence co-occurrence of climate change stressors and their physiological impacts have been in continue study from the past decade, excessive level of biomass generated creates high levels of organic matter which, when respired, promotes hypoxia and acidification [85].

Coastal zones are host to a varied type of aquatic life and are known dynamic ecosystems [86]. Such locations found to be impacted by climate change as several coastal regions are getting warm hastily than the open-ocean [87]. It is also important to note that coastal areas are also prone to eutrophication, acting as stressors, as unnecessary nutrient loading promotes HABs [88]. As result of ecological changes spring diatom blooms within temperate latitudes, surface waters speedily warm and stratify, which isolates bottom waters from surface influxes of dissolved oxygen and lowers CO_2 water, making the condition promoting concurrent hypoxia and acidification [89]. Various HABs flourish in stratified water columns, in late spring and early-summer time's stressor-sensitive, early-life stages of many aquatic genera/species are present in coastal systems [90, 91]. Because of migrating of HABs to new ecosystems native species, experience selective pressures and consequently suffer the greatest population declines [92]. Generally Cyanobacterial HABs are associated with fresh to brackish water, even though blooms of *Trichodesmium* sp. and *Lyngbyaa* sp. in saline tropical and subtropical waters are considered as harmful mainly in Asian and South Pacific nations. Were Cyanobacterial HABs in the marine and freshwater bodies gets worsened due to elevated anthropogenic nutrients that can be the consequences of regional and local population density. Evidence shows that Cyanobacterial HABs are enhanced by elevated temperature [93], Likewise, elevated CO_2 leads to increased growth rates of Cyanobacteria. But surplus inputs of N and P relative to Si shifts the conception from eukaryotic like diatom to Cyanobacteria creation. Noteworthy finding shows that internal loading of phosphorus together with decreasing N:P ratios able to enhance blooms of nitrogen-fixing Cyanobacteria over the other phytoplankton at some area like Baltic Sea.

HABs species too have harmful effects solely on fish other invertebrates. Variety of planktonic algae forms HABs which are associated with killing of fish in nature [94–96]. Example algal blooms of planktonic fish killers haptophyte *Prymnesium parvum,* has caused fish killing blooms worldwide since the first recorded bloom in Danish waters in the 1930s. Some studies show that HABs effects physiology of fish indicating respiratory effect. Evidence shows that on exposure of fish to *P. parvum* reflects toxic effects related to fish gill damage. *P. parvum* exposure may effects fish health as increase in gill permeability found to cause sensitivity to subsequent secondary toxicity, as well as effects of hemolysis and anti-coagulant being noted [97, 98]. Even mammals and birds exposed to Cyanobacterial toxins may become ill or sometimes die. Records show that when other bacteria in the water break-down dead Cyanobacteria, the dissolved oxygen may become depleted, which may responsible to kill fish. Also dense algal blooms in the water column blocks sunlight therefore other organisms cannot survive. Wildlife and pets can become more prone by drinking algal bloom water as very small amount of toxin can also cause illness to some of small animals if ingested. From past few decades, unexpected HAB phenomena have been recognized responsible for eutrophication and ballast water introductions, mean while climate is changing continuously. Changing atmospheric CO_2 concentrations, with rise in global temperatures, melting of glaciers, changing of rainfall and stratification. Seeing that HABs are a global phenomenon requires international understanding, so need has been expressed for generating Global HAB Status.

From last some decade's algal blooms are considered with more importance because of their impact on health and economies around the world [82]. Human modifications of the environmental activities could alter the composition of the phytoplankton community, with varied occurrence and geographic spread of bloom-forming species, also timing of phytoplankton blooms found to changed with increased window each year when blooms can develop [99–102]. Considering example of *Karenia mikimotoi* blooms which are characteristically associated with high rainfall and following low-salinity, high-nutrient run off from land [102]. As temperatures of sea surface in the North Sea have found risen more than the global average over the past 50 years [103]. Practically temperature rise initiates with increase in phytoplankton in the North Sea and North-East Atlantic. Most notably diatoms like *Pseudo-nitzschia* spp. [104, 105]. Increased blooms of *K. mikimotoi* have been seen further in north around the British Isles as compared to past and most potentially linked to changes in duration of stratification [104, 105]. On the other hand, many Dinoflagellates like *Prorocentrum* spp. have decreased in abundance in the North Sea over the last decade, as outcome of increasing temperatures conditions [104–107]. Also shellfish found in Scottish waters have witnessed a decline in the toxins linked with paralytic shellfish poisoning in the last decade [104–107]. These examples show that different species are affected in different ways by changes in environmental conditions. By integrating knowledge of biogeography keen on impact of climate change will be fundamental key for better understanding the effects of change in environment on biodiversity with intention to predict the occurrence and location of an individual bloom event. Now it's time to consider the future directions for HABs and climate change research by bringing together physiologists, ecologists, oceanographers, modelers and climate change specialists to develop consent with priority research for future HABs and climate change effects. In spite how the intensity of HABs changes, the certainty of ecosystems and their toxins creating serious physiological threat to aquatic.

14. Conclusion

The increasing incidences of toxic algal blooms have been reported at international level in the past decades. Which are contributed by various causes including eutrophication, climate changes, upwelling of oceans, including unhealthy coral reefs. All information presented here do recapitulate the current state of knowledge about HABs to better understand how change in climate affecting HABs and also coastal communities worldwide. This chapter highlights environmental factors like temperatures, nutrient and turbulence as scorable aspects for HABs. Also, it is essential to note that these type of change also have the potential ability to decrease magnitude of HABs. Not any of the effects of change in climate discuss at this point are restricted comparatively to few HAB species only. Consequently allowing for the more possibility that in at least some cases several other species could also better exploit to resulting changes in the environmental conditions. Still there is insufficient evidence to resolve this issue. Considering the prediction of outlook HABs, scientists are increasingly being asked to envisage the effects of global change in environments. Now days advances in the understanding and prophecy of HABs is changing worldwide so it's time to formulate international scientific program/committee on harmful algal blooms for providing systematic knowledge to manage and mitigate their impacts.

Author details

Ruby E. Jalgaonwala
Department of Microbiology, Shree Ramkrishna Institute of Computer Education and Applied Sciences, Surat, Gujarat, India

*Address all correspondence to: r_jalgaonwala@yahoo.co.in

IntechOpen

© 2020 The Author(s). Licensee IntechOpen. This chapter is distributed under the terms of the Creative Commons Attribution License (http://creativecommons.org/licenses/by/3.0), which permits unrestricted use, distribution, and reproduction in any medium, provided the original work is properly cited.

References

[1] Glibert P, and Pitcher, G. (eds.),. GEOHAB (Global Ecology and Oceanography of Harmful Algal Blooms Programme Science Plan. Baltimore, MA; 2001.SCOR and IOC

[2] Anderson DM, Burkholder JM, Cochlan WP, Glibert PM, Gobler CJ, Heil CA, et al. Harmful algal blooms and eutrophication: examining linkages from selected coastal regions of the United States. Harmful Algae 8.2008; 1: 39-53.

[3] Anderson DM..Approaches to monitoring, control and management of harmful algal blooms (HABs).Ocean Coast Manag. 2009; 52:7: 342-347.

[4] Berdalet E, Fleming LE, Gowen R, Davidson K, Hess P, Backer LC.et al. Marine harmful algal blooms, human health and wellbeing: challenges and opportunities in the 21st century. J. Mar. Biol. Assoc. U. K. 2016;96:1: 61-91.

[5] Yang Li, Maeda Hiroto, Yoshikawa Takeshi Zhou, Gui-qin. 'Algicidal effect of bacterial isolates of *Pedobacter* sp. against cyanobacterium *Microcystis aeruginosa*.Water Science and Engineering.2012; 5: 375-382.

[6] Nakamura N, Nakano K, Sugiura N, Matsumura M. A novel control process of cyanobacterial bloom using cyanobacteriolytic bacteria immobilized in floating biodegradable plastic carriers. Environ. Technol.2003:24: 1569-1576.

[7] Mankiewicz-Boczek J A Jaskulska, Pawełczyk J, GągałaI, Serwecinska L, Dziadek J. 'Cyanophages infection of Microcystis bloom in lowland dam reservoir of sulejow, Poland'.Microb. Ecol. 2016; 71: 315-325

[8] Pollard Peter C., Young Loretta M. 'Lake viruses lyse cyanobacteria, Cylindro spermopsisraciborskii, enhances filamentous-host dispersal in Australia. Acta Oecol.2010; 36: 114-119.

[9] Zhang Lu Gu, Lei Qian, Wei Zhu Xuexia, Wang Jun Wang, Xiaojun Zhou Yang. 'High temperature favors elimination of toxin-producing Microcystisanddegradation of microcystins by mixotrophic Ochromonas. Chemosphere. 2017: 172: 96-102.

[10] Aljerf L. Biodiversity is Key for more variety for better society. Biodiversity Int J. 2017; 1: (1): 00002.

[11] Liu Lina, Ma Chunzi, HuoShouliang, Xi Beidou, HeZhuoshi, Zhang Hanxiao, Zhang Jingtian, Xia Xinghui. 'Impacts of climate change and land use on the development of nutrient criteria. J. Hydrol .2018;563:533-542.

[12] Wood Susanna A, Borges Hugo, Puddick Jonathan, Biessy Laura, Atalah Javier, Hawes Ian, Dietrich Daniel R, Hamilton David P. Contrasting cyanobacterial communities and microcystin concentrations in summers with extreme weather events: insights into potential effects of climate change. 2017;Hydrobiologia: 785: 71-89.

[13] Paerl HW, Huisman J. Bloomslikeithot.Science. 2008;320:57-58.

[14] PaerlHW,Huisman J.Climate change:acatalyst for global expansion of harmful cyanobacterial blooms.Environ. Microbiol.Reports. 2009; 1:27-37.

[15] HuoShouliang, Ma Chunzi, Xi Beidou, GaoRutai, Deng Xiangzhen, Jiang Tiantian, He Zhuoshi, Su Jing, Wu Feng, Liu Hongliang.'Lake ecoregions and nutrient criteria development in China. Ecol. Indicat. 2014; 46: 1-10

[16] Smayda TJ. Primary production and the global epidemic of phytoplankton

blooms in the sea: a linkage? In: Novel Phytoplankton Blooms. Springer,Berlin, Heidelberg1989; 449-483.

[17] Lin Shengqin, GengMengxin, LiuXianglong, Tan Jing, Yang Hong. 'On the control of Microcystisaeruginosa and Synechococcus species using an algicidal bacterium, Stenotrophomonas F6, and itsalgicidal compoundscyclo-(Gly-Pro) and hydroquinone. J. Appl. Phycol. 2016;28: 345-355.

[18] Anderson DM, Cembella AD, Hallegraeff GM. Annu. Rev. Mar. Sci. 2012; 4:143-176

[19] Scholin C, Doucette G, Jensen S, et al. Oceanogr. 2009; 22:158-167

[20] Campbell L, Olson RJ, Sosik HM, et al. J. Phycol. 2010; 46(1):66-75.

[21] Sarmento, Hugo, Gasol, Josep M., 2012. 'Use of phytoplankton-derived dissolved organic carbon by different types of bacterioplankton. Environ. Microbiol. 14, 2348-2360).

[22] Zurawell Ronald W, Chen Huirong, Janice M Burke, Ellie E Prepas.'Hepatotoxic cyanobacteria: a review of the biological importance of microcystins in freshwater environments. J. Toxicol. Environ. Health, Part B. 2005; 8: 1-37.

[23] Gumbo R Jabulani, Ross Gina, Cloete E Thomas. 'Biological control of Microcystis dominated harmful algal blooms. Afr. J. Biotechnol. 2008;7.

[24] Nakamura N., Nakano K., Sugiura N, Matsumura M. A novel control process of cyanobacterial bloom using cyanobacteriolytic bacteria immobilized in floating biodegradable plastic carriers. Environ. Technol. 2003.24; 1569-1576.

[25] ChoiHee-jin, Kim Baik-ho, Kim Jeong-dong, Han Myung-soo.'Streptomyces neyagawaensis as a control for the hazardous biomass of *Microcystis aeruginosa* (Cyanobacteria) in eutrophic freshwaters. Biol. Contr.2005. 33; 335-343.

[26] LuoJianfei, Wang Yuan, Tang Shuishui, Liang Jianwen, Lin Weitie, LuoLixin. 'Isolation and identification of algicidal compound from Streptomyces and algicidal mechanism to Microcystisaeruginosa.PloS One 8. 2013. e76444.

[27] Kim Jeong-Dong, Kim Bora, Lee Choul-Gyun. 'Alga-lytic activity of *Pseudomonas fluorescens* against the red tide causing marine alga Heterosigmaakashiwo (Raphidophyceae). Biol. Contr. . 2007. 41; 296-303

[28] Su Feng, Jun, Shao Si Cheng, Ma Fang, Jin Suo Lu, Zhang Kai. 'Bacteriological control by Raoultella sp. R11 on growth and toxins production of *Microcystis aeruginosa*. Chem. Eng. J. , 2016.293; 139-150.

[29] Imai I, Kido T, Yoshinaga I, Ohgi K, Nagai S. Isolation of Microcystis-Killer Bacterium Agrobacterium Vitis from the Biofilm on the Surface of the Water Plant EgeriaDensa. Kalliopi A. Pagou, 2010; 150

[30] Pal Mili, Pal Smita, QureshiAsifa, Sangolkar L N. 'Perspective of Cyanobacterial Harmful Algal Bloom (HAB) Mitigation: Microcystis Toxin Degradation by Bacterial Consortia. 2018.

[31] Shunyu Shi, Liu Yongding, ShenYinwu, Li Genbao, Li Dunhai.'Lysis of *Aphanizomenon flos-aquae* (Cyanobacterium) by a bacterium *Bacillus cereus*. Biol. Contr. 2006.39; 345-351

[32] Pei Haiyan, Hu Wenrong.'Lytic characteristics and identification of two alga-lysing bacterial strains. J. Ocean Univ. China. 2006; 5: 368-374.

[33] Zhang Danyang, Qian Ye, Zhang Fuxing, Shao Xueping, Fan Yongxiang, Zhu Xiaoying, Li Yinan, Yao Luming, Tian Yun, ZhengTianling. Flocculating properties and potential of *Halobacillus* sp. strain H9 for the mitigation of *Microcystis aeruginosa* blooms. Chemosphere. 2019;218:138-146.

[34] Suttle Curtis A. Ecological, evolutionary, and geochemical consequences of viral infection of cyanobacteria and eukaryotic algae. Viral ecology . 2000:1: 247-296.

[35] Short, Steven M.The ecology of viruses that infect eukaryotic algae. Environ. Microbiol.2012:14: 2253-2271.

[36] Long, Andrew Milam. Persistence of Algal Viruses and Cyanophages in Freshwater Environments.2017

[37] Rashidan KK, Bird DF. Role of predatory bacteria in the termination of a cyanobacterial bloom.Microb.Ecol. 2001; 41: 97-105.

[38] Shapiro Joseph, Lamarra Vincent A, Lynch Michael.'Biomanipulation: an Ecosystem Approach to Lake Restoration.1975

[39] Loai A,Nuha A. Mercury toxicity: ecological features of organic phase of mercury in biota-Part 1 arc, 3. AOICS. MS. ID, p. 157. Org InorgChem Sci.2018; 3.

[40] Sun Rui, Sun Pengfei, ZhangJianhong, Esquivel-Elizondo Sofia, Wu Yonghong. Microorganisms-based methods for harmful algal blooms control: a review. Bioresour.Technol. 2018; 248: 12-20.

[41] Urrutia-Cordero, PabloMattias, K Ekvall Hansson, Lars-Anders. 'Responses of cyanobacteria to herbivorous zooplankton across predator regimes: who mows the bloom? Freshw.Biol. 2015; 60: 960-972.

[42] Urrutia-Cordero P, Ekvall M K, Hansson LA.Controlling harmful cyanobacteria: taxa-specific responses of cyanobacteria to grazing by large-bodied Daphnia in a biomanipulation scenario.PloS One.2016; 11:4.

[43] Jia Yong, Han Guomin, Wang Congyan, GuoPeng, Jiang Wenxin, Li Xiaona, TianXingjun.'The efficacy and mechanisms of fungal suppression of freshwater harmful algal bloom species. J. Hazard Mater. 2010.183; 176-181.

[44] SalimSina, BosmaRouke, Vermu€e, Marian H, WijffelsRene H. 'Harvesting of microalgae by bio-flocculation. J. Appl. Phycol. 2011. 23; 849-855.

[45] Moore SK, Mantua NJ, Hickey BM, Trainer VL. Recent trends in paralytic shellfish toxins in Puget Sound, relationships to climate, and capacity for prediction of toxic events. Harmful Algae. 2009; 8:3, 463-477.

[46] Gobler CJ, Doherty OM, Griffith AW, Hattenrath-Lehmann TK, Kang Y, Litaker W. Ocean warming since 1982 has expanded the niche of toxic algal blooms in the North Atlantic and North Pacific oceans. Prod Nat. Acad. Sci. 2017; 114: 4975-4980.

[47] Griffith AW, Doherty OM, Gobler CJ. Ocean warming along temperate western boundaries of the Northern Hemisphere promotes an expansion of *Cochlodiniumpolykrikoides*blooms. Prod. R. Soc. B. 2019; 286 (1904): 20190340

[48] Hallegraeff GM. Ocean climate change, phytoplankton community responses, and harmful algal blooms: a formidable predictive challenge. J. Phycol. 2010;46:2, 220-235.

[49] Colin SP, Dam HG. Latitudinal differentiation in the effects of the toxic dinoflagellate *Alexandrium*spp. on the feeding and reproduction of populations of the copepod *Acartiahudsonic*a. Harmful Algae. 2002; 113-125.

[50] Bricelj VM, Connell L, Konoki K, MacQuarrie SP, Scheuer T, Catterall WA, Trainer VL. Sodium channel mutation leading to saxitoxin resistance in clams increases risk of PSP. Nature.2005; 434: 763.

[51] O'Neil JM, Davis T W, Burford MA, Gobler C J. The rise of harmful cyanobacteria blooms: The potential roles of eutrophication and climate change Harmful Algae. 2012; 14: 313-334.

[52] Onderka M, Correlations between several environmental factors affecting the bloom events of cyanobacteria in Liptovska Mara reservoir (Slovakia)—A simple regression model. Ecological Modelling.2007; 209:412-416

[53] Chapra SC, Surface Water-quality Modeling, The McGraw-Hill, New York.1997; 526.

[54] Preece E P, Hardy FJ, Moore BC, Bryan M. A review of microcystin detections in Estuarine and Marine waters: Environmental implications and human health risk, Harmful Algae.2017; 61: 31-45.

[55] Smith, VH, Low nitrogen to phosphorus ratios favor dominance by blue-green algae in lake phytoplankton, Science. 1983; 221:669-671.

[56] Silbergeld EK, Grattan L, Oidach, D, Morris JG, Pfiesteria: harmful algal blooms as Indicator of Human: Ecosystem interactions. Environmental Research Section A. 2000; 82: 97-105.

[57] Semeneh M, Dehairs F, Elskens M, Baumann MEM, Kopezynska EE, Lancelot C, Goeyens L. Nitrogen uptake regime and phytoplankton community structure in the Atlantic and Indian Sectors of the southern ocean. Journal of Marine Systems.1998; 17: 159-177.

[58] Peperzak L, Climate change and harmful algal blooms in the North Sea. Acta.Oecologica. 2003; 24: S139-S144.

[59] Zingone A and Enevoldsen HO. The diversity of harmful algal blooms: challenge for science and management. Ocean and Coastal Management. 2000; 43;725-748..

[60] Carmichael WW, Boyer GL. Health impacts from cyanobacteria harmful algae blooms: Implications for the North American Great Lakes Harmful Algae. 2016; 54: 194-212.

[61] HARRNESS Harmful Algal Research and Response: A National Environmental Science Strategy 2005-2015 (edsRamsdell, J. S., Anderson, D.M., Glibert, P.M.,) Ecological Society of America, Washington DC, 2005; 96.

[62] Fleming LE, Easom J, Baden D, Rowan A, Levin B. Emerging harmful algal blooms and human health: Pfiesteria and related organisms. ToxicolPatho. 1999; 27: 573-581

[63] Sharma GS, Upwelling off the Southwest coast of India. Indian Journal of Marine Sciences.1978; 7: 209-218.

[64] RamanaTV, Reddy MPM, Upwelling and sinking in the Arabian sea along Dakshina Kannada coast. Environment & Ecology.2006; 24: 379-384.

[65] Waldichuk M, Marine biotoxins and human activity. Marine Pollution Bulletin.1990; 21: 215-216.

[66] McQuatters-Gollop A, Raitsos DE, Edwards M, Pradhan Y, Mee LD, Lavender SJ and Attrill MJ. A long-term chlorophyll data set reveals regime shift in North Sea phytoplankton biomass unconnected to nutrient trends. *Limnol. Oceanogr.*2007; 52:2, 635-648.

[67] Edwards M and Richardson AJ. Impact of climate change on marine pelagic phenology and trophic mismatch. *Nature* 2004;430(7002): 881-884..

[68] Davidson K, Gowen RJ, Tett P, Bresnan E, Harrison PJ, McKinney A,

Milligan S, Mills DK, Silke J. and Crooks AM. Harmful Algal Blooms? How Strong is the evidence that nutrient ratios and forms influence their occurrence. *Estuarine Coast.Shelf Sci.* 2012;115:399-413.

[69] Turley C, Findlay HS., Mangi S, Ridgwell A and Schmidt DN. *CO2 and ocean acidification in Marine Climate Change Ecosystem Linkages Report Card 2009*. (Eds. Baxter JM., Buckley P.J. and Frost M.T.) Online Science Reviews.2009 25. www.mccip.org.uk/elr/acidification.

[70] Doney SC, Ruckelshaus M, Duffy JE, Barry JP, Chan F, English CA, Galindo HM, Grebmeier, JM, Hollowed AB, Knowlton N, Polovina J, Rabalais NN, Sydeman WJ, Talley LD. Climate change impacts on marine ecosystems. Annu. Rev. Mar. Sci. 2012;4, 11-37.

[71] Hoegh-Guldberg O, Cai R, Poloczanska ES, Brewer PG, Sundby S, Hilmi K, Fabry VJ, Jung S. The Ocean. In: Barros VR, Field CB, Dokken DJ, Mastrandrea MD, Mach KJ, Bilir TE, Chatterjee M, Ebi KL, Estrada YO, Genova RC, Girma B, Kissel ES, Levy AN. MacCracken S, Mastrandrea PR,White L. (Eds.), Climate Change 2014; Impacts, Adaptation, and Vulnerability. Part B: Regional Aspects. Contribution of Working Group II to the Fifth Assessment Report of the Intergovernmental Panel on Climate Change. Cambridge University Press, Cambridge, United Kingdom and New York, NY, USA,1655-1731.

[72] Donelson JM, Munday PL, McCormick MI, Pitcher CR. Rapid transgenerational acclimation of a tropical reef fish to climate change. Nat. Clim. Change 2,2011;30-32.

[73] Asch RG. Climate change and decadal shifts in the phenology of larval fishes in the California Current ecosystem. Proc. Natl. Acad. Sci. U. S. A. 2015;112; E40,65-74.

[74] Talmage SC, Gobler CJ. The effects of elevated carbon dioxide concentrations on the metamorphosis, size, and survival of larval hard clams (*Mercenaria mercenaria*), bay scallops (*Argopecten irradians*), and eastern oysters (*Crassostrea virginica*). Limnol. Oceanogr. 2009;54, 2072-2080.

[75] Waldbusser GG, Salisbury JE. Ocean acidification in the coastal zone from an organism's perspective: multiple system parameters, frequency domains, and habitats. Annu. Rev.Mar. Sceince. 2014; 6, 221-247.

[76] Burge CA, Mark Eakin C, Friedman CS, Froelich B, Hershberger PK, Hofmann EE, Petes LE, Prager KC, Weil E, Willis BL, Ford SE, Harvell CD. Climate change influences on marine infectious diseases: implications for management and society. Annu. Rev. Mar. Sci. 2014; 6, 249-277.

[77] Breitburg D, Levin LA, Oschlies A, Gregoire M, Chavez FP, Conley DJ, Garcon V, Gilbert D, Gutierrez D, Isensee K, Jacinto GS, Limburg KE, Montes I, Naqvi SWA, Pitcher GC, Rabalais NN, Roman MR, Rose KA, Seibel BA, Telszewski M , Yasuhara M, Zhang J. Declining oxygen in the global ocean and coastal waters. Science . 2018; 359.

[78] Doney SC, Balch WM, Fabry VJ, Feely RA. Ocean acidification: a critical emerging problem for the ocean sciences. Oceanography. 2009;22 :4, 16-25.

[79] Paerl HW, Paul VJ. Climate change: links to global expansion of harmful cyanobacteria. Water Res. 2012; 46:5, 1349-1363.

[80] Raven JA, Beardall J. CO_2 concentrating mechanisms and

environmental change. Aquat. Bot. 2014; 118, 24-37.

[81] Beardall J, Stojkovic S, Larsen S. Living in a high CO_2 world: impacts of global climate change on marine phytoplankton. Plant Ecol Divers. 2009; 2: 2, 191-205.

[82] Anderson CR, Moore SK, Tomlinson MC, Silke J and Cusack CK. Living with harmful algal blooms in a changing world: strategies for modelling and mitigating their effects in coastal marine ecosystems. In Coastal and Marine Hazards, Risks, and Disasters. 2015.Ed. by J. F. Shroder, J. T. Ellis, and D. J. Sherman. Elsevier, The Netherlands.

[83] Berdalet E, Fleming LE, Gowen R, Davidson K, Hess P, Backer LC, Moore SK *et al.* Marine harmful algal blooms, human health and wellbeing: challenges and opportunities in the 21st century. Journal of the Marine Biological Association of the United Kingdom, 2016;96, 61-91.

[84] Giordano M, Beardall J, Raven JA. CO2 concentrating mechanisms in algae: mechanisms, environmental modulation, and evolution. Annu. Rev. Plant Biol. 2005;56, 99-131

[85] Wallace RB, Baumann H, Grear JS, Aller RC, Gobler CJ. Coastal ocean acidification: the other eutrophication problem. Invited Feature Article in Estuar. Coast. Shelf Sci. 2014.148,1-13.

[86] Valiela, I. Global Coastal Change. 2009.John Wiley & Sons.

[87] Baumann H , Doherty O. Decadal changes in the world's coastal latitudinal temperature gradients. 2013 PLoS One 8, e67596.

[88] O'Neil JM, Davis TW, Burford MA, Gobler CJ. The rise of harmful cyanobacteria blooms: the potential roles of eutrophication and climate change. Harmful Algae. 2012; 14, 313-334.

[89] Gobler CJ, Baumann H. Hypoxia and acidification in ocean ecosystems: coupled dynamics and effects on marine life. Biol. Lett. 2016; 12,98.

[90] Green MA, Waldbusser GG, Reilly SL, Emerson K, O'Donnell S. Death by dissolution: sediment saturation state as a mortality factor for juvenile bivalves. Limnol. Oceanogr. 2009;54, 1037-1047.

[91] Talmage SC, Gobler CJ. Effects of past, present, and future ocean carbon dioxide concentrations on the growth and survival of larval shellfish. Proc. Natl. Acad. Sci. 2010;107, 17246-17251.

[92] Bricelj VM, Connell L, Konoki K, MacQuarrie SP, Scheuer T, Catterall WA, Trainer VL. Sodium channel mutation leading to saxitoxin resistance in clams increases risk of PSP. Nature.2005;434,763-767.

[93] Burford MA, Carey CC, Hamilton DP, Huisman J, Paerl HW, Wood SA, Wulff A. Perspective: advancing the research agenda for improving understanding of cyanobacteria in a future of global change. Harmful Algae .2019;91, 101601.

[94] Suikkanen S, Pulina S, Engstrom-Ost J, Lehtiniemi M, Lehtinen S, Brutemark A. Climate change and eutrophication induced shifts in northern summer plankton communities. 2013. PLoS One 8,6.

[95] Visser PM, Verspagen JMH, Sandrini G, Stal LJ, Matthijs HCP, Davis TW, Paerl HW, Huisman J. How rising CO_2 and global warming may stimulate harmful cyanobacterial blooms. Harmful Algae. 2016;54, 145-159.

[96] Vahtera E, Conley DJ, Gustafsson BG, Kuosa H, Pitkanen H, Savchuk OP, Tamminen T, Viitasalo M, Voss M, Wasmund N, Wulff F. Internal ecosystem feedbacks enhance nitrogen-fixing cyanobacteria blooms and complicate management in the Baltic Sea. Ambio 2007; 36,2-3, 186-194.

[97] Nazeer M, Wong MS, Nichol JE. A new approach for the estimation of phytoplankton cell counts associated with algal blooms. Sci. Total Environ. 2017; 590, 125-138.

[98] Yariv J, Hestrin S. Toxicity of the extracellular phase of *Prymnesium parvum* cultures. Microbiology. 1961; 24, 165-175.

[99] Lee K, Ishimatsu A, Sakaguchi H, Oda, T. Cardiac output during exposure to Chattonella marina and environmental hypoxia in yellowtail (*Seriola quinqueradiata*). Mar. Biol. 2003; 142, 391-397.

[100] Berdalet E, Fleming LE, Gowen R, Davidson K, Hess P, Backer LC, Moore SK. *et al.* Marine harmful algal blooms, human health and wellbeing: challenges and opportunities in the 21st century. Journal of the Marine Biological Association of the United Kingdom.2016;96,61-91

[101] Henson SA, Cole HS, Hopkins J, Martin AP and Yool A. Detection of climate change-driven trends in phytoplankton phenology. Global Change Biology. 2017; 1-11.

[102] Moore SK, Mantua N J and Salathé EP. Past trends and future scenarios for environmental conditions favouring the accumulation of paralytic shellfish toxins in Puget Sound shellfish. Harmful Algae. 2011; 10,521-529.

[103] Barnes MK, Tilstone GH, Smyth TJ, Widdicombe CE, Glo¨el J, Robinson C, Kaiser J. *et al*. Drivers and effects of *Karenia mikimotoi* blooms in the western English Channel. Progress in Oceanography. 2015. 137; 456-469.

[104] Hobday AJ, Pecl GT. Identification of global marine hotspots: sentinels for change and vanguards for adaptation action. Reviews in Fish Biology and Fisheries. 2014;24, 415-425.

[105] Bresnan E, Davidson K, Edwards M, Fernand L, Gowen R, Hall A and Kennington K. 2013. Impacts of climate change on harmful algal blooms. MCCIP Science Review. 2013; 236-243.

[106] Hinder S L, Hays GC, Edwards M, Roberts EC, Walne AW and Gravenor MB. Changes in marine dinoflagellate and diatom abundance under climate change. Nature Climate Change. 2012; 2, 271-275.

[107] Hannah L, Midgley GF, Millar D. Climate change-integrated conservation strategies. Global Ecology and Biogeography, 2002; 11, 485-495.

Chapter 5

On the Value of Conducting and Communicating Counterfactual Exercise: Lessons from Epidemiology and Climate Science

Gary Yohe

Abstract

Modeling is a critical part of crafting adaptive and mitigative responses to existential threats like the COVID-19 coronavirus and climate change. The United Nations, in its efforts to promote 17 Sustainable Development Goals, has recognized both sources of risk as cross-cutting themes in part because both expose the wide list of social and economic challenges facing the globe. Here, evidence is presented to encourage the research communities of both topics to work together within and across the boundaries of their international infrastructures, because their modeling approaches, their social objectives, and their desire effectively to bring rigorous science to opinion writers and decision-makers are so similar. Casting decision analysis in terms of tolerable risk, conducting policy relevant counterfactual experiments, participating in organized model comparison exercises, and other research strategies are all part of their common scientific toolsets. These communities also share a responsibility to continue to hone their communication skills so that their insights are more easily understood by the public at large—skills that are also essential to protect their science from attack by groups and individuals who purposefully espouse their own misguided or deliberately misstated perspectives and/or, sometimes, their own corrupted personal agendas.

Keywords: risk, coronavirus, COVID-19, climate change, integrated modeling, model projections, counterfactual experiments, model comparisons, tolerable risk, value of information, sustainable development goals

1. Introduction

There are currently 17 United Nations Sustainable Development Goals, the so-called SDGs, whose content was updated on the United Nations Website [1]. In its preface, the then current (July 1, 2020) collection of SDGs were presented as

> *"the blueprint to achieve a better and more sustainable future for all. They address the global challenges we face, including those related to poverty, inequality, climate change, environmental degradation, peace and justice."*

They are "a call for action by all countries—poor, rich, and middle-income—to promote prosperity while protecting the planet." The SDGs thereby recognize issues that revolve around trying to develop sustainably in a holistic global sense, but that does not mean that they miss the more microscale and pervasive issues where the devil lies in the details. That list is long and growing: ending poverty, building economic growth, and confronting social needs like access to quality education, quality health care, social protection against ordinary and extreme risks, quality opportunities and security in employment, personal security everywhere, food security, promoting equity and justice, and much more. In other words, it is like promoting the public welfare however it is as measured and monitored.

All of this must happen in the context of growing direct and indirect risks from ordinary environmental pollution, extraordinary and sometimes existential risks from climate change, as well as sudden and unrelenting risks from pandemics like COVID-19. While the United Nations asserts accurately that SDGs can "provide a critical framework for COVID-19 recovery," it is also true that pandemics and climate change can expose the extent to which the progress toward achieving any SDGs has not been as significant as one might have hoped or even expected [2]. Both are color-blind, and neither is impressed by social or economic status. In one way or another, both can strike anyone or everyone living anywhere or everywhere.

Coronavirus pandemics and climate change are therefore a cross-cutting theme of enormous concern across the full range of sustainability issues. The very organization of the SDGs shows that this truth has been recognized by the United Nations. "COVID-19 Response" boxes are highlighted close to the tops of the presentations of all 17 of the goals. In addition, climate change has been sustainable development goal for some time; SDG-13, to be specific. Labeled "Take urgent action to combat climate change and its impacts", this goal identifies three critical "targets" for action by decision-makers of all stripes: "strengthen resilience and adaptive capacity to climate-related hazards and natural disasters in all countries, integrate climate change measures into national policies, strategies and planning, and improve education, awareness-raising and human and institutional capacity on climate change mitigation, adaptation, impact reduction and early warning." In addition, it is important to note that the COVID-19 Response Box for SDG-13 calls for: investments that accelerate decarbonization and promote sustainable solutions to energy market distortions, recognition of all climate risks, the creation of green jobs and vibrant employment markets within sustainable and inclusive growth, persistent transitions to more resilient societies that are fair to all, and reliance on international cooperation to most effectively respond to the challenges of climate change, pandemics, and all of the SDGs.

Integrated models are one of the primary tools through which rigorous science can be inserted into deliberations of actions whose goals (social values and costs calibrated in whatever metric is appropriate) extend well into the future—a year or more for viral pandemics up to a century or two for climate change [3–5]. They are, therefore, a means by which decision-makers who are charged with promoting sustainable futures can apply rational and rigorous risk management procedures to their challenges. They are, as well, the means by which decision-makers can organize their thoughts around what emerging data and new science are revealing about the relative likelihoods and fundamental characteristics of possible futures.

This is particularly important because climate change impacts and global pandemics have both shown the tendency of, as put in Flyvbjerg [6], "regressing to the tail" over time. In words, both have shown patterns of never having offered their worst possible outcome; that is, things can always get worse, and there is no reason to believe, ceteris paribus, that that will not always be the case. Technically, this is possible when the tails of distributions are so fat that the mean and variance, among other moments, do not exist; generalized Pareto distributions display this characteristic. **Table 1** in [6] provides a list of the top 10 phenomena (by "tail thickness")

	Number of billion-dollar disasters (average per year)	Associated costs (average per year)	Associated fatalities (average per year)
1980s (1980–1989)	28 (2.8)	$127.7B ($12.8B)	2808 (281)
1990s (1990–1999)	52 (5.2)	$269.6B ($27.0B)	2173 (217)
2000s (2000–2009)	59 (5.9)	$510.3B ($51.0B)	3051 (305)
2010s (2010–2019)	119 (11.9)	$802.0B ($80.2B)	5212 (521)
Last 5 years (2015–2019)	69 (13.8)	$531.7B ($106.3B)	3862 (772)
Last 3 years (2017–2019)	44 (14.7)	$456.7B ($152.2B)	3569 (1190)
Overall (1980–2019)	**258 (6.5)**	**$1.754.6B ($43.9B)**	**13,249 (331)**

Source: [7].

Table 1.
Billion dollar disasters from climate and weather across the US.

and their calibration metric: earthquakes (Richter Scale max), cybercrime (financial loss), wars (per capita death rate), *pandemics (deaths),* IT procurement (percentage cost overrun), *floods (water volume),* bankruptcies (percentage of firms per industry), *forest fires (area burned),* Olympic Games (percentage cost overrun), and blackouts (number of customers affected). Italics, here, put three of the top 10 squarely within the focus of this discussion.

More specifically and less technically, the US National Oceanographic and Atmospheric Administration has observed dramatically increasing trends in the number of billion dollar national catastrophes and the fraction of each year's list that can be attributed to anthropogenic climate change [7]. Incredible episodes of enormous and increasing amounts of rain in one place over consecutive days have, for example, begun to occur because climate change has moved steering wind patterns, such as hurricanes like Harvey in 2017 and Florence in 2018, to suddenly not know where to go. Rapid successions of storms that do not diminish in intensity are now more common around the world because subsurface waters are historically hot in the spawning oceans. Damage records are meant to be broken, but Maria broke the bank for the third storm on the same track in less than one month in 2017. Fires from north to south across all of 2019 brought California more burned area and property than any time in history. **Table 1** shows that these and other climate and weather disasters averaged $80.2 billion with 521 lives lost in the last decade; over the past 2015–2019, the averages were $106.3 billion with 772 lives lost. In addition, COVID-19 indirectly caused economic damages in the US early in its course that were larger than the Great Depression, at least in terms of the rates of unemployment and economic loss [8].

In the face of these kinds of threats, what are the response options that need modeling support? Mitigation is one—slow the pace of the risk so that the spread of the consequences (symptoms) does not overwhelm social capacities to respond and adapt. That is, "flatten the curve" by social distancing, wearing masks, testing, tracking, and quarantining, sheltering at home, locking down nonessential economic activity (that cannot be done remotely), etc. Or, invest in reducing the emissions of greenhouse gases and decarbonizing the macroeconomy and thereby reduce the likelihoods of significant harm. Shrinking the tails of the most extreme consequences is another—invest in new adaptations and response actions (therapeutics and vaccines) that can eradicate the explosive nature of potential outbreaks. That is, invest in the development and distribution of new ways to minimize the ravages of the virus or prevent it from invading human beings. Or, invest in forward-looking or responsive adaptations that reduce the consequences of climate change.

These are abstract issues, of course, but confronting them is critical for efforts to manage the controversies that surround action decisions—controversies that can be born of misinterpretations of modeling results and applications, deliberate distortions designed by unscrupulous agents to promulgate false perceptions, exaggerated foci that obscure social, economic, and political complexities, as well as unfounded assertions that attack the integrity of sound scientific practices [9]. These controversies make it clear that modelers need to work continually to improve the models that they employ to answer comparative policy-relevant questions and to communicate their results effectively. They therefore lead to the conclusion that efforts manage climate and health risks need to include exercising novel and traditional methods for improve modeling practices, the understanding of modeling structures, and the communication of modeling results. These efforts are just as important carefully taking account of more widely expressed modeling concerns: assumptions, bias, framing, and immodesty.

Here, similarities and synergies between epidemiologic models of pandemics like COVID-19 and integrated models of longer-term risks from climate change provide a context for productive suggestions about how to structure these efforts—strategies like policy-relevant counterfactual exercises, structural model comparison experiments, value of information calculations, out-of-scale reality checks, and model updating are all highlighted, here. The goal is to offer some thoughts about how these research activities can support sound communication for sustainable development. This is especially important because systemic social and economic inadequacies have been laid bare by the COVID-19 pandemic and will be exacerbated by the growing global climate crisis [10].

Section 2 provides some context by reviewing briefly the early history of modeling the COVID-19 coronavirus with reference to the needs and challenges of that enterprise—representing the virus, the consequences of exposure, the implications of responding or not, the need for intervening in the workings of the economy, and so on. Section 3 frames the issue of improving the production and communication of modeling results in a skeptical, frightened, and uncertain world. Tools like methods to identify thresholds of tolerable risk, counterfactual modeling exercises, structured model comparisons, and value of information calculations are introduced and discussed briefly with regard to practicality, context, and experience. Concluding and synthetic remarks occupy the last section.

2. The early history of modeling COVID-19 in support of decision-makers

Even as the COVID-19 pandemic evolved through the beginning of its course in early 2020, discussions were underway around the world about preparing for the longer term. In the US, they were based on painful lessons learned from a response often characterized by delays, inefficiencies, a lack of federal coordination, and a pervasive skepticism about the science. Elsewhere, lessons were sometimes more timely and less painful, but the number of cases and deaths continued to climb daily nearly everywhere. Some of these lessons were, of course, obvious. Containment and mitigation can have a positive effect. Creating effective diagnostic tests is difficult. It is even harder to produce and distribute high-quality tests and personal protection equipment in the quantities required. Fast-tracking new therapeutics might become productive, but the real hope probably lies in creating a new and effective vaccine as quickly as possible amidst uncertainties about the character of immunity from the virus and the distribution of the vaccine, itself. Other lessons were more obscure, but one seemed to touch nearly every point where action decisions were required or anticipated: informative modeling results are difficult to communicate and *they are easy to criticize because coping with apparently incomprehensible uncertainty is not a widely distributed skill*.

In the US and many other countries, virus impact projection models played a prominent role in political and public discussions about what it would mean to "flatten the curve" of new COVID-19 infections. Such models were essential to provide insight into the enormous scope of the problem. They became critical tools for planning the timing of efforts to return societies and economies to pre-COVID-19 activities without doing more damage [11]. Many, however, did not provide necessary information on projected uncertainties in the course and severity of the virus, the key determinants of these uncertainties, the information required to reduce them, and/or best practices in conveying all of this to decision-makers, their constituents, and their bosses [12].

As a result, it was challenging for the primary "clients" of modelers' products (decision-makers across governments of all scales, businesses large and small, religious organizations, public and private foundations, individuals, etc.) to be comfortable with the idea of assigning likelihoods or even degrees of confidence to their various outputs—that is, to the varieties of possible futures born of processing results from multiple modeling efforts and/or accommodating deliberately created probability distributions from a single model.

For example, when faced in February with five model results and a consulting firm that produced a "composite" estimate of questionable value, Governor Cuomo of New York ultimately picked the model that produced the projections of hospital demand that matched the maximum number of hospital beds and intensive care beds that his state could make available. The state had determined that it could essentially double its total capacity across its 12 geographic regions (53,000 beds including 26,000 intensive care beds) by manipulating equipment on hand, converting non-treatment rooms into patient rooms, and organizing hundreds of hospitals into a single administrative entity—just barely adequate against the middle scenario that had estimated a maximum need of roughly 120,000 beds including 60,000 ICU beds [13]. Why did he ignore the extreme possibilities? Not because they were totally implausible. "Why waste time", he had thought, "worrying about the two extreme scenarios that would surely overwhelm the entire state hospital system regardless of what we did?"

Governor Cuomo's predicament was a reflection of at least three phenomena that define the communication context of modelers' best efforts. First of all, modeling is an essential tool for understanding the likely outcomes of different strategies for responding to a fast-moving global pandemic like COVID-19 [11] or, as consistently noted by the Intergovernmental Panel on Climate Change (IPCC), a slow but accelerating stressor like climate change [14–18]. Indeed, any phenomenon that produces large, growing, and widespread risk over time can threaten the planet's ability to develop sustainably. However, developing and refining models for any of these threats are very difficult. In most cases, the most useful modeling necessarily involves multidisciplinary collaboration between epidemiologists (climate scientists, natural scientists, etc.), public health experts, mathematicians, statisticians, and economists—the sort of collaboration that cannot be built in a few days and is not possible at all without personal buy-in by willing participants.

Secondly, appropriately displaying uncertainty bands around "best-practice" projections increases the public communication challenges in engaging decision-makers. Such relative likelihood information must be communicated in a responsible, accurate, and understandable way, but also one that minimizes the risk that those who are uncomfortable with probabilistic information will simply throw up their hands and conclude that "Scientists do not know what they are talking about." Care needs to be taken, as well, in communicating the value of looking at the tails of the distributions of results. Speaking of low likelihood extreme events of, for example, very bad outcomes cannot irresponsibly be labeled "fear mongering" if those events have very large consequences. Risk is, after all, the product of likelihood and confidence; and it can be comparatively large and therefore worthy of careful consideration if either factor is large.

Finally, model results and their underlying science are vulnerable to attack by skeptics and partisans who are generally suspicious or, more problematically, possess political agendas [9]. This is particularly concerning when projections honestly change markedly from week to week as new information from around the world becomes available and when results from individual models diverge markedly. It is frequently difficult to explain to decision-makers why they should accept projections of any single, well-described policy scenario when its projected outcomes can differ so widely from model to model. These differences do not mean that any given model or ensemble of models is completely untrustworthy; they mean that the modelers are trying to describe the full range of possible futures as well as they can from difference perspectives of natural and/or human processes. Of course, it was the former impression that undermined trust in published models of COVID-19 course projections, particularly after the "no policy" projections of the Imperial College London model [19] received such widespread public and political attention as a baseline description of the reality and seriousness of the health risks.

Some of the multiple efforts to understand the intricacies of the behavior this virus that blossomed well into the summer are covered briefly in [20]. Pei, et al. [21] is notable in this collection as perhaps the first rigorous counterfactual exercise; it was designed at Columbia University to answer the important question at the time: What would have happened if non-therapeutic interventions in the US had started earlier than March 15? According to their calculations, starting only a week earlier, on March 8, would have saved approximately 35,000 U.S. lives [a 55% reduction (95% CI: 46–62%)] and avoided more than 700,000 COVID-19 cases [a 62% reduction (95% CI: 55–68%)] through May 3. Starting interventions another week earlier could have reduced deaths by more than 50,000 (around 83%) with cases falling proportionately. There were no do-overs, of course. The US was well on its chosen pathway by May, but there would be chances to change course if (not really when) the virus came back. It follows that these published answers to an important "What if we had done X?" question should have become strong reasons to express urgency for renewed action if conditions began to deteriorate sometime downstream. They did with little prompt response, but that is another story.

Before then, on June 8th, *Nature* published two different counterfactual studies that considered the opposite question while including other countries. Hsiang et al. [22] focused on six countries (China, France, Iran, Italy, the UK, and the US) where travel restrictions, social distancing, canceled events, and lockdown orders had been imposed. Their calculations, supported by an estimate that COVID-19 cases had doubled roughly every 2 days starting in mid-January, suggested that as many as 62 million confirmed cases (385,000 in the US) had been prevented or delayed through the first week in April by the actions that had been implemented.

DOI: http://dx.doi.org/10.5772/intechopen.93639

Meanwhile, Flaxman et al. [23] focused on 11 European countries on the same question. They worked with estimated viral reproduction rates between 3 and 5; that is, every infected person was expected to infect between 3 and 5 other people per unit of time (the so called "serial interval"—estimated for COVID-19 in Du et al. [24] to be roughly 4 days). They estimated that a total of 3.1 million deaths (plus or minus 350,000) were avoided through the end of April, and they found that only lockdowns produced statistically significant effects on the number of estimated cases.

Were these high numbers really physically plausible? Yes, but they must be interpreted in their complete and proper contexts. The reported scenarios of all of the virus studies only described trajectories for cases and deaths that could be attributed to COVID-19 given alternative assumptions about the form and timing of any policy or behavioral response. As a result, each imagined path also involved a course of policy intervention that had other economic and social effects that were not captured in the analysis [25]. Ultimately, it is up to decision-makers to ponder the implicit trade-offs between these intertwined impacts, to ferret out joint levels of tolerable risk—a judgment they cannot be made honestly without acknowledging what the science says. Unfortunately, the president of the US called [21] a "political hit job" [26]. Even more troubling, conservatives more generally greeted coronavirus models with the same "detest" that they have voiced about climate models [27].

It is important to note that modeling of the COVID-19 coronavirus was not the first time in recent history that widespread modeling played a significant role in framing global and national responses and communicating their social value. Shortly after the discovery of the Ebola viral disease (EVD) in West Africa, modelers around the world began to work to inform decision-makers about the regional and global risks. Chretien et al. [28] chronical 125 models from 66 publications of trends in EVD transmission (in 41 publications), effectiveness of various responses (in 29), forecasts (projections in 29), spreading patterns across regions and countries (15), the phylogenetics of the disease (9), and the feasibility of vaccine trials (2).

Their takeaway messages include some points that are salient, here. Taken in their order, they began by highlighting the need to understand the influence of increasing awareness of severe infections across various levels of community, to improve the ability to sustain that awareness, and to include its manifestations in the models. They also argued strongly for model coordination and systematic comparison of modeling results to better understand the major sources of uncertainty and how models accommodate their inclusion. Indeed, they encouraged the adoption of ensemble approaches with transparent architectures for easier communication. Finally, drawing on Yozwiak et al. [29], they stress the importance of making data and results available more quickly and effectively to all interested parties. These efforts were part of an enormously successful global response organized by the World Health Organization (WHO) and the US Centers for Disease Control and Prevention (CDC), among others. When EVD subsided in November of 2015, 28,000 cases and 11,000 deaths had been reported in Guinea, Liberia, and Sierra Leone. In the US, the final tally was 4 cases diagnosed among 11 cases recorded and 2 deaths [30].

3. Dealing more effectively with the challenge of communicating new information

The three phenomena noted above are daunting, but the experiences of the virus modelers whose work was criticized unjustly is evidence of the importance of skilled communication that anticipates the dangers of inserting quality science into a political arena. Moreover, of course, improved communication depends in large measure on better modeling—taken one model at a time or together as informative ensemble.

These challenges bring to mind several strategies that can be productive in improving the workings of the models and the supporting of more confidence in their results. Before they are discussed, however, it can be productive to organize thoughts around more practical issues that can productively be considered when framing a complete research plan from creation to dissemination:

1. Models should be designed to produce results that are calibrated in terms of the welfare metrics that decision-makers and/or the public are using to compare possible futures against society's implicit levels of *tolerable risk*.

2. Modelers should expend some significant efforts using their models to answer "What if?" questions that are actually being asked by decision-makers and members of the public (presumably in reference to tolerable risk). What would happen if we did nothing? Or if we did that? Or something else? What variables are most important in determining trends or variability in the answers to these questions? *These are challenges that call for organized counterfactual explorations* to consolidate insights from studies like [21–23].

3. Even more specifically, modelers can find profit in organizing themselves to examine systematically why different models can produce different results. Are the reasons structural, a matter of different assumptions, reflections of different sensitivities to exogenous drivers, and so on? Organizing and participating in *carefully designed model comparison experiments*, conducted as part of routine model development using representations of uncertainty against tolerable risk levels, can build capacity to communicate with some transparency and intuition why the results of a model or an ensemble of models are true and why they should be taken seriously.

4. Time scale matters in these questions, and so modelers should expect to asked about "When?" as well as "How?" and "What?". Do calibrations of risk manifest themselves over short or long term? Immediately, or with a lag? When should decision-makers plan to act, and what metrics should be monitored to best inform evaluations of the efficacy of their decisions. It follows that *answers to counterfactual and model comparison questions can be very time sensitive*.

5. Reporting on *value of information (VOI)* calculations can often support conclusions about which variables are most important in driving the results into the future. This can be important information when it comes to framing plans for the next iteration of the modeling.

These thoughts are clearly interwoven, but the following subsections will provide some annotated descriptions of the italicized concepts and how they support the connections.

3.1 Thresholds of tolerable risk

Limits of tolerable risk reflect the level of "risk deemed acceptable by society in order that some particular benefit or functionality can be obtained, but in the knowledge that the risk has been evaluated and is being managed" (https://www.encyclopedia.com). Starting with its first report, the New York (City) Panel on

Climate Change [31] employed this notion to frame both its evaluation and management of climate change risks to public and private infrastructure. NPCC communicated the concept to planners and decision-makers by pointing out, for example, that building codes imposed across the City did not try to guarantee that a building will never fall down. Instead, they were designed to produce an environment in which the likelihood of the building's falling down was below some X% threshold, that is, risk above X% was not "tolerable." As climate change or a pandemic or any other outside stressor pushes a particular risk profile closer and closer to similarly defined thresholds of social tolerability, it is reasonable to expect that the investment in risk-reducing adaptations can quickly become a critical part of an iterative response strategy over time.

Figure 1 portrays one way by which current and future risk can be evaluated. A smaller version was created to support adaptation considerations in the face of climate change for public and private investment in New York City infrastructure. The idea was to locate infrastructure on the matrix under the current climate—the beginning of the arrow indicates that location. Planners could then envision how the location on the matrix would move as future trajectories of change evolved—upward curving lines, perhaps, that generally move up and to the right at an increasing rate, but drawn as straight lines in **Figure 1** for illustrative simplicity. Green boxes identify low-risk combinations of likelihood and consequence; they are benign and need not be of much worry to the people who manage the facility and the people who benefit from the services that it provides. Yellow and orange boxes identify moderate and significant risk combinations, respectively; they both lie below society's perception of the limit of tolerable risk. Yellow boxes suggest moderate concern, but the orange boxes capture combinations that fall just short of the threshold of tolerability—the boundary between the orange and red boxes.

The arrow in **Figure 1** shows how analysts could, by anticipating a dynamic scenario of climate change, alert decision-makers (as they moved along the arrow into the orange region) about the shrinking proximity of intolerable red combinations to which some reactive or preventative actions would be required. Assume for comparison that it takes 4 units of time to reach the tip of the arrow and that time is linear with the box dimensions. In the iterative response program, passing from green region to the yellow takes one unit of time and puts the risk on somebody's radar screen. Passing from yellow to orange in another 1.25 units of time triggers earnest planning and preparation for adaptive response. Finally, passing into the red region during the final 1.75 units of time identifies the anticipated time for action that would certainly include the implementation of outcome monitoring initiatives.

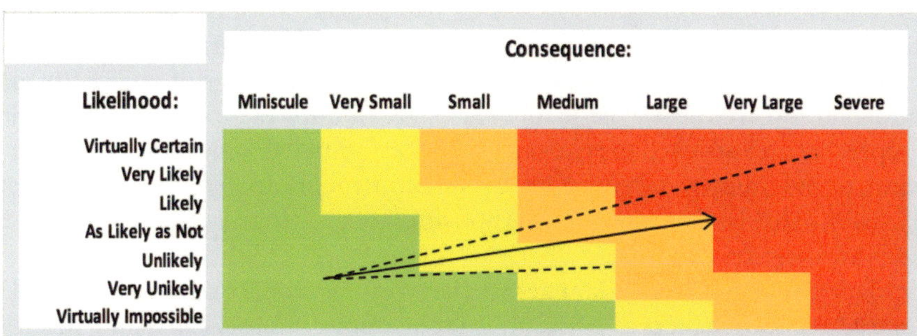

Figure 1.
Risk matrix representation. The formal conceptualization of risk as the product of likelihood and consequence can be portrayed by a two dimensional matrix. Here, subjective calibrations of likelihood and consequence are qualitatively depicted by seven different categories from "Virtually Impossible" to "Virtually Certain" (probabilities close but not equal to zero and close but not equal to one, respectively). Source: Box 4.6 in [32].

Figure 1 also suggests how this conceptual device can be used to insert uncertainty about the future into the depiction and the iterative story. The upper dotted line represents a hypothetical 95th percentile scenario that portends larger consequences with growing likelihood. It starts at the same location as the arrow, but it gets to the red region in just 2.4 units of time and spends the remaining 1.6 units plunging farther into the red area. The lower dotted line represents the 5th percentile trajectory; it is also shorter, because it tracks below the median depicts cases where consequences increase more slowly along climate change scenarios that also proceed at a more leisurely pace. It does not even reach the orange level of risk over 4 units of time. Together, these two pathways bound 90% of possible futures drawn from Monte Carlo simulations of a single model or an ensemble of parallel modeling efforts that are all anchored at current conditions. Decision-makers would expect to accelerate preparation and implementation at the point where the upper boundary of the inner 90% projection region (or any other higher or lower likelihood range determined by social norms) crosses the orange-red boundary as a hedge against a high consequence but lower likelihood risk tail. The reported results could, if this analysis were completed, include a distribution of projected response-action trigger-times rather than a single-valued best guess.

Achieving broad acceptance for any tolerable risk threshold is a huge task for many reasons, of course. For one, risk tolerance varies widely across societies and individuals (the locations of their institutional or personal risk thresholds). For another, the real challenge for governors confronting a pandemic or extreme climate change might be navigating between different, but perhaps strongly contradictory or competing risk management plans. It is possible, though. New York State, for example, relied on science to frame its economic strategies in terms of avoiding futures that would overwhelm its hospital system during a second wave of the virus after what had been a successful first response. It supplemented White House [33] "gating criteria" with two forward-looking thresholds: (1) hold the transmission rate of the virus below 1.0 and (2) keep vacancies of hospital beds and ICU beds across the state above 30% of total bed capacity [13]. These are two tolerable risk thresholds to which results from integrated epidemiological-economic models can certainly speak if they are properly designed.

3.2 Counterfactual exercises

What can be learned when public health and climate change researchers confront the ubiquitous "What if?" questions of science? Recall that Section 2 reported on three COVID-19 counterfactual studies that were of extreme interest to decision-makers and the public at large: "What if we had started sooner?" and "What if we had not shut down the economy?" [21–23]. The results were striking, but plausible. More importantly, all three studies were also direct applications of one of the most fundamental research strategies in all of science. Counterfactual explorations, in fact, represent an approach to rigorous scientific inquiry that defines a research question, a trial group to test an answer and a control group to provide a basis for comparison—that is, the scientific method applied to scenarios with policy interventions and scenarios without.

Similar examples are abundant across the world of climate science, as well. The Summary for Policymakers of IPCC [17], for example, contains an iconic result from a comparison of two extreme assumptions. Figure SPM.4 is replicated here in **Figure 2**; it depicts a result that changed the way the entire world thought about global warming and our confidence in the proposition that it was primarily the product of human activity. The various panels of the figure compare the actual historical global mean surface temperature record (starting in 1910) with distributions

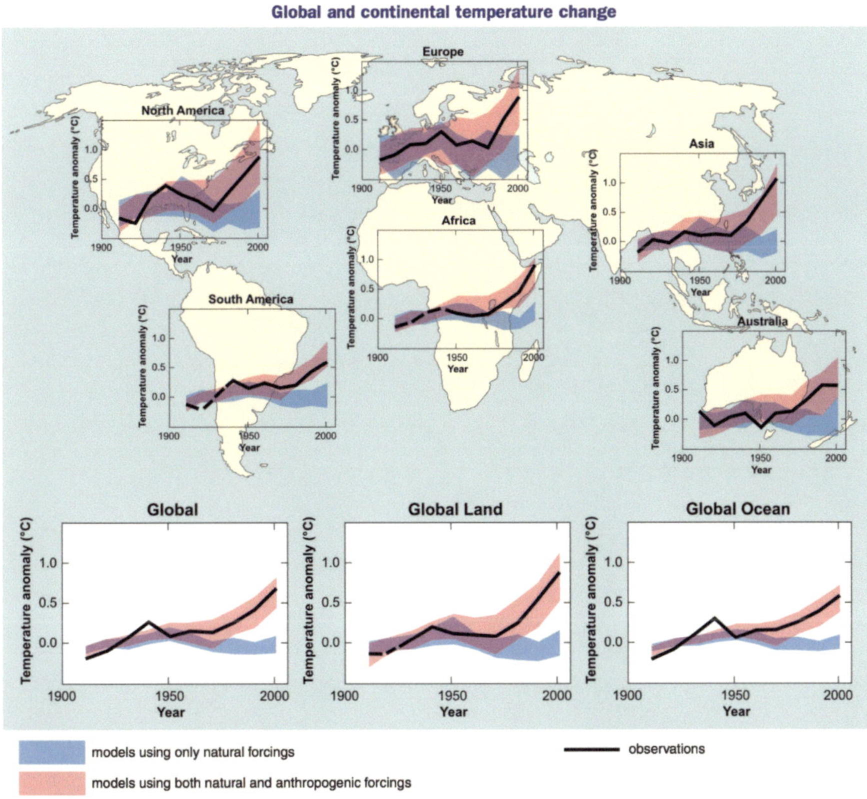

Figure 2.
Comparison of observed continental- and global-scale changes in surface temperature with results simulated by climate models using either natural or both natural and anthropogenic forcings. Decadal averages of observations are shown for the period 1906–2005 (black line) plotted against the center of the decade and relative to the corresponding average for the period 1901–1950. Lines are dashed where spatial coverage is less than 50%. Blue-shaded bands show 5–95% range for 19 simulations from five climate models using only the natural forcings due to solar activity and volcanoes. Red-shaded bands show 5–95% range for 58 simulations from 14 climate models using both natural and anthropogenic forcings. Source: Figure SPM.4 in [17].

of estimated global mean trajectories produced an ensemble of climate models including (trial group) and not including (control group) historically observed carbon emissions and associated forcings. The actual temperature pathway tracks inside only the distributions that include carbon forcings. Moreover, the inner 90-percentile regions of the two distributions around the mean estimates bifurcate around 1980 (earlier for some continents and later for Australia); that is, beyond those bifurcation dates, the likelihood that both distributions are the products of a static climate are virtually nil. Actual temperature tracking therefore combines with the bifurcations to confirm, with very high confidence in 2007, that carbon emissions are a primary cause of observed long term warming globally and across 6 of 7 continents.

Figure 3 shows results from a more recent counterfactual approach that confronts a "try this versus try that" comparison from [20]. The three panels show the results of a modeling exercise designed to produce distributions of economic cost (or benefit) from climate change in 4–20 year climate eras running from 2020 to 2100 for 4 different mitigation (temperature target) futures and 7 geographical regions that cover the contiguous 48 states of the continental US [34]; distributions of transient regional temperature changes were drawn from [35]. Panel A shows estimates for labor costs (in terms of lost annual wages

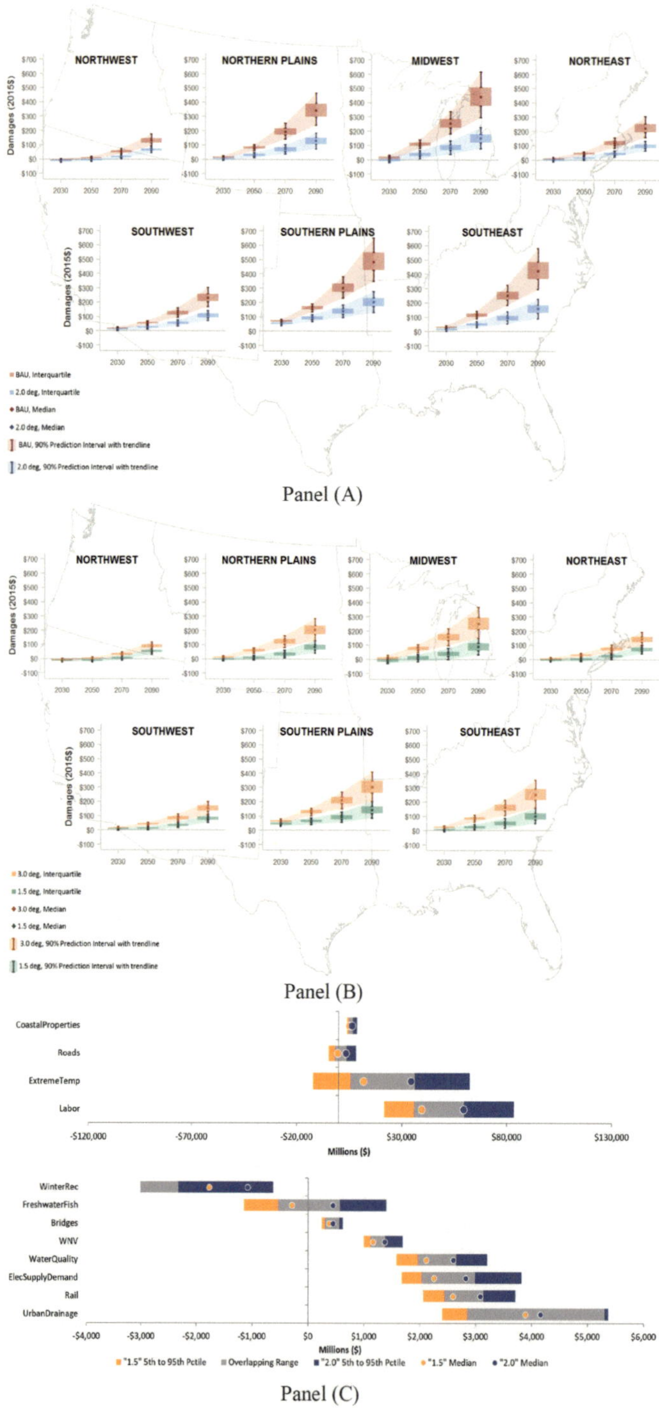

Figure 3.
Selected results from regional transient sectoral damage trajectories. Regional damage trajectories (median, 5th and 95th percentiles and the inner quartile range) are displayed across the contiguous 48 states for the 4 benchmark climate eras along all four of the emissions-driven GMT scenarios. Source: [34] Panel A: Labor damages: Annual lost wages per capita by region and year for the "2.0" and "BAU" scenarios. Panel B: Labor damages: Annual lost wages per capita by region and year for the "1.5" and "3.0" scenarios. Panel C: "1.5" versus "2.0" damages by sector in 2090: 5th to 95th percentile range of total costs (in millions of dollars) across the contiguous 48 states by sector for the "1.5" degree (in orange) and "2.0" degree scenarios (in blue). Overlapping ranges are shown in gray. Median estimates for each sector and scenarios are shown as dots in the color representing the scenario. Note the differences in scales between the two panels due to large variation in magnitude across sectors. Three sectors (aeroallergens, harmful algal blooms, and municipal and industrial water supply) are not shown, as the magnitude of damages is negligible compared to other sectors.

per capita) for two different emissions scenarios—one is a "business as usual (BAU)" scenario, and the other keeps global mean surface temperature (GMST) increases below 2°C through 2100 along the median trajectory. Bifurcations of the inner 90% ranges occur by mid-century; and losses along BAU are uniformly much higher. Panel B replicates A for another two emissions scenarios—one limits the median GMST increase to 1.5°C, and the other, to 3°C. Again, statistically significant bifurcations occur in the mid-century, and losses are higher with warmer temperatures [34].

Loss differences for labor and 15 other sectors were a critical topic of concern when IPCC received an invitation from the members of the United Nations Framework Convention on Climate Change to provide report "on the impacts of global warming of 1.5°C above pre-industrial levels." The IPCC accepted the invitation in April of 2016 when it decided to prepare a "Special Report on the impacts of global warming of 1.5°C above pre-industrial levels and related global greenhouse gas emission pathways, in the context of strengthening the global response to the threat of climate change, sustainable development, and efforts to eradicate poverty" [36]. The headline messages included: "Climate-related risks for natural and human systems are higher for global warming of 1.5°C than at present, but lower than at 2°C (*high confidence*). These risks depend on the magnitude and rate of warming, geographic location, levels of development and vulnerability, and on the choices and implementation of adaptation and mitigation options (*high confidence*). The avoided climate change impacts on sustainable development, eradication of poverty and reducing inequalities would be greater if global warming were limited to 1.5°C rather than 2°C, if mitigation and adaptation synergies are maximized while trade-offs are minimized (*high confidence*)."

When it came to economic damages, though, Yohe [35] suggests that the value of hitting a warming target of 2°C instead 1.5°C might not be as impressive as it is for natural systems and other social systems that are already stressed by confounding factors. Panel C of **Figure 3** makes this point for 16 sectors that were subjected to the same regional analysis as described above. All of the 2°C distributions overlap the 1.5°C distributions in 2090, so no bifurcations can be observed. Any conclusion of higher economic cost for the 2°C target must therefore be offered with at most *medium confidence*, on the basis of a single study, anyway.

These examples show that decision-makers and the public should be happy to see their decisions and perceptions informed by counterfactual experiments designed to identify the *when* differences in the risk profiles of alternative responses become statistically significant in terms of their net social benefit. Plotting the foundational distributions over time for alternative response options allows these experiments quickly to estimate when, in the future, it can be expected that the risk portraits of various policy options will become statistically different with, say, *very high confidence* because the 5th to 95th percentile distribution cones bifurcate—valuable information, no doubt, for designing and implementing an iterative risk management response for a particular decision-making structure (like avoiding (in) tolerable risk).

3.3 Model comparisons

In the climate arena, large groups of willing modelers sometimes all agree to run their models with the same distributions of the same sets of driving variables to explore their models' respective sensitivities or compare response policies' performances across a spectrum projected futures [37–39]. Sometimes, the participants also run contrasting idiosyncratic "modelers' choice" scenarios; and some even run full Monte Carlo analyses across relevant sources of uncertainty. When that happens, scientists can learn something about themselves as well as their topics of interest. The early EMF-12 experiment, for example, displayed a curious result that persists over time—the variances of the output distributions for the modelers' choice runs were significantly smaller than the output variances for the "common inputs" runs. It would seem that integrated assessment teams tended to be uncomfortable if their results were outliers in comparison with competing teams—a cautionary bias for decision contexts where ensemble distributions may be too narrow because thick tails could be catastrophic [37].

The Coupled Model Intercomparison Project (CMIP) was established by the Program for Climate Model Diagnosis and Inter-comparison (PCMDI) at Lawrence Livermore National Laboratories. PCMDI's mission since 1989 has been to develop methods to rigorously diagnose and evaluate climate models from around the world, because the causes and character of divergent modeling results should be uncovered before they are trusted by decision-makers around the world. Over time, it has "inspired a fundamental cultural shift in the climate research community: there is now an expectation that everyone should have timely and unimpeded access to output from standardized climate model simulations. This has enabled widespread scientific analysis and scrutiny of the models and, judging by the large number of resulting scientific publications, has accelerated our understanding of climate and climate change" [38].

CMIP, itself, began in 1995 with the support and encouragement of the World Climate Research Program (WCRP). Its first set of common experiments—comparing model responses to an "Idealized" forcing of 1% per year increase in carbon dioxide emissions. Subsequent experiments expanded continuing idealized forcing work to include parallel investigations historical forcings and comparisons with the observed records of climate variables like global mean surface temperature [39]. CMIP5 and CMIP6, for example, have explored why ensemble results do not track observations perfectly. The reason is uncertainty. Model results reflect uncertainties, of course; but temperature observations are also imprecise. They are not records from a global set of thermometers; they are, instead, the products of model interpretations of remotely sensed data. Understanding why and how the differences occur is especially important because they are the ammunition for attacks by science skeptics and politicians with an anti-climate change perspective [40, 41].

CMIP also sponsors coordinated experiments like the "water hosing" experiments designed to explore the sensitivity of the strength of the overturning of the North Atlantic thermohaline global circulation current to changes in upper ocean salinity. There, climate is held constant except for a simulated influx of un-salty glacial melt water from Greenland. CMIP has, as well and since its inception, focused a lot of attention of making model inter-comparison data available to a wider scientific community than the modelers themselves. Here, a global coordination effort for scientific collaboration is admitting that communication to other research communities, decision-makers at all levels, and private citizens is an important part of their job description; some authors (e.g., [40]) have even included second abstracts in their published versions written in plain language.

Contrasting that approach to public health model comparisons with dramatically different time scales and therefore dramatically different client needs adds diversity to the sources of new knowledge about the models and their relative skills. Shea et al. [42], motivated by the aggressive responses of many modeling groups to "forecast disease trajectory, assess interventions, and improve understanding of the pathogen," expressed concern that their disparate projections might "hinder intervention planning and response by policy-makers." These authors recognized that models do differ widely for a variety of good and not so good reasons. They also noted that relying on one model for authority might cause valuable "insights and information from other models" to be overlooked, thereby "limiting the opportunity for decision-makers to account for risk and uncertainty and resulting in more lives lost." As a result, they advocated a more systematic approach that would use expert elicitation methods to inform a CMIP style model comparison architecture within which decision-theoretic frameworks would provide rigorous access to calibration techniques. While certainly an addition to a long tradition of sometimes sporadic model comparison in public health, NSF [43] notes that this proposal would be the first time modelers would be allowed in the structure itself to see why their models disagree.

3.4 Time scale matters

Taken together, an ensemble of models that were designed to inform COVID-19 response decisions were capable simultaneously and independently to produce estimates at many time scales and different geographic resolutions—daily, monthly, and a few years into the future for a city or town, a state, a region, or the country as a whole. So, too, are ensembles of climate models. Informed by new data and or new understanding of processes which drive component parts of their models, some modelers in either context can publish new sets of estimates for new combinations and permutations of scale and location diversity at the same time. Done often enough over the course of a month or two for pandemics and 5 or 10 years for climate, those modelers could synthesize collections of time series of short-term estimates for any number of important output variables.

Daily recalculations may be excessive for most pandemic models, but surely, on a regular basis, decision-makers, analysts, and media types are anxious to compare the ensemble distributions of these results against the actual historical data. These plots produce insight into the relative near-term skills of the models across different geographic scales. Modelers would surely be interested, as well and as shown by large participation in the CMIP exercises, because they will continue to try to improve their work and make it more valuable and accessible to the decision-makers who use it and the correspondents who interpret it. The point, as described in the mission of the PCMDI, is to generate early confidence in modelers' abilities to project what will likely happen given what just happened and to communicate what that means clearly to the populations that care.

In light of this responsibility, climate scientists and epidemiologists have found it useful to conduct short-run skill tests of their models because they anticipate the need to understand and portray future changes that may happen very quickly. For example, it may become imperative at some point in the future to cope with sudden downstream impacts along an otherwise gradual scenario of change—an impact caused, for example, by crossing some unexpected critical threshold at some unknown date. In other cases, testing near term skill may be important to reassure clients of the quality of model results so that the implications of new and significantly different information can be processed by quickly decision-makers and the public.

3.5 The value of information

In an era of increasingly tight budgets, it is imperative that funders in both the public and private sectors understand the value of investments in different types of information distributed across and within the germane research areas. Climate change research is a case in point; billions of dollars are being spent to improve the knowledge base for future decision-making. A study by the National Research Council [44] called for decision tools to assist in estimating "the value of new information which can help decision makers plan research programs and determine which trends to monitor to best implement a risk management strategy." Identifying the relevant decision-makers measurable priorities is critical, though, because it is their net benefit valuation protocols that produce the VOI metrics with which these calculations can be conducted. The Academy study emphasized that the application of decision theory could provide explicit descriptions of how rigorously to evaluate the appropriate value of perfect and imperfect information, much as done 30 years ago in [45–47].

On the health side of the comparison, VOI estimates need not be calibrated in monetary currency; human lives or other metric can be employed, especially if it can support aggregation across locations. This is one of the major lessons from the "risk to unique and threatened systems" Reason for Concern described in [48], even for the two areas where risks are measured in aggregates. In fact, risks of extreme (weather) events and risks to unique and threatened systems (including human communities) are areas where alternatives to financial currency are preferred.

Assuming access to decision-makers' lists of operative and quantifiable valuation metrics (including confidence in the ability to keep experienced risk below a tolerable maximum), temporal distributions of the value of enacting a re-opening strategy of a locked-down economy relative to a "stay the course" strategy could be available, for example, and the sign and magnitude of valued in differences in lives or jobs or gross domestic product or income inequality or even the likelihood of slowing progress toward an SDG could all be of interest, so, too, would be estimates of distributions of the value of improved (or depreciated) information about driving variables and/or epidemiological-socio-economic specifications.

4. Concluding remarks

The parallel and analogous roles of modeling to support response action in the face of two different sources of global existential risk—global viral pandemics and global human induced climate change—were the motivation for this discussion of the importance of continuing to work to improve multiplicative modeling efforts on both fronts. The rationales for choosing those sources of risk were many. Both are the source of enormous risk with distributions of impacts that are very thick, so "regressing to the tail" is the appropriate frame. Both have adopted similar risk-based approaches to decision making at micro and macro scales [49]. Both have explored similar modeling techniques and have pursued common methods for improvement. Both have faced issues with the communication of difficult subjects and concepts, and both have been subjected to misguided and manipulative attack.

The critical need to continue concerted efforts to improve the science is matched in importance by two other essential components. One is the need to improve communication to decision-makers and the public at large, not only to advance knowledge and understanding of the results at the appropriate decision-making hub and the associated population, but also to defend the results and their communication from misguided and sometime dishonest attack. Both motives are have recently been highlighted by the Working Group on Readying Populations for COVID-19 Vaccine for the Johns Hopkins Center for Health [50] in preparation for achieving wide acceptance of a vaccine that can, when it is created and acclaimed to be safe and effective, be quickly and globally distributed. The other is the recognition that global risks require global responses, and so they require collaborative work across research groups, decision-makers, and populations scattered around the world.

The World Climate Research Program has been devoted to just that for decades, trying to improve both the production of collaborative new scientific results of real social value, but also their communication to positions of power. Climate effort on global scale is impressive so far, but its work is far from done and progress on real action vis-a-vis SDG-13 has been slow. The WCRP mission has not, however, been lost on scholars of the international health community. Chretien et al. [27] posited this assessment of the then current affairs: "New norms for data-sharing during public health emergencies would remove the most obvious hurdle for model comparison. The current situation where groups either negotiate bilaterally with individual countries or work exclusively with global health and development agencies is understandable, but highly ineffective. The EVD outbreak highlights again, after the 2003 Severe Acute Respiratory Syndrome epidemic and the 2009 influenza A (H1N1) pandemic, that an independent, well-resourced global data observatory could greatly facilitate the public health response in many ways, not least of which would be the enablement of rapid, high quality, and easily comparable disease-dynamic studies."

The widely variant COVID-19 coronavirus experiences across the world brought these points to the fore just as they exposed a plethora of social, ethical, and economic realities. In a world moving toward nationalism with persistent racism, growing inequities and threats from the wealthiest nation on the planet to remove itself from the WHO, global welfare as calibrated by the metrics underlying the 17 SDGs is certainly in peril from these two cross-cutting themes. Recognition of common goals, common approaches, and common dedication to the general welfare of the planet across the climate and health science researchers may not be enough. Bringing those communities together through the matching international institutions designed to confront global crises with science and communication may be one of our best and last chances to avoid trusting universal herd immunity to protect us from everything.

Acknowledgements

I gratefully acknowledge their many contributions to this work of Henry Jacoby, Richard Richels, and Benjamin Santer. I benefit and enjoy our weekly phone conversations about climate-related topics of the day. We work together on opinion pieces which we have placed in many venues. What appears here, to some degree, was drawn from the cutting room floor or our discussions, so any errors are certainly mine.

Conflict of interest

The author declares no conflict of interest.

Author details

Gary Yohe
Wesleyan University, Middletown, CT, USA

*Address all correspondence to: gyohe@wesleyan.edu

IntechOpen

© 2020 The Author(s). Licensee IntechOpen. This chapter is distributed under the terms of the Creative Commons Attribution License (http://creativecommons.org/licenses/by/3.0), which permits unrestricted use, distribution, and reproduction in any medium, provided the original work is properly cited.

References

[1] United Nations Sustainable Development Goals. 2020. Available from: https://www.un.org/sustainabledevelopment/poverty/

[2] Yohe G. The Coronavirus Is Showing the Cracks in the Foundation of American Society. Hartford, CT: Hartford Courant; 2020. Available from: https://www.courant.com/opinion/op-ed/hc-op-yohe-revelations-of-coronavirus-0627-20200627-uhmas4jd5neszh5tbgv6ch26he-story.html

[3] Van Elsland S, O'hare R. COVID-19: Researchers model likely impact of public health measures. Medical Xpress. 2020. Available from: https://medicalxpress.com/news/2020-03-covid-impact-health.html [Accessed: 18 March 2020]

[4] Sullivan T. IHME creates COVID-19 projection tool. Policy and Medicine. 2020. Available from: https://www.policymed.com/2020/03/ihme-creates-covid-19-projection-tool.html [Accessed: 18 March 2020]

[5] Cohen J. Scientists are racing to model the next moves of a coronavirus that's still hard to predict. Science. 2020. DOI: 10.1126/science.abb2161. Available from: https://www.sciencemag.org/news/2020/02/scientists-are-racing-model-next-moves-coronavirus-thats-still-hard-predict [Accessed: 07 February 2020]

[6] Flyvbjerg B. The law of regression to the tail: How to mitigate COVID-19, climate change, and other catastrophic risks. Academia. 2020:1-5. DOI: 10.2139/ssrn.3600070. Available from: https://ssrn.com/abstract=3600070

[7] Smith A. 2010-2019: A Landmark Decade of U.S. Billion-Dollar Weather and Climate Disasters. Ashville, NC: National Oceanographic and Atmospheric Administration, National Centers for Environmental Information. 2020. Available from: https://www.climate.gov/news-features/blogs/beyond-data/2010-2019-landmark-decade-us-billion-dollar-weather-and-climate

[8] Pew Research. How U.S. Unemployment during COVID-19 compares with the Great Depression. 2020. Available from: https://www.pewresearch.org/fact-tank/2020/06/11/unemployment-rose-higher-in-three-months-of-covid-19-than-it-did-in-two-years-of-the-great-recession

[9] Howard J, Stracqualursi V. Fauci Warns of 'Anti-Science Bias' Being a Problem in US. Atlanta, GA: CNN; 2020. Available from: https://www.cnn.com/2020/06/18/politics/anthony-fauci-coronavirus-anti-science-bias/index.html

[10] Bowman T, Maibach E, Mann M, Somerville R, Seltser B, Fischhoff BGS, et al. Time to take action on climate communication. Science. 2010;**330**:1044. DOI: 10.1126/science.330.6007/1044. Available from: https://science.sciencemag.org/content/330/6007/1044

[11] Begley S. Disease Modelers Gaze into Computers to See Future of Covid-19. Boston, MA: STAT News; 2020. Available from: https://www.statnews.com/2020/02/14/disease-modelers-see-future-of-covid-19/

[12] Begley S. Influential Covid-19 Model shouldn't Guide U.S. Policies, Critics Say. Boston, MA: STAT News; 2020. Available from: https://www.statnews.com/2020/04/17/influential-covid-19-model-uses-flawed-methods-shouldnt-guide-policies-critics-say

[13] Harris C. Cuomo's Daily Press Briefing on COVID-19 (May 11).

Schenectady, NY: Rochester Health; 2020. Available from: https://blog.timesunion.com/capitol/archives/290108/read-cuomos-daily-briefing-on-covid-19-may-11/

[14] Intergovernmental Panel on Climate Change (IPCC). FAR Climate Change: Synthesis. Cambridge: Cambridge University Press; 1990. Available from: https://www.ipcc.ch/report/ar1/syr/

[15] Intergovernmental Panel on Climate Change (IPCC). SAR Climate Change 1995: Synthesis Report. Cambridge: Cambridge University Press; 1995. Available from: https://www.ipcc.ch/report/ar2/syr/

[16] Intergovernmental Panel on Climate Change (IPCC). TAR Climate Change 2000: Synthesis Report. Cambridge: Cambridge University Press; 2000. Available from: https://www.ipcc.ch/report/ar3/syr/

[17] Intergovernmental Panel on Climate Change (IPCC). AR4 Climate Change 2007: Synthesis Report. Cambridge: Cambridge University Press; 2007. Available from: https://www.ipcc.ch/report/ar4/syr/

[18] Intergovernmental Panel on Climate Change (IPCC). AR5 Synthesis Report: Climate Change. 2014. Cambridge: Cambridge University Press; 2014. Available from: https://www.ipcc.ch/report/ar5/syr/

[19] Imperial College London. Report 12—The Global Impact of Covid-19 and Strategies for Mitigation and Suppression. London, UK: Imperial College London; 2020. Available from: https://www.imperial.ac.uk/mrc-global-infectious-disease-analysis/covid-19/covid-19-reports/

[20] Yohe G, Santer B, Jacoby H, Richels R. Counterfactual experiments are crucial but easy to misunderstand. New York, NY: Scientific American; 2020. Available from: https://www.scientificamerican.com/article/counterfactual-experiments-are-crucial-but-easy-to-misunderstand/

[21] Pei S et al. Differential Effects of Intervention Timing on COVID-19 Spread in the United States. New York, NY: Mailman School of Public Health, Columbia University; 2020. Available from: https://www.medrxiv.org/content/10.1101/2020.05.15.20103655v1.full.pdf

[22] Hsiang S et al. The effect of large-scale anti-contagion policies on the COVID-19 pandemic. Nature Accelerated Article Preview. 2020;**584**:262-267. DOI: 10.1038/s41586-020-2404-8

[23] Flaxman S et al. Estimating the effects of non-pharmaceutical interventions on COVID-19 in Europe. Nature Accelerated Article Preview. 2020;**584**:257-261. DOI: 10.1038/s41586-020-2405-7

[24] Du Z, Xu X, Wu Y, Wang L, Cowling B, Meyers L. Serial interval of COVID-19 among publicly reported confirmed cases. Emerging Infectious Diseases. 2020;**26**(6):1341-1343. DOI: 10.3201/eid2606.200357

[25] Reddy S. How Epidemiological Models Fooled us into Trusting Bad Assumptions. Chicopee, MA: Barrons; 2020. Available from: https://www.barrons.com/articles/the-danger-of-overreliance-on-epidemiological-models-51588179008

[26] Samuels B. Trump Calls Study on Taking Earlier Action against Coronavirus a 'Political Hit Job'. Vol. 2020. Washington, DC: The Hill; 2020. Available from: https://thehill.com/homenews/administration/498985-trump-calls-columbia-study-showing-effects-of-earlier-coronavirus-a-political-hit-job/

[27] Waldman S. U.S. conservatives who detest climate models add a new

target: Coronavirus models. Science. 2020. Available from: https://www.sciencemag.org/news/2020/04/us-conservatives-who-detest-climate-models-add-new-target-coronavirus-models [Accessed: 15 April 2020]

[28] Chretien J-P, Riley S, George D. Mathematical modeling of the West Africa Ebola epidemic. Epidemiology and Public Health. 15 December 2015. DOI: 10.7554/eLife.09186.001

[29] Yozwiak N, Schaffner S, Sabeti P. Data sharing: Make outbreak research open access. Nature. 2015;**518**:477-479. DOI: 10.1038/518477a

[30] United States Centers for Disease Control and Prevention (CDC). Ebola Report: Ebola by the Numbers. Atlanta, GA: Centers for Decease Control and Prevention; 2015. Available from: https://www.cdc.gov/about/ebola/ebola-by-the-numbers.html

[31] New York City Panel on Climate Change (NPCC). Climate change adaptation in New York City: Building a risk management response. Annals of the New York Academy of Sciences. 2010;**1196**:1-354. DOI: 10.1111/j.1749-6632.2009.05415.x (Rosenzweig C, Solecki W, editors) prepared for use by the New York City Climate Change Adaptation Task Force

[32] National Research Council (NRC). Adapting to the Impacts of Climate Change. Washington DC: The National Academies Press; 2010. DOI: 10.17226/12783

[33] White House. Guidelines Opening Up America Again. Washington, DC: U.S. Government Printing Office; 2020. Available from: https://www.whitehouse.gov/openingamerica/

[34] Yohe G, Willwerth J, Neumann J, Kerrich Z. What the Future Might Hold: Regional Transient Sectoral Damages for the U.S.—Estimates and Maps in an exhibition. Middletown, CT: Wesleyan University; 2020

[35] Yohe G. Characterizing transient temperature trajectories for assessing the value of achieving alternative temperature targets. Climatic Change. 2017;**145**:469-479. DOI: 10.1007/s10584-017-2100-3

[36] Intergovernmental Panel on Climate Change (IPCC), 2018, Synthesis Report: Special Report on Global Warming of 1.5°C. Cambridge: Cambridge University Press; 2020. Available from: https://www.ipcc.ch/sr15/chapter/spm/

[37] Energy Modeling Forum 12 (EMF 12), Weyant J. EMF 12: Model comparisons of the costs of reducing CO_2 emissions—Executive summary. In: Weyant J, Gaskins D, editors. Controlling Global Carbon Emissions—Cost and Policy Options. Vol. 1. Stanford, CA: Stanford University; 1993. Available from: https://emf.stanford.edu/projects/emf-12-controlling-global-carbon-emissions-cost-and-policy-options

[38] Program for Climate Model Diagnosis and Inter-comparison (PCMDI). Coupled Model Inter-comparison Program. Geneva, Switzerland: Lawrence Livermore National Laboratories. 2020. Available from: https://pcmdi.llnl.gov/about.html

[39] World Climate Research Program (WCRP) Coupled Model Inter-Comparison Project (CMIP). Geneva, Switzerland: World Climate Research Program; 2020. Available from: https://www.wcrp-climate.org/wgcm-cmip

[40] Kalter J, Collins M, Frankcombe L, England M, Osborn T, Juniper M. Global mean surface temperature response to large-scale patterns of variability in observations and CMIP5. Geophysical Research Letters. 2019;**2015**:2232-2241. DOI: 10.1029/2018GL081462

[41] Neukom R, Schurer N, Steiger N, Hegerl G. Possible causes of data model discrepancy in the temperature history of the last millennium. Nature. 2018;**8**:7572. DOI: 10.1038/s41598-018-25862-2

[42] Shea K, Runge M, Pannell D, Probert W, Li S, Tildesley M, et al. Harnessing multiple models for outbreak management. Science. 2020;**368**(6491):577-579. DOI: 10.1126/science.abb9934. Available from: https://science.sciencemag.org/content/368/6491/577

[43] National Science Foundation (NSF). New Process Considers Numerous Coronavirus Models to Reduce Uncertainty. Washington, DC: NSF Public Affairs; 2020. Available from: https://www.nsf.gov/discoveries/disc_summ.jsp?cntn_id=30057&et_rid=17050839&et_cid=3332201

[44] Manne A, Richels R. Buying Greenhouse Insurance: The Economic Costs of CO_2 Emission Limits. Cambridge: The MIT Press; 1992. p. 182

[45] National Research Council (NRC). America's Climate Choices, Washington, DC: The National Academies Pressl 2011. DOI: 10.17226/12781

[46] Uncertainty YG. Global climate, and the economic value of information. Policy Sciences. 1991;**24**:245-269. DOI: 10.1007/BF00186329

[47] Yohe G. exercises in hedging against extreme consequences of global change and the expected value of information. Global Environmental Change. 1995;**6**:87-101. DOI: 10.1023/B:ENMO.0000004582.29948.d4

[48] O'Neill BC, Oppenheimer M, Warren R, Hallegatte S, Kopp R, Portner H, et al. IPCC reasons for concern regarding climate change risks. Nature Climate Change. 2017;**7**:38-37. DOI: 10.1038/nclimate3179

[49] Yohe G, Ebi KAA. Parallels and contrasts between the climate and health communities. In: Ebi K, Smith J, Burton I, editors. Integration of Public Health with Adaptation to Climate Change: Lessons Learned and New Directions. The Netherlands: Taylor and Francis; 2005

[50] Schoch-Spana M, Brunson E, Long R. Ravi S. Ruth A. Trotochaud M. The Public's Role in COVID-19 Vaccination: Planning Recommendations Informed by Design Thinking and the Social, Behavioral, and Communication Sciences. Baltimore: Johns Hopkins Center for Health Security; 2020. Available from: https://www.centerforhealthsecurity.org/our-work/publications/the-publics-role-in-covid-19-vaccination?utm_source=Public+Health+Updates&utm_campaign=9710f551e2-EMAIL_CAMPAIGN_2020_06_22_05_08_COPY_01&utm_medium=email&utm_term=0_7b4655f81b-9710f551e2-198266756

Chapter 6

Rights and Responsibilities: The Reality of Forest Fringe Communities in the Northern Region of Ghana

Rikiatu Husseini, Stephen B. Kendie and Patrick Agbesinyale

Abstract

The goal for collaborative forest management (CFM) is to attain sustainable management of forest resources for sustainable development. Securing rights and responsibilities of forest fringe communities is central to achieving effective and sustainable management of forest reserves. This article discusses the rights and responsibilities of the forest fringe communities under Ghana's collaborative Forest Management (CFM) in the Northern region and explores the levels of awareness of communities of these rights and responsibilities. The survey employed a mixed method research design with community members and forestry staff as key respondents. We found that although Forest fringe communities are entitled to some admitted rights including access to the reserves and the right to harvest nontimber forest products such as thatch, medicinal plants, dry wood for firewood and edible fruits mainly for domestic use; in reality, access to such rights is somehow restricted by the forestry staff. Fringe communities have limited knowledge about their rights and responsibilities to the forest reserve. For sustainability, educating fringe communities on their rights and responsibilities to forest reserves and involving them in management decisions is recommended as the surest ways of securing their interests in CFM.

Keywords: collaborative forest management, rights, responsibilities, sustainability, northern region

1. Introduction

An important guiding principle of the revised forest and wildlife policy is that it recognizes and confirms the importance of local people in pursuing all other guiding principles of the policy, and therefore proposes to place particular emphasis on the concept of participatory management and protection of forest and wildlife resources and to develop appropriate strategies, modalities and programs in consultation with relevant agencies, rural communities and individuals [1]. The principles and strategies of the policy of participatory management recognizes the rights of local people to have access to natural resources for maintaining a basic standard of living and their concomitant responsibility to ensure the sustainable use of such resources. To this effect, since the adoption of the 1994 Forest and wildlife policy, several operations of the Forestry Commission (FC) have been revised to help meet its aim of achieving equitable sharing of benefits and improved efficiency in management, particularly, in Southern Ghana [1].

For instance, under the Forestry Sector Development Programme (FSDP II) and the High Forest Biodiversity Programme (HFBP), the FC has been providing support toward forest–based livelihood schemes such as grass-cutter rearing, seedling production and snail farming [2]. Although access to NTFP's for domestic use had been enshrined in reserve settlement judgments, foresters had over the years not been fulfilling these rights to land owners. As such all current management plans reassert the rights of communities to harvest NTFP's for domestic use, to have access to fetish sites and other rights as enshrined in original agreements.

In addition to the above, the FC is promoting initiatives to assist forest fringe communities to add value to harvested products through processing and market promotion. This initiative known as Marketing Analysis and Development (MA and D) according to the report is being piloted in three districts of Cape Coast. These are Pra (Suhien forest reserve), Goaso (Bia Tano forest reserve) and Mpreaso (Esukawkaw forest reserve). The ultimate goal is to organize forest fringe communities to form co-operatives to produce items for the export market ([2], p. 7). In terms of integrated use of forest resources, Oduro [3] reports that the collaborative forest management unit (CFMU) of FC has initiated programs that involve helping communities to develop their capacity to manage forest resources in southern Ghana. For instance in Assin Fosu, the author reports that, CFMU has supported communities to manage ancestral forest groves. In the Esen forest reserve at Akyem Oda, the CFMU has involved local communities in devising improved management of NTFPs. The program involved experiments in developing nurseries for the propagation of various NTFPs, using different methods including seed planting, root and stem cuttings. This report has been affirmed by the Forestry Commission of Ghana [2]. Report by Oduro [3] also indicates that the CFMU has carried out a survey of people's attitude in communities near forest reserves which have been proposed for different types of protection: special biological protection areas, hill sanctuaries, and convalescence and fire block areas. The report from the survey showed considerable local support for the continued protection of the forest reserves, particularly for the protection of drinking water supplies, rehabilitation of degraded forests and fire protection belts.

One factor that is worth noting from the literature is that, all the initiatives and successes were recorded in southern Ghana where timber abounds. There are no records of such initiatives or operations by the FC for fringe communities in the timber-poor Northern Region. Being a timber—poor zone, presupposes that communities do not enjoy social responsibility agreement (SRA) as enjoyed by those in Southern Ghana. Ironically, among the challenges that the revised Ghana's forest and wildlife policy sought to address are; the inadequate response to the domestic demand of timber and timber products which has led to increased illegal chainsaw operations in the supply of timber to the market, and the challenges to CFM strategy on how to achieve sustainability in forest management, to integrate local communities into planning and management whilst maintaining a profitable sector. Yet work by [4] found out that participation of fringe communities in the management of forest reserves is passive and tokenistic with local people having no control over access to resources and management. The critical question is, do the fringe communities in the Northern region and for that matter Northern Ghana have any user-rights or obligations to forest reserves at all? Answering this question is the main objective that this article sought to achieve.

2. Theoretical framework interest

Decisions of forest fringe communities may have positive or negative environmental, economic, and social impacts on sustainable development depending on whether it is managed sustainably or not. However, managing forest ecosystems sustainably requires knowledge of their main functions, and the effects of human practices, especially human practices or activities of the communities and/or settlements fringing the forest ecosystems including forest reserves. These practices are often perpetuated with the intension of meeting their needs or wants. Therefore it is important to consider the rights and responsibilities of people living around the forest ecosystems in forest management decisions so as to take onboard those practices that inure to the benefits of the society and the forest environment. This can only be done successfully if the frontiers of forest ecosystems and resource management understand the fringing communities and how they interact with the forest ecosystems. This is because, according to Metz et al. [5] even though over the years scientific literature shows there has been an increasing attempt to understand and integrate long-term effects of current practices of forest management on sustainable development, often, there is no sufficient understanding of the potential long-term impacts of current practices on sustainable development. According to the authors this may stem from the fact that often governing agencies fail to recognize the rights and responsibilities of key stakeholders whose actions and inactions define the forest practices, thereby defeating the purposes of collaborative forest management.

Collaborative forest management (CFM) denotes collective action by multi-stakeholders including local communities for sustainable forest management (SFM) for all. It is premised on the fact that community participation will increase resource flows to local people and help reduce rural poverty by providing them with their livelihoods [6]. According to the principles of CFM, sustainable forest management is the long term aim of CFM. Therefore, aside meeting other aims such as fair benefits to partners and equity in benefit sharing within community, the key objective is sustainability. The Forest Principles adopted at the United Nations Conference on Environment and Development (UNCED) in 1992 specifically states that: "Forest resources and forest lands should be sustainably managed to meet the social, economic, ecological, cultural and spiritual needs of present and future generations. In doing so the interests of Forest-Dependent Communities, security of tenure of forest resources and access to forest land to private and public land holdings, including the rights and obligations of forest owners and local communities must be regarded [7]".

Sustainable development (SD) on the other hand has been defined by FAO Forest Resources Assessment [8] as: "the management and conservation of the natural resources base, and the orientation of technological and institutional change in such a manner as to ensure the attainment and continued satisfaction of human needs for present and future generations" [9, 10].

The essence of this form of development is a stable relationship between human activities and the natural world, which does not diminish the prospects for future generations to enjoy a quality of life as good as the present generation. This implies that, SD can only be achieved through SFM which hinges upon collaborative management of forest resources.

However, because local communities living in or around forests and forest reserves have a traditional dependency upon same, their actions and inaction affects collaborative management decisions and the sustainability of the forest resources. Therefore, respecting the rights and obligations of forest owners and local communities, and enhancement of their well-being are critical to sustainable forest management and development. As emphasized by Metz et al. [5], significant economic, social, and environmental contributions to sustainable development can be gained by involving local people and stakeholders and developing adequate policy frameworks.

Riding on the back of rational choice theory by Buchanan and Tullock [11], this article equates the rights and responsibilities of fringe communities to their expected benefits and costs from forest reserves and discusses these under the current practice of the concept of collaborative forest management in the study area.

2.1 The study area

The region has a total land area of about 70,384 sq. km (7 million ha) which is 29% of the land area of Ghana. Of the total land area of 70,384sq km of the region, 3556.92 sq. km (5.05%) is under reservation [12]. Northern Region is located between latitude 8 30″ and 10 30″ N and lies completely in the savannah belt. It has Togo and La Cote D'Ivoire to the East and West, respectively, as its international neighbors. To the south, the region shares boundaries with Brong Ahafo and the Volta Regions, and to the north, it shares borders with Upper-East and Upper-West Regions. Results of the 2010 population and housing census gave the regional population as 2479, with an intercensal growth rate of 2.9% between 2000 and 2010 [13].

The main vegetation is classified as vast areas of grassland, mainly Guinea savannah interspersed drought-resistant trees such as the acacia, baobab, shea dawadawa, mango, neem Ghana [14]. The region is drained by the Black and white Volta and their tributaries, such as Rivers Nasia and Daka www.ghana.gov.gh/.

3. Research methodology

This study employed a mixed method which combined survey and in-depth interviews. The article is part of a larger study conducted on the fringe communities surrounding forest reserves in four forest districts in the Northern region of Ghana. Two reserves were randomly selected from each of the four forest districts, giving a total of eight sampled forest reserves. Proportionate sampling was then used to select communities whilst simple random sampling was employed in sampling household heads. With a target population of 14,343, a total of 370 households were sampled at 95% confidence level with a 5% margin of error. For detail methodology of the study, see Husseini et al. [4]. **Table 1** shows a summary of the sampled reserve and communities.

Key informants comprised 13 forestry staff, 21 assembly members, 23 women's group leaders (magazias), 23 chiefs, 1 representative from stool lands and the head of the CFM Unit (CFMU) of the Resource Management Support Centre (RMSC) of FC, summing up to 82 key informants.

Quantitative data was collected using structured interview schedule while qualitative data was obtained by in-depth interviews. The quantitative data was analyzed with Statistical Product for Service Solution (SPSS) version 16 software, using descriptive statistics such as frequency tables and percentages. The results from the in-depth interviews were categorized into appropriate themes and analyzed through discourse analysis.

Forest districts	Forest reserves selected	Sampled communities
Tamale	Water works F/R	Yohini, Zogbele, Choggu
	Sinsablegbini	Zakariyili, Zibogu,Tugu
Walewale	Nasia Tributaries	Pigu, Pishigu, Sakpule
	Gambaga scarp West BLK I	Samini, Gbani, Langbinsi
Yendi	Daka head water	Nakoa, Kpatili, Nawuni and Gushiegu
	Kumbo	Kpatugri, Juanayili, Pusuga
Damongo	Yakumbo	Old Buipe and Lito
	Damongo scarp	Damongo and Soalepe
Total	8	23

Table 1.
Forest districts, sampled reserves and communities for the study.

4. Results and discussion

4.1 Awareness of tenure rights and management of forest reserves

Kowero et al. [15] assert that enabling policies, legislation and institutional instruments like clear tenure rights, are important in promoting sustainable management of natural resources. The study revealed that 310 household heads (representing 83.8%) interviewed (**Table 2**) are of the opinion that forest reserves are owned by the state or the government whilst only 38 (10.3%) respondents think that forest reserves are owned by the community.

It was also found that, of the 370 household heads interviewed, 306 of them (representing 82.7%) believe that forest reserves are managed by the Forest Services Division (FSD) staff while 64 of them (representing 17.3%) are of the opinion that forest reserves are either managed by community and FSD, district assembly or traditional rulers (**Table 3**).

The key informants' interview with chiefs revealed that with the exception of three chiefs (Gulkpe-Naa, the Pusuga naa and Kpatugri naa) who knew that forest reserves are owned by the traditional authorities, 17 of the sampled chiefs believe that forest reserves within their communities are owned by the state and managed by the FSD. The other three chiefs are of the opinion that reserves belong to District Assembly and managed by the government. Similarly, with the exception of the

District	Category of ownership				
	Community owned	State owned	NGO owned	The chief	Total
	Frequency/percentage				
Damango	7 (18.4%)	60 (19.4%)	1 (16.7%)	3 (18.8%)	71 (19.2%)
Tamale	22 (57.9%)	175 (56.5%)	3 (50.0%)	9 (56.2%)	209 (56.5%)
Walewale	4 (10.5%)	35 (11.3%)	1 (16.7%)	2 (12.5%)	42 (11.4%)
Yendi	5 (13.2%)	40 (12.9%)	1 (16.7%)	2 (12.5%)	48 (13.0%)
Total	**38 (100.0%)**	**310 (100.0%)**	**6 (100.0%)**	**16 (100.0%)**	**370 (100.0%)**

Table 2.
Households' awareness about ownership of forest reserves.

District	Category of stakeholders managing forest reserve				
	Forest service division	Community and FSD	District assembly	Traditional rulers	Total
	Frequencies/percentages				
Damango	60 (19.6%)	7 (25.9%)	4 (17.4%)	0 (0.0%)	71 (19.2%)
Tamale	175 (57.2%)	12 (44.4%)	13 (56.5%)	9 (64.3%)	209 (56.5%)
Walewale	36 (11.8%)	2 (7.4%)	3 (13.0%)	1 (7.1%)	42 (11.4%)
Yendi	35 (11.4%)	6 (22.2%)	3 (13.0%)	4 (28.6%)	48 (13.0%)
Total	**306 (100.0%)**	**27 (100.0%)**	**23 (100.0%)**	**14 (100.0%)**	**370 (100.0%)**

Table 3.
Household awareness about who manages the forest reserves.

women leader (magazia) for Pusuga and the assembly person for Damongo, who knew that forest reserves are owned by traditional authorities, the rest (22 magazias and 22 assembly person) are of the opinion that forest reserves are owned by the state and managed by the FSD.

These responses are a manifestation of the processes of development planning in Ghana which have generally been top-down and highly centralized. According to Tandoh-Offin [16], while there has been four development plans under the so-called decentralized development planning in Ghana, majority of the decisions and activities that inform all of these plans since 1992 have followed similar approaches as those before, where central government agencies continued to have dominance in the processes and activities. This results affirms Adjei et al. [17] assertion that although Ghana's decentralized forest management intervention recognizes local authorities and creates the requisite democratic space for community representation in forest governance, failure of Forestry Commission (FC) to transfer adequate decision-making power and resources among other factors have collectively undermine local authorities' capacity to be responsive and accountable to the collaborative process in forest management. To the extent that chiefs and assembly members are unaware of the ownership of forest reserves in their localities, tells the un-participatory nature of our so-called decentralized system of development planning.

The above responses on ownership also show that fringe communities of forest reserves in Northern region are unaware of their tenure rights. Forest reserves in Ghana according to Boakye and Baffoe [18], are communally owned, but are held in trust by Government on behalf of the stool or skin landowners through the Forest Ordinance of 1927. According to Asare [19] ownership of forest is closely linked to the indigenous system of landownership. Land is communally owned and held in trust on behalf of the people through the stools and skins. Landowners therefore exert substantial control in deciding whether an area should be set aside for reservation. Though the national law grants the government the authority to constitute a reserve on any land it deems appropriate, landowners must be consulted through an arbitration process to take their concerns into consideration. What this means is that landowners whether stools or skins have immense power on setting aside an area as permanent forest estate and always have rights to revenue from the exploitation of the resource.

This was confirmed by the key informants interview with the head of operations of stool lands in the region, who revealed that, all the forest reserves in the region are situated on skin lands with the overlords being the Yaa Naa (Dagbon land), the Nayiri (Mamprugu land), the Yagbun-wura (Gonja land) and the Bimbila Naa

(Nanumba land). Unfortunately, the reality is that almost all chiefs and community members believe otherwise as there is no legal framework to that effect. The perception of the fringe communities about tenure rights of forest reserves upholds Brown's [20] report that Ghana's forest policies have not any legislative or tenurial change to stimulate the process of community involvement in forest management. It also agrees with the findings of Ahenkan and Boon [21] that consultation processes that led to the 1994 forest and wildlife policy had limited involvement of local communities. Further, it confirms the assertion by Boakye and Baffoe [18] that, even though Ghana's forest reserves are supposed to be managed by both public and communal property regimes, management is leaned more to the former. State control often deprives fringe communities of access to forest resources due to their bureaucratic and centralized processes which distance them from management decisions and access to benefits.

The lack of knowledge of communities about the ownership or tenure rights is indirectly contributing to their exclusion from forest management activities [4]. This may affect their commitment and cooperation toward any collaborative efforts.

4.2 Socioeconomic importance of forest reserves to fringe communities

Collective action in solving natural resource problems is more likely when users are dependent on the resource system for a major portion of their livelihood and when users have a common understanding of the problem [6, 22]. Gibson et al. [23] also assert that the value people place on their benefits and losses from development projects is critical in motivating and increasing their commitments to project sustainability. In this study therefore, we sought the opinions of respondents on the benefits derived by their communities from the forest reserves as well as their use-rights and responsibilities.

The survey revealed major benefit derived from the forest reserve which include; wood for charcoal and firewood, bush meat, herbal medicine, protection from rainstorm and poles for roofing. The least mentioned benefits include ropes, provision of shade, esthetics, and chew stick. **Table 4** shows a summary of the common benefits that are derived from the forest reserves by the fringe communities.

Given the statement by Odera's [24] that, sustained forest benefits to community members guarantees a successful collaborative forest management implementation, the enjoyment of aforementioned benefits by fringe communities in the study area is likely to boost their interest and commitment to any collaborative effort for sustainable management of the forest reserves. Notwithstanding that, the survey also revealed that not all the above benefits are enjoyed legally. Some community members harvest quantities beyond what is enjoyed on them. The study therefore sought views of both household respondents and key informants on communities' rights to use the forest reserves.

4.3 Admitted rights of communities to the forest reserves

Admitted rights are customary rights enjoyed by communities and individuals living close to forest reserve at the time of reservation when they are not seen as harmful to the forest. These rights include cultural and religious rights such as entry into the reserve to perform some cultural rites ([25], p. 29). The household survey revealed that majority 262 of the respondents (70.8%) admitted to having the right to freely enter the forest reserves whilst the remaining 108 (29.2%) said they do not have free access to forest reserves. The most common reasons given by the 29.2%

Major benefits	Least mentioned benefits
Wood for charcoal and firewood	Ropes
Bush meat	Provision of shade
Herbal medicine	Esthetics
Protection from rainstorm	Income
Poles for roofing	Chew stick
Thatch grass	Stimulation of rain or good weather
Grazing grounds for animals	Sand winning for building purposes
Fodder	Forest serving as a hideout for wee smokers
Food (fruits)	
Water	
Farmland	
Honey	
Using the reserve as a place of worship	
Using the forest as a place of convenience	
Using the reserve as recreational grounds	

Table 4.
Summary of benefits derived from the forest reserves.

(108) of household heads who said they are not allowed entry into the forest reserves are that, they are denied because:

Some members destroy the forest by cutting down trees for fire wood; the forest reserve is not for the community; if people are allowed to enter the forest freely, they can destroy the reserve; forest staff feel unsafe to let local people enter freely due to past experience with encroachers; and finally that some members go into the forest reserves to sell illegal drugs like marijuana.

These reasons by those who said they are denied entry into the reserves may suggest that some members are sometimes not allowed to enter the reserve not because they do not have the right, but due to the possible illegal activities they may carry out in the reserve. This is evident in the list of benefits (**Table 4**) enjoyed by communities which included harvesting of wood for charcoal and firewood for sale. As indicated by Marfo [26] the statutory law only recognizes "customary" access and use rights for domestic purposes. Therefore it is illegal for fringe communities to access non-timer forest products for commercial purposes. However, when respondents were asked about their admitted rights (**Table 5**) 78.4% of them admitted to their communities having rights to harvest medicinal plants, 70% admitted to collecting edible fruits like shea and dawadawa, 60.3% admitted to harvesting thatch grass for roofing and 54.6% admitted to harvesting firewood for domestic purposes. **Table 5** shows the admitted rights enjoyed by the fringe communities.

5. Response from Forestry Staff on Admitted Rights of Communities

Like the household heads, the interviews with the district forest managers revealed that fringe communities in the study area have the right of access into the reserve (using the right paths) and the right to harvest non-timber forest products for domestic use such as thatch grass, medicinal plants, dry wood for firewood,

	Harvest firewoodfor domestic use?		**Collect shea and dawadawa fruits?**		**Harvest medicinal plants?**		**Harvest thatch for roofing?**	
	Yes (Freq/%)	**No (Freq/%)**	**Yes (Freq/%)**	**No (Freq/%)**	**Yes (Freq/%)**	**No (Freq/%)**	**Yes (Freq/%)**	**No (Freq/%)**
Damongo	71 (35.1%)	0 (0.0%)	71 (27.4%)	0 (0.0%)	70 (24.1%)	1 (1.2%)	64 (28.7%)	7 (4.8%)
Tamale	77 (38.1%)	132 (78.6%)	106 (40.9%)	103 (92.8%)	131 (45.2%)	78 (97.5%)	77 (34.5%)	132 (89.8%)
Walewale	26 (12.9%)	16 (9.5%)	41 (15.8%)	1 (0.9%)	41 (14.1%)	1 (1.2%)	41 (18.4%)	1 (0.7%)
Yendi	28 (13.9%)	20 (11.9%)	41 (15.8%)	7 (6.3%)	48 (16.6%)	0 (0.0%)	41 (18.4%)	7 (4.8%)
Total	**(54.6%) 202 (100%)**	**168 (100%)**	**(70%) 259 (100%)**	**111 (100%)**	**(78.4%) 290 (100%)**	**80 (100%)**	**(60.3%) 223 (100%)**	**147 (100%)**

Table 5.
Responses on admitted rights enjoined by the fringe communities.

controlled grazing, shea nuts, dawadawa fruits and canes. However, due to abuse of rights for controlled grazing, it is no more allowed in the reserves. Some forest guards believe that communities are entitled to harvest non-timber forest products, but these rights are sometimes abused. One of the forest guards replied as follows:

> *"Community members are entitled to harvest dead wood, thatch grass, fodder, chew stick, and collect shea and dawadawa fruits without any conditions. These rights to some extent boost the interest of some good Samaritans to help in protecting the forest reserve but some community members sometimes abuse the rights" (Forest guard—Yendi district).*

In contrast to the views of the district managers and some forest guards, four of the eight forest guards interviewed are of the opinion that farmers do not have any right to collect any product from the reserves because those rights are confined to only off-reserve woodlands (woodlands outside reserves).

In reality, the responses from these four forest guards only imply that they do not understand what user-rights are, or are unaware of the user-rights of communities over forest reserves. The lack of awareness of forest guards may serve as the basis for abuse of use-rights of communities (by way of access restriction to forest reserves) and that can be a source of conflict between them and community members.

A chi- square test of independence on household responses on admitted rights gave p-value of 0.000. Being smaller than the alpha value of 0.05, a p-value of 0.000 indicate that there is significance differences between the forest districts with regards to respondents' views on their rights over the forest reserves. For instance, **Table 5** shows that for harvesting of fruits and medicinal plants, almost all the respondents in Damongo, walewale and Yendi answered in the affirmative whilst for Tamale 37.3% think otherwise. The trend is different with regards to harvesting of firewood for domestic use, where all the respondents from Damongo district answered in the affirmative with only 36.8% (77) of the respondents in Tamale district answering in the affirmative. This differences are probably because some community members do not know their rights. It may also be due to the over protective attitude of forest guards in the Tamale district as compared to those in other districts. Tamale Metropolis is the most concentrated in terms of population density and also the most urbanized district in the region, it has the highest proportion (14.3%) of the economically active population in the Northern region [13]. As such there is a likely need for more land for development, hence the need for tight precautions against encroachment. This could be a good reason to make forest guards in the Metropolis over protective of the forest reserves.

6. Views of chiefs, magazias and assembly persons on admitted rights

The key informant interview with chiefs partly confirms the responses from the household survey. Sixteen out of the 23 chiefs admitted to their communities having user-rights though sometimes with difficulties. The remaining seven chiefs (six from the Walewale district and one from Tamale district) indicated that their communities do not have any use- rights to the reserves. Similarly, 16 out of the 23 "magazias" (women leaders) interviewed admitted to their community members having rights to collect some firewood and some non-wood forest products for domestic purposes. It was revealed by the "magazias" that the rights of women differ from that of men. Whereas women usually fetch water from the streams in the reserves, gather vegetables and fruits and harvest firewood for domestic use, men are allowed to hunt, harvest termites (for fowls), poles, thatch, as well as harvest firewood for sale.

The responses from some household heads, chiefs and magazias who indicated their communities do not have user-rights to the reserves show they are ignorant of their rights. Their responses could be attributed to their exclusion from management decisions or due to lack of awareness of communities' rights by the forest guards who blatantly restrict communities' access to the reserves. This is manifested in the responses of some forest guards about their knowledge on communities' right to the reserves in the following paragraph.

When asked about the knowledge on user-rights of communities the following were some of the responses from the forest guards:

> *"Community members do not have any rights to the reserves. Farmers only have right to apply for land to farm through the plantation programme" (Forest guard—Walewale district)*

> *"There is no user-rights for communities apart from farming under the national plantation programme. They should go outside the reserve for whatever they want until such a time that it may be possible for us to allow them into the reserve for some resources" (Forest guard-Tamale district).*

The above responses from some forest guards point to the fact that administration of forest reserves in the study area is not participatory. To the extent that frontline staffs of FSD believe that fringe communities do not have any user-rights to forest reserves, shows FSD is still holding onto the "command and control" system of management as was reported by Husseini et al. [4]. Moreover, because some community members are unaware of their rights over the forest reserves, they have come to accept the denial of their rights as the norm and so they do not challenge the status quo. The likely result of this denial is illegal access of the forest resources by community members since there is no motivation for them to protect the forest reserves. A situation which downfalls one of the purposes of the revised

Forest and Wildlife policy (2012) as stated in its policy strategic direction Section 4.1 Subsection 4.1.2, clause f, which seeks to define forest and tree rights in all kinds of forests and ownership systems (2012, p. 28).

6.1 Social responsibility agreement (SRA)

A social responsibility agreement (SRA) may be defined as an agreement capable of being enforced in a court of law which imposes a duty on a timber contractor to provide certain acceptable social amenities to the communities whose forest the contractor operates to the tune of 5% of the annual royalties payable by the contractor. These agreements are ways of ensuring that all Timber Utilization Contract activities are done in a more socially responsible way that respect the rights of the land owners. It is usually attached as a schedule to the contract, which is legally binding. SRAs are negotiated by the FSD with the affected communities in advance of the contract being advertised ([25], p. 33).

When respondents were asked whether they enjoy social responsibility benefits from the reserves, 342 of them (representing 92.4%) admitted they do not benefit whilst 28 (7.6%) indicated they benefit. The reasons given by the 28 (7.6%) respondents, who answered in the affirmative, are that it is their social responsibility to protect the forest from intruders and fire outbreaks. Others think that their SRA is the benefits they get from the reserve like firewood, grazing fields, hunting and football pitches. Certainly, it is clear from the reasons given by the few (7.6%) who claim their communities enjoy SRA that, they do not understand the concept of SRA or the facility does not exist at all as indicated by the majority.

For the 342 (92.4%) who answered in the negative, some of them indicated that it was the first time they were hearing about SRA. Others said that the tree species in the Northern region are not attractive enough for exploitation due to the unfavorable climate, to warrant such social responsibility benefits. Obviously, the latter reason affirms the climate and vegetation of the region, ie. relatively dry with a single rainy season and Guinea savannah [14], which does not support the growth of tall timber tree species. Further, the interview with the forestry staff revealed that, forest reserves in the region were gazetted mainly for protective purposes and so little or negligible exploitation goes on in them. This result also agrees with Mashall [27] that the functions of forest reserves in the Northern territories were for the conservation of water supplies, shelterbelts, and prevention of erosion, shelterbelts and domestic supply of fuel wood, poles and possibly the production of a limited amount of sawn timber. This implies that production of commercial timber was from the unset not the main objective for forest reservation in the study area.

Similar to the views of household heads and the forestry staff, response chiefs, assembly persons and Magazias revealed that fringe communities do not enjoy any social responsibility benefits from the forest reserves. These responses were further confirmed by the head of operations of stool lands in the region, who revealed that due to the non-productive nature of forest reserves in the region, land owners do not receive any royalties or SRA from the reserves. According to him, most revenue from the skin lands in the region come from ground rents, compensation and annual rents. These are fees taken for use of land for farming, residential, commercial and other uses related to physical development. The head of operations of stool lands in the region believes that this situation derails the interest of the chiefs in the reserves.

His response confirms Oduro's [3] observation that the current forest and wildlife policy is silent on how to reward owners of forests, zoned for permanent protection. The author argues that although owners of production forests receive royalties, those whose forests have been designated for permanent protection and for environmental benefits do not receive any. The lack of social responsibility benefits for fringe communities is a hindrance to their allegiance to any effort toward CFM. Among the reasons for community participation in CFM is to secure access to a given forest and use rights as well as create new sources of income for communities [6]. Therefore, the rights of fringe communities in Northern region have to be secured if their commitment in the collaborative management of forest reserves is to be guaranteed.

7. Responsibilities of communities to the management of forest reserves

Fringe communities do not only have rights but also have the duties and roles in protecting forests within their areas, under the law and Constitution of Ghana. Section 19 of the LI 1649 places upon the land owner a responsibility not to allow the use of unregistered chainsaw for cutting trees or sawing timber on his or her land. As such, communities have the obligation to control the extent of forest exploitation so that the very important roles played by the forest resources can continue [25]. Households views were therefore sought on what they think are the responsibilities of community members to the management of forest reserves. **Table 6** shows the responses on what households perceive as responsibilities of their communities toward management of forest reserves.

The study showed that only three management activities namely boundary clearing, fire control and planting of trees in the reserves were admitted by the majority of households' respondents as the responsibilities of their communities toward the management of forest reserves (**Table 6**).

Similarly, responses from the key informants' interviews with the district forest managers, Forest guards, chiefs, assembly members and magazias revealed fringe communities' roles in the management of forest reserves to be provision of labour for plantation establishment and contract boundary clearing. These results are not surprising since these are the activities that FSD usually involves community members as reported by Husseini et al. [4].

Communities seeing these activities as their responsibilities are a positive condition that can be used as a means to awaken their interest and commitment to the collaborative management of forest reserves. That notwithstanding, it can be realized from **Table 6** that majority of the households do not regard the remaining four activities (Weeding, nursing of seedlings, boundary patrol and boundary planting) as their community responsibilities. This mind set defeats the very purpose of the revised forest and wildlife policy (2012, p. 27) which has in its policy strategic direction 4.1 Subsection 4.1.1 clause d; to "support local communities, non-governmental Organizations including women and youth to receive training that allow them meet their objective and assume optimal management responsibilities."

The implication is that in the absence of contract boundary cleaning or fire outbreak, and in the absence of plantation programs like the Modified taungya system in the reserves, communities do not bear any responsibility toward the management of forest reserves. Lack of shared responsibilities among the communities and forestry department coupled with communities' perception that forest reserves belong to the state, is likely to hinder any effort toward collaborative management. Collaborative forest management is most beneficial if both parties take on responsibilities that maximize their capacity ([28, 29], pp. 55–77).

District	Weeding as a responsibility of community members		Boundary clearing as a responsibility of community members		Nursing seedlings as a responsibility of community members		Boundary patrolling as a responsibility of community members		Fire control as a responsibility of community members		Boundary planting as a responsibility of community members		Planting trees as a responsibility of community members	
	Yes (%)	No (%)	Yes (%)	No (%)	Yes (%)	No (%)	Yes (%)	No (%)	Yes (%)	No (%)	Yes (%)	No (%)	Yes (%)	No (%)
Damango	32 (19.5%)	39 (19.0%)	54 (24.2%)	17 (11.6%)	12 (11.8)	59 (22.0%)	22 (15.4%)	49 (21.6%)	71 (24.1%)	0 (0.0%)	26 (17.0%)	45 (20.7%)	67 (24.5%)	4 (4.2%)
Tamale	78 (47.6%)	131 (63.6%)	103 (46.2%)	106 (72.1%)	49 (48.0%)	160 (59.7%)	68 (47.5%)	141 (62.1%) 1	136 46.3%)	73 (96.1%)	72 (47.1%)	137 (63.1%)	123 (44.9%)	86 (89.6%)
Walewale	24 (14.6%)	18 (8.7%)	29 (13.0%)	13 (8.8%)	16 (15.7%)	26 (9.7%)	22 (15.4%)	20 (8.8%)	40 (13.6%)	2 (2.6%)	24 (15.7%)	18 (8.3%)	39 (14.2%)	3 (3.1%)
Yendi	30 (18.3%)	18 (8.7%)	37 (16.6%)	11 (7.5%)	25 (24.5%)	23 (8.6%)	31 (21.7%)	17 (7.5%)	47 (16.0%)	1 (1.3%)	31 (20.3%)	17 (7.8%)	45 (16.4%)	3 (3.1%)

Table 6.
Household perception about communities' responsibilities to forest reserves.

8. Conclusion and Recommendations

We conclude that fringe communities enjoy some benefits and limited access to the forest reserves, but they do not know their tenure rights, user-rights and responsibilities to the reserves. Most front-line staff of FSD are unaware of the user-rights of fringe communities which is the reason for denying access of the reserves to community members. Improving collaborative management means changing the perceptions and attitudes of communities and frontline staff of FSD, respectively, and securing communities rights to the reserves.

8.1 Recommendations

To serve the interest of fringe communities and secure their commitment to responsible collaborative management of forest reserves, we recommend the following: The forestry department should educate community members on their tenure, rights and responsibilities to the reserves and involve them in the processes of decision-making. FSD in collaboration with collaborative forest management Unit (CFMU) of the Ghana forestry commission, should improve the capacity of their frontline staff on the rights and responsibilities of communities in CFM so as to avoid the unlawful denial of fringe communities of what rightfully belong to them.

Forest Fringe communities in the Northern region are not enjoying social responsibility benefits and royalties because the forest reserves were gazetted mainly to protect major rivers within the region. Meanwhile the beneficiaries of these rivers are the Ghana Water Company and the Volta River Authority who are making huge financial gains against the restrictions of right to communities. It is thus recommended that Government ensures that the two beneficiary companies give at least 0.5% of their revenue to FC, fringe communities and land owners as their social responsibility contributions. The part given to the FC could be used to develop the forest reserves through plantation development and to facilitate their activities with communities. That of the communities could be used to provide social amenities for them while the part for the land owners will boost their interest and motivate them to support their communities in sustainable management of forest reserves. This will, in the long term, benefit the two companies since the continuous protection of the rivers depends on the sustainable management of these forest reserves; the success of which in turn depends on the continuous support and cooperation of the fringe communities.

Author details

Rikiatu Husseini[1]*, Stephen B. Kendie[2] and Patrick Agbesinyale[2]

1 Department of Forestry and Forest Resources Management, Faculty of Natural Resources and Environment, University for Development Studies, Tamale, Ghana

2 Department of Integrated Development Studies, School for Development Studies, University of Cape Coast, Cape Coast-Ghana, Ghana

*Address all correspondence to: rikihuss@yahoo.com; rhusseini@uds.edu.gh

IntechOpen

© 2020 The Author(s). Licensee IntechOpen. This chapter is distributed under the terms of the Creative Commons Attribution License (http://creativecommons.org/licenses/by/3.0), which permits unrestricted use, distribution, and reproduction in any medium, provided the original work is properly cited.

References

[1] Ministry of Lands and Forestry. Ghana Forest and Wildlife Policy: Accra Ghana. 2012. Available from: https://www.fcghana.org/library_info.php?doc=43&publication:Forest%20&%20Wildlife%20Policy&id=15 [Accessed: February 5, 2020]

[2] Forestry Commission of Ghana. Forestry Sector Programmes: Savannah Resources Management Project. 2007

[3] Oduro KA. Multi-purpose Rainforest Management in Ghana: An Exploratory Study2002. p. 63

[4] Husseini R, Kendie SB, Agbesinyale P. Community participation in the management of forest reserves in the northern region of Ghana. International Journal of Sustainable Development and World Ecology. 2015;**23**(3):245-256. DOI: 10.1080/13504509.2015.1112858

[5] Metz B, Davidson OR, Bosch PR, Dave R, Meyer LA, editors. Contribution of Working Group III to the Fourth Assessment Report of the Intergovernmental Panel on Climate Change, 2007. Cambridge, United Kingdom and New York, NY, USA: Cambridge University Press; 2007

[6] Carter J, Gronow J. Recent Experience in Collaborative Management. A Review Paper. 2005. 57 p. Published by Center for International Forestry Research. Available from: http://www.cifor.cgiar.org

[7] Food and Agriculture Organization (FAO). Guidelines For the Management of Tropical Forests 1. The Production of Wood (FAO Forestry Paper 135). Based on the Work of Ian Armitage. Forest Resources Division FAO Forestry Department. Food and Agriculture Organiation of the United Nations Rome; 1998

[8] Food and Agriculture Organization. (a) FAO Forest Resources Assessment 2000 definitions; (b) Reports related to Elements discussed by the Inter-Governmental Panel on Forests at its Second Meeting (Geneva, 11–12 March 1996) and Aird, Paul (compiled by). 1994. Conservation for the Sustainable Development of Forests World-wide: A Compendium of Concepts and Term. The Forestry Chronicle Vol. 70(6):666-674; 2000

[9] Forestry Commission of Ghana. Forest and Wildlife Policy, 1994. Accra: Forestry Commission; 1994. pp. 1-7

[10] Krejcie RV, Morgan DW. Determining sample size for research activities. Educational and Psychological Measurement. 1970;**30**:607-610

[11] Buchanan JM, Tullock G. The Calculus of Consent. Michigan: University of Michigan Press; 1962

[12] Nsenkyire EO. Forestry Department's Strategies for Sustainable Savannah Woodland Management1999. p. 11

[13] Ghana Statistical Services (GSS). 2010 Population and Housing Census Regional Report. 2013. Available from: www.statsghana.gov.gh on 26/07/2016 at 13:15 pm

[14] Ghana Statistical Service. Population Dynamics—2010 Population and Housing Census. 2010. Available from: http://www.statsghana.gov.gh/pop_stats.html [Accessed: December 16, 2018]

[15] Kowero G, Campbell BM, Sumaila UR. Policies and Governance Structures in Woodlands of Southern Africa. Bogor: CIFOR; 2003. p. 438

[16] Tandoh-Offin P. Development planning in Ghana since 1992:

Implications for the decentralization process. International Relations and Diplomacy. ISSN: 2328-2134. 2013;**1**(2): 93-107

[17] Adjei PO, Agyei FK, Adjei JO. Decentralized forest governance and community representation outcomes: Analysis of the modified taungya system in Ghana. Environment, Development and Sustainability. 2020;**22**:1187-1209. DOI: 10.1007/s10668-018-0243-7

[18] Boakye KA, Baffoe KA. Trends in Forest Ownership, Forest Resource Tenure and Institutional Arrangements: Case Study from Ghana. 2010. 23 p. Available from: www.fao.org/forestry/12505.01d [Retrieved: October 10, 2011]

[19] Asare A. Operational Guidelines on Community Forest Committee. Ghana: Resource Management Support Centre; 2000. pp. 3-23

[20] Brown D. Principles and Practice of Forest Co-Management: Evidence from West Central Africa. European Union Tropical Forestry Paper 2. London; Brussels: ODI; European Commission; 1999

[21] Ahenkan A, Boon E. Assessing the impact of forest policies and strategies on promoting the development of non-timber forest products in Ghana. Journal of Biodiversity. 2010;**1**(2):85-102

[22] Ostrom E. Self-Governance and Forest Resources. CIFOR Occasional Paper No. 20. Bogor: CIFOR; 1999

[23] Gibson C, Williams JT, Ostrom E. Local enforcement and better forests. World Development. 2005;**33**(2): 273-284

[24] Odera JA. Changing forest management paradigm in Africa: A case for community based forest management systems. Research programme of sustainable use of dry land biodiversity (RPSUD). Discovery and Innovation. 2009;**21**:35

[25] Center for Public Interest Law (CEPIL). Handbook for Paralegals in Forest Communities in Ghana. Prepared by Center for Public Interest Law (CEPIL), Accra, Ghana. London, United Kingdom: International Institute for Environment and Development (IIED); 2009. pp. 1-42

[26] Marfo E. Security of Tenure and Community Benefits under Collaborative Forest Management Arrangements in Ghana. A country Report. CIFOR/RRI Research Report; 2009

[27] Mashall RC. Forestry in the Northern Territories of the Gold Coast. 1945

[28] Diez JJ, Martín-García B. Sustainable Forest Management: Case Studies. BoD—Books on Demand, 11 Apr 2012—Technology & Engineering. 2012. 272 p

[29] Scott P. Collaborative Forest Management—The Process. A Paper at the National Workshop on Community Forestry. Kampala, Uganda. 2000

Section 2

Waste Management

Chapter 7

Treatment of Dairy Wastewaters: Evaluating Microbial Fuel Cell Tools and Mechanism

Aman Dongre, Monika Sogani, Kumar Sonu, Zainab Syed and Gopesh Sharma

Abstract

Pollution caused by chemical and dairy effluent is a major concern worldwide. Dairy wastewaters are the most challenging to treat because of the presence of various pollutants in them. The characteristics of effluent like temperature, color, pH, Dissolved Oxygen, Biochemical Oxygen Demand (BOD), Chemical Oxygen Demand (COD), dissolved solids, suspended solids, chloride, sulfate, oil, and grease depend solely on the volume of milk processed and the form of finished produce. It is difficult to select an efficient wastewater treatment method for the dairy wastewaters because of their selective nature in terms of pH, flow rate, volume, and suspended solids. Thus there exists a clear need for a technology or a combination of technologies that would efficiently treat the dairy wastewaters. This chapter explains the energy-generating microbial fuel cell or MFC technologies for dairy wastewaters treatment having different designs of MFCs, mechanism of action, different electrode materials, their surface modification, operational parameters, applications and outcomes delivered through the technology in reducing the COD, BOD, suspended solids and other residues present in the wastewaters. The chapter also elaborates on the availability of various natural low-cost anode materials which can be derived from agricultural wastes. The current chapter elaborates on MFC technology and its tools used for dairy wastewater treatment, providing useful insight for integrating it with existing conventional wastewater treatment methods to achieve the degradation of various dairy pollutants including emerging micropollutants.

Keywords: dairy wastewaters, chemical oxygen demand, microbial fuel cell, electrode materials, surface modification

1. Introduction

In most countries, the dairy industry has shown tremendous growth in size and volume and is considered to be one of the largest sources of wastewater production [1]. With the swift industrialization that took place in the last century [2] and with the increased milk production rate (approximately 3% annually), dairy processing is generally regarded to be the biggest industrial wastewater source based on food production, especially in European areas [3–5].

The dairy industry is regarded as one of India's prime food industries and India ranked 1st among all the nations for milk produce [6]. The nuanced essence of wastewater from the dairy industry lies in the presence of carbohydrates, proteins, and fats. 2–2.5 L of wastewater is generated during the processing of every liter of milk [7]. A large number of industries are located around river banks and due to lack of stringent rules and regulations, a large volume of dairy wastewater is released without treatment which goes unutilized and pollutes the environment [8]. Dairy industries are also the potent source for various emerging contaminants specifically estrogens which find their way into the environment through wastewater effluents coming out from dairy industries and livestock activities. The fate of these emerging contaminants is recognized as an issue of public health and environmental concern. The current wastewater treatment technologies are not efficient enough for the removal of these pollutants as these are not monitored regularly due to the lack of stringent rules and regulations for these contaminants. Therefore there is a need to find an innovative technology that serves the purpose. Microbial Fuel Cell (MFC) treatment has gained appreciable interest because of its ability to treat wastewaters and simultaneously leading to the generation of power. This property of the MFC technology makes it suitable for the elimination of such recalcitrant pollutants from dairy wastewater making it sustainable in nature.

2. Characteristics of dairy wastewater

Dairy wastewater comprises of compound organic substances like carbohydrates, amino acids, and lipids which get converted into sugars, acids, and fatty acids upon hydrolysis [9]. Milk is a natural supplement for humans and animals. This consists of various nutrients including protein, vitamin, carbohydrate, and fat [10]. Milk is one of the most valuable items that join commerce, and it is vital as an object of food in daily life. Dairy wastewater contains large amounts of milk components like casein, lactose, fat, inorganic salts excluding detergents and sanitizers that accord greatly towards high BOD and COD [11]. In order to increase milk volumes and improve meat quality antibiotics and antimicrobials have been used in dairy animals at the sub-therapeutic level. This does not only harm the animal's health and well-being, but also significantly affects the health and well-being of humans through the intake of animal products like milk and meat, thereby affecting

Sr. no	Details	Value (in mg/L) except for pH
1.	pH	5.4–9.1
2.	Total solids	<2200
3.	Total dissolved solids (TDS)	<2100
4.	Suspended solids (SS)	<100
5.	Total chlorides	<600
6.	Sulfates	<1000
7.	Phosphates	<5
8.	Oil and grease	<10
9.	Chemical oxygen demand	<360
10.	Biological oxygen demand	<30
11.	Nitrates	<10

Table 1.
Standard norms of Central Pollution Control Board of India for dairy effluents (Environment (Protection) Rules, 1986).

public health [12]. According to the Environment (Protection) Rules, 1986 of India, the standard norms and limiting characteristics of dairy effluents as mandated by the Central Pollution Control Board (CPCB) of India are mentioned in **Table 1**.

Effluents from milk production have increased temperatures and varying pH, TSS, biochemical oxygen demand (BOD), chemical oxygen demand (COD), total nitrogen, total phosphorus and fat, oil and grease [3, 5, 13–16]. Generally, dairy wastewater has a white color with an undesirable odor and turbidity [4, 17, 18]. With 16–25°C annual temperatures, dairy effluent waste flows are hotter than urban wastewater (10–20°C), leading to accelerated biological deterioration correlated to other sewage treatment plants. Industrial dairy effluent average temperatures range from 17 to 18°C in winter, and from 22 to 25°C in summer.

3. Factors affecting characteristics of wastewater

3.1 Volume of wastewater

Water has an important role in milk processing. It involves cleaning, washing, disinfection, heating, and cooling in every step of the technologies used. There is a massive requirement for water [19]. A large amount of wastewater is generated through manufacturing processes [20]. Contaminated water from sanitary practices amounts to 50–80% of the actual water utilized in the dairy industry, while the rest of the 20–50% is clean water [20, 21]. It has been measured in volume units stating the quantity of wastewater is around 2.6 times more of the processed milk. The characteristics and the amount of the wastewater generated rely mainly on the size of the factory, technology used, efficacy and convolution of clean-in-place methodologies, good manufacturing practices, and so on [2, 5]. However, the world's mean wastewater volume can be decreased from 0.49–36.0 m^3 to 0.5–2.0 m^3 of effluent per m^3 of milk processed with the introduction of GMP [5, 22]. Nowadays, the volumetric charge designed is 1 m^3 of effluent per ton of milk produced. The instant discharges installed in the washing of tank on transport trucks, mediator pipelines, or machinery after every cycle are a significant aspect of the volume-based loading of wastewater treatment plants designed for dairies. In these cases, the effluent volumes are greater than those of the milk produced [23]. On average, the amount of wastewater discharged is 70% of freshwater being used at the plant [20]. Effluents from dairy products primarily include milk and its products misplaced in the processing cycles (milk spills, skimmed milk, spoiled milk, and curd remnants), inoculums used in processing, byproducts generated by manufacturing techniques (whey, milk and there permeates), and several additives used in manufacturing [16, 21, 24, 25]. Milk lost in wastewater treatment is about 0.49–2.5% of milk processed, which may rise up to 4% [26].

3.2 Categories of wastewater

3.2.1 Processing water

Cooling the milk in separate coolers along with condensation from the evaporation of whey and milk leads to the production of water for fermentation. Vapors are extracted from the milk and whey drying process that after condensation produces the cleanest effluent, but they can also consist of volatile compounds, whey, and milk droplets. Processing waters eliminate toxins, and after minimal pretreatment may be stored or released with stormwater [3]. Water can be reused for systems where the derivative materials are not in close contact. Typical applications involve hot water, steam manufacturing, and membrane washing. After the final flushing of bottles and condensates from secondary vapors created in vacuum installations, water from liquid cooling during pasteurization can be used for room washing, irrigation, and so on.

3.2.2 Cleaning wastewater

Wastewater purification typically benefits from cleaning machinery within close contact with dairy goods. This involves spillage of milk and substance, whey pressing or brine, malfunctioning of the clean in place effluents, or machinery errors. More than 93% of the organic contents contained in the effluent are partly the remnants of milk, cheese, whey, butter, sugar, honey, and fruit concentrate or stabilizers. These effluents are found in significant concentrations and are extremely toxic thereby needing more care.

3.2.3 Sanitary wastewater

Sanitary wastewater is utilized in washrooms, toilets, etc. Sanitary wastewater has parallels with urban wastewater composition and is typically piped straight to sewage facilities. It may be used as a supply of nitrogen for irregular dairy effluents after a secondary aerobic treatment. Furthermore, by-products from agricultural processes like milk, whey, and their permeate can be classified independently if they are segregated individually from other wastewater sources [27, 28].

4. Dairy wastewater treatment

For the dairy industry, common wastewater treatment strategies involve grease traps, oil-water separators to remove floatable solids, flow equalization, and clearers to isolate suspended solids. Biological treatment consists of the aerobic and anaerobic methodologies. Anaerobic treatment accompanied by aerobic treatment is also used to minimize soluble organic matter (BOD), and the reduction of biological nutrients (BNR) is used to increase nitrogen and phosphorus levels. Biological aerobic treatment requires cellular destruction in the presence of oxygen. Conventional aerobic treatment of dairy manure includes procedures such as activated sludge, batch sequencing generator, revolving biological contactors, trickling pipes, aerated lagoons, or a variation of these.

Treatment of anaerobic wastewater has emerged as a feasible and inexpensive alternative particularly for high BOD removal over conventional aerobic treatment. Anaerobic methods of treatment involve up-flow anaerobic sludge blanket or UASB, anaerobic batch sequencing reactors or ASBR, continuous-flow reactor, hybrid anaerobic digesters, up/downflow anaerobic filter, and various 2-stage processes that use acid and methane forming bacteria. **Figure 1** shows the sequential treatment of dairy wastewater through mechanical, physical, chemical and biological treatment methods [20].

4.1 Mechanical treatment

This is the initial phase of dairy wastewater treatment and this includes grit pool, skimming tank, and main clarifiers. During further effluent processing, the large floating material is removed by screens, in-turn avoiding the chocking of pipes. Chambers are used for extracting heavier inorganic substances like sand, gravel, etc. The aim of installing skimming tanks is to extract oil, grease, pieces

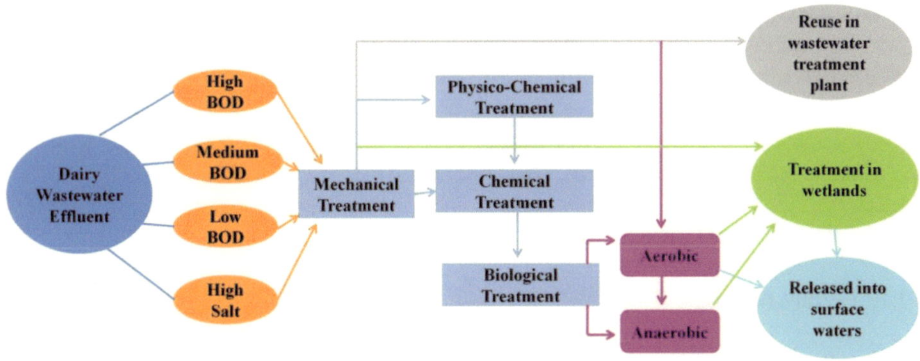

Figure 1.
Dairy wastewater treatment alternates (adapted from [20]).

of wood, skins of fruit; etc. The clarifier helps matter to settle at a very slow rate or sediment at the bottom in the tank. The substance accumulated underneath is known as sludge [29].

4.2 Chemical treatment

Chemical treatment is also recognized as precipitation. This is performed by adding flocculants to wastewater and vigorous mixing with agitators. This method precipitates insoluble phosphate into larger flocks, in the form of small pellets. In pre-sedimentation basins, the greater flocks settle as the main sludge, whereas a clear supernatant fluid overflows into a lake for biological therapies. Sedimentation lagoons are armed with tools to continuously scrape the sediment towards a sump or oblique gutters to keep water away from the clarified surface layers [29].

4.3 Biological treatment

Milk effluent includes organic waste; therefore most viable methods for the elimination of organic content are biological degradation. However, sludge generated may lead to serious and costly problems towards disposal, particularly during the processes of aerobic biodegradation. This can be further worsened due to the tendency of sludge to absorb various organic compounds and poisonous heavy metals also. Nonetheless, biological treatment has the profits of dynamic organic microbial processes and the ability for adsorption of heavy metals effectively. Biological waste management strategies have an immense capacity to incorporate diverse types of biological schemes for selective elimination [30].

4.3.1 Aerobic treatment

Microorganisms cultured in an O_2-rich environment degrade organics by oxidizing matter to CO_2, soil, and cellular material. Aerobic treatment methods include activated sludge reactors, rotating biological reactors, conventional filters for trickling, and so on [30].

4.3.2 Anaerobic treatment

Anaerobic method of treatment is mainly intended for the biological processing of high strength wastewater. It is a process by which microbes are used in the absence of O_2 to digest organic matter by converting it to biogas (CH_4 and CO_2)

and some inorganic contents. 6% of the organic load can be converted into biogas from the wastewater and the rest can be used for cell growth and maintenance. The process reactors are shielded to avoid air obstruction and the release of odors [30].

5. Advanced technologies for the treatment of dairy effluent

5.1 Physio-chemical process

5.1.1 Electrocoagulation (EC)

The electrocoagulation (EC) method could be the alternative treatment option for dairy wastes. Electrocoagulation is an electrolysis process that uses specific electrodes by transferring electrical current via the effluent to extract dissolved organic waste, turbidity, and coloring matter. The method assists in the substantial removal of suspended colloidal particles.

5.1.2 Adsorption

Adsorption was found beneficial among the various physio-chemical treatment methods for removing organic compounds in wastewaters. Activated carbon is mainly used in treating wastewater, among other types of adsorbent materials. Although certain additional adsorbents can also be used to treat streams of wastewater and are cost-effective as well. For instance rice husk ash, coal fly ash, etc. [31].

5.1.3 Membrane treatment

Microfiltration, nanofiltration, ultrafiltration, reverse osmosis, and electrodialysis are typical membrane separation processes. Highly feasible product recovery is possible using these methods and the effluent generated is of high quality which can be used directly [31].

6. MFC in dairy wastewater treatment

The organic contents in wastewater make it a convenient substrate for MFC applications [32]. Various studies have shown that wastewaters from the dairy industry generate significantly less power as compared to the other wastewaters in MFC [33, 34]. Carbohydrates and proteins are among the main components of dairy wastewater. Their influence on the generation of power in MFC along with COD removal by using dairy wastewater as a substrate was mentioned by [35], and was reported that reduction in proteins and carbohydrates does not have a virtuous relation with power generation. The presence and elimination of antibiotics found in dairy wastewaters is a major problem. New technologies need to be employed to solve this problem. Researchers working with dairy wastewaters have concentrated on developing the MFC design that will boost the power generation (**Table 2**). Various surface modifications of the electrode material have improved MFC efficiency by increasing the power output [36].

MFCs are distinctive biofuel cells among the various bio-electrochemical systems that generate electricity by employing microorganisms [41]. For electricity production, hydrogen fuel and oxygen are utilized by the microbial fuel cell. Using bacteria as biocatalyst, MFC converts organic matter into electrical energy [42, 43]. An ideal MFC contains two chambers (cathode and anode), both separated via a proton transfer membrane. The anode chamber consists of the electroactive microorganism, thereby making the chamber biotic whereas the cathode chamber remains abiotic. The available microorganisms in the anode chamber act as the biocatalysts, thereby leading to the degradation of organic matter in order to generate electrons that are transferred to the cathodic chamber via an electric circuit. The free electrons present on the cathode leads to the reduction of oxygen for processing of water as shown in Eqs. (1) and (2).

$$4H^+ + 4e^- + O_2 \rightarrow 2H_2O \quad (1)$$

Or

$$4H^+ + 4e^- + 2O_2 \rightarrow 2H_2O_2 \quad (2)$$

Considering glycerol as an electron donor and oxygen as a terminal electron acceptor, the following reactions occurring in MFCs, shown in Eqs. (3-5).

$$\text{Anode}: C_3H_8O_3 + 3H_2O \rightarrow 3CO_2 + 14H^+ + 14e^- \quad (3)$$

$$\text{Cathode}: 3O_2 + ½O_2 + 14e^- + 14H^+ \rightarrow 7H_2O \quad (4)$$

$$\text{Overall}: C_3H_8O_3 + 3O_2 + ½O_2 \rightarrow 3CO_2 + 4H_2O + \text{Biomass} + \text{Electricity} \quad (5)$$

In biological fuel cells, the catalyst is either an enzyme or the microorganisms as simple as Baker's yeast. Microbial fuel cells convert the chemical energy

S. no.	Types of MFC	System configuration		%COD removal	Maximum surface/volume power density	Refs.
		Anode	Cathode			
1.	Single chamber MFC	Graphite coated SS anode	Carbon cloth	91%	20.2 W/m^3	[36]
2.	Single chamber MFC	SS mesh anode with graphite coating	Carbon cloth	80%	27 W/m^3	[37]
3.	Dual-chamber MFCs	Plain graphite plates	Plain graphite plates	91%	3.2 W/m^3	[8]
4.	Dual-chamber MFCs	Graphite-sprayed SS mesh	Graphite-sprayed SS mesh	91%	5.15 W/m^3	[38]
5.	Dual-chamber MFCs	3D laminated composites	3D laminated composites	81%	122 W/m^3	[39]
6.	Dual-chamber MFCs	Carbon fiber brush	Platinum/ carbon	NA	1056 mw/m^2	[40]

Table 2.
Performance of different types of MFC using dairy wastewater as substrate (authors created).

of carbohydrates present in the substrate, such as alcohol and sugars directly into electrical energy. Currently, efforts have been made towards using MFCs for domestic wastewater treatment and at the same time point, electricity production considering the environmental issues and further reuse of waste [44]. Sewage sludge of anaerobic nature is used to inoculate MFCs, as it is conveniently used from a wastewater treatment plant and it has largely diverse bacterial communities containing electrogenic bacterial strains [45]. MFCs have functional and operational benefits compared with the presently used technologies for producing energy from organic content [46].

7. Comparison of anodic metabolisms in bioelectricity generation by dairy wastewater treatment in microbial fuel cell

The growing concern about environment safety and rapid depletion of energy reserves have made it imperative to update the waste management methods from the mere waste treatment to a novel prospect of waste to energy [47]. Microbial Fuel Cell is a novel technology for electricity generation from organic matter present in wastewater, treating wastewater simultaneously solves energy crisis and environmental damage issues [48]. To generate electricity, Microbial Fuel Cell (MFC) is a

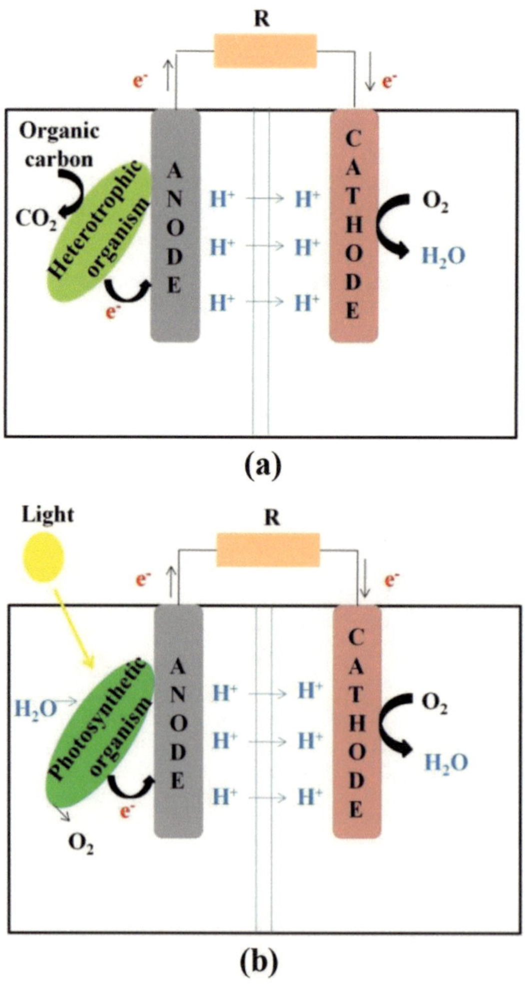

Figure 2.
(a) Anaerobic anodic metabolism in MFC (adapted from [51]). (b) Aerobic anodic metabolism in MFC (adapted from [51]).

bio-electro-chemical system that uses bacterial oxidation of biodegradable organics. The development of bio-potential takes place when organic substances get oxidized to electrons and protons through microbial metabolism. The bacteria transport the electrons to the anode via a variety of mechanisms such as electron shuttles or solid conductive matrix. Then electrons get transported to the cathode via circuit externally [45]. The protons from the anode chamber are transferred to the cathode chamber via passing through the proton exchange membrane, where they form water by combining with the electrons and O_2 in the presence of a mediator. The potential difference between the bacteria's respiratory metabolism and the electron acceptor creates the voltage and current required to produce electricity [45, 49]. In a study, the MFC system is scaled up, consisting of 40 individual cells that have been constructed and evaluated which can generate 4.2 W/m^3 of energy and capable of powering LED panel [50]. Extensive research and scaling up of MFCs will further enable adequate conversion of waste to energy. For long term use, MFCs can be clubbed with the existing technologies for wastewater treatment and electricity generation. MFC uses anaerobic anodic metabolism where it employs bacteria as a substrate for the reduction of COD from wastewaters as shown in **Figure 2(a)**. This technology is further followed by aerobic anodic metabolism where it employs algae as a substrate and under photosynthetic conditions causes the reduction of nitrates and phosphates from wastewaters as shown in **Figure 2(b)**. This combination of treatment with an effective and proper choice of anode material will help in the generation of power followed by the degradation of wastewaters. Further studies need to be carried out for the degradation of antibiotics in such an innovative integrated MFC model for dairy wastewater.

8. Degradation mechanism

The bacteria transfers the electrons to the anode through different mechanisms, including (i) direct bacterial contact via cytochrome, endogenous redox-active based self-mediated electron transfer, such as pyocyanin and conductive pili; (ii) artificial electron shuttles or mediator. Electrons then get transported to the cathode by passing via an external circuit, while the protons are passed through from the anode chamber to the cathode chamber by proton exchange membrane or PEM. At the cathode, the concoction of electron, proton, and O_2 occurs for the production of water. The potential difference between the respiratory metabolism of bacteria and the electron-acceptor creates the voltage and current necessary for electrification.

9. Electron transfer mechanism

The power output of an MFC rests on different aspects including the type of organic content available in wastewater, electron transfer rate from bacteria to the anode, and the membrane ability to carry hydrogen ions [52]. Some micro-organisms are known to transfer electrons to their external environment from their oxidative metabolic pathways, which are called exoelectrogens [53]. Geobacter and Shewanella are the two prime bacterial genera that are known with this ability; the extracellular transportation of electrons to the electrodes occurs through three different ways namely:

1. Direct transfer of electrons

2. Mediator based electron transfer, and

3. Nanowires based electron transfer.

9.1 Direct transfer of electrons

Geobacter and Shewanella sp. use a direct electron transport mechanism where the electrons are dispatched directly to the electrode surface. The outer C-type cytochrome membrane is associated with the direct dispatch of NADH-produced electrons [54].

9.2 Mediator based electron transfer

Some species of bacteria like Shewanella and Pseudomonas secrete certain shuttle molecules like flavins, to pass electrons to electrodes via the cell membrane of the bacteria [55, 56].

9.3 Nanowires based electron transfer

Genera of Geobacter and Shewanella are evident to use conductive auxiliaries for transporting the electrons outside of the cell [57, 58]. Such conductive networks, called nanowires, are cellular outgrowths for as long as 20 μm. These nanowires are claimed to have a substantially higher electrical conductivity than the synthetic metallic nanostructure [59].

10. Anode materials for MFCs

Choosing and designing an anode has a direct effect on the performance parameters which includes the microbial adhesion, transfer of electrons, and oxidation of fuels. An MFC system's achievable power density depends on the selection of an anode that significantly affects the output of an MFC system [60]. As a consequence, achieving higher power density requires the ability to facilitate the improved transfer of electrons from the bacterial cells to the external circuit, thus the anode is of prime importance towards attaining this objective [61]. The electron transfer process necessitates the donation of an electron using extracellular electron transfer (EET) towards the anode surface by the anode respiring bacteria or ARB and, consequently, the current flow in the circuit externally. This mechanism has been interpreted as being similar to transfer electrons to the anode surface from the cell through direct electron transfer mechanism, soluble electron shuttles diffusion, and the transfer of electrons from biofilm via solid component (pili) [61]. Essential features for the anode to attain the best performance include biocompatibility [62–64], corrosion-resistant, low electrical resistance, and high conduction of electricity [62]. The anode must also be of chemically inert in nature that can function in an environment containing diverse biodegradable wastewater composed of variety of organic and inorganic components that are able to react with the anode material causing its deterioration inefficiency.

Lots of anode materials have been used in the last five years to create various anodes for MFCs. The choice of material for the construction of anode, in particular, is significantly influenced by improvement in different MFC system structures. On a particular note, various exotic carbonaceous materials' use is on a hike. This new category includes stainless steel, stainless steel with modified surface, and anodes based on graphene-based carbonaceous anodes. In many recent studies the graphene-based anodes are found very encouraging [65–68]. The grapheme composite anodes have been stated for higher power production [69–71]. Similarly, the use of carbon nanofibers, carbon nanotubes single and multi-walled anodes has also been documented for high-performance MFCs [72]. This chapter has categorized a few of the recent approaches in the configuration of anode materials dividing them into four vast categories, namely modern carbon-based anodes, carbon-based composite anodes, surface-modified and metal-based anodes, and each of these categorized materials are discussed individually in the proceeding sections.

10.1 Modern carbon-based anodes

In MFC systems, various anode materials based on carbon have been used over the last decade. These include carbon cloth, carbon paper, or sheet or graphite plates and graphite rod. Using carbon-based anode materials has the advantages of cost-effectiveness, biocompatible nature, efficient electrical conductivity, and chemical stability [73]. Due to their potentially high-performance enhancement and excellent properties, these have been recognized as being very useful for building MFCs. Accessible surface area is an essential factor that affects the efficiency of these anode materials [74, 75]. Such anodes comprises of natural or synthetic anode materials which are as follows:

10.1.1 Natural anode materials

Synthesis of high-efficiency anode components, by using renewable and recyclable components, provides an outstanding ecological solution including both deriving reusable energy from nature and maintaining biodiversity. An interesting example is the layered corrugated carbon anode production from low priced packaging material through carbonization (LLC). It is important to remember that the LCC's 3D surface is normally tunable by differing the height and layers of the flute. A six times increase in the number of layers resulted in a successive rise in current density because of the potential for biofilm formation in wider surface areas. It is evident that the LCC anode has four times the current density as correlated with the graphite felt anode. Natural anode materials prove to be an ideal option for low priced microbial fuel cells due to their 3-dimensional microporous structures, increased electron transfer rate, and high kinetics of the electrogenic bacterial population. A variety of recently produced highly 3-dimensional porous anode material uses LCC as a low-cost high-performance substitute, usually manufactured from carbonized recycled paper [76, 77]. High performance was obtained from the use of 3-dimensional anodes, based on exoelectrogens' 3-dimensional growth. Stronger anode kinetics can be attained by using maximal anode surface area, but the efficiency only rises gradually as the reaction reaches the triple-phase boundary, i.e. lower inner resistance among anode, cathode, and electrolyte. Interestingly, in comparison with the plane graphite electrode, 8 times better performance is seen with carbonized corn stem. However, few benefits of the aforementioned electrode material include increased biocompatibility, less internal resistance, and rougher surface that facilitated linkage to biofilm. A coated rough electrode, constructed from the carbonization of common packaging materials, was observed to be the highest rated anode of all carbon-based modifications. The current densities achieved were 201 A/m^2 and 391 A/m^2, respectively, from three and six corrugated layers. This is a low-cost material with higher performance for the construction of MFC.

10.1.2 Synthetic anode materials

It is quite evident that 3-dimensional carbon fiber (non-woven) can achieve a maximal current density of up to 31 A/m^2 which is prepared by electrospinning and blowing the solution. The performance and efficiency of MFCs also depends on the system architecture, based on these 3D materials [78]. Double-sided air cathode reduces the boundaries of mass transfer. The stainless steel frame was used for this design as a current assimilator and a carbon fiber support in the 3D matrix. In another study [79], it has been shown that an upgraded adaptation of the carbon-based multi-brush anode achieved admirable power generation. The power generated is similar to that obtained with a carbon anode with a single brush design. Because of cathodic limitations, the MFC system [80] gave a comprehensive comparison of carbon-based material for anodes, like graphite, carbon fiber veil, polycrystalline carbon rod, glossy carbon rod, graphite foil. The maximal current density attainable was calculated using a standardized biofilm grown in domestic wastewater. At 30°C, graphite, and polycrystalline carbon-based rods, both reached catalytic currents peaks of around 501 $\mu A\ cm^{-2}$. By comparison, carbon fiber veil or paper-based material delivered a 40.1% higher current than graphite anode due to its large, microbial rich surface area [80]. In comparison with steady-state reactor, the rotational motion of carbon brush anodes in the tubular microbial fuel cell resulted in a 2.6 times rise in performance. The rotation was adequately mixing the nutrient and minimizing the limitation of mass transport. In general, several studies have shown that the existence and electrode content affected the kinetics of the biocatalyst. It has also been shown that the internal resistance is a major aspect affecting the overall performance. The use of 3-dimensional anode models, like carbon nanotubes (CNTs), nanofibers (CNF), gold/poly (e-caprolactone) microfibers (GPM), and gold/poly (e-caprolactone), to reduce the internal resistance increasingly preferred in microbial fuel cells. 3-dimensional anode material has less internal resistance than two-dimensional anodes. Such anode materials serve to increase the efficiency of nutrients, H^+, and O_2 transfer via biofilm as compared to macroscopic carbon-based paper and planar gold-based anodes. Chemical assisted surface alteration of the CNT/CNF-based anodes has been demonstrated to reduce kinetic losses and cellular toxicity. Ren et al. [81] investigated vertically aligned CNT, randomly aligned CNT, and spin-spray layered CNT. The studied nanotube-materials have a 4000 m^{-1} very large surface area to volume ratio which is very huge. The results showed that CNT-based anodes attracted more electrogenic microbes than bare gold, resulting in a thicker and more stable formation of biofilms. Using CNTs in a miniature MFC device, a maximal power density of 3321 W/m^3 was achieved [81]. This was 8.5 times greater than that attained with the 2D-electrode systems.

10.2 Composite anodes

Composite anodes have intrigued extensive interest recently. These materials were utilized to attain synergistic effects with two or more materials to alter original content, resulting in increased anodic kinetics efficiency.

10.2.1 Graphite-polymer composites

Tang, Yuan, Liu, & Zhou prepared a nano-structured capacitive layer of modified 3D anode consisting of core-shell nanoparticles derived from titanium dioxide (TiO_2) and egg albumin (EWP). This was built into a loofah sponge carbon (LSC) to achieve an efficient 3-dimensional electrode. The LSC's coating with TiO_2 and heat treatment caused tiny particles to cover its entire surface. The resulting altered anode supplied greater power than a graphite anode. The increased power was associated with the increased electrochemical capacity of 3-dimensional anodes and to the synergistic effects of carbon derived TiO_2 and EMP with good characteristics like more surface area, improved biocompatibility, and favorable surface functionality for easier extracellular electron transport [82]. The anodes of open-celled carbon scaffold (CS) and carbon scaffold graphite (CS – GR) were created by carbonizing the microcellular polyacrylonitrile (PAN) and composite PAN/graphite (PAN – GR). The PAN-GR was created by utilizing supercritical carbon dioxide (Sc-CO_2), as a practical foaming agent. The maximal current density achieved with a CS altered anode was 102% greater than that with carbon felt. Improved performance has been referred to as enhanced hydrophilicity and biocompatibility caused by carbonization. Carbon nanofibers with improved graphite fibers and reduced nanotube-coated graphene oxide/carbon scaffold promise new composite anode materials. Using carbon nanofibers as anodes for MFC modified graphite fibers achieved a maximal current density at a peak of 35.8 A/m^2. The nanotube-coated scaffold anode device with reduced graphene oxide/carbon obtained a power density of 335 mW/m^3. Composite graphite fiber brush anode (MFC-GFB) was used in combination with granular graphite (MFC-GG) in a tubular setup to boost the power density 5.2 and 1.3 times greater than that obtained with MFC-GG and MFC-GFB. The improved efficiency of the system was referred to the thick biofilm of the system, and scant internal resistance [83]. Six types of micro or nano-structured anodes utilized in micro-sized MFCs have been compared. The anodes under consideration included carbon nanotubes (CNTs), carbon nanofibers (CNFs), gold or poly (e-caprolactone) microfibers (GPM), nanofibers (GPN), planar gold (PG), and traditional carbon paper (CP). All anode's effectiveness was tested with the use of small and micro-liter sized MFC. A homemade 3-dimensional anode coating has been developed using the iron net as the structural anchor and fastened to a carbon felt layer [82]. The combination of carbon powder and a solution mixture of 30% polytetrafluoroethylene (PTFE) have greatly affected power generation. The performance was assessed using an acetate-fed MFC and the anode coating which improved the power generation considerably. The internal resistance measured in the MFC system was decreased by 59.3% compared to the non-coated iron net, whereas the power density improved by 1.49 times.

10.2.2 Carbon nanotubes composite

Due to their special intrinsic properties, including high conductivity, rust tolerance, high surface area and electrochemical inertness, the usage of CNTs has drawn significant attention lately.

10.2.3 Multi-walled carbon nanotubes composite

Multi-walled carbon nanotubes (MWCNTs) with carboxyl functional groups were utilized for MFC air respiration. It demonstrated a 2-fold improvement in power density relative to the carbon cloth electrode [84]. In a recent report, multi-walled carbon nanotubes/SnO_2 nanocomposite coated on the glass fiber electrode is used [85] producing maximal power densities of 1422 mW/m^2 and 457 mW/m^2, respectively [86]. The use of graphite coated with manganese oxide/multiwalled carbon nanotubes composites has greatly elevated benthic microbial fuel cells in another study. The composite provided greater hydrophobicity, kinetic movement, and power density when opposed to the standard graphite electrode. The shift seen was attributed to the consolidated impact of the Mn ions electron transfer shuttle on the reaction site and its redox reactions (i.e. anode and biofilm) [87].

10.2.4 Graphene anodes

Graphene is an allotrope of 2D crystalline carbon with unusual characteristics such as large surface area (up to 2600 m^2/g), exceptionally high electrical conductivity (7200 S/m), and exceptional tensile strength up to 35 GPa [88]. Graphene-modified stainless steel mesh (GMS) power density was recorded to be 18 times higher than that of a stainless steel mesh anode (SSM) and 17 times higher than that of polytetrafluoroethylene modified SSM (PMS) [68]. The significant improvement was recognized due to increased surface area of the electrodes, improved adhesion of bacterial biofilms, and efficient extracellular electron transfer. The current stainless steel collector (SS) boosts electrical conductivity for electrode, and the overall efficiency of the system is enhanced by the current SS assimilator which reduces internal resistance. Chen et al. [69] used an ice template as an anode to create a versatile macroporous 3D graphene sponge. The microporous 3D graphene allowed the random propagation of bacteria and resulted in a high biofilm span and increased performance [69]. From another study, tin oxide (SnO_2) nanomaterials were utilized on the reduced graphene oxide surface (R-GO-SnO_2) able to generate electricity that was approximately 5 times higher than the use of an unaltered graphene oxide (reduced). Collegial effects among SnO_2 and graphene and strong biocompatibility were liable for the much stable formation of bacterial biofilms and the efficiency of charges transfer [86]. Reduced graphene oxide/carbon nanofibers (R-GO-CNTs sponges) melamine sponges based on dip-coating technique tend to cater to a huge electrically conductive surface area for *Escherichia coli* growth as well as electron transport in MFC [65]. Four R-GO-CNT sponges were tested with varied thicknesses and configurations, but the thinnest one (with a thickness of 1.5 mm) displayed prime efficiency, generating a maximal current density of 336 A/m^3 [65]. The usage of a redesigned anode built from graphene-polyaniline nanocomposite was also found to produce power three times greater than carbon cloth [70]. Often used as an anode for MFC was a 3-dimensional reduced graphene oxide-nickel foam (R-GO-Ni) by accurate deposition of R-GO sheets to the nickel foam substratum. The R-GO thickness may be modified in comparison to the surface region of the electrode by initiation cycles. This macro-porous scaffolding design not only offers a 3-dimensional surface for microbial growth but also promotes the mobility of substrates inside the culture medium. The efficiency was extensively better than with the usage of nickel foam and various graphite materials dependent on anodes [63, 64]. The formation in MFC of highly crystalline graphene or nickel electrode with Shewanella putrefaciens provided the power density of typical MFC carbon cloth anode 13 times greater. Because of the minimal cost of hollow Ni and the low weight percent of graphene (5% w), this composite electrode provides good potential in the development of efficient MFCs for greater power generation [71].

10.3 Surface modified anodes

The electrode surface has a tremendous role in the total anode's efficiency. Currently, several reports have stated that surface alteration is advantageous in actuating increased bacterial adhesion and better biocompatibility that favors electron transfer kinetics. The surface alterations using TiO_2-carbon fabric-based nanofiber usually attain the highest current density of 7.99 A/m^2, whereas a changed surface with carbon nanotubes and coated with conductive polymer had a maximal power density of 1573 mW/m^2. The two broad surface treatments that are most generally used are silicone coating and graphite or carbon surface application. Each of these surface alteration forms is discussed in subsequent subsections.

10.3.1 Conductive polymer coatings

Provided their high conductivity and biocompatibility, conductive polymer coatings have drawn considerable interest [85]. Composite polyaniline (PANI)-mesoporous tungsten trioxide (m-WO_3) had been formed and utilized as a catalyst, free of precious metals [63, 64]. PANI was mounted onto m-WO_3 by the chemical oxidative process. The composite's catalytic nature was elaborated through the application of electrochemical techniques. Significant efficiency changes were observed with the composite based on the-WO_3 and PANI combinations. The m-WO_3 has excellent biocompatibility while PANI has strong electrical conductivity [63, 64]. PANI networks' electrode location on graphene nanoribbons (GNRs)-coated carbon paper (CP/GNRs/PANI) has been found to increase power generation as opposed to GNR and CP usage. The improvement was due to the positively charged PANI backbone which increased the affinity of interaction with negatively charged microbial cells and thus favored direct transfer of electrons through cytochromes. Conductive GNRs significantly enhanced CP/GNRs/ PANI electrode conductivity in neutral environments. This discovery explicitly shows that the synergistic impact of both components was responsible for major energy production changes. In another report, carbon nanotubes/polyaniline carbon paper (CNT/PANI carbon paper) is used and correlated with other conventional carbon paper [63, 64]. The findings revealed that the CNT/PANI carbon paper has obtained a lower ohmic loss and improved power generation. The use of CNTs enhanced the surface area for the biofilm span, as well as achieved a higher electrical conductivity. The achieved maximum power density of 257 mW/m^2 corresponds to an increase of 343% and 186%, respectively, when compared with those achieved with the pristine GF MFC and the PANI/GF MFC, respectively [89].

10.3.2 Graphite/carbon surface modifications

Vertically targeted TiO_2 modified carbon paper shapes vertically breaching pores which offer the bacteria a large area of contact for direct electron transmission. This was particularly useful in a recent study for improving the delivery of nutrients, attaining high biocompatibility, and supporting the electron transport routes [90]. Through using a TiO_2-NSs or CP as a bio-anode, a mixed consortium inoculated MFC's average power production density was improved by 64% relative to using a pure CP as a bio-anode. In a different study, dual nanofiber mats TiO_2 (rutilo)–C (semi-grafito)/C (semi-grafito) were used for MFC anode, one fiber consisting mainly of O, Ti, and C, while the content of the other fiber was predominantly Carbon. The dual nanofiber had stronger efficiency than a single nanofiber. The highest existing density obtained in that analysis was 8 A/m^2 [91]. The activated carbon (AC) with SSM (AcM) and Fe_3O_4 anode was also investigated for MFCs, and capability enhancement was related to device efficiency [92]. Nano-goethite was added with 0, 2.5, 5.0, and 7.5% (mass percentage) to the activated carbon (AC) powder and pressed onto the stainless steel wire. The composite material anodes produced 35 percent more power than a non-modified AC anode. The improved performance was achieved due to reduced transfer charge resistance (Rct) and strengthened the current exchange rate (Io) [92]. Several experiments have shown that start-up time for MFCs in nitric acid or ammonium nitrate can be reduced by electrochemically oxygenated carbon wire. It has been replicated in one report [93] that the coulombic performance of the anodes adjusted by this process was 71 percent. Responsive groups containing oxygen on the carbon surface could be liable for the improved overall efficiency of the system [94].

10.4 Metal-based anode

Many metals such as gold, titanium, and copper have been used as anodes in MFCs for use in the last ten years. Because of their corrosive nature, most of those metals were unsuitable. Conversely, the use of stainless steel as an anode for microbial fuel cells has attracted increasing interest [95].

11. MFC components

A MFC consists of an anode chamber divided by a PEM, and a cathode chamber. By exposing the cathode into the air directly, a mono-compartment MFC eradicates the need for the cathode chamber.

12. Two-compartment MFC systems

Two-compartment MFCs are frequently run in a batch before equilibrium is established to produce energy in the MFC device with a well-defined chemical media such as glucose or acetate. Once the stability is maintained the dairy wastewater is pumped into the anodic chamber continuously through a peristaltic pump, which is currently only being used in the laboratories. A standard two-compartment MFC has two chambers one for the anode and the other for the cathode linked by a PEM or a salt bridge, to enable protons to travel to the cathode whilst preventing oxygen diffusion towards the anode. The compartments would be taking numerous functional forms. Mansoorian et al. [96] constructed non-catalyst and non-mediator membrane microbial fuel cell (CAML-MMFC), as seen in **Figure 3**, for simultaneous treatment of wastewater and bioelectricity production. The CAML-MMFC was equipped with two chambers with an anaerobic anode and aerobic cathode container and divided from one another by a proton exchange membrane. The chambers were constructed of plexiglass sheets 2 cm in diameter, each with an effective volume of 2 L with the gaskets tightly sealed. The anode and cathode electrodes were formed from a graphite plate 14 × 6 × 0.5 cm^3. The electrode in the anode was 5 cm from the membrane, and the electrode in the cathode was 2 cm from the membrane. Via a resistance, the electrodes were attached to copper wire 2 mm in diameter and 35 cm in total.

Jadhav et al. [97] used a cow urine administered another type of dual-chambered MFC with an outer cathodic chamber volume of 2.5 L, made of a plastic bucket and

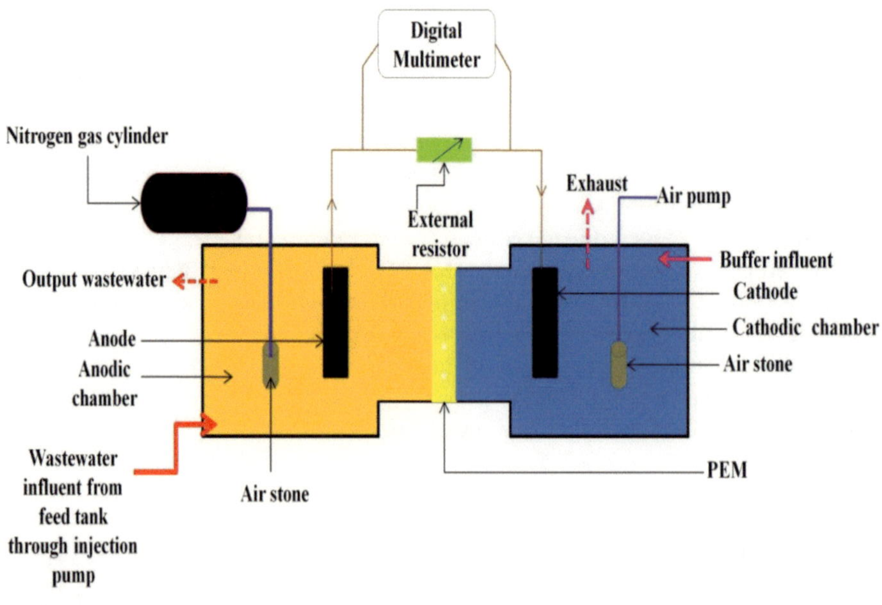

Figure 3.
The schematic view of the CAML-MMFC reactor (adapted from [96]).

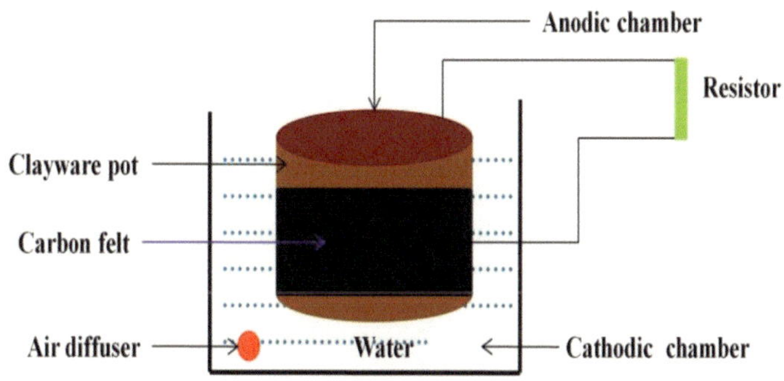

Figure 4.
Dual chambered MFC treating cow urine as a substrate in the anodic chamber (adapted from [97]).

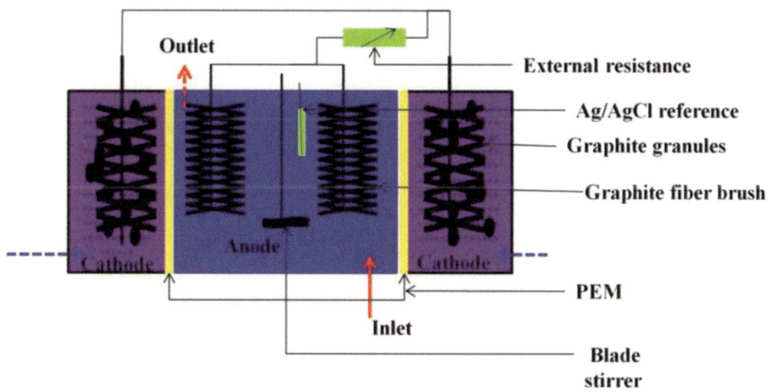

Figure 5.
Schematic drawing of the MFC reactor. (1) Graphite fiber brush; (2) graphite granules; (3) proton exchange membrane (PEM); (4) Ag/AgCl reference; (5) blade stirrer; (6) air; (7) air bubbles; (8) external resistance; (9) inlet; (10) outlet (adapted from [98]).

inner clay container as an anodic chamber with a working volume of 0.4 L as seen in **Figure 4**. The substance of the clayware pot wall itself worked as a separator between the anodized chamber and the cathodic chamber. The anode and cathode are constructed of carbon felt with 394 cm^2 and 755 cm^2 of estimated surface area, respectively.

Zhang et al. [98] constructed a novel design for the treatment of dairy manure as shown in **Figure 5**. The MFC consisted of one cylinder (Ø100 mm × 90 mm, anode compartment with two identical square vision windows (80 mm × 80 mm)) and two rectangular cubes (80 mm × 80 mm × 50 mm, two cathode compartments attached to a Plexiglas conduit (Ø20 mm) and a catholic compartment passing freely between them). The anode and the cathode compartments were divided by two proton exchange membranes (PEM) with the same cross-sectional region (80 mm = 6400 mm^2). The cathode chambers were constantly aerated at 300 ml min^{-1}, to maintain dissolved oxygen at the cathode, and the anolyte was agitated with a blade stirrer (300 rpm) every other hour. The anodic and cathodic chamber had appropriate volumes of 617 ml and 321 ml.

13. Single-compartment MFC systems

Owing to their complicated architectures, two-compartment MFCs are challenging to scale up, but they can be run either in batch or continuous mode. One compartment of the MFCs provides simplified layout and cost savings. Typically they provide just an anodic chamber in a cathodic chamber without aeration need. Mohanakrishna et al. [35] fabricated single-chamber MFC with "perspex" material with a total working volume of 0.54/0.48 L operated under fed-batch mode in an anaerobic microenvironment (**Figure 6**). Plain graphite plates (5 cm × 5 cm; 1 cm thick; surface area 70cm^2) were used as electrodes without coating along with NAFION 117 (Sigma–Aldrich) as proton exchange membrane sandwiched between anode and cathode duly after pre-treatment. Whereas the bottom portion was connected to PEM and exposed to liquid, the top section of the cathode was exposed to sunlight. The anode was mounted below the PEM and submerged in the wastewater absolutely. After sealing with epoxy sealant copper wires were used for contact with electrodes. In order to maintain the anaerobic microenvironment in the anode compartment, leak-proof sealing was provided at the joints. Provisions for the sampling ports, wire input points (top), inlet and outlet ports have been developed.

Mardanpour et al. [36] fabricated a unique annular single chamber microbial fuel cell (ASCMFC) with the spiral anode (**Figure 7**). They used stainless steel mesh coated with graphite as an anode material. The dimensions of the chamber were 3 cm in height, 7.1 cm internal diameter, and 8 cm external diameter. The volume of the anaerobic chamber was 90 cm^3. The anode electrode (63 cm × 2 cm) was composed of stainless steel mesh coated with graphite (mesh 300).

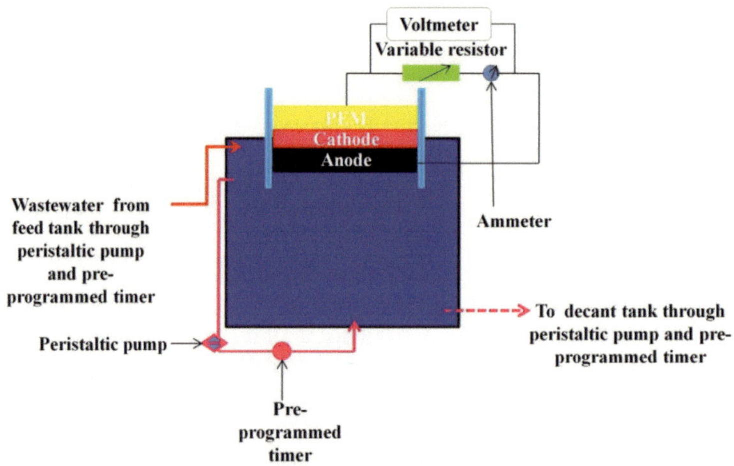

Figure 6.
Schematic details of non-catalyzed single-chambered microbial fuel cell (MFC) used in this study with measurement circuits [FT, wastewater feeding tank; DT, decant tank; VR, variable resister; A, ammeter; V, voltmeter; T, pre-programmed timer; P, peristaltic pump; PEM, proton exchange membrane (NAFION 117)] (adapted from [35]).

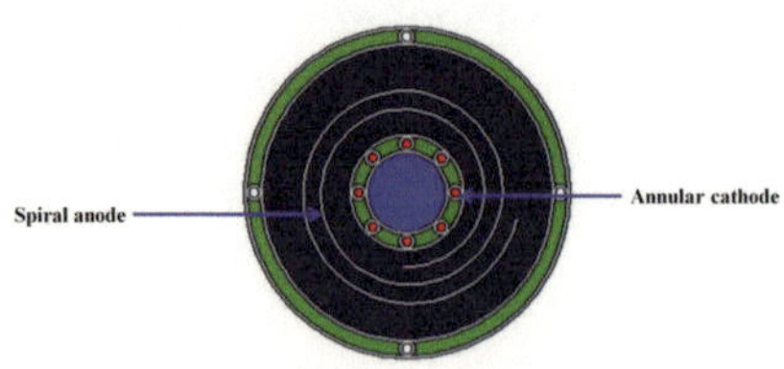

Figure 7.
Schematic diagram of annular single chamber microbial fuel cell (ASCMFC) with the spiral anode (adapted from [36]).

14. Operation parameter

14.1 Performance of MFC under different anodic metabolism

In MFC performance, microbial metabolism at anode plays a significant role. Each metabolism follows its metabolic pathway for generating energy, varying the capacity to generate power. The MFC was maintained at an initial concentration of 1601 mg/L COD and a pH 7 anolyte. Phosphate buffer at 10 mM working concentration was used to control anolyte pH. The voltage could be quickly produced in the MFC during the treatment of aerobic as well as anaerobic anodic metabolism in dairy wastewater. Nearly 760 and 780 mV of OCV was recorded for anaerobic and aerobic metabolism, respectively. Considering both aerobic and anaerobic anodic processes, the maximal OCV was observed from the first cycle of operation. Various studies [36, 99] showed the need of lag phase by microbes after which maximal OCV was obtained. The eradication of requirements for the lag phase may be a determinative result of using inherent microorganism of dairy wastewater which limits the microbial growth adaptation phase. MFC's behavior marks a chance to generate current from the first cycle of operation. However, in power generation there was a clear difference when specific anodic metabolism was used. The polarization data suggests that both the MFCs produced maximal power density of external resistance at 470 ohm; for aerobic and anaerobic metabolism it was recorded as 196 and 162 mW/m^2 respectively. The COD removal efficiency obtained was 91% and 92% for anaerobic and aerobic metabolism in a week's time respectively. The efficiency of conversion of chemical to electrical energy was 3.7 folds lower than anaerobic metabolism with 17.15% efficiency making it the major flaw in the aerobic system. In aerobic mode, oxygen was used by the microbes as terminal electron acceptor, which resulted in the loss of electrons reducing CE. While the CE for aerobic metabolism was much lower than anaerobic metabolism it could generate higher power density, this may be the product of aerobic bacteria's fast growth and rapid metabolic activity, resulting in a higher concentration of protons and production of electrons. The speedier removal of COD by aerobic metabolism results from rapid use of substrates [99].

14.2 Effect of anolyte pH

14.2.1 MFC operation without pH buffer

Anolyte system using a 10 mM concentration phosphate buffer (pH 6.9) reduces the initial anolyte concentration to 7.2 showing a gradual reduction of pH to 6.9 in 8 days. Utilizing orthophosphoric acid, the pH was set to 7 when the device was run in the absence of buffer. The pH variations were found to be crucial in the absence of buffer. In the absence of a buffer system, the MFC pH gradually increased to 7.51 on the 3rd day, and then fell to 7.03 on the 6th day. Though the efficiency of treatment and OCV was the same, a clear difference was observed in system polarization. The MFC's average power density without buffer was 85.97 mW/m^2 which was almost half the system output using a buffer configuration for 161 mW/m^2 of pH maintenance. The requirement of 8-day batch time for both reactors for 90% COD reduction demonstrated that the pH buffer removal did not affect the bacterial activity. In MFC, the citrate and phosphates remain as proton carriers. While for these carriers the diffusion coefficient is smaller, the concentration gradient is higher across the membrane. In cathode chamber, the concentration gradient is higher due to the deficiency of citrate and phosphates. Due to improved proton transfer, the internal resistance was typically reduced due to polarization of the concentration of protons, thereby increasing the output of power in the system using pH buffer. Phosphate buffer system has a wonderful impact on the electricity generation by altering the electrochemical reactions although it has not affected MFC's microbial growth and efficiency in COD removal. The higher anolyte power density may be attained at pH 7 [8].

14.3 Substrate concentration

The concentration of the substrate in the anode chamber has a significant effect on microbial development. The MFCs were run using an anaerobic metabolism buffer system with an initial pH of 7 anolytes. The substrate concentration varied as a function of COD concentration (800, 1600, and 2800 mg/L). A remarkable variation in the overall OCV obtained by the MFC could be observed. MFC having COD concentration of 1600 mg/L reported a maximum OCV of 760 mV. Operating system with 800 and 2800 mg/L COD concentration achieved maximum OCV of 656 and 612 mV. MFC working with COD concentration of 800, 1600, and 2800 mg/L had a batch time requirement of 6, 7, and 11 days. The peak power density (161 mW/m^2) was reported at 1600 mg/L COD concentration and is 2.5 and 1.8 fold lower for 800 and 2800 mg/L COD operating MFCs. The columbic efficiency was 2.6 and 1.7 folds lower for MFC with 800 and 2800 mg/L, respectively, compared to MFC at 1600 mg/L COD concentration having 17.16%. The use of wastewater with higher COD results in a reduction in electricity generation, which may be due to microbial growth inhibition mediated by substrates. A dramatic decrease in power output occurred when 800 mg/L of initial COD concentration was used. Power generation decreased with a decline in the initial concentration of the substrate [99]. The initial COD variance did not influence the effluent quality of the MFC, although the duration of treatment improved with an increased substrate concentration.

14.4 The effect of temperature

The operating time was longer at low temperatures than that at high temperatures, but the voltage generation at high temperatures (30 and 35°C) was higher [100, 101]. The peak current and voltage intensity was measured at 35°C. Decreasing voltage, output and current intensity may occur for a variety of reasons. As temperature rises, the biochemical reactions, bacterial metabolism, and bacterial growth rate increases, leading to rapid bacterial growth and better voltage efficiency. Nonetheless, during long processing periods while bacteria are at high temperatures, essential cell's compounds like nucleic acid and other temperature-sensitive material can be irreversibly impaired, resulting in extreme cell function degradation or death. The voltage and current strength decrease drastically in this case. The slow bacterial growth rate at low temperatures often leads to a reduction in the bacterial population and activity and voltage output decreases [102].

14.5 The effect of organic loading rate (OLR)

A number of studies on the generation of electricity by MFCs have also shown that amount of current generated in both closed and continuous MFC depends upon organic loadings. The MFC research analyzed various organic loadings and measured their effects on current and power during service. During the 30 days of operation, the maximal current and power density was achieved in OLR equal to 53.21 kg COD/m^3d. This is because the MFC requires more time at low OLR to achieve the optimum current and power density. But in greater OLR, maximal current and power density will be attained in a shorter time frame. The other reason is that the microorganisms in inoculated sludge and wastewater are compatible [15, 96].

14.6 The effect of external resistance

Higher external resistance results in diminished power density. Therefore, MFC has to be constructed with lower external resistance for better performance. In other words, the voltage rises as the resistance increases, and the current decreases. The voltage produced decreases from 0.855 to 0.319 V when the external resistance increases from 1 to 25 KΩ. The decrease in voltage indicates that processes other than cathodic reactions used some electrons [1]. Low voltage may be due to a reduced rate of usage of electrons in the cathode with high electrical resistance relative to the rate of transfer from the external circuit. It is acceptable that the ejection of electrons via the circuit reduces as the resistance of a circuit increases. Electrons in the cathode have been used to eliminate other electron receptors from the cathode, like sulfate, permeable oxygen, or nitrate. Electrons quickly pass through the external circuit at lower external resistance and oxidize the electron carriers in the anodic chamber on the external membrane of the microorganism. Maximum power density is also obtained in MFC systems where internal and external resistances are equivalent. Differences in MFC output with varied external resistances can be due to differences in activation losses at the anode, which is a result of the electrochemical behavior of the microorganism-reducing anode [103].

14.7 The effect of hydraulic retention time (HRT)

Hydraulic retention time (HRT) is a critical parameter in the treatment of wastewater and regulates the residual substrate concentration and the amount of dissolved oxygen (DO) in the reactor. When HRT decreases, the concentration of the substrate increases, leading to the utilization of the entire substrate with an improved voltage and power density. On the other hand, higher concentrations of DO in the influent wastewater lead to an increase in the potential for oxidation-reduction (ORP), resulting in a reduction in the voltage and power density generated in the MFC. To understand the impact of HRT on bioelectricity generation, the MFC was run continuously with dairy wastewater at seven different HRTs (2, 3, 4, 5, 6, 7, and 8 days) [96].

The explanation for the rise in voltage as HRT rises may be usually due to the long interaction time between biofilm and organic matter, which may demonstrate the benefit of biofilm, degradation of a substrate, electron output, and transition to the surface of the anode. Despite this, the voltage decreases slightly when HRT increases (8 days). These observations are compatible with the conclusions of single-chamber MFC energy production with the aerial cathode in the existence and exclusion of proton exchange membrane, and also the results of electricity generation and the wastewater treatment utilizing single-chamber MFC [104].

15. Application of MFC

Although a centuries-old technique, initially recognized in the treatment of dairy wastewater, MFC is taking an interest in bioelectricity generation, bio-hydrogen, Nitrogen, and Phosphorus recovery and also used as a biosensor [33, 105–108]. Several issues such as expensive materials, complicated design, and low power output at higher internal resistance needed to be tackled before utilizing MFC for large scale applications.

15.1 Treatment of wastewater

During the early stage of MFC technology, it was considered that this technology could only be used for the treatment of the limited wastewater, but in the recent years, it has been seen that it could be used in the treatment of almost all kinds of industrial, agricultural and municipal wastewater. The most suitable temperature studied for electricity generation via MFC is about 30°C in a regulated climate. Glycerol wastewater, the main source of pollution in the biodiesel industries, has reported a maximum surface power density 600 mW/m^2 [109]. The low cost and the operational stability is an important characteristic for an effective and efficient treatment technology. An earlier study has reported the simultaneous methane and bio-electricity production in the anaerobic digestion process for higher concentrated wastewater at a longer detention time [62]. MFC with certain microbes have the ability for removable of organic matter, sulfides, nitrides, phosphorous, salinity, etc. Do et al. [110] reported the maximum of 90% COD removal and 80% columbic efficiency.

15.2 Bio-electricity

MFC is a wonderful technology in transferring the chemical energy inside the wide varieties of the waste organic matter with the help of the microorganism into bio-electricity. The current MFC technology is capable of producing only low power outputs which are suitable for small telemetry and wireless sensor system with a small power requirement in the remote areas. However, [39] achieved a peak power density of 122 W/m^3 with 81% COD removal using dairy wastewater as a substrate with 3D laminated composites as electrodes [39].

15.3 Biohydrogen

With a minor adjustment, MFCs could also be used to generate biohydrogen instead of bio-electricity that could be extracted and processed for later use. The anode potential is improved with an external voltage of 0.23 V for overcoming the thermodynamic barrier which is much lesser than the conventional fermentation process. The electron and hydrogen ion produced by the microbial activities at the anodic chamber combines at an oxygen devoid cathode chamber generating bio-hydrogen. MFC has a potential of about 8–9 mol H_2/mol glucose in comparison to 4 mol H_2/mol glucose produced from a conventional fermentation process [52]. In order to produce hydrogen gas in a standard MFC, the anodizing potential for an additional voltage must be increased roughly 0.23 V or more.

15.4 Bio-sensor

The MFC is also utilized as an electrochemical biosensor for pollutant analysis. The metabolic activities of the electrogenic microorganisms are highly affected by the sudden change in the concentration of the targeted analyte in the exposed aquatic environment and are reflected as a change of the output electric signal. MFC sensor is a self-sustained sensor unlike other types of the biosensor which require an external source of power. The biofilm-electrode is used as the sensing element in the MFC sensor [67].

16. Conclusion

Anaerobic treatment is most commonly used to treat dairy wastewaters, mainly hybrid anaerobic and UASB digesters. Upstream anaerobic sludge blanket reactors are more commonly used and ideal for the wastewater treatment from the dairy sector since they can handle large amounts of influents within a short period. But, as dairy wastewater, these processes partially degrade wastewater that contains nutrients and fats. Further treatment for anaerobically treated wastewater from the dairy is therefore necessary. The proper selection of anode material it is made from is a key factor in attempts to obtain high-performance MFCs. Selecting the incorrect anode content would make this option obsolete. Since the kinetics of the microbes used in MFCs are far slower than that which can be accomplished with cathode content or cathode catalyst, the use of 3D anodes has so far been seen to be very advantageous and capable of raising power generation by many magnitudes. Developing countries like India who are the leading producers of milk and are among the top world dairy industries rely on the use of antibiotics for enhancing the production of milk in the cows but these antibiotics when finding their way into the water streams, these are very detrimental. Therefore, the adoption of circular practices for the management of the environment is increasing in order to promote the circular economy. From a future perspective, MFCs are the most promising and environmentally friendly approach to the management of environmental pollution. However, scaling up of this technology is an obstacle due to low power outputs but this could be overcome by integrating MFC with other wastewater treatment technologies and a centralized system will solve the problem. Also, various low-cost electrode materials such as ceramics and biological materials make this technology economically sound.

Author details

Aman Dongre[1], Monika Sogani[2*], Kumar Sonu[2], Zainab Syed[1] and Gopesh Sharma[1]

1 Department of Biosciences, Manipal University Jaipur, Jaipur, Rajasthan, India

2 Department of Civil Engineering, Manipal University Jaipur, Jaipur, Rajasthan, India

*Address all correspondence to: monika.sogani@jaipur.manipal.edu

IntechOpen

© 2020 The Author(s). Licensee IntechOpen. This chapter is distributed under the terms of the Creative Commons Attribution License (http://creativecommons.org/licenses/by/3.0), which permits unrestricted use, distribution, and reproduction in any medium, provided the original work is properly cited.

References

[1] El Nadi, M. H, El Sergany, F. A. R., El Hosseiny, O.M. (2016). Industrial wastewater treatment in dairy industry. International Journal of Engineering Sciences & Research Technology, 5(11), 296-301.

[2] Nadais, M. H. G., Capela, M. I. A., Arroja, L. M. G., & Hung, Y.-T. (2010). Anaerobic treatment of milk processing wastewater *Environmental Bioengineering* (pp. 555-627): Springer.

[3] Britz, T. J., van Schalkwyk, C., & Hung, Y.-T. (2006). Treatment of dairy processing wastewaters. Waste treatment in the food processing industry, 1-28.

[4] Carvalho, F., Prazeres, A. R., & Rivas, J. (2013). Cheese whey wastewater: Characterization and treatment. Science of the Total Environment, *445*, 385-396.

[5] Karadag, D., Köroğlu, O. E., Ozkaya, B., & Cakmakci, M. (2015). A review on anaerobic biofilm reactors for the treatment of dairy industry wastewater. Process Biochemistry, *50*(2), 262-271.

[6] Tripathi, B., & Upadhyay, A. R. (2003). Dairy effluent polishing by aquatic macrophytes. Water, Air, and Soil Pollution, *143*(1-4), 377-385.

[7] Ramasamy, E., Gajalakshmi, S., Sanjeevi, R., Jithesh, M., & Abbasi, S. (2004). Feasibility studies on the treatment of dairy wastewaters with upflow anaerobic sludge blanket reactors. Bioresource Technology, *93*(2), 209-212.

[8] Elakkiya, E., & Matheswaran, M. (2013). Comparison of anodic metabolisms in bioelectricity production during treatment of dairy wastewater in microbial fuel cell. Bioresource Technology, *136*, 407-412.

[9] Demirel, B., Yenigun, O., & Onay, T. T. (2005). Anaerobic treatment of dairy wastewaters: A review. Process Biochemistry, *40*(8), 2583-2595.

[10] Potter, N. N., & Hotchkiss, J. H. (1995). Nutritive aspects of food constituents *Food science* (pp. 46-68): Springer.

[11] Marwha, S., Panesar, P., & Singh, B. (1998). Studies on the isolation of efficient yeast strain for the treatment of dairy waste water. Pollution Research, *17*, 51-56.

[12] Sulejmani, Z., Shehi, A., Hajrulai, Z., & Mata, E. (2012). Abuse of pharmaceutical Drugsantibiotics in dairy cattle in Kosovo and detection of their residues in Milk. J Ecosyst Ecogr, *2*(19), 114-120.

[13] Cristian, O. (2010). Characteristics of the untreated wastewater produced by food industry. Analele Universității din Oradea, Fascicula: Protecția Mediului, *15*, 709-714.

[14] Farizoglu, B., Keskinler, B., Yildiz, E., & Nuhoglu, A. (2007). Simultaneous removal of C, N, P from cheese whey by jet loop membrane bioreactor (JLMBR). Journal of Hazardous Materials, *146*(1-2), 399-407.

[15] Mohan, S. V., Babu, V. L., & Sarma, P. (2008). Effect of various pretreatment methods on anaerobic mixed microflora to enhance biohydrogen production utilizing dairy wastewater as substrate. Bioresource Technology, *99*(1), 59-67.

[16] Tawfik, A., Sobhey, M., & Badawy, M. (2008). Treatment of a combined dairy and domestic wastewater in an up-flow anaerobic sludge blanket (UASB) reactor followed by activated sludge (AS system). Desalination, *227*(1-3), 167-177.

[17] Prazeres, A. R., Carvalho, F., & Rivas, J. (2012). Cheese whey management: A review. Journal of Environmental Management, *110*, 48-68.

[18] Qasim, W., & Mane, A. (2013). Characterization and treatment of selected food industrial effluents by coagulation and adsorption techniques. Water Resources and Industry, *4*, 1-12.

[19] Sarkar, B., Chakrabarti, P., Vijaykumar, A., & Kale, V. (2006). Wastewater treatment in dairy industries—Possibility of reuse. Desalination, *195*(1-3), 141-152.

[20] Kolev Slavov, A. (2017). General characteristics and treatment possibilities of dairy wastewater–a review. Food Technology and Biotechnology, *55*(1), 14-28.

[21] Schifrin, S., Ivanov, G., & Mishukov, B. (1981). Feodanov YuA. Wastewaters from dairy industry. *Wastewater treatment of meat and dairy industry. Moscow, Russia: Light and Food Industry*, 11-19.

[22] Authority, E. P. (1997). Environmental guidelines for the dairy processing industry. *State Government of Victoria. (http://www epa. vic. gov. au)*.

[23] Rosenwinkel, K.-H., Austermann-Haun, U., & Meyer, H. (2005). Industrial wastewater sources and treatment strategies. Environmental biotechnology: Concepts and applications, 49-77.

[24] Doble, M., & Kumar, A. (2005). Treatment of waste from food and dairy industries. *Biotreatment of industrial effluents. Burlington, VT, USA: Elsevier Butterworth-Heinemann*, 183-185.

[25] Watkins, M., & Nash, D. (2010). Dairy factory wastewaters, their use on land and possible environmental impacts–a mini review. Open Agric J, *4*, 1-9.

[26] Janczukowicz, W., Zieliński, M., & Dębowski, M. (2008). Biodegradability evaluation of dairy effluents originated in selected sections of dairy production. Bioresource Technology, *99*(10), 4199-4205.

[27] Wang, X., Cheng, S., Feng, Y., Merrill, M. D., Saito, T., & Logan, B. E. (2009). Use of carbon mesh anodes and the effect of different pretreatment methods on power production in microbial fuel cells. Environmental Science & Technology, *43*(17), 6870-6874.

[28] Yang, P., Zhang, R., McGarvey, J. A., & Benemann, J. R. (2007). Biohydrogen production from cheese processing wastewater by anaerobic fermentation using mixed microbial communities. International Journal of Hydrogen Energy, *32*(18), 4761-4771.

[29] Alturkmani, A. (2007). Dairy Industry Effluents Treatment–Anaerobic Treatment of Whey in Stirred Batch Reactor: University of Civil Engineering Bucharest, Romania.

[30] Şengil, İ. A. (2006). Treatment of dairy wastewaters by electrocoagulation using mild steel electrodes. Journal of Hazardous Materials, *137*(2), 1197-1205.

[31] Rao, M., & Bhole, A. (2002). Removal of organic matter from dairy industry wastewater using low-cost adsorbents. Indian Chemical Engineer, *44*(1), 25-28.

[32] Zhang, F., Cheng, S., Pant, D., Van Bogaert, G., & Logan, B. E. (2009). Power generation using an activated carbon and metal mesh cathode in a microbial fuel cell. Electrochemistry Communications, *11*(11), 2177-2179.

[33] Mathuriya, A. S., & Sharma, V. (2010). Bioelectricity production from various wastewaters through microbial fuel cell technology. Journal

of Biochemical Technology, *2*(1), 133-137.

[34] Velasquez-Orta, S., Head, I., Curtis, T., & Scott, K. (2011). Factors affecting current production in microbial fuel cells using different industrial wastewaters. Bioresource Technology, *102*(8), 5105-5112.

[35] Mohanakrishna, G., Mohan, S. V., & Sarma, P. (2010). Bio-electrochemical treatment of distillery wastewater in microbial fuel cell facilitating decolorization and desalination along with power generation. Journal of Hazardous Materials, *177*(1-3), 487-494.

[36] Mardanpour, M. M., Esfahany, M. N., Behzad, T., & Sedaqatvand, R. (2012). Single chamber microbial fuel cell with spiral anode for dairy wastewater treatment. Biosensors and Bioelectronics, *38*(1), 264-269.

[37] Cecconet, D., Molognoni, D., Callegari, A., & Capodaglio, A. G. (2018). Agro-food industry wastewater treatment with microbial fuel cells: Energetic recovery issues. International Journal of Hydrogen Energy, *43*(1), 500-511.

[38] Hasany, M., Yaghmaei, S., Mardanpour, M. M., & Naraghi, Z. G. (2017). Simultaneously energy production and dairy wastewater treatment using bioelectrochemical cells: In different environmental and hydrodynamic modes. Chinese Journal of Chemical Engineering, *25*(12), 1847-1855.

[39] Lai, M.-F., Lou, C.-W., & Lin, J.-H. (2018). Improve 3D electrode materials performance on electricity generation from livestock wastewater in microbial fuel cell. International Journal of Hydrogen Energy, *43*(25), 11520-11529.

[40] Ma, J., Ni, H., Su, D., & Meng, X. (2016). Bioelectricity generation from pig farm wastewater in microbial fuel cell using carbon brush as electrode. International Journal of Hydrogen Energy, *41*(36), 16191-16195.

[41] Shukla, A., Suresh, P., Berchmans, S., & Rajendran, A. (2004). Biological fuel cells and their applications. Current Science, *87*(4), 455-468.

[42] Bond, D. R., & Lovley, D. R. (2003). Electricity production by Geobacter sulfurreducens attached to electrodes. Applied and Environmental Microbiology, *69*(3), 1548-1555.

[43] Wingard, L. B. Jr, Shaw, C. H., & Castner, J. F. (1982). Bioelectrochemical fuel cells. Enzyme and Microbial Technology, *4*(3), 137-142.

[44] Logan, B. (2004). Biologically extracting energy from wastewater: Biohydrogen production and microbial fuel cells. Environmental Science & Technology, *38*(9), 160-167.

[45] Rabaey, K., & Verstraete, W. (2005). Microbial fuel cells: Novel biotechnology for energy generation. Trends in Biotechnology, *23*(6), 291-298.

[46] Niessen, J., Schröder, U., & Scholz, F. (2004). Exploiting complex carbohydrates for microbial electricity generation–a bacterial fuel cell operating on starch. Electrochemistry Communications, *6*(9), 955-958.

[47] Pant, D., Van Bogaert, G., Diels, L., & Vanbroekhoven, K. (2010). A review of the substrates used in microbial fuel cells (MFCs) for sustainable energy production. Bioresource Technology, *101*(6), 1533-1543.

[48] Sedaqatvand, R., Esfahany, M. N., Behzad, T., Mohseni, M., & Mardanpour, M. M. (2013). Parameter estimation and characterization of a single-chamber microbial fuel cell for

dairy wastewater treatment. Bioresource Technology, *146*, 247-253.

[49] Logan, B. E. (2007). Microbial Fuel Cells, a John Wiley & Sons. *Inc., New Jersey*.

[50] Zhuang, L., Yuan, Y., Wang, Y., & Zhou, S. (2012). Long-term evaluation of a 10-liter serpentine-type microbial fuel cell stack treating brewery wastewater. Bioresource Technology, *123*, 406-412.

[51] McCormick, A. J., Bombelli, P., Bradley, R. W., Thorne, R., Wenzel, T., & Howe, C. J. (2015). Biophotovoltaics: Oxygenic photosynthetic organisms in the world of bioelectrochemical systems. Energy & Environmental Science, *8*(4), 1092-1109.

[52] Liu, H., Cheng, S., & Logan, B. E. (2005). Power generation in fed-batch microbial fuel cells as a function of ionic strength, temperature, and reactor configuration. Environmental Science & Technology, *39*(14), 5488-5493.

[53] Reguera, G., McCarthy, K. D., Mehta, T., Nicoll, J. S., Tuominen, M. T., & Lovley, D. R. (2005). Extracellular electron transfer via microbial nanowires. Nature, *435*(7045), 1098.

[54] Lies, D. P., Hernandez, M. E., Kappler, A., Mielke, R. E., Gralnick, J. A., & Newman, D. K. (2005). Shewanella oneidensis MR-1 uses overlapping pathways for iron reduction at a distance and by direct contact under conditions relevant for biofilms. Applied and Environmental Microbiology, *71*(8), 4414-4426.

[55] Schröder, U. (2007). Anodic electron transfer mechanisms in microbial fuel cells and their energy efficiency. Physical Chemistry Chemical Physics, *9*(21), 2619-2629.

[56] Yang, Y., Xu, M., Guo, J., & Sun, G. (2012). Bacterial extracellular electron transfer in bioelectrochemical systems. Process Biochemistry, *47*(12), 1707-1714.

[57] Gorby, Y. A., Yanina, S., McLean, J. S., Rosso, K. M., Moyles, D., Dohnalkova, A., . . . Kim, K. S. (2006). Electrically conductive bacterial nanowires produced by Shewanella oneidensis strain MR-1 and other microorganisms. Proceedings of the National Academy of Sciences, *103*(30), 11358-11363.

[58] Yuzvinsky, T., El-Naggar, M., Wanger, G., Leung, K. M., Southam, G., Yang, J., . . . Gorby, Y. (2011). Electrical transport along bacterial nanowires. *Biophysical Journal, 100*(3), 132a.

[59] Malvankar, N. S., Vargas, M., Nevin, K. P., Franks, A. E., Leang, C., Kim, B.-C., . . . Johnson, J. P. (2011). Tunable metallic-like conductivity in microbial nanowire networks. Nature Nanotechnology, *6*(9), 573.

[60] Xie, X., Hu, L., Pasta, M., Wells, G. F., Kong, D., Criddle, C. S., & Cui, Y. (2010). Three-dimensional carbon nanotube- textile anode for high-performance microbial fuel cells. Nano Letters, *11*(1), 291-296.

[61] Torres, C. I., Marcus, A. K., Lee, H.-S., Parameswaran, P., Krajmalnik-Brown, R., & Rittmann, B. E. (2010). A kinetic perspective on extracellular electron transfer by anode-respiring bacteria. FEMS Microbiology Reviews, *34*(1), 3-17.

[62] Rahimnejad, M., Adhami, A., Darvari, S., Zirepour, A., & Oh, S.-E. (2015). Microbial fuel cell as new technology for bioelectricity generation: A review. Alexandria Engineering Journal, *54*(3), 745-756.

[63] Wang, H., Wang, G., Ling, Y., Qian, F., Song, Y., Lu, X., . . . Li, Y. (2013a). High power density microbial fuel cell with flexible 3D graphene–nickel

foam as anode. Nanoscale, *5*(21), 10283-10290.

[64] Wang, Y., Li, B., Zeng, L., Cui, D., Xiang, X., & Li, W. (2013b). Polyaniline/mesoporous tungsten trioxide composite as anode electrocatalyst for high-performance microbial fuel cells. Biosensors and Bioelectronics, *41*, 582-588.

[65] Chou, H.-T., Lee, H.-J., Lee, C.-Y., Tai, N.-H., & Chang, H.-Y. (2014). Highly durable anodes of microbial fuel cells using a reduced graphene oxide/ carbon nanotube-coated scaffold. Bioresource Technology, *169*, 532-536.

[66] Xie, X., Ye, M., Hu, L., Liu, N., McDonough, J. R., Chen, W., . . . Cui, Y. (2012). Carbon nanotube-coated macroporous sponge for microbial fuel cell electrodes. Energy & Environmental Science, *5*(1), 5265-5270.

[67] Yuan, Y., Zhou, S., Liu, Y., & Tang, J. (2013). Nanostructured macroporous bioanode based on polyaniline-modified natural loofah sponge for high-performance microbial fuel cells. Environmental Science & Technology, *47*(24), 14525-14532.

[68] Zhang, Y., Mo, G., Li, X., Zhang, W., Zhang, J., Ye, J., . . . Yu, C. (2011). A graphene modified anode to improve the performance of microbial fuel cells. Journal of Power Sources, *196*(13), 5402-5407.

[69] Chen, W., Huang, Y.-X., Li, D.-B., Yu, H.-Q., & Yan, L. (2014). Preparation of a macroporous flexible three dimensional graphene sponge using an ice-template as the anode material for microbial fuel cells. RSC Advances, *4*(41), 21619-21624.

[70] Hou, J., Liu, Z., & Zhang, P. (2013). A new method for fabrication of graphene/polyaniline nanocomplex modified microbial fuel cell anodes. Journal of Power Sources, *224*, 139-144.

[71] Qiao, Y., Wu, X.-S., Ma, C.-X., He, H., & Li, C. M. (2014). A hierarchical porous graphene/nickel anode that simultaneously boosts the bio-and electro-catalysis for high-performance microbial fuel cells. RSC Advances, *4*(42), 21788-21793.

[72] Shen, Y., Zhou, Y., Chen, S., Yang, F., Zheng, S., & Hou, H. (2014). Carbon nanofibers modified graphite felt for high performance anode in high substrate concentration microbial fuel cells. *The Scientific World Journal, 2014*.

[73] Peng, X. H., Chu, X. Z., Huang, P. F., & Shan, K. (2015). *Improved Power Performance of Activated Carbon Anode by Fe2O3 Addition in Microbial Fuel Cells.* Paper presented at the Applied Mechanics and Materials.

[74] Chen, S., Liu, Q., He, G., Zhou, Y., Hanif, M., Peng, X., . . . Hou, H. (2012). Reticulated carbon foam derived from a sponge-like natural product as a high-performance anode in microbial fuel cells. Journal of Materials Chemistry, *22*(35), 18609-18613.

[75] Wei, J., Liang, P., & Huang, X. (2011). Recent progress in electrodes for microbial fuel cells. Bioresource Technology, *102*(20), 9335-9344.

[76] Chen, X., Cui, D., Wang, X., Wang, X., & Li, W. (2015). Porous carbon with defined pore size as anode of microbial fuel cell. Biosensors and Bioelectronics, *69*, 135-141.

[77] Karthikeyan, R., Wang, B., Xuan, J., Wong, J. W., Lee, P. K., & Leung, M. K. (2015). Interfacial electron transfer and bioelectrocatalysis of carbonized plant material as effective anode of microbial fuel cell. Electrochimica Acta, *157*, 314-323.

[78] Chen, S., Hou, H., Harnisch, F., Patil, S. A., Carmona-Martinez, A. A.,

Agarwal, S., . . . Greiner, A. (2011). Electrospun and solution blown three-dimensional carbon fiber nonwovens for application as electrodes in microbial fuel cells. Energy & Environmental Science, *4*(4), 1417-1421.

[79] Logan, B., Cheng, S., Watson, V., & Estadt, G. (2007). Graphite fiber brush anodes for increased power production in air-cathode microbial fuel cells. Environmental Science & Technology, *41*(9), 3341-3346.

[80] Liu, Y., Harnisch, F., Fricke, K., Schröder, U., Climent, V., & Feliu, J. M. (2010). The study of electrochemically active microbial biofilms on different carbon-based anode materials in microbial fuel cells. Biosensors and Bioelectronics, *25*(9), 2167-2171.

[81] Ren, H., Pyo, S., Lee, J.-I., Park, T.-J., Gittleson, F. S., Leung, F. C., . . . Chae, J. (2015). A high power density miniaturized microbial fuel cell having carbon nanotube anodes. Journal of Power Sources, *273*, 823-830.

[82] Tang, J., Yuan, Y., Liu, T., & Zhou, S. (2015). High-capacity carbon-coated titanium dioxide core–shell nanoparticles modified three dimensional anodes for improved energy output in microbial fuel cells. Journal of Power Sources, *274*, 170-176.

[83] Fraiwan, A., Adusumilli, S., Han, D., Steckl, A., Call, D., Westgate, C., & Choi, S. (2014). Microbial power-generating capabilities on micro-/Nano-structured anodes in micro-sized microbial fuel cells. *Fuel Cells, 14*(6), 801-809.

[84] Thepsuparungsikul, N., Phonthamachai, N., & Ng, H. (2012). Multi-walled carbon nanotubes as electrode material for microbial fuel cells. Water Science & Technology, *65*(7).

[85] Mehdinia, A., Dejaloud, M., & Jabbari, A. (2013). Nanostructured polyaniline-coated anode for improving microbial fuel cell power output. Chemical Papers, *67*(8), 1096-1102.

[86] Mehdinia, A., Ziaei, E., & Jabbari, A. (2014). Multi-walled carbon nanotube/SnO2 nanocomposite: a novel anode material for microbial fuel cells. Electrochimica Acta, *130*, 512-518.

[87] Fu, Y., Yu, J., Zhang, Y., & Meng, Y. (2014). Graphite coated with manganese oxide/multiwall carbon nanotubes composites as anodes in marine benthic microbial fuel cells. Applied Surface Science, *317*, 84-89.

[88] Xiao, L., Damien, J., Luo, J., Jang, H. D., Huang, J., & He, Z. (2012). Crumpled graphene particles for microbial fuel cell electrodes. Journal of Power Sources, *208*, 187-192.

[89] Cui, H.-F., Du, L., Guo, P.-B., Zhu, B., & Luong, J. H. (2015). Controlled modification of carbon nanotubes and polyaniline on macroporous graphite felt for high-performance microbial fuel cell anode. Journal of Power Sources, *283*, 46-53.

[90] Yin, T., Lin, Z., Su, L., Yuan, C., & Fu, D. (2014). Preparation of vertically oriented TiO2 nanosheets modified carbon paper electrode and its enhancement to the performance of MFCs. ACS Applied Materials & Interfaces, *7*(1), 400-408.

[91] Garcia-Gomez, N. A., Balderas-Renteria, I., Garcia-Gutierrez, D. I., Mosqueda, H. A., & Sánchez, E. M. (2015). Development of mats composed by TiO2 and carbon dual electrospun nanofibers: A possible anode material in microbial fuel cells. Materials Science and Engineering: B, *193*, 130-136.

[92] Peng, X., Yu, H., Wang, X., Gao, N., Geng, L., & Ai, L. (2013). Enhanced anode performance of microbial fuel cells by adding nanosemiconductor

goethite. Journal of Power Sources, *223*, 94-99.

[93] Cai, H., Wang, J., Bu, Y., & Zhong, Q. (2013). Treatment of carbon cloth anodes for improving power generation in a dual-chamber microbial fuel cell. Journal of Chemical Technology & Biotechnology, *88*(4), 623-628.

[94] Luo, J., Chi, M., Wang, H., He, H., & Zhou, M. (2013). Electrochemical surface modification of carbon mesh anode to improve the performance of air-cathode microbial fuel cells. Bioprocess and Biosystems Engineering, *36*(12), 1889-1896.

[95] Mathuriya, A. S., & Yakhmi, J. (2014). Microbial fuel cells to recover heavy metals. Environmental Chemistry Letters, *12*(4), 483-494.

[96] Mansoorian, H. J., Mahvi, A. H., Jafari, A. J., & Khanjani, N. (2016). Evaluation of dairy industry wastewater treatment and simultaneous bioelectricity generation in a catalyst-less and mediator-less membrane microbial fuel cell. Journal of Saudi Chemical Society, *20*(1), 88-100.

[97] Jadhav, D. A., Jain, S. C., & Ghangrekar, M. M. (2016). Cow's urine as a yellow gold for bioelectricity generation in low cost clayware microbial fuel cell. Energy, *113*, 76-84.

[98] Zhang, G., Zhao, Q., Jiao, Y., Wang, K., Lee, D.-J., & Ren, N. (2012). Biocathode microbial fuel cell for efficient electricity recovery from dairy manure. Biosensors and Bioelectronics, *31*(1), 537-543.

[99] Mohan, S. V., Mohanakrishna, G., Velvizhi, G., Babu, V. L., & Sarma, P. (2010). Bio-catalyzed electrochemical treatment of real field dairy wastewater with simultaneous power generation. Biochemical Engineering Journal, *51* (1-2), 32-39.

[100] Jadhav, G., & Ghangrekar, M. (2009). Performance of microbial fuel cell subjected to variation in pH, temperature, external load and substrate concentration. Bioresource Technology, *100*(2), 717-723.

[101] Wei, L., Han, H., & Shen, J. (2013). Effects of temperature and ferrous sulfate concentrations on the performance of microbial fuel cell. International Journal of Hydrogen Energy, *38*(25), 11110-11116.

[102] Jana, P. S., Behera, M., & Ghangrekar, M. (2010). Performance comparison of up-flow microbial fuel cells fabricated using proton exchange membrane and earthen cylinder. International Journal of Hydrogen Energy, *35*(11), 5681-5686.

[103] Shimoyama, T., Komukai, S., Yamazawa, A., Ueno, Y., Logan, B. E., & Watanabe, K. (2008). Electricity generation from model organic wastewater in a cassette-electrode microbial fuel cell. Applied Microbiology and Biotechnology, *80*(2), 325.

[104] Liu, H., & Logan, B. E. (2004). Electricity generation using an air-cathode single chamber microbial fuel cell in the presence and absence of a proton exchange membrane. Environmental Science & Technology, *38*(14), 4040-4046.

[105] Call, D., & Logan, B. E. (2008). Hydrogen production in a single chamber microbial electrolysis cell lacking a membrane. Environmental Science & Technology, *42*(9), 3401-3406.

[106] Cheng, S., Liu, W., Sun, D., & Huang, H. (2017). Enhanced power production of microbial fuel cells by reducing the oxygen and nitrogen functional groups of carbon cloth anode. Surface and Interface Analysis, *49*(5), 410-418.

[107] Du, Z., Li, H., & Gu, T. (2007). A state of the art review on microbial fuel cells: A promising technology for wastewater treatment and bioenergy. Biotechnology Advances, *25*(5), 464-482.

[108] Zhuang, L., Zhou, S., Yuan, Y., Liu, T., Wu, Z., & Cheng, J. (2011). Development of Enterobacter aerogenes fuel cells: From in situ biohydrogen oxidization to direct electroactive biofilm. Bioresource Technology, *102*(1), 284-289.

[109] Nimje, V. R., Chen, C.-Y., Chen, C.-C., Chen, H.-R., Tseng, M.-J., Jean, J.-S., & Chang, Y.-F. (2011). Glycerol degradation in single-chamber microbial fuel cells. Bioresource Technology, *102*(3), 2629-2634.

[110] Do, M., Ngo, H., Guo, W., Liu, Y., Chang, S., Nguyen, D., . . . Ni, B. (2018). Challenges in the application of microbial fuel cells to wastewater treatment and energy production: A mini review. Science of the Total Environment, *639*, 910-920.

Chapter 8

Analysis of Municipal Solid Waste Generation in Dir City

Shakeel Mahmood

Abstract

The study is an attempt to analyze municipal solid waste generation Dir City, District Dir Upper Khyber Pakhtunkhwa (KP), Pakistan. This study has utilized primary data collected through a semi-structured questionnaire and direct waste sampling as primary research. Mathematical analysis and descriptive statistical analysis is applied and generation of municipal solid waste at different scales is estimated. Results indicated that the total waste generated was 16.65 million kg/annum (18356.5 tons) or 45624 kg/day (50.29 tons), or 0.37 kg/capita. Average waste produced by residential, commercial, educational and health sectors was 3.3 kg, 21 kg, 12 kg and 7 kg, correspondingly. Among all, residential sector was the leading producer with 40738 kg (89%) follow by commercial sector 4321 kg (9%) per day while remaining in fraction. High income households and large size families were producing average waste of 5.6 kg/day and 4.9 kg/day, respectively. The main components of waste generated in the study area included paper (8%), organic matter (53%), plastics (12%), clay, pebbles, gravels, ashes and broken ceramic objects (24.8%). The spatial distribution of waste generation varies across the city, high rate of generation was found Rehankot and Shaow whereas Fringe areas were characterized by low generation rate.

Keywords: solid waste, income, family size, waste generation, Dir City

1. Introduction

Worldwide, environmental problems are increasing with negatives consequences on human life and environment. Municipal solid waste is one of the current environmental problems particularly in developing countries [1]. Different human activities at domestic, commercial, industrial and agricultural level, as well as construction work are generating solid waste [2]. The quantity of municipal solid waste is increases with increasing population [3]. Improved living standards have and urban living style has intensified the problem of waste generation [4]. Likewise super packing form of various products ready to use and of fast food products has changed waste composition [5]. The population growth and haphazard expansion also contribute in a straight line to waste generation and urban areas are facing environmental problems and public health issues [3, 6]. The solid wastes produced by any urban societies contain rubbish, construction material, leaf litter and other constituents in a fraction [7]. The physical constituents of solid wastes included "food waste, yard waste, wood, plastics, papers, metals, leather, rubbers, inert materials, batteries, paint containers, textiles, construction and demolishing materials and many others" [8]. Various studies indicate that in developing countries 60–85 percent of the municipal solid waste is generated by residential sector

IntechOpen

followed by commercial activities with heterogeneous nature and quantity [9, 10]. The focus of this study is the analysis of solid waste generation by residential, commercial, health, and educational sectors of Dir City.

2. Methods and material

2.1 The study area

The district of Upper Dir is situated in the North-west of Pakistan with a total geographical area of 3,699 sq.km [11]. The total population of the district was enumerated as 946,421 with 120,228 households as in 2018. The population density is 156 persons/sq.km [12]. The elevation of study area varies from 5577 meters above mean sea level in the north to 844meters in the south. River Panjkora, fed by rain and melt water, is the main source of water for various purposes particularly at domestic level. The annual rainfall in the area varies from 823 to 2149 mm [13–14].

The target community is Dir City- the oldest settlement with high population density in the entire district. The estimated population of the target area is 121893 persons with 12345 households. Average family size is about 8 persons [15]. Dir City is further divided into many communities like Main Bazaar, Rehankot, Shaow, Kaas, College Colony and Bijli Ghar. Most of the municipal solid waste and entire liquid waste is persistently dumped haphazardly in open spaces and into Dir River which is a source of fresh water. Such anthropogenic activity is polluting precious fresh water resource.

2.2 Data collection and analysis

For achievement of this micro-level research work objectives, primary data is collected using questionnaire based households survey and direct field measurements. The field work was conducted in September, 2020. A detailed semi-structured questionnaire was developed containing questions regarding family size, monthly income, daily solid waste generation in Kilograms (Kg), effects of open dumping and caused of inappropriate disposal as suggested by [16]. The surveys were conducted in the target community using systematic sampling techniques. A total of 112 household's head were interviewed. Population data and households data was acquired from the Tehsil Municipal Authority (TMA), District Upper Dir.

The data regarding monthly income and family size were processed and classified using frequency distribution. The monthly income of the surveyed household was arranged into three classes i.e. "*low income class*" <35,000 in Pakistani Rupees (PKR; 1US$ =160 PKR, 2020), "*middle income class*" ranging from 35,000–70,000 PKR, and "*high income class*" >70,000 PKR. These income classes were used to find out variations in generation of solid waste at household level among various segments of the community. In the same way, family size of the surveyed households was arranged into three groups; *small family* (<7 persons), *medium family* (7–12 persons) and *large family* (>12 persons).

The average solid waste generation (Kg/day) for each income and family size class was calculated by using Eq. (1):

$$\mathbf{SW}_{\mathbf{average}} = \sum \mathbf{N} / \mathbf{n} \tag{1}$$

In the given equation "$\mathbf{SW}_{\mathbf{average}}$" is the average solid waste generation, "N" numerical value of each observation and "n" is the total number of observations. While average solid waste per person/day was calculated using Eq. (2):

$$\mathbf{SW_{pc} = SW_{average} / FS_{average}} \quad (2)$$

In the given equation "$\mathbf{SW_{pc}}$" is the solid waste generation per capita and "$\mathbf{FS_{average}}$" is the average family size. The total solid waste generated by residential sector is calculated by using Eq. (3). In the same manner solid waste generation per day for each sector is calculated and then by adding all sectors a grand total "T" for all sectors is estimated.

$$\mathbf{SW_{residential} = (p) * (SW_{pc})} \quad (3)$$

In the given equation "$\mathbf{SW_{residential}}$" is the residential solid waste generated per day, and "p" is the total population. The annual solid waste generation is estimated using the Eq. (4).

$$\mathbf{Annual = [(T) \, x \, (365)]} \quad (4)$$

The results are visualized in the form of tables and graphs.

3. Results and discussion

The total population of the 112 surveyed households was counted as 1442 persons. Family size of the surveyed households has divided into three classes. The family included parents, their sons, daughters, nephews, grandfather and grandmother. Medium size families were around 33 percent, though small and large size families were 17% and 50%, respectively (**Table 1**). Average family size of the surveyed households was 9 persons. Solid waste generated by the small, medium and large families was 1.8 Kg/day, 3.2 Kg/day and 4.9 Kg/day, respectively.

Similarly, the monthly income of the surveyed household head was also classified into three groups out of which about 32 percent were low income with a monthly income of less than 35,000 PKR, around 44 percent income was ranging from 35,000 to 70,000 PKR, and about 24 percent falls in high income group having monthly income more than 70,000 PKR (**Table 2**). Daily waste generation increases with the increase in household monthly income. Low, medium and high monthly income households have been generating 1.3 Kg/day, 3.1 Kg/day and 5.6 Kg/day, respectively.

3.1 Municipal waste generation and composition

The rapid population growth, rising urbanization and consumption patterns led to the production of more solid waste [17]. Municipal authorities have to manage

Family Size	Percentage	Kg/day
Small	17	1.8
Medium	33	3.2
Large	50	4.9
Average		3.3

Source: Field Survey September, 2020.

Table 1.
Solid waste generation per day by various size families in (kg/day).

Income Groups	Percentage	Kg/day
Low income	32	1.3
Middle income	44	3.1
High income	24	5.6
Average		3.3

Source: Field Survey September, 2020.

Table 2.
Solid waste generation various income groups in (kg/day).

the solid waste arising from residential, commercial, health and educational activities along with the waste collected from the streets [18]. Normally the municipal authorities manage all type of wastes dropped in the community bins located at street level in the city [19]. In the study area, Tehsil Municipal Authority (TMA) is not working properly and the residents are also disposing the wastes directly in the streets, drains, open spaces, vacant plots and river. The major source of municipal solid waste production is residential sector. The average wastes produced by commercial, educational and health sectors per day were 3.3 kg, 21 kg, 12 kg and 7 kg, correspondingly (**Table 3**). The fruit and vegetable market was generating waste of about 300 kg/day.

Results indicated that the per capita generation of solid waste is 0.37 kg/day. The total waste generated by the entire studied community is 45624 kg/day (50.29tons) whereas total 16.65 million kg/annum (18356.5tons) is the estimated figure for one year. Residential sector was the leading producer with 40738 kg/day (89%) followed by commercial sector 4321 kg/day (9%) presented in **Figure 1**.

The composition of the waste generated by the studied community has different constituent elements. The average physical ingredient of municipal solid waste produced by Dir City comprised of paper (8%), organic matter (53%), plastics (12%), soil, pebbles, gravels, ashes and broken ceramic objects (23.3%) and others things (3.5%; **Figure 2**). The organic matter is one the major constituent because of the use of fresh vegetables, fruits, other food wastes, wood and leaves at household level, and kitchen remains. These results are very near to the findings of [16, 20]. Spatial analysis of results indicates that waste generation rate is highest in Rehankot followed by Shaow. High population density, monthly income and family size are the major factors of more waste generation. The commercial activities are concentrated in a narrow belt along the main road where fruit and vegetable market "*Sabzi Mandi*", hotels and restaurants are located. Therefore, it forms a separate zone of waste generated by commercial activities. Spatially, this zone is extending from north to south in city center covering the entire main market "Main Bazaar". The waste generated in Rehankot, Shaow and Main Bazaar is higher in the city whereas the outskirts are producing low waste because low income group and small to medium size families are settled there.

The major constituent of solid waste in the Dir City is organic matter (53%). The same is found in the previous studies [4, 16, 21] that municipal solid waste is dominated by organic and recyclable materials.

3.2 Community perception

Community perception on the subject of open dumping of municipal solid waste is also been investigated. The perception across the study area was different about negative outcomes of dumpling waste openly. Results indicated that most of

S.No.	Sources	Average Solid Waste
1	*Residential Area*	
	Households	3.3
2	*Commercial Areas*	
	Hotels	8.5
	Shops	1
	Fruit Market	300
3	*Medical facilities*	
	Hospitals	12
	clinics	1.5
4	*Educational Institutions*	
	Private schools	12
	Govt. schools	14
	Private College	7
	Govt. College	14
5	Parks & grounds	8
6	*Offices*	
	Private	1.2
	Government	3

Table 3.
Sector wise average solid waste generation in (kg/day).

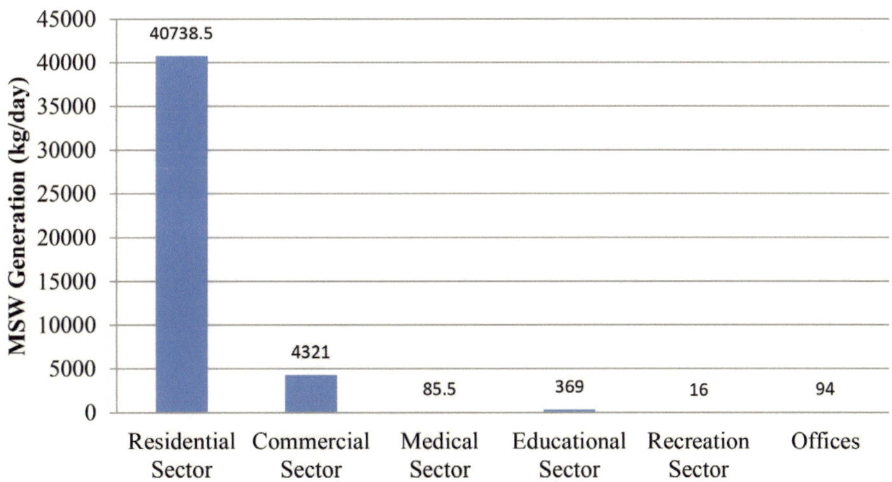

Figure 1.
Sector wise municipal solid waste generation (kg/day).

the residents (68%) were aware of the negative consequences of solid waste open dumping. There view point was that open dumping of solid waste is polluting the environment and causing bad smell and may cause different diseases because it provides breeding grounds for mosquitoes. The remaining (32%) respondents were of view that there is no effect of open dumping of solid waste on health of the environment and people.

The community perception concerning the causes of open dumping of solid waste was uneven. About 63% of the studied population considered that TMA employees are not working properly in residential sector. There is lack of bins at street level. Similarly, there is no one to collect waste from door to door. They just came on request and remove the waste from drains. In some places across the study area, they are unloading solid wastes from hand trolleys directly in the open spaces or in river because there is no waste dumping site. The function of District Government is also poor because the growth of population and expansion of built up land of city has been occurred but there is no improvement has been seen in management of municipal solid waste. The perception of about 37% of the respondents was that Tehsil Municipal Authority employees and residents of the area are accountable for dumping (**Figure 3**). The residents are also throwing the domestic wastes direct in the drains, streets or open spaces. The haphazard dumping is more hazardous for the community. In the study area, drains are not covered and people are throwing waste into it leading to drains obstruction. The blockage further intensifies the problem. The treatment of solid waste is relatively hard subsequent to production.

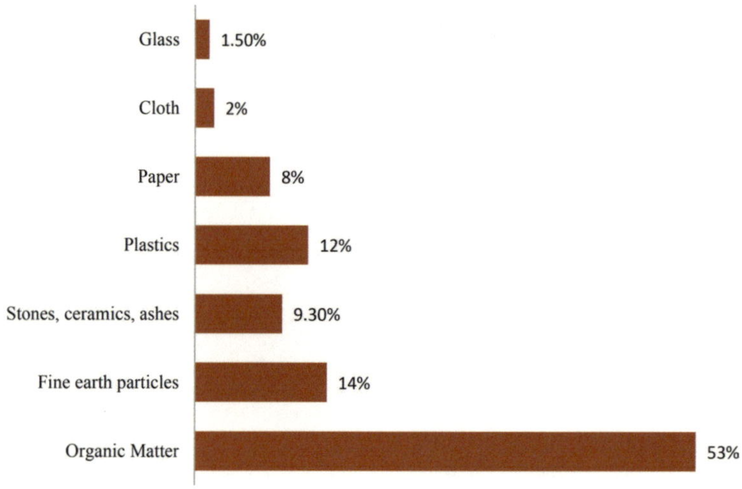

Figure 2.
Composition of the sample solid waste at domestic level.

Figure 3.
Community perception.

Well planned mechanism for collection and disposal is required to dump the waste in landfill site [22, 23]. Both the land filling and open dumping is causing leaching. This may pollute the fresh water resources. Polluted water is causing the accumulation of harmful substances in aquatic animals. Consequently affect the aquatic life negatively. In the same manner it can cause human health problem [24].

4. Conclusions and recommendations

It is concluded from the analysis that about 89% of the solid waste is generated by residential sector. The major constituent elements of sampled wastes were organic matter, plastic and paper.

The related authority and departments has poor performance to manage solid waste properly because of limited available resources. Dumping in drains, open spaces, and streets is very common and most of the community is unaware of its negative consequences on environmental health and human health. Similarly, dropping the waste direct in the river is also one of hazardous activity because it pollutes river's water and may lead to aquatic life. Hazardous environmental and health impacts might be the fate residents of Dir City, if the issue is not managed properly. It is the demand of time to design solid waste management plan for Dir City in order to reduce the risk environmental and health problems.

Future Prospects.

Municipal solid Waste management is a challenge for waste managers and dealing departments/authorities. In this regard, development of proper waste management system is highly required. It will not only reduce risk of environmental problem but also generate revenue. Alongside site suitability analysis for damping of waste is also needed. It will protect the rivers. Similarly, awareness campaigns regarding reuse, recycle and reduce strategies is also highly required at household level.

Author details

Shakeel Mahmood
Department of Geography, GC University Lahore, Pakistan

*Address all correspondence to: shakeelmahmoodkhan@gmail.com

IntechOpen

© 2020 The Author(s). Licensee IntechOpen. This chapter is distributed under the terms of the Creative Commons Attribution License (http://creativecommons.org/licenses/by/3.0), which permits unrestricted use, distribution, and reproduction in any medium, provided the original work is properly cited.

References

[1] Zhang , D. Q., Tan, S. K., & Gersberg, R. M (2010). Municipal solid waste management in China: status, problems and challenges. *Journal of Environmental Management*, *91*(8), 1623-1633.

[2] Karak, T., Bhagat, R. M., & Bhattacharyya, P. (2012). Municipal solid waste generation, composition, and management: the world scenario. *Critical Reviews in Environmental Science and Technology*, *42*(15), 1509-1630.

[3] Muttalib, O. A., & Mohammed Mozaffar Hossain, A. (2016). Quantification and Physical Composition of Household Municipal Solid Waste and People's Attitudes towards its Final Disposal–Chuadanga Municipality, Khulna. *Global Journal of Research In Engineering*, *16*(1).

[4] Trang, P. T. T., Dong, H. Q., Toan, D. Q., Hanh, N. T. X., & Thu, N. T. (2017). The Effects of Socio-economic Factors on Household Solid Waste Generation and Composition: A Case Study in Thu Dau Mot, Vietnam. *Energy Procedia*, *107*, 253-258.

[5] Bufoni, A. L., Oliveira, L. B., & Rosa, L. P. (2015). The financial attractiveness assessment of large waste management projects registered as clean development mechanism. *Waste Management*, *43*, 497-508.

[6] Singh, R. P., Singh, P., Araujo, A. S., Ibrahim, M. H., &Sulaiman, O. (2011). Management of urban solid waste: Vermi composting a sustainable option. *Resources, Conservation and Recycling*, *55*(7), 719-729.

[7] Younes, M. K., Nopiah, Z. M., Basri, N. A., Basri, H., Abushammala, M. F., &Maulud, K. N. A. (2015). Prediction of municipal solid waste generation using nonlinear autoregressive network. *Environmental monitoring and assessment*, *187*(12), 753.

[8] Valkenburg, C., Gerber, M. A., Walton, C. W., Jones, S. B., Thompson, B. L., & Stevens, D. J. (2008). Municipal solid waste (MSW) to liquid fuels synthesis, volume 1: Availability of feedstock and technology. *Richland, WA (US): Pacific Northwest National Laboratory.*

[9] Nabegu, A. B. (2010). An analysis of municipal solid waste in Kano metropolis, Nigeria. *Journal of Human Ecology*, *31*(2), 111-119.

[10] Miezah, K., Obiri-Danso, K., Kádár, Z., Fei-Baffoe, B., & Mensah, M. Y. (2015).Municipal solid waste characterization and quantification as a measure towards effective waste management in Ghana. *Waste Management*, *46*, 15-27.

[11] GoP (Government of Pakistan), (2000). District census report of Dir, 1998. Population census organization, Islamabad.

[12] GoP (Government of Pakistan), (2018). Population census organization of Pakistan, Islamabad.

[13] Mahmood, S., Rahman, A & Shaw, R. (2019). Spatial appraisal of flood risk assessment and evaluation using integrated hydro-probabilistic approach in Panjkora River Basin, Pakistan. *Environmental Monitoring and Assessment*, *191*, 573-583.

[14] Mahmood, S. Khan, A.U. and Mayo, S.M., (2016). Exploring underlying causes and assessing damages of 2010 flash flood in the upper zone of Panjkora River. *Natural Hazards*, *83*(2), pp.1213-1227.

[15] GoP (Government of Pakistan), (2019). Tehsil Municipal Authority (TMA), District Dir Upper, Khyber Pakhtunkhwa.

[16] Mahmood, S., Sharif, F., Rahman, A. U., & Khan, A. U. (2018). Analysis and forecasting of municipal solid waste in Nankana City using geo-spatial techniques. *Environmental monitoring and assessment*, *190*(5), 275.

[17] Ogwueleka, T. C. (2013). Survey of household waste composition and quantities in Abuja, Nigeria. *Resources, Conservation and Recycling*, *77*, 52-60.

[18] Marshall, R. E., & Farahbakhsh, K. (2013). Systems approaches to integrated solid waste management in developing countries. *Waste Management*, *33*(4), 988-1003

[19] Batool, S. A., & Chuadhry, M., N. (2009).Municipal solid waste management in Lahore city district, Pakistan. *Waste management*, *29*(6), 1971-1981.

[20] Suthar, S., & Singh, P. (2015). Household solid waste generation and composition in different family size and socio-economic groups: A case study. *Sustainable Cities and Society*, *14*, 56-63

[21] Jadoon, A., Batool, S. A., & Chaudhry, M. N. (2014).Assessment of factors affecting household solid waste generation and its composition in Gulberg Town, Lahore, Pakistan. *The Journal of Material Cycles and Waste Management*, *16*(1), 73.

[22] Asim, M., Batool, S. A., & Chaudhry, M. N. (2012). Scavengers and their role in the recycling of waste in Southwestern Lahore. *Resources, Conservation and Recycling*, *58*, 152-162.

[23] Ali, S. M., Pervaiz, A., Afzal, B., Hamid, N., & Yasmin, A. (2014). Open dumping of municipal solid waste and its hazardous impacts on soil and vegetation diversity at waste dumping sites of Islamabad city. *Journal of King Saud University-Science*, *26*(1), 59-65.

[24] Maiti, S. K., De, S., Hazra, T., Debsarkar, A., & Dutta, A. (2016). Characterization of Leachate and Its Impact on Surface and Groundwater Quality of a Closed Dumpsite–A Case Study at Dhapa, Kolkata, India. *Procedia Environmental Sciences*, *35*, 391-399.

Chapter 9

Valorization of Rapeseed Waste Biomass in Sorption Processes for Wastewater Treatment

Irina Morosanu, Carmen Teodosiu, Lavinia Tofan, Daniela Fighir and Carmen Paduraru

Abstract

Circular economy provides an efficient framework for effective biomass valorization, through strategic use and processing of resources and waste reuse. Being the second largest energetic crop, rapeseed (RS) presents a high potential in this sense. However, good management of the large quantity of generated wastes from agro-industrial activities is required. The most common management strategies in this sense refer to the reuse of RS wastes (mainly stems and press-cake) for animal feed, compost, soil amendment and fertilizer. Valorization of RS wastes as adsorbent for wastewater treatment is attractive. Despite the fact that only few articles on this subject exist in literature, they are sufficient to reflect the potential of this adsorbent to remove both inorganic and organic compounds from aqueous phase. The rapeseed wastes were used in native form (for diluted effluents) or modified by chemical or thermal treatment (for concentrated effluents or large molecule contaminants). This chapter will provide a review on the RS wastes management strategies, highlighting the applications for removing contaminants from wastewater in single and multi-component systems, in static or continuous operation mode.

Keywords: rapeseed, canola, biomass, wastewater treatment, adsorption, biosorption, pollutants removal

1. Introduction

A sustainable growth of our society implies a continual and efficient (re)use of the available resources. At the European Union (EU) level, great efforts are made to move to a circular economy with an efficient use of resources and zero waste generation. In the latest report, member states view food, waste processing and mobility among the priority sectors in the circular economy strategies [1]. Waste from one part of the system may be a resource in other sector, matching demand and supply, while biofuels obtained from the high-growing biomass and biological wastes tackles the problem of renewable energy.

Rape or rapeseed (*Brassica napus* L. and its varieties) currently occupies the second place in the world production of oilseed and meal [2]. EU is the second major producer of rapeseed, after Canada. In Europe, the main oilseed culture consists of rapeseed, followed by sunflower seeds and soya beans. Romania is among the top seven major producers, being responsible for almost 5.5% of the EU total RS production [3]. Crushing of oilseeds produces RS oil (for human consumption or biodiesel production) and RS meal. The latter represents almost 57% of the world total RS production [2]. Within the scope of this chapter, the terms "rape" or "rapeseed" will be used when referring to other common names or varieties, such as canola, colza, swede, swede rape, summer rape, winter rape, annual rape. Another mention is about the methods of oil extraction from rape seeds (RSs). This can be done by mechanical pressing, when RS meal is produced, with 8–20% residual oil content. The fat content could be further lowered by solvent extraction to 1–3%; then the solid waste obtained is RS cake [4]. Because we have found a great number of articles in literature where no distinction between RS meal (RSM) and RS cake (RSC) was made, we will be using these terms interchangeably here.

Valorization options for RS meal are based predominantly on the use as animal feed. Although a recognized feedstock for protein extraction, RS is still underutilized for production of commercially available protein products [5, 6]. Besides meal, other solid residues result from RS harvesting (stems and leaves). They are primarily used to obtain energy by combustion or fermentation [7] and soil amendment and fertilizer [8]. Currently at EU level, lignocellulosic and agricultural biomass (including rapeseed wastes) are the subject of some Bio-Based Industries Joint Undertaking projects [9].

An emerging valorization alternative consists of using RS wastes for the removal of pollutants from wastewater by adsorption. In order to lower the cost of activated carbon (AC) processes, abundant and readily available agricultural wastes were tested in native form or after a treatment as presented in various reviews [10–13]. The process is called *biosorption* when the waste is used in either its natural form or after some physical or chemical modification. At present, most of the work is done at laboratory scale. Although activated carbon process is an established technology at industrial scale, not many ventures can be encountered for the commercialization of biosorption [14].

This chapter aims to dive into the rapeseed waste management practices and strategies, specifically on the opportunity of valorization as a sorbent in wastewater treatment. Firstly, the sources of different rape waste biomass are identified and their valorization options are discussed from the circular economy perspective. The second part of the chapter will focus on the relation between adsorption and RS waste. After a short description of the adsorption process as a wastewater treatment technology, the characteristics that make RS a potentially suitable biosorbent are highlighted. Finally, an overview of the limited number of studies found in literature dealing with RS-based sorbents will be focusing on the types of pollutants and wastewater matrix investigated and the adsorption system configuration employed.

2. Rape waste biomass sources and management strategies

2.1 Sources

Rape is a multifunctional oily plant with yellow flowers and thin, long and branched stems. The many RS varieties are remarkable by extensive biomass, easiness in harvesting and adaptability to climatic change, their cultivation being estimated as one of the most sustainable oil crops [15]. The main applicability of the harvested component of the rape crop, the seeds, targets vegetable oils production (**Figure 1**). Rape seeds contain compounds of nutritional value (proteins and oil) and anti-nutrients, namely erucic acid and glucosinolates. The two varieties of *Brassica napus* seeds frequently cultivated - industrial rapeseed and canola- have

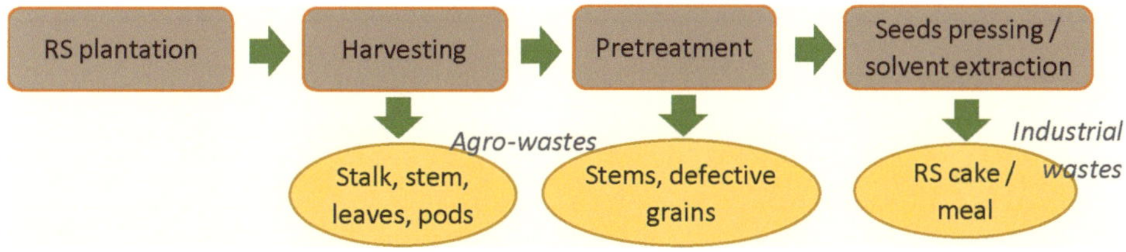

Figure 1.
Sources of wastes from the RS oil production process.

as distinguishing feature the erucic acid content in the corresponding oils. Unlike traditional varieties of rapeseed that give oils that contain 22–60% erucic acid, the cultivars of canola produce oils with low erucic [5].

The main sources of RS waste are agricultural activities and production of oil and biodiesel (**Figure 1**). Field residues, present after RS crop harvesting, consist of stems, stalks, leaves and seed pods. From the technological process before seed storing result impurities, broken and immature grains, stems, rotten grains etc. [16, 17]. The total RS biomass consists of 28–50% seeds, while the rest is crop residues, mainly stalks [18]. The agricultural wastes resulting in large amounts from the harvesting and postharvest of the seeds of rape are lignocellulosic materials: straws and stalks contain 15–36% cellulose, 18–25% hemicelluloses and 14–31.6% lignin [19, 20], while seeds husks contain: 13.7% cellulose, 19% hemicellulose and 25.5% lignin [21]. The processing of the rape seeds for vegetable oils yields press-cake or meal as industrial residue, which account for about 60% by weight of the input seeds [21, 22]. The RSC obtained by mechanical pressing of oleaginous seeds contains 30–40% proteins and 9.0–12.60% crude fibers [16, 23]. On the other hand, RSM resulted after the solvent extraction of the oil from the rape seeds has a content of about 37–40% proteins and 10–17.5% crude fibers [22, 24]. Authors [25] have determined the composition of deoiled canola meal (CM): 34.5% lignin, 33.5% hemicellulose and 30.2% cellulose. The RSC/RSM are currently important sources of organic matter and energy.

The wide availability, low-cost, renewability, versatility, unique structure and interesting technological properties make these residual materials more than just wastes. Their resource potential for sustainable products with multi-faceted applications is still undervalued.

2.2 The circular economy approach and management of rape biomass

Circular economy can be described as an industrial system that is restorative or regenerative by intention and design, aiming for the elimination of waste through the superior design of materials, products, systems and business models [26]. The recovery of valuable by-products can contribute to circular economy transition by reducing waste generation, maximizing resources potential and also leading to cost reduction [27]. The management of RS wastes with the possibility of their reuse in different forms is presented in **Figure 2**. Rapeseed meal/cake, the main by-product of vegetable oil and biodiesel production, has a high potential for an integrated valorization scheme [28]. For example, RSM can be transformed into a hydrolysate and used with crude glycerol to produce poly (3-hydroxybutyrate) [29]. RSM contains bioactive constituents, such as phenolic sinapinic acid and protocatechuic acid, which can be used as functional food ingredients and for use in cosmetic and pharmaceutical applications [27, 30]. Its application for animal feed is limited however due to the presence of anti-nutritional compounds (e.g. glucosinolates, phytic acid, synapine, erucic acid, tannins) and high fiber contents. Treatment with ethanol reduces phenols and glucosinolates content, while increasing the protein

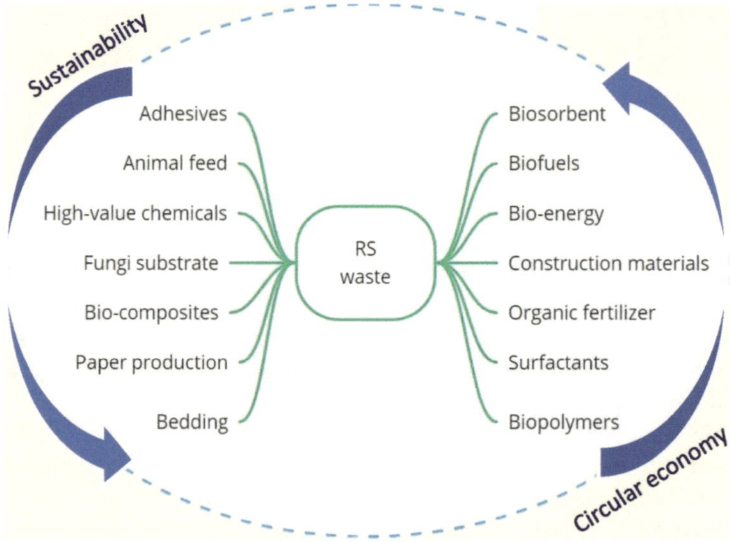

Figure 2.
Rape waste biomass as resourceful raw material in circular economy.

level, and makes possible RSM use as feed additive or as a source for production of protein-rich ingredients with specific value and functionality [31]. The biotransformation of RSM using bacteria increases its nutritional value and enriches it with a variety of additives, including polymers, bio-surfactants and enzymes [32]. RSM has proved to be a plant-derived alternative for development of bio-plastic materials [33] and new polyurethane composites [23].

The lignocellulosic biorefinery strategies integrate physical, chemical, thermophysical, thermochemical or biological processes for the pretreatment and conversion of biomass into bio-based products [34]. In the case of RS, these processes are adapted to the characteristic content of cellulose, hemicellulose and lignin that are the main components responsible for biorefinery. The use of the whole plant of RS for production of biodiesel, bioethanol and methane into the frame of biorefinery concept resulted in a 3 times increase of the efficiency of energy recovery as compared to conventional process of biodiesel production [35–37]. RS straws, containing >50% of carbohydrates, are an interesting source of biomass for biorefineries, by conversion into bioenergy and high-value chemicals. It is also an attractive source of fermentable sugars for bioethanol production [19]. More than 50% of RS straw could be recovered as xylan, lignin and nanocellulose [38].

RS stalk and straw also present interest in pulping and papermaking industries [39–41]. The potential of RS straws as source of lignocellulosic fibers can also be valorized for the production of biocomposite materials [42, 43]. The beneficial effects of RS stalks use on the humus and nutrients content of some damaged soils have been pointed out [44, 45]. Polyphenols and proteins were extracted from rapeseed stems and leaves by pulse electric fields [46]. Another potential use for canola leaves is as annual forage for field-raised swine and poultry. RS leaves and hulls can be used in livestock (rabbits, swine, poultry, fish) feeding [17, 47], or substrate for fungi production [48]. RS shells can be used as precursors for activated carbon materials as cathode in lithium-sulfur batteries [49]. Other applications of RS wastes include the use as soil amendments for increasing crop growth, usually in biochar form [8, 50, 51].

Another interesting possibility of recycled–value added application of RS wastes involves their ability to act as efficient biosorbent for the removal of heavy metals and organic pollutants from environmental aqueous media, which will be discussed in the second part of this chapter.

3. Adsorption on rape waste biomass

3.1 Adsorption/biosorption processes

Among the numerous wastewater treatment processes, adsorption distinguishes by efficiency, design simplicity and flexibility, operation easiness, insensitivity to toxic pollutants and economic feasibility [52]. Adsorption refers to the retention of a chemical species (adsorbate) on the surface of a solid substance (adsorbent) by means of physical and chemical interactions. The existence of weak van der Waals interactions determines the fast kinetics, low heat, monolayer or multilayer coverage, non-selectivity and reversibility of the physical adsorption. A chemisorption mechanism reaches equilibrium slower due to creation of covalent bonds, which causes a high activation energy, monolayer coverage and irreversibility. The adsorption of inorganic and organic pollutants from wastewater is most often the result of both types of mechanisms overlapping. The significance of adsorption for wastewater treatment is highlighted by the increasing range of materials used as adsorbents. The materials that can act as adsorbents are remarkable by the variety of structures and properties. They can be raw and modified materials of mineral, organic or biological origin, natural materials, synthetic materials, industrial and agricultural wastes and biomasses [53].

The "green" subcategory of adsorption, biosorption, can be defined as the low-cost and low-tech concentration of pollutants from aqueous media on the solid surface of a biological matrix (biosorbent), achieved through a passive mechanism [54]. As a physico-chemical process, biosorption works by a combination of different interactions ranging from hydrogen forces to covalent bonds through which the targeted toxic species is retained on the biosorptive materials surface. The key concepts of biosorption have been fully decrypted by means of a large number of laboratory studies addressing issues of fundamental research (**Table 1**).

Due to its quasi-perfect framing into the sustainable development coordinates, biosorption has received considerable acceptance in removing heavy metals and organic pollutants from wastewater [54, 55]. Besides the ecologic and economic advantages, biosorption is also challenging by its applicability over a wide array of operational conditions, adaptability to varied designs of systems, possibility of sequential or simultaneous removal of pollutants from large volumes of wastewaters. Biosorption is a propriety characteristic to a broad spectrum of natural or waste bio-origin materials that are cheap, abundant, ready available, renewable, recyclable and versatile [55]. The biosorption potential of biomass is mainly due to their surface functional groups (hydroxyl, carboxyl, amino, sulfhydryl, carbonyl, phosphate) able to cope with the pollutants' toxicity. Due to the functional groups, these materials developed a wide range of uptake mechanisms (electrostatic interaction, ion exchange, precipitation, complexation, chelation, reduction) that ensure high pollutants removal efficiencies from aqueous media [13, 14, 56]. Various biological materials were tested for the development as biosorbents, including: microorganisms and algae, plant materials, agro-industrial wastes and other polysaccharides materials. These categories of green adsorbents have been almost exclusively investigated from the perspective of their application for removal of heavy metals and/or textile dyes from synthetic wastewaters. The promising results have opened the way to develop environmentally friendly technologies for removal – recovery – recycling of rare earths and precious metals [57, 58]. Biosorbents must

Targeted issues	Relevance
Batch studies	
Effect of experimental parameters: pH, initial pollutant concentration, biosorbent dose, contact time, temperature	Optimization of the biosorption process
Isotherm modeling: Langmuir, Freundlich, Dubinin-Radushkevich, Tempkin, Elovich etc.	Quantification of the interactions. Evaluation of the maximum biosorption capacity
Kinetics modeling: Lagergren (pseudo-first order), Ho (pseudo – second order); diffusion models - intraparticle, film	Determination of uptake rate. Insights into the mechanism of biosorption reactions
Thermodynamic parameters	Biosorption energy (heat)
Fixed – bed column studies	
Parameters process: initial concentration of adsorbate, pH, flow rate, bed height Breakthrough curve and its modeling	Valuable information for design of wastewater treatment for continuous operation in real conditions
Desorption studies	
Desorption agent Minimum number of reused cycles	Biosorbent regeneration and recyclability

Table 1.
Description of biosorption process and its characteristics.

exhibited high capacity and rate of biosorption, increased selectivity and multiple recyclability. Unlike algal biosorbents that have significant pollutant uptake capacity, fungi and some agricultural wastes show moderate capacity of biosorption [59]. Due to the adjustable surface chemistry of biomass, the essential features of biosorption materials can be significantly improved or tailored to practical applications by way of adequate chemical modification procedures [13, 14, 56, 60]. The stringent necessity for the near future is the transposition of biosorption processes performances to pilot and industrial scale.

3.2 Characteristics of rape waste

Rape waste biomass shows interesting properties that promote its biosorbent function for pollutants' removal, as another prospective way of waste reuse and recycling. The features of RS wastes are determined by factors correlated with the raw material (source, geographical region and environmental conditions), types of products and processes. RS wastes are vegetable materials with lignocellulosic composition of high degree of heterogeneity, as mentioned in Section 2.1. They have been assimilated with multi chromatographic systems carrying very different supports of polarity [61]. This heterogeneity is due to their complex structure and composition. For instance, the structure of the RSs encompasses three main structural components: (1) the embryo that in turn, is formed by cotyledon, hypocotyl and radicle; (2) the endosperm; (3) the coat of seed [62]. The seed flesh contains lipids (essentially residual oil) in the form of triacylglycerols and lipids associated with cell membranes, proteins (oleosins make up to 20% of total seed proteins) and fibers, composed from lignin and polysaccharides (cellulose, hemicellulose and pectin) [21]. The chemical composition of RS agro-wastes (stalk, straw, leaves) reveals a high content of carbon (457–465 mg/g) and nitrogen (1.9–6.7 mg/g), together with elements like Ca, Mg, K, Na and P [63, 64]. Deoiled CM contains

44.21% C, 6.3% H, 5.55% N and 0.37% S [25], while the following elemental analysis of RSC was reported: 77.82% C, 15.05% O, 5.48% N, 0.65% Ca, 0.48% S and 0.54% P [65].

The surface characteristics are of major importance for the biosorption potential of a material. One of them is the specific surface area assessed by Brunauer-Emmet-Teller (BET) method. For example, a BET area of 5.6 m^2/g was determined for RSC by N_2 adsorption analysis at 77 K [66]. The surface area of RS waste from a local unit of biodiesel production has been evaluated at 107.32 m^2/g by dynamic water vapor sorption [65]. A higher value was obtained for RS stalk - 43.21 m^2/g [67].

The surface charge is expressed in terms of point of zero charge pH (pH_{PZC}), representing the pH value at which the surface of biosorbent is neutral from electric point of view. The pH_{PZC} of a RS waste has been reported as being 5 [68]. Thus, the surface of RS is positively charged at $pH < 5$ and favorable for anions biosorption. Meanwhile, for $pH > 5$, the surface of biosorbent is negatively charged and has affinity for cationic pollutants. More basic pH_{PZC} values were obtained for canola stalk (5.7) [69], canola stalk and leaves (6.1) [63] and canola hull (7.0) [70].

The morphological features of the biosorbents are usually studied by means of scanning electron microscopy (SEM). From **Figure 3a**, it may be observed that rapeseed waste has an uneven and porous structure that seems to be very adequate for the biosorption of pollutants [71, 72]. RS stalk, straw and hull present a rough surface, with regular tunnel-like structure (remains of cell wall) [70, 73–75]. The small pores on the surface had an average pore diameter of 1.09 ± 0.13 μm [73].

The Fourier transform infrared spectroscopy (FTIR) features are valuable source of information related to the functional groups playing a key role in the biosorption process. FTIR studies revealed that the surface of RS waste contains valuable functional groups playing a key role in the biosorption process, such as amino, hydroxyl and carbonyl groups [65, 70–72, 76, 77]. The main peaks in the FTIR spectrum of RS waste are presented in **Figure 3b**.

Thermal stability and degradation behavior of RS have been assessed by thermogravimetric analysis (TGA). Thermal decomposition of RS biomass has been described as a three stages process: moisture evaporation (up to 120°C), hemicellulose decomposition (200–250°C), degradation of cellulose and lignin (300–450°C) [25, 68]. The high thermal stability indicated by the TGA suggests that the RS biosorbents yielding as wastes from the treatment of wastewaters could be reused for energy recovery purposes.

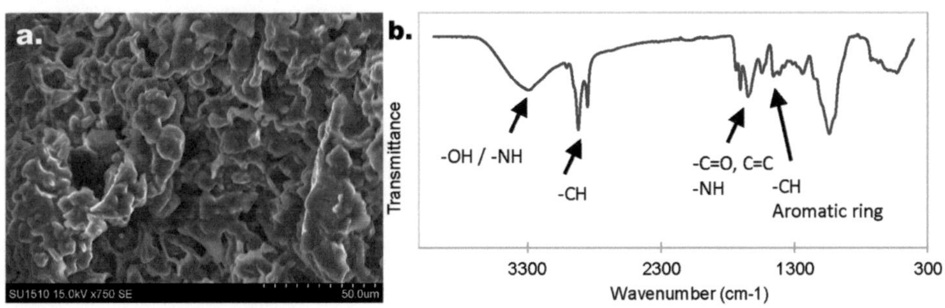

Figure 3.
SEM image (a) and FTIR spectra (b) of RS waste.

4. Pollutants removal and system configuration

4.1 Types of pollutants adsorbed and wastewater characteristics

A systematic adsorption investigation starts at laboratory scale, when the interaction between a single target pollutant and the adsorbent is studied. This fundamental set-up is called a mono-component system, consisting from a single pollutant-model (usually, its salt form) dissolved in high-grade purified water. The complexity of the system will grow with two or more target pollutants to be removed from the same aqueous media. The multi-component system study is necessary in order to see the possible effects (competitive or synergic) generated by the presence of another compound (possible interference) on the uptake by the adsorbent. The ultimate goal is to test the adsorbent in a real aqueous media, i.e. wastewater, which is a more complex system, containing many dissolved (and in many cases, not individually known) compounds.

To the authors' best knowledge, the first studies using RS biomass-based adsorbents, i.e. canola meal, were reported over two decades ago by Al-Asheh and Duvnjak [24, 78, 79]. After 2010 (**Figure 4a**), RS waste has again attracted attention in the research community, as a result of worldwide increased production of rape cultures and waste management regulatory pressures.

4.1.1 Mono-component systems: inorganics adsorption

Figure 4b presents the distribution of model pollutants reported in literature, by the number of RS-derived adsorbents investigated for the individual uptake of a certain pollutant (i.e., in mono-component system). Among inorganic compounds, the prevalence of heavy metals removal from wastewater is justified by their high occurrence, persistence in the environment and high toxicity. Numerous articles have reported the use of RS-based adsorbents for the abatement of Pb and Cd removal, followed by Cu, Ni and Zn (**Figure 4b**). It is interesting that most fractions of rape biomass were studied for Cu adsorption, in natural or modified state (**Table 2**): from sprouts to stalks and leaves resulted from harvesting and finally, to rapeseed press-cake. A quite similar variability can be observed for cadmium. An

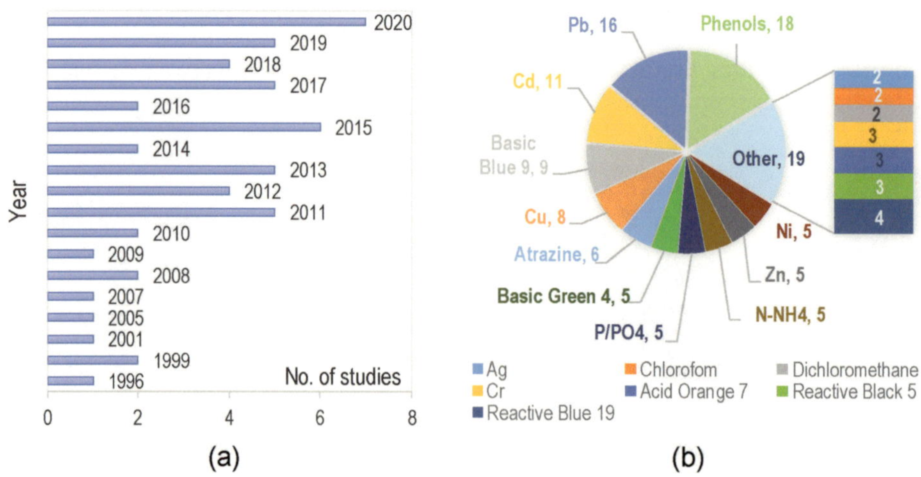

Figure 4.
Distribution of adsorption studies using rapeseed biomass per years (a) and tested RS-based adsorbents (except the 22 cases of 1 adsorbent per pollutant) on different wastewater contaminants (b).

Adsorbent	Efficiency	Adsorbent	Efficiency
Canola meal [24]	36.747 mg Cu/g*	RSC [68]	13.858 mg Zn/g*
Canola meal [78]	22.69 mg Zn/g*, 89.6% Cd, 67.2% Cu, 40.3% Ni, 92.3% Pb	*Brassica* straw [char, magnetic-gelatin] [85]	Cr*: 35.1971 mg/g char; 434.85 mg/g magnetic-gelatin char
RSC, husks, WS, ground seeds [21]	Cu*: 13.4 mg/g RSC; 36.6 mg/g husk; 8.6 mg/g WS; 10.7 mg Cu/g seeds	Canola stalk and leaves [75]	62.5 mg Fe/g*, 40.0 mg Mn/g*, 41.7 mg Zn/g*, 20.8 mg Ni/g*, 35.7 mg Cu/g*, 71.4 mg Cd/g*
RSM [71]	18.35–22.70 mg Pb/g*	Canola straw [char] [64]	30.50–37.49 mg Cu/g*
RS pellet cellulose [citric acid] [86]	40% Cu	RS oil cake [char] [87]	129.87 mg Pb/g*, 133.33 mg Ni/g*
RSM [77]	15.43 mg Cu/g*, 21.72 mg Cd/g*	Deoiled RSM [88]	97.09 mg Pb/g*
Brassica campestris waste stem [82]	40% Ni, 98% Pb, 91.8% Cr	Canola straw [char] [84]	Pb*: 84–108 mg/g char; 72–195 mg/g steam-AC
Canola straw [char] [83]	14.56 mg/g* Cr	Expired rapeseeds [89]	4.65–45.38 mg Hg/g
Canola residues [81]	90–99% Cd	Canola shoot [char] [80]	4.14 mg Cd/g, 15.52 mg Cu/g
RS pomace [sunflower husks, char] [90]	26.9 mg Ag/g*, 17.1 mg Cu/g*	RS stalk from 2 cultivars [NaOH, enzymatic hydrolysis] [67]	Cd*: 10.93–25.19 mg/g stalks; 18.15–27.40 mg/g fermentation residues

Notes: "[X]" indicates that the native biomass has undergone significant structure modification, while X can be the chemical agent used, the final adsorbent or other mixture component; char – carbonized material (e.g. biochar).
**Langmuir maximum sorption capacity.*

Table 2.
Efficiency of RS-based adsorbents for heavy metals removal from liquid phase.

AC prepared from canola shoot showed maximum sorption capacities of 15.52 mg Cu/g and 4.14 mg Cd/g [80]. Similar efficiency for Cu adsorption was observed for RSM, i.e. 15.43 mg/g [77].

The sorptive potential of RS agro-wastes was commonly assessed (**Table 2**). In many cases, the residues were used after minimal pre-treatment, which usually involves the removal of impurities by several washings and drying for a certain period of time, at room temperature, in sunlight or in an oven. Washed and dried canola agro-residues from Iran were used for adsorption of cadmium ions from aqueous solution [81], whilst a mixture of stalk and leaves was used for the removal of several metals in the sequence of sorption capacities: Cd > Fe > Zn > Mn > Cu > Ni [75]. Untreated stalks have been investigated in the adsorption process of Cr, Cd, Ni and Pb [82]. Reference [67] used several cultivars of RS to assess the ethanol production after a mild alkali pretreatment (1% NaOH, 50°C). The solid residues obtained after yeast fermentation exhibited higher Cd adsorption capacities than the raw stalks (**Table 2**). In the last years, RS straw was used as feedstock for biochar production at laboratory scale [64, 83–85]. Although the adsorption capacities of these materials are usually higher than the precursors (**Table 2**), the feedstock particles size and preparation conditions vary.

According to **Table 2**, the most popular bio-material for heavy metals adsorption is RS meal (or cake, press-cake). This complex lignocellulosic material is comprised of a water-soluble fraction (e.g., phytic acid, proteins, glucosinolates etc.) and a solid fraction, formed from husks (hulls) and the flesh of seeds. Authors [21] made a systematic research regarding the component of RSC responsible for metal binding. By comparing the adsorption capacity of Cu for press-cake, husks, white sediment (WS, i.e. flesh of seeds) and ground seeds, under the same experimental conditions, they observed that husks are the most efficient fraction. Based on the removal efficiency, RSC presents higher affinity for Pb, followed by Cd, Cu and Ni [78]. The values of metal biosorption capacity reported in literature aren't higher than 40 mg/g. Meanwhile, the ACs obtained from RSM can easily achieve adsorption capacities of around 130 mg/g (**Table 2**), by creating a microporous structure and a high surface area.

Nutrients were also under investigation for adsorption on agricultural RS residues. Native and modified canola stalks and leaves were used for the removal of phosphorus from aqueous solutions [63]. According to Langmuir sorption capacity (q_L), sorbents efficiency followed the sequence: *native* (4.3 mg/g) < *modified by* $CaCl_2$ (6.6 mg/g) < *modified by urea* (8.5 mg/g) < *modified by* $FeCl_3$ (9.0 mg/g). A biochar prepared from RS leaves and stems was combined with Mg-Al layered double oxides and tested for the adsorption of phosphate from water [91]. The phosphate removal efficiency remained above 92% at a pH range of 2–10, for an initial pollutant concentration (C_i) of 50 mg/L, while q_L reached a value of 132.8 mg/g. Adsorption of ammonium nitrogen from diluted aqueous solutions was studied using natural mineral and organic adsorbents [76]. The authors observed that the canola agro-residues presented an adsorption capacity comparable to that of zeolite and bentonite. The organic spent adsorbent can be safely used afterwards as soil fertilizer. q_L of ammonium ion for several ACs from CM varied between 17.9 and 148.9 mg/g [92]. The low cost of the KOH treated AC was determined.

A single study was found with regards to the adsorption of fluoride using canola stalk treated with bicarbonate, reporting a removal efficiency of 79% for C_i of 10 mg F/L [93].

4.1.2 Mono-component systems: organics adsorption

To the authors' knowledge, adsorption/biosorption studies using rape-derived sorbents involved the following categories of organic compounds: textile dyes, phenolic compounds, organochloride compounds, pesticides and herbicides. Phenolic compounds and textile dyes were the organic pollutants with the highest interest for removal from aqueous phase by RS biomass (**Figure 4b**).

Various dyestuffs, including acid, basic, direct and reactive, were used as model pollutants in the adsorption experiments. From **Table 3**, higher sorption capacities for cationic dyes (13.22–836.2 mg/g) were observed, when compared to those for anionic dyes (2.01–11.81 mg/g). This is mainly because of the different treatments (chemical or thermal) applied to the rape biomass. Among the various dyes, malachite green (MG) and methylene blue (MB) are preferred as model contaminants. Extensive research was done using stalk adsorbents, in different forms: native, chemically treated, biochar or activated form (**Table 3**).

Other studies involving RS meal adsorbents (**Table 3**) deal with the removal of chloroform and dichloromethane, atrazine, phenolic compounds and dyes. In addition, there is a study from Canada reporting acyclovir adsorption on powdered AC prepared from deoiled CM with a removal efficiency of 39.5% at C_i = 400 mg/L [25]. RS cake was used many times as precursor for AC production, which was then used

Adsorbent	Efficiency	Adsorbent	Efficiency
Defatted seeds [94]	68.6% chloroform, 70.4% dichloromethane, 78.6% trichloroethylene	Defatted seeds [95]	71.9% chloroform, 69% dichloromethane, 46.8% benzene
RSM [magnetic NPs, polypyrrole] [96]	MG*: 836.2 mg/g RS-magnetic NPs, 93.3 mg/g RS-polypyrrole	Waste of RS after microbial culture medium [48]	17.857 mg MG/g*
RS straw-based compost [97]	2.15 mg Reactive Yellow 84/g*, 4.78 mg Reactive Black 5/g*, 26.41 mg Basic Green 4/g*, 27.19 mg Basic Violet 10/g*	Laccase immobilized with RS press cake [98]	74% Amaranth, 81% Acid Orange 7, 50% Acid Blue 113, 83% Trypan Blue, 57% Sunset Yellow FCF
RSC [61]	58.2% atrazine	RS [AC] [99]	70–95% phenol
RSC [alginate] [100]	Atrazine: 70% for beads form; 96% for rods form	Canola stalk [101]	6.73 mg Methylene blue/g**
RS meal [72]	11.81 mg Reactive Blue 19/g*	RSC [AC] [102]	332 mg phenol/g, 482 mg p-cholorophenol/g
RS stalk [AC] [103]	0.079 mg bromopropylate/g*; 90–100%	RSC [AC] [104]	Phenol: 88 mg/g steam-AC, 68 mg/g CO_2-AC
Canola hull [70]	67.56 mg Basic Blue 41/g*, 49.01 mg Basic Red 46/g*, 25.0 mg Basic Violet 16/g*	Canola hull [105]	63% Reactive Red 198, 70% Reactive Blue 19, 80% Direct Red 79, 81% Direct Red 80
Swede rape straw native, [oxalic acid] [73]	MB*: 143 mg/g native, 432 mg/g modified	Swede rape straw native, [tartaric acid] [74]	MB*: 128.2 mg/g native, 246.4 mg/g modified
Canola straw [char] [106]	102 mg Methyl violet/g	Canola stalk [char] [107]	93.4 mg MB/g
Canola stalk [69]	32.8 mg Remazol Black B/g*	Canola residue [108]	Acid Orange 7
Canola stalk [20]	25.06 mg Acid Orange 7/g*, 32.79 mg Remazol Black 5/g	Swede rape hull [microwave] [109]	272 mg MB/g*
RSM [110]	78 mg MG/g*, 122 mg MB/g*	Canola stalk [AC] [111]	135.8 mg 2,4-dichlorophenoxyacetic acid/g

Notes: "[X]" indicates that the native biomass has undergone significant structure modification, while X can be the chemical agent used, the final adsorbent or other mixture component; char – carbonized material (e.g. biochar).
**Langmuir sorption capacity.*
***Sips sorption capacity.*

Table 3.
Efficiency of RS-based adsorbents for organics removal from liquid phase.

for phenolic compounds abatement (**Table 3**). Moreover, pesticides of moderately to highly hydrophobic nature, like atrazine, have shown fairly good removal efficiencies when RS cake was used (yet, mainly due to the absorption in the oil droplets that remain trapped in the matrix after seed pressing) [61]. Higher efficiencies than powdered AC were obtained for volatile organic compounds, where some intracellular fat particles named spherosomes are responsible for their uptake [94, 95].

4.1.3 Multi-component systems

There are few studies involving RS sorbents that report simultaneous adsorption experiments. Firstly, Al-Asheh et al. [24, 78] investigated the single, binary, ternary and quaternary adsorption of some heavy metals using CM. They observed the same succession in single system and mixture based on the molar sorption capacities for: Zn > Cu > Cd [24]. In a later study, the same authors noticed Ni was strongly inhibited by the presence of Cu and Pb in the same solution [78]. In binary and tertiary metal systems, inhibition of Pb was manifested by Cu, Cd and/or Ni, whereas Cd uptake was higher in binary mixture with Ni or Pb. Copper biosorption was restricted by Pb only in binary mixtures, while in any other combination with Cd and Ni, it was promoted. In all cases, copper exhibited the highest molar biosorption capacity, followed by Cd, Ni and then Pb in mono-, bi- and tri-component systems. In a quaternary mixture, the following order (molar basis) was obtained: Cu > Cd > Pb > Ni.

The efficiency of canola residues (stalk and leaves) in the competitive biosorption of Cd, Cu, Ni, Zn, Fe and Mn was investigated by means of equilibrium isotherms [75]. The authors mention that: "The sorption isotherm of heavy metals in single and competitive systems were studied using batch technique. Sorbents were allowed to equilibrate with solutions at different initial metal concentrations (0, 5, 10, 30, 50, 100, 150, 200, and 300 mg/L)." However, it is not clearly stated for competitive systems if the mentioned initial concentrations are for each metal (and the highest total C_i would be 300 mg/L times 6 metals = 2400 mg/L) or the values are cumulated (the highest C_i of each metal would be 300 mg/L divided by 6 metals = 50 mg/L). In any case, the biosorption capacities of all metals have decreased in multi-component systems with more than 67% as compared to the individual biosorption (**Table 2**), in the following order of metal sorption: Ni (6.6 mg/g) < Zn (9.4 mg/g) < Fe (10.7 mg/g) < Mn (10.2 mg/g) < Cu (11.6 mg/g) < Cd (14.7 mg/g).

To the authors' knowledge, the only article reporting simultaneous biosorption of pollutants of different type, i.e. Pb and Reactive blue 19 (Rb19) dye, is reference [112]. In the absence of a rigorous experimental framework for multi-component biosorption study, the authors have tried multiple strategies to study the biosorption of binary system using RS meal. These involved: (i) influence of Pb:Rb19 molar ratio (range of 0.8–6.0), (ii) equilibrium studies by varying the initial concentration of one pollutant (15–150 mg/L), while maintaining a fixed C_i (50 mg/L) of the second contaminant, (iii) kinetics modeling at various pollutant molar ratios, and (iv) selectivity tests. The biosorption profile of the binary system was found to be versatile. At low C_i, dye biosorption was promoted by the presence of metal ions. However, at high C_i of dye, lead uptake was inhibited.

Studies on sorption processes with rape biomass involving real effluents were reported by few authors [71, 80, 94, 98, 111]. Heavy metals have been successfully removed from industrial effluents: Cu from smelting wastewater in Canada using CM [78], Pb from spiked industrial wastewater in Romania (94% efficiency in biosorption column with RS meal) [71] and Cd (20% reduction) and Cu (95% removal) from acid mine water in Australia by using biochar obtained from canola shoot [80]. Dichloromethane was removed (90%) from chemical wastewater on defatted seeds from oil extraction in Japan, while total elimination of an herbicide from drainage water from sugarcane fields in Iran using canola stalk-based AC was obtained [111].

4.2 Batch and dynamic process operation

Current research regarding adsorption as a wastewater treatment technology is focused on trials of a large and diverse range of materials that could become suitable adsorbents for different pollutants. This could be easily done at laboratory scale by using batch testing. The batch operation is also favored for obtaining fundamental information about the adsorption process, like the adsorption capacity in optimum working conditions. A summary of the best adsorption conditions by using RS biomass is presented in **Table 4**. Among the factors influencing the sorption process, solution acidity affects the pollutant speciation, the charge of functional groups on the sorbents surface and the ions competition for the binding sites. As **Table 4** shows, metals usually adsorb at acidic pH (precipitation of metal hydroxides at pH > 6 is also avoided). Organic contaminants, like volatile compounds or phenols, mostly favor neutral to alkaline conditions. On the other hand, pH values of 6–8 are optimal for cationic dyes, while acidic medium is best for anionic dyes. The amount of available sorption sites is directly dependent on the amount of adsorbent used and its granulometry. Native biosorbents, which have low specific area, impose the use of a higher dose, whereas a lower dosage is necessary for chemically modified or pyrolised adsorbents. However, a too high dose may lead to particle agglomeration and low access to the sorbent. The rapidity with which the sorption equilibrium is reached depends on the contact time and agitation speed. The average time when using RS adsorbents was reported to be a few hours (**Table 4**). Temperature influences the sorption capacity and biosorbent structural stability. An endothermal process is favored at high temperatures, involving heating costs and a possible biosorbent structural damage. However, many studies have reported high adsorption capacities close to room temperature (**Table 4**), which is important for practical reasons.

The biosorption equilibrium can be modeled by using equilibrium and kinetics experimental data. The most frequently used isotherms are Langmuir and Freundlich. The wide applicability of Langmuir isotherm model in case of heavy metals on native RS biosorbents and dyestuffs (**Table 4**) indicates the monolayer uptake on a homogenous surface without interaction between adsorbed molecules [48]. When using ACs, the metals sorption conformed to the assumptions of the Freundlich model – multilayer uptake occurring on a heterogeneous surface [85]. Phenol and organochloride compounds adsorption also follow the Freundlich model. In some cases, Freundlich and Langmuir models were both good models to describe the system at equilibrium conditions, indicating the complexity of the process. Kinetics of adsorption using RS biomass widely conforms to the pseudo-second order model (**Table 4**), implying that the rate-limiting step is a chemical sorption between the adsorbent and pollutant [73].

Because it is inconvenient to have a one-time use sorbent, regeneration of the spent sorbent by means of desorption is necessary. The eluents used for desorption of metal and dyes can be either acids, alkalis or some other chemical compounds (**Table 4**). The observed trend is that the pH can act like a switch for the selective desorption of pollutants (acidic medium for metals, basic medium for dyes). After desorption, the recovered rape-based adsorbent can be re-used in a new sorption process. The number of cycles of sorption–desorption indicate the reusability adsorbent potential (**Table 4**). Some sorbents, including untreated RS meal, maintain a decent sorption efficiency after several cycles of adsorption–desorption. After 3 cycles, the drop in efficiency was between <5% and 22.5% [48, 88]. Some studies reported up to 5–6 cycles of biosorbent reuse, and the decrease in the removal efficiency was found between 16.2% and 43% [85, 111]. Another practical aspect of the type of eluent used is the indication about the sorption mechanism. For example, a pH-dependent desorption suggests the involvement of electrostatic interactions in the sorption process. Or if water is a successful eluent, then the pollutant uptake is predominantly based on physisorption [21]. Several researchers have made efforts to elucidate the main sorption mechanism(s) (**Table 4**). Nevertheless, the adsorption

Ref.	Optimum parameters	Best fit model	Desorption	Proposed mechanism
[95]	pH 7, dose 10 g/L, 6 h	F	- Chloroform, dichloromethane, benzene	Uptake by spherosomes
[21]	pH 5, dose 10 g/L, 1 h, 120rpm	L	HCl 0.1 M; 102.6% Cu	Proton & Ca exchange, chemisorption
[99]	pH 7.5, dose 1 g/L, 7 days, 25°C	F	- Phenol	π–π dispersion interaction, electrostatic interaction
[113]	pH 2.5, dose 1 (RR198, RB19) - 2 (DR79, DR80) g/L, 60 min, 200 rpm	T; PSO	H2SO4; 88% RR198, 86% RB19, 91% DR79, and 95% DR80 at pH 12	Electrostatic interaction
[64]	pH 4.5–5, dose 8 g/L, 25°C, 2 h	L	$NaNO_3$ 1 M; 45.7% Cu @ pH 3.5	Electrostatic interaction, formation of surface complexes
[20]	pH 2.5, dose 7.5 g/L, 25°C, 120min, 100 rpm	L; PSO	- Acid orange 7, Remazol black 5	Electrostatic attraction, chemisorption
[74]	pH 8, dose 1 g/L, 40–60 min	L; PSO	HCl 0.01 M; 91.01% MB	Electrostatic attraction, chemisorption, particle diffusion
[73]	pH 8, dose 1 g/L, 60–180 min	L; PSO	HCl 0.01 M; 68.6% MB for SRS and 12.4% for SRSOA	Electrostatic attraction, chemisorption, diffusion
[48]	pH 6.5, dose 2.5 g/L, 180 min, 120 rpm	L; PSO; endothermal	NaOH 0.1 M; 94.5% MG; 95% of MG uptake capacity in the next adsorption cycle was achieved	Electrostatic attraction
[83]	pH 4, dose 4 g/L, 25°C, 2 h	F, L	- Cr	Formation of surface complexes, hydrolysis reactions
[96]	pH 6, dose 1 g/L, 25°C, 120 min (RM-MNs) - 150 min (RM-PPy)	S; SD (RM-MNs), ANN (RM-PPy); endothermal	NaCl 0.05 M at pH 3; MG: 93% (RM-MNs) - 71% (RM-PPy); 3 reuse cycles with 22.5% decrease of dye removal for RM-MNs and 11.2% for RM-PPy	Electrostatic interactions; more complex mechanism for RM-PPy
[71]	pH 5.2, dose 10 g/L, 20 °C, 3 h	L; PSO; endothermal	- Pb	Electrostatic interaction, complexation reaction, ion-exchange
[88]	pH 5.5, dose 8 g/L, 22 °C, 30 min	L; PSO	HNO3 0.1 M; 98.2% Pb; min. 3 reuse cycles with <5% decrease of biosorption efficiency	Ion-exchange

Ref.	Optimum parameters	Best fit model	Desorption	Proposed mechanism
[91]	pH 2, dose 2.5 g/L, 30 min, 200 rpm	L, F; PSO	- Phosphate	"Memory effect," electrostatic attraction, surface complexation, anion exchange
[111]	pH 2, dose 0.33 g/L, 25°C, 45–60 min, 120 rpm	PSO, IPD	Acetone; 83.79% 2,4-dichlorophenoxyacetic acid adsorption efficiency after 5 cycles	Aromatic ring interaction
[85]	pH 1, dose 1 g/L, 25°C, 12 h, 160 rpm	F; PSO; endothermal	NaOH 1 M; Cr: 57% sorption capacity after 6 cycles	Electrostatic interaction, redox reaction, surface complexation

*Notes: Adsorbents corresponding to each reference can be found in **Tables 2 and 3**; L (Langmuir), F (Freundlich), L-F (Langmuir–Freundlich), S (Sips), T (Tempkin) isotherm models; PFO (pseudo-first order), PSO (pseudo-second order), IPD (intraparticle diffusion), SD (surface diffusion) kinetics models; ANN – artificial neural network.*

Table 4.
Optimum conditions of adsorption/desorption for pollutant uptake on RS-based adsorbents.

mechanism is characterized by a high degree of complexity, especially when natural lignocellulosic biosorbents are involved.

In a single biosorption run, it is quite often that the sorbent does not reach the maximum sorption capacity (e.g., given by the Langmuir isotherm model) for a certain pollutant. Nevertheless, there will not be any further noticeable uptake of the respective pollutant even if the contact time is prolonged. Then, the spent sorbent is not sent to regeneration, but instead to a new sorption run involving a different target pollutant. And then in a third run of adsorption and so on. This concept is called an alternating or sequencing sorption. The main idea is to load the biosorbent as much as possible before its disposal, which could be practical for a low capacity biosorbent. This concept was studied by Morosanu et al. [65, 114] using RS meal as adsorbent and they have achieved 4 sequential adsorptions. The research was done considering two directions: (a) the biosorption of Rb19 dye followed by lead ions - RS-Rb19/Pb biosorption system, and (b) the biosorption of Pb followed by Rb19 dye - RS-Pb/Rb19 system. The authors observed that: (i); Pb uptake at higher concentrations is impeded by the presence of Rb19 on RS; (ii) dye sorption is favored by Pb presence; (iii) for the system RS-Rb19/Pb, pollutant desorption is selective, as a function of pH (**Table 4**); (iv) desorption was <7% in case of RS-Pb/Rb19 system. The experimental data suggests that the succession of pollutant biosorption matters. However, the biosorbent reuse in a new sorption cycle in order to determine the pollutants' uptake was not done.

At larger scale, continuous sorption processes are preferred. However, we have found only two studies using RS adsorbents in column tests. Amiri et al. [111], using a fixed-bed column (30 cm length, 2.5 cm inlet diameter) filled with canola stalk-derived AC (height of 20 cm) to adsorb 2,4-dichlorophenoxyacetic acid, obtained maximum sorption capacities comparable with the batch data. The intraparticle diffusion coefficient from batch experiments was used for column modeling. Lead uptake in a fixed-bed column with RS meal (bed height 6 cm) was reported [71]. A faster column saturation was observed at higher pollutant concentration, while the maximum sorption capacities were higher than the one provided by Langmuir model. The authors also tested an industrial wastewater containing lead ions in column configuration.

Considering the adsorbent's life cycle, when its regeneration is not economical anymore or it's not possible due to a previous chemisorption mechanism, the sorbent must be disposed of in such a manner that secondary pollution is avoided. In this sense, several authors proposed that exhausted RS meal could be used as a substrate for microbial colonization [48, 61]. Other practices involved biochar production from dye-loaded rape straw (modified with oxalic acid) [73], soil fertilizer [76] and using depleted biochars as biofuel [106]. To avoid leaching, a metal contaminated CM biochar was stabilized using phosphate binders [115]. Recovery of heavy metals from RS biomass can be done by electrochemical methods [116].

5. Conclusions

The wastes derived from rapeseed cultivation and production of oil and biodiesel are of interest in the context of circular economy. According to the reviewed literature, there exists valorization options for each rapeseed waste (stems, stalks, leaves, hulls, meal/cake). Major applications of these wastes include the use as cover crop for agricultural residues (stems and leaves) and animal feed for rapeseed meal. Rapeseed wastes contain valuable constituents and nutrients, making them of relevant nutritional and economic importance. Protein, pectin and polyphenols can be extracted from stems, leaves and meal. Besides the use of animal feed, the RS meal has great potential for obtaining high-value products for human consumption.

A less popular valorization option is the use of rapeseed waste as adsorbents for wastewater treatment. The literature survey presented in this chapter has revealed the existence of sufficient RS-derived adsorbents that have a stable structure and proved significant organic and inorganic removal efficiencies. However, many studies were done in batch operation, at laboratory scale. Very few researchers reported the use of fixed-bed column and/or real wastewater containing the target pollutants. Practical application of RS waste can sometimes be difficult. For example, RS meal forms a slurry when in sufficient contact time with water, which leads to difficult separation of phases or column clogging. This problem ca be tackled by mixing the biosorbent with some inert material (e.g., ceramic rings) or immobilization in a matrix (e.g. alginate). The use of stalks or husks is another solution, due to their lower protein content. In any case, chemical or thermal modification of natural RS waste can be also an alternative, especially when a higher sorption capacity is desired. Regeneration of the adsorbent and its subsequent use in a new sorption cycle is also possible. The exhausted adsorbent can be valorized as substrate for microbial growth, biochar or biofuel production.

Acknowledgements

This study was supported by a grant of the Romanian Ministry of Research and Innovation, CCCDI-UEFISCDI, project number 26PCCDI/01.03.2018, "*Integrated and sustainable processes for environmental clean-up, wastewater reuse and waste valorisation*" (SUSTENVPRO), within PNCDI III.

Author details

Irina Morosanu, Carmen Teodosiu*, Lavinia Tofan, Daniela Fighir and Carmen Paduraru
Department of Environmental Engineering and Management, "Cristofor Simionescu" Faculty of Chemical Engineering and Environmental Protection, "Gheorghe Asachi" Technical University of Iasi, Iasi, Romania

*Address all correspondence to: cteo@ch.tuiasi.ro

IntechOpen

© 2020 The Author(s). Licensee IntechOpen. This chapter is distributed under the terms of the Creative Commons Attribution License (http://creativecommons.org/licenses/by/3.0), which permits unrestricted use, distribution, and reproduction in any medium, provided the original work is properly cited.

References

[1] Salvatori G, Holstein F, Böhme K. *Circular economy strategies and roadmaps in Europe: Identifying synergies and the potential for cooperation and alliance building*. European Economic and Social Committee. DOI: 10.2864/554946.

[2] USDA. Oilseeds: World Markets and Trade. *United States Department of Agriculture* 2020; 39.

[3] European Commission. *Oilseeds and Protein Crops Market Situation*, https://ec.europa.eu/info/food-farming-fisheries/farming/facts-and-figures/markets/overviews/market-observatories/crops (2020).

[4] Mosenthin R, Messerschmidt U, Sauer N, et al. Effect of the desolventizing/toasting process on chemical composition and protein quality of rapeseed meal. *J Anim Sci Biotechnol* 2016; 7: 36.

[5] Mupondwa E, Li X, Wanasundara JPD. Technoeconomic Prospects for Commercialization of Brassica (Cruciferous) Plant Proteins. *J Am Oil Chem Soc* 2018; 95: 903-922.

[6] Campbell L, Rempel C, Wanasundara J. Canola/Rapeseed Protein: Future Opportunities and Directions—Workshop Proceedings of IRC 2015. *Plants* 2016; 5: 17.

[7] Jiang Y, Havrysh V, Klymchuk O, et al. Utilization of Crop Residue for Power Generation: The Case of Ukraine. *Sustainability* 2019; 11: 7004.

[8] Yang W, Zhou H, Gu J, et al. Application of rapeseed residue increases soil organic matter, microbial biomass, and enzyme activity and mitigates cadmium pollution risk in paddy fields. *Environ Pollut* 2020; 264: 114681.

[9] Bio-based Industries Joint Undertaking. *2020*, https://www.bbi-europe.eu/projects.

[10] Sud D, Mahajan G, Kaur MP. Agricultural waste material as potential adsorbent for sequestering heavy metal ions from aqueous solutions - A review. *Bioresour Technol* 2008; 99: 6017-6027.

[11] Argun Y, Karacali A, Calisir U, et al. Biosorption method and biosorbents for dye removal from industrial wastewater. A review. *Int J Adv Res* 2017; 5: 707-714.

[12] Ramírez Calderón OA, Abdeldayem OM, Pugazhendhi A, et al. Current Updates and Perspectives of Biosorption Technology: an Alternative for the Removal of Heavy Metals from Wastewater. *Curr Pollut Reports* 2020; 6: 8-27.

[13] Beni AA, Esmaeili A. Biosorption, an efficient method for removing heavy metals from industrial effluents: A Review. *Environ Technol Innov* 2020; 17: 100503.

[14] de Freitas GR, da Silva MGC, Vieira MGA. Biosorption technology for removal of toxic metals: a review of commercial biosorbents and patents. *Environ Sci Pollut Res* 2019; 26: 19097-19118.

[15] Forleo MB, Palmieri N, Suardi A, et al. The eco-efficiency of rapeseed and sunflower cultivation in Italy. Joining environmental and economic assessment. *J Clean Prod* 2018; 172: 3138-3153.

[16] Sadh PK, Duhan S, Duhan JS. Agro-industrial wastes and their utilization using solid state fermentation: a review. *Bioresour Bioprocess* 2018; 5: 1.

[17] Kormanjos S, Popovic S, Kostadinovic L, et al. Valorization of

rapeseed grain by-products. *Food Feed Res* 2016; 43: 51-56.

[18] Rathke G, Behrens T, Diepenbrock W. Integrated nitrogen management strategies to improve seed yield, oil content and nitrogen efficiency of winter oilseed rape (*Brassica napus* L.): A review. *Agric Ecosyst Environ* 2006; 117: 80-108.

[19] Wang ZW, Zhu MQ, Li MF, et al. Effects of hydrothermal treatment on enhancing enzymatic hydrolysis of rapeseed straw. *Renew Energy*. DOI: 10.1016/j.renene.2018.11.019.

[20] Hamzeh Y, Ashori A, Azadeh E, et al. Removal of Acid Orange 7 and Remazol Black 5 reactive dyes from aqueous solutions using a novel biosorbent. *Mater Sci Eng C* 2012; 32: 1394-1400.

[21] Boucher J, Chabloz C, Lex O, et al. Oleaginous seeds, press-cake and seed husks for the biosorption of metals. *J Water Supply Res Technol* 2008; 57: 489-499.

[22] Carré P, Quinsac A, Citeau M, et al. A re-examination of the technical feasibility and economic viability of rapeseed dehulling. *OCL* 2015; 22: D304.

[23] Paciorek-Sadowska J, Borowicz M, Isbrandt M, et al. The use of waste from the production of rapeseed oil for obtaining of new polyurethane composites. *Polymers (Basel)*. DOI: 10.3390/polym11091431.

[24] Al-Asheh S, Duvnjak Z. Adsorption of copper by canola meal. *J Hazard Mater* 1996; 48: 83-93.

[25] Jain S, Kumar P, Vyas RK, et al. Adsorption optimization of acyclovir on prepared activated carbon. *Can J Chem Eng* 2014; 92: 1627-1635.

[26] EMF. *Towards the Circular Economy. Economic and Business Rationale for an Accelerated Transition*, https://www.ellenmacarthurfoundation.org/publications (2013).

[27] Moreno-González M, Keulen D, Gomis-Fons J, et al. Continuous adsorption in food industry: The recovery of sinapic acid from rapeseed meal extract. *Sep Purif Technol*. DOI: 10.1016/j.seppur.2020.117403.

[28] Wongsirichot P, Gonzalez-Miquel M, Winterburn J. Rapeseed meal valorization strategies via nitrogen- and oxygen-limited production of polyhydroxyalkanoates with Pseudomonas putida. *Waste Manag* 2020; 105: 482-491.

[29] Salakkam A, Webb C. Production of poly(3-hydroxybutyrate) from a complete feedstock derived from biodiesel by-products (crude glycerol and rapeseed meal). *Biochem Eng J* 2018; 137: 358-364.

[30] Quinn L, Gray SG, Meaney S, et al. Sinapinic and protocatechuic acids found in rapeseed: Isolation, characterisation and potential benefits for human health as functional food ingredients. *Irish Journal of Agricultural and Food Research*. DOI: 10.1515/IJAFR-2017-0012.

[31] Kalaydzhiev H, Ivanova P, Stoyanova M, et al. Valorization of Rapeseed Meal: Influence of Ethanol Antinutrients Removal on Protein Extractability, Amino Acid Composition and Fractional Profile. *Waste and Biomass Valorization*. DOI: 10.1007/s12649-018-00553-1.

[32] Konkol D, Szmigiel I, Domżał-Kędzia M, et al. Biotransformation of rapeseed meal leading to production of polymers, biosurfactants, and fodder. *Bioorg Chem* 2019; 93: 102865.

[33] Delgado M, Felix M, Bengoechea C. Development of bioplastic materials:

From rapeseed oil industry by products to added-value biodegradable biocomposite materials. *Ind Crops Prod*. DOI: 10.1016/j.indcrop.2018.09.013.

[34] Putro JN, Soetaredjo FE, Lin SY, et al. Pretreatment and conversion of lignocellulose biomass into valuable chemicals. *RSC Advances*. DOI: 10.1039/c6ra09851g.

[35] Luo G, Talebnia F, Karakashev D, et al. Enhanced bioenergy recovery from rapeseed plant in a biorefinery concept. *Bioresour Technol* 2011; 102: 1433-1439.

[36] Gaballah ES, Abomohra AEF, Xu C, et al. Enhancement of biogas production from rape straw using different co-pretreatment techniques and anaerobic co-digestion with cattle manure. *Bioresour Technol*. DOI: 10.1016/j.biortech.2020.123311.

[37] Antonopoulou G, Stamatelatou K, Lyberatos G. Exploitation of rapeseed and sunflower residues for methane generation through anaerobic digestion: The effect of pretreatment. In: *Chemical Engineering Transactions*. 2010. DOI: 10.3303/CET1020043.

[38] Svärd A, Moriana R, Brännvall E, et al. Rapeseed Straw Biorefinery Process. *ACS Sustain Chem Eng* 2019; 7: 790-801.

[39] Mazhari Mousavi SM, Hosseini SZ, Resalati H, et al. Papermaking potential of rapeseed straw, a new agricultural-based fiber source. *J Clean Prod*. DOI: 10.1016/j.jclepro.2013.02.016.

[40] Kiaei M, Mahdavi S, Kialashaki A, et al. Chemical composition and morphological properties of canola plant and its potential application in pulp and paper industry. *Cellul Chem Technol*.

[41] Tofanica BM. Rapeseed – a valuable renewable bioresource. *Cellul Chem Technol* 2019; 53: 837-849.

[42] Yousefi H. Canola straw as a bio-waste resource for medium density fiberboard (MDF) manufacture. *Waste Manag*. DOI: 10.1016/j.wasman.2009.06.018.

[43] Balo F. Characterization of green building materials manufactured from canola oil and natural zeolite. *J Mater Cycles Waste Manag* 2015; 17: 336-349.

[44] Bernesson S, Nilsson D, Hansson PA. A limited LCA comparing large- and small-scale production of rape methyl ester (RME) under Swedish conditions. *Biomass and Bioenergy*. DOI: 10.1016/j.biombioe.2003.10.003.

[45] Bhupinderpal-Singh, Rengel Z, Bowden JW. Carbon, nitrogen and sulphur cycling following incorporation of canola residue of different sizes into a nutrient-poor sandy soil. *Soil Biol Biochem*. DOI: 10.1016/j.soilbio.2005.03.025.

[46] Yu X, Bals O, Grimi N, et al. A new way for the oil plant biomass valorization: Polyphenols and proteins extraction from rapeseed stems and leaves assisted by pulsed electric fields. *Ind Crops Prod* 2015; 74: 309-318.

[47] Yun HM, Lei XJ, Lee SI, et al. Rapeseed meal and canola meal can partially replace soybean meal as a protein source in finishing pigs. *J Appl Anim Res* 2018; 46: 195-199.

[48] Jasińska A, Bernat P, Paraszkiewicz K. Malachite green removal from aqueous solution using the system rapeseed press cake and fungus Myrothecium roridum. *Desalin Water Treat* 2013; 51: 7663-7671.

[49] Zheng M, Hu Q, Zhang S, et al. Macroporous Activated Carbon Derived from Rapeseed Shell for Lithium–Sulfur Batteries. *Appl Sci* 2017; 7: 1036.

[50] Liu T, Yang L, Hu Z, et al. Biochar exerts negative effects on soil fauna

across multiple trophic levels in a cultivated acidic soil. *Biol Fertil Soils* 2020; 56: 597-606.

[51] Cen Y, Guo L, Liu M, et al. Using organic fertilizers to increase crop yield, economic growth, and soil quality in a temperate farmland. *PeerJ* 2020; 8: e9668.

[52] Crini G, Lichtfouse E, Wilson LD, et al. Adsorption-Oriented Processes Using Conventional and Non-conventional Adsorbents for Wastewater Treatment. In: Crini G, Lichtfouse E (eds) *Green Adsorbents for Pollutant Removal: Fundamentals and Design*. Cham: Springer International Publishing, pp. 23-71.

[53] Tofan L. *Heavy metal removal from wastewaters by sorption processes*. "Gheorghe Asachi" Technical University, 2017.

[54] Derco J, Vrana B. Introductory Chapter: Biosorption. In: *Biosorption*. InTech. DOI: 10.5772/intechopen.78961.

[55] Singh S, Kumar V, Datta S, et al. Current advancement and future prospect of biosorbents for bioremediation. *Sci Total Environ* 2020; 709: 135895.

[56] Vijayaraghavan K, Balasubramanian R. Is biosorption suitable for decontamination of metal-bearing wastewaters? A critical review on the state-of-the-art of biosorption processes and future directions. *J Environ Manage* 2015; 160: 283-296.

[57] Anastopoulos I, Bhatnagar A, Lima EC. Adsorption of rare earth metals: A review of recent literature. *Journal of Molecular Liquids*. DOI: 10.1016/j.molliq.2016.06.076.

[58] Costa TB da, Silva MGC da, Vieira MGA. Recovery of rare-earth metals from aqueous solutions by bio/adsorption using non-conventional materials: a review with recent studies and promising approaches in column applications. *Journal of Rare Earths*. DOI: 10.1016/j.jre.2019.06.001.

[59] Gupta VK, Nayak A, Agarwal S. Bioadsorbents for remediation of heavy metals: Current status and their future prospects. *Environmental Engineering Research*. DOI: 10.4491/eer.2015.018.

[60] Asgher M. Biosorption of reactive dyes: A review. *Water Air Soil Pollut* 2012; 223: 2417-2435.

[61] Boucher J, Steiner L, Marison IW. Bio-sorption of atrazine in the press-cake from oilseeds. *Water Res* 2007; 41: 3209-3216.

[62] Hu ZY, Hua W, Zhang L, et al. Seed Structure Characteristics to Form Ultrahigh Oil Content in Rapeseed. *PLoS One*. DOI: 10.1371/journal.pone.0062099.

[63] Feizi M, Jalali M. Sorption of aquatic phosphorus onto native and chemically-modified plant residues: modeling the isotherm and kinetics of sorption process. *Desalin Water Treat* 2014; 57: 3085-3097.

[64] Tong X, Li J, Yuan J, et al. Adsorption of Cu(II) by biochars generated from three crop straws. *Chem Eng J* 2011; 172: 828-834.

[65] Morosanu I, Teodosiu C, Coroaba A, et al. Sequencing batch biosorption of micropollutants from aqueous effluents by rapeseed waste: Experimental assessment and statistical modelling. *J Environ Manage* 2019; 230: 110-118.

[66] Sokołowska Z, Bowanko G, Boguta P, et al. Characteristics of rapeseed oil cake using nitrogen adsorption. *Int Agrophysics* 2013; 27: 329-334.

[67] Xu C, Xia T, Wang J, et al. Selectively Desirable Rapeseed and

Corn Stalks Distinctive for Low-Cost Bioethanol Production and High-Active Biosorbents. *Waste and Biomass Valorization*. DOI: 10.1007/s12649-020-01026-0.

[68] Paduraru C, Tofan L, Teodosiu C, et al. Biosorption of zinc(II) on rapeseed waste: Equilibrium studies and thermogravimetric investigations. *Process Saf Environ Prot* 2015; 94: 18-28.

[69] Ashori A, Hamzeh Y, Azadeh E, et al. Potential of canola stalk as biosorbent for the removal of Remazol Black B reactive dye from aqueous solutions canola stalks for removal of RBB. *J Wood Chem Technol* 2012; 32: 328-341.

[70] Mahmoodi NM, Arami M, Bahrami H, et al. Novel biosorbent (Canola hull): Surface characterization and dye removal ability at different cationic dye concentrations. *Desalination* 2010; 264: 134-142.

[71] Morosanu I, Teodosiu C, Paduraru C, et al. Biosorption of lead ions from aqueous effluents by rapeseed biomass. *N Biotechnol* 2017; 39: 110-124.

[72] Morosanu I, Gilca A-F, Paduraru C, et al. Valorisation of rapeseed as biosorbent for the removal of textile dyes from aqueous effluents. *Cellul Chem Technol* 2017; 51: 175-184.

[73] Feng Y, Dionysiou DD, Wu Y, et al. Adsorption of dyestuff from aqueous solutions through oxalic acid-modified swede rape straw: Adsorption process and disposal methodology of depleted bioadsorbents. *Bioresour Technol* 2013; 138: 191-197.

[74] Feng Y, Zhou H, Liu G, et al. Methylene blue adsorption onto swede rape straw (*Brassica napus* L.) modified by tartaric acid: Equilibrium, kinetic and adsorption mechanisms. *Bioresour Technol* 2012; 125: 138-144.

[75] Feizi M, Jalali M. Removal of heavy metals from aqueous solutions using sunflower, potato, canola and walnut shell residues. *J Taiwan Inst Chem Eng* 2015; 54: 125-136.

[76] Zarabi M, Jalali M. Competitive Removal of Ammonium-Nitrogen from Aqueous Solutions by Mineral and Organic Adsorbents. *Commun Soil Sci Plant Anal* 2018; 49: 1129-1143.

[77] Tofan L, Paduraru C, Volf I, et al. Waste of rapeseed from biodiesel production as a potential biosorbent for heavy metal ions. *BioResources*. DOI: 10.15376/biores.6.4.3727-3741.

[78] Al-Asheh S, Duvnjak Z. Sorption of Heavy Metals by Canola Meal. *Water Air Soil Pollut* 1999; 114: 251-276.

[79] Al-Asheh S, Duvnjak Z. Sorption of Heavy Metals from Synthetic Metal Solutions and Industrial Wastewater Using Plant Materials. *Water Qual Res J* 1999; 34: 481-504.

[80] Bandara T, Xu J, Potter ID, et al. Mechanisms for the removal of Cd(II) and Cu(II) from aqueous solution and mine water by biochars derived from agricultural wastes. *Chemosphere* 2020; 254: 126745.

[81] Amouei AI, Amooey AA, Asgharzadeh F. Cadmium Removal from Aqueous Solution by Canola Residues: Adsorption Equilibrium and Kinetics. *Iran J Chem Eng*; 10.

[82] Baby Shaikh R, Saifullah B, Rehman F, et al. Greener Method for the Removal of Toxic Metal Ions from the Wastewater by Application of Agricultural Waste as an Adsorbent. *Water* 2018; 10: 1316.

[83] Pan J, Jiang J, Xu R. Adsorption of Cr(III) from acidic solutions by crop straw derived biochars. *J Environ Sci* 2013; 25: 1957-1965.

[84] Kwak J-H, Islam MS, Wang S, et al. Biochar properties and lead(II) adsorption capacity depend on feedstock type, pyrolysis temperature, and steam activation. *Chemosphere* 2019; 231: 393-404.

[85] Luo M, Huang C, Chen F, et al. Removal of aqueous Cr(VI) using magnetic-gelatin supported on Brassica-straw biochar. *J Dispers Sci Technol* 2020; 0: 1-13.

[86] Németh D, Labidi J, Gubicza L, et al. Comparative study on heavy metal removal from industrial effluents by various separation methods. *Desalin Water Treat* 2011; 35: 242-246.

[87] Uçar S, Erdem M, Tay T, et al. Removal of lead (II) and nickel (II) ions from aqueous solution using activated carbon prepared from rapeseed oil cake by Na2CO3 activation. *Clean Technol Environ Policy* 2015; 17: 747-756.

[88] Arsenie T-D, Nemeş L, Bulgariu D, et al. Alternative use of biomass waste from biofules production as biosorbents for Pb(II) removal from aqueous effluents. In: *Proceedings of VENICE2018 Symposium, the 7th International Symposium on Energy from biomass and waste*. 2018.

[89] Arsenie T, Nemes L, Nacu G, et al. Quantitative removal of Hg(II) ions from aqueous media by biosorption on rape waste biomass. In: *2017 E-Health and Bioengineering Conference (EHB)*. IEEE, pp. 89-92.

[90] Tomczyk A, Sokołowska Z, Boguta P. Biomass type effect on biochar surface characteristic and adsorption capacity relative to silver and copper. *Fuel* 2020; 278: 118168.

[91] Zhang Z, Yan L, Yu H, et al. Adsorption of phosphate from aqueous solution by vegetable biochar/layered double oxides: Fast removal and mechanistic studies. *Bioresour Technol* 2019; 284: 65-71.

[92] Rambabu N, Rao BVSK, Surisetty VR, et al. Production, characterization, and evaluation of activated carbons from de-oiled canola meal for environmental applications. *Ind Crops Prod* 2015; 65: 572-581.

[93] Zazouli MA, Mahvi AH, Mahdavi Y, et al. Isothermic and kinetic modeling of fluoride removal from water by means of the natural biosorbents sorghum and canola. *Fluoride* 2015; 48: 37-44.

[94] Adachi A, Komiyama T, Tanaka T, et al. Removal Efficiency of Defatted Seed for Organochlorine Compounds. *J Heal Sci* 2001; 47: 54-59.

[95] Adachi A, Hamamoto H, Okano T. Use of lees materials as an adsorbent for removal of organochlorine compounds or benzene from wastewater. *Chemosphere* 2005; 58: 817-822.

[96] Podstawczyk D, Witek-Krowiak A. Novel nanoparticles modified composite eco-adsorbents—A deep insight into kinetics modelling using numerical surface diffusion and artificial neural network models. *Chem Eng Res Des* 2016; 109: 1-17.

[97] Jóźwiak T, Filipkowska U, Rodziewicz J, et al. Zastosowanie kompostu jako taniego sorbentu do usuwania barwników z roztworów wodnych. *Rocz Ochr Sr* 2013; 15: 2398-2411.

[98] Jasińska A, Góralczyk-Bińkowska A, Soboń A, et al. Lignocellulose resources for the Myrothecium roridum laccase production and their integrated application for dyes removal. *Int J Environ Sci Technol* 2019; 16: 4811-4822.

[99] Nabais JMV, Gomes JA, Suhas, et al. Phenol removal onto novel activated carbons made from lignocellulosic precursors: Influence of surface properties. *J Hazard Mater* 2009; 167: 904-910.

[100] Breguet V, Boucher J, Pesquet F, et al. Immobilization of rapeseed press-cake in an alginate matrix for the sorption of atrazine. *Water Res* 2008; 42: 1606-1612.

[101] Balarak D, Jaafari J, Hassani G, et al. The use of low-cost adsorbent (Canola residues) for the adsorption of methylene blue from aqueous solution: Isotherm, kinetic and thermodynamic studies. *Colloids Interface Sci Commun* 2015; 7: 16-19.

[102] Pstrowska K, Walendziewski J, Szary J, et al. Adsorption of phenols on activated carbons prepared using rapeseed meal. *Przem Chem* 2015; 94: 823-827.

[103] Ioannidou OA, Zabaniotou AA, Stavropoulos GG, et al. Preparation of activated carbons from agricultural residues for pesticide adsorption. *Chemosphere* 2010; 80: 1328-1336.

[104] Smets K, De Jong M, Lupul I, et al. Rapeseed and Raspberry Seed Cakes as Inexpensive Raw Materials in the Production of Activated Carbon by Physical Activation: Effect of Activation Conditions on Textural and Phenol Adsorption Characteristics. *Materials (Basel)* 2016; 9: 565.

[105] Mahmoodi NM, Salehi R, Arami M. Binary system dye removal from colored textile wastewater using activated carbon: Kinetic and isotherm studies. *Desalination* 2011; 272: 187-195.

[106] Xu R, Xiao S, Yuan J, et al. Adsorption of methyl violet from aqueous solutions by the biochars derived from crop residues. *Bioresour Technol* 2011; 102: 10293-10298.

[107] Salimi M, Balou S, Kohansal K, et al. Optimizing the Preparation of Meso- and Microporous Canola Stalk-Derived Hydrothermal Carbon via Response Surface Methodology for Methylene Blue Removal. *Energy & Fuels* 2017; 31: 12327-12338.

[108] Balarak D, Abasizadeh H, Yan J-K, et al. Biosorption of Acid Orange 7 (AO7) dye by canola waste: equilibrium, kinetic and thermodynamics studies. *Desalin WATER Treat* 2020; 190: 331-339.

[109] Feng Y, Xue L, Duan J, et al. Purification of Dye-stuff Contained Wastewater by a Hybrid Adsorption-Periphyton Reactor (HAPR): Performance and Mechanisms. *Sci Rep* 2017; 7: 9635.

[110] Li GL, Li S, He DL, et al. Adsorption of Cationic Dyes from Aqueous Solution onto Rapeseed Meal. *Adv Mater Res* 2012; 550-553: 1550-1555.

[111] Amiri MJ, Roohi R, Arshadi M, et al. 2,4-D adsorption from agricultural subsurface drainage by canola stalk-derived activated carbon: insight into the adsorption kinetics models under batch and column conditions. *Environ Sci Pollut Res* 2020; 27: 16983-16997.

[112] Morosanu I, Teodosiu C, Fighir D, et al. Simultaneous biosorption of micropollutants from aqueous effluents by rapeseed waste. *Process Saf Environ Prot* 2019; 132: 231-239.

[113] Mahmoodi NM, Arami M, Bahrami H, et al. The effect of pH on the removal of anionic dyes from colored textile wastewater using a biosorbent. *J Appl Polym Sci* 2011; 120: 2996-3003.

[114] Morosanu I, Tofan L, Teodosiu C, et al. Equilibrium studies of the sequential removal of Reactive Blue 19 dye and lead (II) on rapeseed waste. *Rev Chim* 2020; 71: 162-174.

[115] Devi P, Kothari P, Dalai AK. Stabilization and solidification of arsenic and iron contaminated canola meal biochar using chemically modified phosphate binders. *J Hazard Mater* 2020; 385: 121559.

[116] Delil AD, Köleli N, Dağhan H, et al. Recovery of heavy metals from canola (*Brassica napus*) and soybean (*Glycine max*) biomasses using electrochemical process. *Environ Technol Innov* 2020; 17: 100559.

Chapter 10

Hazardous Waste Management

Krishnaswamy Kanagamani, P. Geethamani and M. Narmatha

Abstract

Waste management is one of the vital environmental issues since last few decades. It has been noted that the generation of waste increases with increasing population, industrialization and urbanization etc. The waste management strategy includes both non-hazardous and hazardous waste management. Non-hazardous waste does not cause potential threat to environment but instead hazardous waste is the waste that poses substantial or potential threats to public health and the environment. Rapidly growing industrial sector has contributed to the generation of large quantity of hazardous waste material. Therefore, to reduce environmental hazard, proper attention is required during storage, segregation, transportation and disposal of hazardous waste, because it cannot be disposed as off in the environment. This study explains about hazardous wastes, types and management.

Keywords: hazardous waste, types and management

1. Introduction

Industries play a vital role in the economic aspect of modern society and hazardous waste production is an inevitable outcome of developmental activities and industrialization. A material becomes waste when it is discarded without expecting to be compensated for its inherent value [1]. Hazardous wastes that are disposed off causes potential hazard to human health or the environment (soil, air, and water) when it is not properly managed. They are non-biodegradable, persistent in the environment and are deleterious to human health or natural resources. The management of hazardous waste is a process which includes the collection, recycling, treatment, transportation, disposal, and monitoring of wastes disposal sites. In the current scenario of developing countries, hazardous wastes are often disposed directly into the environment posing health and environmental risk. On the other hand, governments and international agencies are taking steps for controlling the growing problem of hazardous substances in the environment which appears to be a difficult process because the wastes are from many sources. Toxic and hazardous substances from these sources contaminate the land, air, and water [2]. The potential health risk associated with these substances vary from minor, short term discomforts, such as headaches and nausea to serious health problems, such as cancers and birth defects, to major accidents that cause immediate injury or death [3]. It is therefore important to take necessary steps in managing the waste. In view of this, management of hazardous wastes including their disposal in an environment friendly and economically viable way is very important and therefore suggestions are made considering the waste types and states [4–6]. Hence in this chapter we will discuss about hazardous waste, types and management.

2. Classification of solid wastes

Solid waste are classified into different types based on their source as shown in **Figure 1**

2.1 Non-hazardous waste

Non-hazardous waste is any waste that does not cause harm to people or the environment, and regulations for safe disposal of non-hazardous waste.

2.2 Hazardous waste

Hazardous waste is waste that is dangerous or potentially harmful to our health or the environment. Hazardous wastes can be liquids, solids, gases, sludge's, discarded commercial products (e.g., cleaning fluids or pesticides), or the by-products of manufacturing processes.

2.2.1 Classification of hazardous wastes

According to EPA more than 450 listed wastes which are known to be hazardous are grouped as F-List, K-List, P-List and U-List

2.2.1.1 F-list

The F-list contains hazardous wastes originated from a nonspecific source that includes various industrial processes leading to generation of these wastes. The list mainly incudes the solvent used in degreasing, metal treatment baths and sludge's, wastewaters from metal plating operations and dioxin containing chemicals or their precursors. The F-list are categorized depending upon industrial operations generating the wastes.

They can be divided into seven groups depending on the type of manufacturing or industrial operation generating the waste.

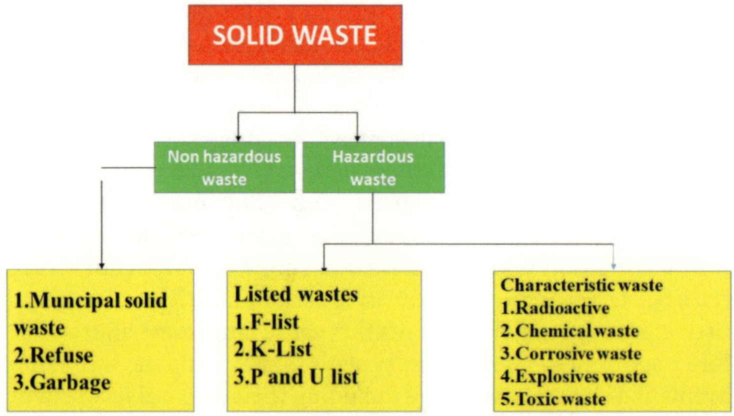

Figure 1.
Classification of solid waste.

- Solvent wastes
- Metal finishing wastes
- Dioxin-contaminated wastes
- Chlorinated aliphatic hydrocarbons production
- Wood preserving wastes
- Waste from petroleum refinery
- Multisource leachate.

2.2.1.2 K-list

The K-list contains hazardous wastes generated as a result of specific industrial processes and are considered as source-specific wastes. The classification of K-listed hazardous waste must fit into one of the 13 categories mentioned below

- Wood preservation
- Organic chemicals manufacturing
- Pesticides manufacturing
- Petroleum refining
- Veterinary pharmaceuticals manufacturing
- Inorganic pigment manufacturing
- Inorganic chemicals manufacturing
- Explosives manufacturing
- Iron and steel production
- Primary aluminum production
- Secondary lead processing
- Ink formulation
- Coking (processing of coal to produce coke)

2.2.1.3 P and U lists

The unused chemicals of pure and commercial formulations that are being disposed come under P and U lists. For a P- or U-listed waste it requires the following three criteria:

- The waste must contain one of the chemicals listed on the P or U list
- The chemical in the waste must be unused
- The chemical in the waste must be in the form of a commercial chemical product.

3. Characteristics of hazardous waste

3.1 Ignitability

A waste is considered to be an ignitable hazardous waste if its flash point is less than 60°C, readily catches fire and burns vigorously as a hazard; or is an ignitable compressed gas or an oxidizer. Ex: Naphtha, lacquer thinner, epoxy resins, adhesives, and oil based paints etc.

3.2 Corrosivity

Any type of liquid waste whose pH is less than or equal to 2 or greater than or equal to 12.5 is considered to be corrosive hazardous waste. Sodium hydroxide (High pH) and hydrochloric acid (Low pH) is often used in many industries to clean or degrease metal parts. Prior to painting disposed solvents without any treatment contributes to corrosive hazardous waste.

3.3 Reactivity

A material is considered as reactive hazardous waste, if it is unstable, reacts violently with water, and generates toxic gases when exposed to water or corrosive materials, or explodes when exposed to heat or a flame.

Examples of reactive wastes would be waste gunpowder, sodium metal or wastes containing cyanides or sulphides.

3.4 Toxicity

Toxicity of a hazardous waste can be determined by taking a representative sample of the material and subjected to a test conducted in a certified laboratory and toxic characteristics can be determined.

4. Categories of hazardous wastes

4.1 Radioactive substance

Radioactive waste is the type of hazardous waste that contains radioactive material. Radioactive waste is a by-product of various nuclear technology processes, industries based on nuclear medicine, nuclear research, nuclear power, manufacturing, construction, coal and rare-earth mining and nuclear weapons reprocessing. Any substances capable of emitting ionizing radiation are said to be radioactive and are hazardous because prolonged exposure often results in damage to living organisms. Radioactive substances attract special concern because they persist for a long period and disposal depends upon half-life period of the radioactive substance.

For example, uranium compounds have half-lives that range from 72 years for U232 to 23,420,000 years for U236.

4.2 Chemicals

The hazardous chemical wastes can be categorized into five group's namely synthetic organics, inorganic metals, salts, acids and bases, and flammables and explosives. Some of the chemicals are hazardous because they threaten human lives.

4.3 Bio-medical wastes

The main sources of hazardous biological wastes are from hospitals and biological research facilities. The biological waste has the capability of infecting other living organisms and has the ability to produce toxins. Biomedical waste mainly includes malignant tissues discarded during surgical procedures and contaminated materials, such as hypodermic needles, bandages and outdated drugs.

4.4 Flammable wastes

The hazardous waste category also includes flammable wastes. This grouping is necessary because of risk involved in storage, collection and disposal of flammable wastes. The flammable wastes may be of solid, liquid or gaseous form. Examples of flammable waste include organic solvents, oils, plasticizers and organic sludge's.

4.5 Explosives

Explosive hazardous wastes are mainly ordnance (artillery) materials. Explosives also involve high potential for hazard in case of storage, collection and disposal. These types of wastes may exist in solid, liquid or gaseous form.

5. Principles and methods of hazardous waste management

5.1 Principles

Hazardous waste management is the general term associated with procedures and policies of hazardous waste management that it does not cause any potential threat to man and the environment. Traditionally, hazardous wastes are disposed by dumping in open space and burning. Open dumping results in soil and water pollution and open burning and incineration contribute to air pollution in the form of particulates, nitrogen oxides, noxious odors, and other constituents. After solid waste residues disposed leads to water pollution. Municipal incineration with sophisticated energy recovery systems were popular in large European and American cities at the turn of the century, but became extinct due to high operating costs. In recent years, for hazardous solid waste management incineration has become less popular because of risk associated with increased air pollution control requirements. Because of rapid industrialization the concern of hazardous waste management is increasing [7]. The waste generated from various industrial and domestic activities can result in severe health hazards and also leads to negative impact on the environment. The following procedure illustrates the standard waste management strategy in a developed society. Various steps involved in hazardous waste management was shown in **Figure 2**.

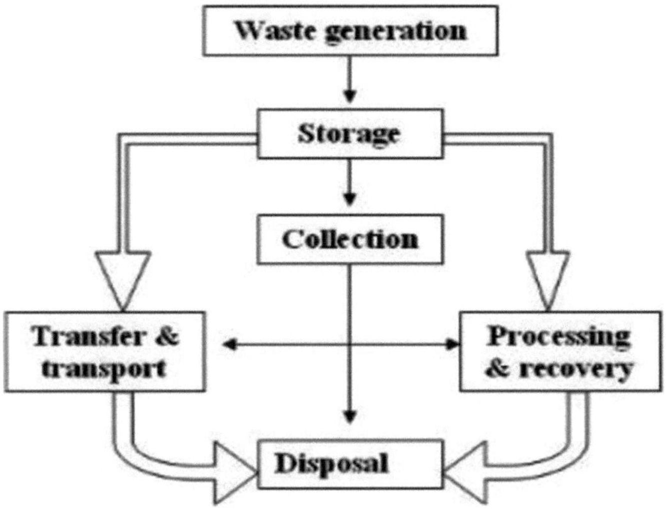

Figure 2.
Steps involved in hazardous waste disposal.

5.2 Handling of hazardous wastes

Persons handling hazardous wastes are advised to have protective precautions to protect themselves from health effects. Exposure of hazardous waste leads to dermatitis in the skin, asthma on long exposure, eye irritation and also tightening of the chest.

5.3 Transport of hazardous waste

Hazardous waste generated often requires transport to a particular site for an approved treatment, storage, or disposal facility (TSDF). Because of potential threats to public safety and the environment, transport is given special attention by governmental agencies to avoid any occasional accidental spill [8].

5.4 Disposal

Disposal of hazardous waste is the final stage of a hazardous waste management system. The different waste disposal methods includes secure landfill, deep well and bedrock disposal [9].

5.4.1 Secure landfill

Disposal of some hazardous wastes in regular landfills resulted in unfavorable amounts of hazardous materials seeping into the ground. These chemicals eventually enter natural hydrologic systems. So to prevent the chemicals entering the soil, landfill requires a barrier for collecting hazardous substances that may remain in the disposed waste. Now, hazardous wastes are stabilized and made into solid and placed in landfill and this process depends upon the type of hazardous waste. A landfill is a disposal facility where hazardous wastes are placed into and stored in the soil [10]. An example of a recommended design is shown in **Figure 3**. The wastes are dumped in sealed drums before disposal. The hazardous-waste landfill setup consists of two impermeable liners and also includes leachate collection

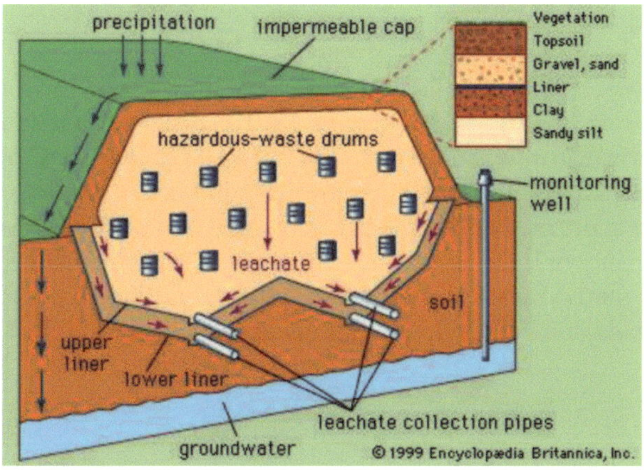

Figure 3.
Secure land fill method.

systems. Double leachate collection system is made up of network of pipes placed above each liner. The upper layer reduces the accumulation of leachate trapped in the fill, and the lower layer acts as a backup. The leachate collected is transferred to treatment plant for further process. An impermeable cap or cover is placed over a finished landfill is placed to reduce the amount of leachate in the fill and minimize the potential for environmental degradation.

The main components in the leachate from landfill sites are grouped as follows

- Major elements and ions such as calcium, magnesium, iron, sodium, ammonia, carbonate, sulphate and chloride.
- Trace metals such as manganese, chromium, nickel, lead and calcium
- Wide variety of organic compounds
- Biological agents

Hazardous waste mainly from industries will give rise to leachate. Heavy metals concentration in the leachate is of greater concern compared to other components of leachate.

5.4.2 Deep well disposal

Another alternative disposal of liquid industrial waste is injection into deep well as shown in the **Figure 4**. Deep well injection is a liquid waste disposal technology. This alternative uses injection wells to place treated or untreated liquid waste into geologic formations that have no potential to allow migration of contaminants into potential potable water aquifers. In order to force the liquid into the pores and fissures of the rock, high pressures are applied. The rock unit selected are of porous and permeable (commonly, sandstone or fractured limestone), and must be separated by low permeability layers (for example, shale) above and below. Deep-well injection is a cost effective and requires little or no pretreatment of the waste, but it poses a danger of leaking hazardous waste and eventually polluting underground water resources.

5.4.3 Bedrock disposal

Bedrock disposal is mainly meant for solid hazardous waste and a variety of bed rock types are being investigated as host rocks. The design of a bedrock disposal site or repository for hazardous wastes is shown in **Figure 5**. It is based on the multiple barrier (or multi barrier) concept: surrounding solid hazardous waste sealed with several different types of materials to prevent waste leakage or invasion by ground water. A major concern is the nature of the host rock as well as some potential drawbacks. The method is widely used for high-level radioactive wastes. Sealed into stainless steel canisters, or spent fuel rods encapsulated in corrosion resistant metals

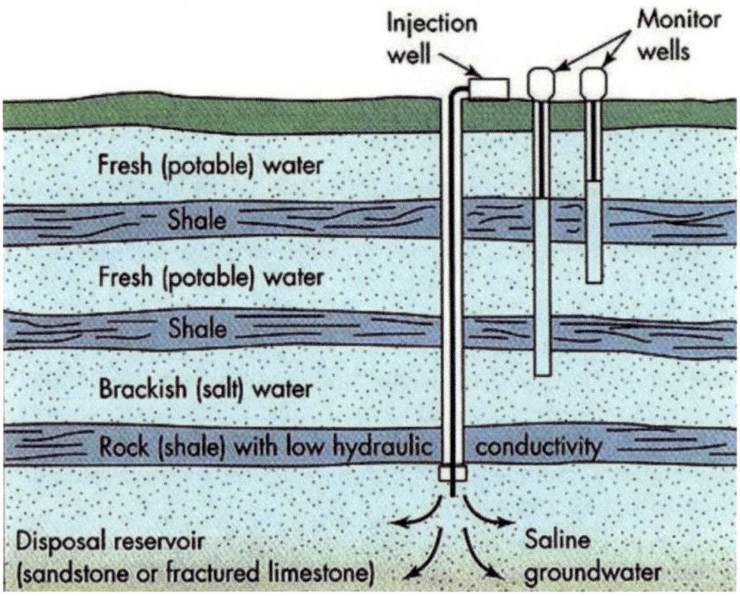

Figure 4.
Deep well disposal method.

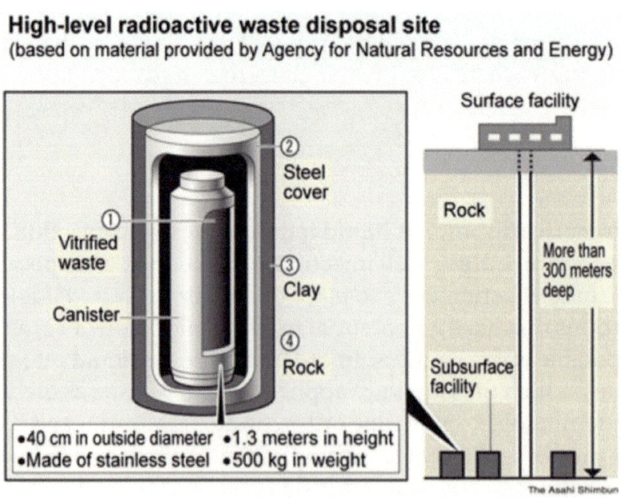

Figure 5.
Bedrock disposal method.

such as copper or stainless steel and buried in stable rock structures deep underground. Many geological formations such as granite, volcanic tuff, salt, thick basalts such as the Columbia River plateau basalt or shale will be suitable [11].

6. Waste management: Indian scenario

Hazardous waste is any substance in solid, liquid or gaseous form, because of physical, chemical, reactive, toxic, flammable, explosive, corrosive, radioactive or infectious characteristics causes threat to human health and environment.

The amount of hazardous waste generated per annum is found to be 4.4 million tonnes as per organization of economic cooperation and development (OECD). This estimate of about 4.4 million is based on the 18 categories of wastes which appeared in the Hazardous waste management (HWM) rules first published in 1989. Among this 38.3% is recyclable, 4.3% is incinerable and the remaining 57.4% is disposable in secured landfills. Nearly about 13 States of the country (Maharashtra, Gujarat, Tamil Nadu, Orissa, Madhya Pradesh, Assam, Uttar Pradesh, West Bengal, Kerala, Andhra Pradesh, Telangana, Karnataka and Rajasthan) contributes for about 97% of total hazardous waste generation. The top five states include Maharashtra, Gujarat, Andhra Pradesh, Telangana and Tamil Nadu. If the hazardous waste is not properly maintained, severe pollution of land, surface and ground water will occur [12–13]. As per industrial requirement category in India, every industry should have enough land available within its premises for the treatment and disposal and or reuse/recycling of the wastes generated from it [14]. There is a major concern all over the world for the safe disposal of hazardous waste. Hazardous Wastes (HWs) can be disposed off at Treatment, Storage and Disposal Facility (TSDF) as it is one of the centralized location for treatment of wastes. The TSDF helps small and medium scale industries generating hazardous waste [15–16].

6.1 Characterization of hazardous waste

The Hazardous Wastes are categorized into three groups namely Recyclable, Incinerable, and Disposable. The disposable Hazardous Wastes category (inorganic in nature to be disposed off in landfill) is high compared to the other two categories [17].

6.2 Quantification

In India the amount of hazardous waste generated is 4,415,954 TPA covering 373 districts out of 525 districts. With reference to the cited literature [18] the land required to dispose 5.3 million tons of hazardous wastes in an engineered landfill with the density of waste (1.2 tonnes/m3) with the depth of the landfill 4 m is 1.08 km^2 every year.

6.3 Integrated sustainable waste management

Integrated sustainable waste management is defined as selection and application of suitable techniques, technologies and management approaches to achieve specific objectives and goals. This system ensures the integrity of all the systems to work with compatibility and allows rational planning and execution [19]. It consists of four basic principles and three components.

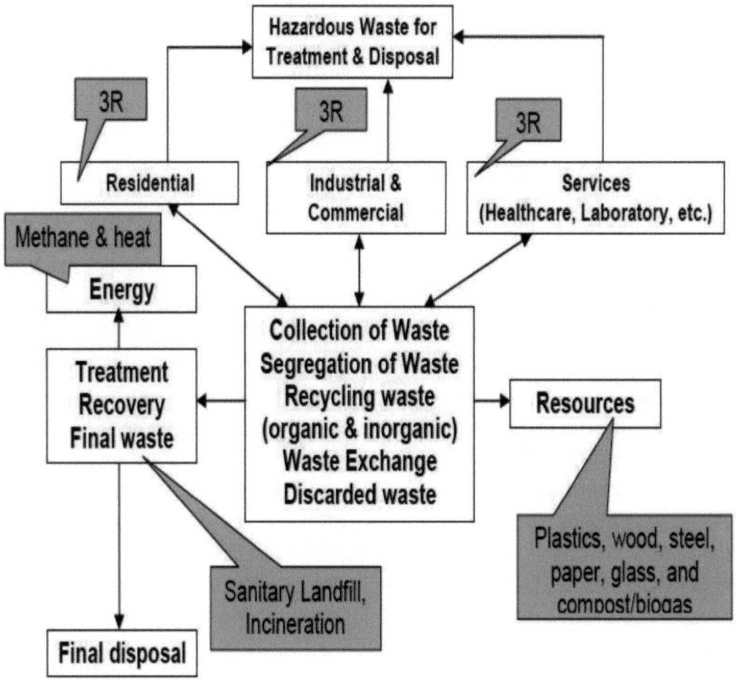

Figure 6.
Integrated sustainable waste management.

6.3.1 Principles of integrated sustainable waste management

6.3.1.1 Equity

All citizens should be exposed to appropriate waste management system for environmental health reasons.

6.3.1.2 Effectiveness

The waste management model should ensure safe removal of waste.

6.3.1.3 Efficiency

The major concern of waste management is to maximize the benefits, lower the costs and optimize the use of resources, taking into account, equity, effectiveness and sustainability.

6.3.1.4 Sustainability

The waste management system is appropriate to the local conditions and feasible from a technical, environmental, social, economic, financial, institutional and political perspective. It can maintain itself overtime without exhausting the resources upon which it depends.

6.3.2 Components of integrated sustainable waste management

1. The stakeholders

2. The (practical and technical) elements of the waste system

3. The aspects of the local context for assessing and planning waste management system.

ISWM includes elements such as collection, transportation and disposal or treatment. and also gives equal importance to waste minimization, reuse, recycling and composting. The concept of integrated sustainable waste management was shown in **Figure 6**.

Sustainable hazardous waste management is of prime importance for proper health, protection of environment on and resource management towards sustainability. Prevention of the generation of hazardous wastes and the rehabilitation of contaminated sites are the key elements, and both require knowledge, experienced people, facilities, financial resources and technical and scientific capacities.

7. Conclusion

The main prospective of hazardous waste management program is to change the way of managing hazardous waste so that they can be stored, transported and dispose in an environmentally safe manner. The focus of managing hazardous waste comes in an effort to address potential threats to public health and environment. Hazardous waste management must have an initiative beyond disposing directly into the land surface. Industries are encouraged to generate less amount of hazardous waste as a part of manufacturing process. Because the toxic wastes cannot be completely eliminated and only possible way is to minimizing, recycling, and treating wastes. So steps should be taken to use the modern technology without causing any threat to environment. Minimizing, recycling, and treating wastes.

Author details

Krishnaswamy Kanagamani*, P. Geethamani and M. Narmatha
Department of Chemistry, SNS College of Technology, Coimbatore, India

*Address all correspondence to: kanagamanichem@gmail.com

IntechOpen

© 2020 The Author(s). Licensee IntechOpen. This chapter is distributed under the terms of the Creative Commons Attribution License (http://creativecommons.org/licenses/by/3.0), which permits unrestricted use, distribution, and reproduction in any medium, provided the original work is properly cited.

References

[1] V. Misra, S.D. Pandey, Hazardous waste, impact on health and environment for development of better waste management strategies in future in India. Environment International. 2005,31(3), 417-435. https://doi.org/10.1016/j.envint.2004.08.005

[2] E.D.Enger, B.F.Smith, A study of interrelationships. Environmental Science. Edward E. Bartell. California, USA, 2004.

[3] B. Roger, E.S.James, & D.David The safe disposal of Hazardous wastes: The special needs and problems of developing countries, A world Bank Technical paper 1989,1 (93),154

[4] C.C. Amadi, O.C. Okeke & D.C. Amadi, Hazardous waste management: A review of principles and methods, International Journal of Advanced Academic Research Sciences, Technology & Engineering, 2017, 3 (8), 1-20.

[5] L. Fazzo, F. Minichilli, M. Santoro, A. Ceccarini, M. Della Seta, F. Bianchi, P. Comba & M. Martuzzi, Hazardous waste and health impact: a systematic review of the scientific literature, Environmental Health, 2017, 16 DOI 10.1186/s12940-017-0311-8.

[6] Vandana bharati, Jaspal singh, A.P.Singh, A Review on Solid Waste Management Methods and Practices in India, 2017, 4065-4067.

[7] V.M. Iyyanki & M.Vali, Science and Engineering for industry, Environmental Management 1st Edition, Elsevier. Inc, 2017.

[8] A.N.Jerry, Encyclopedia Britannica, Hazardous Waste management,2015

[9] C.Visvanathan , Hazardous waste disposal, Resources, Conservation and Recycling.1996,16, 201-212. https://doi.org/10.1016/0921-3449(95)00057-7

[10] Encyclopedia Britannica, Hazardous Waste Disposal,2016, Retrieved from https://www.britannica.com/technology/hazardous-waste-management

[11] Rajkumar Joshi, Sirajuddin Ahmed, Status and challenges of municipal solid waste management in India: A review, Cogent Environmental Science 2016, 2, 1139434.

[12] V.Ramakrishna and B.V. Babu, "Fresh water depletion – a crisis: Causes & remedies", Environment & People.1999a, 6(1), 33-39.

[13] J. Parsa., H.M. Stuart and R. Steiner, Stabilization /solidification of hazardous wastes using fly as, J. Environ. Engg, ASCE, 1996,122 (10), 935-940.

[14] Leelavathy Karthikeyan , Venkatesan Madha Suresh , Vignesh Krishnan , Terry Tudor and Vedha Varshini, The Management of Hazardous Solid Waste in India: An Overview, Environments, **2018**, 5, 103.

[15] B.V. Babu and V. Ramakrishna, Mathematical modeling of Site sensitivity indices in the site selection criteria for hazardous waste treatment, storage and disposal facility, Journal of the Institution of Public Health Engineers India, 2000, 2000 (1), 54-70.

[16] R. Lakshmi, Remote Sensing application in siting of waste disposal facilities with special reference to hazardous wastes", in Remote Sensing Applications in Applied Sciences, edited by Saumitra Mukherjee, Manak Publications Pvt. Ltd., New Delhi, 1999, 141-179.

[17] A. Agarwal., M. Agarwal, A. Mehta, and M. Bajpai. A review on current status of municipal solid waste management in India, MSSRGIJCE3, 2016, (5):122-125.

[18] SDNP. Hazardous waste: special reference to municipal solid waste management, 2003.

[19] A.V. Shedkar, Sustainable solid waste management: An integrated approach for asian countries, Waste Manage., 2009, 29(4), 1438-1448.

Chapter 11

Soil Genesis of Histosols and Gelisols with a Emphasis on Soil Processes Supporting Carbon Sequestration

Michael T. Aide, Christine Aide and Indi Braden

Abstract

Based on the U.S. Soil Taxonomy Histosols are soils that have a histic epipedon, which is a surface horizon that exhibits a sufficient abundance of soil organic matter to be distinctively different than other soil orders predominantly composed of clastic materials. Gelisols are soils that have permafrost, with histels being a suborder that is dominated by organic materials. Collectively, these soil orders are abundant in peatland ecosystems. The abundance of soil organic material is primarily a consequence of climate, topography, hydrology, vegetation. Peatland ecosystems have been a major research arena; however, added research attention is being directed to the potential release of carbon because of accelerated climate change. This review focuses of the structure and dynamics of organic soils and an understanding of their creation, evolution and ultimate fate. Attention is focused on degraded peatland net primary productivity because of potential forthcoming differences attributed to rainfall, temperature, vegetation, hydrology and permafrost disappearance.

Keywords: peatlands, net primary productivity, climate change, soil organic matter, soil respiration

1. Introduction (Histosols)

Organic soils are soils which have diagnostic horizons with more than 20% organic matter and essentially reside in marshes, bogs, and swamps where anaerobic soil conditions support a low rate of organic matter decomposition relative to the rate of organic matter production. Thus, organic soils are observed to have a carbon input rate that is initially greater than the carbon loss rate resulting in an annual carbon accumulation, then with continued soil genesis the rate of carbon input approximately equals the carbon loss rate and a carbon quasi-equilibrium is attained.

These organic soils are frequently associated with extremely wet landscapes, or extremely acidic soils, or soils lacking available nutrients or some combination of these influences. Organic soils (Histosols) as defined in the United States [1] are soils that have an abundance of organic soil materials with additional criteria specifying that they lack sufficient andic properties and lack permafrost plus these soils possess certain thickness, water saturation duration, and decomposition status associated with their fresh and rubbed fiber contents. According to the United States Keys of Soil Taxonomy [1], organic soil horizons have (i) 12% organic carbon (approximately 21% soil organic matter) if the clay content is 0% and (ii) 18% organic carbon if the clay content is 60% or greater. For horizons that have clay contents between 0 and 60% the organic carbon content is a linear relationship to clay content involving the 12% organic carbon if the clay content is 0% and 18% organic carbon if the clay content is 60%.

Histic epipedons are surface organic horizons that are water saturated for at least 30 days in most years (typically an aquic soil moisture regime) are generally 0.2 to 0.4 m thick and have sufficient organic carbon as a function of clay content. Folistic epipedons are surface horizons that are not water saturated for at least 30 days in most years (not artificially drained), typically are more than 0.20 m thick, and are largely composed of 75% or more sphagnum fibers or have a bulk density of less than 0.1 g cm^{-3}. The Keys of Soil Taxonomy [1] partition histic epipedons into fibric, hemic and sapric materials. Fibric materials (Of) are minimally decomposed where three quarters or more of its volume is made up of fibers after rubbing the sample. Sapric materials (Oa) are highly decomposed; less than one-sixth of the volume of sapric material contains fibers after a sample is rubbed. Hemic materials (Oe) are intermediate with respect to decomposition. In general, fibric materials possess a very low bulk density (0.05 to 0.15 Mg m^{-3}), a large total pore space (85%) with a high distribution of large pores spaces, a low bearing capacity, and a hydraulic conductivity ranging from 1.6 to 30 m day^{-1}.

Generally, the Histosol soil order is recognized if more than half of the upper 0.8 m of the soil profile is organic or if organic soil material rests on rock or fragmental material showing interstices filled with organic material. In colloquial terms the Histosol order contains soils formally described as bogs, moors, peatlands, muskegs, fens or are composed of peats and mucks. Histosols make up about 1% of the world's glacier-free land surface (325 to 375 million ha). Suborders of Histosol order are based on the degree of organic material decomposition and the length of water saturation. The Histosol suborders are: Fibrists, Hemists, Saprists and Folists. The World Reference Base for soil resources [2] states that Histosols are soils having a histic or folic horizon either 0.1 m or more thick from the soil surface to a lithic or paralithic contact or 0.4 m or more thick and starting within 0.3 m from the soil surface, and having no andic or vitric horizon starting within 0.3 m of the soil surface.

2. Histosol soil forming processes

Histosols occur in all latitudes; however, Histosols are particularly common in the boreal zone, a feature Histosols share with Spodisols. The dominant feature of Histosols is the accumulation of organic materials, which may be characterized as:

$$\text{Organic material content} = \text{organic matter input} - \text{organic matter loss} \qquad (1)$$

The rate of organic matter decomposition in Histosols is usually very slow, a feature attributed to specific conditions of climate, topography and hydrology. In boreal biomes, cool summer temperatures restrict microbial activity, with biologic zero being approximately 4 to 5°C. Low soil temperatures must be further associated with anoxic soil conditions to support Histosol genesis. In tropical climates, warmer temperatures support greater ecosystem productivities; however, the combined effects of precipitation, topography and hydrology may create anoxic soil conditions for a sustained time interval to restrict soil organic matter decomposition. Topography influences Histosol formation by directing water flux within the landscape position. Lateral groundwater may create seepage on sideslopes, whereas peatlands may form in poorly-drained basins. Fens occur where surface water inflow or groundwater discharge concentrates nutrient rich water. Pocosins or bogs on coastal plains or interior flatlands are frequently located on slightly raised interfluvial positions.

The degree of soil organic matter decomposition has a significant influence on soil properties. Buol et al. [3] reviewed literature to describe the soil genesis and classification of Histosols. Key soil properties that are influenced based on the degree of soil organic matter decomposition include: organic carbon, total nitrogen, carbon to nitrogen ratio, cellulose content, pH, cation exchange capacity, bulk density, water contents at field capacity and permanent wilting point, hydraulic conductivity. Upon transition from fibric to sapric soil conditions the following properties typically increase in magnitude: total nitrogen, pH, cation exchange capacity, bulk density, and the water contents at field capacity and permanent wilting point. Most notably the vertical and horizontal hydraulic conductivities decrease on transition from fibric to sapric soil conditions. However, many Histosols exhibit greater soil organic matter decomposition with increasing soil profile depth, thus the corresponding reduced hydraulic conductivity and increased water content at greater soil profile depth support continuance of the sapric condition.

Buol et al. [3] alluded to two adjacent Histosols in Michigan that differ in nutrient sources. The Napoleon soil series (dysic, mesic Typic Haplohemists) receives nutrients only from precipitation and dry deposition, whereas the Houghton (euic, mesic Typic Haplosaprists) primarily receives nutrients from seepage water that transverses calcareous sandy glacial till. The Napoleon mucky peat has an Oa1-Oa2-Oe1-Oe2 horizon sequence, with all horizons having a pH near 4, whereas the Houghton muck has an Oa1-Oa2-Oa3-Oa4-Oa5-Oa6 horizon sequence with all horizons having a pH near 7. Vegetation associated with the Napoleon mucky peat comprised various maples, swamp white oak, and dogwood, whereas the Houghton muck is vegetated with marshy grasses. Thus, water chemistry dramatically influences the soil's pH and exchangeable cation expression and coupled with hydrology influences vegetation establishment.

Aide and Aide (two authors of this manuscript) have unpublished field data of several soil series in northeastern Wisconsin. The Lupton series (Euic, frigid Typic Haplosaprists) are very deep, very poorly-drained organic soils formed in depressions on lake and outwash plains. The horizon sequence is Oa1-Oa2-Oa3-Oa4-Oa5 and has little inorganic material, a very low bulk density, a pH in 0.01 M $CaCl_2$ of 5.7 to 6.0 and a cation exchange capacity ranging from 107 to 199 cmol kg^{-1} across multiple pedons. The dominant surrounding soil consists of pedons of the Padus series (coarse-loamy, mixed, superactive, frigid Alfic Haplorthods). The tupical Padus horizon sequence is A-E-Bs1-Bs2-E/B-B/E-2C. The texture is sandy loam above the lithologic discontinuity and sandy textured at greater depths (2C). These very deep, well-drained and very strongly acidic pedons are moderately deep to stratified sandy outwash with an abundance of clay films in the B material of the E/B and B/E horizons. The organic carbon content of the A horizon is less than 2% and the cation exchange capacity is very low, reflecting the sandy loam texture and diminished quantity of soil organic matter. Water extracts from both soils show an abundance of calcium, reflecting that calcium is the dominant exchange cation. These two soils have very distinctive profiles, whose properties are directly related to the contrasting oxidation–reduction environments imposed by the local hydrology.

Parent materials for Histosols are mostly hydrophytic plants [1]. Sphagnum consists of both living and dead tissue from the genus Sphagnum, with approximately

380 species. Sphagnum leaf tissue consists of chlorophyllose and hyaline cells, with the former having photosynthetic activity and the latter consisting of larger, clear and non-living cells with a large capacity to hold and store water. The cell walls contain an abundance of phenolic compounds that are resistant to decomposition. Sphagnum also has a substantial uptake capacity for calcium, magnesium and other nutrients, predisposing the underlying mineral soil to an acidic reaction. Typically, Sphagnum is the dominant plant genus in mires, raised bogs and blanket bogs. Other plant species commonly associated with Sphagnum include sedges, various dwarf shrubs, *Betula nama* (Dwarf birch) and *Salix* spp. (Willows).

Paludification or the geologic accumulation of organic materials across a landscape is influenced by soil pH, soil temperature, microbial activity, nutrient availability, oxidation–reduction and vertebrates (example: beavers or *Castor canadensis*). One criterion for paludization is the maintenance of anaerobic soil conditions sufficient to inhibit plant material decomposition. In glacial lake settings or ox-bows in fluvial systems, sediment infusion may occur resulting in lacustrine sediment accumulation. When sediment accumulation is sufficient to permit acceptable light levels to penetrate to the submerged sediment surface and if the water oxygen levels are appropriately anaerobic then plant material preservation prevails. When Histosols evolve because of sediment deposition with subsequent soil organic matter accumulation then this process is termed terrestrialization.

3. Gelisols

In the United States the Keys of Soil Taxonomy support 12 soil orders at the highest level of soil taxonomy [1]. Gelisols (Cryosols in the World Reference Base of Soil Resources [2]) are soils that have permafrost within two meters from the soil surface. Permafrost is a soil climatic condition where soil material has continuous temperatures at or below 0°C. Because of the permafrost requirement, Gelisols occur extensively in boreal, subarctic and arctic environments and comprise approximately 18 km^2 (13.4%) of the ice-free land area [1]. Gelisols having a short period of seasonal thawing have an upper zone that thaws, creating an "active layer" approximately a few cm to 1.5 m thick. This active layer may experience soil forming processes, including sufficient biotic activity to form histic epipedons (suborder histels) [3].

The boundary between the active layer and permafrost is termed the "permafrost table". In moist soil and with the return of winter conditions, soil freezing begins at the permafrost table and also at the soil surface, which subsequently finalizes in the active layer. Thus, the active layer experiences freezing fronts from both the soil surface and from the permafrost table, giving rise to compaction and a loss of any soil structure. In the active layer of many Gelisols, dark streaks of organic matter that are distinguished from the soil matrix colors, suggesting soil material redistribution because of cryoturbation. The permafrost table is frequently impermeable to percolating water and therefore develops an accumulation of soil organic matter.

In very cold and low precipitation areas Gelisols are mostly shallow and relatively featureless soils; however, where temperatures are relatively mild and precipitation is more extensive, Gelisols are deeper and likely have an active layer that exhibits accumulation of soil organic matter. Gelisol vegetation includes lichens, moss, liverwort, sedge, grass and boreal forest species. Soil inhabiting organisms include prokaryotes (most notably N-fixing Azotobacter), fungi, actinomycetes, anthropoids, nematodes, protozoa and algae [1, 3].

Solifluction may occur on sloping landscapes. Cryopedogenic processes include cryoturbation causing a reduction in soil profile horizonation (Haploidization), soil structure formation, seasonal ice lens formation above the permafrost table, landscape collapse (thermokarst), and the formation of redoximorphic features. Additionally, soil carbon pool sizes, redistribution within the soil profile, and bioavailability are strongly affected by (1) cryoturbation, which is the soil-mixing action of freeze/thaw processes, and (2) by the presence of permafrost itself, which has strong controls over soil temperature and moisture and runoff. Overall, permafrost affected soils represent 16% of all soils on the globe, and contain up to 50% of the global belowground soil carbon pool [4]. Histels are Gelisols consisting of organic materials, with suborder groups listed as: (i) Folistels, (ii) Glacistels [have the upper boundary of a glacic layer (75% or more visible ice)], (iii) Fibristels, (iv) Hemistels, and (v) Sapristels.

Tarnocai et al. [4] performed an extensive review of carbon pools in the northern permafrost region, noting that approximately 3.56 x 10^6 km^2 in this region at peatlands. These authors provided data illustrating that Histels (66.6 kg m^{-2}) and Histosols (69.6 kg m^{-2}) have the highest soil organic carbon contents. Histels alone are estimated to contain 184 Pg C, whereas histosols contribute 94.3 Pg C. Turbels show extensive soil organic carbon incorporation to deeper soil depths because of cryoturbation.

4. Organic carbon and peatlands

Peatland ecosystems are well represented in the majority of the world's biomes. In this manuscript we define a biome as a community of associated ecosystems characterized by their prevailing vegetation and by organism adaptation to that particular environment. Different sources define the types and number of biomes differently; herein, we specify six biomes: (i) tundra, (ii) taiga, (iii) grassland, (iv) deciduous forest, (v) desert, and (vi) tropical rainforest. Tundra, taiga and tropical rainforests are commonly accepted biomes having considerable expanses of peatlands; however, examples do exist in grassland and deciduous forest biomes.

Peatlands, as defined by the National Working Group (Canada), are wetlands containing more than 0.4 m thickness of peat [5]. Ombrotrophic peatlands or oligotrophic peatlands include soil and vegetation which receive water and nutrients primarily from precipitation, thus they are environments isolated hydrologically from the surrounding landscape. Given that rainfall is acidic because of equilibrium with the partial pressure of CO_2 and the rainfall nutrient composition is relatively low, ombrotrophic peatlands are typically considered nutrient deficient and exhibit reduced microbial activity. Frequently the vegetation is dominated by Sphagnum mosses. Minerotrophic peatlands are wetlands whose water availability comes mainly from nutrient-enriched surface waters that have neutral to alkaline pH reactions. Typically, minerotrophic wetlands have a high-water table, low internal drainage and exhibit moderately-well to well-decomposed sedges, brown mosses and related vegetation.

Carbon content is variably defined to represent the carbon concentrations on a surface area basis or a soil volume basis. Typically, carbon content defined as the mass of carbon per unit land area (kg carbon m^{-2}) is presented to indicate landscape variability, whereas carbon content on a volume basis (kg carbon m^{-3}) is presented to indicate intra-pedon or inter-pedon differences. Carbon content as expressed as the carbon concentration per volume is a soil or landscape property influenced by bulk density and horizon depth. Carbon accumulation is the net gain or loss of carbon content, typically at century or millennial scales. Peatlands reside on nearly

2.7% of the global land surface, yet peatlands possess a significant portion of the terrestrial soil carbon pool with deep soil organic matter accumulations created over millennia. Estimates suggest that boreal and subarctic peatlands contain 455 Pg C [6] and 462 Pg [7], repectively. Boreal peat deposits tend to be deeper than subarctic peatlands, a feature attributed to long carbon accumulation intervals [8].

Peat-forming systems have been partitioned into acrotelm and catotelm zones [9]. The acrotelm portion of a peat-forming soil system is defined as the relatively more oxygenated (oxic) upper portion of the peat forming soil system, where aerobic decomposition is comparatively greater, the hydraulic conductivity is more rapid and the bulk density typically ranges from 0.1 to 0.4 g cm^{-3}. Conversely the catotelm is the suboxic to anoxic lower portion of the peat-forming soil system that is characterized by a comparatively slower hydraulic conductivity and a bulk density typically ranging from 0.8 to 1.2 g cm^{-3}.

Soils being open thermodynamic systems receive water and particulate soil organic matter and energy at their boundaries, most notably at the soil-atmosphere interface. Matter and energy may also be transferred by lateral flow at the pedon-pedon interface or vertical flow at the soil-sediment interface. Water infiltration and percolation within the acrotelm is rapid; however, percolation slows substantially in the catotelm, creating the upper oxic and deeper anoxic oxidation–reduction regimes within the soil profile. As soil organic matter decomposition progresses at the base of the acrotelm, the resulting loss of pore space, attributed to an increase in the bulk density, supports water retention and conversion of the lowermost portion of the acrotelm into that of the catotelm, thus elevating the acrotelm-catotelm boundary with progressive soil development.

The primary vegetation productivity (P [=] g cm^{-2}) is the annual production of particulate organic matter and its subsequent incorporation in the soil's surface horizons. The transformation of particulate matter to humus is predicated on soil temperature, microbial acidity, the soil's oxidation–reduction status, pH and nutrient availability. The rate of organic matter accumulation per unit surface area (x) is the difference between the annual production of particulate organic matter per unit area and the rate of soil organic matter loss per unit area, expressed as a first-order linear ordinary differential equation:

$$dx / dt = P - \alpha x, \tag{2}$$

where α is the decay coefficient, and t is time (years). Integration using an integration factor provides a solution:

$$x = (P / \alpha)\left(1 - e^{-\alpha t}\right). \tag{3}$$

From Clymo [9] typical decay constant values include α = 0.05 and 0.15 $year^{-1}$. Also, from Clymo [9] typical annual production of particulate organic matter values includes: 150 and 450 g m^{-2} $yr.^{-1}$. Using Eq. 3, The mass accumulation is presented for two scenarios: (i) P = 450 g m^{-2} $yr.^{-1}$ and α = 0.15 $year^{-1}$ (upper line in **Figure 1**) and (ii) P = 150 g m^{-2} $yr.^{-1}$ and α = 0.05 $year^{-1}$ (lower line in **Figure 1**). The scenario (i) P = 450 g m^{-2} $yr.^{-1}$ and α = 0.15 $year^{-1}$ provides a greater annual production of particulate organic matter and a faster rate of decay, such that the ratio P/α is a limit point as t approaches infinity. The asymptotic approach to P/α as a limit point implies that the net annual accumulation of organic matter ultimately becomes constant.

Street et al. [10] in Svalbard considered the influence of phosphorus (P) on the decomposition potential of carbon stocks. Nitrogen additions supported carbon stock reductions because of enhanced soil organic matter decomposition; however, the combination of added nitrogen and phosphorus supported an increase in the

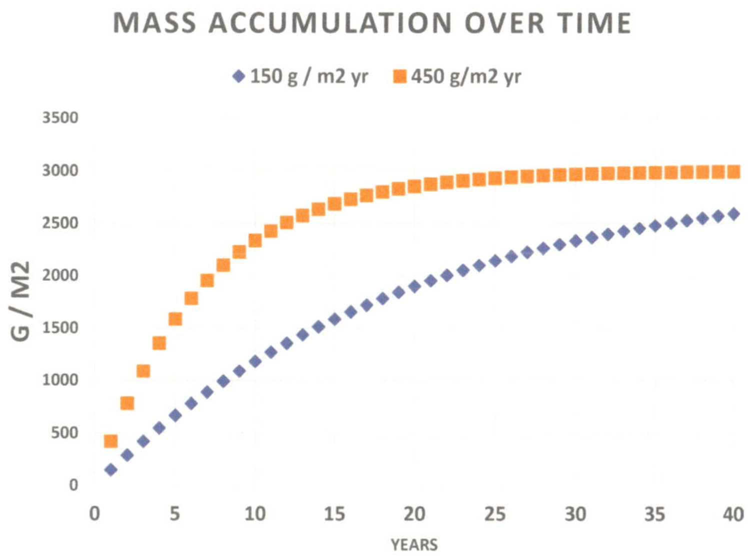

Figure 1.
Illustration of mass accumulation per year (0 to 3500 g m^{-2} yr.$^{-1}$) versus time (40 years) using Eq. (2) . The primary vegetation productivity was 150 and 450 g m^{-2} yr.$^{-1}$ and the decay coefficients were 0.05 and 0.15 year^{-1}, respectively.

carbon stocks because of stimulated plant production. In Poland, Sienkiewicz et al. [11] investigated Histosol soil organic carbon and its relationship to total nitrogen, dissolved organic carbon and dissolved organic nitrogen. Carbon and nitrogen loss rates were independent, and soil organic carbon losses were dependent on the soil organic carbon content. The ratio of dissolved organic carbon to soil organic carbon increased with respect to the intensity of soil organic matter decomposition. Turunen et al. [12] investigated wet deposition of nitrogen (0.3 to 0.8 g nitrogen m^{-2} yr.$^{-1}$) in ombrotrophic peatlands in eastern Canada, noting that nitrogen additions supported a greater diversity of vascular plants.

Qui et al. [13] modeled northern peatland areas and carbon changing aspects during the Holocene. They recognized that the net primary production (NPP) and heterotrophic respiration increased over the past century in response to climate change and increased atmospheric CO_2 activity. In their study net primary productivity was a greater influence than heterotrophic respiration, with 11.1 Pg C accumulated carbon storage since 1901, with the majority of the carbon storage increase occurring after 1950.

5. Research studies focusing on soil chemistry with emphasis on low molecular weight carbon species

The literature is replete with compelling research documenting biologically mediated geochemical pathways that are instrumental in creating vibrant biomes that have substantial accumulations of soil organic matter. Microbial populations secrete extracellular enzymes that are specific for degrading organic functional groups. The effectiveness of these extracellular enzymes is a complex function of (i) peat chemistry and litter quality, (ii) nutrient status, (iii) moisture content, (iv) plant community composition, (v) microbial community representation, and (vi) temperatures [14]. The absence of oxygen may also result in the accumulation of phenolic compounds that impost a negative feedback on microbial activity. Key enzyme activities important to mineralization include: (i) alpha-glucosidase, (ii) beta-glucosidase, (iii) cellobiohydrolase, (iv) N-acetylglucosaminidase, (v) acid phosphatase, and (vi) leucine aminopeptidase.

Fox [15] reviewed literature involving low-molecular-weight organic acids. Low-molecular weight organic acids are approximately 10% of a typical forest soil's dissolved organic carbon pool, but they may have a disproportionate influence on soil processes, including metal complexation. Common low molecular weight organic acids include: acetic, aconitic, benzoic, cinnamic, citric, formic, fumaric, gallic, lactic, malic, maleic, malonic, p-hydroxybenzoic, phthalic, protocatechuic, oxalic, salicylic, succinic, tartaric, and vanillic. Common functional groups include (i) acidic groups [carboxylic (R-COOH), enolic (R-CH=CH-OH), phenolic (Ar-OH) and quinones (Ar = O)], (ii) neutral groups [alcoholic OH ($R\text{-}CH_2OH$), ethers ($R\text{-}CH_2\text{-}O\text{-}CH_2\text{-}R$), ketones (R-C=O (−R)), aldehydes (R-C=O(-H)) and esters (R-C=O(-OR))] and (iii) neutral nitrogen-bearing amines ($R\text{-}CH_2\text{-}NH_2$) and amides (R-C=O(NH-R)). When considering root extracts oxalic, citric and malic are quite abundant. Sources of low molecular weight organic acids are root respiration, leaching from the litter floor, decomposition of soil organic matter, and rainfall. Herbert and Bertsch [16] further detailed dissolved and colloidal organic matter in the soil solution. Based on their review of literature dissolved organic matter is primarily composed of hydrocarbons, chlorophyll, carotenoids, phospholipids and long-chain fatty acids, tannins, flavonoids and other polyphenols, fulvic and humic acids, aromatic and aliphatic acids, and proteins /amino acids. In most studies the dominant organic materials were humic substances.

Kane et al. [17] measured pore water chemistry associated with an artificially-induced warming of a nutrient poor fen. The dissolved organic carbon (DOC) concentration was greater in the warmed fen (73.4 ± 3.2 mg L^{-1}) compared to the untreated check (63.7 ± 2.1 mg L^{-1}). The amount of dissolved organic nitrogen (DON) was greater in the warmed fen; however, the DON/DOC ratio was smaller. The reduced DON/DOC ratio was primarily attributed to a smaller capacity of the microbial community to yield labile nitrogen via the decomposition process and the greater utilization efficiency of the nitrogen by the microbial community. In Manitoba (Canada) Aide and Cwick [18] studied Eluviated Eutric Brunisols having an Of-Bm-C horizon sequence and Orthic Eutric Brunisols having an Oh or Of-Bm-C horizon sequence. Located in the glacial Lake Agassiz these soils formed in fine-graine lacustrine sediments interspersed with organic soils and fens. The surface horizons of the Eluviated Eutric Brunisols possessed organic carbon contents ranging from 19.8 to 29.4% with C/N ratios of 29.5 to 27.4, whereas the surface horizons of the Orthic Eutric Brunisols possessed organic carbon contents ranging from 27.3 to 41.7% with C/N ratios of 39.5 to 25.4. The C/N ratios and associated nitrate-N concentrations suggests that nitrogen limits the rates of soil mineralization. In a near companion manuscript Aide et al. [19] documented that the silty sediments were dominated by hydroxy Al-interlayered vermiculite, smectite, hydrous mica, and kaolinite in the clay separate. The potential for potassium fixation by vermiculite was reduced by Al-interlayering.

Van Cleve and Powers [20] isolated state factors involved in carbon storage in forest soils, noting the role of climate, parent material, topography, vegetation, and soil organisms. The chemistry of soil organic carbon, including root exudates and leachates, strongly influence the microbial processing of detritus, the materials synthesized in this process and the intensity of the roles that low and high molecular weight organic acids have in soil development. Observed effects show that synthesized products are more resistant to further decomposition and possessed smaller nitrogen contents, which over time supports soil organic matter accumulation.

6. Research studies having a focus on carbon loss as greenhouse gas emissions

Peatlands are an important terrestrial carbon sink and any increased microbial activity may result in soil organic matter oxidation, with subsequent CO_2 release. Northern peatlands historically have had the benefit of cool to frigid temperatures that limit microbial activity. Low oxygen activity attributed to water saturation further limits mineralization. Climate change may result in warmer soils, with the cavate that the effective length of the increasingly warmer summer interval is also increased. The encroachment of vascular plants will be expected to proceed, leading to a positive feedback on microbial activity. Thus, studies on peatland functioning in higher latitudes and their potential to accelerate climate change are becoming commonplace [14].

In Canada, Dieleman et al. [21] established mesocosms, where peat production of dissolved organic carbon was measured. The production of dissolved organic carbon from peat was estimated to be a function of temperature, CO_2 concentration and the influence of the water table, wherein increased temperatures increased the dissolved organic carbon contents, lowered water tables increased decomposition rates and reduced pore water dissolved organic carbon concentrations. In the Alaskan arctic Euskirchen et al. [22] established eddy covariance flux towers across various ecosystems for three years to document peak CO_2 uptake patterns. Peak CO_2 uptake centered from June to August at a mean of 51 to 95 g C m^{-2} across the various ecosystems. Warmer spring seasons promoted greater CO_2 uptake patterns, whereas warmer late seasons supported greater soil respiration rates, reducing the Net Ecosystem Exchange (NEE).

In Canada, Frolking et al. [23] employed the Holocene Peat Model to simulate the vegetation community composition and the annual net primary productivity. Northern peatlands take up CO_2 at rates of 40 to 80 g carbon m^{-2} $yr.^{-1}$, with carbon leaching as DOC at rates of 10–20 g DOC m^{-2} $yr.^{-1}$. Decomposition was estimated to be 95% of the Net Primary Productivity. Similarly, Frolking et al. [23] observed undisturbed Canadian peatlands and determined that these peatlands were a weak sink for carbon and a moderate source of methane emission. McLoughlin and Webster [24] performed a review of peatland dynamics, primarily within the Hudson Bay Lowlands. Long term carbon accumulation, CO_2 sequestration, peat depth and land age were positively correlated. Carbon dioxide sequestration showed the greatest variability, with bogs (−1.7 to 1.5 g carbon m^{-2} day^{-1}), fens (−4.3 to 1.6 g carbon m^{-2} day^{-1}), and palsa peat (−0.8 to 1 g carbon m^{-2} day^{-1}). Methane and evapotranspiration were greater in the wettest ecosystems, with methane emission for bogs (3.3 to 28 mg carbon m^{-2} day^{-1}), fens (0.1 to 204 mg carbon m^{-2} day^{-1}), and palsa peat (−1.6 to 24 mg carbon m^{-2} day^{-1}).

On paludified soils Schneider et al. [25] measured methane (CH_4) flux for forest and peatland areas. Open peatlands exhibited a methane emission rate of 21.9 ± 1.6 g m^{-2} $yr.^{-1}$ in contrast with forested peatland transition zones (7.9 ± 0.5 g m^{-2} $yr.^{-1}$). The forested peatland transition zones demonstrated an inflow of less acidic surface water that supported a higher biological diversity and greater plant productivity. These authors noted that methane emission was more influenced by increased temperatures than the water table depths. In Sweden, Sagerfors et al. [26] established eddy covariance measurements across oligotrophic mires. Based on the vertical exchange of CO_2 their sites were a net sink for carbon (55 ± 7 g carbon m^{-2} $yr.^{-1}$). The non-growing seasons exhibited a carbon loss; however, the growing season sequestration of carbon more than compensated for the non-growing season carbon loss.

Wickland et al. [27] observed changes in CO_2 and methane exchanges on a black spruce (*Picea mariana*) lowland experiencing permafrost melting. Sites were partitioned as peat soils having permafrost, thermokarst wetlands, and thermokarst edges, with thermokarst edges having greater methane emissions. Ernakovich et al. [28] measured greenhouse gas emissions from thawed permafrost with simulated oxic and anoxic redox environments. Carbon dioxide emission was supported by an active microbial community and a labile dissolved organic carbon pool. Increased methane production was related to soils with a labile litter pool. Carbon dioxide emission was 30 to 450 times the methane production in an anoxic soil and carbon dioxide emission was 500 to 2500 times the methane production in an oxic soil.

In Canada, Webster et al. [29] investigated net ecosystem exchange and methane emissions for bogs, nutrient-poor fens, intermediate-rich fens across seven ecozones. During the growing season, the net ecosystem exchange, per season, was -108 ± 41.3 Mt. CO_2 and the methane emissions were 4.1 ± 1.5 Mt. CH_4. Converting methane to CO_2 global warming potential for a 25 to 100-year event, the total sink was -7 ± 77.6 Mt. CO_2e. The boreal plain peatlands exhibited the greatest net ecosystem exchange, whereas the boreal shield peatlands exhibited the highest methane emissions. In the discontinuous permafrost zone of western Siberia, Shirokova et al. [30] showed that permafrost thaw supported an increase in soil subsidence and the development of thermokarst lakes. Soil subsidence was related to soil carbon decomposition and mobilization to water resources.

Jackowicz-Korczynski et al. [31] observed methane emission from subarctic Swedish mires. A permafrost free mire having tall graminoid vegetation showed methane emission rates of 6.2 ± 2.6 mg CH_4 m^{-2} $hr.^{-1}$. The annual emission was 24.5 to 29.5 g CH_4 m^{-2} $yr.^{-1}$, with most of the emission during the summer months. In Wales (UK), Fenner et al. [32] investigated ombrotrophic peat or acid mires. Artificially enhanced CO_2 and warming produced increased concentrations of dissolved organic carbon. Higher concentrations of phenolic compounds were associated with the increase in dissolved organic carbon. The influence of increased temperature promoted microbial activity, whereas increased CO_2 content increased the supply of photosynthate to the soil because of greater root exudates. The effect of the temperature and elevated CO_2 were to synergistically decrease the C/N of the dissolved organic carbon. In Indonesian tropical peatlands, Uda et al. [33] noted that land drainage influenced CO_2 emissions from drained oil palm landscapes.

Aurangojeb et al. [34] contrasted a drained Histosol and an adjacent mineral soil in Sweden, noting that the Histosol N_2O emissions were 49.9 ± 3.3 μg N_2O m^{-2} $hr.^{-1}$, whereas the adjacent mineral soil N_2O emission was 8.0 ± 3.3 μg N_2O m^{-2} $hr.^{-1}$. The N_2O difference was attributed to the mineral soil having greater mycorrhizal N demand reducing the N availability. Leifeld et al. [35] investigated four temperate ombrotrophic peatlands across central Europe and determined that ash content is related to land drainage and land management, thus ash may be an indicator of historical decomposition but this protocol should be used only in pristine study areas.

7. Peatlands, net primary productivity and climate change

Net primary production is critical to developing large carbon contents in peatlands. Net primary production is a function of climate, vegetation, topography, the natural of the parent materials, and land use. Investigating Swedish peatlands, Chaudhary et al. [36] investigated drivers of biotic and abiotic peatland dynamics. For patterned ground they noted that plant species, hydrology, nutrient status, plant productivity and decomposition rates vary between hummock and hollow positions. Typically hollows possessed taller productive graminoid species that showed faster decomposition rates than sphagnum. Hummock positions possessed more shrub species that preferentially lowered the water table. In interior Alaska, O'Donnell et al. [37] studied Gelisols having a 30-day enhanced temperature incubation period, noting that the dissolved organic carbon concentration and its associated aromaticity increased at higher incubation temperatures. At these higher temperatures the dissolved organic materials contained more hydrophobic organic acids, polyphenols, and condensed aromatics and smaller concentrations of low-molecular weight hydrophilic and aliphatic compounds. Dissolved labile organic materials were preferentially mineralized, with the dominant kinetic controls being temperature and substrate lignin contents.

Wang et al. [38] correlated that increased mean annual air temperature was associated with increased active layer thickness. In a Siberian low arctic landscape, Frost et al. [39] documented seasonal and long-term changes to active layer temperatures and noted that vegetation and snow cover were important predictors of active layer thickness. Summer soil temperatures decreased with increasing shrub cover and soil organic matter thickness. Compared with open tundra, mature shrubs depressed summer soil temperatures; however, mature shrubs altered the insulative snowpack and fostered warmer winter soil temperatures.

In Canada Kroetsch et al. [5], working with the National Wetlands Working Group, noted that peatlands were routinely identified when peat depths exceeded 0.40 meters. Fibrisol, Mesisol and Humisol great groups were partitioned based on rubbed fiber content, von Post scale, pyrophosphate and depth of the surface, middle and bottom tiers. The key diagnostic genetic processes of organic soils included: (i) additions from litter, fine roots, soil organic matter deposition and low molecular weight organic acid exudation from sphagnum, feather mosses and related plant species, (ii) losses attributed to decomposition, (iii) transfers of dissolved organic carbon because of fluctuating water tables, leaching and burrowing organisms, (iv) transformations attributed to soil organic matter decomposition, O_2 status, nutrient availability, and toxins.

Glaser et al. [40] observed Hudson Bay Lowlands peatland development from a chronological perspective, relating the length of time for isostatic rebound to elevate the landscape and developing a transect of peatland sites ranging from comparatively younger to older sites. They observed that the resulting transects consisted of a sequence consisting of (i) basal tidal marshes in the youngest sites, (ii) Larix (Larches) dominated swamp forests, (iii) Picea (Spruce) forested bogs, and ending with (iv) non-forested bogs in the oldest sites. This sequence of peatlands was viewed as a predictable vegetation succession influenced by changes in hydrology and other factors derived from continuing isostatic rebound. Conversely, in western Siberia, peatlands demonstrated an increase in carbon accumulation upon transition from the northern region to the southern region [41]. The northern peatlands exhibited a carbon content of 7–35 kg carbon m^{-2}, whereas the southern peatlands exhibited a carbon content range of 43–88 kg carbon m^{-2}. The carbon content was estimated to be a complex function of soil organic matter quality (lignin content) and the predominant vegetation (vascular plants versus bryophytes).

8. Peatlands and their conservation

Karofeld et al. [42] noted Estonia's decline of pristine mires and investigated a method for mire reconstruction, involving the removal of oxidized peak layer followed by the spreading of plant fragments to increase the effective development of bryophyte and vascular plants. Along with maintaining the presence of a highwater table, the reconstruction effort was deemed successful.

Miettinen et al. [43] employed satellite images to document the role of fire and logging on the loss of Sumatra's pristine peat swamps. In Indonesia, Swails et al. [44] investigated soil respiration as a climatic driver in undrained forest settings and adjacent oil palm plantations. They documented that oil palm plantations with a reduced water table exhibited a higher soil respiration rate (0.71 ± 0.04 g CO_2 m^{-2} h^{-1}) than forested sites (0.58 ± 0.04 g CO_2 m^{-2} h^{-1}).

Across Poland, Grzywna [45] documented drainage-induced Histosol subsidence ranges from 9 to 33 cm. Nicia et al. [46] demonstrated that restoration of peatlands in Poland has potential to increase the organic carbon content, the C/N ratio and increase the pH in acidic fens. Richardson [47] noted the development sequence of alkaline mires (fens) in the Everglades (Florida) and the role of changing hydrology during the Holocene. In Wisconsin, Adhikari et al. [48] used digital maps and soil profile data to spatially quantify carbon stocks and subsequently estimated the fate of carbon stocks with improved land use management. The average baseline soil organic carbon stock was 90 mg ha^{-1} and with improved land management the soil across the state could increase the carbon stocks by 20 mg ha^{-1}. Mollisols were predicted to have the greatest potential for increasing carbon stocks, whereas Histosols and Spodisols were likely to lose carbon stock. Frazier and Lee [49] investigated Wisconsin Histosols partitioned as fibrists, hemists and saprists. Saprists possessed the highest carbon content, whereas the fibrists possessed the least carbon content, a feature related to chemical changes associated with the humification process.

9. Future possibilities

The fate of peatland ecosystems is integral to global sustainability. As scientists, we are acutely aware that carbon stored in peatland ecosystems may be released to the atmosphere, contributing to climate change acceleration. The precise drivers of peatland respiration, the role of the microorganism communities, organic acid leaching, soil mineralization, and other soil carbon pathways are reasonably well understood, but they are not sufficiently formalized into a coherent and interconnected model to provide detailed information concerning near-term peatland degradation [50–55]. Thus, a critical need exists to predict on a regional level specific changes to peatland dynamics because of the multi-faceted nature of accelerated climate change. With this process focus on peatland dynamics, best management practices are slow carbon de-sequestration.

Author details

Michael T. Aide*, Christine Aide and Indi Braden
Department of Agriculture, Southeast Missouri State University, United States

*Address all correspondence to: mtaide@semo.edu

IntechOpen

© 2020 The Author(s). Licensee IntechOpen. This chapter is distributed under the terms of the Creative Commons Attribution License (http://creativecommons.org/licenses/by/3.0), which permits unrestricted use, distribution, and reproduction in any medium, provided the original work is properly cited.

References

[1] Soil Survey Staff. 2014. Keys to Soil Taxonomy, 12th ed. USDA-Natural Resources Conservation Service, Washington, DC.

[2] World Reference Base (WRB) is the international standard for soil classification system endorsed by the International Union of Soil Sciences. http://www.fao.org/soils-portal/soil-survey/soil-classification/world-reference-base/en/ [verified July 2020]

[3] Buol SW, Southard RJ, Graham RC, and McDaniel. 2003. Soil Genesis and Classification. Iowa State University Press. Ames, IA. ISBN 0-8138-2373-2.

[4] Tarnocai G, Canadell JG, Schuur EAG, Kuhry P, Mazhitova G, and Zimov S. 2009. Soil organic carbon pools in the northern circumpolar permafrost region. Glob. Biogeochem. Cycles 23: GB2023. doi:10.1029/2008GB003327

[5] Kroetsch DJ, Geng X, Chang SX, and Saurette DD. 2011. Organic soils of Canada: Part 1. Wetland organic soils. Can. J. Soil Sci. 91:807-822. Doi:10.4141/CJSS10043.

[6] Gorham E. 1991. Northern peatlands: Role in the carbon cycle and probable responses to climatic warming. Ecol. Appl. 1: 182-195.

[7] Bridgham S, Megonigal J, Keller J, Bliss N, and Trettin C. 2006. The carbon balance of North American wetlands. Wetlands 26(4): 889-916.

[8] Kolka RK, Rabenhorst MC, and Swanson D. 2011. Histosols. Chapter 33.2. In P. M. Huang, Y. Li, and M. E. Sumner (Eds.) Handbook of Soil Sciences Properties and Processes, 2nd ed. CRC Press, Boca Raton, FL. pp. 33.8-33.29.

[9] Clymo RS. 1884. The limit to peat bog growth. Philosophical Transactions of the Royal Society London. Series B-Biological Science 303:605-654.

[10] Street LE, Mielke N, and Woodin SJ. 2018 Phosphorus availability determines the response of tundra ecosystem carbon stocks to nitrogen enrichment. Ecosystems 21:1155-1167. https:// doiI.org/10.1007/s10021-017-0209-x

[11] Sienkiewicz J, Porębska G, Ostrowska A, and Gozdowski D. 2019 Indicators of peat soil degradation in the Biebrza valley, Poland. Vol. 30 No 2(80):41-51 DOI 10.2478/oszn-2019-0009

[12] Turunen J, Roulet NT, and Moore TR. 2004: Nitrogen deposition and increased carbon accumulation in ombrotrophic peatlands in eastern Canada. Global Biogeochemical Cycles, 18: GB3002, doi: http://dx.doi.org/10.1029/2003GB002154.

[13] Qui C, Zhu D, Ciaia P, Guenet B, Peng S, Krinner G, Tootchi A, Ducharne A, and Hastie A. 2019. Moddelling northern peatland re and carbon dynamics with the ORCHIDEE-PEAT land surface model (SVN r5488). Geosci Model Dev. 12:2961-2982. https://doi.org//10.5194/gmd-12-2961-2019

[14] Rewcastle KE, Moore JAM, Henning JA, Mayes MA, Patternson CM, Wang G, Metcalfe DB, and Classen AT. 2020. Investigating drivers of microbial activity and respiration in a forested bog. Pedosphere 30:135-145.

[15] Fox TR. 1995. The influence of low-molecular-weight organic acids on properties and processes in forest soils. Pages 43-62. In Bigham JM (editor) Carbon forms and functions in forest soils. Soil Science Soc. America. Madison, WI.

[16] Herbert BE and Bertsch PM. 1995. Characterization of dissolved

and colloidal organic matter in soil solution. Pages 63-88. In Bigham JM (editor) Carbon forms and functions in forest soils. Soil Science Soc. America. Madison, WI.

[17] Kane ES, Mazzoleni LR, Kratz CJ, Hribljan JA, Johnson CP, Pypker TG, and Chimner R. 2014. Peat porewater dissolved organic carbon concentration and lability increasing with warming: a field temperature manipulation experiment in a poor-fen. Biogeochemistry 119:161-178.

[18] Aide MT, and Cwick GJ. 2002. Elemental distributions in eutric brunisols from the northern Glagial Lake Agassiz region of Manitoba. Transactions Missouri Academy Science 36: 49-54.

[19] Aide MT, Cwick GJ, and Cummings M. 1999. Clay mineralogy and potassium status of selected soils in the glacial Lake Agassiz region of central Manitoba. Canadian J Soil Science 79:141-148.

[20] Van Cleve K and Powers RF. 1995. Soil carbon, soil formation and ecosystem development. Pages 115-200. In Bigham JM (editor) Carbon forms and functions in forest soils. Soil Science Soc. America. Madison, WI.

[21] Dieleman CM, Lindo Z, McLaughlin JW, Craig AE, and Branfireun BA. 2016 Climate change effects on peatland decomposition and porewater dissolved organic carbon biogeochemistry. Biogeochemistry 128:385-396 DOI 10.1007/s10533-016-0214-8

[22] Euskirchen ES, Bret-Hart MS, Scott GJ, Edgar C, and Shaver GR. 2012: Seasonal patterns of carbon dioxide and water fluxes in three representative tundra ecosystems in northern Alaska. Ecosphere, 3: article 4, doi: http://dx.doi.org/10.1890/ES11-00202.1.

[23] Frokling S, Roulet NT, Tuittila E, Bubier JL, and Quillet A. 2010: A new model of Holocene peatland net primary production, decomposition, water balance and peat accumulation. Earth Systems Dynamics, 1, 1-21, 2010, doi:10.5194/esd-1-1-0210.

[24] McLaughin J, and Webster K. 2014 Effects of climate change on peatland in the far north of Ontario, Canada: a synthesis. Arctic, Antarctic, and Alpine research, Vol. 46, No. 1, 2014, pp. 84-102

[25] Schneider J, Ťupek B, Lukasheva M, Gudyrev V, Miglovets M, and Jungkunst H. 2018 Methane emissions from paludified boreal soils in European Russia as measured and modelled. Ecosystems 21:827-838 DOI: 10.1007/s10021-017-0188-y

[26] Sagerfors J, Lindroth A, Klemedtsson L, Weslien P, and Nilsson M. 2008: Annual CO2 exchange between a nutrient poor, minerotrophic, boreal mire and the atmosphere. Journal of Geophysical Research, 113: G01001, doi: http://dx.doi.org/10.1029/2006JG000306.

[27] Wickland KP, Striegl RG, Neff JC, and Sachs T. 2006: Effects of permafrost melting on CO2 and CH4 exchange of a poorly drained black spruce lowland. Journal of Geophysical Research, 111: G02011, doi: http://dx.doi.org/10.1029/2005JG000099.

[28] Ernakovich JG, Lynch LM, Brewer PE, Calderon FJ, and Wallenstein MD. 2017 Redox and temperature-sensitive changes in microbial communities and soil chemistry dictate greenhouse gas loss from thawed permafrost. Biogeochemistry 134:183-200 DOI 10.1007/s10533-017-0354-5

[29] Webster KL, Bhatti JS, Thompson DK, Nelson SA, Shaw, CH,

Bona KA, Hayne SL, and Kurz WA. 2018 Spatially-integrated estimates of net ecosystem exchange and methane fluxes from Canadian peatlands. Webster et al. Carbon Balance Manage 13:16 https://doi.org/10.1186/s13021-018-0105-5

[30] Shirokova LS, Pokrovsky OS, Kirpotin SN, Desmukh C, Pokrovsky BG, Audry S, and Viers J. 2013 Biogeochemistry of organic carbon, CO2, CH4, and trace elements in thermokarst water bodies in discontinuous permafrost zones of western Siberia. Biogeochemistry 113:573-593 DOI 10.1007/s10533-012-9790-4

[31] Jackowicz-Korczyski, M, Christensen TR, Bäckstrand K, Crill P, Friborg T, Mastepanov M, and Ström L. 2012: Annual cycle of methane emission from subarctic peatland. Journal of Geophysical Research, 115: G03009, doi: http://dx.doi.org/10.1029/2008JG000913.

[32] Fenner N, Freeman C, Lock MA, Harmens H, Reynolds B and Sparks T. 2007. Interactions between elevated CO2 and warming could amplify DOC exports from peatland catchments. Environ Sci and Technol 41: 3146-3152. Doi:10/1021/es061765v.

[33] Uda SK, hein L, and Sumarga E. 2017 Towards sustainable management of Indonesian tropical peatlands. Wetlands Ecol Manage 25:683-701 DOI 10.1007/s11273-017-9544-0

[34] Aurangojeb M, Klemedtsson L, Rütting T, He H, Weslien P, Banzhaf S, and Kasimir A. 2017 Nitrous oxide emissions from Norway spruce forests on drained organic and mineral soil. Can. J. For. Res. 47:1482-1487 dx.doi.org/10.1139/cjfr-2016-0541

[35] Leifeld J, Gubler L, and Grünig A. 2011 Organic matter losses from temperate ombrotrophic peatlands: an evaluation of the ash residue method. Plant Soil 341:349-361 DOI 10.1007/s11104-010-0649-y

[36] Ghaudharry N, Miller PA, and Smith B. 2018 Biotic and abiotic drivers of peatland growth and microtopography: a model demonstration. Ecosystems 21:1196-1214 https://doi.org/10.1007/s10021-017-0213-1

[37] O'Donnell JA, Aiken GR, Butler KD, Guillemette F, Podgorski DC, and Spencer RGM. 2016. DOM composition and transformation in boreal forest soils: The effects of temperature and organic-horizon decomposition state. J. Geophys. Res. Biogeosci. 121:2727-2744. Doi:1002/2016JG003431

[38] Wang C, Wu D, Kong Y, Li R, and Shi H. 2017 Changes of soil thermal and hydraulic regimes in northern hemisphere permafrost regions over the 21st century. Arctic, Antarctic, and Alpine Research, Vol. 49, No. 2, 2017, pp. 305-319 DOI: http://dx.doi.org/10.1657/AAAR0016-026

[39] Frost GV, Epstein HE, Walker DA, Matyshak G, and Ermokhina K. 2018 Seasonal and long-term changes to active-layer temperatures after tall shrubland expansion and succession in arctic tundra. Ecosystems 21:507-520 DOI: 10.1007/s10021-017-0165-5

[40] Glaser PH, Hansen BSC, Siegel DI, Reeve AS, and Morin PJ. 2004: Rates, pathways and drivers for peatland development in the Hudson Bay Lowlands, northern Ontario, Canada. Journal of Ecology, 92: 1036-1053.

[41] Beilman DW, MacDonald GM, Smith LC, and Reimer PJ. 2009: Carbon accumulation in peatlands of West Siberia over the last 2000 years. Global biogeochemical Cycles, 23: GB1012, doi: http://dx.doi.org/10.1029/2007GF003112

[42] Karofeld E, Müür M, and Vellak K. 2016 Factors affecting re-vegetation

dynamics of experimentally restored extracted peatland in Estonia. Environ Sci Pollut Res 23:13706-13717 DOI 10.1007/s11356-015-5396-4

[43] Miettinen J, Hooijer A, Wang J, Shi C, and Liew SC. 2012 peatland degradation and conversion sequences and interrelations in Sumatra. Reg Environ Change 12:729-737 DOI 10.1007/s10113-012-0290-9

[44] Swails E, Hertanti D, Hergoualc'h K, Verchot L, and Lawrence D. 2019 The response of soil respiration to climatic drivers in undrained forest and drained oil palm plantations in an Indonesian peatland. Biogeochemistry 142:37-51 https://doi.org/10.1007/s10533-018-0519-x

[45] Grzywna A. 2017 The degree of peatland subsidence resulting from drainage to land. Environ Earth Sci. 76:559 DOI 10.1007/s12665-017-6869-1

[46] Nicia P, Bejger R, Zadrożny P, and Sterzyńska M. The impact of restoration processes on the selected soil properties and organic matter transformation of mountain fens under Caltho-Alnetum community in the Babiogórski National Park in Outer Flysch Carpathians, Poland. Journal of Soils and Sediments 18:2770-2776 https://doi.org/10.1007/s11368-017-1909-8

[47] Richardson CJ. 2010 The everglades: North America's subtropical wetland. Wetlands Ecol Manage 18:517-542 DOI 10.1007/s11273-009-9156-4

[48] Adhikari K, Owens PR, Libohova Z, Miller DM, Wills SA, and Nemecek J. 2019. Assessing soil organic carbon stock of Wisconsin, USA and its fate under future land use and climate change. Sci Total Environ 667:833-845. Doi.org/10.1016/j.scitotenv.2019.02.420.

[49] Frazier, BE, and Lee GB. 1971. Characteristics and Classification of Three Wisconsin Histosols1. Soil Sci. Soc. Am. J. 35:776-780. doi:10.2136/sssaj1971.03615995003500050040x

[50] Bunbury J, Finkelstein SA, and Bollman J. 2012: Holocene hydroclimate and effects on carbon accumulation inferred for a peat bog in the Attawapiskat River watershed, Hudson Bay Lowlands, Canada. Quaternary Research, 78: 275-284.

[51] Kurhyr P. 2008: Palsa and peat plateau development in the Hudson Bay Lowlands, Canada: timing, pathways and causes. Boreas, 37: 316-327.

[52] Lafleur PM, Roulet NT, Bubier JL, Frolking S, and Moore TR. 2003: Interannual variability in the peatland-atmosphere carbon dioxide exchange at an ombrotrophic bog. Global Biogeochemical Cycles, 17: 1036, doi: http://dx.doi.org/10.1029/2002GB001983.

[53] Robinson SD. 2006: Carbon accumulation in peatlands, southwestern Northwest Territories, Canada. Canadian Journal of Soil Science, 86: 305-319.

[54] Webster, K. L., and McLaughlin, J. W., 2010: Importance of water table in controlling dissolved carbon along a fen nutrient gradient. Soil Science Society of America Journal, 74: 2254-2266.

[55] Wickland KP, Neff JC, Aiken GR. 2007. Dissolved organic carbon in Alaskan boreal forest: Sources, chemical characteristics, and biodegradability. Ecosystems 10:1323-1340. doi:10.1007/s10021-007-9101-4

Section 3

Climate Change

Chapter 12

Impact of Climate Change on Life

Hassan M. Heshmati

Abstract

Climate is changing in an accelerating pace. Climate change occurs as a result of an imbalance between incoming and outgoing radiation in the atmosphere. The global mean temperatures may increase up to 5.4°C by 2100. Climate change is mainly caused by humans, especially through increased greenhouse gas emissions. Climate change is recognized as a serious threat to ecosystem, biodiversity, and health. It is associated with alterations in the physical environment of the planet Earth. Climate change affects life around the globe. It impacts plants and animals, with consequences for the survival of the species. In humans, climate change has multiple deleterious consequences. Climate change creates water and food insecurity, increased morbidity/mortality, and population movement. Vulnerable populations (e.g., children, elderly, indigenous, and poor) are disproportionately affected. Personalized adaptation to the consequences of climate change and preventive measures are key challenges for the society. Policymakers must implement the appropriate strategies, especially in the vulnerable populations.

Keywords: climate change, global warming, ecosystem, animal survival, human health, vulnerable populations, adaptation, prevention

1. Introduction

Climate change has always happened on Earth but its rapid rate and important magnitude occurring now are of great concern. Climate change occurs as a result of an imbalance between incoming and outgoing radiation in the atmosphere. The global warming associated with climate change is different from past warming in its rate. It is anticipated that there will be a rise in global mean temperatures of up to 5.4°C by 2100. There is overwhelming evidence showing that human activities have contributed to climate change over the past century while changes in solar activity and volcanic eruptions have played a minor role. Over the last several decades, humans have engaged in large-scale transformation of natural systems causing a net accumulation of carbon dioxide in the atmosphere [1–5].

Climate change is recognized as a serious threat to ecosystem, biodiversity, and health. It is associated with alterations in the physical environment of the planet Earth and affects life around the globe [1–37].

Adaptation to the consequences of climate change and prevention of aggravation of climate change are key challenges for the society. Policymakers must implement personalized strategies, especially in the vulnerable populations [1, 2, 5, 30–32, 35–37].

IntechOpen

2. Climate

Climate, from Ancient Greek "klima" (meaning inclination), is defined as the weather averaged over a long period (the standard period is 30 years).

The instrumental record of climate change is based on thousands of temperature and precipitation recording stations around the world.

3. Climate change versus global warming

Climate change and global warming are often used interchangeably but have distinct meanings and refer to different physical phenomena. Climate change includes warming and side effects of warming (e.g., heavy precipitation and increased wind speeds) while global warming refers only to long-term Earth's rising global mean surface temperature.

4. Climate change causes

Climate change occurs as a result of an imbalance between incoming and outgoing radiation in the atmosphere. The increase in heat-trapping greenhouse gases (e.g., carbon dioxide, methane, and nitrous oxide) in the atmosphere raises Earth's mean surface temperature. The levels of greenhouse gases are higher now than at any time in the last 800,000 years. As temperature increases, more water evaporates from the oceans and other water sources into the atmosphere, causing further increase of the temperature [1–5].

Atmospheric carbon dioxide comes from two primary sources, natural and anthropogenic (human-induced). Natural sources of carbon dioxide include most animals which exhale carbon dioxide as a waste product. Anthropogenic sources of carbon dioxide have been primarily driven by human activities since the early 20th century (industrial revolution), mainly fossil fuel burning (e.g., burning coal, oil, and natural gas), but also agricultural emissions and deforestation. The top 5 countries responsible for emissions of carbon dioxide are China, United States of America (USA), India, Russia, and Japan [4]. In 2017, the USA emitted approximately 5.1 billion metric tons of energy-related carbon dioxide for a global worldwide emission of approximately 32.5 billion metric tons. Deforestation of the Amazon in Brazil (loss of the equivalent of almost one million soccer fields of forest cover each year), mainly for agricultural purposes, is significantly contributing to climate change.

5. Climate change consequences

Climate change causes a cascade of side effects for the physical environment of the planet Earth and the living organisms on the globe (**Figure 1**). All the changes in the physical planet Earth's environment affect the life of plants, animals, and humans. Coral reefs, forests, and coastal human communities are particularly vulnerable to climate change. Some of the effects of climate change may be through the enhancement of the susceptibility to chemical pollution [1–37].

Although most impacts of climate change are likely to be adverse, some health benefits may result in some regions. For example, warmer winters may reduce the number of temperature-related health events and death.

Figure 1.
Climate change causes global changes of the planet.

5.1 Physical planet Earth's environment

According to the core accretion theory, planet Earth formed around 4.54 billion years ago (approximately one-third the age of the universe) by accretion from the solar nebula [38].

Planet Earth has faced climate change throughout its long history. The current climate change has multiple negative impacts on the physical planet Earth's environment. It affects the frequency and severity of extreme events and natural disasters [1, 4, 6–13, 19].

5.1.1 Temperature

Temperature records from modern thermometers (with temperature scales) have been available only since early 18th century. By studying indirect parameters (chemical and structural signatures), scientists can infer past temperatures.

At the creation of the universe, the temperature of the universe at 10^{-35} second old was around 1 octillion°C. Within less than 2 minutes, the universe temperature cooled down to around 1 billion°C. Over at least the last several million years, planet Earth shifted between ice ages facing long cold periods (glacial) and warm periods (interglacial), on 100,000-year cycles.

The current climate change is associated with increased Earth's temperature (land surfaces and upper layers of the ocean) (**Figure 2**) [1, 4]. Land surfaces are heating faster than ocean surfaces. A warmer atmosphere can hold more water vapor, leading to increased overall average precipitation [4]. Over the past 70 years, the Earth's temperature has increased by approximately 0.7°C [4]. Since 1950, the number of cold days and nights has decreased while the number of warm days and nights has increased. Since 1976, the rate of warming has been greater than at any other time during the last 1,000 years. For any given period, there are extreme temperatures. In the past 20 years, Earth's lowest air temperature was −94.7°C (recorded in Antarctica in 2010) and hottest air temperature was 70.7°C (recorded in Iran's Lut Desert in 2005). The present global mean temperature is around 15.0°C. Currently, the surface temperatures are rising by approximately 0.2°C per decade [6]. According to the Intergovernmental Panel on Climate Change (IPCC) and based on different emissions scenarios, there will be a rise in global mean temperatures of 0.9 to 5.4°C by 2100 [4].

Figure 2.
Climate change is associated with increased Earth's temperature.

The rise in global mean temperature is not the same everywhere. There are regional variations in Earth's temperature. Some areas will not even get warmer and may actually get cooler in the short term [4]. Warming is more pronounced at higher latitudes. The North Pole and Northern Hemisphere have warmed much faster than the South Pole and Southern Hemisphere. Greater temperature increases are expected in winter compared to summer and in nighttime versus daytime. Springs occur earlier and winters are milder.

5.1.2 Mountain glaciers and lakes

Climate change causes mountain glaciers to melt and accelerates the rate of ice loss on Earth in Greenland and Antarctica (**Figure 3**). Some glaciers are sites of

Figure 3.
Climate change causes melting of mountain glaciers.

powerful sacred and symbolic meanings for local communities (e.g., in the Peruvian Andes, the Nepalese Himalayas, and the Chinese Meili Snow Mountains) [7].

Lakes around the world are freezing less and for a shorter duration. In few decades, thousands of lakes may lose their winter ice cover.

5.1.3 Sea levels

Climate change triggers rise in sea levels. The sea levels rise following either an increase in the volume of the water already in the ocean as water warms and expands or an increase in the mass of the water in the ocean mainly due to melting glaciers [4]. Since 1900, global mean sea level has increased by approximately 0.20 meter [4]. Over the last 25 years, the global mean see level rose on average by 0.003 meter per year [8]. By 2100, based on different emissions scenarios, sea levels are predicted to rise between 0.40 and 1.50 meters [4]. The sea-level rise will lead to disappearance of some islands and flooding with invasion of cities by water, leading to homelessness and population movement (**Figure 4**).

The salty ocean water will challenge native plants and animals to adapt to the changing conditions. For humans, it causes salination of freshwater supplies and loss of productive farmlands [8]. Low-income countries (e.g., Bangladesh) are particularly impacted.

Figure 4.
Climate change triggers rise in sea levels.

5.1.4 Hurricanes and rainstorms

Climate change promotes more dangerous hurricanes and heavier rainstorms due to warmer ocean water temperature (**Figure 5**) [4, 9]. The proportion of Category 4 and 5 hurricanes has increased at a rate of 25–30% per 1.0°C of global warming [9]. Hurricane Katrina (Category 5, New Orleans, USA, 2005) was one of the deadliest hurricanes in recent USA history. The total number of direct or indirect fatalities following hurricane Katrina was 1,833 (reports from state and local officials in five states). The 2019 North Atlantic hurricane season had six hurricanes (including three major hurricanes, e.g., Category 3 or higher).

Figure 5.
Climate change promotes more dangerous hurricanes.

5.1.5 Wildfires

Climate change causes more frequent wildfires. The dry, hot weather has increased the intensity and destructiveness of forest fires in several countries (e.g., Brazil, USA, and Australia) (**Figure 6**) [10, 11]. Wildfires can cause deforestation, serious property damage, exposure of large populations to prolonged periods of polluted and toxic air with potential health impacts (e.g., respiratory diseases), and death. Amazon (Brazil) has become more flammable and vulnerable to wildfires during recent droughts [10]. California (USA) has experienced devastating autumn wildfires in recent years [11]; over 100 fatalities were directly attributed to the most destructive and deadliest wildfires that occurred in 2017 and 2018.

Figure 6.
Climate change causes more frequent wildfires.

5.1.6 Droughts

Drought is a complex and multivariate phenomenon influenced by diverse physical and biological processes. Drought is among the most expensive natural disasters. Climate change is responsible for more frequent and severe droughts (especially in subtropical regions), promoting the expansion of deserts (**Figure 7**) [4, 12]. This will lead to misery, hunger, starvation, and population movement.

Figure 7.
Climate change is responsible for more frequent and severe droughts.

5.1.7 Ocean acidity

The ocean provides most of the life-supporting environment on planet Earth. The abundance of carbon dioxide in the atmosphere is causing the surface waters of the oceans to become more acidic as some carbon dioxide dissolves into ocean water forming carbonic acid [4]. Ocean acidification can alter marine ecosystems with damage to coral reefs (source of many benefits for human communities), fish, and other aquatic species [4, 13].

5.2 Plants

Climate change impacts plant phenology. Different climate change components are involved including atmospheric carbon dioxide level, temperature, sea level, rainfall, weeds, and pests or microbes [14–19].

5.2.1 Survival

Plant survival is affected by climate change (**Figure 8**) [14–16]. The increased land surface temperature with the resulting mild winters promoting pest proliferation (e.g., allowing more pine beetles to survive), the invasion of farmlands by salty water, the wildfires, and the droughts compromise life of plants and lead to destruction of forests and damage to human agriculture. According to some reports,

Figure 8.
Climate change challenges plant survival.

agriculture is the most endangered activity adversely affected by climate change. The decreased farming activity will lead to food insecurity.

5.2.2 Blooming, pollination, and fructification

Plant growth, blooming, pollination, and fructification are impacted by climate change [17–19]. With the occurrence of shorter winters and warmer springs, plants bloom earlier for a shorter period and die younger (**Figure 9**). Winter chill is essential for several fruit-producing trees. Insufficient chilling due to climate change can affect the productivity of fruit trees (e.g., less fruits, smaller fruits, and changes in color, texture, and taste of fruits) [17, 18]. Around 75% of the production of seeds and fruits for human consumption depend on pollinators. Pollinators, especially bees, are facing unprecedented challenges for survival. With the lack of synchrony between plants and pollinators due to shift in seasons and the decline in the number of pollinators, the production of fruits is decreasing while the cost is significantly increasing.

Figure 9.
Climate change is responsible for earlier blooming time of plants.

5.3 Animals

Climate change exposes animals to a variety of stressors, influencing metabolic and endocrine functions, with potential consequences for the survival of species [14, 20–28]. With climate change, more animal species are going extinct every year. Approximately 700 mammals and birds are impacted. The degree of vulnerability varies by the type of animal and different species will be affected in different ways. Species with low tolerance for rising temperature are vulnerable to extinction. The vulnerable/endangered animals include polar bears, koalas, elephants, sea turtles, cheetahs, panda bears, and penguins (non-exhaustive list).

Species affected by climate change will either need to move to more suitable locations (e.g., higher elevations and latitudes) or to adapt to changes at their current locations (e.g., habitat, feeding and breeding patterns). If unable, they may perish and become extinct.

5.3.1 Habitat

Climate change can cause habitat degradation or loss for several species (e.g., polar bears, koalas, and birds). Polar bears are dependent on sea ice. The increased temperature is causing the arctic sea ice to melt, damaging the polar bears' habitat (**Figure 10**) [23]. Koalas are dependent on eucalyptus tree. The increased temperature and drought are causing wildfire, destroying the koalas' habitat [24]. Lake Urmia (Iran) is a bird habitat and used to be a popular tourist destination. The lake is drying up mainly because of climate change.

Figure 10.
Climate change causes loss of habitat for polar bear.

5.3.2 Nutrition

Survival of species can be affected by water/food availability/quality beyond those that species can tolerate. Unpredictability/shortage of water and food caused by climate change may lead to greater prevalence of torpor and hibernation in small mammals and hypometabolism in large mammals.

Polar bears will have trouble finding food as the sea ice thins and melts earlier. With limited food supply, the polar bears rely on their stored fat. They have to swim longer distances in the water and many young cubs die because of their inability to swim. Koalas' main food source is eucalyptus leaves. Each koala eats approximately 1 kg of eucalyptus leaves per day. Climate change reduces the amount of water in the eucalyptus tree. The increased carbon dioxide level causes decrease protein levels in the tree affecting plant nutritional quality. All these changes create dehydration, malnutrition, and starvation. Koalas are risking their lives by climbing down from their trees in search of water and food. This leaves them vulnerable to predators and the risk of being hit by cars. Koalas' population has declined by more than 30% over their last three generations (**Figure 11**) [24]. Elephants require 150–300 liters of water per day for drinking in addition to the amount needed for bathing and playing. Droughts can cause population decline (**Figure 12**) [25].

Figure 11.
Climate change is responsible for dehydration and malnutrition of koala.

Figure 12.
Climate change causes decline in elephant population.

5.3.3 Migration, breeding, and gender determination

Warmer springs have promoted advanced timing of migration and breeding in most avian species in the last decades (**Figure 13**) [26]. Rising sea levels threaten the sea turtle eggs as most turtles lay their eggs on beaches. Climate change can affect sex determination in several animals [27, 28]. The sex of the sea turtles is determined by the nest temperatures. Cool temperatures produce more males while warm temperatures produce more females. Climate change alters the sea turtles' gender population (females outnumbering males). Certain areas could end up producing only female turtles, with the possibility of local species extinction since there will be no mating partners for female turtles (**Figure 14**).

Figure 13.
Climate change promotes early avian migration.

Figure 14.
Climate change leads to female sea turtle overpopulation and domination.

5.4 Humans

Climate change is a major threat to human existence. It has multiple deleterious health consequences leading to increased morbidity and mortality [1–3, 5, 8, 29–37].

5.4.1 Temperature

The human core temperature averages 37.0°C and is tightly controlled within a range of 33.2°C and 38.2°C to ensure optimal physiological function. Extreme deviations from the normal core temperature, i.e., a decrease below 27.0°C (hypothermia) or an increase above 42.0°C (hyperthermia) can be fatal [5]. Climate change is resulting in increased exposures to intense heat in many parts of the world. With increase temperature, there are physiological reactions in humans creating risks for some organs and exposing individuals to increased morbidity and mortality (e.g., reduced performance and work productivity, behavioral changes, heat exhaustion, heat stroke, respiratory failure, myocardial infarction, stroke, and death) (**Figure 15**) [5, 29–31]. The reduced work productivity (up to 10% in some hot areas) has large economic consequences. Without adaptation, the economic losses of reduced work productivity could be more than 20% of the gross domestic product by 2100. Children, elderly people, poor people, outdoor workers, workers required to wear protective clothing and/or personal protective equipment, and subjects with chronic health conditions are at higher risk when facing heat stress. In the USA, the annual heat-related death is approximately 1,500. The European heat wave during the summer of 2003 caused as many as 70,000 deaths.

On the upside, increased temperatures by allowing milder winters can lower the incidence and mortality of some winter-related events such as myocardial infarction and stroke. Also, hotter and drier conditions can reduce the incidence of some infectious diseases (e.g., malaria).

Figure 15.
Climate change through heat wave can cause increased morbidity and mortality.

5.4.2 Nutrition

Climate change creates water and food insecurity/shortage with significant impact on hygiene, nutrition, and food safety in several countries (**Figure 16**) [1, 8, 32, 33]. In the absence of proper desalination of drinking water impacted by increased salinity following sea-level rise (especially in low-income countries like Bangladesh), the high exposure to salt through drinking water, food, and bathing can lead to several health problems (e.g., hypertension and skin diseases) [8]. In many regions, food production systems are negatively impacted by climate change [1]. According to the International Rice Research Institute in the Philippines, 1.0°C rise in night-time temperature can reduce rice yields by 10%. With the ocean temperature rise, several fish populations may move to higher latitudes, affecting dietary protein supplies of millions of people.

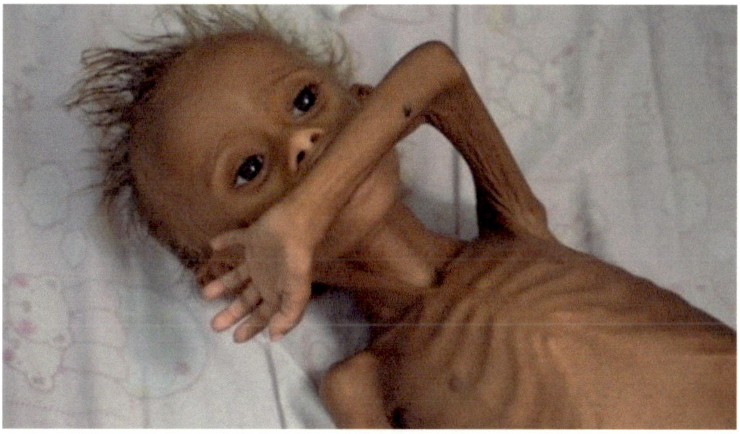

Figure 16.
Climate change can create human undernutrition.

5.4.3 Infection

Climate change through variations in temperature, precipitation/humidity, wind, and solar radiation influences the spread of some infectious diseases since these variations may impact the survival, reproduction, and distribution of disease pathogens and vectors/hosts as well as their transmission environment. Several infectious diseases are involved including malaria, dengue, and Lyme disease (**Figure 17**) [3, 34].

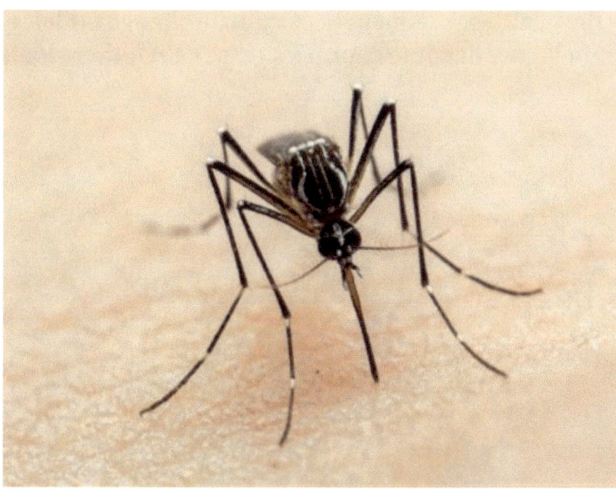

Figure 17.
Climate change favors spread of infectious diseases.

5.4.4 Population movement

Climate change by creating unsuitable living conditions (e.g., desertification, sea-level rise, decline in freshwater availability, food shortage, health issues) will move many people (forced displacement, planned resettlement, migration). Poor communities are particularly impacted by the human movement. It is estimated that by 2050, up to several hundred million persons will be moved (**Figure 18**) [32]. Population movement will expose countries to multiple challenges (e.g., social, health, and financial consequences and violent conflicts).

Figure 18.
Climate change causes population movement.

5.4.5 Vulnerable populations

Overall, children, elderly, indigenous groups, poor individuals, outdoor workers, remote populations, and subjects with pre-existing conditions are disproportionately affected by climate change (**Figure 19**) [1, 2, 5, 30–32, 35–37].

Low-income and geographically vulnerable countries (e.g., Bangladesh) are most affected by the health consequences of climate change (at least in its earlier stages). However, in higher-income countries (e.g., USA), there is also a high

Figure 19.
Climate change disproportionately impacts vulnerable populations.

vulnerability in some ethnic and socio-economic groups as demonstrated by the Chicago heatwave of 1995 and the New Orleans hurricane Katrina of 2005. According to the World Health Organization, the global mortality in 2004 as a result of climate change was around 141,000 of which 85% were children. The mortality of the European heat wave of 2003 affected mainly the elderly.

6. Climate change adaptation in animals

Adaptive evolution of phenotypes to climate change has been the subject of several investigations [26, 39].

Animals react to climate change in three ways: to move, to adapt, or to die. Moving to a new territory is not always a simple solution and can create new challenges (e.g., interaction with unfamiliar species and more competition for food).

Some animals can adapt to changing conditions. An interesting example of adaptation to climate change is the case of polar bears. With the change in climate, polar bears who usually used seal pubs and other marine mammals as food, have started hunting animals available on land (e.g., snow geese and caribou). However, there is no proof that the change in diet can support the polar bear population in the long run. Another example of adaptation to climate change is with migrating birds. As spring arrives earlier, insects emerge earlier. Some migrating birds are laying their eggs earlier to match insect availability for their young.

7. Climate change adaptive and preventive strategies

Adaptation to deleterious consequences of climate change and prevention of aggravation of climate change are important components of the global response of the society [1–3, 5, 16, 18, 31, 32, 35–37, 40].

Adaptation (spontaneous or planned) is especially important in developing countries. Policymakers must implement personalized adaptive strategies, especially in the vulnerable populations. The risk control to population health cannot be implemented efficiently at the local level alone. It requires coordinated international policy. Human beings rely on biodiversity and functioning ecosystems for water, food, and health. If other species are unable to adapt to climate change, the consequences for humans could be extremely serious. Adaptive strategies require investment and skills. Society needs to implement strategies to help wildlife adapt to the impacts of climate change (e.g., wildlife overpass and drinking stations). Identification of traits contributing to resilience and vulnerability of species will allow the development of efficient conservation action plans.

Prevention (long-term strategies) is a key approach. To spare species and protect humans, the greenhouse gas emissions should be reduced as soon as possible. If we drastically reduce greenhouse gas emissions, our climate may reach a new and potentially acceptable equilibrium. Development and deployment of low-carbon energy technologies, policies to reduce fossil fuel burning, forest preservation, and reforestation should be promoted. Carbon sequestration, by capturing and storing atmospheric carbon dioxide, can decrease the amount of carbon dioxide in the atmosphere and reduce climate change. More energy-efficient homes and vehicles using alternative energies from sun, wind, and waves are needed. Increased use of public transportation, cycling, and walking should be promoted. It is also helpful if humans could reduce the consumption of animal-based food (red meat) and switch to plant-based diet (fruits and vegetables). This type of dietary change can have multiple health, environmental, and economic benefits.

Numerous countries work together under the umbrella of the United Nations Framework Convention on Climate Change. The recommendation of the IPCC is to keep the global warming below 1.5°C to avoid irreversible damages. Unfortunately, in some countries, extensive political lobbying denying the contribution of humans to climate change and creating political barrier to pro-environmental policies has emerged. In 2015, all United Nations countries negotiated the Paris Agreement aiming to keep global warming well below 2.0°C [41]. Almost all countries signed the treaty. However, in 2017, the USA decided to withdraw from the Paris Agreement.

8. Climate change cost

Climate change, through its multiple consequences, has a very high cost for the society and significantly affects the economic growth.

The estimates of total direct damage of hurricane Katrina were up to $125 billion and the cost of California wildfires of 2017 and 2018 exceeded $40 billion. It is estimated that the cost of climate change for USA economy can reach hundreds of billions of dollars a year by 2090.

Adaptive and preventive strategies need important financial investments. The cost of halting global warming and reducing greenhouse gas emission to very low levels by 2050 will be around $50 trillion. At the current greenhouse gas emission rate, the budget for keeping the global warming below 1.5°C would be exhausted by 2028.

9. Climate change and future of life on planet Earth

Climate change is a serious threat for our planet. The number of relatively undisturbed ecosystems is decreasing rapidly. Climate change seriously affects the viability of many plant and animal species, and human health. Climate change may become one of the major drivers of species extinction in the 21st century.

The Intergovernmental Science-Policy Platform on Biodiversity and Ecosystem Services (IPBES) releases regular reports on biodiversity written by hundreds of experts from all regions of the world. The reports found that biodiversity is declining in every region of the world, endangering economies, livelihoods, food security, and quality of life. In the words of the IPBES chair, "the time for action was yesterday or the day before".

According to scientists, we have approximately a decade to keep carbon dioxide from reaching catastrophic levels that can cause irreversible damages. If no efficient preventive action is undertaken, by the year 2050, 15 to 37% of existing plant and animal species are predicted to become extinct and by the year 2100, half of all species may experience extinction.

10. Conclusions

It is widely accepted that the climate is changing in an accelerating pace. Climate change is affecting every aspect of life. It is recognized as a serious threat to ecosystem, biodiversity, and health.

Adaptation to health consequences of climate change and prevention of aggravation of climate change are key challenges for the society. The health sector should promote research, education (for health personnel), and information (for public and policymakers) on climate change and its consequences.

Adaptation requires multiple measures at various levels. Policymakers must implement personalized adaptive strategies, especially in the vulnerable populations.

Climate change impacts can be mitigated by reducing greenhouse gas emissions and by enhancing the capacity of Earth's land surface to absorb greenhouse gases from the atmosphere. Long-term investment in renewable energy and energy efficiency is urgently needed.

Conflict of interest

The author declares no conflict of interest.

Author details

Hassan M. Heshmati
Endocrinology Metabolism Consulting, LLC, Anthem, AZ, USA

*Address all correspondence to: hassanheshmati@yahoo.com

IntechOpen

© 2020 The Author(s). Licensee IntechOpen. This chapter is distributed under the terms of the Creative Commons Attribution License (http://creativecommons.org/licenses/by/3.0), which permits unrestricted use, distribution, and reproduction in any medium, provided the original work is properly cited.

References

[1] McMichael AJ, Lindgren E. Climate change: Present and future risks to health, and necessary responses. Journal of Internal Medicine. 2011;**270**:401-413. DOI: 10.1111/j.1365-2796.2011.02415.x

[2] McMichael AJ. Globalization, climate change, and human health. The New England Journal of Medicine. 2013;**368**:1335-1343. DOI: 10.1056/NEJMra1109341

[3] Wu X, Lu Y, Zhou S, Chen L, Xu B. Impact of climate change on human infectious diseases: Empirical evidence and human adaptation. Environment International. 2016;**86**:14-23. DOI: 10.1016/j.envint.2015.09.007

[4] Hsiang S, Kopp RE. An economist's guide to climate change science. Journal of Economic Perspectives. 2018;**32**:3-32. DOI: 10.1257/jep.32.4.3

[5] Ahima RS. Global warming threatens human thermoregulation and survival. The Journal of Clinical Investigation. 2020;**130**:559-561. DOI: 10.1172/JCI135006

[6] Sobrino JA, Julien Y, García-Monteiro S. Surface temperature of the planet Earth from satellite data. Remote Sensing. 2020;**12**:218. DOI: 10.3390/rs12020218

[7] Allison EA. The spiritual significance of glaciers in an age of climate change. WIREs Climate Change. 2015;**6**:493-508. DOI: 10.1002/wcc.354

[8] Vineis P, Chan Q, Khan A. Climate change impacts on water salinity and health. Journal of Epidemiology and Global Health. 2011;**1**:5-10. DOI: 10.1016/j.jegh.2011.09.001

[9] Holland G, Bruyère CL. Recent intense hurricane response to global climate change. Climate Dynamics. 2014;**42**:617-627. DOI: 10.1007/s00382-013-1713-0

[10] Brando P, Macedo M, Silvério D, et al. Amazon wildfires: Scenes from a foreseeable disaster. Flora. 2020;**268**:151609. DOI: 10.1016/j.flora.2020.151609

[11] Goss M, Swain DL, Abatzoglou JT, et al. Climate change is increasing the likelihood of extreme autumn wildfire conditions across California. Environmental Research Letters. 2020;**15**:094016. DOI: 10.1088/1748-9326/ab83a7

[12] Cook BI, Mankin JS, Anchukaitis KJ. Climate change and drought: From past to future. Current Climate Change Reports. 2018;**4**:164-179. DOI: 10.1007/s40641-018-0093-2

[13] Hoegh-Guldberg O, Poloczanska ES, Skirving W, Dove S. Coral reef ecosystems under climate change and ocean acidification. Frontiers in Marine Science. 2017;**4**:158. DOI: 10.3389/fmars.2017.00158

[14] Wiens JJ. Climate-related local extinctions are already widespread among plant and animal species. PLOS Biology. 2016;**14**:e2001104. DOI: 10.1371/journal.pbio2001104

[15] Karimi V, Karami E, Keshavarz M. Climate change and agriculture: Impacts and adaptive responses in Iran. Journal of Integrative Agriculture. 2018;**17**:1-15. DOI: 10.1016/S2095-3119(17)61794-5

[16] Raza A, Razzaq A, Mehmood SS, et al. Impact of climate change on crops adaptation and strategies to tackle its outcome: A review. Plants. 2019;**8**:34. DOI: 10.3390/plants8020034

[17] Rai R, Joshi S, Roy S, Singh O, Samir M, Chandra A. Implications

of changing climate on productivity of temperate fruit crops with special reference to apple. Journal of Horticulture. 2015;**2**:1000135. DOI: 10.4172/2376-0354.1000135

[18] Houston L, Capalbo S, Seavert C, Dalton M, Bryla D, Sagili R. Specialty fruit production in the Pacific Northwest: Adaptation strategies for a changing climate. Climatic Change. 2018;**146**:159-171. DOI: 10.1007/s10584-017-1951-y

[19] De LC. Impact of climate change on floriculture and landscape gardening. International Journal of Agriculture Sciences. 2018;**10**:6253-6256

[20] Jenssen BM. Endocrine-disrupting chemicals and climate change: A worst-case combination for arctic marine mammals and seabirds. Environmental Health Perspectives. 2006;**114**(Suppl 1):76-80. DOI: 10.1289/ehp.8057

[21] Noyes PD, Lema SC. Forecasting the impacts of chemical pollution and climate change interactions on the health of wildlife. Current Zoology. 2015;**61**:669-689

[22] Fuller A, Maloney SK, Blache D, Cooper C. Endocrine and metabolic consequences of climate change for terrestrial mammals. Current Opinion in Endocrine and Metabolic Research. 2020;**11**:9-14. DOI: 10.1016/j.coemr.2019.12.003

[23] Wilson RR, Regehr EV, Rode KD, St Martin M. Invariant polar bear habitat selection during a period of sea ice loss. Proceedings of the Royal Society B. 2016;**283**:20160380. DOI: 10.1098/rspb.2016.0380

[24] Narayan EJ, Williams M. Understanding the dynamics of physiological impacts of environmental stressors on Australian marsupials, focus on the koala (*Phascolarctos cinereus*). 2016;**1**:2. DOI: 10.1186/s40850-016-0004-8

[25] Ngcobo JN, Nedambale TL, Nephawe KA, Sawosz E, Chwalibog A. The future survival of African elephants: Implications for conservation. International Journal of Avian & Wildlife Biology. 2018;**3**:379-384. DOI: 10.15406/ijawb.2018.03.00123

[26] Charmantier A, Gienapp P. Climate change and timing of avian breeding and migration: Evolutionary versus plastic changes. Evolutionary Applications. 2014;**7**:15-28. DOI: 10.1111/eva.12126

[27] DeCourten BM, Brander SM. Combined effects of increased temperature and endocrine disrupting pollutants on sex determination, survival, and development across generations. Scientific Reports. 2017;**7**:9310. DOI: 10.1038/s41598-017-09631-1

[28] Jensen MP, Allen CD, Eguchi T, et al. Environmental warming and feminization of one of the largest sea turtle populations in the world. Current Biology. 2018;**28**:154-159. DOI: 10.1016/j.cub.2017.11.057

[29] Huang C, Barnett AG, Wang X, Vaneckova P, FitzGerald G, Tong S. Projecting future heat-related mortality under climate change scenarios: A systematic review. Environmental Health Perspectives. 2011;**119**:1681-1690. DOI: 10.1289/ehp.1103456

[30] Lundgren K, Kuklane K, Gao C, Holmér I. Effects of heat stress on working populations when facing climate change. Industrial Health. 2013;**51**:3-15

[31] Kjellstrom T, Briggs D, Freyberg C, Lemke B, Otto M, Hyatt O. Heat, human performance, and occupational health: A key issue for the assessment

of global climate change impacts. Annual Review of Public Health. 2016;**37**:97-112. DOI: 10.1146/annurev-publhealth-032315-021740

[32] McMichael C, Barnett J, McMichael AJ. An III wind? Climate change, migration, and health. Environmental Health Perspectives. 2012;**120**:646-654. DOI: 10.1289/ehp.1104375

[33] Lake IR, Hooper L, Abdelhamid A, et al. Climate change and food security: Health impacts in developed countries. Environmental Health Perspectives. 2012;**120**:1520-1526. DOI: 10.1289/ehp.1104424

[34] Liang L, Gong P. Climate change and human infectious diseases: A synthesis of research findings from global and spatio-temporal perspectives. Environment International. 2017;**103**:99-108. DOI: 10.1016/j.envint.2017.03.011

[35] Sheffield PE, Landrigan PJ. Global climate change and children's health: Threats and strategies for prevention. Environmental Health Perspectives. 2011;**119**:291-298. DOI: 10.1289/ehp.1002233

[36] Ford JD. Indigenous health and climate change. American Journal of Public Health. 2012;**102**:1260-1266. DOI: 10.2105/AJPH.2012.300752

[37] Lesnikowski AC, Ford JD, Berrang-Ford L, Paterson JA, Barrera M, Heymann SJ. Adapting to health impacts of climate change: A study of UNFCCC Annex I parties. Environmental Research Letters. 2011;**6**:044009. DOI: 10.1088/1748-9326/6/4/044009

[38] Co'Neill HS. The origin of the moon and the early history of the earth – A chemical model. Part 2: The earth. Geochimica et Cosmochimica Acta. 1991;**55**:1159-1172

[39] Merilä J, Hendry AP. Climate change, adaptation, and phenotypic plasticity: The problem and the evidence. Evolutionary Applications. 2014;**7**:1-14. DOI: 10.1111/eva.12137

[40] Springmann M, Godfray HCJ, Rayner M, Scarborough P. Analysis and valuation of the health and climate change cobenefits of dietary change. PNAS. 2016;**113**:4146-4151. DOI: 10.1073/pnas.1523119113

[41] Dimitrov RS. The Paris Agreement on climate change: Behind closed doors. Global Environmental Politics. 2016;**16**:1-11. DOI: 10.1162/GLEP_a_00361

Chapter 13

Climate Change Implications to High and Low Potential Zones of Tanzania

Msafiri Yusuph Mkonda

Abstract

This chapter presents the findings from a literature review distinguishing the levels of vulnerability and resilience between the people who live in high potential zone areas and low potential zone areas. High potential zones are natural-resourced areas, while low potential zones are less-resourced areas. The refereed resources include fertile soil, water sources, vegetation, and landscape just to mention a few. Predictions from global circulation models confirm that global warming will have substantial impacts to biodiversity and agricultural systems in the most developing countries, including Tanzania. These impacts are severe, significant, and more pronounced in low potential zones where the poor people always dwell. High potential zones are less vulnerable to these impacts due to resources endowments. These impacts are mainly exacerbated by anthropogenic activities like overgrazing, burning of the ecosystem, and monoculture to mention a few. The increase in stress to the already affected areas increases the vulnerability of the poor and thus squeezing the threshold of livelihood options. This chapter focuses on climate change and biodiversity (i.e., soil, landscape, and vegetation) and agricultural biodiversity for climate change adaptations. Therefore, coping and adaptation strategies, particularly economic and technological adaptations, are relented as they significantly reduce the vulnerability of the livelihoods.

Keywords: adaptation, agriculture, biodiversity, climate change, high and low potential zones, Tanzania, vulnerability

1. Introduction

This chapter aimed at viewing the differences in vulnerability levels between the people living in high potential zones and those living in low potential zones [1, 2]. The vulnerability refereed is that caused by stress and shocks caused by the impacts of climate change [3]. The global weather change has determined the livelihood setups in most developing countries [4]. In the countries with varied ecological gradients and agroecological zones, we expect diverse impacts in the livelihood systems [5]. Tanzania has seven agroecological zones with different soils, rainfalls, temperatures, vegetations, locations, and altitudes just to mention a few [6]. Some of these zones are endowed with diverse natural resources (high potential zones) like fertile soil, water sources, and favorable climate to mention a few, while other zones are poorly endowed (low potential zones). Therefore, the people in diverse zones have different entitlements. Their responses to stress are varied depending on the livelihood assets

IntechOpen

and vulnerability [7]. In this aspect, vulnerability may refer to lack of asset to absorb shocks and recover from stress. Some of these assets include human, capital, physical, and technology just to mention few. Over the past two decades, most marginal areas (low potential areas) have been experiencing regular food insecurity due to poor crop yields [8]. This situation has been exacerbated by the rainfall variability, that is, change in seasons, erratic rainfalls, and increased droughts, which affects agricultural systems and reduces crop yields. According to Afifi et al. [9], climate change contributes up to 80% of crop failure in most vulnerable agricultural systems in Tanzania.

Since the 1990s, a number of wealth research findings have been done in Tanzania to address climate change impacts and its vulnerability. Among these studies are the following: Ahmed et al. [1], Paavola [3], Rowhani et al. [4], Yanda [5], Agrawala et al. [2], Mkonda and He [8], and Afifi et al. [9]. Despite addressing the temporal and spatial variability of climate change, most of these studies have limited focus on the ground exploration between the people living in low potential zones and those in high potential zones. The studies generally execute on how these impacts affect livelihoods but with little magnitudes on the comparison between groups. Climate change is expected to affect African countries in a variety of ways. For example, temperatures in Tanzania and the whole East African region are expected to rise by between 2 and 4°C by 2100, thus shifting agroecological zones in most areas [5, 10]. However, the impacts will be more pronounced in the already affected areas, especially in the semiarid agroecological zones and other marginal areas.

Predictions from global circulation models confirm that global warming will have a substantial impact on biodiversity and agricultural systems in Tanzania [11]. The changing weather patterns such as less predictable seasons, increasing events of erratic rainfall, and prolonged drought will stress on the already stressed areas and will threaten the sustainability of agriculture and food security in most parts of Tanzania [12]. Tanzanian rainfall is predicted to increase in areas with bimodal rainfall pattern from 5 to 45%, while decreasing in those with unimodal rainfall patterns from 5 to 15% [4, 13].

The vulnerability is going to increase in areas experiencing decreased rainfall, thus affecting livelihood systems of the dwellers [14, 15]. Soil replenishment through organic matter decomposition cannot simply take place in these areas [16]. Some areas with increasing rainfall may experience temporary floods and loss of soil fertility through leaching and runoff [5]. Under normal conditions, most of the poor people are squeezed in low potential zones due to entitlement failure [17]. As a livelihood strategy, some of these people living in marginal areas migrate to other areas.

They migrate (some with their herds of cattle) to areas with suitable agricultural systems and economic diversification [6, 18–20]. A good example is Usangu valleys (alluvial plain agroecological zone) which act as a destination of different people, especially pastoralists from other region with stressed environments.

Although the impacts of climate change have been globally established, there is a need to assess the magnitude of these effects in local conditions and diverse ecological gradients. Therefore, this chapter establishes the differential resiliences to climate impacts based on high and low potential zones. This will even enable climate practitioners and policy analysts to estimate the level of adjustments needed to curb climate impacts [21].

2. Location

Tanzania is located on the eastern coast of Africa, south of the equator, between latitudes 1° 00′ S and 11° 48′ S and longitudes 29° 30′ E and 39°45′. The eastern side of Tanzania is a coastline of about 800 km long marking the western side of

DOI: http://dx.doi.org/10.5772/intechopen.93384

Zone	Sub-zones	Soil and topography	Altitude	Rainfall (mm/yr)	G/season
1. Coast	North: Tanga (except Lushoto), Coast, and Dares Salaam	Infertile sands on gently rolling uplands Alluvial soils in Rufuji sand and infertile soils	Under 3000 m	North: bimodal, 750–1200 mm	North: October–December and March–June
	South: eastern Lindi and Mtwara (except Makonde plateau)	Fertile clays on uplands and river flood plains		South: unimodal, 800–1200 mm	South: December–April
2. Arid lands	North: Serengeti, Ngorogoro Parks, and part of Masailand	North: volcanic ash and sediments. Soils are variable in texture and very susceptible to water erosion	North: 1300–1800 m	North: unimodal, unreliable, 500–600 mm	March–May
	Masai Steppe, Tarangire Park, Mkomazi Reserve, Pangani, and Eastern Dodoma	South: rolling plains of low fertility susceptible to water erosion Pangani river flood plain with saline and alkaline soil	South: 500–1500 m	South: unimodal and unreliable, 400–600 mm	
3. Semiarid lands	Central Dodoma, Singida, Northern Iringa, some of Arusha, and Shinyanga	Central: undulating plains with rocky hills and low scarps. Well-drained soils with low fertility. Alluvial hardpan and saline soils in eastern rift valley and Lake Eyasi Black cracking soils in Shinyanga	Central: 1000–1500 m	Central: unimodal and unreliable: 500–800 mm	December–March
	Southern: Morogoro (except Kiliombero and Wami Basins and Uluguru Mts.) and also Lindi and Southwest Mtwara	Southern: flat or undulating plains with rocky hills, moderate fertile loams and clays in South (Morogoro), and infertile sand soils in center	Southeastern: 200–600 m	Southeastern: unimodal: 600–800 mm	
4. Plateaux	Western: Tabora, Rukwa (north and center), and Mbeya	Western: wide sandy plains and rift valley scarps	800–1500 m	Western: unimodal, 800–1000 mm	November–April
	North: Kigoma, part of Mara	Flooded swamps of Malagarasi and Ugalla rivers have clay soil with high fertility			
	Southern: Ruvuma and Southern Morogoro	Southern: upland plains with rock hills Clay soils of low to moderate fertility in south, and infertile sands in north		Southern: unimodal, very reliable, 900–1300 mm	

Zone	Sub-zones	Soil and topography	Altitude	Rainfall (mm/yr)	G/season
5. Southern and western highlands	Southern: a broad ridge from N. Morogoro to N. Lake Nyasa, covering part of Iringa, Mbeya	Southern: undulating plains to dissected hills and mountains. Moderately fertile clay soils with volcanic soils in Mbeya	Southern: 1200–1500 m	Southern: unimodal, reliable, and local rain shadows, 800–1400 mm	Northern: December–April
	Southwestern: Ufipa plateau in Sumbawanga	Southwestern: undulating plateau above rift valleys and sand soils of low fertility	Southwestern: 1400–2300 m	Southern: unimodal, reliable, and 800–1000 mm	Southwestern: November–April
	Western: along the shore of Lake Tanganyika in Kigoma and Kagera	Western: North-south ridges separated by swampy valleys, loam and clay soils of low fertility in hills, with alluvium and ponded clays in the valleys	Western: 100–1800 m	Western: bimodal, 1000–2000 mm	Western: October–December and February–May
6. Nothern highlands	Northern: Foot of Mt. Kilimanjaro and Mt. Meru Eastern rift valley to Eyasi	Northern: volcanic uplands, volcanic soils from lavas and ash. Deep fertile loams. Soils in dry areas prone to water erosion	Northern: 1000–2500 m	Northern: bimodal, varies widely between 1000 and 2000 mm	Northern: November–January and March–June
	Granite Mts. Uluguru in Morogoro, Pare Mts. in Kilimanjaro and Usambara Mts. in Tanga, Tarime highlands in Mara	Granite steep mountain side to highland plateaux. Soils are deep, arable, and moderately fertile on upper slopes, shallow and stony on steep slopes	Granitic Mts.: 1000–2000 m	Granitic Mts.: bimodal and very reliable 1000–2000 m	Granitic Mts.: October–December and March–June
7. Alluvial plains	K—Kilomberao (Morogoro)	K—cental clay plain with alluvial fans east and west		K—Unimodal, very reliable, 900–1300 mm	K—November–April
	R—Rufuji (Coast)	R-wide mangrove swamp delta, alluvial soils, sandy upstream, loamy down steam in floodplain		R—Unimodal, often inadequate 800–1200 mm	R—December–April
	U—Usangu (Mbeya)	U—seasonally flooded clay soils in north, alluvial fans in south		U—Unimodal, 500–800 mm	U—December–March
	W—Wami (Morogoro)	W—moderately alkaline black soils in east, alluvial fans with well-drained black loam in west		W—Unimodal, 600–1800 mm	W—December–March

Source: URT [7].

Table 1.
Agroecological zones of Tanzania.

the Indian Ocean. Tanzania has a total of 945,087 km^2, and out of this area, water bodies cover 61,495 km^2 which is equivalent to 6.52% of the total area.

The country has about 44 million hectares of arable land. Tanzania has seven agroecological zones (**Table 1**). Eastern plateau and mountain blocks; southern highlands; northern highlands/northern rift valley and volcanic high lands, arid lands/central plateau; alluvial Plains/Rukwa-Ruaha rift zone; and semiarid lands/ inland sedimentary plateau.

Therefore, this study aimed to distinguish the level of vulnerability and proper adaptation strategies between the high and low potential areas of Tanzania [14].

3. Climate change and biodiversity

It is obvious that the impact of climate change will continue to affect the biodiversity in most developing countries [22]. These effects are more pronounced and significant in vulnerable agro-biodiversity. IPCC 2014 reports that Tanzania is among the 13 countries in the world which are affected and most vulnerable to the impact of climate change [23]. This is evidenced by the reality seen on the ground. In this sense, climate change has impacted crop production, forest ecology, fishery industry, and livestock just to mention a few [4, 20–22].

Furthermore, climate change has affected crop genetics, the functioning of the soil microbial (due to drought), landscape, and the entire livelihood systems of 75% of the Tanzanian population (i.e., farmers). Basing on our discussion, the people and biodiversity found in low/marginal areas are more stressed than those in high potential zones. The livelihood options of the poor people in the marginal areas are too limited as they entirely depend on the environment [5].

Currently, the environment is stressed and has failed to support the people, thus the people are further subjected into distress. Prospectively, climate change will affect the ecosystem services and agricultural biodiversity, and the magnitude of the impacts will differ according to biophysical characteristics of the particular area [13].

3.1 Climate change impact on crop production

The increase in temperature and decrease in rainfall (including the shift of rainfall pattern) have significant impact to crop production in most developing countries [1–5]. In most areas of the country, there is significant correlation between the trend of crop production and that of rainfall [3–5]. In the years with poor yields, there have been incidences of low rainfall.

Agricultural systems are affected by drought and erratic rainfall, and therefore, the condition cannot support crop production. Specifically, crop failure has been more pronounced in the semiarid (i.e., Dodoma, Singida, Tabora, Manyara, and Shinyanga regions) due to prolonged drought and poor soil replenishment [2, 13]. Therefore, semiarid is among the marginal areas with excessive drought, crop failure, and food insecurity [3, 24]. As adaptation measure, farmers are advised to use drought-resistant crops and diverse crop varieties which are tolerant to drought [7, 14].

For example, SARO 5 rice varieties have been adopted in some rice-producing areas (such as Kilombero and parts of Kilosa districts) that face frequent droughts. Agronomic practices done in most marginal areas provide insights on how to optimize climate resilience in these areas. The dominant agricultural systems in these areas are monoculture, shifting cultivation, and extensive livestock rearing just to mention a few [21]. These practices have significant impacts to soil and its ingredients [21, 22, 24, 25].

However, there are limited soil management practices that are sustainably done in these areas [3]. Comparatively, the high potential zones experience little impacts than their counterparts. According to IPCC 2014, Tanzania will experience diverse impacts of climate change in the agriculture sector [23]. It is predicted that rainfall will increase in bimodal rainfall pattern (high potential zone) and decrease in unimodal rainfall pattern (low potential zone), therefore affecting the already stressed areas (low potential zone). In the high potential zone, especially in Eastern Arc Mountain and alluvial plain just to mention few, the natural replenishment of soil fertility through litter and/or organic matter decomposition is high because the microbial processes such as mycorrhizae can adequately perform their functions [26, 27]. Subsequently, carbon sequestration seems to be more significant in these areas [28, 29]. Therefore, these areas become potential for crop production and other livelihood patterns as they support diverse production systems.

3.2 Climate change impact on the soil

Climate is among the significant factors in the formation of the soil. Specifically, temperature, rainfall, and atmospheric carbon have specific function in the decomposition of litter and other plant biomass to organic matter [30]. The concentration of atmospheric CO_2 increases the growth rate and water-use efficiency of crops and natural vegetation [5]. Subsequently, the increased microbial activity in the soil always leads to the increase in the rates of plant nutrient release (e.g., C, K, Mg, and trace nutrients just to mention a few) from weathering of soil minerals. Similarly, the mycorrhizal activity leads to better phosphate uptake [31].

Subsequently, the increase in soil temperature creates a favorable condition for microbial activity. In turn, this increases the rate of organic matter and litter decomposition for forming soil fertility. Among the soil nutrients formed in this process are soil organic carbon, total nitrogen, and soil Olsen-P [27, 30, 31]. These nutrients are significant for plant uptake for growth and increased production. These processes are more pronounced in the high potential zone than in the low potential zone [5–7].

Therefore, high potential zones can produce more crop yields than low potential zones and therefore, the peoples' livelihoods in these areas are potentially better [3–8]. For instance, in the northern highland of Tanzania, granite soil is dominant, and this soil is useful for plant growth and improvement of agricultural systems in those areas. Therefore, these two zones have distinct characteristics and they offer diverse livelihood options [15].

3.3 Effects of rainfall on the landscape

The increase and decrease in rainfall have diverse impacts to different landscapes. This brings insight that different landscapes may have different ways to adapt to climate change impacts [7–9]. Geographically, highland areas have different biophysical characteristics from lowland areas. It is noted that landscape determines the flow of water runoff and infiltration [6]. It is expected that in plain areas with well-drained soil, there will be loss of soil nutrient through infiltration, while in steep slope with compact soil, nutrient will get lost through water runoff [5–10].

This scenario is expected to be significant in bimodal rainfall where rainfall is expected to increase [6]. In Mvomero and Kilosa districts of Morogoro region, there have been frequent occurrences of floods due to heavy rains [5]. This hazard is propagated by the characteristics of the landscape, that is, highland and lowland. Similarly, landslides and mudflow have been occurring and are significantly expected to occur in these areas [5].

Besides, drought is expected to be pronounced in areas with unimodal rainfall pattern [6]. And this will pose effects depending on the landscape of the area. In this aspect, steep slope will experience poor soil formation and thus the area is not favorable for agriculture. Lowland areas may experience less impacts of drought than highland areas [5]. And this brings insights that agricultural potentials may differ between the two areas.

Basing on the potentiality of the area (high and low potential zones), lowland areas often receive nutrients and water from highland areas through runoff and therefore improve the agricultural systems of the locality [1–3]. Highland and steep slope areas might be vulnerable to environmental stress, thus providing less potentials in agricultural systems unless there are other sources of resources, that is, water and soil fertility [6–10]. To control this, some farmers and institutions have been practicing some farming systems that are ecologically significant to adapt to climate change and impacts related to environmental stresses [1–6]. Preferably, conservation agriculture has been opted as a possible absorber of these stresses and shocks. The “Matengo” farming systems in Ruvuma region and the “Ngitiri” pasture farming in Shinyanga, just to mention a few, are some good examples of the mentioned conservation agriculture [5–9].

3.4 Climate change impact on agricultural systems

The increase in temperature at both global and local levels is predicted to impact a wide range of biodiversity, including the extinction of some animals and plant species [7]. The predicted increase in temperature by 1.5–2.5°C will increase the concentration of atmospheric carbon dioxide and eventually affect the ecosystem functions, biotic species, ecological interactions, and water supply. IPCC 2014 predicts that by 2100, the threshold of resilience of most ecosystems is going to be reduced and narrowed naturally [23].

Agricultural systems (animal and crop production) are most concerned in this case. Temperature will increase incidences of drought, flooding, wildfire, ocean acidification, eutrophication (especially in Lake Victoria), and pollution just to mention a few. As a response to this, farmers engage in land-use changes and overexploitation of resources to meet their needs [6].

Besides, ecosystem services, particularly sources, will be severely affected. However, the magnitude of these impacts will differ depending on the level of vulnerability, that is, high and low potential zones [10]. There will be relief to some agroecological zones (with high potentials) and severe impacts to low potential zones [12–16]. This will also be based on the ecological gradient and landscape of the area. Losses of biodiversity (agroecological systems) will automatically affect food security and socioeconomic challenges caused by ecological challenges.

Livestock rearing, on the other hand, will experience similar impacts. Some genetic breeds which are vulnerable to climate change impacts will be substituted by drought-resistant breeds. In most drought areas of Tanzania, drought-resistant animals have been replacing the vulnerable ones. Camels (i.e., though few) have been adopted instead of goat, sheep, and cow just to mention a few.

Basing on the actual and potential impacts of climate change on resources, some adaptation strategies and mechanisms have been adopted to reduce the magnitude of the impacts [3]. Similarly, landscapes have been determining the best use of the land [3–8]. Previously, highland areas (southern highland of Tanzania) have been used for tea and coffee plantations. However, due to the changing climate, these areas have become warmer than before and therefore are not conducive for these crops.

Instead, maize, beans, and other moderate crops have been grown in these areas as paradigm shift [3–6]. And thus, coffee, tea, and pyrethrum have been grown in small scale or are totally redundant due to change of weather.

4. Agricultural biodiversity for climate change adaptation

Adaptive capacity to climate change impacts is varied over space and time. People have diverse capacity to adapt to climate change impacts [15–20]. Some are vulnerable, while others are resilient and they can recover soon from the impacts. Similarly, the thresholds of adaptive capacity is subject among other things to resource entitlements, that is, human asset, financial asset, physical asset, and technological asset just to mention a few [21, 22, 24].

Tanzania has identified a wide range of adaptation strategies through National Adaptation Program for Action [6]. The identified adaptations were based on location (ecological gradients), resource endowments, livelihood options, financial assets, and agroecological zone just to mention a few.

Altitude and climate were among the other significant factors in this chapter. The main aim of the program was to identify and recommend proper adaptation strategies that would reduce the vulnerability and increase the resilience of the farmers. Meanwhile, the program comes up with the wide range of adaptation option based on the aforementioned factors [24–26].

The recommended adaptation strategies include the growing of drought-resistant crops such as cassava (*Manihot esculenta* C.), sesame (*Sesamum indicum* L.), sweet potatoes (*Ipomea Batatas* L.), and pigeon peas (*Cajanus cajan* L.). Further, crop diversification was another adaptation strategy. This involved the growth of different types of crops (both food and cash crops) in order to avoid total loss.

Modern farming techniques, changing cropping calendar, and involvement of nonfarming activities were other adaptation strategies. All these are done to curb food security in the country [5–8]. Subsequently, the program report shows that there is spatial and temporal variation of onset and cessation of rain and dry seasons [15–18]. The trend of rainfall and dry season during 1980–2010 shows that it is not statistically significant different ($P > 0.05$). Thus, erratic rainfall and rain patterns are significant in determining climate impacts.

Similarly, agricultural and research institutes are responsible to review on the current changes and current recommended adaptation strategies. Policies, plans, frameworks, and projects related to agriculture and environment are keen to accommodate adaptation strategies in their action and implementation for sustainable development of both agriculture and environment. Likewise, enhancing ecosystem services (management and payment of ecosystem services) is a suitable approach of strengthening the adaptation strategies [5–8].

Both abiotic and biotic factors need to be well accommodated in the planning in order to reduce the magnitudes of climate change impacts [26–29]. Abiotic factors may range from heat, salinity, floods, and drought to mention a few, while biotic factors are all aspects of living organisms found in the environment [6–8]. For more explanation, see the subsections below which describe specific adaptation approaches.

4.1 Animal genetic resource

About 30% of the Tanzanian land is under arid and semiarid climates, of which its main activities are extensive livestock keeping and some mixed farming [6, 13]. Therefore, livestock is among the major livelihoods and is a tool of increasing resilience from the stress caused by climate change [21]. However, the impacts of climate change have subjected livestock into stress and will continue affecting it. This is more pronounced in most central regions of Tanzania.

This situation dries water sources and affects grasses in the pasture and range land required for animal grazing [26–29]. In turn, the situation affects most animals, and most of them die due to shortage of pasture and water. From 2008 to date, thousands of animals have died in Manyara (i.e., Kiteto District), Arusha, Shinyanga, Dodoma, and Singida regions due to drought [13–18]. In this stance, evidences show that cows have been more vulnerable than goats and sheep. Similarly, the increase in temperature stresses the already affected areas and catalyzes the outbreak of disease and pests which affect the animals [5–10]. As a result, a number of animals have been dying due to diseases and pest [6–8]. The effects have been more severe to some types of animal breeds/or and species due to differences of the level of tolerance.

Some measures have been taken by the government and local people to adjust to stress. The government has been advocating intensive livestock keeping for the purpose of increasing quality and quantity of the product and reducing overgrazing on the already stressed areas [6, 13]. Pastoralists have been shifting from the stressed environment (low potential zone) to areas with pasture and water (high potential zone). The Usangu valley in Mbeya region (high potential zone) has been the actual and potential destination of most pastoral societies [6–10].

These pastoralists are after water and pasture for feeding their herds. Therefore, planners and policy makers need to integrate this challenge in order to rescue environmental degradation by pastoral societies as well as to reduce the disturbances to pastoralists.

4.2 Crop genetic resources

It is obvious that crop production can be the most affected sector by stresses and shocks of climate change [5–8]. Increased incidences of drought have reduced crop yield massively. A number of studies show that crop production has been significantly affected by climate change impacts [3–5]. Crop species that need more moisture are more vulnerable than those which need little. Hybrid maize is among those which are less resistant to drought due to that factor.

Therefore, a number of crop species have been lost because they can no longer tolerate to the present climate change impacts. As adaptation strategies, resistant crops such as SARO 5 rice species have been adopted to reduce the vulnerability of rice crop [7–10]. Otherwise, irrigation agriculture has been recommended as a solution to accommodate a wide threshold of crop species.

In Kilombero, Mtibwa, Usangu, and Ruvu Basin, rice production has been growing due to irrigation. However, only 2% of the Tanzanian land potential for irrigation agriculture has been harnessed. Therefore, the vulnerability of crop species varies depending on where it is grown. In high potential zones, the crop breed may have a wide chance to survive than in low potential zones [15].

4.3 Adaptation in agricultural systems

Agriculture provides full livelihoods to more than 75% of the Tanzanians and most of them are living in rural areas [5–8]. Therefore, it is very important to make sure that adaptation strategies and coping mechanisms to the impacts of climate change are taken into full consideration [1–4]. Different agroecological zones may have diverse adaptation measures depending on the climate, soil, financial asset, and human asset just to mention a few. It is obvious that low potential areas are the most fragile ecosystems and when mismanaged even the little potentials may get lost [5–8].

Therefore, a wide range of adaptation measures are considered in various areas of the country [5–10]. Some of the general adaptation measures taken across the country includes shifting cultivation (to more potential areas), adopting drought-resistant crops like cassava (*Manihot esculenta* C.), sesame (*Sesamum indicum* L.), and sweet potatoes (*Ipomea Batatas* L.), rice (*Oryza sativa L.*), banana (*Musa* Spp.), and maize (*Zea mays* L.) should be incorporated in irrigation agriculture to reduce their vulnerability and increase yields [31–33].

Another adaptation related to agricultural system is the change of agronomic practices [5–12]. In this aspect, the adaptation of conservation agricultural practices such as agroforestry, better crop rotation, mixed farming, and intercropping [15–20] will help to improve organic soil fertility, preferably soil carbon. This will increase crop yields and carbon sequestration of greenhouse gases. This goes together with the adoption of modern farming techniques, particularly irrigation [21, 22, 24–26]. Tanzania has done very little in irrigation agriculture because it has harnessed only 2% of the total irrigable land.

Therefore, there is a need to work on it and increase the land under irrigation in order to curb all aspects of food insecurity in the country and increase the export of agricultural products. Similarly, early planting is adopted to curb the variation of onset and cessation of both rainy and dry seasons [26–29]. Erratic rainfall and the shift of onset has been a key problem in most areas in the country [15–18]. Despite the prediction that rainfall will increase in areas with bimodal rainfall pattern, these areas suffer the same problem of paradigm shift of the growing season.

In has been noted that most of the bimodal rainfall pattern have been experiencing unimodal rainfall with a great shift [4–8]. Meanwhile, experience from the field shows that the amount of rainfall has been changing in a roughly regular pattern. There have been roughly rotating patterns, that a year with low rainfall is followed by the year with high rainfall and vice versa [15–20]. Therefore, further adaptation strategies are needed to be accommodated as climate continues to change. We need to incorporate strong adaptation measures in the policy in order to curb food insecurity in the country.

Nonfarming practices can also help to strengthen the resilience of the people [26–29]. Diversified sectors such as commercial enterprises and employment just to mention a few, can help to reduce the dependence on the already stressed agroecosystems [30–33]. Therefore, diversification will enable the replenishment of the soil resources tenable for crop production.

4.4 Changes in agricultural practice

Traditional agriculture has been in practice even before the Tanzanian independence [5–8]. Indigenous knowledge has been limited to solve complex challenges posed by climate change. It is obvious that the number of people has been increasing every year and the demand of food has been accruing too [8–11]. Sustainable agriculture is currently advocated in order to get duo benefits (environmental conservation and increased crop yields) at the same time [1–6]. It is a great challenge for the country with about 44 million hectares of fertile land; less than 24% of this resource is harnessed while the country experiences usual food shortage [6–8].

The adoption of modern farming methods especially irrigation agriculture can increase crop yield to curb food insecurity. Agroforestry system is less adopted in the country, compared to its needs. The Eastern Arc Mountain in Tanzania has the potential for agroforestry but it is least harnessed [27].

In addition, Tanzania has a number of hydroecological zones such as the Ruaha, Rufiji, Ruvu, Wami, Ruvuma, Usangu, Pangani, Kilombero, and Malagarasi valleys just to mention a few [6–10]. These areas have potential for irrigation agriculture, but the actual situation reveals that there is underutilization and mismanagement of these resources [6]. Instead, these valleys have been sources of conflicts between resource users, therefore posing no or little benefit to users [3–8].

Therefore, good agricultural practices need to be adopted to increase crop yields in various areas. It has been obvious that traditional, rain-fed agriculture is a major production technique to the people [27–30]. Rain-fed agriculture has been vulnerable to the impact of climate change since the 1980s to date [31–33]. The adoption of sustainable agriculture countrywide can help to reduce the vulnerability and calibrate a quick recovery of the affected areas.

5. Conclusion

Tanzanian agroecological zones (i.e., high and low potential zones) experience the impacts of climate change differently. Semiarid areas experience the impacts of climate change more severely than the alluvial plains. This happens because the former is a low potential zone while the latter is a high potential zone. The vulnerability of the people also depends on the resource entitlements and assets they possess. Overall, poor people have little options than the rich people.

The two categories are differentiated by financial assets. It has been obvious that the poor always live in the low potential zone where they get more challenges and therefore they need a quick rescue; otherwise, their livelihood options are limited. Similarly, they can seek livelihood options by inserting more stress to the already affected environments. They move from the stressed areas to other areas where they end up degrading too.

This study recommends that farmers with weak adaptive capacity should be carefully and immediately attended to; otherwise, their livelihood options can further destroy the environment. The increase in awareness to local farmers in searching for sustainable livelihood options would be more secure to the environment. Similarly, relevant policies should clearly include practical adaptations of the vulnerable societies.

Conflict of interest

The author declares no conflict of interest.

Author details

Msafiri Yusuph Mkonda
Department of Geography and Environmental Studies, Solomon Mahlangu College of Science and Education, Sokoine University of Agriculture, Morogoro, Tanzania

*Address all correspondence to: msamkonda81@yahoo.co.uk

IntechOpen

© 2020 The Author(s). Licensee IntechOpen. This chapter is distributed under the terms of the Creative Commons Attribution License (http://creativecommons.org/licenses/by/3.0), which permits unrestricted use, distribution, and reproduction in any medium, provided the original work is properly cited.

References

[1] Ahmed S, Deffenbaugh N, Hertel T, Lobell D, Ramankutty N, Rios A, et al. Climate volatility and poverty vulnerability in Tanzania. Global Environmental Change. 2011;**21**:46-55

[2] Agrawala SA, Moehner A, Hemp M, Van Aalst S, Hitz J, Smith H, et al. Development and Climate Change in Tanzania: Focus on Kilimanjaro. Paris: Organisation for Economic Co-operation and Development; 2003

[3] Paavola J. Livelihoods, vulnerability and adaptation to climate change in Morogoro, Tanzania. Environmental Science & Policy. 2008;**11**:642-654

[4] Rowhani P, Lobell DB, Linderman M, Ramankutty N. Climate variability and crop production in Tanzania. Agricultural and Forest Meteorology. 2011;**15**:449-460

[5] Yanda PZ. Climate change implications for management and use of agricultural biodiversity resources in Africa. Environment and Ecology Research. 2015;**3**(2):35-43

[6] URT, United Republic of Tanzania, National Adaptation Programme of Action (NAPA). Dar es Salaam: Division of Environment, Vice President's Office; 2007

[7] Challinor AJ, Wheeler TR, Garforth C, Craufurd P, Kassam A. Assessing the vulnerability of food crop systems in Africa to climate change. Climatic Change. 2007;**83**:381-399

[8] Mkonda MY, He XH. Climate variability, crop yields and ecosystems synergies in Tanzania's semi-arid agro-ecological zone. Ecosystem Health and Sustainability. 2018;**4**(3). DOI: 10.1080/20964129.2018.1459868

[9] Afifi T, Liwenga E, Kwezi L. Rainfall-induced crop failure, food insecurity and out-migration in same-Kilimanjaro, Tanzania. Climate and Development. 2014;**6**(1):53-60. DOI: 10.1080/17565529.2013.826128

[10] Easterling WE, Aggarwal PK, Batima P, Brander KM, Erda L, Howden SM, et al. Food, fibre and forest products. Climate Change (2007). Impacts, Adaptation and Vulnerability. In: Parry ML, Canziani OF, Palutikof JP, van der Linden PJ, Hanson CE, editors. Contribution of Working Group II to the Fourth Assessment Report of the Intergovernmental Panel on Climate Change. Cambridge, UK: Cambridge University Press; 2007. 273-313

[11] Mkonda MY. Impacts of climate change and variability on crop production and its implications to food security a case of Mvomero District, Tanzania [Master's dissertation]. Dar-Es-Salaam: University of Dar-Es-Salaam; 2011

[12] Mkonda MY, He XH, Festin ES. Comparing smallholder farmers' perception of climate change with meteorological data: Experiences from seven agro-ecological zones of Tanzania. Weather, Climate, and Society. 2018;**10**(3):435-452. DOI: 10.1175/WCAS-D-17-0036.1

[13] United Republic of Tanzania. National Strategy for Growth and Reduction of Poverty. Dar es Salaam, Tanzania: Vice President's Office, United Republic of Tanzania. 2005. Available from: <www.tanzania.go.tz/pdf/nsgrptext.pdf> [Accessed: 20 September 2018]

[14] Etzold B, Ahmed A, Hassan S, Neelormi S. Clouds gather in the sky, but no rain falls. Vulnerability to rainfall variability and food insecurity in northern Bangladesh and its effects on migration. Climate and Development. 2014;**6**(1):18-27. DOI: 10.1080/17565529.2013.833078

[15] Balama C, Augustino S, Eriksen S, Makonda FSB, Amanzi N. Climate change adaptation strategies by local farmers in Kilombero District, Tanzania. Ethiopian Journal of Environmental Studies and Management. 2013;**6**

[16] Lobell DB, Burke MB, Tebaldi C, Mastrandrea MD, Falcon WP, Naylor RL. Prioritizing climate change adaptation needs for food security in 2030. Science. 2008;**319**:607-610

[17] Kangalawe R. Climate change impacts on water resource management and community livelihoods in the southern highlands of Tanzania. Climate and Development. 2016;**9**(3):1-16. DOI: 10.1080/17565529.2016.1139487

[18] Mkonda MY, He XH. Yields of the major food crops: Implications to food security and policy in Tanzania's semi-arid agro-ecological zone. Sustainability. 2017;**9**(8):1490. DOI: 10.3390/su9081490

[19] Mkonda MY, He XH. Are rainfall and temperature really changing? Farmer's perceptions, meteorological data, and policy implications in the Tanzanian semi-arid zone. Sustainability. 2017;**9**(8):1-16. DOI: 10.3390/su9081412

[20] Mkonda MY. Rainfall variability and its association to the trends of crop production in Mvomero District, Tanzania. European Scientific Journal. July 2014;**10**(20):363-273

[21] Davoudi S, Shaw K, Haider J, Quinlan A, et al. Resilience: A bridging concept or a dead end? "Reframing" resilience: Challenges for planning theory and practice interacting traps: Resilience assessment of a pasture management system in northern Afghanistan urban resilience: What does it mean in planning practice? Resilience as a useful concept for climate change adaptation? The politics of resilience for planning: A cautionary note. Planning Theory & Practice. 2012;**13**(2):299-333. DOI: 10.1080/14649357.2012.677124

[22] Eriksen S, Aldunce P, Bahinipati C, Martins R, et al. When not every response to climate change is a good one: Identifying principles for sustainable adaptation. Climate and Development. 2011;**3**(1):7-20. DOI: 10.3763/cdev.2010.0060

[23] Intergovernmental Pannel on Climate Change. Climate change 2014 impacts, adaptation, and vulnerability. Part A: Global and sectoral aspects. In: Field CB, Barros VR, Estrada, Genova RC, Girma B, Kissel ES, Levy AN, MacCracken S, Mastrandrea PR, White LL, editors. Contribution of Working Group II to the Fifth Assessment Report of the Intergovernmental Panel on Climate Change. Cambridge, United Kingdom and New York, NY, USA: Cambridge University Press; 2014

[24] Eriksen S, Brown K. Sustainable adaptation to climate change. Climate and Development. 2011;**3**(1):3-6. DOI: 10.3763/cdev.2010.0064

[25] Brown K. Sustainable adaptation: An oxymoron? Climate and Development. 2011;**3**(1):21-31. DOI: 10.3763/cdev.2010.0062

[26] Milan A, Ho R. Livelihood and migration patterns at different altitudes in the central highlands of Peru. Climate and Development. 2014;**6**(1):69-76. DOI: 10.1080/17565529.2013.826127

[27] Haoa Q, Jianga C, Chaia X, Huanga Z, Fana Z, Xiea D, et al. Drainage, no-tillage and crop rotation decreases annual cumulative emissions of methane and nitrous oxide from a rice field in Southwest China. Agriculture, Ecosystems & Environment. 2016;**233**:270-281

[28] Munishi PK, Shear TH. Carbon storage in Afromontane rain Forest of the eastern Arch Mountain of Tanzania. Their net contribution to atmospheric carbon. Journal of Tropical Forest Science. 2004;**16**(1):78-93

[29] Challinor AJ, Watson J, Lobell DB, Howden SM, Smith DR, Chhetri N. A meta-analysis of crop yield under climate change and adaptation. Nature Climate Change. 2014;**4**:287-291. DOI: 10.1038/nclimate2153

[30] Hertel TW, Burke MB, Lobell DB. The poverty implications of climate-induced crop yield changes by 2030. Global Environmental Change. 2010;**20**(4):577-585. DOI: 10.1016/j.gloenvcha.2010.07.001

[31] Lobell DB, Field CB. Global scale climate-crop yield relationships and the impacts of recent warming. Environmental Research Letters. 2007;**2**:1-7

[32] Malviya S, Priyanka N, Irfan-Ullah M, Davande S, Joshi PK. Distribution potential of 563 simarouba glauca under climate change—Strategizing rural livelihood adaptation. International Journal of Geoinformatics. 2013;**9**(1):31-37

[33] Morton J. Livestock and climate change: Impacts and adaptation. Agriculture for development. Rome, Italy: Tropical Agriculture Association Report No 17; 2012. pp. 17-20

Chapter 14

Impact of Climate Change on Maize and Pigeonpea Yields in Semi-Arid Kenya

Kizito Musundi Kwena, G.N. Karuku, F.O. Ayuke and A.O. Esilaba

Abstract

The objective of this study was to assess the impact of climate change on intercrops of maize and improved pigeonpea varieties developed. Future climate data for Katumani were downscaled from the National Meteorological Research Centre (CNRM) and Commonwealth Scientific and Industrial Research Organization (CSIRO) climate models using the Statistical Downscaling Model (SDSM) version 4.2. Both models predicted that Katumani will be warmer by 2°C and wetter by 11% by 2100. Agricultural Production Systems Simulator (APSIM) model version 7.3 was used to assess the impact of both increase in temperature and rainfall on maize and pigeonpea yield in Katumani. Maize crop will increase by 141–-150% and 10–-23 % in 2050 and 2100, respectively. Intercropping maize with pigeonpea will give mixed maize yield results. Pigeonpea yields will decline by 10–20 and 4–9% by 2100 under CSIRO and CNRM models, respectively. Intercropping short and medium duration pigeonpea varieties with maize will reduce pigeonpea yields by 60–80 and 70–90% under the CSIRO and CNRM model, respectively. There is a need to develop heat and waterlogging-tolerant pigeonpea varieties to help farmers adapt to climate change and to protect the huge pigeonpea export market currently enjoyed by Kenya.

Keywords: climate change impacts, semi-arid, adaptation, maize yields, pigeonpea varieties

1. Introduction

Kenya is the world's fourth largest producer of pigeonpea after India, Myanmar and Malawi, of which 99% is produced in semi-arid eastern Kenya, especially Machakos, Kitui, Makueni, Meru, Lower Embu, and Tharaka-Nithi Counties. It is also grown in the drier parts of Kirinyaga, Murang'a, and Kiambu Counties in Central Kenya; and some parts of Lamu, Kilifi, Kwale, Tana River, and Taita-Taveta Counties at the Coast; mainly by small-scale resource-poor farmers [1–6]. Most farmers intercrop pigeonpea with maize or sorghum on the same land, either in alternate or multiple rows, as a form of security against total crop failure [7].

Pigeonpea provides multiple benefits to the rural poor. Firstly, its protein-rich grain can be consumed both fresh and dry and provides a cheap source of protein for the poor farmers in the drylands. Secondly, its leaves and hulls are used as livestock feeds and the stem as fuelwood. Thirdly, it has the ability to enrich the soil through di-nitrogen fixation [8], litter fall and being a deep-rooted crop, to mobilize nutrients, particularly phosphorus, from the deep soil horizons [9–11]. Fourthly, intercropping pigeonpea with cereals enhances soil coverage, reduces soil erosion, and boosts cereal yields [9, 10]. Finally, the crop provides an assured source of income for farm families and foreign exchange for Kenya. About 7000 ton of dhal (dehulled pigeonpea) and 15,000 ton of whole grain are exported annually to Europe, North America, the Middle East, and India, but this figure represents just 30% of Kenya's export potential [1, 4–6, 12]. Thus, pigeonpea has immense untapped potential which if fully exploited could transform the lives of many communities and economies of many countries in the East African region. Maize on the other hand is the staple food for over 90% of Kenya's population and accounts for 56% of cultivated land in Kenya [13].

Despite the importance of maize-pigeonpea intercropping system in semi-arid Kenya and elsewhere in the region, their productivity has continued to decline. Maize and pigeonpea yields on farmers' fields are low, averaging 300–500 kg ha^{-1} against a yield potential of 2.5 t ha^{-1}, mainly due to non-use of improved varieties and poor farming practices, low soil fertility and climate variability [2, 6, 14]. The situation is bound to worsen in future with the expected change in climate. Temperatures and rainfall in Kenya and the rest of East Africa are expected to increase by about 2°C and 11%, respectively, by 2050 due to climate change [15–18]. However, the rise in temperature may cause a substantial increase in evaporation rates, which are likely to balance and exceed any benefit from the predicted increase in precipitation [19]. Thus, if not checked, climate change will undermine agricultural productivity and expose millions of people to hunger and poverty, especially in semi-arid areas where temperatures are already high and rainfall low and unreliable, agriculture is predominantly rain-fed and adoption of modern technologies is low [20, 21].

A lot of work has been done to quantify some of the agricultural impacts associated with projected changes in future climate using a variety of simulation models, but most of it has been carried out at global, regional and country levels hence not applicable to community-based adaptation planning [20, 22–24]. Similarly, despite the importance of pigeonpea in Kenya and elsewhere in the region, few studies have assessed the impact of climate change on its performance. Most studies have focused on staple and commercial crops such as maize, tea, wheat, rice, beans and groundnuts [20, 21, 25–27], and tomatoes [28]. There is a need for more detailed information on the impacts of climate change on pigeonpea-maize intercropping systems to guide in formulating appropriate adaptation measures that will increase their productivity, ensure food security in future, and safeguard pigeonpea's niche markets. Therefore, the objective of this study was to assess the impact of climate change under a range of scenarios on intercrops of maize and improved pigeonpea varieties developed and released in Kenya in recent times.

2. Materials and methods

2.1 Study area

The study was conducted at the Kenya Agricultural and Livestock Research Organization (KALRO) Katumani Research Centre in Machakos County, 80 km south-east of Nairobi (37°14′E and 1°35′S). Katumani has bimodal rainfall pattern and receives an average of 711 mm annually. The long rains (LR) occur from March to May and the short rains (SR) from October to December with peaks in April and November, respectively [7, 29]. Inter-seasonal rainfall variation is large with coefficient of variation ranging between 45 and 58% [30]. Temperatures range between 17 and 24°C with February and September being the hottest months. The mean annual temperature is 20°C. Evaporation rates are high and exceed the amount of rainfall, most of the year, except in the month of November. The mean potential evaporation is in the range of 1820–1840 mm per year whilst evapotranspiration is estimated at 1239 mm [31] giving an r/ETo ratio of 0.57. Katumani is 1600 m asl and the terrain ranges from flat to hilly with slopes varying from 2 to 20% [32]. It falls under agro-climatic zone IV which has a low potential for rain-fed agriculture [29]. The dominant soils are chromic Luvisols [33, 34], which are low in organic C, highly deficient in N and P and to some extent Zinc and generally have poor structure [35].

Mixed farming systems involving food crops and livestock are characteristic of the region. Crops grown are predominantly drought-escaping or early maturing varieties of pigeonpea, maize, beans, sorghum, and millet [29]. Due to the erratic nature of rainfall, most farmers around Katumani and the larger semi-arid Eastern Kenya prefer to intercrop maize with at least a legume (pigeonpea, beans, or cowpeas) on the same land. This is often done either in alternate or multiple rows and is seen by many farmers as a form of security against total crop failure [7]. Long duration pigeonpea is normally planted during SR in October–November and harvested in August–September the following year. Medium and short duration varieties can be planted and harvested in one season. Crop combinations, planting patterns, and plant populations of pigeonpea and other crops vary considerably, depending on the soil type, climate, and farmer's preferences. However, dominant pigeonpea cropping systems practiced in the region include: pigeonpea intercropped with maize, sorghum, millets, cowpea and green gram; pigeonpea and cowpea intercrops; and maize/bean/pigeonpea intercrops [1, 4–6].

2.2 Long-term simulation

Agricultural Production Systems Simulator (APSIM) version 7.3 was used to predict the impact of climate change on maize and pigeonpea yields in Katumani and similar areas in eastern Kenya. APSIM was preferred due to its user-friendliness, widespread application in the region and ability to make highly precise simulations/predictions once properly initialized [16, 36–40]. The APSIM has the capacity to predict the outcome of diverse range of farming systems and management practices under variable climatic conditions, both short and long term [39, 41–44]. It also simulates growth and yield of a range of crops in response to a variety of management practices, crop mixtures, and rotation sequences, including pastures and livestock [44]. The model runs with a daily time step and has four key components: (1) a set of biophysical modules that simulate biological and physical processes in farming systems, (2) a set of management modules that allow the user to specify the intended management rules that characterize the scenario being simulated and controls the conduct of the simulation, (3) various modules that facilitate data input and output to and from the simulation, and (4) a simulation engine that drives the simulation process and controls all messages passing between the independent modules [44, 45]. It has a user interface which allows selection of input data (climate, soil, crop, and management), output data from modules of interest (e.g., water balance, carbon, nitrogen and phosphorus balances, and crop growth and yield) management of simulation scenarios (saving, running, retrieving, and deleting), error checking (summary of scenario set-up inputs and run time operations), and output analysis via software links for viewing output data in text file, Excel, or graphs [44].

APSIM requires site-specific data on latitude and longitude, soil texture and depth (m), slope (%) and slope length (m); climate (daily maximum and minimum temperature [°C], daily solar radiation [MJ/m^2] and daily rainfall [mm]); crop growth and phenology (crop type and cultivar name, maturity type, date of 50% flowering and total number of leaves, total biomass at harvest (kg ha^{-1}), grain yield (kg ha^{-1}), final plant population (plts m^{-2}), N and P contents of plant parts, biomass at anthesis (kg ha^{-1}), population at thinning (plts m^{-2}), date of physiological maturity (black layer) and maximum leaf area index (LAI); soil water, nitrogen and phosphorus; residues and manure (crop and manure type, dry weight [kg ha^{-1}], N, C and P content [%], ash content, and ground cover [%]); and management (date of all operations e.g. sowing, harvest, thinning, weeding, tillage and fertilizer applications, sowing depth and plant population, type, rate and depth of fertilizer application, and type (hoe, disc, harrow, etc.) and depth of tillage) to run. These data can be obtained from field trials or secondary sources. However, this study used the APSIM that had been calibrated and validated for Katumani semi-arid area by Okwach and Simiyu [46] and Okwach [47].

Daily minimum and maximum temperature, solar radiation and rainfall data for Katumani for the near (2050) and far (2100) future scenarios were downscaled from the National Meteorological Research Centre (CNRM) and Commonwealth Scientific and Industrial Research Organization (CSIRO) climate models using the Statistical Downscaling Model (SDSM) version 4.2 [48] and uploaded in APSIM. Both models, CNRM and CSIRO, have predicted a 1–2.5°C and 10% increase in temperature and rainfall, respectively, by the end of the century (2100) which is consistent with the Intergovernmental Panel on Climate Change (IPCC)'s prediction of 3.2°C and 11% rise in temperature and rainfall, respectively, for Kenya and the rest of East Africa by 2100. SDSM is a decision support tool for assessing local climate change impacts using a robust statistical downscaling technique. It is a hybrid of a stochastic weather generator and regression-based downscaling methods and facilitates the rapid development of multiple, low-cost, single-site scenarios of daily surface weather variables under current and future climate [49]. The tool has been used extensively with remarkable success [49–55].

The following eight cropping systems were simulated using the downscaled climate data: (1) Sole short duration maize crop, (2) Sole short duration pigeonpea crop, (3) Sole medium duration pigeonpea crop, (4) Sole long duration pigeonpea crop, (5) Short duration pigeonpea-maize intercrop, (6) medium duration pigeonpea-maize intercrop and (8) long duration pigeonpea-maize intercrop. The model was run to simulate 50 and 100 years under these cropping systems. The growing season was defined to start after 5 consecutive days with volumetric soil water content in the top 100 cm above 70%. The end of the season was deemed to occur when soil water content fell below 50% for 8 consecutive days. KDVI maize variety was used to represent all early maturing (120–150 days to mature) and high yielding maize varieties recommended for semi-arid conditions. Similarly, Mbaazi I, Kat 60/8 and Mbaazi II pigeonpea varieties were used to represent short (100 days to mature), medium (150 days to mature) and long (180–220 days to mature) duration pigeonpea varieties, respectively. Pigeonpea was planted at spacings of 90 cm × 60 cm, 75 cm × 30 cm and 50 cm × 25 cm for the long, medium and short duration varieties, respectively, whilst maize was planted with Triple Super Phosphate (TSP) fertilizer at the recommended rate of 40 kg P_2O_5 ha^{-1} at spacing of 90 cm × 30 cm. Other agronomic practices were adopted as currently practiced by farmers such as early planting, timely weeding and thinning.

3. Results and discussion

3.1 Maize yields

Long-term yields of maize under variable and changing climate in Katumani are presented in **Figure 1**. Prospects for increased maize production under sole maize crop in Katumani (Machakos County) are high, both in the near (by 2050) and far (2100) future scenarios under the two climate models, CNRM and CSIRO models. Relative to baseline yield of 500 kg ha^{-1}, maize yields are expected to increase by 141 and 10% in 2050 and 2100, respectively, under the CSIRO model. The CNRM model was more optimistic and predicted maize yield increases of 150 and 23% in 2050 and 2100, respectively, under maize sole crop. The increase in yield could be attributed to the projected increase in rainfall of 20–40 mm per year by 2100. The predictions corroborate reports by Waithaka et al. [56] that Kenya's bread basket could shift from the Rift Valley to semi-arid eastern and north-eastern Kenya by 2050. Intercropping maize with pigeonpea will give mixed results. According to the CSIRO model, maize yield will increase by 18 and 15% under maize/Mbaazi I and maize/Mbaazi II intercrops, respectively, in 2050. However, yields under maize/Kat 60/8 intercrop will decline by 4% in the same period. A similar trend will be observed in 2100 where intercropping maize with pigeonpea will reduce maize yields by 10–20% under the CSIRO model. The projected decline in maize yield could be attributed to high evapotranspiration due to anticipated rise in temperature. According to Thornton et al. [18], high evapotranspiration is bound to cause water scarcity which will adversely affect maize growth. These results agree with Herrero *et al.* [20] who predicted maize yield losses of upto 50% in the ASALs due to climate change, albeit under the Hadley model. Thornton et al. [18], Jones and Thornton [25], and Downing [57] have also predicted a significant decline in yields of maize and other food crops in the East African region due to the same phenomenon. However, the decline in maize yield could be arrested by encouraging farmers to adopt irrigation, conservation agriculture, seed priming, and in-situ water harvesting among other adaptation measures [58].

Conversely, according to the CNRM model, intercropping will increase maize yields by 28 and 11% under maize/short duration pigeonpea and maize/medium

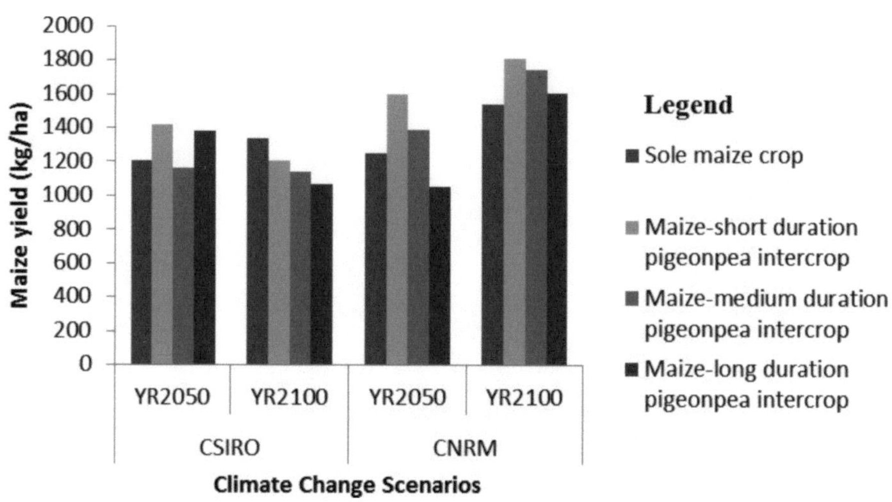

Figure 1.
Long-term effect of pigeonpea on maize yield in Katumani under variable and changing climate.

duration pigeonpea intercrops, respectively, by 2050. Maize yields under maize/long duration pigeonpea intercrop will declined by 16%. However, maize yields will increase by 18, 13, and 4% under maize/short duration pigeonpea, maize/medium duration pigeonpea and maize/long duration pigeonpea intercrops, respectively, in the far future (2100). Because of these conflicting results, it is difficult to generalize the impacts of climate change on maize yields from maize/pigeonpea intercrops in Katumani and similar areas in the country. Further simulations involving many GCM model X scenario combinations are therefore required to establish the correct direction of change in maize yields under these systems, whether they will increase or decrease. Meanwhile, the results corroborate observation by Herrero et al. [20] that climate change impacts on maize yields depend on the emission scenario, crop model and the Global Climate Change Model (GCM) used.

3.2 Pigeonpea yields

Long-term yields of pigeonpea under variable and changing climate in Katumani are presented in **Figure 2**. Unlike maize, both CSIRO and CNRM models predicted decreased pigeonpea yields in Katumani in the near and far future. Yields from sole pigeonpea crop will decline by 10–20% and 4–9% under CSIRO and CNRM models, respectively, by 2100. Intercropping short and medium duration pigeonpea varieties with maize will reduce pigeonpea yields by 60–80% and 70–90% under the CSIRO and CNRM model, respectively. However, long duration varieties will yield highest under the two Global Climate Change Models (GCMs) irrespective of the cropping system, but the yields will be much lower than the potential yield of over 2 t ha^{-1} obtained from research experiments and large-scale commercial farms in the region. The decline in pigeonpea yields could be attributed to the projected 2°C and 11% increase in temperature and rainfall, respectively. Pigeonpea is a Carbon-3 (C3) plant and is highly sensitive to waterlogging; therefore, existing pigeonpea varieties may not thrive in the predicted hotter and wetter conditions [59, 60]. High temperatures reduce the rate of photosynthesis in legumes due to their C3 photosynthesis cycle leading to low yields [61, 62]. Waterlogging blocks oxygen supply to roots which hamper permeability [63], delays flowering and reduces vegetative growth, photosynthetic rate, biomass and grain yield in pigeonpea [64, 65]. Short duration

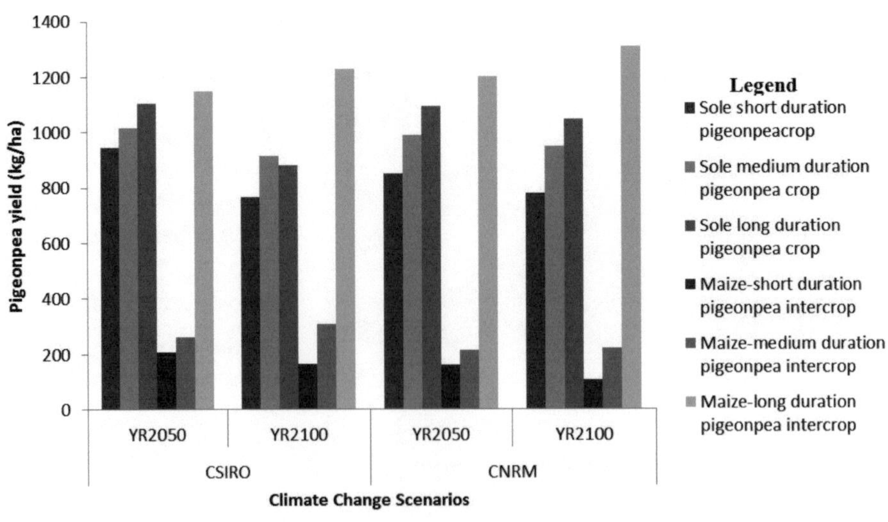

Figure 2.
Projected pigeonpea yields for Katumani in the near and far future.

pigeonpea varieties like Mbaazi I are more prone to the risk of yield reduction due to waterlogging compared to the medium and long duration varieties such as Kat 60/8 and Mbaazi II, respectively [66]. Therefore, farmers in Katumani and similar areas in the country may have to rethink their dependence on pigeonpea going into the future. Scientists also need to start breeding for more heat and waterlogging-tolerant varieties to save the livelihoods of thousands of resource-poor households in ASALs and safeguard the huge pigeonpea export market that Kenya currently commands.

4. Conclusion

Prospects for growing maize in Katumani are high both in the near (2050) and far (2100) future. However, pigeonpea production will be negatively affected by climate change going forward due to pigeonpea's susceptibility to high temperatures and waterlogging. Therefore, farmers in the ASALs need to rethink their dependence on pigeonpea while national plant breeding programs need to start developing heat and waterlogging-tolerant varieties to help thousands of resource-poor households in ASALs to adapt to climate change and protect the huge pigeonpea export market that Kenya currently enjoys.

Acknowledgements

We are grateful to the Kenya Agricultural and Livestock Research Organization (KALRO) for allowing us to conduct this study. We also thank the Department of Land Resource Management and Agricultural Technology (LARMAT) of the University of Nairobi, KALRO's Natural Resources Management (NRM) Programme and the Kenya Meteorological Service (KMS) office in Machakos County for their technical support.

Author details

Kizito Musundi Kwena[1,2*], G.N. Karuku[1], F.O. Ayuke[1] and A.O. Esilaba[3]

1 Department of Land Resource Management and Agricultural Technology (LARMAT), University of Nairobi, Nairobi, Kenya

2 Kenya Agricultural and Livestock Research Organization (KALRO), Katumani Research Centre, Machakos, Kenya

3 Kenya Agricultural and Livestock Research Organization (KALRO), Nairobi, Kenya

*Address all correspondence to: kwenakizito@yahoo.com

IntechOpen

© 2020 The Author(s). Licensee IntechOpen. This chapter is distributed under the terms of the Creative Commons Attribution License (http://creativecommons.org/licenses/by/3.0), which permits unrestricted use, distribution, and reproduction in any medium, provided the original work is properly cited.

References

[1] Audi P, Nagarajan L, Jones Rl. Seed interventions and cultivar diversity in pigeonpea: A farmer-based assessment in eastern Kenya. Journal of New Seeds. 2008;**9**:111-127

[2] Gwata ET, Shimelis H. Evaluation of Pigeonpea Germplasm for Important Agronomic Traits in Southern Africa. 2013. Available form: http://dx.doi.org/10.5772/56094

[3] Høgh-Jensen H, Myakka FA, Sakala WD, Kamalongo D, Ngwira A, Vesterager JM, et al. Yields and qualities of pigeonpea varieties grown under smallholder farmers' conditions in eastern and southern Africa. African Journal of Agricultural Research. 2007;**2**(6):269-278

[4] Nagarajan L, Audi P, Jones R. Supply of Pigeonpea Genetic Resources in Local Markets of Eastern Kenya. International Food Policy Research Institute (IFPRI) Discussion Paper 00819; 2008

[5] Shiferaw B, Okello J, Muricho G, Omiti J, Silim S, Jones R. Unlocking the Potential of High-Value Legumes in the Semi-Arid Regions: Analyses of the Pigeonpea Value Chains in Kenya. Research Report No. 1. Nairobi: International Crops Research Institute for the Semi-Arid Tropics; 2008

[6] USAID. Staple Foods Value Chain Analysis: Country Report—Kenya. 2010. pp 126-150. Avaialble from: http//pdf.usaid.gov/pdf_doc/Pnadw641.pdf

[7] Recha J, Kinyangi J, Omondi H. Climate Related Risk and Opportunities for Agricultural Adaptation and Mitigation in Semi-Arid Eastern Kenya. Nairobi, Kenya: Climate Change, Agriculture and Food Security (CCAFS) Program, ILRI; 2012. p. 42. Available from: https://ccafs.cgiar.org/sites/default/files/assets/docs/climate_related_risk_and_opportunities.pdf

[8] Kumar RR, Karjol K, Naik GR. Variation of sensitivity to drought stress in pigeonpea (*Cajanus cajan* (L.) Millsp.) during seed germination and early seedling growth. World Journal of Science and Technology. 2011;**1**:11-18

[9] Adu-Gyamfi JJ, Myakka FA, Sakala WD, Odgaard R, Vesterager JM, Hogh-Jensen H. Biological nitrogen fixation and nitrogen and phosphorus budgets in farmer-managed intercrops of maize-pigeonpea in semi-arid southern and eastern Africa. Plant and Soil. 2007;**295**:127-136

[10] Myakka FA, Sakala WD, Adu-Gyamfi JJ, Kamalongo D, Ngwira A, Odgaard R, et al. Yields and accumulations of N and P in farmer-managed maize-pigeonpea intercrop in semi-arid Africa. Plant and Soil. 2006;**285**:207-220

[11] Snapp SS, Silim SN. Farmer preferences and legume intensification for low nutrient environments. Plant and Soil. 2002;**245**:181-192

[12] Simtowe F, Shiferaw B, Kassie M, Abate T, Silim S, Siambi M, et al. Assessment of the Current Situation and Future Outlooks for the Pigeonpea Sub-Sector in Malawi. Working Paper. Nairobi: ICRISAT; 2008

[13] Kirimi L, Sitko N, Jayne TS, Karin F, Muyanga M, Sheahan M, et al. A Farm Gate-to-Consumer Value Chain Analysis of Kenya's Maize Marketing System. The Michigan State University (MSU). International Development Working Paper No. 111; 2011

[14] Ngome AF, Mtei MK, Becker M. Leguminous cover crops differentially affect maize yields in Western

Kenya. Journal of Agriculture and Rural Development in the Tropics. 2011;**112**:1-10

[15] Christensen JH, Hewitson B, Busuioc A, Chen A, Gao X, Held I, et al. Regional climate projections. In: Solomon S, Qin D, Manning M, Chen Z, Marquis M, Averyt KB, et al., editors. Climate Change 2007: The Physical Science Basis. Contribution of Working Group I to the Fourth Assessment Report of the Intergovernmental Panel on Climate Change. Cambridge, UK: Cambridge University Press; 2007

[16] Cooper PJM, Dimes J, Rao KPC, Shapiro B, Shiferaw B, Twomlow S. Coping better with current climatic variability in the rain-fed farming systems of sub-Saharan Africa: An essential first step in adapting to future climate change? Agriculture, Ecosystems and Environment. 2008;**126**:24-35

[17] Doherty RM, Sitch S, Smith B, Lewis SL, Thornton PK. Implications of future climate and atmospheric CO2 content for regional biogeochemistry, biogeography and ecosystem services across East Africa. Global Change Biology. 2009. DOI: 10.1111/j.1365-2486.2009.01997. x

[18] Thornton PK, Jones PG, Alagarswamy G, Andresen J. Spatial variation of crop yield response to climate change in East Africa. Global Environmental Change. 2009;**19**(1):54-65

[19] Osbahr H, Viner D. Linking Climate Change Adaptation and Disaster Risk Management for Sustainable Poverty Reduction. Kenya Country Study. A study carried out for the Vulnerability and Adaptation Resource Group (VARG) with support from the European Commission; 2006

[20] Herrero M, Ringler C, van de Steeg J, Thornton P, Zhu T, Bryan E, et al. Climate Variability and Climate Change and their Impacts on Kenya's Agricultural Sector. Nairobi, Kenya: ILRI; 2010

[21] Ochieng J, Kirimi L, Mathenge M. Effects of climate variability and change on agricultural production: The case of small-scale farmers in Kenya. Wageningen Journal of Life Sciences. 2016;**77**:71-78

[22] Cline WR. Global Warming and Agriculture: Impact Estimates by Country. Washington DC: Center for Global Development, Peterson Institute for International Economics; 2007. p. 7

[23] Lobell DB, Burke MB, Tebaldi C, Mastrandrea MD, Falcon WP, Naylor RL. Prioritizing climate change adaptation needs for food security in 2030. Science. 2008;**319**:607-610

[24] Parry ML, Rosenzweig C, Iglesias A, Livermore M, Fischer G. Effects of climate change on global food production under SRES emissions and socio-economic scenarios. Global Environmental Change. 2004;**14**:53-67

[25] Jones PG, Thornton PK. The potential impacts of climate change on maize production in Africa and Latin America in 2055. Global Environmental Change. 2003;**13**(1):51-59. DOI: 10.1016/S0959-3780(02)00090-0

[26] Kabubo-Mariara J, Karanja FK. The economic impact of climate change on Kenyan crop agriculture: A Ricardian approach. Global and Planetary Change. 2007;**57**(3):319-330. DOI: 10.1016/j.gloplacha.2007.01.002

[27] Food and Agriculture Organization of the United Nations (FAO). Climate Change and Tea in Kenya: Impact Assessment and Policy Response. 2014. Available from: http://www.fao.org/fileadmin/templates/est/Climate change/kenya/Project brief Kenya-EN FINAL.pdf

[28] Karuku GN, Gachene CKK, Karanja N, Cornelius W, Verplancke H. Use of CROPWAT model to predict water use in irrigated tomato (*Lycopersicon esculentum*) production at Kabete, Kenya. East African Agricultural and Forestry Journal. 2014;**80**(3):175-183

[29] Jaetzold R, Schmidt H, Hornet ZB, Shisanya CA. Farm Management Handbook of Kenya. Natural Conditions and Farm Information (Eastern Province). Vol. 11/C. 2nd Ed. Nairobi, Kenya: Ministry of agriculture/GTZ; 2006

[30] Keating BA, Siambi MN, Wafula BM. The impact of climatic variability on cropping research in semi-arid Kenya between 1955 and 1985. In: Probert ME, editor. Sustainable Dry Land Cropping. ACIAR Proceedings No.41. Australia: Canberra; 1992. pp. 16-25

[31] Gicheru PT. Detailed Soil Survey of Three Newly Opened Farms in Kathekakai Co-Operative Society Farm (Section B) in Konza Region, Machakos District. Report No.D73. Kenya Soil Survey, Nairobi, Kenya; 1996

[32] Gicheru PT, Ita BN. Detailed Soil Survey of Katumani National Dryland Farming Research Station Farms (Machakos District). Report No. D43. Kenya Soil survey, Ministry of Agriculture; 1987

[33] Food and Agriculture Organization of the United Nations (FAO)/UNESCO. Soil Map of the World. Revised Legend. World Soil Resources. Report 60. Rome, Italy: FAO; 1997. p. 41

[34] WRB. World Reference Base for Soil Resources 2006. World Soil Resources Report No. 103. Rome: Food and Agriculture Organization of the United Nations; 2006. ISBN-10: 9251055114

[35] NAAIAP. Soil suitability evaluation for maize production in Kenya. A report by National Accelerated Agricultural Inputs Access Programme (NAAIAP) in collaboration with Kenya Agricultural Research Institute (KARI) Department of Kenya Soil Survey, Kilimo, Nairobi, Kenya; 2014

[36] Cooper PJM, Rao KPC, Singh P, Dimes J, Traore PS, Rao K, et al. Farming with current and future climate change risk: Advancing a – "Hypothesis of Hope" for rainfed agriculture in semi-arid tropics. Agricultural Research. 2009;**7**:1-19

[37] Dixit PN, Cooper PJM, Rao KP, Dimes J. Adding value to field-based agronomic research through climate risk assessment: A case study of maize production in Kitale, Kenya. Experimental Agriculture. 2011;**47**:317-338

[38] Challinor A, Wheeler T, Garforth C, Craufurd P, Kassam A. Assessing the vulnerability of food crop systems in Africa to climate change. Climate Change. 2007;**83**(3):381-399

[39] Dimes JP. Application of APSIM to evaluate crop improvement technologies for enhanced water use efficiency in Zimbabwe's SAT. In Management for Improved Water Use Efficiency in the Dry Areas of Africa and West Asia: Proceedings of a Workshop organized by the Optimizing Soils Water Use (OSWU) Consortium, April 2002, Ankara, Turkey. 2005. pp. 203-214

[40] Micheni A, Kihanda F, Irungu J. Soil organic matter (SOM): The basis for improved crop production in arid and semi-arid climates of eastern Kenya. In: Bationo, A, Managing Nutrient Cycles to Sustain Soil Fertility in Sub-Saharan Africa. Nairobi, Kenya: Academy Science Publishers (ASP); 2004. pp. 239-248

[41] Keating BA, Carberry PS, Hammer GL, Probert ME, Robertson MJ, Holzworth D, et al.

An overview of APSIM, a model designed for farming systems simulation. European Journal of Agronomy. 2003;**18**:267-288

[42] Whitbread AM, Robertson MJ, Carberry PS, Dimes JP. How farming systems simulation can aid the development of more sustainable smallholder farming systems in southern Africa. European Journal of Agronomy. 2010;**32**:51-58

[43] Holzworth DP, Huth NI, de Voll PG, Zurcher EJ, Hermann NI, McLean G, et al. APSIM-evolution towards a new generation of agricultural systems simulation. Environmental Modeling Software. 2014;**62**:327-350

[44] APSIM. An Overview. 2017. Available from: https://www.researchgate.net/publication/263238329 [Accessed: 21 June 2017]

[45] Wang EH, Cresswell H, Paydar Z, Gallant J. Opportunities for manipulating catchment water balance by changing vegetation type on a topographic sequence: A simulation study. Hydrological Processes. 2008;**22**:736-749

[46] Okwach GE, Simiyu CS. Evaluation of long-term effects of management on land productivity in semi-arid areas of Kenya using simulation models. East African Agricultural and Forestry Journal. 1999;**65**:143-155

[47] Okwach GE. Developing an Appropriate Tool for Managing Runoff, Erosion and Crop Production in Semi-Arid Eastern Kenya: A Case for APSIM Model. CARMASAK Technical Report No. 3. Kenya Agricultural Research Institute; 2002. p. 97. ISBN: 9966-879-47-1

[48] Wilby RL, Dawson CW. SDSM 4.2-A Decision Support Tool for the Assessment of Regional Climate Change Impacts. Version 4.2 User Manual; 2007

[49] Wilby RL, Dawson CW, Barrow EM. SDSM—A decision support tool for the assessment of regional climate change impacts. Environmental Modelling and Software. 2002;**17**:145-157

[50] Brown TJ, Hall BL, Westerling AL. The impact of twenty-first century climate change on wildland fire danger in the Western United States: An applications perspective. Climatic Change. 2004;**62**:365-388. DOI: 10.1023/B:CLIM.0000013680.07783.de

[51] Goldstein J, Milton J, Major N, Gachon P, Parishkura D. Climate Extremes Indices and Their Links with Future Water Availability: Case Study for Summer of 2001. In: Proceeding of the 57th Annual Conference of the Canadian Water Resources Association, 16-18 June 2004, Montréal, Canada. 2004. p. 7

[52] Nguyen VTV, Nguyen TD, Gachon P. On the linkage of large-scale climate variability with local characteristics of daily precipitation and temperature extremes: An evaluation of statistical downscaling methods. Advances in Geosciences. 2006;**4**(16):1-9

[53] Dibike Y, Gachon P, Hilaire A, Ouarda TBMJ, Nguyen VTV. Uncertainty analysis of statistically downscaled temperature and precipitation regimes in northern Canada. Theoretical and Applied Climatology. 2007 (in press)

[54] Nguyen TD, Nguyen VTV, Gachon P. A spatial-temporal downscaling approach for construction of intensity-duration-frequency curves in consideration of GCM-based climate change scenarios. In: Park et al., editors. Advances in Geosciences Vol. 6: Hydrological Sciences. World Scientific Publishing Company; 2007. pp. 11-21

[55] Rakhshandehroo GR, Afrooz AH, Pourtouiserkani A. Climate Change Impact on Intensity-Duration-Frequency

Curves in Chenar-Rahdar River Basin. ASCE Watershed Management 2015. 2015. pp. 48-61. Available from: https://www.researchgate.net/Publication/271515213

[56] Waithaka M, Nelson GC, Thomas TS, Kyotalimye M. East African Agriculture and Climate Change: A Comprehensive Analysis. Washington, DC, USA: IFPRI; 2013

[57] Downing TE. Climate Change and Vulnerable Places: Global Food Security and Country Studies in Zimbabwe, Kenya, Senegal, and Chile. Research Paper No. 1, Environmental Change Unit, University of Oxford, Oxford, United Kingdom, 1992. pp. 54

[58] Government of Kenya (GoK). National Climate Change Action Plan 2013-2017. Nairobi, Kenya: Ministry of Environment and Mineral Resources; 2013. pp. 59-60

[59] Chauhan YS, Silim SN, Kumar Rao JVDK, Johansen C. A pot technique to screen pigeonpea cultivars for resistance to water logging. Journal of Agronomy and Crop Science. 1997;**178**:179-183

[60] Perera AM, Pooni HS, Saxena KB. Components of genetic variation in short duration pigeonpea crosses under water logged conditions. Journal of Genetics and Plant Breeding. 2001;**55**:21-38

[61] Black C, Ong C. Utilisation of light and water in tropical agriculture. Agriculture and Forest Meteorology. 2000;**104**:25-47

[62] Lindquist JL, Arkebauer TJ, Walters DT, Cassman KG, Dobermann A. Maize radiation use efficiency under optimal growth conditions. Agronomy Journal. 2005;**97**:72

[63] Else MA, Davies WS, Malone M, Jackson MS. A negative hydraulic message from oxygen-deficient roots of tomato plant? Plant Physiology. 1995;**109**:1017-1024

[64] Sarode SB, Singh MN, Singh UP. Genetics of water logging tolerance in pigeonpea (*Cajanus cajan* (L.) Millsp). Indian Journal of Genetics and Plant Breeding. 2007;**67**:264-265

[65] Takele A, Mcdavid CR. The response of pigeonpea cultivars to short durations of water logging. African Crop Science Journal. 1995;**3**:51-58

[66] Matsunaga R, Ito O, Tobita S, Rao TP. Response of the pigeonpea (*Cajanus cajan* (L.) Millsp.) to nitrogen application and temporary waterlogging. In: Kutschera L, Hubl E, Lichtenegger E, Persson H, Sobotic M, editors. IRR Symposium Wien University. Klagenfurt: Bodenkultur; 1991. pp. 183-186

Section 4

Sustainability

Chapter 15

Spatial Carrying Capacity and Sustainability: Cities, Basins, Regional Transformation

Tao Ma, Nairong Tan, Xiaolei Wang, Fanfan Zhang and Hui Fang

Abstract

This chapter focuses on the spatial carrying capacity of different types of space units. Based on the characteristics of different units, it discusses how resource carrying capacity, environmental carrying capacity, ecological carrying capacity, and infrastructure carrying capacity together affect the spatial carrying capacity and allocation efficiency of space units. Cities need agglomeration of economic and demographic elements to expand the scale of spatial carrying capacity. Basins need to allocate water resources rationally under the condition of limited water resources for the sustainable development of river basin ecosystem. Regions need to explore regional comparative advantages and transformation paths from regional industries. The case studies discuss how the spatial carrying capacity of cities, river basins, and regional transformation adapt to environmental changes and the direction of carrying capacity improvement.

Keywords: spatial carrying capacity, cities, basin, regional transformation

1. Introduction

Environmental change is having a huge impact on human society, how to optimize, adjust and reconstruct the interaction between human and natural systems, and how to provide urban residents with a high-quality living environment [1], has become the critical issues faced by human society. At present, it has exceeded that China's population is more than 1.5 billion, and in the future, economic and demographic factors will continue to gather in the medium and long term. Meanwhile, a series of issues such as food security, water resource security, ecological load, and air pollution will be highlighted. From the perspective of the relationship between spatial carrying capacity and sustainability in China, cities, basins and regions are not adapted to resource and environmental carrying capacity. The economically dense megacities such as the Beijing-Tianjin-Hebei Region, Yangtze River Delta, and Guangdong-Hong Kong-Macao Greater Bay Area are closed to or exceed their carrying capacity. It is necessary to coordinate and improve the comprehensive carrying capacity of upper and lower reaches about the river basins [2], due to the Yangtze River, Yellow River, Pearl River, and other river basins connect ecologically fragile highly dense economic areas to many provinces and cities in in China.

This chapter focuses on the relationship between the carrying capacity of different types of space and sustainability, taking the spatial carrying capacity of Chinese cities, river basins and regions under the influence of changes in resource and environmental elements as the research object, and discussing the direction on the improvements on different units adapted to environmental changes.

2. Spatial carrying capacity and sustainability

2.1 The analytical framework of spatial carrying capacity

Carrying capacity originally refers to the mechanical or engineering characteristics of manufactured objects or systems. It appears in the shipping field with steam power as a sign, and is used to evaluate wind and steam power [3]. In the 1870s, when carrying capacity was first applied to biological and natural systems, it was used to measure the maximum amount of animals and food from natural system extremes. The evolution of carrying capacity is the inevitable result of human transformation and development in nature. From the initial biosphere consideration of the maximum of individuals or populations to the planet-scale development, sustainability research on carrying capacity is playing an increasingly important role under the constraints of global environmental change.

China is one of the most populous countries in the world. The degree of governance of climate change and environmental degradation has a profound impact on the process of global sustainable development. Therefore, the establishment of carrying capacity as the core analysis tool selects three levels of cities, basins and regions, and through multi-scale and multi-level element coupling, respectively proposes promotion strategies and spatial layout models, in order to achieve the realization of China's economic society sustainable development goals. Cities are relatively small carrying capacity units, river basins are secondary carrying capacity units. The basic urban units constitute the spatial carrying capacity unit at the basin scale. The basin carrying capacity unit belongs to the regional carrying capacity unit.

2.2 The spatial carrying capacity of cities

A city is a multi-dimensional carrying space consisting of resources, environment, ecology, population, economy, and society, which are the foundation of sustainability. A city is an important carrying space not only consisting of population, ecosystems, industrial clusters, but also for resource consumption and environmental pollution. The space provided by the urban unit is a construction and industrial development space, such as economic output, city scale, traffic capacity, land resources, etc. The spatial scale and growth boundary are affected by the interaction of resources, environment and technology, human activity and environmental sustainability, which is coordinated to the ultimate goal, so that it can be protected and improved the resources for the survival of humans.

The preconditions oriented in multi-element expansion of urban space are spatial carrying capacity for the development of sustainable. Sustainability of urban units is the foundation of social economic development, which lie both in regional and higher levels of units. They are the fundamental area for various aggregation factors of production, which carry more and more efficient production through the expansion of space scale, population size, industry, transportation and urban infrastructures. Despite that, sustainability is the precondition for expansion of units, setting goals within the boundaries of spatial carrying capacity and taking baseline of resources and environment, in such a way as to facilitate comprehensive benefits.

2.3 The spatial carrying capacity of River Basin

Basin scale is a spatial unit divided by natural geographical ecosystem. Due to the sharing of water resources in the basin, the upstream and downstream water resources competition is fierce, and the water resources carrying capacity of each city forms a common support and constraint, the total amount is fixed, and the relationship between this and the other changes. It is characterized by linking different administrative units and stakeholders through water resources. The sustainable development of river basin mainly focuses on the rational allocation of water resources and maximizes the economic, social and ecological conditions within the threshold value of water resources carrying capacity.

The basin carrying capacity should be innovated in management mode in upstream and downstream. In the new stage of coordinated development of river basin, it is necessary to take full account of the disharmonious separation of basin units, the limited overall development space of the basin, the enhancement of the correlation between the development activities of different units in the same basin and the constraint of the total amount threshold of the carrying capacity of resources and environment, so it is necessary to carry out fine management of water resources in the basin. The current basin development model still has many problems, such as low efficiency of water resources utilization, fierce competition between upstream and downstream water resources, and low overall water quality. Therefore, it is necessary to coordinate the cooperation among different units in the basin to enhance the overall carrying capacity of the basin.

2.4 The comprehensive carrying capacity of regional function division

The comprehensive carrying capacity of a region is different in space and changes dynamically with time. The comprehensive carrying capacity of the region is the sum of all resources in a specific space (material resources, energy resources, information resources, space resources, human resources, social resources, etc.), which can provide the comprehensive development capacity of the region. On one hand, Because of the difference of economic development level and resource endowment in each region, the comprehensive carrying capacity of each region is different. On the other hand, the spatial carrying capacity of a region changes dynamically with time. In some resource-based urban areas, the development of natural resources will generally promote the development of industry and the growth of population, bringing about the improvement of carrying capacity. However, When the stock of natural resources to reduce or dried up, there will be a leading industry gradually decline, the ecological environment is destroyed, social problems highlight contradictions.

To promote the coordinated development of regions, it is necessary to concentrate population and economic activities in regions with high carrying capacity according to the differences of core functions of each region, while reducing the scale of population aggregation and economic activities in ecologically fragile regions. The connotation of regional coordinated development is to comprehensively coordinate the relationship among economy, society, population, resources and environment, and guide the economic layout and population distribution to adapt to the carrying capacity of resources and environment. In order to reduce the imbalance of regional development is to promote regional harmonious development, according to different regional development potential and the resource environmental carrying capacity, according to the regional division of labor and coordinated development of the principle of overall consideration the future population distribution, economic layout, land use and urbanization pattern, reverse the regional resources excessive development for a long time, the regional ecological environment has become increasingly serious phenomenon.

3. Environmental changes and sustainable development of cities

3.1 The impact of environmental changes on spatial carrying capacity of cities

Natural resource and environment are the basic elements of urban spatial carrying capacity, which determine the degree of urban industrialization and expansion. Understanding the great changes in the spatial and material relationship between human and nature are the key determinant factor of sustainable development [4]. The natural environment can provide humans with the greatest degree of carrying capacity, and the environmental resource basing on which all human economic activities ultimately depend include ecosystems that produce various services [5]. As a result of the interaction between human activities and the natural environment, different natural landscapes, economic patterns, and temporal and spatial dynamic characteristics are produced. It can examine the maximum carrying capacity under the action of man-land relationship, including the upper limit of population, natural resource (water, atmosphere, animals and plants, minerals), and the characteristics of the dynamic changes on the spatial and temporal scales. There has a significant impact on social and economic activities about geographical environment and climatic conditions. China has abundant natural resources, including coal, crude oil, natural gas, pyrite, bauxite, copper, etc., which have promoted the development of manufacturing in coastal and inland area. The difference in factor supply brought by regional resource endowments, which the fundamental reason that determines the continuous development and spatial expansion. Furthermore, the development of urban spatial carrying capacity has gradually shifted to regional division of labor basing on comparative advantages, the man-land relationship shifts to a larger-scale study of the ecological environment, economy and society.

The carrying capacity dominated by environmental changes is transformed into a spatial constraint factor as the urban expansion reaches to the certain threshold. The urban spatial carrying capacity under the background of environmental changes focuses on physical geography, resource endowment, and extreme carrying limit. However, when the urban expansion approaches the carrying threshold, the laws of ecological economy such as total withdrawal, structural optimization, and restoration of ecological system functions begin to affect the efficiency of urban economic and social development, and the ecological carrying function is transmitted to the ecological restraint function. At this time, the spatial carrying capacity should be expanded from the original regional scale to the planetary boundary frame below the global scale, emphasizing that the urban economic and social activities should maintain a sufficient safe distance from the threshold of the earth's ecosystem [6]. The concept of planetary boundaries provides a starting point to understand the natural resources and processes on which human sustainable development depends [7], and set up ecological carrying functions of different regions and scales through a global top-down perspective. Based on this, with the development of urban land resources and the expansion of urban space in China, the ecosystem and ecological environment has gradually become the constraining functional bearer of sustainable urban development. Because of negative economic-environmental externalities, when the threshold is approaching, the urban expansion and efficiency increase gradually show rigid constraints.

3.2 The unsustainable problems in urban development

The unsustainable problems in the process of urban development are mainly embodied in the spatial carrying capacity of economic society, population, resource endowments, environmental capacity and various urban service facilities. With the continuous expansion of cities and the rapid growth of population, the carrying capacity on resources and environment has gradually attracted widespread attention. In the process of large-scale industrialization and urbanization in China, the land element, as the basic element of spatial carrying capacity, is the direct element of population, industry and life community of mountains, rivers, forests, fields, lakes and grasses. Due to rapid consumption of land resources, the supply structure and allocation efficiency of land resources show long-term flexibility. China has a large number of resource-based cities dominated by coal, steel, and oil. At the same time, Beijing and Shanghai are also core cities with severe water shortages. In the long run, the structural scarcity of land resources, water resources, and mineral resources will further affect the sustainable development of cities. In the process of urbanization, a large number of populations have been concentrated, especially in rapidly developing global cities in China, where the floating population is huge, consequently a large number of resource consumption, energy consumption, and environmental pollution problems arise. The urban environmental capacity is close to saturation, smog and automobile exhaust pollution, which also common problems in the process of urban development. In addition, the allocation of urban infrastructure and public service facilities are unreasonable, especially the various urban service facilities of large cities have been overloaded, which are also an important issue that restricts the sustainable development.

3.3 Improvement of cities carrying capacity under the sustainable development goals

The spatial carrying capacity transmitted from the planetary boundary scale to the national downscaling is increased to achieve the sustainable development goals. Sustainable development requires the use of natural resources by humans to be kept within environmental limits [8], this means that on the basis of recognizing that human activities continue to cause major global environmental changes. As a criterion and important influencing factor of carrying capacity, it is necessary to fully account for the various public, exclusive and irreversible risks arising from the ever-increasing global climate change, water resource changes, and the fragility of ecosystems. In particular, the global climate change caused by the spatial diffusion of carbon dioxide-based greenhouse gases, which determining to environmental governance should shift from the original biosphere level to the global level planetary scale. The sustainable development and other national decomposition of goals can be achieved to need a multi-scale systematic approach [9]. Downscaling transmission from the planetary boundary scale to the national level can be realized by means of consume of good and services basing on carbon footprint [10].

The coordinated resource and environmental carrying capacity provide best standards of practice for China. In 2019, the "Several opinions on establishing spatial planning system and supervising its implementation" clarified the basic role of the evaluation of "resources and environmental carrying capacity and spatial suitability" based on bottom-line management and control [11]. In 2020, "Resources and Environment Carrying Capacity and Space Development Suitability Evaluation

Technical Guidelines (Trial Version)" established standards of practice in provinces, cities (districts) in China. Delineate urban growth boundaries, baseline of farmland, resource and environment through the evaluation system to achieve management and control of urban units; through the economic scale, population forecast and demand update in urban development, and at the same time integrate ecosystem units to achieve urban identity flexible management and control; by responding to the spatial layout of various elements in different scales of space, it can be achieved to realized the carrying capacity and scale of elements to sustainable development nationally.

The technological innovation should be used to improve the carrying capacity of resources and environment. A basic assumption of economics is the scarcity of resources, as the supply of resources is limited to the needs of human beings, mainly including the limitation of quantity, quality, time, space, structure, capital and environmental capacity, there is no exception for both natural and social resources. However, technological innovation can improve the utilization efficiency of resources, which alleviating the scarcity of resources to a certain extent, reducing the dependence on natural resources, damaging to the ecological environment, and improving the carrying capacity of resources and environment.

4. Environmental change and sustainable development of river basin

As an important typical spatial unit, basin has the characteristics of coordinating the upstream and downstream subsystems and coordinating the resource elements of each unit. There is a close relationship between the fluctuations of water resources in the basin. Under the condition that the total amount of water resources is fixed, it is of great significance to play the role of overall planning and unified allocation for the basin as a whole and each economic unit.

4.1 The impact of environmental change on spatial carrying capacity of River Basin

Environmental changes have intensified the vulnerability and instability of the whole basin space, and the spatial carrying pressure in the basin is increasing. With the continuous development of the resources in the basin, the vulnerability of the basin environment is increasing. The reserve of resource elements in the basin has become a huge constraint on the carrying capacity of the basin, especially the shortage of water resources has a great impact on the development of the basin. As an important area of ecological security, energy security, food security and economic security in China, the Yellow River Basin has serious problems such as low water use efficiency, shortage of water resources and serious water pollution in some provinces and regions. The imbalance of water supply and demand has become a serious challenge to the sustainable economic and social development of some provinces [12].

From the perspective of water carrying capacity, the total water load of the basin is too large. Gansu, Ningxia, Inner Mongolia. The water carrying capacity of Shaanxi and Shanxi provinces is in the state of overload and serious overload. Except for Qinghai Province and Gannan Prefecture of Gansu Province, the per capita water resources of other cities are in low and very low levels. The water consumption of ten thousand yuan industrial added value, groundwater exploitation coefficient and ecological environment water use rate are all in low and very low levels. Among them, the groundwater in Inner Mongolia except Alxa League is in low and very low level. The exploitation coefficient is above 15. The development and utilization degree of groundwater is very high. The irrigation water takes up 72.5% of the total water, and the ecological environment water consumption rate is only 4.7% [13].

In terms of water quality carrying capacity, the water quality of the middle and lower reaches of the Yellow River is poor. The water quality carrying capacity of Qinghai Province is mostly in the state of overload, while Xining city is in the state of overload; the water quality carrying capacity of some cities in Ningxia, Inner Mongolia and Shanxi Province is seriously overloaded, and the water quality standard rate and per capita pollutant discharge of water functional areas are in low and very low levels.

4.2 The unsustainable problems in the utilization of water resources in River Basin

The lower reaches of the Yellow River are frequently cut off, resulting in serious water shortage. The Yellow River has been cut off since 1972, and the time and frequency of the water cut-off are getting higher and higher. The Yellow River almost becomes a seasonal river, and the supply of water resources has exceeded its carrying capacity. The Yellow River Basin is a typical monsoon climate region. The runoff is mainly formed by rainfall [14]. The temporal and spatial distribution is extremely uneven, and the rainfall in flood season is abundant, which makes the contradiction between supply and demand of water resources more prominent in non-flood season.

The phenomenon of waste and low utilization of water resources is prominent. Taking Shandong as an example, the irrigation water from the Yellow River accounts for about 90% of the total water diversion in Shandong Province, and the main way is flood irrigation and string irrigation. The lining rate of the Yellow River diversion channel is only 7.5%. The irrigation area is short of supporting facilities and serious leakage. The irrigation water utilization coefficient is only about 0.4, compared with 0.7–0.8 in advanced countries, the waste is very serious [15].

The water ecosystem is destroyed, the water quality is deteriorated and the function of water body is reduced. With the continuous growth of population and the rapid development of industry and agriculture, the amount of sewage discharge has increased sharply. The increase of sewage discharge and the discharge of sewage exceed the standard, which makes the water pollution of the Yellow River become more and more serious. The pollution has developed from the tributary to the main stream, and the pollution of the main stream has also spread from the upper reaches to the middle and lower reaches.

4.3 Improvement of basin carrying capacity under sustainable development goals

The natural ecological background of the Yellow River Basin is fragile and the amount of water resources is limited. Due to the sharing of water resources in the Yellow River Basin, the water resources carrying capacity of each city forms a common support and constraint, the total amount is fixed, and the relationship between this and the other is ebb and flow. Ecological protection and high-quality development of the Yellow River Basin is a major national strategy. In order to implement this strategy, we should give full play to the leading role of central cities in the Yellow River Basin, enhance the comprehensive carrying capacity and resource allocation efficiency of the Yellow River Basin, and form a regional layout with complementary advantages and high-quality development.

Central cities play an important role in promoting regional development. Central cities and urban agglomerations have become the main spatial forms of carrying development elements. For example, with its unique geographical location, Jinan will play an important strategic role in the development of the central city of the Yellow River Basin, whether it is ecological protection and high-quality development of the Yellow River Basin or energy conversion, and its development vision will be highly consistent with the direction and implication of the national strategy. Therefore, it is an important way to promote the development of the carrying capacity of the Yellow River Basin. We should make use of the central city construction to improve the spatial ecological governance pattern of the Yellow River Basin. Taking the central city as the core, through coordinating the development orientation of the city, we can form an orderly urban development pattern and establish a multi-centers, network-based regional ecological governance structure. In this regional ecological governance structure, each region not only seeks its own interests independently, but also adjusts and adapts to each other under the framework of economic zone, realizing the coordination of economic boundary and governance boundary, thus promoting the optimization of spatial water resources governance pattern in the Yellow River Basin.

To promote the cooperation and linkage between the upper and lower reaches of the Yellow River Basin, and promote the urban water resources carrying capacity of the Yellow River Basin. We should strengthen the scientificity of the land and space planning of the central cities in the Yellow River Basin, make full use of the water resources to study and judge the future development direction of the city, promote the rational distribution of industry and population in the central city, and effectively play the role of scientific guidance and macro-control of urban planning. Promote the integration of multiple plans and establish a unified urban space planning system. In addition, it is also necessary to carry out accurate policies on the classification of different main functional areas such as key development areas, prohibited development areas and ecologically fragile areas, so as to continuously improve the spatial governance pattern of water resources in the Yellow River Basin. We should adhere to the principle of determining the city by water, land, people and production by water. The middle reaches of the region should further enhance the ability of energy development, utilization and allocation, strengthen the ecological environment governance and restoration, and actively cultivate the continuous alternative industries. The downstream areas should adhere to the intensive development, continuously transform the development momentum, and enhance the carrying capacity of population and industry. It is important to note, however, that the effectiveness of multi-level governance depends on the smooth realization of collaboration between governments and between governments and external actors, but there is a lack of analysis of how vertical and horizontal governance models empower each other rather than constrain each other.

5. Environmental change and sustainable development of regional function division

5.1 The impact of resource and environment changes on regional comprehensive carrying capacity

Many resource-based cities are facing the problem of resource exhaustion. According to the National Sustainable Development Plan for Resource-based Cities

(2013–2020), there are 262 resource-based cities in China. Among them, there are 126 prefecture-level administrative regions, 62 county-level cities, 58 counties and 16 municipal districts. In Northeast China, the industry started earlier and concentrated about one-sixth of the country's resource-based cities (21 prefecture-level cities in the three northeastern provinces). Many of these resource-based cities are facing the risk of resource depletion. Economic development in these regions is lagging behind, people's livelihood problems are prominent, and the ecological environment is under great pressure. Take Heilongjiang Province as an example. With the depletion of natural resources in Heilongjiang Province, 16 of the 33 major mines in the province have been depleted. The available resources of the forest industry system are only 19 million cubic meters, down 97.3% compared with the early days of the People's Republic of China. There are 40 forestry bureaus in the province, 2/3 of which have no forest to harvest. The Daqing oilfield has only 30 per cent of recoverable reserves.

Resource-exhausted cities bring about the reduction of population and industrial carrying capacity. For cities in northeast China, from 2014 to 2018, the urban population of some cities has decreased significantly, such as Anshan city by 19,700, Fushun city by 104,700, Daqing city by 91,400 and Benxi city by 89,000. Among the 19 resource-based cities available (the data of Greater Khingan Mountains and Yanbian Korean Autonomous Prefecture are not available among the 21 prefecture-level cities mentioned above), the urban population of 13 cities is decreasing, with a total decrease of 662,400 people [16]. On the whole, the population of resource-based cities in Northeast China is decreasing. Among the 19 prefecture level cities, only Daqing City (5.21%), Heihe City (0.38%) and Yichun City (0.16%) increased the proportion of mining industry employees in the whole city. The proportion of mining industry employees in other cities decreased, especially Qitaihe City (down 20.11%), Fuxin City (down 18.15%), Jixi City (down 13.31%). The employment proportion of mining industry in the city decreased the most.

5.2 The unsustainable problems in the current regional function division

The industry is relatively simple and the economic transformation is difficult. The economic decline of northeast China in recent years is closely related to the "single structure" of northeast China's industries. The proportion of energy and raw materials industries is too large, and modern manufacturing and modern service industries are underdeveloped. Due to the oversupply of bulk products in the international market, the domestic production of bulk product industry has been affected. Therefore, although there are many reasons for the economic downturn in northeast China, the "single structure" of the industry is undoubtedly one of the important reasons.

Excessive exploitation of resources results in serious environmental damage. Large-scale and extensive exploitation of natural resources is bound to cause serious damage to the ecological environment. In pursuit of wealth accumulation and economic growth, mining enterprises in areas with good resource endowments have risen to prominence, forming a large-scale, high-intensity and group-oriented resource development situation. Many resource-based cities thrive on mining, with cities built on top of mines and mining under cities. In recent years, the externalities of resource-based industries, such as environmental pollution, ecological decline and resource depletion, have become prominent. In particular, the process of resource utilization will cause environmental deterioration of atmosphere, water and soil, and at the same time, it will also give rise to a series of ecological environmental problems.

5.3 Improvement of regional carrying capacity under sustainable development goals

Use comparative advantage, guide population and industry to move to the area with higher carrying capacity. Northeast China is rich in resources and has the resource base to develop the primary industry and the secondary industry. However, after the service industry of the tertiary industry has become the main engine of economic development, most areas in northeast China are affected by natural and climatic conditions, which makes it difficult for them to gather and attract more population and industries, and resource-based cities that used to absorb a large number of jobs are gradually facing the pressure of population outflow. In the future, it needs to guide the migration of population and industries to the big cities in northeast China, improve the core carrying capacity of big cities, and develop the industries of higher education, scientific research, military industry and heavy industry with northeast characteristics in big cities. In other large areas, at least in the short term, resource-based cities in northeast China, as an important energy supply base, still need to continue to assume the responsibility and pressure of supplying resources and energy in order to ensure the rigid demand for resources and energy and national strategic security.

In the long run, we should strengthen the endogenous driving force of economic growth in resource-exhausted cities by cultivating diversified industrial systems. Utilize local advantages to develop diversified industries. Take Fuxin, a coal city in Liaoning province, as an example, it has vast land and great agricultural development potential, and the agricultural products processing industry is booming. Fuxin is rich in fluorite resources, and the fluorine chemical industry based on this raw material has begun to develop. Taking coal gangue produced in coal mining process as raw material, a number of building materials enterprises are emerging gradually. In view of the increasingly depleted resources, we should plan ahead to promote the development of emerging industries. For example, Volvo's plant in Daqing, is a model for the introduction of new industries. Daqing, which has no automobile industry base at all, has initially set up a high-end automobile factory, injecting new vitality into this increasingly exhausted resource-based city. In 2017, Daqing exported more than 25,000 vehicles, with an export volume of $897 million, accounting for 74% of the city's total exports. Therefore, it is feasible to construct capital intensive industries such as automobiles in remote, cold and remote areas due to their low labor cost, high degree of automation and low transportation cost.

Author details

Tao Ma*, Nairong Tan, Xiaolei Wang, Fanfan Zhang and Hui Fang
Harbin Institute of Technology, Harbin, China

*Address all correspondence to: matao@hit.edu.cn

IntechOpen

© 2020 The Author(s). Licensee IntechOpen. This chapter is distributed under the terms of the Creative Commons Attribution License (http://creativecommons.org/licenses/by/3.0), which permits unrestricted use, distribution, and reproduction in any medium, provided the original work is properly cited. (cc) BY

References

[1] Guiyou Zhang, Shuai Luo, Zhuowei Jing, Shuo Wei, Youhua Ma. Evaluation and Forewarning Management of Regional Resources and Environment Carrying Capacity: A Case Study of Hefei City, Anhui Province, China. Sustainability,2020,12(4). DOI:RePEc:gam:jsusta:v: 12:y:2020:i:4:p:1637-:d:323764

[2] FENG Z M, LI P. The genesis and evolution of the concept of carrying capacity: A view of natural resources and environment. Journal of Natural Resources, 2018, 33(9): 1475-1489(in Chinese).

[3] Nathan F. Sayre. The Genesis, History, and Limits of Carrying Capacity. Annals of the Association of American Geographers,2008,98(1). DOI:https://doi. org/10.1080/00045600701734356.

[4] Liyin Shen, Tianheng Shu, Xia Liao, Nan Yang, Yitian Ren, Mengcheng Zhu, Guangyu Cheng, Jinhuan Wang. A new method to evaluate urban resources environment carrying capacity from the load-and-carrier perspective. Resources, Conservation & Recycling,2020,154. DOI:10.1016/j.resconrec.2019.104616

[5] Rees W, Wackernagel M. Urban Ecological Footprints: Why Cities Cannot be Sustainable—and Why They are a Key to Sustainability. Environmental Impact Assessment Review, 2008. DOI:10.1007/978-0-387-73412-5_35

[6] K, Arrow, B., et al. Economic Growth, Carrying Capacity, and the Environment. Science, 1995. DOI:10.1126/science.268.5210.520

[7] FANG K, HEIJUNGS R, SNOO G R D. Understanding the complementary linkages between environmental footprints and planetary boundaries in a footprint-boundary environmental sustainability assessment framework. Ecological Economics, 2015, 114: 218-226. DOI:10.1016/j. ecolecon.2015.04.008

[8] Raworth Kate. A Safe and Just Space for Humanity: Can we live within the doughnut. Oxfam Policy and Practice: Climate Change and Resilience, 2012. DOI:10.5822/978-1-61091-458-1_3

[9] Tiina Häyhä, Paul L. Lucas, Detlef P. van Vuuren, Sarah E. Cornell, Holger Hoff. From Planetary Boundaries to national fair shares of the global safe operating space — How can the scales be bridged?. Global Environmental Change,2016,40. DOI:10.1016/j. gloenvcha.2016.06.008

[10] Daniel W. O'Neill, Andrew L. Fanning, William F. Lamb, Julia K. Steinberger. A good life for all within planetary boundaries. Nature Sustainability,2018,1(2). DOI:10.1038/ s41893-018-0021-4

[11] GU Chaolin. Scientific "Dual-Evaluation" as the Key and Foundation for Territorial Spatial Planning in the New Era. Journal of Urban and Regional Planning,2019,11(02):1-4 (in chinese).

[12] Xinhao Huang,Meng Sun.Stochastic Frontier Analysis of economic Growth Factors in Northeast China . Economic Review,2018(12):112-118.

[13] Yan Chen,Lin Mei .Quantitative Analysis of population distribution and Influencing Factors in resource-based cities in Northeast China. Geographic Science, 2008,38(03):402-409. DOI:10.13249/j.cnki.sgs.2018.03.010

[14] Shiwei Cheng , Yuwen Li. Environmental Governance and Development Strategies for Coal-resource-Exhausted Cities in Heilongjiang Province.Inner

Mongolia Science, Technology and Economy,2011(10):74-76.

[15] Shouting lu. New theory on urbanization development in northeast China. Journal of liaoning normal university (social science edition),2010,33(01):21-23.

[16] Xinying Zhang, Lianjun Tong. Analysis on the Construction of ecological Economy in resource-exhausted Cities. Ecological Economy,2005(01):59-63.

Chapter 16

Sustainability and Livelihoods

Chinta Srinivas

Abstract

The word environmental sustainability of late has been used as catch word for illustrating the climate change and subsequent sequential impact of various aspects of environmental landscape that include soil management, gaseous exchange, nutrient cycling, carbon emission, rainfall etc., Interpretation of environmental changes are interpreted based on very few trends which need not necessarily cause short term or long term impacts. The impact assessment of a region fundamentally depends on region specific history of habitat management, human interference, agricultural practices, Economic livelihood activities which depend on available natural resources and seasonality of intensity of activities. In the present study efforts are made to indentify the major NTFP based livelihood economic activities and relate the habitat management aspects along with commercial invasion that became detrimental to environmental threshold to call for sustainability alarm. The livelihoods in various developing economies have different environmental impacts. Such assessment of economic activities have any real environmentally detrimental consequences or is it being essentially over emphasizing to create such fears have been analyzed.

Keywords: sustainability, ecology, non timber forest economic activities, threshold

1. Introduction

Rural economic development being the focal point of many of the developing economies all over the world, livelihood opportunities is an inseparable entity. Livelihoods comprise the capabilities, assets (including both material and social resources) and activities for means of living [1]. A Livelihood is well-defined as the events, assets and the admittance which together defines the living multiplied by a single individual or family [2]. The three essential elements of life i.e. food, shelter and clothing are to be sourced or earned by any human being for sustaining his life and his family members. Therefore all such activities that involves means of finding food, water, shelter, clothing for self and his dependants can be referred to as livelihoods.

United Nations Sustainability Goals are to be addressed of which goal ending everywhere in all forms we see poverty. Culmination of starvation, accomplishing food security and better-quality Nutrition in addition to support and uplift Sustainable agriculture. Safeguard, renovate and encourage sustainable usage of earthly networks, sustainably be able to manage forests, fight against desertification as well as converse land degradation and halt biodiversity loss are the major direct impactful goals that can be addressed while indirectly combat the other sustainable goals during this study. Various studies have been reported on livelihood and sustainability [3], defined livelihood as a wealth of attainment of living. United

IntechOpen

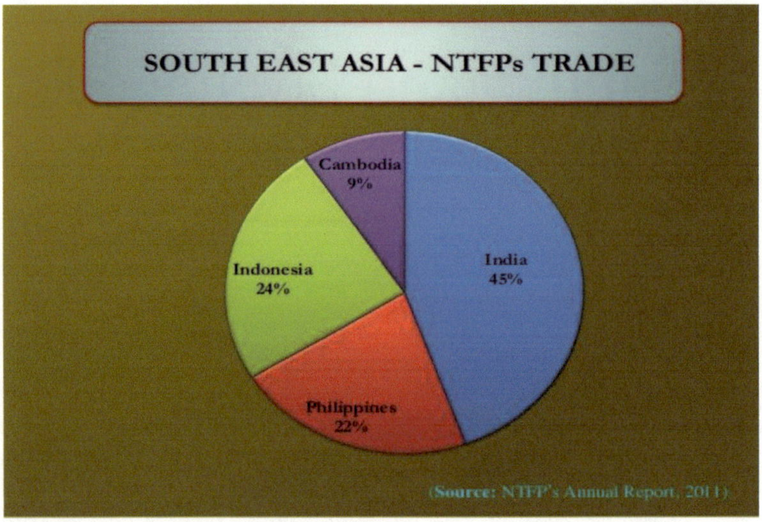

Figure 1.
Proportion of NTFP trade among representative countires of South East Asia.

Kingdom's Department of International Development (DFID) and the United States agency for International Development (USAID, 2005), more appropriately defines "Livelihoods are the means by which households obtain and maintain admittance to the possessions essential to ensure their immediate and long term survival". Approximately 90% of farming activities are carried by rural of rural families [4]. Whereas in Africa, 70% of income is achieved through farming activities. And in Asia and Latin America, 50% of the household income is achieved by farming [4]. Among these the rural populace practice fishery, livestock raising and also small-scale farming activities apart from these other non-farming activities for their survival and for source of income (**Figure 1**). Many studies are being carried through various angles on the livelihoods worldwide. The village studies tradition, dominated by economists, but not exclusively so, was an important, empirically-based alternatives to other economic analyses of rural situation [5]. In India, studies were made on diverse impacts of Green revolution [6, 7].

Studies on classic examination of rural change in Nigeria have been carried and also had studied the livelihood strategies in Zambia. Different people respond to changes in livelihoods differently, but the most common response seems to be that individuals and nations buoy their access to resources thus creating conditions for competition and conflict over those scare resources. The present paper enumerates the status of native population and various influencing factors in divergence ineffective sustainable development strategies compromising the livelihoods of indigenous people. This paper addresses the limitations of governmental imposition of laws and break-even point for co-existence of indigenous habitants to harness available resources for their own sustenance.

2. NTFP trade

Livelihoods while traversing over a long period has attained commercial proportions globally. Demand and supply determines the dynamics of production for example forest wood is estimated at 3469 million M3 in 2011, of which 1891Mn Cu.m is fuel wood and 1578 Mn cu.m is industrial round wood. Of the Forest fuel wood produced apart from consumption for domestic use, about 10 percent of

(115 Mn cu.m) is marketed internationally. Similarly of the 406 Mn cu.m sawn wood produced, 120 Mn cu.m internationally marketed throughout the world. Similarly such higher consumption patterns have been observed globally for various other forest products such as wood panels 288 Mn cu.m, of which 71 Mn cu.m is traded globally. Paper and Paperboard production out of 403 Mn cu.m of which 112 Mn cu.m was exported into global markets. Estimated value of $ US 246 billion forest products are globally traded in 2011 FAO (FAOSTAT, 2013). Production of tropical industrial logs of round wood among ITTO member countries increased from 40.4 million m3 in 2009 to 141.4 million m3 in 2010, which dropped to 137.7 million m3 in 2011. Indonesia, Brazil, India and Malaysia are the four major countries that accounted for almost three quarters of total production in 2010 and an estimated 63 percent of production was in the Asia Pacific, reduction of production by over 18% by Malaysia resulted in drastic decline in production [8]. It is also reported that Forestry & logging contributes to 1.2% of India's GDP (Economic Survey, Ministry of Finance, 2011). At the rate of 5.5 (CAGR) between 2007 and 2011 the Indian forest products industry had total revenue of $65,844.6 million in 2011 similarly Consumption by industries in terms of volume, increased at the rate of CAGR of 0.2 percent between 2007–2011, to reach a total of 355.4 million cubic meters in 2011. Projection based on performance of the industry is to accelerate, with an anticipated CAGR of 7.7 percent for the five-year period 2011–2016, which is expected to value US $ 95,467 million industry by the end of 2016. With the demand growth for forest based raw materials, resulting in drastic increase in harvest at a rate of CAGR of 5.5 percent calls for restraint and stricter forest policy and efforts to escalate sustainability to protect the livelihoods of generations to come while evolving strategies forest succession based on natural habitat supporting diverse products.

The trades between South East countries are given below as on 2011 (**Table 1**).

2.1 Supply chain of NTFP

The general pathways of supply chain of NTFP will illustrate the intricacies of each segment of raw material base. **Figure 2** depicts the schematic representation of supply chain of NTFP. Market access and strategic market interventions would determine the vertical and horizontal expansion of successful business enterprise. This can be achieved by facilitating through governmental interventions through its network of stakeholders and collaborating with national and international agencies as well as development projects [9, 10], however, demand for such forest based non-timber products will only be viable in which suitable initiatives would be beneficial

South – East Asia – NTFPs Trade				
Country	**Number of enterprises**	**Number employed**	**Number of villages**	**Sales (in Euros)**
India	27	2232	370	181594
Indonesia	29	1452	58	99838
Phillipines	64	1946	68	88417.8
Cambodia	38	7400	81	38344.2
Total	**163**	**7400**	**600**	**408196**

Source: *NTFF'S ANNUAL REPORT 2011.*

Table 1.
Comparative trade pattern among the south East Asian countries and their share in total NTFP trade.

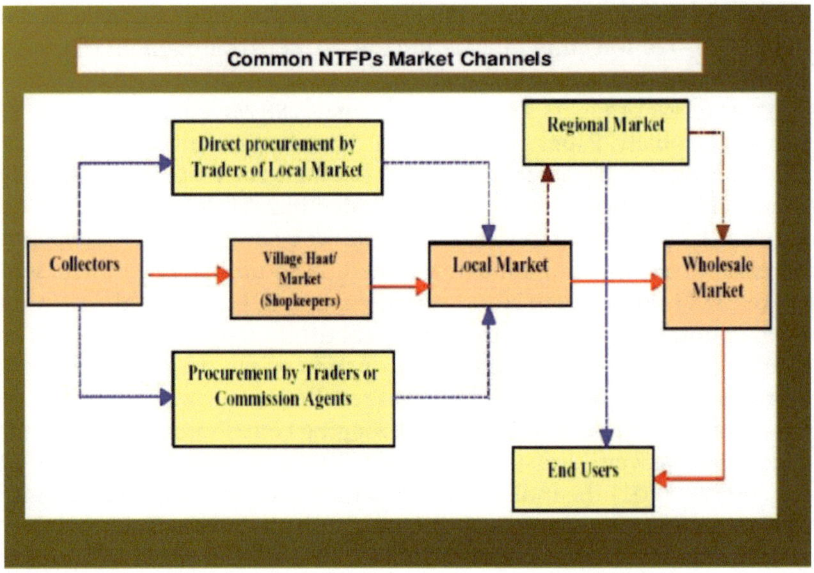

Figure 2.
Schematic representation supply Chain of NTFP.

to the livelihoods of people who depend on such products. High demand is a prerequisite for NTFP business establishment, as seen for instance for Tropical Tasar silkworm rearing on *Terminalia arjuna* trees and Temperate Tasar Silkworm rearing on *Quercus serrata* and *Quercus accutissima* or oak trees the cocoons of which are the raw material for silk industry in India, charcoal [11], brooms [12], amarula products [13] or agar oil. Renewed exerted pressure for demand often invites professional and intense marketing strategies, in particular for exceptionally innovative products introduced into international markets [14, 15], funds for which are frequently not freely available. Nevertheless, studies have demonstrated that demand potential for NTFP products can be considerable, with quality and environmental friendliness being the most important attributes [16, 17].

Business enterprises and projects based on NTFP business development models without considering the market consumption of product may fail since the increased supply of products cannot be absorbed, resulting in low prices of the products [10, 14, 18–21]. Markets and Prices being dynamic and volatile, NTF products will have to face hurdles in gaining foothold many a times [18, 22, 23], like many other commercial products, market slump and boom-bust cycles, or the sudden hibernation and limited or few buyers [13, 14] under such conditions, small-scale producers should be skillfully equipped with product diversification options readily in place within the NTFP enterprises and forsake other income-generating opportunities [24].

Certain value chain setups have been demonstrated to fetch larger benefits for NTFP-processing enterprises. Short value chains are seen as beneficial, since the role of middlemen is restricted and producers can potentially obtain higher prices [1, 21, 25]. Furthermore, shorter chains may also ease implementation and control of standards [14]. The unorganized nature of NTFP becomes vulnerable to exploitative role of intermediaries, who misappropriate accrued benefits that have a cascading effect contributing towards poor marketing margins for producers has often been demonstrated [24, 26, 27]. However, lack of market information, poor infrastructure and financial constraints, intermediaries may sometimes be the only pathway for producers to market their products. The NTFP when takes the shape of organized and structured system, the value chains with close cooperation among members are also commonly associated with economic benefits. Close networking and cooperation between collectors and processors might result in cost effectiveness and ensure that high-quality raw material is sourced through integrating modern technological interventions, for instance, via setup of collection centers, buyer–seller meets or pick-up events [1, 28]. With modern technologies of SMS services Market, product and prices are available on finger tips. Such information dissemination services and networking among NTFP collectors can also provide collectors with assured market openings [29] via contracts; linkage of producers of limited capacity to international markets with higher profitable prices would improve their income [14, 30]. Such mutually co-existing cooperative system may also occur via groups of informal social norms, integrating value added supply chain members together, and providing accrued benefits.

Though, partnership among value chain members should not be seen as a highly lucrative proposition, but are inter-dependant mutualism depends on the respective posturing. For example, small-scale producers may be limited in their financial flexibility that allow economic freedom and are relegated to disadvantageous position depending on the conditions existing or set [18]. Furthermore, they may be restricted with little elbow room to exhibit higher value addition without scope for value-added NTFP development, whereas groups further downstream may accrue higher profits [20]. The livelihoods thus sustained by means of the NTFP are to be used judiciously to uphold the balance of harvesting and regeneration of forest resources made available for consumption on its own over a period of time.

The increased rate of demand and supply increasing at the rate of 5.5% have implications on, the imminent danger of depletion of NTFP and its cascading effect on livelihoods and unemployment. The rights of livelihoods and employment are undermined of aboriginals or actual inhabitants of the forest areas. The sustainability backed by stringent forest laws has implicit political maneuvering to displace original inhabitants with settlers resulting in ethnic conflict as observed in north eastern India.

2.2 Aboriginals and livelihoods

Forest deprivations as well as deforestation are serious threats to sustainable development; their exponential rate of growth poses a severe risk to the world's ecosystems. Forests are common property resources in many parts of the world. As [31] argued, open access to forests, without restriction, can be subjected to indiscriminate harvesting leading to degradation of forests. Various non-timber forest products (NTFPs) manufactures drive their operations in unbarred or with limited self -restraint access systems of resource occupancy, resulting in misuse of NTFPs [12]. Aimed at the imperishable harvest of NTFPs, land and resource occupancy are crucial [32] quick expansion of market of NTFP products with little or no proprietorship security leads to over-harvesting [33]. However, the institutional interventions, policies, and law enforcement at the various levels both at local and international strata could help reduce the cataclysm of multitudes [14] and lead to the judicious utilization of quotidian resources.

Millions of people who depend directly or indirectly on forests for their livelihoods or forest produces either entirely or partially along the entire segments of supply chain for either goods or service facilities at regional or international level will critically get affected due to forest degradation (FAO, 2011). The impact of forest degradation which result in reduced forest productivity which has a cascading detrimental effect on the livelihood of forest-dependent communities. The reasons for forest degradation often is attributed intricate complex interplay between forces of direct influences functioning at the local or provincial levels and ancillary influencing forces functioning at the local, regional, national and international levels [7]. In general reasons for forest degradation is primarily attributed to interference of extreme anthropogenic factors in developing countries, while in developed countries natural events are usually the reasons for genesis of degradation (FAO, 2011). Fuel wood collection, charcoal making, and timber logging are the most severe problems fostering forest degradation in Africa and subtropical Asia, while timber logging and uncontrolled fires are the main drivers of degradation in Latin America [34, 35].

The main direct drivers of forest degradation in Myanmar are illegal logging, overexploitation of forest resources, fuel wood collection, and shifting cultivation [35]. Conventionally, the major contributing factor for forest degradation in Myanmar is attributed to excessive human infringement and exploitative activities, specifically the overexploitation of forest resources. However, very little is known about the reasons behind these activities driving forest degradation. It is of utmost importance to understand the degree of needs for survival of local population on forest resources of NTFPs and to recognize the contributing factors affecting this dependence. Reducing Emissions from Deforestation and Forest Degradation (REDD+) is an international voluntary mechanism under the United Nations Framework Convention on Climate Change (UNFCCC) designed to mitigate climate change by reducing greenhouse gases (GHG) emissions (UNFCCC Report, 2007).

The influencing factors which are attributed to forest degradation as well as deforestation by considering both social and natural systems are at the fundamental base by understanding the underlying mechanisms behind the forces of forest degradation is imperative to achieve the UN sustainable development goals. Utilization of forest resources in excess resulting from over dependence of the communities are the causative attributes which mainly lead to forest degradation. Thus, by understanding influences of critical factors of survival on NTFPs would help blueprint and/or strategize to constitute to inscription on impediments on various characteristics by analyzing NTFPs for their livelihoods of such forest-dependent communities and their potential for developing policies and strategic interventions or measures (PAMs) that could mitigate in reducing forest degradation and restore or otherwise reestablish and improved forest management techniques. Policies measures thus enacted by countries undertake to address the grounds for deforestation and forest degradation nationally to mitigate the dangers of emerging environmental issues [32, 36]. Multipronged approach of in combinations of new policy and measures from different sources are required to collectively address priority issues confronting the region specific measures to implementation, in a coherent way [REDD+ Programme. 2018). Depending on the country specific (i.e., priority, political preference, capacity, and stakeholders involved), policy measures may be a mixture of legal and institutional reforms, regulatory measures, and incentives taking social and environmental safeguards into account as well as capacity building [37]. Strategically South Asian countries need to ensure policy measures that address the priority drivers of forest degradation and deforestation and also to overcome the barriers to the sustainable management of forests (REDD+ Program. 2017). A balance needs to be made when Policy measures being contemplated, such as legal or regulatory reform need to be implemented at the national level while some should be implemented at the local level (REDD+ Programme, 2017). This present status underscores the need to further assess the fundamental rationale of depletion of forests and forest degradation and the dependency of local population on forest resources when the REDD+ plan is executed in a specific region. Strategies to reduce excessive exploitation of NTFPs, a policy structure could be evolved based on a close evaluation of the issues that affect aboriginal community dependent on Non-Timber Forest Products (NTFPs).

The term **Indigenous peoples**, besides recognized in some areas as **First peoples**, **First Nations**, **Aboriginal peoples** or **Native peoples** or **autochthonous peoples**, are ethnic groups who are the original or earliest known inhabitants of an area, Groups usually are described as indigenous when they practice and continue to practice same traditions or other characteristics of an initial culture that is associated with a designated region. Many indigenous people do not practice this characteristic, as most people have imbibed substantial components of a colonial culture, such as attires, religious beliefs or languages and dialects. Indigenous peoples may have adopted themselves in a given region (sedentary) or might have relocating lifestyle across a large territory, but they generally establish linkages to their ancestry by descent co-existing with a specific region on which they dwell. Indigenous societies are found in every inhabited climate zone and continent of the world where human settlements are known to exist. The inter-relationship of habitants and their means of living have been debated in many international forums and commissions. It was specified that four criterions must be fulfilled in order to qualify for aboriginal subsistence whaling as part of International Whaling Commission proceedings [35]. The descendant of the first known inhabitants of an area, be of any origin, be dominated politically by out-siders and depend on simple technologies without being properly involved in the world economy.

The studies and surveys conducted in the tribal areas of Chhattisgarh state of India where forest stands are utilized by the aboriginal population for their livings are conserved by means of apportioning the available resources for self sustenance and for small portion of the products for commercial purposes to earn money for their living. The sustainability concept is inherent in their life style and religiosity attached to the nature by the aboriginals has gone a long way in protecting their livelihoods as well as the produce that they depend on for their survival. Depicting and showcasing native people in scantily clad, feathers in their head gear in international events are the norms in several parts of the world forums. Such show casing of exhibits of indigenous people was important for NGOs "Fund Raising, Eco Factories, environmental activists in the name of eco-tourists are fundamentally thrusting their limited knowledge on locally solvable issues into politically and socially squeezable entities. The most aptly the phrase of [21] "Think Locally, Act Globally" is relevant to the present scenario for many developing economies where forest resources such as Amazonian, Australian, South African, Asian countries like India, Nepal, Vietnam and many more needs to adopt strategies to conserve the aboriginal evidence of people who are dependent on the indigenous resources. The focuses of development politics by colonial and post colonial governments have not only been economically unsuccessful more often than not, but they have also frequently been harmful to the environment. A schematic representation depicting different economic activities of Income generation in a tribal family is given in **Figure 3**.

More than 50% of the income generated in a tribal family is from Non-timber Forest Produce while Agriculture other employments contributes (18%) each and cattle breeding 14% respectively. In such a scenario, the value system for preservation and sustained production chain is inherent to the indigenous habitants of the region. Generally prevailing scheme of natural resources and operating mechanism worldwide is shown in the **Figure 4**. NTFP resources are under the control of government is managed through Forest Department by inviting highest bidder the harvesting rights permitted by the local government authority. The agents of bidder and sub – agents in turn assign the task to Tribal collector. The over harvesting and exploitation and chain of corruption initiated in the process becomes detrimental to the livelihoods of the local people as the commercial exploitation set in through this process resulting in pushing the indigenous and poor people to

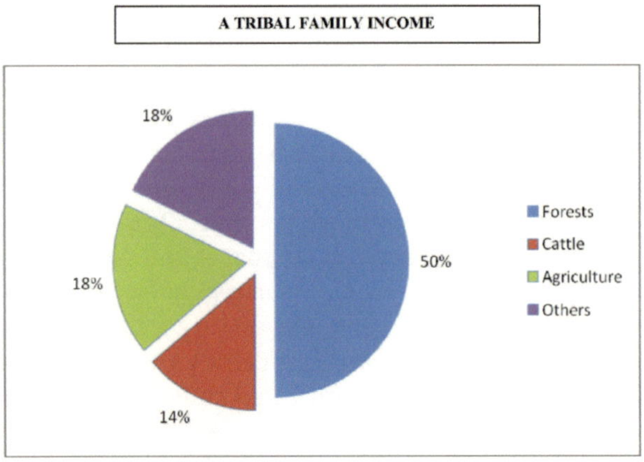

Figure 3.
A schematic representation of economic activities in a tribal family.

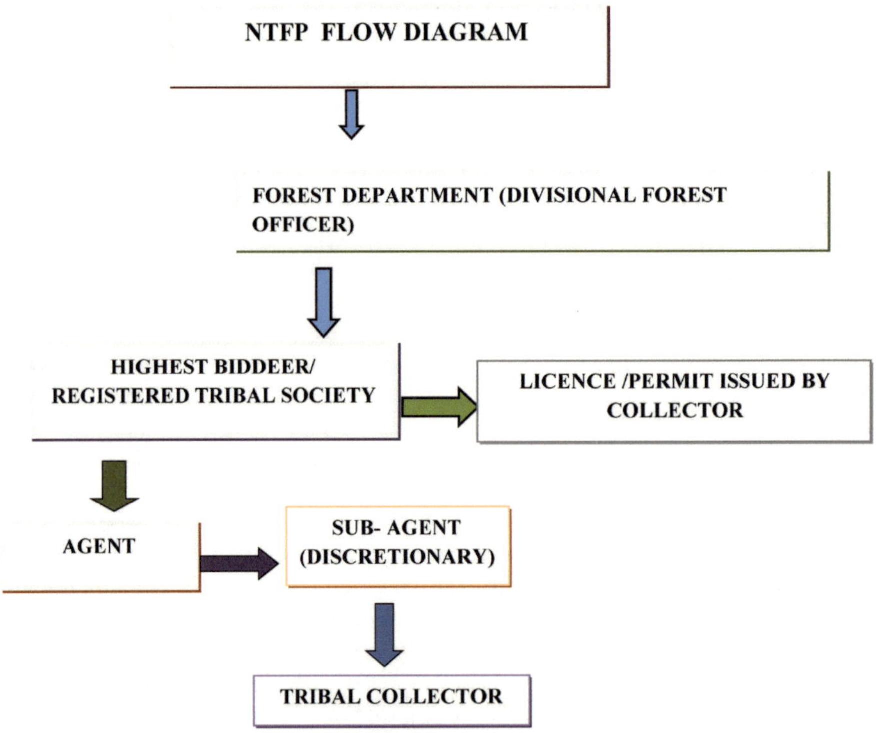

Figure 4.
Flow chart of process of NTFP allocation.

lowest socioeconomic strata. Such experiences are recorded in a number of studies [13] studied in Northern Mexico, [14] in Khunjerab National Park (KNP) where he highlights the "exclusionary principle is neither new nor the environmental agencies and NGOs intervention, part of the blame for the failure of the KNP must fall on IUCN, the WWF and other organizations whose global mission for protecting wildlife could not contain or tackle the needs of local people who mostly involuntarily become involved in wildlife conservation. [38] while analyzing the Ngorongoro Conservation Area (NCA) in northern Tanzania in which International

Wildlife Conservation lobby was expelling huge number of pastoralists and their livestock because of environmental degradation and their impact on conservation values. Similarly [5] described the shortcomings in attending the combination of pastoral development and wildlife conservation using the case of the Amboseli Park in southern Kenya. In the present studies conducted in India exhibited over harvesting, over stocking and exploitation resulting in desertification and diminishing economic returns over a period of 5–10 years for a particular Forest Produce. Similar observations were also made, where overstocking, over grazing and desertifications have become self –reinforcing concepts, and the general rangelands have been expropriated for exclusive wild life conservation use [38]. The universal applicability of the concepts of overgrazing and desertification has been seriously questioned. [39], shows convincingly how an opportunistic strategy in tropical Savannah areas is economically more efficient in terms of returns to farmers, than a governmental strategy based on the concept of carrying capacity. He concludes that evaluations

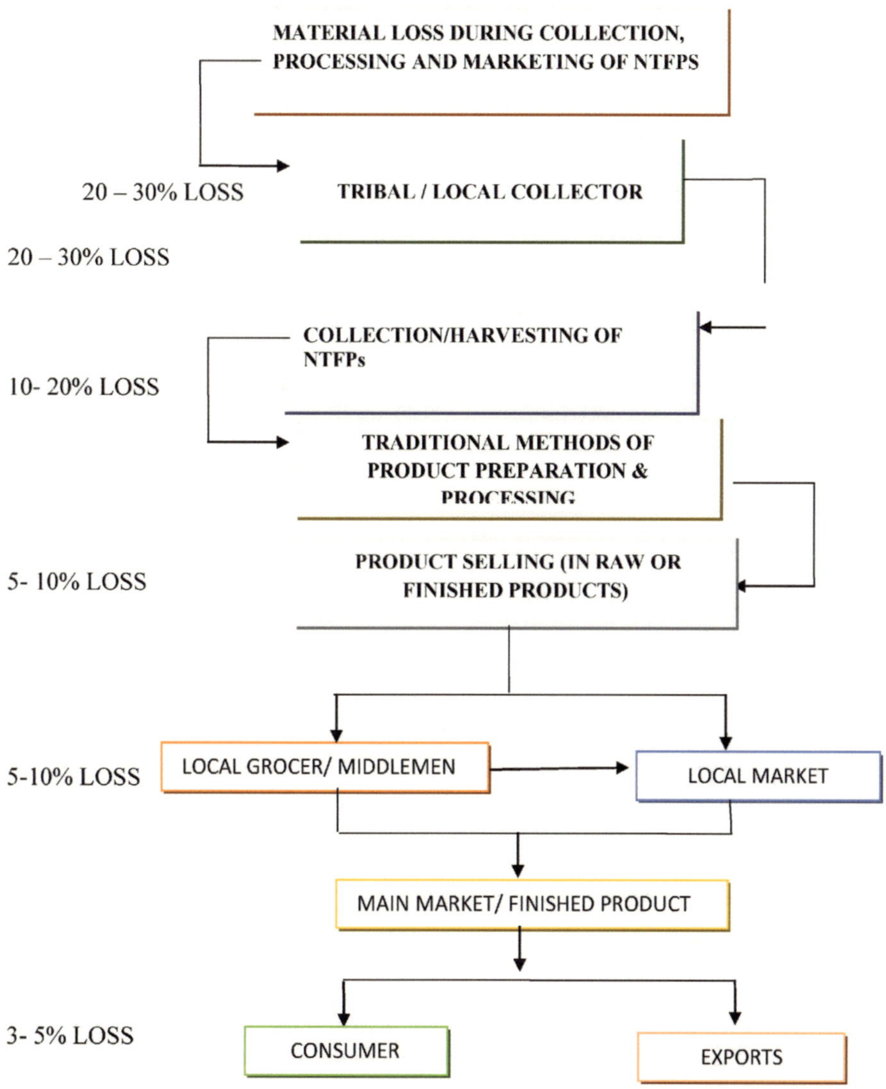

Figure 5.
Flow chart of loss of material loss.

of conflicting perspectives thus becomes both political and technical and demands that more serious consideration is given to farmer's knowledge.

Drastic commercialization and greed for quick buck coupled with amassing wealth in the shortest possible time, the livelihood resources mostly of NTFPs are harvested rapidly rendering depletion of basic material for rejuvenation and succession of plant biomass in different strata of forests. A study conducted in India indicates substantial loss of natural resources at various stages of supply chain which is depicted in the **Figure 5**. It may be observed that the highest loss of harvested product loss is in the first phase of product collection itself (20–30%). The impact of such a huge loss has a cascading effect on the rejuvenation of forests and their succession in the long run. However, frequency of harvesting activities should not deplete the resource base, should have minimal or no immediate environmental impact. Livelihood of local population should not be compromised by NTFP harvesting at commercial magnitude [40]. Unfortunately, resource extracted in excess resulting depletion and unsustainable scavenging practices is predominantly a common system in the sector. Although the thrust of the article identified other than environmental implications of NTFP harvesting and processing, over 40% broach negative ecological effects most commonly, over exploitation of the resource that become scarce. Uncontrolled and excessive harvesting due to high demand of the resource and unsustainable and primitive techniques of harvesting which leads to destructive harvesting [7, 41] or harvesting before sexual reproduction is reached [42], can lead to an overall of the resource crunch and a lower rate of forest regeneration and productivity of the NTFP species. The aggravated harvesting pressure leads to likely considerable post-harvest losses caused by a lack of or inadequate storage facilities which may lead to insect infestation or microbiological and fungal contamination. Indirect negative environmental implications can occur as well, such as the need for other natural resources, in particular firewood, for processing activities [43] or pollution and hunting during NTFP harvesting process [36] leading to further environmental degradation.

3. Threshold indicator

Critical analysis of degraded forests is essential to know if forests are being degraded and, if so, the reasons and the measures that could be taken to stop and restore the process forests regeneration has be put in place. Comprehensive knowledge on forest status and the degree of damage inflicted on forest resulting in degradation essentially is required to prioritize manual work force and financial resources to arrest further deterioration of inflicted damage and to re-establish and rehabilitate degraded forests.

The level and status of forest degradation can be categorized as either degraded or non-degraded and a process where the forests are at a threshold along a stretch of continuum of such degradation. Thresholds or reference points are needed to estimate the status of a forest, or the magnitude of disturbance caused along a sequence, and they may vary between countries and even within countries. Forests continuum changes due to natural procedure and human activity. However, when a boundaries of forests change modifying beyond a certain limit or amount, the forests may be classified to be degraded. Tipping point is another word used similar to the concept of threshold to describe the point at which the activity of degradation mortification becomes unrepairable (without intervention), leading to the changes to a permanent state.

3.1 Components of SFM

We can deduce a few thematic components of SFM, such as the quantum of forest resources dimension; biological diversity within the forest ecosystem; forest robustness and exuberance; resource productivity and functional attributes of forest; Safeguarding responsibility of forest resources; socio-economic concomitant of forests; and legal, policy and organizational scaffolding (United Nations, 2007). A thematic variables component, or variations of them, stands the grounds for all the forest-related regional and international Criteria & Indicator (C&I) processes (FAO, 2003). Forests monitoring and reporting and appraising the status of forest management practices are fundamentally governed by the C&I designed and developed solely for this purpose. The C & I processes can be employed to audit purpose of evaluation SFM at different levels like national, sub-national and forest management unit (FMU) levels. They also provide suitable structural boundaries for critical analysis of status of forest degradation (FAO, 2009).

In a larger context, the SFM components circumscribe advantages placed on forest resources; therefore, forest degradation can be evaluated in terms of the amplitude of a forest to bestow those economic advantages. The major impediment in quantifying forest degradation is the inexplicit, conglomerate and often prejudiced interpretations of the concept (FAO, 2009). Any suggested procedure or technique must prescribe for and recognize various perceptions of it. Four key selection criteria have been used from the SFM components based on the indicators identified for each and that they are quantifiable. The four criteria are: forest biological diversity; biomass, growing stock and carbon; assessing forest degradation 6 productive functions; protective functions. However SFM criterion of 'legal, policy, and institutional framework', indicators of forest degradation have proven less uncomplicated to identify. The applicability of the criterion 'proportion of forest resources' was ambiguous; therefore, neither of these is talked about in this analytical review. To some portion, the criterion 'socio-economic functionality of forests' is covered by the criterion 'productive functional attributes of forest resources' as loss of forest productivity would have profuse bearing for many of the socio-economic linked benefits of forests. Hence, this indicator has been included, for forest produces. On the other hand, it was considered that the quantified measurement of all forest services is a very complex process it would be inappropriate and comprehensive detailing is beyond the scope of this paper. Since many forest benefits are of directly derived, such direct benefits could be measured in quantified terms with the changes in the supply of forest goods, while many services can only be measured indirectly. Plant Biomass, Net Primary Productivity resulting growing stock and carbon can be grouped separately where its impact or changes can measured in quantified terms that can feature as an indicator. Enumerating the biomass in quantified terms and its importance being recognized can be obtained through the measurement of growing stock or directly through biomass measures, and measures of carbon storage can be obtained using such as Vegetation carbon storage estimates, soil carbon storage estimation and litter carbon storage estimate are some standard methods adopted. Soil health or status as an indicator presents the condition of soil erosion as factor that impacts and regulates the sustained supply of forest goods and services that requires stable and fertile soils. The other determining factors such as soil salinity, soil structural variations or modifications, loss of organic matter, aspects of soil degradation, such as salinization, soil structure decline, organic matter loss, soil nutrient status and contamination are some of the other edaphic factors that determine sustainability of forests which are not considered within the scope of this paper.

4. Conclusion

The importance of NTFPs in rural sustainable livelihoods are directly proportional to the conservation interventions of forest wealth which in turn have an impact on poverty reduction. The communities engaged in doing NTFPs value addition as an enterprise will be benefited with uninterrupted supply of raw materials thus strengthening the NTFP raw material base, simultaneously the processing units of these NTFPs quality will improve which have a cascading effect on rural livelihoods. But they people benefiting from the NTFP dependent enterprises should know and mitigate the negative impact on environment. Evolve and reinforce efforts of various projects and programs to achieve food security, escalate cash flow through income and conserve forests through NTFP related interventions. To achieve the UN Development goals during the course of present investigation, a comprehensive approach to have to be adopted which are enumerated as follows;

a. Using the present technology of satellite imaging mapping the of deforested areas that are to be restored, forest areas that put under the danger of destruction and lands which have degraded and are catchment areas which needs to be sustained for mitigating climate change should be made a priority for each country by the UNEP and mandatory for every country to follow.

b. National level Forest inventory of NTFPs are to be made and categorizing the consumption pattern of NTFPs such as (i) high commercial value products and high demand, (ii) moderate value season based demand (iii) high value but low demand products.

c. High commercial value and high in demand NTFPs should be shifted to cultivable category in degraded zones so that the supply of products would not be affected and employment is generated to the native population away from conservation areas. For example in India Temperate and Tropical Tasar silkworms feeding on *Terminalia arjuna, Terminalia tomentosa, Quercus accutissima, Quercus serrata* which are basically product of non-timber forest based activity has been now made a commercially viable income generating activity forest dwelling of the based on volume of production and demand for silk yarn production.

d. The conservation along with native biodiversity should invariably brought under the irrigated forest land without access for a longer durations not less than five years except for native population who have land tending rights to maintain those irrigated forest land. Such delimitation would safeguard the sustenance rights of the local population by cultivating the high value – high demand product on commercial scale while protecting the forest lands for conservation would enable succession of forests in their natural form. The rejuvenation of such forest should be expanded slowly to contiguous areas so that the impact of deforestation and climate change can be mitigated faster without sacrificing the living rights of local population without compromising the environmental safety and balance of climate changes.

Such comprehensive and broader efforts globally could escalate and impact on achieving sustainability goals and reinforce the national and international conglomeration to respond proactively to contain poverty and secure livelihoods of local communities of their respective countries as a responsible welfare state.

DOI: http://dx.doi.org/10.5772/intechopen.96158

Acknowledgements

The author acknowledges the fellow scientists, technical assistants and other para forces helping in collection of data and other support rendered during course of the investigation in various states of India and analytical team which has put its efforts in interpretation of data who directly or indirectly supported in the investigation.

Author details

Chinta Srinivas
Central Silk Board, Ministry of Textiles, Government of India,
Bilaspur, Chhattisgarh State, India

*Address all correspondence to: csrinivas@nic.in

IntechOpen

© 2021 The Author(s). Licensee IntechOpen. This chapter is distributed under the terms of the Creative Commons Attribution License (http://creativecommons.org/licenses/by/3.0), which permits unrestricted use, distribution, and reproduction in any medium, provided the original work is properly cited.

References

[1] Secco, L.; Pettenella, D.; Maso, D. 'Net-System' Models Versus Traditional Models in NWFP Marketing: The Case of Mushrooms. Small-Scale For. Econ. Manag Policy 2009, 8, 349-365.

[2] Ellis F., (1998) Household strategies and rural livelihood diversification. J Dev Stud 35(1):1-38.

[3] Chambers, 1995. Poverty and livelihoods: whose reality counts? ID discussion paper, 347. Brighton: IDS.

[4] Davis B, Winters P, Carletto G, Covarrubias K, Quiñones EJ, Zezza A, DiGiuseppe S (2010a) A cross-country comparison of rural income generating activities. World Dev 38(1):48-63.

[5] Lindsay, W.K. 1987. Integrating Parks and Pastoralists: Some lessons from the Amboseli. In D. Anderson & R. Grove (eds.). Conservation in Africa: People, Policies and Practice. Cambridge: Cambridge university press.

[6] Farmer, 1997, Green revolution. London:MacMillan.

[7] Vormisto, J. Making and Marketing Chambira Hammocks and Bags in the Village of Brillo Nuevo, Northeastern Peru. Econ. Bot. 2002, 56, 27-40.

[8] Weaver, T. 2000. Changes in Forest Policy, production, and the Environment in the Northern mexico: 1960-2000. Journal of Political Ecology 7:1-17.

[9] Pereira, T.; Shackleton, C.; Shackleton, S. Trade in reed-based craft products in rural villages in the Eastern Cape, South Africa. Dev. S. Afr. 2006, 23, 477-495.

[10] Rasul, G.; Choudhary, D.; Pandit, B.H.; Kollmair, M. Poverty and Livelihood Impacts of a Medicinal and Aromatic Plants Project in India and Nepal: An Assessment. Mt. Res. Dev. 2012, 32, 137-148.

[11] Bennett-Curry, A.; Malhi, Y.; Menton, M. Leakage effects in natural resource supply chains: A case study from the Peruvian commercial charcoal market. Int. J. Sustain. Dev. World Ecol. 2013, 20, 336-348.

[12] Shackleton, S.; Delang, C.O.; Angelsen, A. From Subsistence to Safety Nets and Cash Income: Exploring the Diverse Values of Non-timber Forest Products for Livelihoods and Poverty Alleviation. In Non-Timber Forest Products in the Global Context; Shackleton, S., Shackleton, C., Shanley, P., Eds.; Springer: Berlin/Heidelberg, Germany, 2011; p. 289, ISBN 9783642179822.

[13] Weatherley-Singh, J.; Gupta, A. Drivers of deforestation and REDD+ benefit-sharing: A meta-analysis of the (missing) link. Environ. Sci. Policy 2015, 54, 97-105.

[14] Knudsen, A. 1999. Conservation and Controversy in the Karakoram: Khunjerab National park,Pakistan. Journal of Political Ecology 56:1-29.

[15] Lipton and Moore, 1972. The methodology of village studies in less developed countries.Brighton:IDS, University of Sussex.

[16] Kissinger, G.; San, P.P.; Arnold, F.; Mon, M.S.; Min, N.E.E. Identifying Drivers of Deforestation and Forest Degradation in Myanmar; Myanmar REDD Programme: Yezin, Myanmar, 2017.

[17] Seeland, K.; Kilchling, P.; Hansmann, R. Urban Consumers' Attitudes Towards Non-wood Forest Products and Services in Switzerland and an Assessment of Their Market Potential. Small-Scale For. Econ. Manag. Policy 2007, 6, 443-452.

[18] Quaedvlieg, J.; García Roca, I.M.; Ros-Tonen, M.A.F. Is Amazon nut certification a solution for increased smallholder empowerment in Peruvian Amazonia? J. Rural Stud. 2014, 33, 41-55.

[19] Egelyng, H.; Bosselmann, A.S.; Warui, M.; Maina, F.; Mburu, J.; Gyau, A. Origin products from African forests: A Kenyan pathway to prosperity and green inclusive growth? For. Policy Econ. 2017, 84, 38-46.

[20] Lacuna-Richman, C. Using suitable projects in adding value to non-wood forest products in the Philippines: The copal (Agathis philippinensis) trade in Palawan. Econ. Bot. 2004, 58, 476-485.

[21] UNFCCC. Report of the Conference of the Parties on its Thirteenth Session, Held in Bali from 3 to 15 December 2007. 2007, pp. 1-60. Available online: http://Unfccc.Int/Resource/Docs/2007/Cop13/Eng/06a01.Pdf (accessed on 2 May 2019).

[22] Da Silva, R.R.V.; Gomes, L.J.; Albuquerque, U.P. What are the socioeconomic implications of the value chain of biodiversity products? A case study in Northeastern Brazil. Environ. Monit. Assess. 2017, 189, 64.

[23] Ingram, V. Savannah Forest Beekeepers in Cameroon: Actions to Reduce Vulnerability. In Dryland Forests: Management and Social Diversity in Africa and Asia; Bose, P., van Dijk, H., Eds.; Springer International Publishing: Cham, Switzerland, 2016; pp. 139-163.

[24] Rahman, M.; Nath, N.M.; Sarker, S.; Adnan, M.; Islam, M. Management and Economic Aspects of Growing Aquilaria agallocha Roxb. in Bangladesh. Small-Scale For. Econ. Manag. Policy 2015, 14, 459-478.

[25] Sousa, F.F.; de Vieira-da-Silva, C.; Barros, F.B. The (in) visible market of miriti (Mauritia flexuosa L.f.) fruits, the "winter acai", in Amazonian riverine communities of Abaetetuba, Northern Brazil. Glob. Ecol. Conserv. 2018, 14

[26] Abtew, A.A.; Pretzsch, J.; El-Sheikh Mohmoud, T.; Adam, Y.O. Commodity Chain of Frankincense from the Dry Woodlands of Nuba Mountains, South Kordofan State, Sudan. Small-Scale For. Econ. Manag. Policy 2012, 11, 365-388.

[27] Krause, T.; Ness, B. Energizing agroforestry: Ilex guayusa as an additional commodity to diversify Amazonian agroforestry systems. Int. J. Biodivers. Sci. Ecosyst. Serv. Manag. 2017, 13, 191-203.

[28] Wynberg, R.; Cribbins, J.; Leakey, R.; Lombard, C.; Mander, M.; Shackleton, S.; Sullivan, C. Knowledge on Sclerocarya birrea subsp. caffra with emphasis on its importance as a non-timber forest product in South and southern Africa: A summary: Part 2: Commercial use, tenure and policy, domestication, intellectual property rights and benefit-sharing. S. Afr. For. J. 2002, 67-77.

[29] Murphy, D. Safeguards and Multiple Benefits in a REDD+ Mechanism; International Institute for Sustainable Development: Winnipeg, MB, Canada, 2011; pp. 1-29.

[30] Girma, J.; Gardebroek, C. The impact of contracts on organic honey producers' incomes in southwestern Ethiopia. For. Policy Econ. 2015, 50, 259-268.

[31] Hardin, G. The Tragedy of the Commons. Science 1968, 162, 1243-1248. [PubMed]

[32] Angelsen, A., Wunder, S. Exploring the Forest—Poverty Link: Key Concepts, Issues and Research Implications, Occasional paper 40, Center for International Forestry Research: Bogor, Indonesia, 2003, ISSN 0854-9818.

[33] Alcorn, J.B. Economic Botany, Conservation, and Development: What's the Connection? Ann. Missouri Bot. Gard. 1995, 82, 34-46.

[34] Hosonuma, N.; Herold, M.; De Sy, V.; De Fries, R.S.; Brockhaus, M.; Verchot, L.; Angelsen, A.; Romijn, E. An assessment of deforestation and forest degradation drivers in developing countries. Environ. Res. Lett. 2012, 7, 4009.

[35] Kalland, A. 1993. Whale politics and Green Legitimacy. A Critique of anti-whaling campaign. Anthropology Today 9(2): 3-7.

[36] Matias, D.M.S.; Tambo, J.A.; Stellmacher, T.; Borgemeister, C.; von Wehrden, H. Commercializing traditional non-timber forest products: An integrated value chain analysis of honey from giant honey bees in Palawan, Philippines. For. Policy Econ. 2018, 97, 223-231.

[37] Hugel, B.; Devalue, K.; Scriven, J.; Halverson, L.; Labbate, G.; Hicks, C.; Walcott, J.; Chiu, M.; Vickers, B.; Eggerts, E. Redd+ Academy Learning Journal, Module 7: Policies and Measures for REDD+ Implementation, 2; United Nations Enviornment Program, Châtelaine: Geneva, Switzerland, 2017; ISBN 9789280736472.

[38] Homewood, K. and Rodgers, W.A. 1987. Pastoralism, Conservation and the overgrazing controversy. In D. Anderson & R. Grove (eds.). Conservation in Africa: People, Policies and Practice. Cambridge: Cambridge university press

[39] Stanford, S. 1983. Management of pastoral Development in the third world Chichester John willey & Son.

[40] Buchmann, C., Prehsler, S., Hartl, A., Vogl, C.R., The Importance of Baobab (Adansonia digitata L.) in Rural West African Subsistence—Suggestion of a Cautionary Approach to International Market Export of Baobab Fruits. Ecol. Food Nutr. 2010, 49, 145-172.

[41] Runk, J.V. Wounaan and Emberá use and management of the fiber palm Astrocaryum standleyanum (Arecaceae) for basketry in eastern Panamá. Econ. Bot. 2001, 55, 72-82. [CrossRef] .

[42] Delgado-Lemus, A., Casas, A., Téllez, O. Distribution, abundance and traditional management of Agave potatorumin the Tehuacán Valley, Mexico: Bases for sustainable use of non-timber forest products. J. Ethnobiol. Ethnomed. 2014, 10, 63.

[43] Jasaw, G.S.; Saito, O.; Takeuchi, K. Shea (Vitellaria paradoxa) Butter Production and Resource Use by Urban and Rural Processors in Northern Ghana. Sustainability 2015, 7, 3592-3614.

Chapter 17

How to Design Sustainable Structures

Kazutoshi Fujihira

Abstract

Achieving sustainability is the ultimate goal-oriented challenge. Control science can be applied to all goal-oriented tasks. Accordingly, utilizing control science, we have been progressing in research on sustainability and sustainable design. Here this chapter illustrates the methodology for designing sustainable structures with two examples. In this context, "structures" include various city components, such as buildings, roads, and parks, as well as the whole city. First, this chapter illustrates the control system for promoting sustainable structure design. Next, it shows the process of producing and revising sustainable structure design guidelines. Based on this process, Section 4 demonstrates how to produce and revise sustainable housing design guidelines, with the completed guidelines' extracts. Moreover, Section 5 outlines a way of producing sustainable urban design guidelines. Designing the whole city needs extensive spatial planning; therefore, the guidelines consist of three parts: (1) development allowable areas, (2) spatial relationships among city components, (3) principles of designing city components. This methodology's characteristics include visualization of the whole picture for promoting sustainable design, user-friendliness, comprehensiveness, and adaptability to different and changing situations.

Keywords: sustainable structure, system control, design guidelines, housing design, urban design, sustainable design, climate change

1. Introduction

Cities are becoming increasingly related to environmental change and sustainability. Since 2007, more than half of the world's population has been living in urban areas; that share is projected to rise 60% by 2030 [1]. A vast number of buildings, transport systems, and other facilities occupy cities, where intense socio-economic activities are performed. On the other hand, there have been various urban problems, including sprawl, traffic congestion, environmental pollution, waste, unemployment, and crimes. World cities are responsible for up to 70% of harmful greenhouse gases [2]. Furthermore, cities lie near waters, such as seas and rivers; therefore, urban areas are at increased risk from flooding and sea-level rise caused by climate change.

Cities, as well as various city components, need to be designed and implemented toward sustainability. The Sustainable Development Goals (SDGs) set by the United Nations in 2015 also refer to cities, housing, and infrastructure. Typically, Goal 11 demands to make cities and human settlements inclusive, safe, resilient, and sustainable. Meanwhile, Goal 9 requires people to build resilient infrastructure [3].

As the term "goal" indicates, achieving sustainability is the ultimate goal-oriented challenge. The science of control can be applied to all goal-oriented tasks

[4]. Besides, control science has produced remarkable results in many fields, particularly engineering [4]. Accordingly, utilizing control science, we have been progressing in research on sustainability and sustainable design.

Based on our accomplished research results, this chapter illustrates the methodology for designing sustainable structures with two examples. First, it shows the "control system for promoting sustainable structure design" and "process of producing and revising sustainable structure design guidelines." Following these basic schemes, Section 4 demonstrates a way of producing and revising sustainable housing design guidelines. Furthermore, Section 5 outlines how to produce sustainable urban design guidelines.

2. Control system for promoting sustainable structure design

The "control system for promoting sustainable structure design" is demonstrated in **Figure 1**. The upper and lower areas divided by the dotted line represent the "theoretical world" and the "practical world," respectively.

In this control system, "controlled objects" are structures, which include both new and existing structures. In this context, "structures" include various city components, such as houses, other buildings, roads, and parks, as well as the whole city.

"Disturbances" mean harmful influences on controlled objects resulting from environmental, social, or economic problems. Instances of the disturbances are adverse effects due to environmental pollution and a variety of impacts caused by climate change. The course from "disturbances" to "sustainability" means "adaptation." This course has been added, on the basis of the current scientific understanding that achieving sustainability also needs adaptation measures to climate change impacts [5–8].

The purpose of control is the accomplishment of "sustainability." The model of sustainability (**Figure 2**) demonstrates that sustainability requires both fundamental stability and internal stability, to achieve the long-term well-being of all humankind, within the finite global environment and natural resources [9]. Fundamental stability means environmental stability and a stable supply of necessary goods; the conditions for fundamental stability are "environmental preservation" and "sustainable use of natural resources" [9]. Meanwhile, internal stability is social and economic stability; the

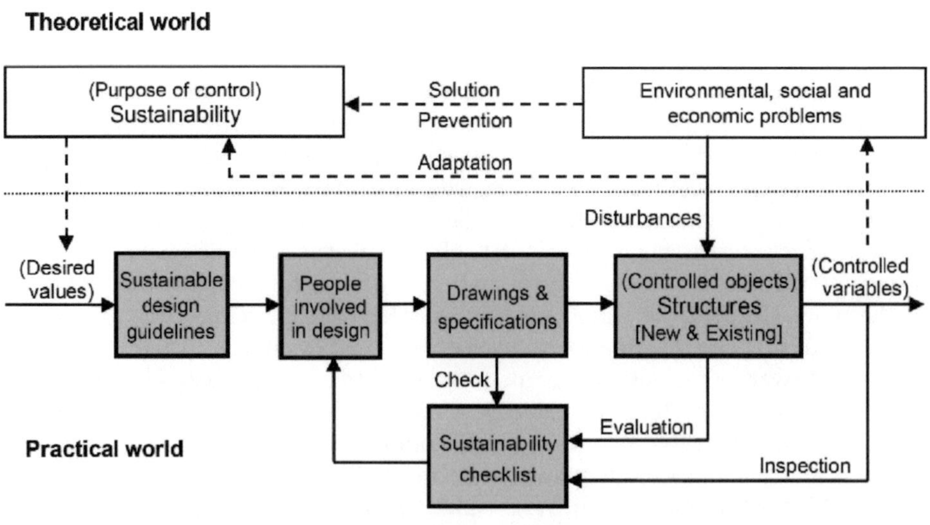

Figure 1.
Control system for promoting sustainable structure design.

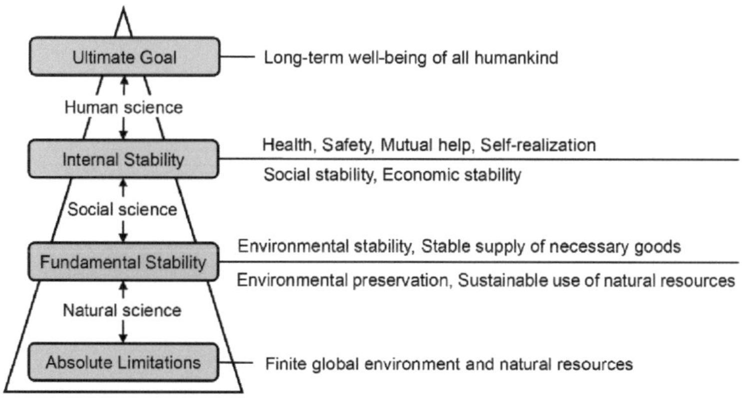

Figure 2.
Model of sustainability [9].

conditions for internal stability are "health," "safety," "mutual help," and "self-realization," which are essential for the humans' well-being [9].

"Controlled variables" mean the variables that relate to controlled objects and are necessary to be controlled for chiefly solving or preventing the problems or adapting to disturbances [10, 11]. On the other hand, "desired values" are extracted from the purpose of control, that is, sustainability. The control objective of this control system is to adjust the controlled variables to their desired values.

In the practical world, the subjects of control are "people involved in design." The subjects vary depending on types of structures. For example, if controlled objects are houses, people involved in design are homeowners, architects, designers, and homebuilders. Meanwhile, in case of the whole city, people involved include city planners, administrative staff, and representatives of the city residents.

In this control system, people involved in design adjust the controlled variables to their desired values, by using the "sustainable design guidelines" and "sustainability checklist." The design guidelines and checklist have nearly the same expressions, that is, elements, variables, and desired values. But the checklist is formed to smoothly compare measured or estimated variables to the desired values and search for controlled variables [10, 11].

When new structures are objects, information about the desired values first reaches "people involved in design" through the "sustainable design guidelines." People involved prepare "drawings and specifications," so that the variables of structure's elements can satisfy their desired values to the maximum. At significant phases in the design process, people involved in design check the drawings and specifications by seeing the "sustainability checklist" [10, 11].

In the case where objects are existing structures, the design process starts with "inspection" on the structure as an object. Referring to the "sustainability checklist," the "people involved in design" measure or estimate each element's variables of that structure. After finishing the inspection, the people involved mostly prepare "drawings and specifications" for improvement, so that controlled variables meet their desired values to full potential [10, 11].

3. Process of producing and revising sustainable structure design guidelines

The process of producing and revising the sustainable structure design guidelines and sustainability checklist is demonstrated in **Figure 3**. The upper area of the figure is the theoretical world; the lower area is the practical world.

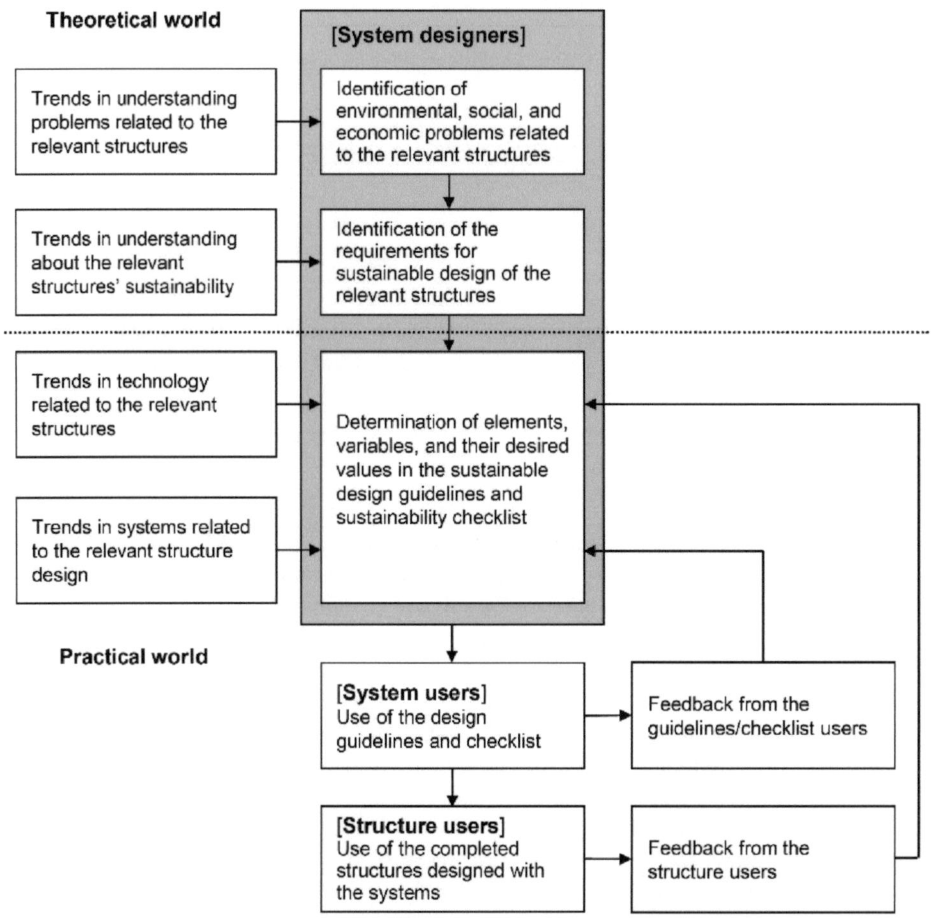

Figure 3.
Process of producing and revising the sustainable structure design guidelines and sustainability checklist.

The middle part shows the route of preparing and utilizing the "sustainable design guidelines" and "sustainability checklist." System designers first produce or revise the design guidelines and checklist through the process of three stages. After that, system users employ the design guidelines and checklist. Subsequently, structure users utilize the completed structures that have been designed with the guidelines and checklist.

The four blocks on the left side demonstrate the items to check when producing or revising the design guidelines and checklist. The contents of these four blocks can change over time. On the other hand, the two blocks at the lower right demonstrate the items to check when revising the systems, on the basis of the feedbacks from the guidelines/checklist users and the structure users.

3.1 Production process of the design guidelines and checklist

The production process of the design guidelines and checklist is composed of three stages: (1) identification of environmental, social, and economic problems related to the relevant structures, (2) identification of the requirements for sustainable design of the relevant structures, (3) determination of elements, variables, and their desired values in the design guidelines and checklist [12].

3.1.1 Identification of problems related to the relevant structures

In the first stage, system designers identify environmental, social, and economic problems related to the relevant structures, while observing trends in understanding such problems. The basis for the identification is that the problems affect the total six stability conditions shown in **Figure 2**, such as health, safety, and environmental preservation. When identifying problems, system designers take up local/particular problems in their country or region, in addition to global/general problems [12].

3.1.2 Identification of the requirements for sustainable design

Next, based on the specified problems, system designers identify the requirements for sustainable design of the relevant structures. For example, if "global warming and climate change" are specified as problems in the first stage, "energy saving," "use of renewable energy," and "conservation of green spaces" can be specified as the requirements.

3.1.3 Determination of elements, variables, and their desired values

In the third stage, system designers convert the requirements for sustainable design into the framework of "element-variable-desired value," which can be found in the design guidelines and checklist. The aim of this conversion is the convenience of system users. The framework of "element-variable-desired value" concretely shows design targets of each part of the relevant structures; thus, it enables the system users to quickly find what should be designed and the design courses [12].

First, system designers determine "elements," considering both the standard structures and the requirements for sustainable design. Structures in one category consist of almost the same component parts; accordingly, system designers can select important parts of the standard structures as elements. Moreover, they may add necessary elements to cover all of the requirements for sustainable design. For example, when "use of renewable energy" is identified as one of the requirements, "equipment for harnessing renewable energy" should be added as an element, even if it is not common in current ordinary structures [9].

Next, system designers determine "variables" by examining the relationships between each element and the relevant stability condition(s), as well as the related requirement(s) for sustainable design. For instance, if "equipment for harnessing renewable energy" is an element, its relationships with the relevant stability conditions, namely environmental preservation and sustainable use of natural resources, as well as the related requirement, namely use of renewable energy, should be examined. Consequently, "harnessed renewable energy" can be determined as its variable.

After that, system designers set the variables' "desired values" to meet the relevant stability conditions. If "harnessed renewable energy" is the variable, its desired value can be set at "100% or more of the total energy usage." When determining "desired values," system designers also consider trends in technology and systems related to the relevant structures.

3.2 Revision process of the design guidelines and checklist

The "sustainable design guidelines" and "sustainability checklist" need to be revised, adjusting to changing situations, and higher user-friendliness and accuracy. The revision process can be divided into three spheres: (1) changes in the theoretical world, (2) changes in the practical world, (3) feedback from the users [12]. After making preparations from the above three perspectives, system designers modify the guidelines and checklist tables.

3.2.1 Changes in the theoretical world

Obvious changes over time in the theoretical world need to be reflected into the design guidelines and checklist [12]. First of all, searching for recent changes in environmental, social, and economic problems, system designers can modify the list of problems related to the relevant structures. Based on the modified list of problems, the system designers can also amend the list of the requirements for sustainable design of the relevant structures. When amending these two lists, it is also necessary to observe the latest trends in "understanding problems related to the relevant structures" and "understanding about the relevant structures' sustainability." Subsequently, system designers examine amendments to the "element-variable-desired value" expressions of the design guidelines and checklist.

3.2.2 Changes in the practical world

Changes over time in the practical world are also necessary to be reflected in the guidelines and checklist. Changes in the practical world include "changes in technology related to the relevant structures" and "changes in systems related to the relevant structure design" [12].

3.2.3 Feedback from the users

"Feedback from the guidelines/checklist users" and "feedback from the structure users" also need to be examined, as shown at the lower right of **Figure 3** [12]. The feedback from the guidelines/checklist users is information on reactions to the guidelines and checklist, such as comments about the user-friendliness and validity of these systems. Such information is utilized as a foundation for the improvement of the systems. On the other hand, the feedback from the structure users is information on reactions to the completed structures designed with the guidelines and checklist. Such information, including comments on the structures' amenities and sustainability performance, is also useful for improving the systems.

4. Sustainable housing design guidelines

We produced the sustainable housing design guidelines and sustainability checklist, mainly for use in Japan. After that, we made revisions on the design guidelines and checklist. This section briefly explains the process of producing and revising the sustainable housing design guidelines, anew following the procedure demonstrated in **Figure 3**. In addition, this section has been organized based on Section 4 of our latest study results, "Comprehensive strategy for sustainable housing design."

4.1 Sustainable housing design guidelines produced in Japan

4.1.1 Identification of problems related to housing

Producing the design guidelines begins with identifying environmental, social, and economic problems related to houses. In this case, we selected global/general problems and local/particular problems observed in Japan. Significant problems are shown in the second column of **Table 1**. Global/general issues include global warming and climate change, and increased medical and nursing care expenses due to aging population. Meanwhile, Japan's local/particular problems include poor indoor thermal performance, and earthquake damage.

4.1.2 Identification of the requirements for sustainable housing design

After specifying the housing-related problems, we identified the requirements for sustainable housing design. For instance, "poor indoor thermal performance" requires "improvement of indoor thermal performance." In addition, relevant stability conditions are demonstrated in the right column of **Table 1**.

4.1.3 Determination of elements, variables, and their desired values

In the third stage, we first specified "elements," considering both the standard housing and the requirements for sustainable housing design. When considering the standard housing, we analyzed two factors: "material" and "space" [10, 11]. "Material" regards housing as the complexity of material elements, such as framework, exterior, thermal insulation, windows and doors, interior, and piping. "Space" considers housing as the complexity of spatial elements, such as rooms and areas

Type of problems	Main environmental, social, and economic problems related to housing	Requirements for sustainable housing design	Stability conditions
Global/ general problems	• Global warming and climate change	• Energy saving • Use of renewable energy • Conservation of green spaces	• Enviro-preservation • Sustainable resources
	• Depletion of natural resources • Waste	• Extension of housing lifespan • Use of resource-saving or waste-prevention materials	• Sustainable resources
	• Harmful influences caused by climate change	• Adaptation measures	• Health • Safety
	• Flood risks due to rainwater flowing out • Water shortage risks	• Rainwater permeation into the ground • Water saving • Use of rainwater	• Enviro-preservation • Sustainable resources • Health • Safety
	• Increased medical and nursing care expenses due to aging population	• Accessible and universal design	• Health • Safety
Local/ particular problems (in Japan)	• Poor indoor thermal performance	• Improvement of indoor thermal performance	• Health • Enviro-preservation • Sustainable resources
	• Earthquake damage	• Higher resistance to earthquakes	• Safety

Table 1.
Problems related to housing and requirements for sustainable housing design identified for the design guidelines produced in Japan [extracts] [12].

[10, 11]. Moreover, in order to cover all of the requirements for sustainable housing design, we added necessary elements, such as "equipment for harnessing renewable energy."

After specifying the elements, we identified the variables and their desired values. Choosing one element, namely "thermal insulation," the rest of this section explains the details of identifying the variable and its desired value. First of all, we determined "thermal insulation performance" as the variable, considering two requirements, that is, "energy saving" and "improvement of indoor thermal performance," as well as the relevant stability conditions. Higher thermal insulation performance contributes to "environmental preservation" and "sustainable use of natural resources" due to a decrease in energy usage for air-conditioning and heating, as well as residents' better "health."

When specifying the desired value, we observed trends in technology and systems related to housing thermal insulation performance. Japanese housing thermal performance has traditionally been low. Japan's building codes have not stipulated the standards of housing thermal insulation performance. Meanwhile, since 2000, a national voluntary system, namely the Japan Housing Performance Indication Standards (JHPIS), have provided four-level thermal insulation performance grades. Consequently, we determined the desired value to be the highest level in the thermal insulation performance grades of the JHPIS.

4.2 The latest revision of the design guidelines

The above sustainable housing design guidelines produced in Japan have recently been revised. This latest revision has dealt with the three aspects as mentioned before: (1) changes in the theoretical world, (2) changes in the practical world, (3) feedback from the users.

4.2.1 Changes in the theoretical world

First of all, observing recent trends in understanding problems related to houses, we have searched for problems which affect stability conditions. Consequently, as shown in the second column of **Table 2,** we have specified additional problems that

Type of problems	Environmental, social, and economic problems related to housing	Requirements for sustainable housing design	Stability conditions
Global/ general problems	• Breakdown risks in electricity systems due to increasing wind and solar power generation	• Storage of electricity	• Sustainable resources • Health (in crises) • Safety (in crises)
	• Insufficient considerations for homeworking, telecommuting, and lifelong learning	• Considerations for homeworking, telecommuting, and lifelong learning	• Self-realization
Local/ particular problems (in Japan)	• Problems resulting from insufficient communication	• Floor planning suitable for good communication among residents	• Mutual help • Self-realization

Table 2.
Additional problems and requirements for sustainable housing design identified for the latest revision of the design guidelines [extracts] [12].

should be dealt with. Based on these problems, additional requirements for sustainable housing design have also been identified. After that, these additional requirements have been incorporated into the framework of "element-variable-desired value."

Choosing one requirement, namely "storage of electricity," the following describes the essentials of the identification and incorporation processes. In order to curb global warming, the utilization of renewable energy, particularly wind and solar power generation, is quickly increasing in many countries [13]. But the quantity of electricity extracted from solar and wind sources varies chiefly with the time of day, weather, and season. Therefore, a surge in wind and solar power generation is also raising the risks of power failures [14, 15]. In order to cope with such changing circumstances, we have added "storage of electricity" as a requirement for sustainable housing design. Besides, storing electricity leads to securing an emergency power source, which is one of the adaptation measures against climate change.

When incorporating the "storage of electricity" into the guidelines, we have added "storage battery" as a new material element. Subsequently, we have identified two variables of this new element: "type" and "linkage." The desired value of "type" has been specified as "stationary battery or electric vehicle battery." Meanwhile, the desired value of "linkage" has been determined to be "interconnection with the home electrical system."

4.2.2 Changes in the practical world

Observing recent trends in housing-related technology and systems, we have found noticeable changes, mainly in thermal insulation performance. Japanese housing thermal performance has been gradually improving, due to progress in technology and requirements for energy saving and occupants' health. As a result, recently, a new national voluntary system, the "net-zero energy house (ZEH) certification standards," has emerged and shown higher thermal performance criteria than usual criteria [16]. Recognizing these changes, we have lifted the desired value of "thermal insulation performance" of the two material elements: "thermal insulation" and "windows and doors." To be concrete, we have revised the desired value from the highest level in the JHPIS's thermal insulation performance grades to the relevant criterion stipulated in the ZEH certification standards.

4.2.3 Feedback from the users

After finding a constructive opinion in recent feedback from the system users, we have determined to include it in the latest revision. This opinion's gist is that lighting fixtures utilized in living spaces should be products with brightness and color adjustment functions, for energy conservation and residents' health. The necessary brightness of indoor artificial lighting changes depending on circumstances, including residents' visual comfort and natural lighting through windows. Meanwhile, exposure to bright lights and blue light before bedtime suppresses melatonin secretion and can affect sleep and potentially cause diseases [17, 18]. Accordingly, especially in living spaces, lighting fixtures fitted with brightness and color adjustment functions are beneficial for energy conservation and residents' health. Therefore, when revising the guidelines this time, we have added an explanatory note to "LED," the desired value of lighting fixtures' type, saying "lighting fixtures used in the living spaces are fitted with brightness and color adjustment functions."

Finally, all of the above revision items have been incorporated into the table of the "element-variable-desired value" framework. The final revised version of the guidelines has been shown in **Table 3** in our latest study results, "Comprehensive

Element	Variable	Desired value
Framework	Resistance to earthquakes	JHPIS 1–1: Grade 2 or over
	Durability	JHPIS 3.1: Grade 3
	Materials	CASBEE LR_H2 1.1: Level 4 or over
Exterior (outer wall, roof, etc.)	Fire resistance (outer wall)	JHPIS 2–6: Grade 3 or over
	Shape and color	Consideration for the landscape
Thermal insulation	Thermal insulation performance	*Thermal performance criteria stipulated in the net zero energy house (ZEH) certification*
Windows and doors	Thermal insulation performance	*Thermal performance criteria stipulated in the ZEH certification*
	Sunlight adjustment capability	CASBEE Q_H1 1.1.2: Level 4 or over
	Protection of glass against impacts	With shutters
Piping	Measures for maintenance	JHPIS 4.1: Grade 3
Lighting fixtures	Type of light	LED *(lighting fixtures used in the living spaces are fitted with brightness and color adjustment functions)*
Equipment for harnessing natural energy	Harnessed natural energy	100% or more of the total energy usage
Storage battery	*Type*	*Stationary battery or electric vehicle battery*
	Linkage	*Interconnection with the home electrical system*
Specified bedroom (Bedroom for elderly and wheelchair users)	Routes to toilet and bath area, dining room, kitchen, and entrance	Accessible without steps
Living/dining room and kitchen area	*Place in the home*	*Between the entrance and private room area*
	Type of kitchen	*Open or semi-open*
Area(s) for working and learning	*Place(s) in the home*	*In or near the living/dining room and kitchen area*
Areas relating to water use and hot-water supply	Areas in the home	Placing them closer
Position and area of windows	Natural ventilation	CASBEE Q_H1 1.2.1: Level 5
Doorways	Differences in level	No differences
	Width	75 cm or more (Bath: 60 cm or more)
Garden area	Ratio of the garden area to the exterior area	40% or more

(1) Material elements are from "framework" to "storage battery;" spatial elements are from "specified bedroom" to "garden area."
(2) JHPIS means the Japan Housing Performance Indication Standards (for new homes).
(3) CASBEE means CASBEE for Detached Houses (for new construction) – Technical Manual 2018 Edition.

Table 3.
The latest revised version of the sustainable housing design guidelines [extracts] [12].

strategy for sustainable housing design." Extracts from this latest revised version are demonstrated in **Table 3**. The added and modified descriptions in the latest revision are written in *italics*.

5. Sustainable urban design guidelines

This section outlines how to produce sustainable design guidelines for the whole city. **Figure 4** shows the process of producing and revising sustainable urban design guidelines. This diagram has been drawn based on **Figure 3** in Section 3. First, the descriptions of "relevant structures" in **Figure 3** have been replaced with "cities" or "urban." Moreover, three items have been added to the box of "Determination of elements, variables, and their desired values in the design guidelines and checklist."

5.1 Problems related to cities and requirements for sustainable urban design

5.1.1 Problems related to cities

As shown in the upper central part of **Figure 4**, producing the design guidelines starts with identifying environmental, social, and economic problems related to

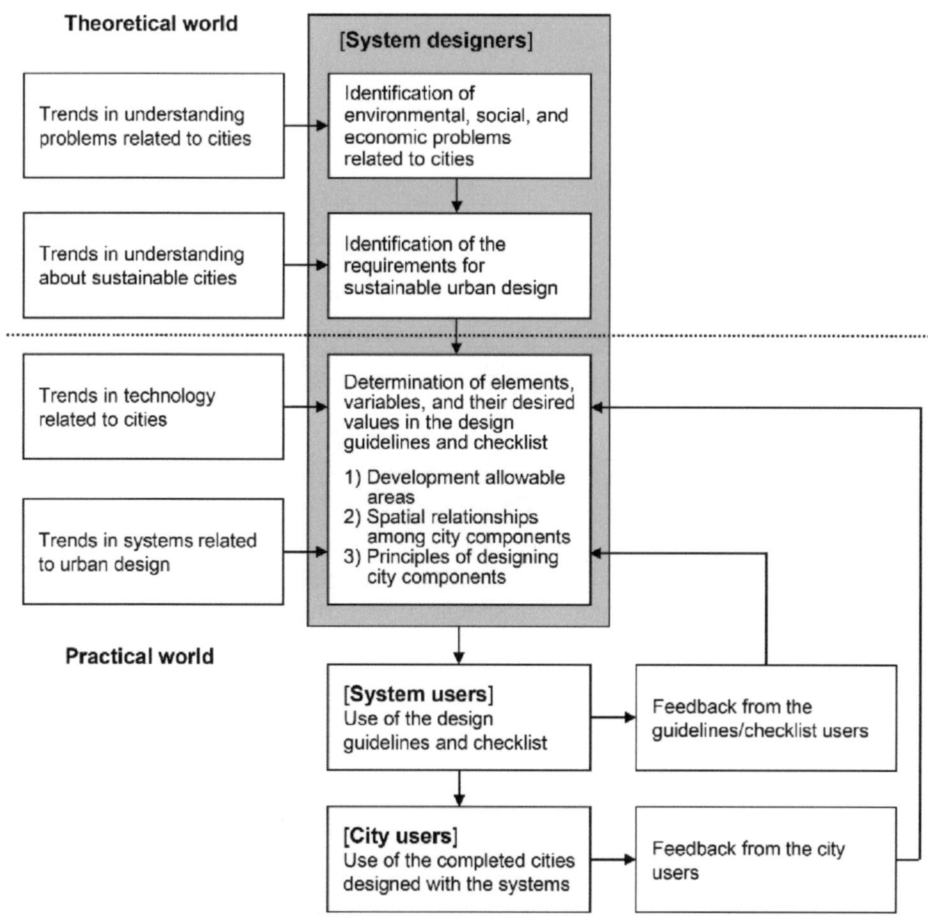

Figure 4.
Process of producing and revising the sustainable urban design guidelines.

Environmental, social, and economic problems related to cities (Main global/general problems)	Requirements for sustainable urban design	Stability conditions
• Urban sprawl • Environmental destruction • Biodiversity loss	• Prevention of urban sprawl • Environmental protection • Biodiversity conservation	• Enviro-preservation
• Global warming and climate change	• Energy saving • Use of renewable energy • Conservation of green spaces	• Enviro-preservation • Sustainable resources
• Damage caused by natural disasters • Harmful influences caused by climate change	• Exclusion of natural disaster danger areas from development areas • Measures for disaster damage prevention or reduction	• Safety • Health
• Urban heat island	• Increase in green spaces • Reduction in waste heat from buildings, vehicles, etc.	• Enviro-preservation • Health
• Depletion of natural resources • Waste • Environmental pollution	• Extension of the lifespan of constructions and products • Use of resource-saving or waste-prevention materials • Proper waste management	• Enviro-preservation • Sustainable resources
• Traffic congestion • Automobile pollution	• Shifts from automobile to mass transit, walking and biking	• Enviro-preservation • Sustainable resources • Health
• Lack of physical activity	• Inducement to walking and biking • Safe streets • Recreational facilities and places	• Health • Safety
• Sluggish economy • Less social cohesion • Crimes	• Consideration for increasing economic vitality • Consideration for encouraging social interaction • Increase in people's "eyes on the street"	• Safety • Mutual help • Self-realization
• Increase of medical and nursing care expenses due to aging population	• Accessible and universal design	• Health • Safety

Table 4.
Main global/general problems related to cities and requirements for sustainable urban design.

cities. While observing trends in understanding city-related problems, system designers search for the problems that should be identified. In this section, only typical global/general problems have been extracted and demonstrated in **Table 4**.

5.1.2 Requirements for sustainable urban design

In the second stage, based on the selected problems related to cities, system designers identify the requirements for sustainable urban design. Identified requirements for sustainable urban design are demonstrated in the second column of **Table 4**. For example, "damage caused by natural disasters" and "harmful influences caused by climate change" require "exclusion of natural disaster danger areas from development areas" and "measures for disaster damage prevention and reduction."

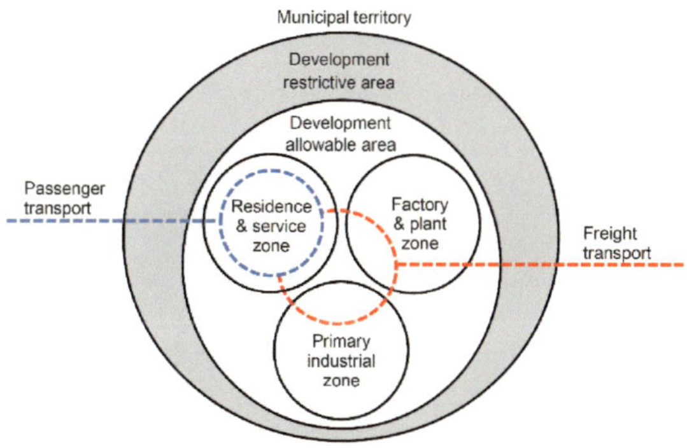

Figure 5.
Concept diagram for considering sustainable urban design.

Element	Variable	Desired value	Remarks
Development allowable areas	Risk of biodiversity loss	Lower risk of biodiversity loss	
	Risk of natural disasters	Lower risk of natural disasters	• Examples of natural disasters: flood damage, landslides, drought damage, and forest fires.
	Gradient of the topography	Flat or gently-sloping topography	

Table 5.
Sustainable urban design guidelines (1) development allowable areas [essentials].

5.2 Sustainable urban design guidelines

In the third stage, the requirements for sustainable urban design are converted into the "element-variable-desired value" framework of the design guidelines. When designing the whole city, people involved must consider the extent of land development areas, the placement of city components, and city components' design principles. The requirements in **Table 4** also extend over these three spheres. Therefore, as shown in **Figure 4**, we have divided the third stage into three steps: (1) development allowable areas, (2) spatial relationships among city components, (3) principles of designing city components.

5.2.1 Development allowable areas

The first step focuses on the relationship between land development and natural features. As demonstrated in **Figure 5**, a municipal territory can be divided into development restrictive areas and development allowable areas. "Development allowable areas" are areas where land development can be permitted.

Table 5 shows the essentials of the first part of the sustainable urban design guidelines. At first, we have identified "development allowable areas" as the element. Next, we have determined its three variables: (1) risk of biodiversity loss, (2) risk of natural disasters, (3) gradient of the topography. When defining "development allowable areas," it is necessary to select areas where all these three variables meet their desired values.

Element	Variable	Desired value	Remarks
Residence and service zones	Facilities placed in the residence and service zones	Facilities for people's use and related facilities	• Examples of facilities for people's use: housing, buildings for various services, streets, and parks.
	Extent of the residence and service zone from a station of passenger transport	1. Within walking distance of an interurban railway station 2. Within short walking distance of a local transport (tram/bus) line's station	• At least one of the two desired values must be satisfied. • Walking distance should be set at 1000 m or less. • Short walking distance should be set at 500 m or less.
Main streets	Layout	Well-connection to essential facilities	• Examples of essential facilities: interurban railway stations, and large-scale public facilities.
Residential streets	Access to main streets	Convenient	
Routes of local public transport (tram/bus)	Relation with streets	On main streets, in principle	
Lots for larger buildings	Relation with streets	Connected to main streets	
Lots for smaller buildings	Relation with streets	Connected to residential streets	
Lots for frequently used facilities	Relation with passenger transport	In close vicinity to passenger transport stations	
Factory and plant zones	Facilities placed in the factory and plant zones	Facilities for large-scale production and related facilities	• Examples of the facilities for large-scale production: manufacturing factories, and power plants.

Table 6.
Sustainable urban design guidelines (2) spatial relationships among city components [extracts].

The first variable, "risk of biodiversity loss," is mainly related to two requirements shown in **Table 4**, namely "environmental protection" and "biodiversity conservation." Considering these two requirements and their related stability condition, namely "environmental preservation," we have determined its desired value as a "lower risk of biodiversity loss." This means that areas with a higher risk of biodiversity loss, such as Key Biodiversity Areas, must be excluded from development allowable areas. According to the International Union for Conservation of Nature (IUCN), Key Biodiversity Areas are sites contributing significantly to the global persistence of biodiversity [19].

The second variable, "risk of natural disasters," is connected with another requirement in **Table 4**, "exclusion of natural disaster danger areas from development areas." Considering this requirement and its related stability conditions, "safety" and "health," we have specified its desired value as a "lower risk of natural disasters." Examples of natural disasters are flood damage, landslides, drought damage, and forest fires. When estimating natural disaster risks, system designers should also consider future risks caused by climate change, in addition to current risks.

Element	Variable	Desired value	Remarks
Main streets	Main divisions of the street surface	Sidewalk, planting zone, bike lane, roadway	
	Design of spaces for pedestrians	Accessible and universal design	
	Roadway space	Considerations for the passage of public transport (tram/bus)	
Residential streets	Passage	Pedestrians, bicycles, vehicles for the residents	• Priority to pedestrians
Larger buildings	Energy usage of the building	Net zero energy building	• High energy efficiency • Use of renewable energy
	Height limits for construction	Not high	• Hight for several-floor buildings at the maximum
	Uses of the building's street-level floor	Priority to service uses	
Smaller buildings	Energy usage of the building	Net zero energy building	• High energy efficiency • Use of renewable energy
	Height limits for construction	Low	• Hight for a-few-floor buildings
Public open spaces (parks, etc.)	Green coverage ratio	High	
Manufacturing factories	Raw materials used for manufacturing	Priority to locally produced materials and used materials	
Energy production plants	Type of energy resources	Renewable energy	

Table 7.
Sustainable urban design guidelines (3) principles of designing city components (extracts).

Meanwhile, the third variable, "gradient of the topography," is associated with two requirements in **Table 4,** "environmental protection" and "accessible and universal design." Considering these requirements and their related stability conditions, namely "environmental preservation," "health," and "safety," we have determined its desired value as "flat or gently-sloping topography." When steep slopes are disturbed by removing vegetation and developing the hillside or mountainside, significant environmental issues can arise. Potential consequences can include soil erosion, landslides, an increase in downstream runoff, and flooding [20–22]. Moreover, slopes become steeper, the provision of infrastructure and accessible design becomes more difficult and expensive [21]. Accordingly, areas with steep slopes should be excluded from development allowable areas.

5.2.2 Spatial relationships among city components

The second step, spatial relationships among city components, focuses on the placement of land development sites and facilities. Land development sites need to be situated in development allowable areas. As shown in **Figure 5**, land development sites can be divided into three major zones: (1) residence and service zone,

(2) factory and plant zone, (3) primary industrial zone. The "residence and service zone" contains facilities for people's use, such as housing, buildings for various services, streets, and parks. The "factory and plant zone" contains facilities for large-scale industrial production, such as manufacturing factories and power plants. The "primary industrial zone" includes farmlands and planted forests. In addition, the "factory and plant zone" and "residence and service zone" are closely connected to the "secondary industry" and "tertiary industry," respectively. Meanwhile, facilities for interurban and local transport are also significant as city components. Accordingly, we have added typical transport routes to **Figure 5**, dividing them into passenger transport and freight transport.

Bearing standard cities in mind, we have specified important spatial relationships among city components. Extracts of such relationships are shown in **Table 6**. Choosing one element, that is, "residence and service zone," the rest of this section explains a key variable and its desired value. First, we have identified "extent of the residence and service zone from a station of passenger transport" as the key variable. Next, we have determined its two desired values: (1) within walking distance of an interurban railway station, (2) within short walking distance of a local transport (tram/bus) line's station. At least one of the two desired values need to be met.

Satisfying the above desired value contributes to meeting many of the requirements shown in **Table 4**. First, limiting the residence and service zones within walking distances of public transportation stations leads to environmental protection by preventing urban sprawl. It also promotes the shift from automobile to mass transit systems, walking, and biking, which reduces traffic congestion, pollution, and CO_2 emissions. Meanwhile, an increase in walking and biking leads to better health. Furthermore, lively pedestrian traffic contributes to increasing economic vitality and social interaction, as well as preventing crimes through an increase in people's "eyes on the street" [23–25].

5.2.3 Principles of designing city components

The third step shows the principles of designing city components. In this step, first, main city component types are identified as elements. Next, items that strongly influence urban sustainability are determined as variables. Part of such elements and variables are demonstrated in **Table 7**.

Choosing one element from this table, that is, "larger buildings," the rest of this section comments on the selected three variables and their desired values. Meeting these desired values helps to fill various requirements for sustainable urban design.

Concerning the first variable, "energy usage of the building," we have identified its desired value as "net-zero energy building." Achieving this desired value requires buildings' high-level energy efficiency and the use of renewable energy. In addition, installing equipment for using renewable energy, such as solar panels, is a measure for disaster damage reduction, since such equipment can provide emergency electricity.

Meanwhile, we have determined the desired value of "height limits for construction" to be "not high," more specific "height for several-floor buildings at the maximum." There are many disadvantages in constructing tall buildings, including skyscrapers. The taller the buildings become, the more difficult they achieve net-zero energy buildings. Installing solar panels on the roof is a common way to use renewable energy at building sites; however, high-rise buildings inevitably increase the ratio of total floor area to the roof area. Besides, high-rise buildings often block surrounding buildings from the sun and make it difficult to use renewable energy. Furthermore, controlling buildings' height uniform with neighbors also contributes to better landscapes.

Regarding the third variable, "uses of the building's street-level floor," we have identified its desired value as "priority to service uses." If the street-level floor of residential buildings facing main streets is allocated for service uses, such as shops, pedestrian traffic can increase. Lively pedestrian traffic helps economic vitalization, social interaction, and crime prevention [23–25].

6. Conclusion

This chapter illustrated the system-control-based methodology for sustainable structure design, with the examples of housing and urban design. Section 2 showed the "control system for promoting sustainable structure design." The third section demonstrated the "process of producing and revising sustainable structure design guidelines." The fourth section included the extracts of the sustainable housing design guidelines produced and revised in Japan. Lastly, Section 5 outlined a way of producing sustainable urban design guidelines. Unlike the design of city components, such as houses, the design of the whole city needs extensive spatial planning. Accordingly, the final stage of producing sustainable urban design guidelines consists of the three steps: (1) development allowable areas, (2) spatial relationships among city components, (3) principles of designing city components.

As already shown in our previous studies, this methodology has the following four characteristics: (1) visualization of the whole picture for promoting sustainable design, (2) user-friendliness, (3) comprehensiveness, (4) adaptability to different and changing situations [26]. The first characteristic originates in the schematization of the control system (**Figure 1**) and the process of producing and revising the design guidelines (**Figure 3**). Besides, this chapter has included two new diagrams, namely **Figure 4** and **Figure 5**, which are expected to help understand the whole picture for promoting sustainable urban design.

The second feature, "user-friendliness," originates from the "element-variable-desired value" framework in the sustainable design guidelines. Elements in the design guidelines are equivalent to actual parts of structures. Therefore, the system users can smoothly design the structures by comparing the actual structure or drawings with the design guidelines. Meanwhile, the third feature, "comprehensiveness," means that this methodology can deal with various environmental, social, and economic issues. This feature results from the model of sustainability (**Figure 2**), which has been incorporated in the control system for promoting sustainable structure design (**Figure 1**).

The fourth characteristic, "adaptability to different and changing situations," originates in the process of producing and revising the design guidelines. As demonstrated in **Tables 1** and **2**, local/particular problems in a country or region can be included in producing and revising the design guidelines. As a result, the produced and revised guidelines naturally become adaptable to that country's or region's situation. Meanwhile, Section 3.2 and Section 4.2 have shown the process of revising the design guidelines and its concrete instance, respectively. These study results include theoretical and practical ways to adapt the guidelines to changing situations over time.

Our main future work is further research on sustainable urban design. First, we must complete the sustainable urban design guidelines for practical use. After that, it is also necessary to revise the design guidelines by following the revision process shown in **Figure 4**. Through such future work, we are aiming to refine this methodology for designing sustainable structures.

Author details

Kazutoshi Fujihira
Institute of Environmentology, Inagi, Tokyo, Japan

*Address all correspondence to: fujihira@kankyogaku.com

IntechOpen

© 2020 The Author(s). Licensee IntechOpen. This chapter is distributed under the terms of the Creative Commons Attribution License (http://creativecommons.org/licenses/by/3.0), which permits unrestricted use, distribution, and reproduction in any medium, provided the original work is properly cited.

References

[1] United Nations Department of Economic and Social Affairs. World Urbanization Prospects 2018 [Internet]. 2018. Available from: https://population.un.org/wup/ [Accessed: 2020-09-07]

[2] United Nations Human Settlements Programme (UN-Habitat). Cities and Climate Change: Global Report on Human Settlements 2011. London, Washington DC: Earthscan; 2011. 300 p.

[3] United Nations. Resolution adopted by the General Assembly on 25 September 2015, Transforming our world: the 2030 Agenda for Sustainable Development [Internet]. 2015

[4] Osuka K, Adachi S. Approach to Systems Control (in Japanese). Tokyo: Corona Publishing; 1999 177 p

[5] IPCC. Climate Change 2007: Synthesis Report. Contribution of Working Groups I, II and III to the Fourth Assessment Report of the Intergovernmental Panel on Climate Change. Geneva: IPCC; 2007. 104 p

[6] IPCC. Climate Change 2014: Synthesis Report. Contribution of Working Groups I, II and III to the Fifth Assessment Report of the Intergovernmental Panel on Climate Change. Geneva: IPCC; 2014. 151 p

[7] Denton F, Wilbanks T, Abeysinghe A, Burton I, Gao Q, Lemos M, et al. Climate-resilient pathways: Adaptation, mitigation, and sustainable development. In: Field C et al., editors. Climate Change 2014: Impacts, Adaptation, and Vulnerability. Part a: Global and Sectoral Aspects. Contribution of Working Group II to the Fifth Assessment Report of the Intergovernmental Panel on Climate Change. Cambridge. New York: Cambridge University Press; 2014. pp. 1101-1131

[8] Fujihira K. Requirements for sustainable housing design. In: Fujihira K, editor. Sustainable Home Design by Applying Control Science. Rijeka: IntechOpen; 2017. DOI: 10.5772/intechopen.71322 Available from: https://www.intechopen.com/books/sustainable-home-design-by-applying-control-science/requirements-for-sustainable-housing-design

[9] Fujihira K. Basic schemes: Preparations for applying control science to sustainable design. In: Fujihira K, editor. Sustainable Home Design by Applying Control Science. Rijeka: IntechOpen; 2017. DOI: 10.5772/intechopen.71325 Available from: https://www.intechopen.com/books/sustainable-home-design-by-applying-control-science/basic-schemes-preparations-for-applying-control-science-to-sustainable-design

[10] Fujihira K. Methodology of applying control science to sustainable housing design. In: Fujihira K, editor. Sustainable Home Design by Applying Control Science. Rijeka: IntechOpen; 2017. DOI: 10.5772/intechopen.71324 Available from: https://www.intechopen.com/books/sustainable-home-design-by-applying-control-science/methodology-of-applying-control-science-to-sustainable-housing-design

[11] Fujihira K. System control for sustainability: Application to building design. In: Thomas C, editor. Complex Systems, Sustainability and Innovation. Rijeka: IntechOpen; 2016. DOI: 10.5772/65875 Available from: https://www.intechopen.com/books/complex-systems-sustainability-and-innovation/system-control-for-sustainability-application-to-building-design

[12] Fujihira K. Comprehensive strategy for sustainable housing design. In: Cakmakli A, editor. Different Strategies of Housing Design. London:

IntechOpen; 2019. DOI: 10.5772/intechopen.86278 Available from: https://www.intechopen.com/books/different-strategies-of-housing-design/comprehensive-strategy-for-sustainable-housing-design

[13] International Energy Agency. Key Renewables Trends 2016 Excerpt from: Renewables Information [Internet]. 2016. Available from: https://docs.wind-watch.org/IEA-Key-Renewables-Trends-2016.pdf [Accessed: 2020-09-15]

[14] U.S. Department of Energy. Grid Energy Storage [Internet]. 2013. Available from: https://www.energy.gov/sites/prod/files/2014/09/f18/Grid%20Energy%20Storage%20December%202013.pdf [Accessed: 2020-09-15]

[15] European Commission Directorate General for Energy. DG ENER. Working Paper: The Future Role and Challenges of Energy Storage [Internet]. Available from: https://ec.europa.eu/energy/sites/ener/files/energy_storage.pdf [Accessed: 2020-09-15]

[16] Energy Efficiency and Conservation Division Agency for Natural Resources and Energy Ministry of Economy, Trade and Industry. Definition of ZEH and Future Measures Proposed by the ZEH Roadmap Examination Committee [Internet]. 2015. Available from: https://www.enecho.meti.go.jp/category/saving_and_new/saving/zeh_report/pdf/report_160212_en.pdf [Accessed: 2020-09-15]

[17] Gooley J, Chamberlain K, Smith K, Khalsa SB, Rajaratnam S, et al. Exposure to room light before bedtime suppresses melatonin onset and shortens melatonin duration in humans. Journal of Clinical Endocrinology & Metabolism. 2011; **96**(3):E463-E472. DOI: https://doi.org/10.1210/jc.2010-2098

[18] Harvard Health Publishing. Blue Light has a Dark Side: What is Blue Light? The Effect Blue Light has on Your Sleep and More [Internet]. 2012–2020. Available from: https://www.health.harvard.edu/staying-healthy/blue-light-has-a-dark-side [Accessed: 2020-09-15]

[19] IUCN. A Global Standard for the Identification of Key Biodiversity Areas, Version 1.0. First Edition. Gland: IUCN; 2016 46 p

[20] Southern Tier Central Regional Planning and Development Board. Steep Slopes and Land Use Decisions [Internet]. 2012. Available from: http://www.stcplanning.org/usr/Program_Areas/Flood_Mitigation/SCAP_steepslopes%202010_02_21_CR.pdf [Accessed: 2020-09-15]

[21] Lehigh Valley Planning Commission. Steep Slopes: Guide, Model Regulations. [Internet]. 2008. Available from: https://www.lvpc.org/pdf/SteepSlopes.pdf [Accessed: 2020-09-15]

[22] Land-of-Sky Regional Council. Mountain Ridge and Steep Slope Protection Strategies. Asheville: Land-of-Sky Regional Council; 2008. 76p.

[23] Jacobs J. The Death and Life of Great American Cities. New York: Random House; 1992 458 p

[24] Gehl J. Cities for People. Washington DC: Island Press; 2010 288 p

[25] Long Y, Huang CC. Does block size matter? The impact of urban design on economic vitality for Chinese cities. Environment and planning B: Urban Analytics and City Science. 2019;**46**(3): 406-422. DOI: 10.1177/2399808317715640 (First published: 2017)

[26] Fujihira K. Discussion and conclusion: Effectiveness, characteristics and future prospects of the methodology. In: Fujihira K, editor. Sustainable Home Design by Applying Control Science. Rijeka: IntechOpen;

2017. DOI: 10.5772/intechopen.71321 Available from: https://www.intechopen.com/books/sustainable-home-design-by-applying-control-science/discussion-and-conclusion-effectiveness-characte ristics-and-future-prospects-of-the-methodology

Section 5

Pollution Management

Chapter 18

Possibility of Complexation of the Calix[4]Arene Molecule with the Polluting Gases: DFT and NCI-RDG Theory

Bouzid Gassoumi, Fatma Ezzahra Ben Mohamed, Houcine Ghalla and Rafik Ben Chaabane

Abstract

The calix[4]arenes (abbreviated as CX[4]) are characterized by a specific hydrophobic cavity formed by a four cyclically phenol groups to encapsulate a gas or small molecules. Recently, the CX[4] molecule is used in a specific media and in pharmaceutical drug delivery. The pollution problem will be a vital subject in the future because the increase of the explosions of the gaseous pollutants in the environment. In this report, we have encapsulated the polluting gases NO_3, NO_2, CO_2 and N_2 by the calix[4]arene molecule. In this work, The binding energies of the CX[4]-gas has been calculated including the BSSE (Basis Set Superposition Error) counterpoise (CP). The red-shift of the O-H bonding interactions obtained by adding the gas in the sensitive area of calix[4]arene is clearly explained by the infrared spectrum analysis. The Molecular electrostatic potential (MEP) of the stable CX[4]-gas complexes have been investigated in the endo-vs. exo-cavity regions. Finally, the non-covalent interactions analyses of the stable host-guests complexes have been estimated by using DFT calculations.

Keywords: complexation, specific gases, H-bonding, molecular electrostatic potential and binding energy

1. Introduction

The recognition of the electrostatic and magnetic properties in the selective guest in microscopic systems facilitates to know several anionic cationic or neutral guests' complexes [1–5]. In this work, the CX[4] molecule is specified by its own chemical composition and the hydrophobic cavity form [6]. This molecule is characterized by specific parameters such as the diameter and the height, which facilitates the encapsulation of the cationic, anionic, neutral guests or small molecules [7–9]. Also, the cavity of the CX[4] molecule have attracted the researchers to test a new guest materials to be functional in the medical [10–12] or micro-biological field [13, 14]. In literature, we have noted that there are some works which discuss the encapsulation of the CX[4] with gases molecules (CH_4, NH_3 and C_2H_2) [15–18]. In our work, we have studied the photo-physical properties of the CX[4]-gas complexes (CX[4]-NO_3, CX[4]-NO_2, CX[4]-CO_2 and CX[4]-N_2). We discuss the possibility of the encapsulation of these gases by the CX[4] molecule to show the sensibility of this molecule to the polluting gases outside or inside the cavity. We have chosen the NO_3, NO_2, CO_2 and N_2 gas as guest's because they can be formed a dipole-dipole interactions and a CH...π hydrogen-bonding with the CX[4] molecule. By using the density functional theory (DFT) calculations, we have described the dynamic stabilities of the endo-vs. exo-cavity of the CX[4]-gas complexes. The vibrational properties of the CX[4]-gas complexes have been studied. The Molecular electrostatic potential studies of these host-guests complexes have been performed. The Non-covalent interaction via RDG function are very important to know the nature of the interactions between the specific guests and the CX[4] molecule.

2. Computational method

The stable structures of the studied systems (CX[4] and CX[4]-gas) have been calculated with the DFT method by using the B3LYP [16, 19–21] coupled to the D3BJ (empirical Becke and Johnson damping dispersion corrections) in combination with the 6-31 + G(d) basis set, as implemented in GAUSSIAN 09 package [22] and the Gauss View [23] as a visual program. We have been calculated the binding energies of the CX[4]-gas take into account the Basis Set Superposition Error (BSSE) counterpoise (CP) correction energy of Boys and Bernardi [24].

The binding energies are given by the following formula:

$$\ddot{A}E_{CX[4]-gas} = E_{CX[4]-gas} - E_{CX[4]} - E_{gas} + BSSE \quad (1)$$

where $E_{CX[4]\text{-}gas}$, $E_{CX[4]}$ and E_{gas} are the total energies of host-guest and host or guest molecules. The electronic parameters of the studied complexes are very effective to show the sensibility of the specific gas inside or outside the cavity. We analyzed then the infrared spectrum of these complexes using the DFT/B3LYP-D3 method. The nature of the interaction between the CX[4] molecule and the pollutant gases is better explained using the Non covalent interaction via RDG analysis [25].

3. Results and discussions

3.1 Geometry optimizations

The CX[4]-gas complexes have been optimized at the DFT/B3LYP-D3 (**Figure 1**). In this study, we have placed the NO_3, NO_2, CO_2 and N_2 gas in the exo or endo-cavity positions. **Table 1** presents the Binding energy E_b (in (kcal/mol)) of CX[4]-gas complexes. The binding energy value of the CX[4]-CO_2 is equal to 21.33 kcal/mol (see **Figure 1**). We show that, the CX[4]-$CO_{2(endo)}$ complex is more stable than that of CX[4]-$CO_{2(exo)}$. In addition, from the CX[4]-NO_3 complex, the NO_3 gas has placed in the endo or the exo-cavity position. In this situation, we have obtained a divergence in the case of the interaction of CX[4] with NO_3 outside the cavity that is why, we have tested the case where the NO_3 gas perpendicular to the 4-fold axis of CX[4] and a parallel position of the NO_3 (NO_3 parallel to the 4-fold axis). We have been noted a very weak energy of the CX[4]-$NO_{3(perp.)}$ complex in comparison with the CX[4]-$NO_{3(paral.)}$ complex. Moreover, we have noted that the interaction between the CX[4] molecule and the $NO_{3(paral\cdot)}$ is stabilized by a low dipole moment. We have calculated

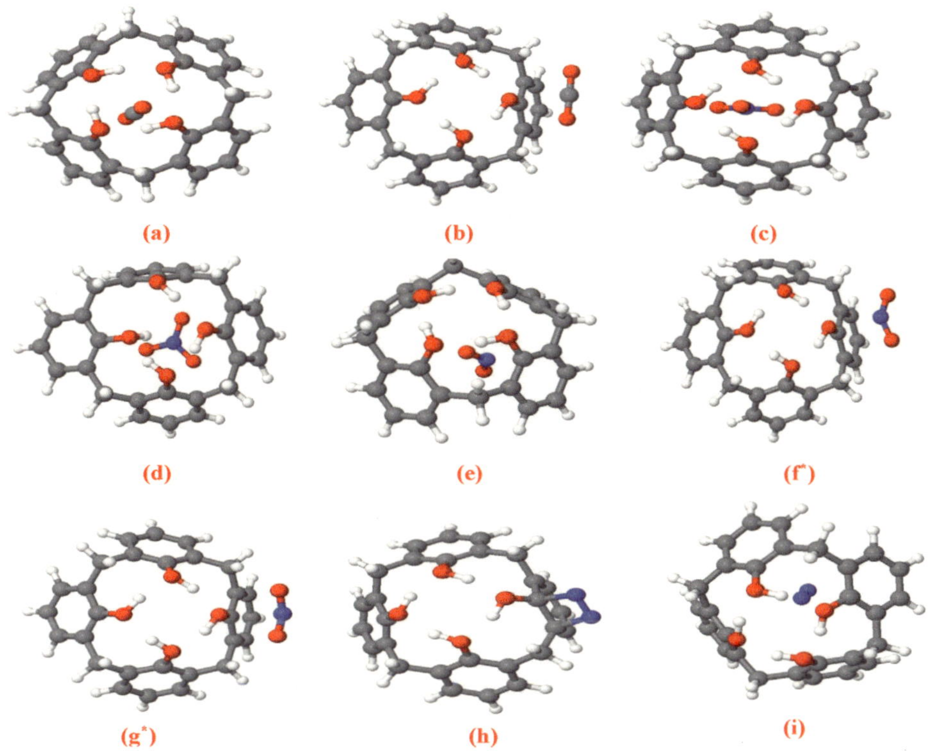

Figure 1.
Optimized geometries of the CX[4]-$CO_{2(endo)}$ (a), CX[4]-$CO_{2(exo)}$ (b), CX[4]-$NO_{3(paral.)}$ (c), CX[4]-$NO_{3(perp.)}$ (d), CX[4]-$NO_{2(endo)}$ (e), CX[4]-$NO_{2(exo)}$ (f), CX[4]-$NO_{2(exo)}$ (g*), CX[4]-$N_{2(endo)}$ (h) and CX[4]-$N_{2(exo)}$ (i) complexes using B3LYP-D3BJ/6-31 + G(d) method (top view).*

Complexes	E_b	BSSE	E_b (with BSSE)
CX[4]-$NO_{3\,(paral.)}$	24.62	6.17	
CX[4]-$NO_{3(perp.)}$	16.51	6.05	22.56
CX[4]-$N_{2(exo)}$	16.89	1.70	18.59
CX[4]-$N_{2(endo)}$	16.90	1.80	18.70
CX[4]-$NO_{2(exo)f^*}$	18.17	1.82	19.99
CX[4]-$NO_{2(exo)g^*}$	18.11	1.80	19.91
CX[4]-$NO_{2(endo)}$	17.83	2.71	20.54
CX[4]-$CO_{2(endo)}$	18.62	2.71	21.33
CX[4]-$CO_{2(exo)}$	18.10	2.71	20.81

Table 1.
Binding energy E_b (in (kcal/mol)) of CX[4]-gas complexes.

two positions for the guest N_2: the N_2 gas located on the outside of cavity and this gas located perpendicular to the 4-fold axis of CX[4] molecule. We have shown that the CX[4]-$N_{2(endo)}$ has a very strongest energy, which explain that this geometry is more stable than CX[4]-$N_{2(exo)}$ (see **Table 1**). The binding energy (E_b) of the stable complex is equal to 18.90 kcal/mol. Finally, from the CX[4]-$NO_{2(exo)}$ complex, we note that the NO_2 gas is located in the outside of the H-link network of the phenolic hydroxyl groups. The binding energy of the CX[4]-$NO_{2(endo)}$ complex is equal to 20.54 kcal/mol (see **Table 1**). As we see, The binding energy of the CX[4]-$NO_{2(endo)}$

complex is higher than that of CX[4]-$CO_{2(exo/endo)}$. Therefore, The CX[4]-$NO_{2(endo)}$ complex is more stable than others, which is explained by the lowest dipole moment.

3.2 Red-shifted of O-H bonds

The reorganization of the O...H stretching vibration has been calculated after the system perturbation with the pollutant gases. Moreover, The IR spectrum calculation of the four stable complexes is given in **Figure 2**. In literature, Furel et al. have been studied the experimental infrared spectrum of the CX[4] molecule. In this work, we have analyzed the stretching region of the IR spectrum between 2900 and 3500 cm^{-1}, respectively 3254 (OH), 3168(OH asymmetric), 3045($C_{ar.}$H), 2951 (asym. CH2), 2916 cm^{-1}(sym.CH2). The infrared spectrum of the CX[4]-gas have been compared to the IR spectra of the free CX[4] molecule (See **Figure 2**). In addition, to take into account the an-harmonic effect our calculated frequencies scaled by 0.956. However, we have noted that, the CX[4]-CO_2 is characterized by two peaks located in the vicinity of 3177 cm^{-1} and 3181 cm^{-1}respectively. The CX[4]-N_2 complex have the same results. These tow peaks are specified by the O-H asymmetric stretching vibration. We have shown that the frequency band located at 3160 cm^{-1} is corresponding to the O-H stretching vibration of the phenol O-H groups. Concerning the CX[4]-NO_2 complex, we have noted the appearance of the two peaks in the neighborhood of 3170 cm^{-1} and 3193 cm^{-1}. These peaks are corresponding to the vibrations of the O-H and O-H asymmetric bonds. Finally, we have shown a burst of the OH peak in the CX[4]-NO_3 gas what form four peaks located in the vicinity of 2928 cm^{-1} (asym.CH2), 3100 cm^{-1}(asym.OH), 3204 cm^{-1}(OH) and 3298 cm^{-1}(free OH) respectively. The noted values for the comparing of the red-shifted O-H vibration between the CX[4]-gas and the free CX[4]molecule are 44 cm^{-1}, 24 cm^{-1} and 9 cm^{-1} for CX[4]-NO_3, CX[4]-NO_2, CX[4]-CO_2 and CX[4]-N_2 successively.

3.3 Molecular electrostatic potential study

In **Figure 3(a–d)**, we have been created the MEP map of the stable host-guests. These graphs indicate the relation between the supra-molecular structure and the physic-cal-chemical properties of the CX[4]-gas complexes. In this work, we have explained the more nucleophile or electrophile sites in these stable host-guests. The color code of the maps varying from −0.005 to 0.005 (isoval = 0.001). From **Figure 3**, we show that the electrophilic sites surrounded by N atoms and the nucleophilic sites surrounded by O atoms. In addition, these host-guests complexes are characterized by the existence of the positive charges located at the level of the phenolic branch.

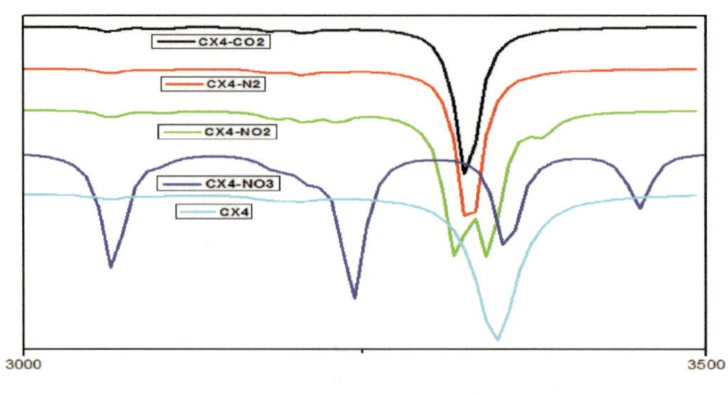

Figure 2.
Infrared spectrum of the stable host-guests complexations (H-bonding region (the unit is cm^{-1})).

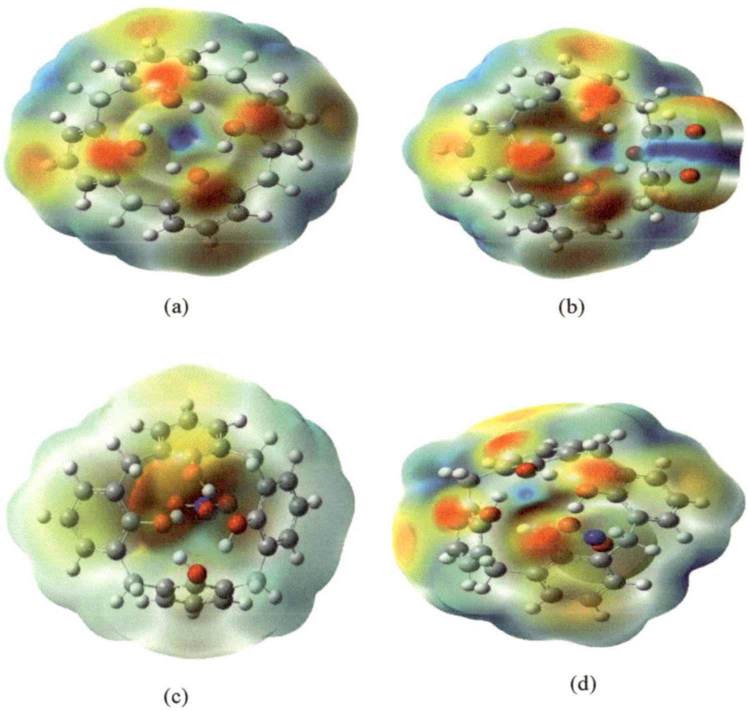

Figure 3.
Molecular electrostatic potential analysis of the CX[4]-CO_2 (a), CX[4]-N2 (b), CX[4]-NO_2 (c) and CX[4]-NO_3 (d) complexes calculated by B3LYP-D3/6–31 + G(d) level.

This part demonstrates how the MESP can explore the region of the unravel molecular interactions between the CX[4] molecule and these hosts.

3.4 Non covalent interactions analysis

Figure 4(a) shows the existence of a weak van der Waals (VdW) type interactions between CO_2 gas and CX[4]. Concerning the CX[4]-N_2 complex (**Figure 4(b)**), we show a green color between the guest and the host that indicates the existence of the weak Van der Waals interactions and the blue color at the lower edge level indicates the existence of the O-H-bonding type interactions. Also, we have shown clearly a red color located in the center of the phenol rings indicates a strong repulsion. The NCI-plots have been confirmed these results (see **Figure 4**). In addition, from CX[4]-NO_2 (**Figure 4(c)**) complex, we find the existence of a red color which explain the steric effect interactions, blue color (hydrogen bonds type interactions) and a green color (week van der Waals type interactions). The type of majority bonds of the links between the NO_3 gas and the CX[4] molecule is the weak VdW type interactions. The NCI-RDG analysis shows that the VdW type interactions and the hydrogen bonding interactions between the guest and the host are very necessary for the stability of the encapsulated complexes.

4. Conclusion

The CX[4] and the CX[4]-gas complexes have been optimized using the density functional theory (DFT). Our work has clearly explained the sensibility of the pollutant gas inside the cavity, which is very important in comparison with the gas

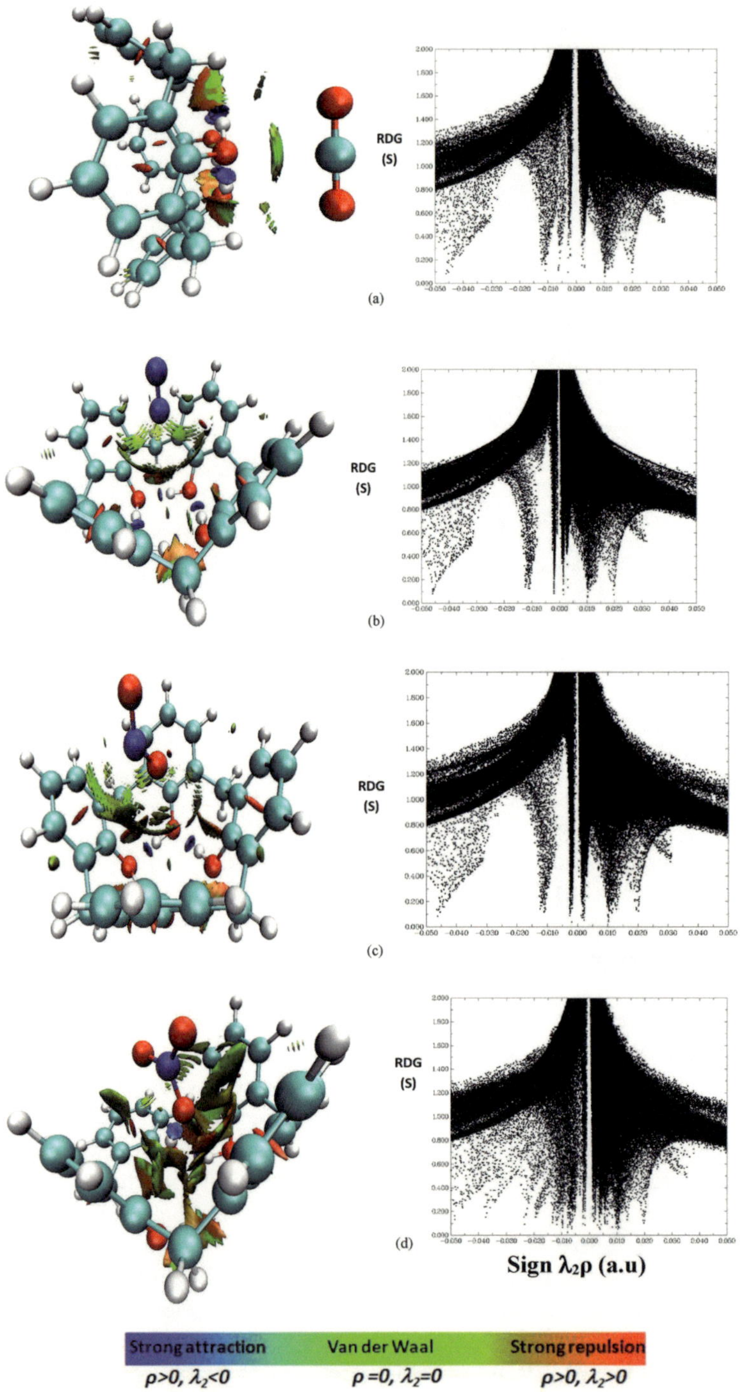

Figure 4.
NCI-RDG plots of the electron density and its reduced gradient of the inclusion complexes for CX[4]-gas (CX[4]-CO_2(a), CX[4]-N_2(b), CX[4]-NO_2(c) and CX[4]-NO_3(d)). The iso-surfaces were constructed with RGD = 0.5a.u and the colors scaling from −0.01 to −0.01 a.u.

located outside the cavity. The IR spectrum study has explained the role of the NO_3 gas in the red-shifted of the O-H bonds in comparison with the other gases. The MEP results is clearly explained the charge distribution reactivity. The NCI-RDG analysis clearly shows the strong interactions of the gas NO_3 and NO_2 with the endo-cavity environments of the CX[4] molecule. Finally, the non-covalent interactions analyses show that the calix[4]arene maybe useful for encapsulated the pollutant gas in the future. The sensitivity of the calix[4]arene molecule for these polluting gases opens a way to test the interaction of CX[4] with other types of biological molecules (proteins).

Acknowledgements

The authors acknowledge financial support from the Tunisian's Ministry of high education and scientific research. In this work, we were granted access to the HPC resources of the FLMSN, 'Fédération Lyonnaise de Modélisation et Sciences Numériques', partner of EQUIPEX EQUIP@MESO and to the 'Centre de calcul CCIN2P3' at Villeurbanne, France.

Author details

Bouzid Gassoumi[1,3*], Fatma Ezzahra Ben Mohamed[2], Houcine Ghalla[3] and Rafik Ben Chaabane[1,3]

1 Laboratory of Advanced Materials and Interfaces (LIMA), University of Monastir, Faculty of Science of Monastir, Avenue of Environment, Monastir, Tunisia

2 Department of Physics, Faculty of Arts and Sciences of AlMikhwah, Al-BAHA University, Kingdom of Saudi Arabia

3 University of Monastir, Quantum and Statistical Physics Laboratory, Faculty of Science, Monastir, Tunisia

4 Institute of Light and Matter, UMR5306 University of Lyon 1-CNRS, University of Lyon, Villeurbanne Cedex, France

*Address all correspondence to: gassoumibouzid2016@gmail.com

IntechOpen

© 2020 The Author(s). Licensee IntechOpen. This chapter is distributed under the terms of the Creative Commons Attribution License (http://creativecommons.org/licenses/by/3.0), which permits unrestricted use, distribution, and reproduction in any medium, provided the original work is properly cited. (cc) BY

References

[1] Athar, M., Lone, M.Y., Jha, P.C.: Recognition of anions using urea and thiourea substituted calixarenes: A density functional theory study of non-covalent interactions. Chemical Physics. 501, 68-77 (2018). doi:10.1016/j.chemphys.2017.12.00

[2] Kumagai, S., Hayashi, K., Kameda, T., Morohashi, N., Hattori, T., Yoshioka, T.: Identification of number and type of cations in water-soluble Cs+ and Na+ calix[4]arene-bis-crown-6 complexes by using ESI-TOF-MS. Chemosphere. 197, 181-184 (2018). doi:10.1016/j.chemosphere.2018.01.040

[3] Arena, G., Contino, A., Gulino, F.G., Magrì, A., Sciotto, D., Ungaro, R.: Complexation of small neutral organic molecules by water soluble calix[4]arenes. Tetrahedron Letters. 41, 9327-9330 (2000). doi:10.1016/S0040-4039(00)01687-7

[4] Ortolan, A., Oestroem, I., Caramori, G., Parreira, R., Muñoz-Castro, A., Bickelhaupt, F.M.: Anion Recognition by Organometallic Calixarenes: Analysis from Relativistic DFT Calculations. Organometallics. 37, (2018). doi:10.1021/acs.organomet.8b00292

[5] Cabral, B.J.C., Coutinho, K., Canuto, S.: Dynamics of endo- vs. exo-complexation and electronic absorption of calix[4]arene-Ar2. Chemical Physics Letters. 612, 266-272 (2014). doi:10.1016/j.cplett.2014.08.036

[6] Haino, T., Rudkevich, D.M., Shivanyuk, A., Rissanen, K., Jr, J.R.: Induced-Fit Molecular Recognition with Water-Soluble Cavitands. Chemistry – A European Journal. 6, 3797-3805 (2000).doi:10.1002/1521-3765(20001016)6:20<3797::AID-CHEM3797>3.0.CO;2-1

[7] Wei, A.: Calixarene-encapsulated nanoparticles: self-assembly into functional nanomaterials. Chem Commun (Camb). 1581-1591 (2006). doi:10.1039/b515806k

[8] Wang, J.-F., Huang, L.-Y., Bu, J.-H., Li, S.-Y., Qin, S., Xu, Y.-W., Liu, J.-M., Su, C.-Y.: A fluorescent calixarene-based dimeric capsule constructed via a M II –terpyridine interaction: cage structure, inclusion properties and drug release. RSC Advances. 8, 22530-22535 (2018). doi:10.1039/C8RA02146E

[9] Atwood, J.L., Koutsantonis, G.A., Raston, C.L.: Purification of C60 and C70 by selective complexation with calixarenes. Nature. 368, 229-231 (1994). doi:10.1038/368229a0

[10] Da Silva, E., Lazar, A.N., Coleman, A.W.: Biopharmaceutical applications of calixarenes. Journal of Drug Delivery Science and Technology. 14, 3-20 (2004). doi:10.1016/S1773-2247(04)50001-1

[11] Fahmy, S.A., Ponte, F., Abd El-Rahman, M.K., Russo, N., Sicilia, E., Shoeib, T.: Investigation of the host-guest complexation between 4-sulfocalix[4]arene and nedaplatin for potential use in drug delivery. Spectrochimica Acta Part A: Molecular and Biomolecular Spectroscopy. 193, 528-536 (2018). doi:10.1016/j.saa.2017.12.070

[12] Schühle, D.T., Peters, J.A., Schatz, J.: Metal binding calixarenes with potential biomimetic and biomedical applications. Coordination Chemistry Reviews. 255, 2727-2745 (2011)

[13] Balasaheb Nimse, S., Kim, T.: Biological applications of functionalized calixarenes. Chemical Society Reviews. 42, 366-386 (2013). doi:10.1039/C2CS35233H

[14] Hua, B., Shao, L., Zhang, Z., Sun, J., Yang, J.: Pillar[6]arene/acridine orange

host–guest complexes as colorimetric and fluorescence sensors for choline compounds and further application in monitoring enzymatic reactions. Sensors and Actuators B: Chemical. 255, 1430-1435 (2018). doi:10.1016/j.snb.2017.08.141

[15] B.J.C. Cabral, K. Coutinho, S. Canuto, Dynamics of endo- vs. exo-complexation and electronic absorption of calix[4]arene-Ar2, Chemical Physics Letters. 612 (2014) 266-272. https://doi.org/10.1016/j.cplett.2014.08.036.

[16] B. Gassoumi, H. Ghalla, R.Ben. Chaabane, DFT and TD-DFT investigation of calix[4]arene interactions with TFSI− ion, Heliyon. 5 (2019) e02822. https://doi.org/10.1016/j.heliyon.2019.e02822.

[17] Y. Inokuchi, K. Soga, K. Hirai, M. Kida, F. Morishima, T. Ebata, Ultraviolet Photodissociation Spectroscopy of the Cold K+·Calix[4]arene Complex in the Gas Phase, J. Phys. Chem. A. 119 (2015) 8512-8518. https://doi.org/10.1021/acs.jpca.5b05328.

[18] S. Kaneko, Y. Inokuchi, T. Ebata, E. Aprà, S.S. Xantheas, Laser spectroscopic and theoretical studies of encapsulation complexes of calix[4]arene, J Phys Chem A. 115 (2011) 10846-10853. https://doi.org/10.1021/jp204577j.

[19] L.I. Shamova, G.A. Shamov, I.S. Antipin, A.I. Konovalov, Modeling K+ and Ag+ Complexation by Thiacalix[4]arene Amides Using DFT: The Role of Intramolecular Hydrogen Bonding, J. Phys. Chem. A. 113 (2009) 5691-5699. https://doi.org/10.1021/jp810947g.

[20] G. Mazzone, M.E. Alberto, F. Ponte, N. Russo, M. Toscano, Anion-π weak interactions in a heteroaromatic calixarene receptor. A theoretical investigation, Inorganica Chimica Acta. 470 (2018) 379-384. https://doi.org/10.1016/j.ica.2017.05.033.

[21] B. Gassoumi, M. Chaabene, H. Ghalla, R.B. Chaabane, Role of hydrogen bonding interactions within of the conformational preferences of calix[n = 4,6,8]arene: DFT and QTAIM analysis, J Mol Model. 26 (2019) 12. https://doi.org/10.1007/s00894-019-4255-5.

[22] G09 | Gaussian.com, http://gaussian.com/glossary/g09/

[23] Dennington RI, Keith T, Millam J, GaussView Version 5.0.8. Semichem Inc.

[24] S.F. Boys, F. Bernardi, The calculation of small molecular interactions by the differences of separate total energies. Some procedures with reduced errors, Molecular Physics. 19 (1970) 553-566. https://doi.org/10.1080/00268977000101561.

[25] Johnson ER, Keinan S, Mori-Sánchez P, et al (2010) Revealing Noncovalent Interactions. J Am Chem Soc 132:6498-6506. https://doi.org/10.1021/ja100936w

Chapter 19

Apatite/Salt Slurry Emission Control of Post Combustion Flue Gas of Lignite and Coal in Fluidized Bed - Double Circulation Microwave Column Adsorber

Yildirim İsmail Tosun

Abstract

Heated Ca apatite slimes in microwave radiated salt slurries are one of the most promising technologies for advanced fuel energy storage with favorable economic potential and intrinsic properties. The development of solid pellet technology for molten salt is a key issue in the heat transport processing. The apathite phosphate, slurry salt in the slime-salt bath mixes was investigated under microwave radiation heating to result in insoluble sorbent fines dissolved in porous basket. The insoluble consists of noble metal fission products, such as Pb, Zn, Cu. In this study, there have been very few transport studies of wet steam alkali slurry (metal fines-molten alkali salt mixture). Bath ferrite/apatite particle size changed the heat conductivity to salt bath. A major reason is that the retention time in fixed film processes is longer than in solid–gas processes. This allows more time to the heat absorption for cracking to the desorbed persistent compounds. Furthermore, radiated ferrite by microwave allows a sufficient intimate contact between coal and biomass surface pores and gas atmosphere in the furnace due to more pyrolysis gas desorption. Bubbling slurry of sorbent porosity decreases while temperature decreases. There was a critical porous structure of bubbling sorbent bath which is a factor that determines to a great extent both the sorbent rate and degree of boiling it was found that, a porous slurry bath over 45% was more efficient with radiated a low amount ferrite below weight rate of 15% in microwave column.

Keywords: apatite, Ca phosphate, microwave radiation, salt slurries, metal sorption, energy, risk assessment, hybrid sorbent, apatite compost, salt slurries, microwave, column adsorber, toxic emission, phosphate composts

1. Introduction

Exhaust toxic gases coming out of the chimneys in the highly industrialized locations cause hazardous environmental issue. The factories using combustion boilers pollute the fresh air in nature. The industrial development and urbanization and transportation opportunities harm the environment and living things due to combusted fuels. In many countries, power generation is the leading source of air pollution. While thermal power plants using coal make a significant contribution part of air pollution, diesel generators are also another major ecological concern. Industrial processes in the chemical and mining industries are related with use of solvents producing hazardous emissions as a result of the volatile properties of those chemicals and the combustion outputs pollute the air. In Turkey, The policies and programs that aimed to increase energy efficiency and production from renewable sources have a direct impact on a country's air quality [1].

In environmental impact assessment processes since 2012, the Turkish Ministry of Environment and Urbanization request risk assasment supported financially the project owners to make calculations using owning and operating modeling programs that take into account the long-range and cumulative reducing effects on air pollution in the country [2].

Privatized owning resources for 50 years period income owing and tax free ıncome quarentee for renewable resource use was eliminating incentive uses for fossil fuels, especially coal, and developing policies and incentive mechanisms to prioritize other alternative energy sources instead of fossil fuels.

2. Pollution control on post combustion shower sorption

Conventional coal combustion systems using Stokers or grate chambers are not designed to treat potentially low quality coal and waste in combustion [3–12]. In order to prevent air pollution, combusted boilers with post combustion was become the potential choice eliminate to spread of toxic emissions of coal and wastes [13–15]. The polluting matter of combusted emissions in stack should be controlled for Pb and Hg flue emissions, even as radioactive dust control. Sorbent use as the charcoal was offered and the sorptive property on porosity and the effect of char content was advantageous. The toxic waste and the reactive washing solutions utilized active carbon which resulted in the followed washing equations as below: [6–8].

The dissolution kinetics of sludge/mud particle for Pb heavy metal is followed by equation

$$\frac{dP_{Pb}}{dt} = k_i e^{-tic} dc \tag{1}$$

Where c_{Pb} Lead contamination mg/l, k the rate of dissolution of lead, i is the reaction style, t is time, Lead matter of coal would affect mainly emission increase pressure content.

The different type of solid sorbents such as Tatvan Pumice, salted pumice and borax, the popped borax soaked CaO were studied in elimination of toxic emissions in high sulfur asphaltite coal combustion [15, 16]. It was found that the reduction of toxic gas emissions can reach as high as 94.52% with soaking CaO and 90% with soaking CaO and oil slurry after 1 h combustion at 750°C, with a 100:1 weight ratio of clay pellet to fuel, 21 wt. % CaO/borax.

2.1 Sorption matter

The large surface used for industrial purposes natural materials [17–20]. Absorbents and adsorbents generally used bentonite; Simectite, Atapulgite, Sepiolite. It can be classified as montmorillonite. The smectite group is one of clay minerals or fire clay activated more called bentonite. Bentonite base mineral montmorillonite is common for the killer and is a commercially used term, at least soft, containing 85% montmorillonite, is an aluminum hydrosilicate with a colloidal property. When mixed with water, density of a few solid swelling bentonite about 2.5 g/cm^3. Montmorillonite is calcium clay in common use. Bentonite is a given name on the main content which cation of montmorillonite change mainly with Ca; Atapulgite, $2MgSi_8O_{20}$ $4(H_2O)$ (OH). The palygorskite expressed by the formula $4H_2O$ aqueous magnesium, aluminum silicate. Sepiolite is (OH) 6 Mg_9 Si_{12} $O_{30}(OH)_4$ $6H_2O$ group is aqueous Mg silicate. In these clay minerals, the channel-shaped pore water bound to crystal structure with layered silicate molecules. The activated clay minerals by deydrated crystal cavities contain micropores and channels and large surface area due to the possession of various cavity surfaces adsorbing heavy metals and high adsorbing capacities [20–30].

2.2 Sorbent type and utility

The diffusion rate of combustion gases with solid sorbents may influence the adsorption of toxic emissions amount. Especially, increased combustion temperature will reduce the time of solid sorbent diffusion [13–20].

The gas stream amendments, such as shale char carbonized from Şırnak asphaltite containing 52–60% shale by columns under microwave radiation as geo material composted for waste gas treatment should control contaminated effluents concentration. The field studies to evaluate the stability of heavy Hg and Pb SO_x concentrations and salts were balanced as weight increase. The initial objective of this study was to determine the effects of gas flow to sorbent column from the industrial discharge under certain pressure and temperature. In this study, important investigations have been made on composite granules production with Şırnak shale char and apatite ore of Mazıdağ, Mardin, as Ca phosphate feed in order to salt slurry shower in microwave oven 2 M HCl dissolution. The double stage compost sorbent for high level high gas sorption in laboratory water packed bed column adsorption compost system. Although the changes in the structural properties of bentonite after acid activation have been studied extensively in the literature, the studies on Pb adsorption of these samples are rather limited [30–33]. For this reason, the aim of this study is to investigate the thermal Pb and Hg washed adsorption properties of shale after acid modification and microwave activation.

In this study, bentonite and other clays, shale and marly shale of Şırnak utilized regarding absorbance properties, areas of use, production and market conditions. The bulk density of absorbent apatite phosphate changed the amount of moisture and the absorbent capacity. Bentonite and atapulgite absorbance by passing through certain processes was performed and the absorbance was measured at the mechanical strength change has been studied [25–30].

Bentonite with desired surface properties, porosity and hence retention capacity was mainly produced by dry or wet acid activation using mineral acids such as H_2SO_4 and HCl [31–34]. The main purpose in acid activation is to reach the desired structure without disrupting the layered crystal structure of the clay. For this reason, the acid/clay ratio, temperature, acidity, acid concentration, type and duration of activation, clay type and physical properties and amount of activation were important considerations to be taken into account when performing the appropriate activation [35–40].

2.3 Phosphate - clay compost

The Mazıdağı phosphate waste was Ca salt form of the phosphate mineral and lımestones with even fluorine apatite [41–45]. The dust waste of calcinations was utilized as necessary to prevent the joint reactive of CaO and F in order to sorptive washing process The obtained slurries at 10% waste dust by using such as CaO $2HPO_4$ 5OH.

xP_2O_5 and $NaCO_3$. The calcinations product is subjected to acid treatment for artificial fertilizer fabrication. The acid dissolution characteristics after calcinations, Mazıdağı apatite phosphate was mostly acid-soluble in their natural state compared to other phosphate minerals. The study utilized the fine waste, compost 32.81% P_2O_5–30.98% P_2O_5, soluble% P_2O_5 27.16%% P_2O_5 parts - calcination at 625°C at last 1/2 hour [38–40].

2.4 Ca phosphate/Asphaltite shale char composite

In this study, bentonite type clay is used as salt slurry with char fine for emission control. The substrate fine of the bentonite/P_2O_5 granules use as absorbent in 2020s show improved treatment [24–30]. The industrial waste sludges in some tanning and wood board plants, airplane hangars, ship building bench, other production facilities required neutralization and further treatment. In the workshops, grease, oil, water, chemicals and other undesirable substances absorbed by compost of apatite waste/zeolite and char and cleaned [31–37].

2.5 Microwave treated biomass char/apatite phosphate compost

Washing of hazardous waste waters by microwave action efficiencies exceeding the total Fe Pb and Hg contents of sludge increased fast on coal char and wood char were also reported by Tosun [6–10]. Material to be used as powder at porous granule at ultrafine grain size, basic as absorption capacity by the gas emission and other fluids reactive and solvents. High absorption capacity having clay, only to absorb the urea not ventilated, but bad reduce smell and bacteria should avoid. The packed grain size distribution of clay granules it is important that it is usually between 1 and 6 mm is required.

3. Material and methods

3.1 Physical surface properties of sorbent/char

BET specific surface areas of sorbent as tested by N2 gas permeability. The sorbent was critical on the base of surface properties such as total surface activity, oxygen functional groups, total surface impurities, metal concentrations, dielectric value, free radical concentration and reactivity. The main chemical texture was related to the stimulation of oxidation reactivity. However, in some investigations, the pore size distribution of activated carbon is also likely to affect desorption kinetics.

The salt slurries were mixed with activated clay bentonite at weight rates of 1/8. The head tests are caried out by CaCl2 adde 10000ppm slurries to 80 gr bentonite solid. The suspension of 80 gr slurry of clay and apatite was mixed in 1lt water as slurry and give through shower in 5 cm diameter glass columns. Finally microwave radiated glass showered to flue gas compressed at 2 bar retained by exposure to at 160 °C for 4 hours. In addition, these samples were further dried at the same temperature for 1 hour to remove vapor species. The experimentation unit as shown in **Figure 1**. The microwave salt slurry washing tests are followed by flowsheet as seen in **Figure 2**. The surface areas of the apatite, coal char, activated compost and shale clay samples were measured with a Quanta Chromosorb surface analyzer. The surface area was determined by measuring the thermal conductivity using a gas mixture prepared in N2 and Ar composition and taking into account the BET equation. The sorbent solids compositions and physical quality are given in **Tables 1** and **2**.

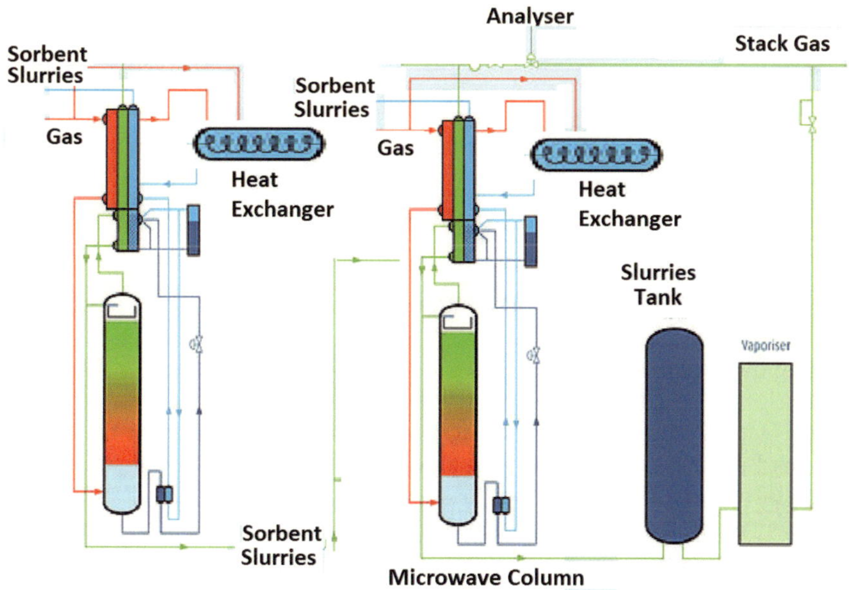

Figure 1.
The schematic view of an washing with microwave recycled by microwave sorption technique.

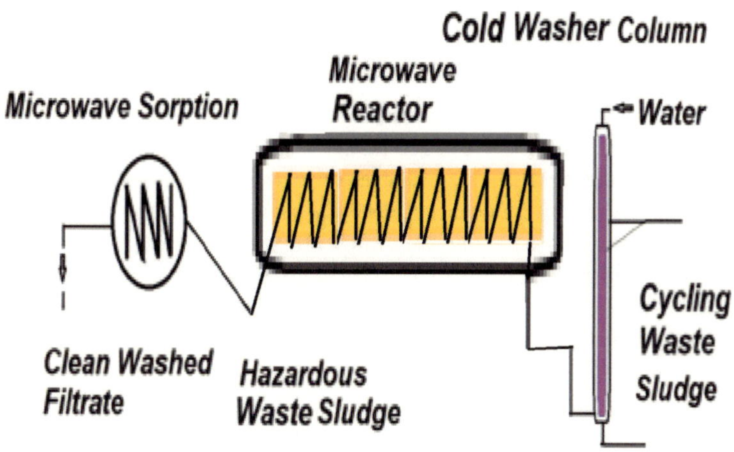

Figure 2.
Studied washing by microwave sorption technique.

	SiO_2	Al_2O_2	Fe_2O_2	MgO	K_2O	CaO	P_2O_5	TiO_2	LOI*
Kaolin (%)	47.85	37.60	0.83	0.17	0.97	0.57	0.2	0.2	11.27
Şırnak Asphaltite Char Shale	27,4	7.70	10.83	2.17	1.97	10.5	1.4	1.74	5.47
Bentonite	50.45	17.80	6.83	12.17	4.97	3.57	0.1	0.4	7.37
Marly Shale	17.85	11.60	0.83	5.17	3.97	20.57	0.2	0.4	5.27
Fly ash	27.8	13.60	17.83	4.17	2.97	10.7	1.6	1.4	17.27
Apatite Phosphate	0,2	0,1	2,3	2,3	4,3	11,3	23,5	0,1	6,5

**LOI: Loss on Ignition at 1000°.*

Table 1.
Sorbent types for washing treatment.

Waste Sorbent Granule	Active Matter,%	BET Area, density
Bentonite	CaO, 23	122, 800–980 kg/cm^3
Sepiolite	NaO, 12	45, 400–700
Apatite Phosphate	P2O5, 16	23, 700

Table 2.
Phosphate, shale and Marly shale granules, physical packed properties.

3.2 Ca phosphate/carbon compost sorbent applications

During the experimental studies bentonite and phosphate samples, Ünye region, was investigated with intermediate type bentonite; pure, purified, tap water and $CaCl_2.2H_2O$, NaCl, $MgCl_2$, KCl, $FeCl_3$ at concentrations ranging from 125 mg to 1000 ppm. Bentonite suspensions prepared by adding waters such as suspensions decanted by sedimentation method for 30 minutes in a 2 lt scale and bentonite slurries were obtained and then necessary test and characterization procedures were applied afterwards.

Decantation was carried out in 2000 ml mills by adding 75 gr bentonite to 1900 ml of water. For a homogeneous suspension mortar, the bentonite water mixture was first subjected to salt slurry mixing cell for 5 minutes.

After the scurvy, the suspension was allowed to stand for 30 minutes after being agitated so that the impurities were precipitated. At the end of the period, suspended bentonite concentrate was removed by titration method and etch was dried.

The same procedure was repeated with synthetic waters prepared by adding salts at concentrations ranging from 125 ppm to 1000 ppm, until the bentonite slurry were obtained in sufficient quantities with salt slurry mixing water.

The layout of the washing cycle is somewhat simpler than that of the lime slurry: there was no water–compost washing column towers connected to the waste sludge, and the washing unit contained one single microwave radiation column can be used to perform the three decantation washing phases: roughing, scraping and cleaning. The variation of the third cycle washing was also more limited recycled by decantation.

The simple production presented as adapted and optimized depending on the target application. The main applications are briefly described in the following sections. Although this review only focuses on state-of-the art commercially available pellet plants, it should be noted that some prospective advanced applications for heat melting of binder are currently being studied, mainly in the form of prototypes proposed as seen in **Figure 3**. These innovative applications include:

- Compost systems, in which the extrusion mold system takes advantage of temperature gradients in wet gradient.

- Compression press systems, where the high load press is used to drive the forming sludge in plant.

- Continuous conversion systems, utilizing the high temperature binding gradients and amounts (of at least 20 C) in slurries to drive a recycle.

- Hot production, where the scraping power of the load system is used to drive the compressive form of hot system.

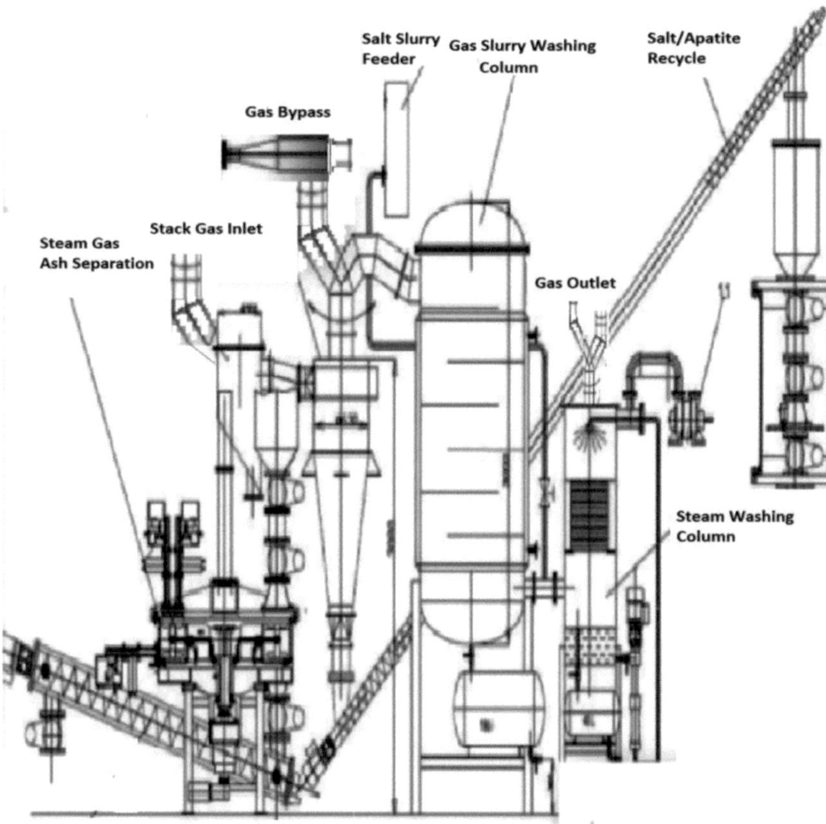

Figure 3.
Apatite and salt slurry gas washing plant for emission control of flue gas, proposed for silopi power plant.

4. Langmuir absorption model

For an overview of these more innovative and prospective applications, the general common method can be given in first order linear concentration change. However sequential sorption cycles changed that trend in sorption of heavy metal contents of gases.

The first order sorption concentration at three stage cycling counted as t time depended by the Eq. 3 below:

$$\ln c_{Pb}^{(Ca,PO3,S2O3)} = a + b\left(\frac{k_{1Ca}t}{1!} + \frac{k_{2PO3}t^2}{2!} + \frac{k_{3S2O3}t^3}{3!}\right. \quad (2)$$

$$\frac{dQ}{dt} = k^{(Ca,,PO3,S2O3)}(Qe - Q) \quad (3)$$

$$Q = Qe(1 - e^{-kt}) \quad (4)$$

Qe: Equilibrium adsorption capacity (mg/g)
Q: Time adsorption capacity (mg/g)

t: Time (min)

k1: First-order rate coefficient (l/min)

Apatite phosphate was known to react easily at low pH of 5–6 by a considerable dependence on the layer charge and edge charge pH. Therefore, a decrease in the cation exchange capacity should be expected in locked cavity texture of char with the decrease in pH. Acidic washing was so efficient reaching by Fe holdup of 70 ppm and Lead holdup of 65 ppm with 55% highest yield at 18 hours (**Figure 4**).

Cation exchange ability was so effective in metal sorption manner. The acidic pH was efficient at criteria in the washing column sorption. It can be seen in the above graph, the pH decreases inversely proportional to the amount of salt added to bentonite suspension, which is much more noticeable when FeCl3 as activation cavity sites developed.

Bentonite is known to have a considerable dependence on the layer charge and edge charge pH. Therefore, a decrease in the cation exchange capacity should be expected in parallel with the decrease in pH. Acidic washing was so efficient reaching by Fe holdup of 60 ppm and Lead holdup of 41 ppm with 45% highest yield at 18 hours (**Figure 5**).

The FeCl3 20 mg added bentonite solutions showed the change in cation exchange capacity (CEC, milliequivalent gram/100gr) found in the bentonite concentrates and suspensions obtained using the precipitation-siphoning technique, depending on the salt concentration added.

Zeolite exchange ability was so effective in metal sorption manner. The pH was efficient criteria in the washing column sorption. It can be seen in the above graph, the pH decrease improved the amount of lead and Hg char suspension, pH 4 was more noticeable when Pb 65 ppm at high cavity sites developed (**Figure 6**).

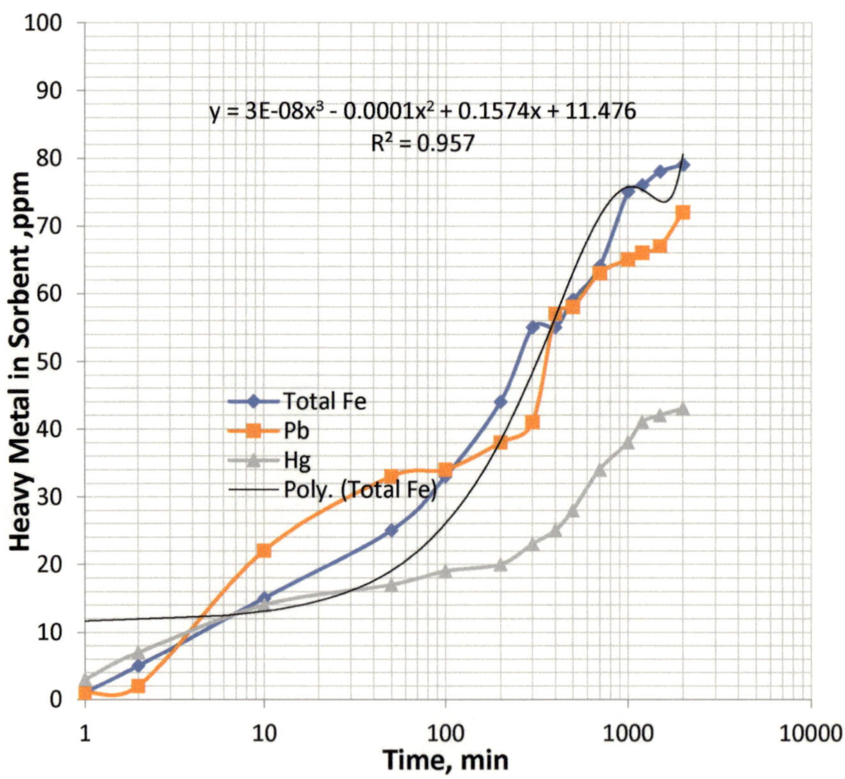

Figure 4.
The change in metal sorption depending on the metal concentration incorporated in the phosphate char suspensions.

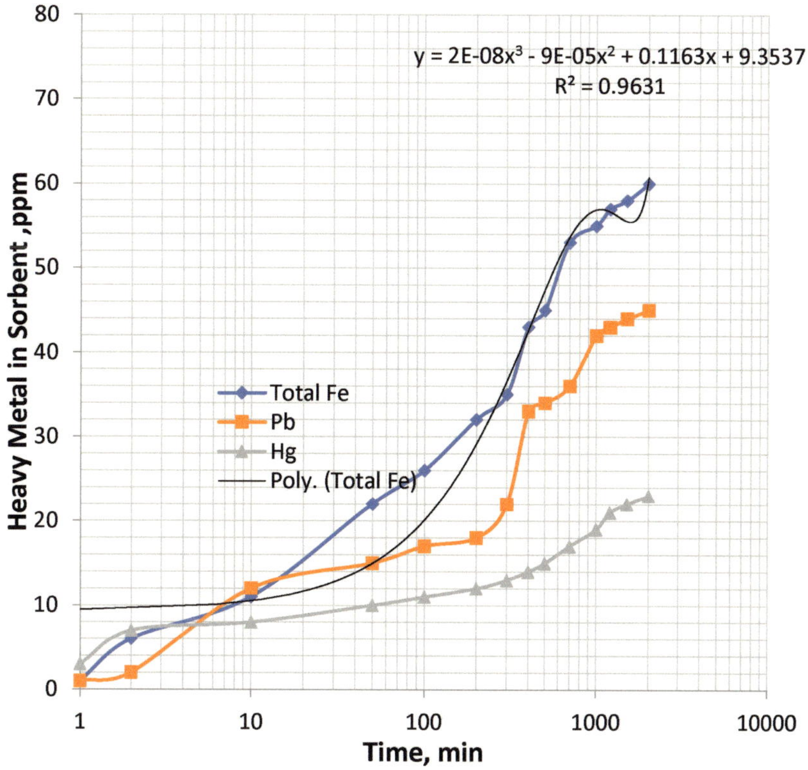

Figure 5.
The change in metal sorption depending on the metal concentration incorporated in the bentonite char suspensions.

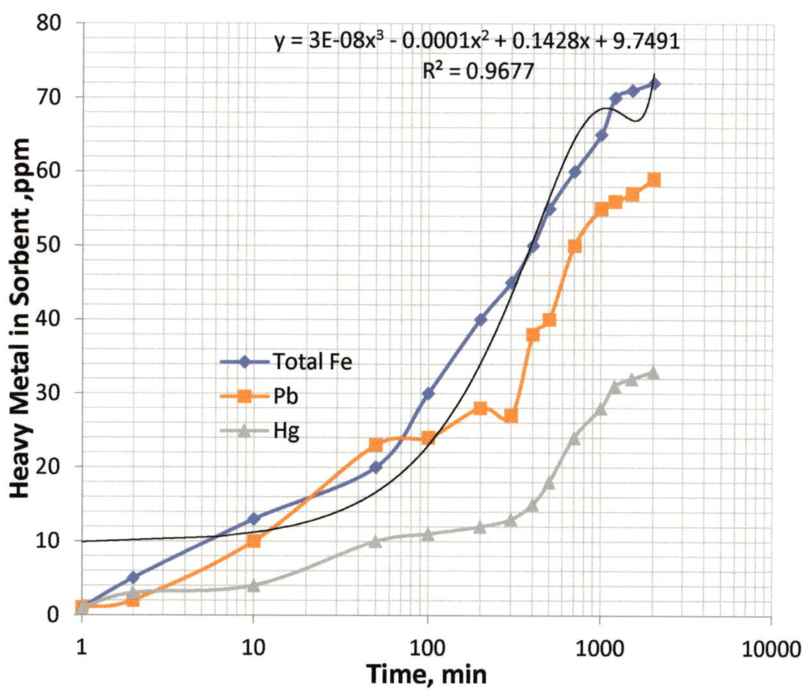

Figure 6.
The change in metal sorption depending on the metal concentration incorporated in the zeolite char suspensions.

Zeolite was known to have a considerable dependence on the layer charge and a decrease in the cation exchange capacity should be expected in parallel with the decrease in pH. Acidic washing was so efficient reaching by Fe holdup of 60 ppm and Lead holdup of 65 ppm with 45% yield at 18 hours.

4.1 Double shower by microwave radiation

The bentonite sample was sieved and a small part of 45 μm was used for the operation. Bentonite samples were activated with 1 and 2 M HCl solutions for 2 h at 90° C using the Batch method (using 100 ml acid solution for 5 g sample). The acid-treated samples were washed with hot deionized water to remove Cl-ions and dried in room condition. 125-1000 ppm salt $CaOH_2$, $CaCl_2$, NaOH, NaCl, KCl, $FeCl_3$ was mixed by activated clay samples are mixed in 2 lt slurry mixing cells by tap water.

5. Results and discussion

The current use of absorbent bentonite and new areas of use increase in demand due to outflow. The phosphate resources of Mazıdağı Mardin was gaining in sorbent production and phosphoric acid use in copper ore leaching recently inTurkey, The local sobent alkali and reactive alkali matters is limited due to instead of clay consumption. For this purpose, apathite resources as high rock salt reserves existing in Turkey provided high advantage in use as absorbent and waste mixtures with clay beds. These phosphate waste materials must be fully identified, potential sources should be determined, absorbent purpose should be investigated. In this market, the country economy will provide significant benefits in desulphurization and air pollution control in terms of apathite phosphate instead of fertilizer acid production.

Effective sorptive char in pyrolysis process depend on numerous factors including coal rank in carbonization, the volatile gaseous matter of coal such as presence of hydrogen, carbonyl gas. Char oxidation rate was so stabilizing the desorbence, the settings of optimal diffusion conditions including structure defects (nitrogen, phosphorus, sulfur, etc.), temperature, oxygen content of coal. The optimization of reactivity and cavity concentration ratios improved the adsorption–desorption balance, the residence time and the reactive spatial distribution of sorbent molecules in coal amorph texture. The acidified washing was other parameter determining the sorbent efficiency of carbonized char. The extent of carbonization was much dependent on the site activation affecting sorption rate, its desorption properties and bed meso porosity. As seen in **Figures 3–5**, the carbonized char was a prerequisite step for sorption substrate.

The apathite content rate was widely used to improve the adsorption and catalytic properties of natural bentonites. The impurities, such as calcite and dolomite, are removed from the structure by the treatment of montmorillonite with inorganic acids, the interchangeable cations are replaced by hydrogen ions, and some of the Al ions in the tetrahedral layer dissolve certain cations of Fe, Al and Mg in the octahedral layer.

As a result, acid activation increases the pore diameters of the bentonite surface and the surface area and adsorption capacity up to a certain amount of this application. If the amount of acid used during the acid activation process is excessively high, the Al ions found in the octahedral layer dissolve more and as a result, the mineral structure collapses, leaving a skeleton structure composed of silica solids. This reduces the adsorption capacity of the clay and disrupts its selectivity. Pb is a colorless and Hg. The main sources are fossil fuels such as Pb, acidic mine waters and toxic metal sludges, which are industrial plants and industrial steel washings. During the metal smelting processes and other industrial processes.

The compost of apatite, char and salts has substantially oxidized, resistant to forming crystal crack underway service. This pressurized fluid provides precise, uniform temperature control to 500°C in closed-loop microwave systems where the heat transfer fluid is more than occasionally exposed to air. The fluid is comprised of a unique high-stability base plus high-performance oxidation inhibitor/stabilizer.

5.1 Carbon surface activation

In the sorbent size distribution, 80% of weights of samples were less than 3 mm. The lignite samples were mainly distributed between 1 mm and 3 mm size fractions. The effect of particle size of solid sorbents were investigated over the combustion of Şırnak Asphaltite char shale and bentonite carried out well on acidic mine water of copper mine in Siirt substance subjected to reaction with salt/char slurry in sorption, as shown in **Figure** 7.

Although metal diffusion on sorbent from salt slurry was believed to be the primary mass transport process in the absorption chamber, complex reactions proliferated the alkali clusters below 1-2 mm size and exothermic oxidation reactions increased toxic substances in the effluent form, a relatively porous structure of bentonite clay interstitial spaces and cracks reduced below 1 mm size. The hazardous heavy metal concentrations reacted adsorbate then adsorbs to the sorbent in a certain amount that is equal to the amount of previous adsorbate that was partially degraded on the surface of the bentonite clay and stuck covered toxins, along with avoiding chelating organic matter related carbonyl and amine.

Initially, most of the toxin removal occurs through chemical adsorption of the toxins to the apatite fine at weight rate of 5 % in fluidized bed where the combustion temperature was in the combustion phase below 750°C that lasts approximately 2–3 mins.The removal efficiency of 40–90% were reported during this temperature range. Total organic toxin substances were completely slightly at efficiencies of 75–90% in the late combustion phase. A common industrial combustion to control the emissions pro combustion stage lime washing involves backwashing with air and hydrated lime water rinse. Process variables include the control backwash rate,

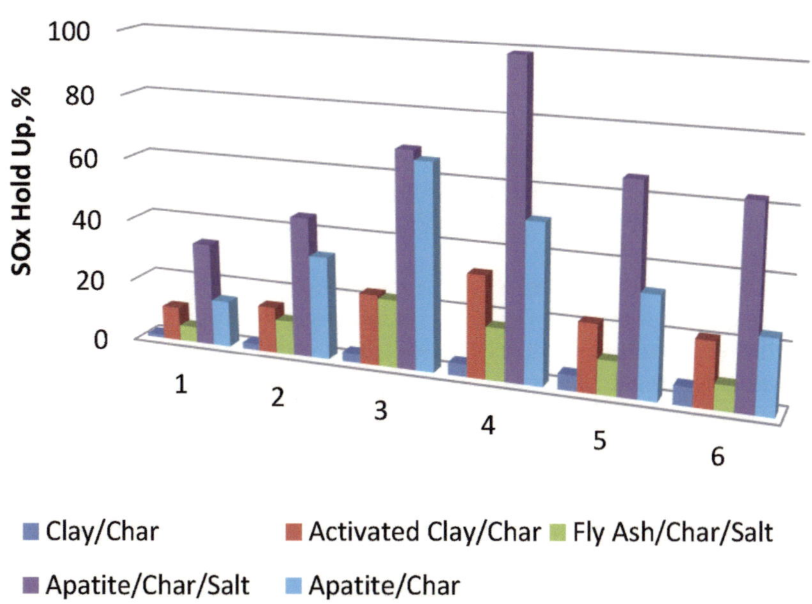

Figure 7.
Apatite and salt act on emission control for flue gas.

surface wash rate/duration, time sequence and duration of backwash. Clean filtrate is pumped back into the bottom of the column during backwashing.

6. Conclusions

The stack gas washed and ESP dust controlled exhaust gas given to vertical column washing by the slurry salt providing toxic metal washing on based acidified digestive mass transfer. This was provided by microwave heating on reactivity of different absorbent materials and amount conditions on activated cavity at Langmuir linear trend. The same situation was also available in the case of other sorbent char lead and CS, COS gas. The apathite material improved packed bed sorption reaction rate. The zeolite activated cage was influenced by the unit surface area, which varied with the internal pore type of the zeolite sorption reaction and the adsorption metal washing cycle.

The power plants using Şırnak asphaltite in fluidized bed combustion chamber produced fly ash slurries contaminated water control, management practices and emission control water washings and metal solutions in treatment system.

The column activated by microwave dissolved washing of exhaust gas at atmospheric pressure happened in porous basket column. The insoluble consists of metal outputs, such as Pb, Zn, Cu. In this study, there have been very few transport studies of apatite char salt slurry (exhaust gas- salt mixtures. There is a great green concern prompting clean air in order to control air and washing waters so that the research study controlled and avoided hazardous toxicity limits of residual gas streams and contaminants of heavy streams by sorption local clay and Ca phosphate compost. The contamination rate changes to those based on weight concentrations and wetness.

In the pH measurements made, the pH value of 5–3 in washing hazardous waste water finally at the last washing column decreased to 5, depending on the concentration of salt content of sorbents in the water.

In the three cycled stage microwave activated washing test measurements made with tap water, it was found that 73 mg/l(ppm) in apatite salt slurries/asphaltite char shale decreased to 53 mg/l(ppm)/in last column output. Likewise, the washed waste waters obtained after 100 min washing by microwave activity using sodium salts softened flow with below 1 mm sized sorbent packages showed reductions in Pb,Hg and Fe at 47% performance.

In water aliquate had the 24 ppm Pb,5 ppm Hg and 57 Fe values, which Pb reduction rates of sorption at Langmuir model with nitrate washing rate was 0,73 ppm/min.l, Hg and total Fe reduction rate decreased to 0,43 ppm/min.l and 0,23 ppm/min.l,respectively.

The pH increased at washing was efficient in heavy metal sorption, the swelling index decreased, the loss of filtration increased negatively, and viscosity decreased by the addition of sodium. In the obtained data, it was observed that sorption manner of bentonite negatively affected by foreign ions in washing water for the activation especially total iron ion.

Abbreviations

Greek symbols

a	affinity parameter of the Langmuir isotherm (L mg^{-1})
b	stoichiometric constant defined by

B	reactant solid defined
Bi_m	Biot number for mass transfer
C_i	concentration of manganese in the bulk external phase of stage i (mg L^{-1})
C_0	feed concentration of manganese in the column (mg L^{-1})
D_{ef}	effective diffusion coefficient (m^2 s^{-1})
F	objective function
h	fixed bed height (m)
k_e	mass transfer coefficient in the bulk external phase (m s^{-1})
k_r	reaction rate constant for heterogeneous systems (m s^{-1})
N	number of stages
Q	volumetric flowrate (m^3 s^{-1})
q_i	concentration of immobilized manganese within the adsorbent particle at stage i (mg g^{-1})
q_m	theoretical maximum adsorption capacity of the Langmuir isotherm (mg g^{-1})
r	radial distance from the center of the particle, $0 < r < R_p$(m)
R	radius of column (m)
R_p	radius of adsorbent particle (m)
R^2	determination coefficient (–)
$r_{c,i}$	unreacted core radius at stage i (m)
t	time (s)
V_i	volume of stage i (L)
α	backmixing coefficient (–)
φ	column hold-up (–)
ρ	density of adsorbent particle (g m^{-3})
τ	mean residence time of fluid in the column (s)

Author details

Yildirim İsmail Tosun
Şırnak University, Engineering Faculty, Mining Engineering, Department, Şırnak, Turkey

*Address all correspondence to: yildirimismailtosun@gmail.com

IntechOpen

© 2020 The Author(s). Licensee IntechOpen. This chapter is distributed under the terms of the Creative Commons Attribution License (http://creativecommons.org/licenses/by/3.0), which permits unrestricted use, distribution, and reproduction in any medium, provided the original work is properly cited. CC BY

References

[1] Anonymous, 2018, TC Çevre ve Şehircilik Bakanliği, Çevre Yönetimi Genel müdürlüğü, Bati akdeniz havzası kirlilik önleme eylem plani, https:// cygm.csb.gov.tr/

[2] Anonymous, 2018, TC Çevre ve Şehircilik Bakanliği, Çevre Yönetimi Genel müdürlüğü, Guideline for Energy Efficiency in Wastewater Treatment, https:// cygm.csb.gov.tr/

[3] Tosun,Y.I., 2014, Shale stone and Fly ash Landfill Use in Land-slide Hazardous Area in Sirnak City with Foam Concrete, GM Geomaterials Journal, Vol 4, issue 4, pp 141-150 DOI: 10.4236/gm.2014.44014

[4] Tosun, Y.I., 2014, Benefaction from Carbonation of Flue Gas CO2 as Coal Mining Filling, GM Geomaterials Journal, Vol 4, issue 2, pp 64-73, DOI: 10.4236/gm.2014.42007

[5] Tosun, Y.I., 2014, Benefaction and Pyrolysis of Şırnak Aspaltite and Lignite, IJCCE International Journal of Clean Coal and Energy, Vol 3, issue 2, pp 13-18, DOI: 10.4236/ijcce.2014.32002

[6] Tosun, Y İ., 2015, Co-gas production from pyrolysis and gasification of agricultural biowaste of sorghum root with waste wood and turkish coals in retort and biogas, 15th International Multidisciplinary Scientific GeoConference SGEM 2015, www.sgem.org, SGEM2015 Conference Proceedings, ISBN 978-619-7105-38-4 / ISSN 1314-2704, June 18-24, 2015, Book4, 91-98 pp, DOI: 10.5593/SGEM2015/B41/S17.012, Albena Resort, Bulgaria

[7] Tosun, Y İ., 2015, Ferrite nano fill catalyst clay pellet production, 15th International Multidisciplinary Scientific GeoConference SGEM 2015, www.sgem.org, SGEM2015 Conference Proceedings, ISBN 978-619-7105-42-1 / ISSN 1314-2704, June 18-24, 2015, Book6 Vol. 1, 61-68 pp, DOI: 10.5593/SGEM2015/B61/S24.009, Albena Resort, Bulgaria

[8] Tosun, Y İ., 2017, Microwave plasma combustion of coal with maize slush and waste cardboard, wood in modified tube furnace, 17th International Multidisciplinary Scientific GeoConference SGEM 2017, www.sgem.org, SGEM2017 Conference Proceedings, ISBN 978-619-7408-07-2 / ISSN 1314-2704, 29 June - 5 July, 2017, Vol. 17, Issue 42, 429-436 pp, DOI: 10.5593/sgem2017/42/S17.054. Albena Resort, Bulgaria

[9] Tosun, Y İ., 2018, Thickener Water Neutralization by Mid-Bottom and Fly Ash of Thermal Power Plants and CO_2: Organic Humate Mud of AMD Treatment for Remediation of Agricultural Fields, Chapter 8, pp141-170, DOI: 10.5772/intechopen.69927, *Coal Fly Ash Beneficiation - Treatment of Acid Mine Drainage with Coal Fly Ash*, Edited by Segun A. Akinyemi and Mugera W. Gitari, ISBN 978-953-51-3753-5, Print ISBN 978-953-51-3752-8, 208 pages, Publisher: InTech, Chapters published January 31, 2018, DOI: 10.5772/65147

[10] Tosun, Y İ, 2020, Microwave Radiated Sorption-Hazardous Emission Control by Popped Borax and Salted Pumice for Coal Combustion in Thermal Power Plants, *Sorption in 2020s*, editor Dr. George Kyzas and Prof. Nikolaos Lazaridis, Published: March 11th 2020, ISBN: 978-1-83880-114-4, Print ISBN: 978-1-83880-113-7, eBook (PDF) ISBN: 978-1-78985-565-4, DOI: 10.5772/intechopen.89370.

[11] Christidis, G.E., Scott, P.W., Dunham, A.C. 1997. Acid activation and bleaching capacity of bentonites from the islands of Milos and Chios, Aegean, Greece. Applied Clay Science, 12, 329-347.

[12] Gregg, S.J., Sing, K.S.W. 1982. Adsorption, surface area and porosity, Academic Press, London, 52 pp.

[13] Lopez-Gonzalez, J.D., Deitz, V.R. 1952. Surface changes in an original and activated bentonite. Journal of Research of the National Bureau of Standards, 48, 325-333.

[14] Murray, H.H. 1999. Applied clay mineralogy today and tomorrow. Clay Minerals, 34, 39-49.

[15] Murray, H.H. 2000. Traditional and new applications for kaolin, smectite and palygorskite: a general overview, Applied Clay Science, 17, 207-221.

[16] Nguetnkam, J.P., Kamga, R., Villieras, F., Ekodeck, G.E., Razafitianamaharavo, A., Yvon, J. 2005. Assessment of the surface areas of silica and clay in acid-leached clay materials using concepts of adsorption on heterogeneous surfaces. Journal of Colloid and Interface Science, 289, 104-115.

[17] Novak, I., Cicel, B. 1978. Dissolution of smectites in hydrochloric acid; II, Dissolution rate as a function of crystallochemical composition. Clays and Clay Minerals, 26, 341-344.

[18] Önal, M., Sarıkaya, Y., Alemdaroğlu, T., Bozdoğan, İ. 2002. The effect of acid activation on some physicochemical properties of a bentonite. Turkish Journal of Chemistry, 26, 409-416

[19] Srasra, E., Bergaya, F., van Damme, H., Arguib, N.K. 1989. Surface properties of an activated bentonite. Decolorization of rape-seed oil. Applied Clay Science, 4, 411-421.

[20] Srivastava, R.V. 2003. Controlling of SO2 Emissions, A Review of Technologies, Nova Science Publishers, Inc., New York, 1 pp.

[21] Venaruzzo, J.L., Volzone C., Rueda M.L., Ortiga J. 2002. Modified bentonitic clay minerals as adsorbents of CO, CO2 and SO2 gases. Microporous and Mesoporous Materials, 56, 73-80.

[22] Volzone, C., Ortiga, J. 2009. Adsorption of gaseous SO2 and structural changes of montmorillonite. Applied Clay Science, 44, 251-254

[23] Tosun, Y.I., 2018, Sorbtions of Toxic Emissions of Flue gas on Active carbon of Microwave acted in Post combustion, GCGW 2018, 29 Haziran

[24] Tosun, Y.I., 2018, Investigation on the adsorption quality of biochar for waste water treatment by carbonized biomass waste and coal slimes, Carbon 2018, 29 Haziran, Madrid

[25] Alemdaroğlu, T., Akkuş, G., Önal, M., Sarıkaya, Y. (2003). Investigation of the Surface Acidity of a Bentonite Modified by Acid Activation and Thermal Treatment. *Turk. J. Chem.,* 27, 675-681.

[26] Benesi, H.A. (1956). Acidity of Catalyst Surfaces I. Acid Strength from Colors of Adsorbed Indicators. *J. Phys. Chem.,* 78, 5490-5494.

[27] Benesi, H.A. (1957). Acidity of Catayst Surfaces II. Amine Titration Using Hammett Indicators. *J. Phys. Chem.,* 61, 970-973.

[28] Caglar, B., Afsin, B., Tabak, A. (2007). Benzamide Species Retained by DMSO Composites at a Kaolinite Surface. *J. Therm. Anal. Cal.,* 87, 429-432.

[29] Caglar, B., Afsin, B., Tabak, A., and Eren, E. (2009). Characterization of Cation Exchanged Bentonites by XRPD, ATR, DTA/TG and BET measurement Investigation of. *Chemical Engineering Journal*, 149, 242-248.

[30] Chitnis, S.R., Sharma, M.M. (1997). Industrial Applications of Acid-Treated Clays as Catalyst. *React. Funct. Polym.,* 32, 93-115.

[31] Christidis, G.E., Scott, P.W., Dunham, A.C. (1997). Acid Activation and Bleaching Capacity of Bentonites from the Islands of Milos and Chios, Aegean, Greece. *Appl. Clay Sci.,* 12, 329-347.

[32] Flessner, U., Jones, D.J., Roziere, J., Zajac, J., Storaro, L., Lenarda, M., Pavan, M., Lopez, A.J., Castellon, E.R., Trombetta, M., Busca, G. (2001). A Study of the Surface Acidity of Acid-Treated Montmorillonite Clay Catalyst. *J. Mol. Catal. A: Chemical*, 168, 247-256.

[33] Heyding, R.D., Ironside, R., Norris, A.R., ve Prysiazniuk, R.Y. (1960). Acid Activation of Montmorillonite. *Can. J. Chem.,* 38, 1003-1016.

[34] Hutson, N.D., Hoekstra, M.J., Yang, R.T. (1999). Control of Microporosity of Al2O3-Pillared Clays: Effect of pH, Calcination Temperature and Clay Cation Exchange Capacity. *Micropor. Mesopor. Mater.,* 28, 447-459.

[35] Jankovich, L., Komadel, P. (2003). Metal Cation-Exchanged Montmorillonite Catalyzed Protection of Aromatic Aldehydes with Ac2O. *J. Catal.,* 218, 227-233.

[36] Koh, S.M., Dixon, J.B. (2001). Preparation and Application of Organo-Minerals as Sorbents of Phenol, Benzene and Toluene. *App. Clay Sci.,* 18, 111-122.

[37] Kurian, M., Sugunan, S. (2005). Characterization of the Acid-Base Properties of Pillared Montmorillonites. *Micropor. Mesopor. Mater.,* 83, 25-34.

[38] Tosun, Y.I., 2012, Kısmi Ergiyik Kostik Liç Yöntemi İle Türk Linyitlerinin Kükürtsüzleştirilmesi-Mermer Atık Tozu Kullanımı, S. Demirel Üniversitesi Fen Bilimleri Enst. Dergisi, Ocak 2012.

[39] Tosun, Y.İ., Çiçek, F., 1997, Ergiyik Kostik Liç Yöntemi ile Türk Linyit ve Taşkömürlerinin Kükürtsüzleştirilmesi, Madencilik Dergisi, TMMOB Maden Mühendisleri Odası, Vol.36, Sy.4, Ankara.

[40] Tosun, Y.İ., 1995, "Reduction of Sulfurdioxide Emission by Solid Basic Filters after Coal Burning", 4th Int. Conf. on Combustion, Bursa.

[41] Tosun, Y.I., 2012, "Semi-fused Salt-Caustic Mixture Leaching of Turkish Lignites - Sorel Cement Use for Desulfurization", Proceedings of XIIIth International Mineral Processing Symposium – Bodrum-Turkey

[42] Tosun, Y.I., 2014, Use of Turkish Geothermal Hot Waters in CO_2 Mineral Sequestration, ICCE 2014, 1st İnternational Conference Clean Energy 2014, 21-24 Sept 2014, 8-12 June 2014, İstanbul

[43] Tosun, Y.I., 2014, Investigation on Flue Gas CO_2 Sequestration by Turkish Coal Fly Ashes, ICCE 2014, 1st İnternational Conference Clean Energy 2014, 8-12 June 2014, İstanbul

[44] Tosun, Y.I., 2018, Simulatıon of gas sorbtion kinetıcs on active carbon - regressed model for control toxic emissions of flue gas, IMSMATEC 2018, 2nd International conference on material scince engineering, 10-12 Nisan, Karabük

[45] Tosun, Y.I., 2018, Simulation microwave radiation - temperature regressed model in combustion act, IMSMATEC 2018, 2nd International conference on material scince engineering, 10-12 Nisan, Karabük

Chapter 20

Numerical Modelling of Fouling Process in EGR System: A Review

Concepción Paz, Eduardo Suárez, Jesús Vence and Adrián Cabarcos

Abstract

In order to combat climate change, the new rigorous standards for pollutant reduction have shone a light on the use of exhaust gas recirculation system in order to minimize the NOx emissions of vehicles. For this reason, the fouling problem that appears on the exhaust gas recirculation line, caused by the deposition of soot particles and hydrocarbons that are part of the exhaust gas, has become particularly relevant in the last few years. In this field, researches have proposed numerical models in order to estimate and predict the deposit formation and growth. Using various numerical techniques, they intend to determine and reproduce the fouling layer buildup considering the different mechanisms that are involved in the deposit formation. This chapter provides a detailed and comprehensive account of the numerical approaches that have been proposed to analyze the fouling phenomenon that occurs inside the exhaust gas system. The main characteristics of each numerical model, as well as their main strengths and weaknesses, are exposed and evaluated, and their simulation capabilities are examined in detail.

Keywords: EGR, fouling, soot agglomerates, thermophoresis, hydrocarbon condensation, erosion, CFD, numerical simulation

1. Introduction

The Sustainable Development Goals (SDG), known as the 2030 Agenda for Sustainable Development, have been adopted by 193 countries since 2015 [1]. Reducing air pollution, development of sustainable cities, and combating climate change are some of the main goals of this plan of action, and, within that context, the reduction of pollutant emissions from vehicles is an important activity to be faced.

In order to minimize greenhouse gas emissions, vehicle emissions for passenger cars have been regulated worldwide by means of several standards, such as the Euro emission standards in Europe or the Tier standards in the USA [2–4]. These successive standards, which define more stringent acceptable limits for polluting emission and fuel economy, push car manufacturers to use the best technology available for vehicle emission control, and this is one of the biggest technical challenges that the automotive industry faces.

The public concern about diseases derived from air pollution and recent emissions scandals, like *dieselgate*, have shone a light on vehicle emissions, particularly in terms of nitrogen oxides (NOx) and particulate matter emissions [5, 6].

IntechOpen

In this context, since 2014, the EURO 6 emission standard set the emissions limit for nitrogen oxides (NOx) in 60 and 80 mg/km for gasoline and diesel light-duty vehicles, respectively [7]. This fact has extended the use of techniques like the exhaust gas recirculation (EGR) system, which have proven to be an effective way of reducing NOx formation. Nowadays, the EGR system is used together with other systems, such as diesel oxidation catalyst (DOC), lean NOx trap (LNT), or selective catalytic reduction (SCR), to fulfill the NOx emissions in internal combustion engines [8, 9].

The EGR system, whose main components are the EGR pipe, the EGR valve, and the EGR cooler, is a technique in which a portion of exhaust gas is returned to the intake manifold, reducing the oxygen content inside the cylinder—oxygen-poor environment [10]. Since the NOx formation is increased in an exponential function with a temperature increase, lower oxygen content of the diluted fresh charge leads to a cooler combustion process that drastically reduces the NOx formation [11]. To increase its effectiveness, the EGR cooler—a compact heat exchanger that uses engine coolant—is in charge of reducing the exhaust gas temperature prior to entering the combustion chamber [12]. The quantity of EGR is regulated by controlling the EGR valve, which manages the EGR rate required under the different work conditions of the engine.

One of the problems encountered in EGR systems is the fouling of the heat exchanger walls. The carbonaceous soot particles and condensable hydrocarbons derived from the combustion process lead to the formation of a highly porous deposit with low thermal conductivity that can cause the degradation in heat transfer performance in the range of 20–30% [13], as **Figure 1** shows. The accumulation of this unwanted material also causes the increase of the pressure drop along the heat exchanger, adversely affecting the control of the EGR rate and decreasing the fuel efficiency due to the increased pumping work [14]. Under significant fouling conditions, the massive increase of the thickness of the deposit can clog some tubes of the heat exchanger, as **Figure 2** shows, hampering the full normal functioning of the device [15].

In the last few decades, numerous investigations have been focused on the study of the fouling process that takes place on the heat exchanger walls of the EGR system. Numerous attempts in analysis, measurement, and prediction of the deposit have contributed to increase the knowledge of the deposit formation, and many of them have pointed out the complexity of the dynamics of this phenomenon. These

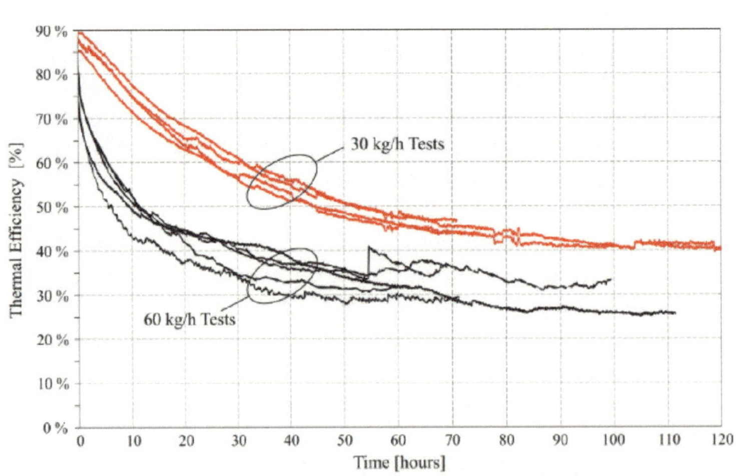

Figure 1.
Thermal efficiency evolution of an EGR cooler [16].

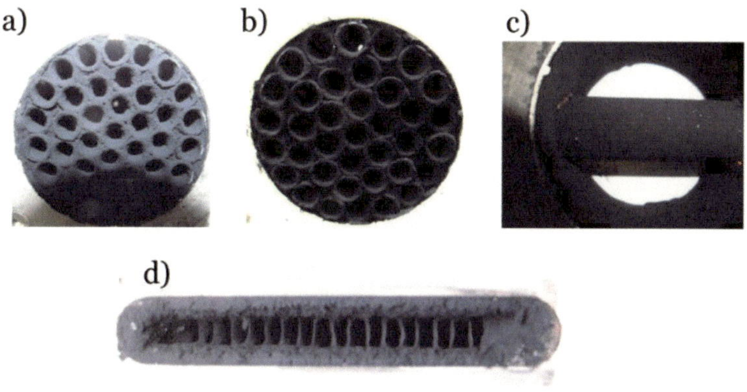

Figure 2.
Photographs of different fouling layers: (a) and (b) show deposits generated by diesel particulate matter inside shell-and-tube heat exchangers, (c) depicts the fouling layer generated on a cylindrical probe which is positioned transverse to the diesel exhaust, and (d) shows the deposit formed by dry soot particles on a tube-and-fin heat exchanger.

studies fall into two broad categories: one group intends to determine and analyze the deposit growth using in situ measurements, i.e., employing experimental procedures to quantify the morphology and characteristics of the fouling layer [17, 18], whereas the second intends to reproduce and recreate the fouling formation employing numerical approaches. The studies of this second category encompass the analysis of the EGR deposit using different numerical models like zero-dimensional (0-D) models, one-dimensional (1-D) models, or advanced computational fluid dynamics (CFD) simulations, which have been created to simulate and reproduce the behavior of the fouling layer that appears inside the EGR technology.

In the following sections, specific features of the different types of numerical approaches used to study the fouling in the EGR system are presented in detail. The functions offered by the several numerical models are examined, and their implementation and results are thoroughly analyzed. In this context, both the composition and characteristics of the particulate matter and the fouling mechanisms involved in this process are briefly presented in advance.

2. Particulate matter involved in EGR fouling

The exhaust gas flow emitted from internal combustion engines has been categorized as dilute flow, where the low concentration of particulate matter (PM) makes negligible the effect of particles on gas flow [19]. Several factors, such as the air-fuel ratio, the EGR rate, the engine load, or the cylinder temperature, can alter the particulate loading in the exhaust flow, and, in the same way, they can influence the formation, agglomeration, and growth of the particles [20].

According to the size of the particulate matter, the nanoparticles emitted from internal combustion engines can be classified into three modes: nucleation, accumulation, and coarse. Nucleation mode is formed by particles that are less than 50 nm in diameter, and, according to the number distribution, most of the particles reside in this mode, as **Figure 3** reports. In the accumulation mode, the agglomerates consist of a collection of much smaller particles, and the size of these aggregates ranges from 50 nm to 1 μm, and particle mass distribution highlights that accumulation mode accounts the largest portion. The biggest particles—diameters between 1 μm and 10 μm—represent only a small fraction of the number of particles, and they belong to the coarse mode [21–23].

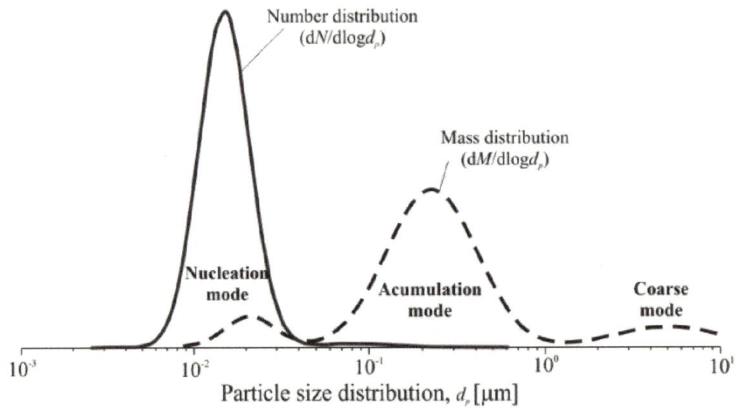

Figure 3.
Generalized size distribution for typical particles emitted by internal combustion engines.

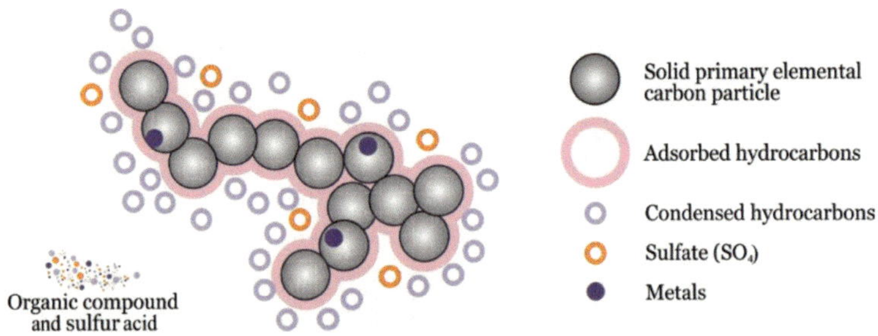

Figure 4.
Agglomerate diesel particle.

Analyzing the composition of the PM of the exhaust gas, the particles are a product of a mix of volatile and nonvolatile species. Volatile faction is composed by sulfates (SO_4^{2-} + metal sulfate), nitrates (NO_3^- + metal nitrate), and organic elements (—CH_2 + N, O and S). Nonvolatile fraction is composed by carbonaceous particles, commonly referred to as soot, and ash, formed by metals (Fe, Cr, Cu, Zn, Ca) and nonmetals (Si, P, S, Cl) [24]. Several factors, such as fuel and lubricant characteristics or engine work conditions, can influence the composition and proportion of these species, however, in most cases, elemental carbon accounts for around 90% of PM mass [25]. The primary particles—sizes typically between 15 and 30 nm—are composed by carbon and traces of metallic ash, and they aggregate forming complex irregular clusters together with adsorbed and condensed hydrocarbons (HC) [26, 27]. As **Figure 4** shows, the agglomeration of the primary particles causes the formation of clusters with a complex structure with nonuniform shape and compactness [28].

When this particulate matter is deposited on the heat exchanger walls, it forms a fouling layer which coats the heat exchanger surface. The interaction between the particles and the metal surface during the early stages of the deposit formation, and the particle-particle interaction during fouling layer growth, leads to the accumulation of amorphous aggregates on the heat exchanger walls, causing a highly porous deposit (around 98% [18]). This fouling layer, with a complex nanostructure with multiple pores between the deposited aggregates, functions as an insulator between the gas flow and the heat transfer surface. According to the experimental measurements of Lance et al. [18], the fouling layer generated from the deposition of diesel particulate matter has a density around 0.035 g/cm^3 and a low thermal conductivity that is around 0.041 W/mK. However, in some cases, different phenomena, such as the condensation of hydrocarbons and water or the spallation of the deposit, can collapse the nanostructure of the fouling layer, slightly modifying its thermal properties [20, 29–33]. It is no easy task to determine and quantify the deposit's chemical and physical characteristics due to the fragile nature of the structure, but it is an essential step to provide accurate inputs to the numerical models.

3. Fouling mechanisms in the EGR system

The gas-particle multiphase flow and the formation of fouling layer inside the EGR system are complex phenomena in which several mechanisms are involved. Thermophoresis, diffusion, inertial impact, hydrocarbon condensation, gravitational settling, removal due to shear force, water vapor condensation, or turbulent burst are the main mechanisms that engage in the fouling process.

Excluding the thermal effects, other parameters, such as the particle diffusion, the gravitational settling, the inertial impact of the turbophoresis, play an important role in the EGR fouling formation. The particle diffusion is the dominant mechanism for the small particles, particles with dimensionless relaxation times (t_p^+) less than 0.1, while the transport of large particles, particles with dimensionless relaxation times (τ_p^+) more than 0.1, is dominated by inertial and gravitational effects [34].

Inside the EGR cooler, thermophoresis—induced by the temperature gradient—drives the nanoparticles from the bulk gas flow to the near cool walls, causing the deposition of the soot particles over the heat exchanger surfaces. It has been reported by several authors that under non-isothermal conditions, thermophoresis is the primary mechanism of soot deposition in the particle size typically encountered in exhaust gas, 10 nm to 1 μm, and some correlations from literature, such as Brock-Talbot or Cha-McCoy-Wood, have been used to determine the thermophoretic velocity as a function of the particle diameter [13, 35–38].

The condensation of HC and acids, which are part of the exhaust flow, is significant on a mass basis compared to soot deposition, and it is an important issue in the deposit formation [39]. As exhaust gas is diluted and cooled, the condensation of hydrocarbons is particularly important inside the EGR system. Condensate, which is mixed with soot particles inside the fouling layer, modifies the microstructure of the soot deposit and changes the characteristics of the deposit, leading to an increase of the density and the thermal conductivity of the fouling layer [40].

The effect of shear force of the gas flow over the deposited particles, the turbulent burst, or the water vapor condensation have been identified as potential mechanisms that cause the removal of particles from the fouling layer [41, 42]. When the drag force over the particle is larger than the adhesion force, removal occurs. In the same way, the condensed water droplets can interact with the deposited particles, causing a washout of the dry soot deposit [43].

It has been extensively reported in literature that the formation of the fouling deposits depends on two simultaneous phenomena: the deposition and the removal of particles [13, 44–48]. Such categorization usually selects thermophoresis, particle diffusion, gravitational drift, inertial impact, or hydrocarbon condensation as deposition mechanisms. On the contrary, water vapor condensation, the shear force, or the turbulent burst are usually classified as removal mechanisms.

4. Numerical approaches

In the study of the fouling process of the EGR system, both experimental and numerical investigations have been carried out in order to analyze the effects of the

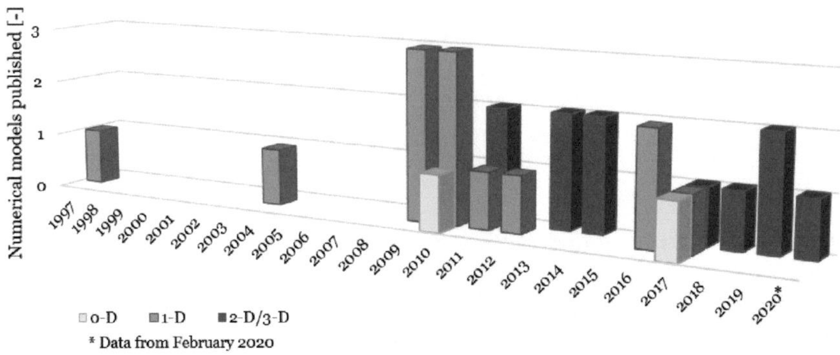

Figure 5.
Main numerical models published from 1997 to 2020.

deposit that grows on the heat exchanger walls. Although the amount of experimental studies have been larger and more frequent, the numerical models have become relevant since 2009, as **Figure 5** depicts, due to the increase in NOx emission regulation requirements.

The numerical approaches intend to reproduce and simulate the formation and evolution of the deposit inside the EGR system recreating the different mechanisms involved in the fouling process. Because of their significance in the prediction of the deposit, the deposition mechanisms have been implemented in 76.9% of the main numerical models that analyze the deposit formation inside the EGR system. By contrast, the numerical approaches that recreate removal mechanisms are slightly lower (50.0%), and only the 30.8% of the models are focused on the study of the condensation of volatile species. In many cases, several kinds of mechanisms are implemented and coupled in one single numerical approach, in order to achieve more complete simulation frameworks.

According to the complexity of the formulation of the models, they can be divided into three principal categories: the zero-dimensional (0-D), the one-dimensional (1-D), and the multidimensional models.

The zero-dimensional models are focused on an overall heat and material balance of the system, and they do not include any analysis of the fluid dynamics. Following several assumptions and simplifications, they evaluate the overall fouling effects, and, although these numerical approaches avoid any spatial resolution of the variables involved in the process, they can give a fair indication about the fouling phenomenon.

The one-dimensional approach is the next level of complexity. In these models, only one spatial dimension is considered, dividing the fluid zone in different regions and analyzing the properties of the system in each region separately. Although this approach simplifies the number of equations, it can give a detailed evolution of the spatial changes of the fouling parameters.

The multidimensional models require the spatial discretization of the volume of the region and can provide a thorough analysis of the variables of the process. In this field, the use of computational fluid dynamics simulations has been increasing steadily since the 1990s, due to the availability of high-performance computing hardware and the development of user-friendly interfaces. The computer-based simulations make it possible to obtain a detailed solution of the fluid flow, both in two-dimensional (2-D) and three-dimensional (3-D) domains, and they can reproduce the evolution and formation of fouling layers.

5. 0-D models

Table 1 summarizes the 0-D models that have been proposed to analyze the fouling layer effect in the EGR system.

Abarham et al. [49] proposed an analytical model for thermophoretic particle deposition that solves the mass conservation of particles and the energy equation of the gas flow for a single turbulent pipe flow. This approach considers the submicron particle deposition due to the thermophoretic effect, neglecting the diffusion and other deposition mechanisms. The model takes into consideration the pipe diameter reduction due to the growth of the fouling layer and considers different boundary conditions, such as the inlet temperature and mass flow rate of the gas, the inlet particle concentration, or the wall temperature. In this study, the properties of the soot layer, i.e., density, porosity, and thermal conductivity, have been taken from the experimental measurements of Lance et al. [18], and the soot particle diameter has been set at 57 nm, based on the study of Maricq and Harris [51]. This model computes the total mass deposited on the tube and evaluates the degradation of the heat transfer effectiveness over time. To verify the results of this numerical approach, the data were compared with the experimental measurements obtained by the Oak Ridge National Laboratory, and an acceptable agreement was achieved between both methods.

Garrido et al. [50] presented a theoretical analysis of the thermodynamics of exhaust gas condensation. They analyzed the condensation of different species that are part of the exhaust gas produced by gasoline engines, such as water vapor, ammonium, and sulfuric, nitrous, nitric, and chloric acids. The examination of the chemical reactions that takes place along the exhaust line and the analysis of the vapor-liquid equilibrium of the condensable species under different temperatures allow the study of their behavior and the calculation of their dew point. The experimental validation of the model showed that, although the collected condensate amount was slightly lower than the model predicted results, the general tendencies were verified.

Since the 0-D models do not provide any spatial resolution of the fouling parameters, their scope is deliberately more concise. Nevertheless, they can be used as essential tools in guiding the study of the fouling phenomenon.

Authors	Mechanisms modeled	Main fouling equations	Parameters analyzed	Model—experiment	Remarks
Abarham et al. [49]	Thermophoresis	$K_{th} = \frac{2C_s C_c}{1+3C_m K_n} \frac{k_g/k_p + C_t K_n}{1+2k_g/k_p+2C_t K_n}$	• Deposited soot mass • Cooler effectiveness • Pipe diameter reduction	In reasonable agreement	An analytical solution for thermophoretic deposition of submicron particles
Garrido et al. [50]	• Water vapor condensation • Acid condensation	$\dot{m}_{cond} = \dot{m}_g (w_{i,initial} - w_{i,end})$	• Saturation temperature • Condensation flux	General tendencies validated	Theoretical analysis of the thermodynamics of gasoline engine exhaust condensation

Table 1.
0-D model.

6. 1-D models

According to the mechanisms considered by the 1-D models, they can be categorized in five groups, as **Table 2** summarizes. The first group covers those models that only analyze the condensation of water or hydrocarbons. The second group is formed by those studies that investigate the fouling layer formation solely by considering the effect of particle deposition mechanisms. The third group, which combines the characteristic of the two previous groups, contains those models that take into account both the prediction of the HC condensation and the deposition of particulate matter. The fourth group includes those models that, in addition to simulating the particulate matter deposition, also discuss the removal mechanisms. And the fifth group is composed of those investigations that take into consideration all of the mechanisms mentioned above: deposition of particulate matter, removal of particles from the deposit, and condensation of hydrocarbons.

The 1-D models included in the first group are exclusively focused on the analysis of the condensation mechanisms that occur inside the exhaust system. When the temperature of the EGR line drops below the dew point of the condensable species, the condensate—made up of water, HC, and acids—appears. This condensate interacts with the soot-deposited particles, modifying the physical structure of the fouling, and it may corrode the walls of the heat exchanger when the acid amount is high enough.

On the one hand, when the fuel sulfur content is rather high, the detection of the sulfuric acid condensation becomes relevant, and, in this field, McKinley et al. [52] proposed a 1-D model that predicts the condensation of the acid. This numerical approach allows to compute the sulfuric acid dew point considering the coolant temperature, the concentration of the acid, and the engine operating point. The acid condensation rate is calculated assuming that condensate is formed due to direct condensation on the wall and due to formation in a portion of the boundary layer. In addition, the model estimates the condensate composition inside the EGR cooler, taking into account the sulfuric acid and water vapor condensation fluxes. All of these parameters allow the analysis and detection of the sulfuric acid condensation inside the EGR cooler, and, although this is an unvalidated model, it represents an essential step in understanding the effects of the acid condensation on the fouling process.

On the other hand, during the starting of a cold engine—in the first few hundred seconds—the water condensation and evaporation can interact with the existing deposit on the EGR cooler walls and can alter the normal functioning of other exhaust after-treatment devices, such as the catalyst. Although it is a process that occurs mainly during the first few seconds of an engine service, it can cause a severe effect on the deposit evolution. Within this framework, Sharma et al. [53] proposed a 1-D model that simulates the condensation and evaporation of water inside the exhaust line. This is a mathematical model that computes the condensation and evaporation rate of water and that calculates the gas flow temperature considering the heat transfer due to phase change processes. The model provides more accurate simulations of the evolution of the temperature of the gas flow than previous models that do not consider the effect of water condensation and evaporation, and it was validated with experimental results, achieving a high level of agreement.

The second group is formed by the 1-D models that investigate the fouling layer formation solely by considering the effect of soot particle deposition mechanisms. For the sake of simplicity, these numerical approaches intend to compute the fouling buildup taking into account only the effect of particulate matter deposition mechanisms, neglecting both the removal mechanisms and the presence of

Authors	Mechanisms modeled	Main fouling equations	Parameters analyzed	Model—experiment	Remarks
McKinley [52]	Acid condensation	$\dot{m}_{cond} = \rho_g h A \frac{MW_i}{MW_g}\left(y_i - \frac{P_i(T_s)}{P_g}\right)$	• Dew point • Condensation flux	—	Prediction of condensation rate and condensate composition to minimize EGR cooler corrosion
Sharma et al. [53]	Water vapor condensation	$R_{cond} = k_{cond}\, y_{water}(1-\theta)$ $R_{evap} = k_{evap}\,\theta$	Condensation evaporation fluxes	Close agreement observed	Simulation of temperature profiles inside after-treatment devices considering water condensation and evaporation
B. Ismail [54]	• Thermophoresis • Diffusion	$G_{th} = -2C_s \frac{\left(\frac{k}{k_p}+C_t K_n\right)}{(1+3C_m K_n)} \frac{\left[1+K_n\left(1.2+0.41e^{-0.88K_n}\right)\right]}{\left(1+2\frac{k}{k_p}+2C_t K_n\right)} \frac{\nu_g}{T_g}$	• Soot layer thickness • Effectiveness degradation • Pressure drop evolution	—	Calculation of the coupling between the gas and particle phases to compute the soot deposition in diesel EGR cooling devices
Abarham et al. [55]	Thermophoresis	$V_{th} = -K_{th}\frac{\nu_g}{T_g}\vec{\nabla}T$	• Tube diameter reduction • Soot layer thickness • Deposit interface temperature • Effectiveness degradation • Pressure drop	Significant differences observed	Prediction of EGR cooler fouling amount and distribution across a concentric tube heat exchanger with a constant wall temperature
Abarham et al. [56]	• Thermophoresis • HC condensation	$V_{th} = -K_{th}\frac{\nu_g}{T_g}\vec{\nabla}T$ $j_i = K_g \rho_g \ln\left(\frac{y_{interface}}{y_o}\right)$	• Tube diameter reduction • Deposit interface temperature • Mass gain • Pressure drop • HC condensed mass	Significant differences observed	Simulation of soot and HC deposition on a concentric tube EGR cooler with a constant wall temperature

Authors	Mechanisms modeled	Main fouling equations	Parameters analyzed	Model—experiment	Remarks
Teng and Regner [57]	• Thermophoresis • Removal	$\dot{m}_{dep} = K_1 \eta_{dep} U \rho_g C$ $\dot{m}_{rem} = K_2 \rho_g U^2 \delta_d$	Cooler effectiveness degradation	Good agreement observed	Prediction of the cooler effectiveness deterioration considering the characteristics of the soot deposit
Teng and Regner [58]	• Thermophoresis • Removal	$\dot{m}_{dep} = K_1 \eta_{dep} U \rho_g C$ $\dot{m}_{rem} = K_2 \rho_g U^2 \delta_d$	Cooler effectiveness degradation	Good agreement observed	Calculation of soot particle accumulation employing heat, mass, and momentum transfer theories for the particle-gas system
Teng [59]	• Thermophoresis • Removal	$V_{th} = -K_{th} \frac{\nu_g}{T_g} \vec{\nabla} T$ $\Delta p = K_f \frac{(\rho_g U)^2}{2\rho_f}$	• Cooler effectiveness degradation • Pressure drop	Good agreement observed	Semiempirical model that predicts cooler effectiveness degradation and pressure drop over fouled EGR coolers
Mehravaran and Brereton [60]	• Thermophoresis • Diffusion • Removal	$J_r = -(D_B + D_t)\frac{\partial C}{\partial r} + V_{th} C$ $\dot{m}_{rem} = b\, m_{dep}$ $b \propto \frac{\bar{\tau}_w}{\varphi}$	Deposit thickness	Good conformity with literature results	Prediction of soot layer formation based on existing experimental and numerical observations
Reza Razmavar and Reza Malayeri [61]	• Thermophoresis • Removal • Sticking probability	$V_{th} = -K_{th} \frac{\nu_g}{T_g} \vec{\nabla} T$ $J_{rem} = K\left(\frac{U}{U_{Cr}}\right) \rho_f k_f R_f$	• Fouling thermal resistance • Deposition flux • Removal flux • Total mass deposited	Good agreement observed	Analysis of soot particle deposition and three potential removal mechanisms
Sul et al. [62]	• Thermophoresis • Removal	$V_{th} = -K_{th} \frac{\nu_g}{T_g} \vec{\nabla} T$ $\dot{m}_{rem} = \frac{1}{\Delta t\, A} f(\delta, T, \Delta P, \Delta P^2)$	• Thermal effectiveness • Trapped soot mass • Deposit thickness • Deposit surface temperature • Pressure drop	Good correspondence	Simulation of EGR cooler fouling considering thermophoretic equation and an empirically derived removal function

Authors	Mechanisms modeled	Main fouling equations	Parameters analyzed	Model—experiment	Remarks
Kuan et al. [63]	• Thermophoresis • Removal	$V_{th} = -K_{th}\frac{\nu_g}{T_g}\vec{\nabla}T$ $If: \Delta P < c_0 T_s + c_1$ $\dot{m}_{rem} = 0$ $Else:$ $\dot{m}_{rem} = e^{(c_2 + c_3 T_s + c_4\delta + c_5\Delta P)}$	• Exhaust outlet temperature • Fouling factor • Deposit thickness	Close agreement observed	Prediction of the long-term fouling behavior of EGR coolers on a medium-duty diesel engine for steady-state conditions
Warey et al. [64]	• Thermophoresis • Diffusion • Inertial impaction • Gravitational drift • Removal • HC condensation	$V_{th} = -K_{th}\frac{\nu_g}{T_g}\vec{\nabla}T$ $V_d = 0.057u^*\left(\frac{3\pi\mu_g^2 d_p}{\rho_g k_b T C_c}\right)^{-\frac{2}{3}}$ $V_i = 4.5\,10^{-4}u^*\left(\frac{\tau_p u^{*2}}{\nu_g}\right)^2$ $V_g = \left(1 - \frac{\rho_g}{\rho_p}\right)g\tau_p$ $\dot{m}_{rem} = \frac{K\tau_w m_{dep}}{\psi}$ $j_i = K_g\rho_g \ln\left(\frac{y_{interface}}{y_o}\right)$	• Deposit thickness • Condensed HC mass • Deposit surface temperature • Total soot mass • Cooler effectiveness reduction • Fouling thermal resistance	Reasonably good agreement	Calculation of soot deposition, soot removal, and condensation of several HC species in a circular tube with turbulent gas flow at constant wall temperature

Table 2.
1-D models.

hydrocarbon and water condensates. These simplified models are based on the assumption that thermophoretic effect is three to four orders of magnitude bigger than other deposition mechanisms, and during the first stages of the deposit growth, the removal of particles does not take place [65].

The investigations of B. Ismail [54] and Abarham et al. [55], which proposed 1-D models that investigate the soot deposit evolution considering only the effect of particulate matter deposition mechanisms, are included in this category.

Ismail [54] developed a simplified model, based on two-phase gas-particle conservation equations, which simulates the heat transfer, pressure drop, and soot deposition in EGR cooling devices. This model takes into consideration the particle transport due to the effect of diffusion and thermophoresis and employs a quasi-steady-state formulation that computes the incremental deposited layer thickness along the heat exchanger. It allows the prediction of the change in soot layer thickness, the evolution of the temperature at the outlet of the heat exchanger, and the increase in pressure drop across the EGR cooling device. The weak point of this simplified model is that, although it allows the prediction of the main effects of the soot deposit on the cooler performance, its results were not validated with experimental data.

In the same way, the model presented by Abarham et al. [55] permits to simulate the cooler effectiveness degradation and pressure drop along the EGR cooler, taking into account the particulate matter deposition caused by the thermophoretic effect. This numerical approach allows the calculation of the reduction of the cross sectional area of the tube and estimates the evolution of the temperature of the soot layer interface. In this case, the results of this 1-D model were verified using the experimental measurements of a controlled EGR cooler fouling test, and, although the predicted values for the EGR cooler effectiveness were in agreement with experimental data, the values expected in pressure drop differed significantly from the experimental measurements.

The analysis of the performance of the models of the second group shows that the simulation of the fouling process solely by considering the deposition mechanisms does not bring about the expected results regarding the evolution of the pressure drop along the EGR cooler. As Abarham et al. [55] detailed, although these simplified 1-D models reproduce the fouling growth yielding positive results, it should be expected that the addition of removal mechanisms may improve the predictive capabilities of these models.

In order to complete the features of the abovementioned numerical approach, Abraham et al. [56] added to their model the simulation of the HC condensation, and this new model belongs to the third group, i.e., the category of 1-D models that take into account both the prediction of the HC condensation and the deposition of soot particles. This numerical approach incorporates, coupling with the soot particle deposition equations, the calculation of the dew point and the total mass flux of HC that condenses and becomes part of the deposit. As their other model, it allows to compute the cooler efficiency degradation and the pressure drop evolution neglecting the changes in the physical structure and the chemical reactions that occur in the fouling layer due to the presence of condensate.

Despite the fact that another mechanism was added to the model, the comparison between experimental data and the results of the new model showed a certain mismatch. Although the predicted cooler effectiveness degradation was in agreement with the experimental measurements, the calculated pressure drop continued to display certain differences with the experimental data, and no improvements were seen in this field.

The fourth category comprises the higher number of 1-D numerical approaches, and it covers those models that, in addition to simulating the particulate matter deposition, also discuss the removal mechanisms. Following the assumption of Kern and Seaton [66], which determined that the net growth of the fouling layer depends on two opposing simultaneous processes of deposition and removal, the models of this category recreate the effects of the fouling deposit on the EGR cooler performance.

The models proposed by Teng and Regner [57, 58], Teng [59], Mehravaran and Brereton [60], Reza Razmavar and Reza Malayeri [61], Sul et al. [62], and Kuan et al. [63] belong to this fourth category. These models compute the deterioration of the heat exchanger effectiveness caused by the fouling layer growth and calculate the increase in pressure drop along the device.

On the one hand, with regard to the particle deposition process, thermophoresis is, in the majority of cases, the only referred deposition mechanism. Although some of these numerical approaches take into consideration the deposition of particulate matter due both to diffusion and thermophoretic effect, such as the model of Mehravaran and Brereton [60], the simulation of the deposition phenomenon of the remaining models is, on an exclusive basis, the calculation of the thermophoretic coefficient.

On the other hand, the removal of soot particles from the deposit is computed using different methodologies. One of these is based on the simulation of the different mechanisms that produce the erosion of the particles, i.e., calculating the physical phenomena that is potentially responsible for the removal of deposited particles. This physical approach, as used by Reza Razmavar and Reza Malayeri [61], simulates removal mechanisms such as the shear force, the effect of incident particle impact, or the particle rolling, allowing to estimate the gas maximum critical velocity to compute the particle removal flux. The other removal approach is quite different, and it is based on empirically derived removal functions that allow the estimation of the removal trend. In this removal approach, as the one proposed by Sul et al. [62], the equation that computes the removal rate is a function of different parameters, such as the deposit thickness, the temperature, or the pressure drop, and it was derived from the data of experimental tests that cover a wide range of fouling conditions.

All numerical models of this fourth category were validated with experimental data. The evolution of the overall parameters of the EGR cooler undergoing a fouling process was compared with the models' results, and, in general, they were in agreement. Although the lack of detailed information prevents a full appraisal of the performance of each mechanism involved in the process, it may be concluded that the combination of deposition and removal mechanisms is expected to provide accurate simulations of the fouling process caused by soot particles.

Finally, the fifth category of 1-D models covers the numerical approaches that take into consideration the deposition mechanisms, the removal mechanisms, and the condensation of hydrocarbons. In addition to the features of the models of the previous group, the approaches of this category include the simulation of the hydrocarbon condensation, implementing the three phenomena in a comprehensive model.

It is worth stressing that, following the methodology of the previous models, the numerical implementations of this category also assume that the deposit, which is formed by soot particles and condensates, has uniform properties. Although, as has been mentioned, the presence of condensate can alter the physical structure of the deposit changing its properties, the density and thermal conductivity of the modeled fouling layer do not change over time, regardless of the amount of condensate expected.

The model proposed by Warey et al. [64] belongs to this fifth category, and it is able to compute the total mass deposited and the fouling layer resistance over time.

The model predictions were validated, and they were in reasonably good agreement with experimental data.

7. Multidimensional models

According to the methodology used to study the fouling process, the multidimensional models can be categorized in five groups, as **Table 3** summarizes. The first category covers those numerical studies that analyze the exhaust gas flow and its effects on the deposit formation, neglecting the simulation of any fouling layer inside the heat exchanger. The second group is formed by those models that, using Eulerian–Lagrangian approach, determine the soot particle deposition on the walls of the EGR system. The third group contains those models that, using a species transport modeling approach, compute the condensation of different hydrocarbons. The fourth category includes those models that intend to reproduce the effects of the deposit, modifying the heat exchange properties of the EGR cooler surface. And the fifth group is composed of those investigations that recreate the real growth of the deposit on the walls of the EGR cooler.

The multidimensional models included in the first category are focused on the analysis of the exhaust gas flow to assess how changes in heat exchanger shape characteristics can reduce or minimize the fouling layer formation. Knowing that, in most cases, the removal process is caused by shear force, these numerical simulations intend on determining which EGR surface structures increase the shear stress and, thus, lead to an effective deposit suppression. Analyzing different parameters, such as the wall shear stress, the velocity field, or the temperature profile along the EGR cooler, these models intend to determine the fouling propensity of several heat exchanger configurations, as Lee and Min [31] and Mohammadi and Malayeri [67] shown.

Since, in the majority of cases, these models are single-phase numerical simulations, where only the gas flow is taken into consideration, the simplicity of these models allow a detailed examination of all the gas parameters involved in the fouling process. Therefore, they provide an exhaustive examination of the gas variables that can be induced or reduce the fouling layer growth. By contrast, these numerical approaches do not bring any information about the fouling mechanisms. They do not provide the estimation of deposited particulate matter, the number of removed particles, or the amount of condensate that will be generated. For this reason, although these models give an initial estimation of the fouling phenomenon, they have a limited scope of application.

The second category is formed by those models that reproduce the soot particle deposition using an Eulerian-Lagrangian approach. Employing the Lagrangian framework, these models track the trajectory of each soot particle in order to determine the regions where they can be deposited. Computing the particle transport equation, which takes into consideration the forces of the gas flow acting on a single particle, these numerical approaches determine the movement of the particulate matter inside the EGR cooler. Considering different soot particle diameters, these models offer an in-depth analysis of the particle deposition and allow the computing of the deposition efficiency inside different EGR cooler configurations.

Just like the models of the previous group, which only analyze the gas phase, the numerical approaches of this category do not provide any information about the growth and evolution of the fouling deposit, and, although they give relevant data about the regions where deposition will occur, they do not reproduce the interaction between the soot deposit and the exhaust gas flow.

Authors	Mechanisms modeled	Main fouling equations	Parameters analyzed	Model—experiment	Remarks
Lee and Min [31]	—	—	• Exhaust gas velocity • Exhaust gas temperature • Exhaust gas pressure	—	Analysis of the gas phase
Mohammadi and Malayeri [67]	—	—	Wall shear stress	—	Study of various tube structures that encourage the deposit suppression
Xu et al. [68]	• Thermophoresis • Diffusion • Inertial impaction	$\frac{du_p}{dt} = \frac{C_d Re_p}{24\tau_p}(u_g - u_p) + \frac{g(\rho_p - \rho_g)}{\rho_p} + F_B + F_S + F_{th}$	• Deposition efficiency • Deposition velocity • Particle deposition distribution	Good conformity with literature results	Simulation of soot particle deposition inside a plate-fin heat exchanger
Nagendra et al. [69]	• Thermophoresis • Diffusion	$\frac{du_p}{dt} = F_{drag} + F_{th} + F_{others}$	• Forces acting on particles • Deposition fraction • Exhaust gas velocity	Good conformity with literature results	Calculation of soot particle deposition on wavy-fin EGR coolers
Yang et al. [70]	• Water vapor condensation • Acid condensation	$\dot{m}_{cond}\pi d = \frac{\tau_i}{2\nu_{film}}\delta_{film}^2$	• Dew point • Condensation flux	Close agreement observed with literature results	Prediction of condensation of water vapor, sulfuric acid, and nitric acid formed in the exhaust gases of diesel engines
Gonçalves Guedes [71]	• Deposition • Removal • Condensation	$V_{th} = -K_{th}\frac{\nu_g}{T_g}\vec{\nabla}T$ $V_d = 0.057u^*\left(\frac{3\pi\mu_g{}^2 d_p}{\rho_g k_b T C_c}\right)^{-\frac{2}{3}}$	• Deposit thickness • Deposition efficiency	Differences observed with data from literature	Evaluation of temperature evolution inside a cooler, changing the dependence of the deposit thermal conductivity

Authors	Mechanisms modeled	Main fouling equations	Parameters analyzed	Model—experiment	Remarks
		$V_i = 4.5\,10^{-4}u^*\left(\frac{\tau_p u^{*2}}{\nu_g}\right)^2$ $log_{10}P_{vap} = AA - \frac{BB}{T_s+CC}$	• Outlet gas temperature • Condensation rate		
Paz et al. [72]	• Thermophoresis • Diffusion • Inertial impaction • Removal	$u_{di}^+ = 0.057\,Sc^{-\frac{2}{3}} + 4.5\,10^{-4}\tau_p^{+2}$ $u_{th}^+ = -\frac{2C_s}{1+3C_m K_n}\frac{\frac{k}{k_p}+C_t K_n}{1+2\frac{k_g}{k_p}+2C_t K_n}\frac{\nu C_c \nabla T}{u^* T}$ $u_{rem}^+ = \frac{\tau_w \delta_d}{\psi u^*}$	• Deposit thickness evolution • Deposited mass	Good agreement observed	Simulation of the real depth of the fouling layer and its effects on the hydrodynamic of the flow
Abarham et al. [73]	• Thermophoresis • Diffusion	$\frac{\partial(\rho_g Y)}{\partial t} + \nabla\left(\rho_g(\tilde{v} + V_{th})Y\right) = \nabla\left(\rho_g D_B \nabla Y\right) + \nabla\left(-\rho_g\left(v''Y'' + V_{th}''Y''\right)\right)$	• Effectiveness degradation • Deposited mass • Deposit thickness	Good agreement observed	2-D axisymmetric model that computes the growth of the deposit using dynamic grids
Paz et al. [74]	• Thermophoresis • Diffusion • Inertial impaction • Removal	$\Delta\delta_d = \left(\frac{S_d(u_{di}+u_{th})C}{\rho_f} - \frac{\tau_w \delta_d}{\psi}\right)\Delta t$	Deposit thickness	—	3-D model that computes the fouling layer evolution, considering the movement of the fouling-gas interface
Paz et al. [75]	• Thermophoresis • Diffusion • Inertial impaction • Removal	$\dot{m}_{dep} = S_d(V_{th} + V_d + V_i)C$ $\dot{m}_{rem} = K\hat{\tau}_w \delta_d$	• Thermal efficiency degradation • Pressure drop • Outlet gas temperature • Deposit thickness	Good agreement observed	Detailed experimental validation of the local fouling thickness

Authors	Mechanisms modeled	Main fouling equations	Parameters analyzed	Model—experiment	Remarks
Paz et al. [76]	• Thermophoresis • Diffusion • Inertial impaction • Removal • HC condensation	$\Delta\delta_d = \left(\frac{S_d(u_{di}+u_{th})C}{\rho_f} - \frac{\tau_w\delta_d}{\psi}\right)\Delta t$ $j_i = K_g\rho_g \ln\left(\frac{1-y_i}{1-y_o}\right)$	• Condensation flux • Condensed mass • Deposit surface temperature • Areas where condensation occurs	Good conformity with literature results	Calculation of the HC condensation process considering local scale effects

Table 3.
Multidimensional models.

The models proposed by Xu et al. [68] and Nagendra et al. [69] use this technique in order to compute the submicron particle deposition inside plate-and-fin heat exchangers. They evaluated the particle deposition under different boundary conditions and validated their results, achieving a good agreement with the experimental measurements taken from literature.

The third category includes the multidimensional models that use the species transport modeling approach to compute the condensation of different condensable species. Considering convection, diffusion, or even the chemical reactions that take place in the exhaust gas mixture, these numerical approaches compute the partial pressure of each species to determine their dew temperature. The corresponding condensation flux is calculated in the presence of non-condensable gases, and the thin liquid film of condensate that appears on the walls of the heat exchanger is simulated.

An example that uses this modeling approach is the study proposed by Yang et al. [70]. In order to estimate the corrosion inside the EGR system of heavy-duty trucks, they developed a numerical technique that determines the condensation of nitric and sulfuric acid. The model allows the carrying out of three-dimensional simulations, computes the heat and mass transfer processes, and calculates the amount of condensate formed on the heat exchanger walls. Using the Ansys Fluent CFD code, it computes the condensation flux of water vapor, sulfuric acid, and nitric acid, providing results under different operating conditions. Results of this numerical approach were validated, and they were in close agreement with the data from literature.

These kinds of models are based solely on the study of the condensation of acid and hydrocarbon species, generating detailed reports about the condensation process and neglecting the study of the particulate matter deposition and removal processes that occur along the EGR system. For this reason, they are suitable means to find the regions where acid condensation takes place and to detect the zones of the EGR system where corrosion problems may occur.

The fourth category is formed by the numerical models that reproduce the effects of the fouling layer, modifying the heat exchange properties of the wall. Computing the fouling thermal resistance that opposes the cooling of the flow, these numerical approaches allow the simulation of the evolution of the temperature of the gas flow inside the EGR cooler. After resolving the exhaust gas flow inside the EGR cooler, the model calculates the thickness of a virtual fouling layer and adjusts the thermal resistance of the heat exchanger surface, achieving a steady-state solution of the temperature field.

Changing the properties of the virtual fouling layer according to the computed deposit thickness, these models, as the evaluated in the study of Gonçalves Guedes [66], allow the simulation of the evolution of the exhaust gas temperature. However, their main disadvantage is that they provide poor results in the calculation of different parameters, such as the pressure drop along the heat exchanger, because they avoid the simulation of the real growth of the fouling layer inside the tube. That is why employing these models, the simulation of the changes in the hydrodynamics of the exhaust gas flow caused by the fouling layer and the local parameters of the deposit cannot be estimated reliably.

Finally, the models of the fifth category intend to recreate the real growth of the deposit on the walls of the EGR cooler. To that end, they simulate the movement of the fouling-gas interface, after computing the nonuniform thickness of the deposit. Thus, taking into consideration the local-scale effects involved in the fouling phenomenon, these numerical approaches reproduce the real formation of the fouling deposit on the heat exchanger walls, causing the reduction of the cross-sectional area of the tube.

According to the methodology used, the numerical models of this fifth group can be divided into two subcategories: those that convert fluid cells into solid cells and those that use the dynamic mesh methodology to recreate the growth of the fouling layer.

On the one hand, the first subcategory includes those models that, to simulate the growth of the deposit, transform the fluid cells of the domain into fouling cells, as **Figure 6a** illustrates. When the thickness of the fouling layer is larger than the height of the fluid cell, this is converted into a solid cell, and it becomes part of the fouling layer domain. These numerical approaches, as the proposed by Paz et al. [72], couple the gas flow solution and the fouling layer growth and provide a local final thickness of the deposit considering the hydrodynamics of the flow.

On the other hand, to recreate the fouling layer growth, the models of the second subcategory employ the dynamic mesh methodology, as the 2-D axisymmetric model proposed by Abarham et al. [73] or the 3-D model proposed by Paz et al. [74–76]. After the fouling thickness calculation, these numerical approaches adjust the thickness of the deposit moving the fouling-fluid interface, as **Figure 6b** shows. At every time-step of the simulation, they estimate the position of the nodes of the mesh and update the fouling layer domain, allowing the possibility to determine the deposit growth evolution.

As **Figure 7** shows, the main advantage of these numerical approaches is that they simulate the evolution of the fouling layer in a local manner. Considering the local properties of the exhaust gas flow and taking into account the mechanisms involved in the fouling process, they provide a comprehensive solution of the fouling layer and recreate its real growth inside the heat exchanger. In contrast, these kinds of models have higher computational costs than other multidimensional

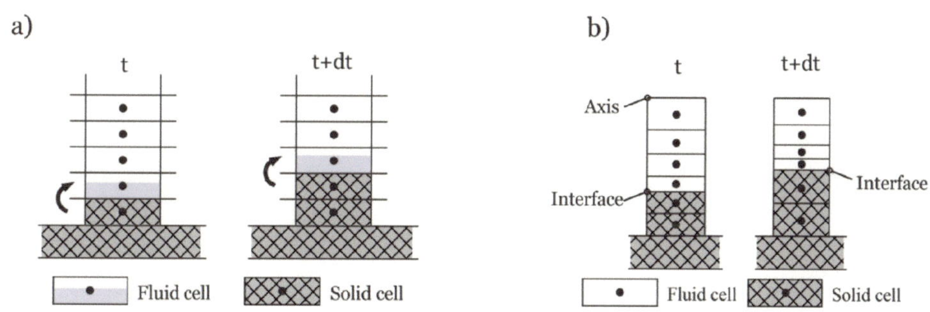

Figure 6.
Scheme of the fouling growth: (a) converting fluid cells into solid cells and (b) using the dynamic mesh methodology.

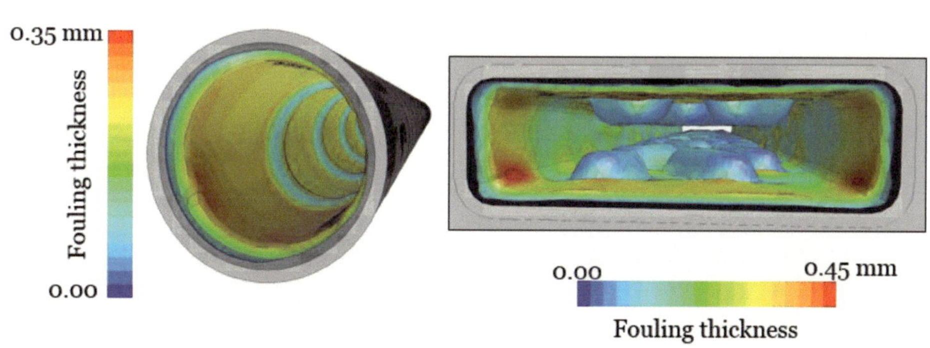

Figure 7.
Fouling thickness computed using dynamic mesh methodology.

models, and, although they provide detailed information about the fouling phenomenon, they demand more computational resources.

8. Concluding remarks

This chapter compiles and analyzes the main numerical approaches that have been proposed to predict and reproduce the fouling phenomenon that takes place inside the EGR system. Features of each option, its range of applicability, as well as their main strengths and weaknesses have been highlighted. The fouling prediction capabilities of each numerical approach have been analyzed in detail with the aim of reviewing the most relevant numerical approaches used in the study of the fouling process that occurs in the EGR system.

The stringent construction requirements of new EGR technologies and the development of new numerical techniques, and more particularly the use of computational fluid dynamics codes, have contributed to the creation of more sophisticated models that allow the simulation of the fouling phenomenon considering a large number of parameters and mechanisms. Nevertheless, the simulation of the deposit formation and evolution involves intricate matters, such as the particle-fluid interaction, agglomerate formation, or the physicochemical reactions that take place inside the deposit, which make the fouling process a complex phenomenon that needs to be addressed coherently across all its parameters.

The information and knowledge about the numerical modeling of the fouling process in the EGR system collected in this study may help EGR designers and manufactures to improve and develop new vehicle emissions control techniques, which contribute to meet the Sustainable Development Goals.

Acknowledgements

The authors are grateful for the financial support from the Spanish Ministry of Economy, Industry, and Competitiveness through the ENE2017-87855-R project.

Nomenclature

0-D	zero-dimensional
1-D	one-dimensional
2-D	two-dimensional
3-D	three-dimensional
A	surface area
AA	Antoine coefficient
BB	Antoine coefficient
CC	Antoine coefficient
C	soot concentration
c_{0-5}	constant coefficients
CFD	computational fluid dynamics
C_c	Stokes-Cunningham slip correction factor
C_D	drag coefficient
C_m	thermophoretic constant
C_s	thermophoretic constant
C_t	thermophoretic constant
D_B	molecular diffusivity

d	tube diameter
d_p	particle diameter
D_t	mean effect of velocity and concentration fluctuations
DOC	diesel oxidation catalyst
EGR	exhaust gas recirculation
F_B	Brownian force
F_{drag}	drag force
F_S	Saffman lift force
F_{th}	thermophoretic force
g	gravitational acceleration
G_{th}	dimensional thermophoretic parameter
h	mass transfer coefficient
HC	hydrocarbon
J	mass flux
j_i	mass condensation flux of the ith species
K	proportionality constant
K_1	cooler structure-related parameter
K_2	parameter characterizing the dispersion of the soot particles removed from the deposit
k_{cond}	condensation rate constant
k_{evap}	evaporation rate constant
K_f	overall pressure loss factor
k_f	fouling layer thermal conductivity
K_g	mass transfer coefficient
k_g	gas thermal conductivity
K_n	Knudsen number
k_p	particulate matter thermal conductivity
K_{th}	thermophoretic coefficient
LNT	lean NOx trap
m	mass
$\dot{m}$	mass flow
MW	molecular weight
NOx	nitrogen oxides
P_g	pressure of the gas flow
P_i	vapor pressure of the ith species
P_{sat}	saturation pressure
P_{vap}	vapor pressure
PM	particulate matter
R_{cond}	condensation rate
R_{evap}	evaporation rate
R_f	fouling resistance
Re_p	particles' Reynolds number
SCR	selective catalytic reduction
SDG	sustainable development goals
S_d	particle sticking probability
T_g	gas temperature
T_s	surface temperature
U	mean velocity
U_{C_r}	critical velocity
u^*	friction velocity
u_{di}	isothermal deposition velocity
u_{di}^+	dimensionless isothermal deposition velocity

u_{th}	thermophoretic deposition velocity
u_{th}^{+}	dimensionless thermophoretic deposition velocity
u_{rem}^{+}	dimensionless removal velocity
u_g	gas velocity
u_p	particle velocity
$\tilde{v}$	time average velocity vector
V_d	drift velocity due to diffusion
V_g	gravitational drift velocity
V_i	drift velocity due to inertial impaction
V_{th}	thermophoretic drift velocity
Y	particle mass fraction
y_i	mole fraction of the ith species
$y_{interface}$	mole fraction of vapor at interface
y_o	mole fraction of vapor in bulk mixture
w_i	mass fraction of the ith species
Greek	
δ_d	deposit thickness
δ_{film}	liquid film thickness
η_{dep}	deposition efficiency
θ	fractional surface coverage of water
μ_g	gas dynamic viscosity
ν_g	gas kinematic viscosity
ν_{film}	kinematic viscosity of the liquid film
ρ_f	fouling density
ρ_g	gas density
τ_i	liquid-gas interface shear stress
τ_p	particle relaxation time
τ_p^{+}	dimensionless particle relaxation time
τ_w	wall shear stress
$\hat{\tau}_w$	normalized wall shear stress
φ	surface bonding force
ψ	strength of deposit

Author details

Concepción Paz*, Eduardo Suárez, Jesús Vence and Adrián Cabarcos
CINTEXT, Universidade de Vigo, Vigo, España

*Address all correspondence to: cpaz@uvigo.es

IntechOpen

© 2020 The Author(s). Licensee IntechOpen. This chapter is distributed under the terms of the Creative Commons Attribution License (http://creativecommons.org/licenses/by/3.0), which permits unrestricted use, distribution, and reproduction in any medium, provided the original work is properly cited. CC BY

References

[1] G. Assembly. Resolution adopted by the General Assembly on 19 September 2016. A/RES/71/1, 3 October 2016 (The New York Declaration); 2010

[2] Anenberg SC, Miller J, Minjares R, Du L, Henze DK, Lacey F, et al. Impacts and mitigation of excess diesel-related NOx emissions in 11 major vehicle markets. Nature. 2017;**545**(7655):467–471. DOI: 10.1038/nature22086

[3] Joshi A. Review of vehicle engine efficiency and emissions. In: SAE Technical Paper Series. 2019. DOI: 10.4271/2019-01-0314

[4] Vestreng V, Ntziachristos L, Semb A, Reis S, Isaksen ISA, Tarrasón L. Evolution of NOx emissions in Europe with focus on road transport control measures. Atmospheric Chemistry and Physics. 2009;**9**(4):1503–1520. DOI: 10.5194/acp-9-1503-2009

[5] Rissler J, Swietlicki E, Bengtsson A, Boman C, Pagels J, Sandström T, et al. Experimental determination of deposition of diesel exhaust particles in the human respiratory tract. Journal of Aerosol Science. 2012;**48**:18–33. DOI: 10.1016/j.jaerosci.2012.01.005

[6] Brand C. Beyond 'Dieselgate': Implications of unaccounted and future air pollutant emissions and energy use for cars in the United Kingdom. Energy Policy. 2016;**97**:1–12. DOI: 10.1016/j.enpol.2016.06.036

[7] May J, Favre C, Bosteels D. Emissions from Euro 3 to Euro 6 light-duty vehicles equipped with a range of emissions control technologies. In: Internal Combustion Engines: Performance, Fuel Economy and Emissions. London: Elsevier; 2013. pp. 55–65. DOI: 10.1533/9781782421849.2.55

[8] Jacobs T, Assanis D, Filipi Z. The Impact of Exhaust Gas Recirculation on Performance and Emissions of a Heavy-Duty Diesel Engine. In: SAE 2003 World Congress & Exhibition. Detroit, Michigan, USA: SAE Technical Paper; 3-6 March 2003. DOI: 10.4271/2003-01-1068

[9] Deppenkemper K, Lng ME, Schoenen M, Koetter M. Super ultra-low NOX emissions under extended RDE conditions - evaluation of light-off strategies of advanced diesel exhaust aftertreatment systems. In: SAE Technical Paper Series. 2019. DOI: 10.4271/2019-01-0742

[10] Wei H, Zhu T, Shu G, Tan L, Wang Y. Gasoline engine exhaust gas recirculation – A review. Applied Energy. 2012;**99**:534–544. DOI: 10.1016/j.apenergy.2012.05.011

[11] Agarwal D, Singh SK, Agarwal AK. Effect of exhaust gas recirculation (EGR) on performance, emissions, deposits and durability of a constant speed compression ignition engine. Applied Energy. 2011;**88**(8):2900–2907. DOI: 10.1016/j.apenergy.2011.01.066

[12] Resitoglu IA. NOx pollutants from diesel vehicles and trends in the control technologies. In: Richard Viskup, editor. Diesel and Gasoline Engines. IntechOpen; 2018.

[13] Hoard J, Abarham M, Styles D, Giuliano JM, Sluder CS, Storey JME. Diesel EGR cooler fouling. SAE International Journal of Engines. 2008;**1**(1):1234–1250. DOI: 10.4271/2008-01-2475

[14] Ismail BI, Zhang R, Ewing D, Cotton JS, Chang J-S. The heat transfer characteristics of exhaust gas recirculation (EGR) cooling devices. In: Proceedings of the ASME 2002 International Mechanical Engineering Congress and Exposition. Vol. 7.

New Orleans, Louisiana, USA: ASME; 17-22 November 2002. p. 539-546. DOI: 10.1115/imece2002-39559

[15] Kim HM, Park SK, Choi K-S, Wang H-M, Lee DH, Lee DK, et al. Investigation on the flow and heat transfer characteristics of diesel engine EGR coolers. International Journal of Automotive Technology. 2008;**9**(2): 149–153. DOI: 10.1007/s12239-008-0019-4

[16] Paz C, Suárez E, Eirís A, Porteiro J. Experimental evaluation of the critical local wall shear stress around cylindrical probes fouled by diesel exhaust gases. Experimental Thermal and Fluid Science. 2012;**38**:85–93. DOI: 10.1016/j.expthermflusci.2011.11.011

[17] Abarham M, Chafekar T, Hoard JW, Salvi A, Styles DJ, Sluder CS, et al. In-situ visualization of exhaust soot particle deposition and removal in channel flows. Chemical Engineering Science. 2012;**87**:359–370. DOI: 10.1016/j.ces.2012.09.025

[18] Lance MJ, Sluder CS, Wang H, Storey JME. Direct Measurement of EGR Cooler Deposit Thermal Properties for Improved Understanding of Cooler Fouling. In: SAE 2009 World Congress & Exhibition. Detroit, Michigan, USA: SAE Technical Paper; 20-23 April 2009. DOI: 10.4271/2009-01-1461

[19] Elghobashi S. On predicting particle-laden turbulent flows. Applied Scientific Research. 1994;**52**(4):309–329. DOI: 10.1007/bf00936835

[20] Teng H, Barnard M. Physicochemical characteristics of soot deposits in EGR coolers. In: SAE Technical Papers. 2010. DOI: 10.4271/2010-01-0730

[21] Bika AS, Warey A, Long D, Balestrino S, Szymkowicz P. Characterization of soot deposition and particle nucleation in exhaust gas recirculation coolers. Aerosol Science and Technology. 2012;**46**(12):1328–1336. DOI: 10.1080/02786826.2012.712730

[22] Eastwood P. Particulate Emissions from Vehicles. Chichester: John Wiley and Sons Ltd; 2008

[23] Lapuerta M, Armas O, Gómez A. Diesel particle size distribution estimation from digital image analysis. Aerosol Science and Technology. 2003; **37**(4):369–381. DOI: 10.1080/02786820300970

[24] Raza M, Chen L, Leach F, Ding S. A review of particulate number (PN) emissions from gasoline direct injection (GDI) engines and their control techniques. Energies. 2018;**11**(6):1417. DOI: 10.3390/en11061417

[25] Fushimi A, Kondo Y, Kobayashi S, Fujitani Y, Saitoh K, Takami A, et al. Chemical composition and source of fine and nanoparticles from recent direct injection gasoline passenger cars: Effects of fuel and ambient temperature. Atmospheric Environment. 2016;**124**:77–84. DOI: 10.1016/j.atmosenv.2015.11.017

[26] Maricq MM. Chemical characterization of particulate emissions from diesel engines: A review. Journal of Aerosol Science. 2007;**38**(11):1079–1118. DOI: 10.1016/j.jaerosci.2007.08.001

[27] Myung CL, Park S. Exhaust nanoparticle emissions from internal combustion engines: A review. International Journal of Automotive Technology. 2011;**13**(1):9–22. DOI: 10.1007/s12239-012-0002-y

[28] Brasil AM, Farias TL, Koylu UO, Carvalho MG. A recipe for image characterization of fractal-like aggregates. Journal of Aerosol Science. 1998;**29**:S1275–S1276. DOI: 10.1016/s0021-8502(98)90820-5

[29] Hong K, Park J, Lee K. Experimental evaluation of SOF effects on EGR cooler

fouling under various flow conditions. International Journal of Automotive Technology. 2011;**12**(6):813–820. DOI: 10.1007/s12239-011-0093-x

[30] Lance MJ, Sluder S, Lewis S, Storey J. Characterization of field-aged EGR cooler deposits. SAE International Journal of Engines. 2010;**3**(2):126–136. DOI: 10.4271/2010-01-2091

[31] Lee J, Min K. A study of the fouling characteristics of EGR coolers in diesel engines. Journal of Mechanical Science and Technology. 2014;**28**(8):3395–3401. DOI: 10.1007/s12206-014-0752-8

[32] Lee Y, Hong KS, Song S, Chun KM, Lee KS, Min S, et al. Evaluation of SOF effects on deposit characteristics of the EGR cooler using a PM generator. In: SAE Technical Papers. 2011. DOI: 10.4271/2011-01-1156

[33] Salvi A, Hoard J, Bieniek M, Abarham M, Styles D, Assanis D. Effect of volatiles on soot based deposit layers. Journal of Engineering for Gas Turbines and Power. 2014;**136**(11):111401. DOI: 10.1115/1.4027460

[34] Young J, Leeming A. A theory of particle deposition in turbulent pipe flow. Journal of Fluid Mechanics. 1997; **340**:129–159. DOI: 10.1017/s0022112097005284

[35] Abarham M, Hoard J, Assanis D, Styles D, Curtis EW, Ramesh N. Review of soot deposition and removal mechanisms in EGR coolers. SAE International Journal of Fuels and Lubricants. 2010;**3**(1):690–704. DOI: 10.4271/2010-01-1211

[36] Chunhong He GA. Particle deposition with thermophoresis in laminar and turbulent duct flows. Aerosol Science and Technology. 1998; **29**(6):525–546. DOI: 10.1080/02786829808965588

[37] Epstein N. Elements of particle deposition onto nonporous solid surfaces parallel to suspension flows. Experimental Thermal and Fluid Science. 1997;**14**(4):323–334. DOI: 10.1016/S0894-1777(96)00135-5

[38] Talbot L, Cheng RK, Schefer RW, Willis DR. Thermophoresis of particles in a heated boundary layer. Journal of Fluid Mechanics. 1980;**101**(4):737–758. DOI: 10.1017/s0022112080001905

[39] Mulenga MC, Chang DK, Tjong JS, Styles D. Diesel EGR cooler fouling at freeway cruise. In: SAE Technical Paper Series. 2009. DOI: 10.4271/2009-01-1840

[40] Lance MJ, Storey J, Sluder CS, Meyer Iii H, Watkins B, Kaiser M, et al. Microstructural analysis of deposits on heavy-duty EGR coolers. In: SAE Technical Papers. Vol. 2. 2013. DOI: 10.4271/2013-01-1288

[41] Cleaver JW, Yates B. Mechanism of detachment of colloidal particles from a flat substrate in a turbulent flow. Journal of Colloid and Interface Science. 1973;**44**(3):464–474. DOI: 10.1016/0021-9797(73)90323-8

[42] Warey A, Bika AS, Long D, Balestrino S, Szymkowicz P. Influence of water vapor condensation on exhaust gas recirculation cooler fouling. International Journal of Heat and Mass Transfer. 2013;**65**(0):807–816. DOI: 10.1016/j.ijheatmasstransfer.2013.06.063

[43] Warey A, Bika AS, Vassallo A, Balestrino S, Szymkowicz P. Combination of pre-EGR cooler oxidation catalyst and water vapor condensation to mitigate fouling. SAE International Journal of Engines. 2014; 7(1):21–31. DOI: 10.4271/2014-01-0636

[44] Abd-Elhady MS, Malayeri MR. Asymptotic characteristics of particulate deposit formation in exhaust gas recirculation (EGR) coolers. Applied Thermal Engineering. 2013;**60**(1–2):96–104. DOI: 10.1016/j.applthermaleng.2013.06.038

[45] Epstein N. Particulate fouling of heat transfer surfaces: Mechanisms and models. In: Melo LF, Boot TR, Bernardo CA, editors. Fouling Science and Technology. Dordrecht: Springer; 1988. pp. 143-164. DOI: 10.1007/978-94-009-2813-8_10

[46] Freeman WB, Middis J, Müller-Steinhagen HM. Influence of augmented surfaces and of surface finish on particulate fouling in double pipe heat exchangers. Chemical Engineering and Processing: Process Intensification. 1990;**27**(1):1–11. DOI: 10.1016/0255-2701(90)85001-K

[47] Paz C, Suárez E, Concheiro M, Porteiro J. Experimental study of soot particle fouling on ribbed plates: Applicability of the critical local wall shear stress criterion. Experimental Thermal and Fluid Science. 2013;**44**(0): 364–373. DOI: 10.1016/j.expthermflusci.2012.07.008

[48] Tang S-Z, Wang F-L, Ren Q, He Y-L. Fouling characteristics analysis and morphology prediction of heat exchangers with a particulate fouling model considering deposition and removal mechanisms. Fuel. 2017;**203**: 725–738. DOI: 10.1016/j.fuel.2017.03.049

[49] Abarham M, Hoard J, Assanis D, Styles D, Sluder C, Storey J. An analytical study of thermophoretic particulate deposition in turbulent pipe flows. Aerosol Science and Technology. 2010;**44**(44):785–795. DOI: 10.1080/02786826.2010.491841

[50] Garrido Gonzalez N, Baar R, Drueckhammer J, Kaeppner C. The thermodynamics of exhaust gas condensation. SAE International Journal of Engines. 2017;**10**(4):1411-1421. DOI: 10.4271/2017-01-9281

[51] Harris SJ, Maricq MM. The role of fragmentation in defining the signature size distribution of diesel soot. Journal of Aerosol Science. 2002;**33**(6):935–942. DOI: 10.1016/S0021-8502(02)00045-9

[52] McKinley TL. Modeling sulfuric acid condensation in diesel engine EGR coolers. In: SAE Technical Papers. 1997. DOI: 10.4271/970636

[53] Sharma M, Laing P, Son S. Modeling water condensation in exhaust A/T devices. In: SAE Technical Paper Series. 2010. DOI: 10.4271/2010-01-0885

[54] Ismail B. The Heat Transfer and the Soot Deposition Characteristics in Diesel Engine Exhaust Gas Recirculation Cooling Devices [thesis]. Hamilton: McMaster University; 2004

[55] Abarham M, Hoard J, Assanis D, Styles D, Curtis EW, Ramesh N, et al. Numerical modeling and experimental investigations of EGR cooler fouling in a diesel engine. In: SAE 2009 World Congress & Exhibition. Detroit, Michigan, USA: SAE Technical Paper; 20-23 April 2009. DOI: 10.4271/2009-01-1506

[56] Abarham M, Hoard J, Assanis DN, Styles D, Curtis EW, Ramesh N, et al. Modeling of thermophoretic soot deposition and hydrocarbon condensation in EGR coolers. SAE International Journal of Fuels and Lubricants. 2009;**2**:921–931. DOI: 10.4271/2009-01-1939

[57] Teng H, Regner G. Characteristics of soot deposits in EGR coolers. Society of Automotive Engineers. 2009;**01–2671** (2):81–90. DOI: 10.4271/2009-01-2671

[58] Teng H, Regner G. Particulate fouling in EGR coolers. SAE International Journal of Commercial Vehicles. 2010;**2**(2):154–163. DOI: 10.4271/2009-01-2877

[59] Teng H. A semi-empirical model for predicting pressure drops of fouled EGR coolers. SAE International Journal of Commercial Vehicles. 2010;**3**(1):156–163. DOI: 10.4271/2010-01-1948

[60] Mehravaran M, Brereton G. Modeling of Thermophoretic Soot Deposition and Stabilization on Cooled Surfaces. In: Commercial Vehicle Engineering Congress. Rosemont, Chicago, Illinois, USA: SAE Technical Paper; 13-14 September 2011. DOI: 10.4271/2011-01-2183

[61] Reza Razmavar A, Reza Malayeri M. A simplified model for deposition and removal of soot particles in an exhaust gas recirculation cooler. Journal of Engineering for Gas Turbines and Power. 2016;**138**(1):011505. DOI: 10.1115/1.4031180

[62] Sul H, Han T, Bieniek M, Hoard J, Kuan C-K, Styles D. The effects of temperature, shear stress, and deposit thickness on EGR cooler fouling removal mechanism - part 2. SAE International Journal of Materials and Manufacturing. 2016;**9**(2016–01–0186): 245–253. DOI: 10.4271/2016-01-0186

[63] Kuan C-K, Styles D, Bieniek M, Hoard J. An EGR cooler fouling model: Experimental correlation and model uses. SAE International Journal of Engines. 2017;**10**(2):541–549. DOI: 10.4271/2017-01-0535

[64] Warey A, Balestrino S, Szymkowicz P, Malayeri MR. A one-dimensional model for particulate deposition and hydrocarbon condensation in exhaust gas recirculation coolers. Aerosol Science and Technology. 2012;**46**(2):198–213. DOI: 10.1080/02786826.2011.617400

[65] Housiadas C, Drossinos Y. Thermophoretic deposition in tube flow. Aerosol Science and Technology. Apr. 2005;**39**(4):304–318. DOI: 10.1080/027868290931069

[66] Kern DQ, Seaton RE. A theoretical analysis of thermal surface fouling. British Chemical Engineering. 1959; **4**(5):258–262

[67] Mohammadi K, Malayeri MR. Model-based performance of turbulence induced structures in exhaust gas recirculation (EGR) coolers. Heat Transfer Engineering. 2014;**36**(7–8): 706–714. DOI: 10.1080/01457632.2015.954949

[68] Xu Z, Sun A, Han Z, Yu X, Zhang Y. Simulation of particle deposition in a plate-fin heat exchanger using a particle deposition model with a random function method. Powder Technology; 2019;**355**:145-156. DOI: 10.1016/j.powtec.2019.07.031

[69] Nagendra K, Tafti DK, Viswanathan AK. Modeling of soot deposition in wavy-fin exhaust gas recirculator coolers. International Journal of Heat and Mass Transfer. 2011; **54**(7–8):1671–1681. DOI: 10.1016/j.ijheatmasstransfer.2010.10.033

[70] Yang B-J, Mao S, Altin O, Feng Z-G, Michaelides EE. Condensation analysis of exhaust gas recirculation system for heavy-duty trucks. Journal of Thermal Science and Engineering Applications. 2011;**3**(4):041007. DOI: 10.1115/1.4004745

[71] Golçalves Guedes de Pinho Guerra, Sara Raquel. Fouling of Exhaust Gas Recirculation Coolers [thesis]. Porto: Universidade do Porto; 2017

[72] Paz C, Suárez E, Eirís A, Porteiro J. Development of a predictive CFD fouling model for diesel engine exhaust gas systems. Heat Transfer Engineering. 2013;**34**(8–9):674–682. DOI: 10.1080/01457632.2012.738321

[73] Abarham M, Zamankhan P, Hoard JW, Styles D, Sluder CS, Storey JME, et al. CFD analysis of particle transport in axi-symmetric tube flows under the influence of thermophoretic force. International Journal of Heat and Mass Transfer. 2013;**61**(0):94–105. DOI: 10.1016/j.ijheatmasstransfer.2013.01.071

[74] Paz C, Suárez E, Conde M, Vence J. Development of a computational fluid dynamics model for predicting fouling process using dynamic mesh model. Heat Transfer Engineering. 2020;**41**(2): 199-207. DOI: 10.1080/01457632.2018.1522108

[75] Paz C, Suárez E, Vence J, Cabarcos A. Fouling evolution on ribbed surfaces under EGR dry soot conditions: Experimental measurements and 3D model validation. International Journal of Thermal Sciences. 2020;**151**:106271. DOI: 10.1016/j.ijthermalsci.2020.106271

[76] Paz C, Suárez E, Vence J, Gil C. CFD study of the fouling layer evolution due to soot deposition and hydrocarbon condensation inside an exhaust gas recirculation cooler. In: 13th International Conference on Heat Exchanger Fouling and Cleaning. 2019

Chapter 21

Fate and Occurrences of Pharmaceuticals and Their Remediation from Aquatic Environment

Ardhendu Sekhar Giri

Abstract

Pharmaceuticals have been present in our world's waters since humans began experimenting with medicines; however, product propagation and ready access to pharmaceuticals coupled with burgeoning human population have significantly increased the loading of these compounds into the environment. Pharmaceutically active compounds (PhACs) are considered to produce a biological activity on humans and animals. Drugs manufacturing processes lead to release of toxic organic compounds and their metabolites into the environment. Safety and toxicology studies have used to investigate the side effects of pharmaceuticals on human and animal health. Treatment processes can and do reduce the concentrations of pharmaceuticals in water, however, the degree of efficacy is often a function of chemical structure, cost, and energy. All treatment processes have some degree of side effects, such as generation of residuals or by-products. This paper provides a concise report on removal of PhACs by recent advances oxidation processes (AOPs) where hydroxyl radicals (HO.) acts as a common oxidant and the improvement of biodegradability to a level amicable for subsequent biological treatment.

Keywords: pharmaceuticals, metabolites, toxicity, wastewater, biological treatment

1. Introduction

Pharmaceutical compounds are released widely into the environment without proper treatment. Proper elimination of Pharmaceutically active compound (PhACs) present in aquatic system plays an important role for preventing of diseases both in humans and animals. PhACs are structurally complex in nature and these organic compounds have some intrinsic characteristics so that treatment of drug contaminated water using conventional treatment processes namely, membrane-based separations, adsorption, ion-exchange and biological treatment are not that efficient for the industrial applications [1]. Researchers have been continuously working to progress technically, environmentally and economically comprehensive treatment techniques.

To quantify the impact of PhACs on the environment several attempts have been made in the past few years. Low levels of PhACs including antibiotics, analgesics, anti-depressants, beta-blockers, and hormones & hormone mimics are detected in

 IntechOpen

Parameters	Typical values
pH	6.5–7.0
BOD, mg/L	1,200–1,700
COD, mg/L	2,000–3,000
BOD/COD	0.57–0.6
Suspended solids, mg/L	300–400
Volatile acids, mg/L	50–80
Alkalinity as $CaCO_3$, mg/L	50–100
Phenols, mg/L	65–72

Table 1.
Characteristics of pharmaceutical industry wastewater producing allopathic medicines [2].

surface, ground and drinking water resources apart from wastewater effluent Globe [2]. However, the removal efficiency is highly variable, and it can be substantially less than 100%. Carballa et al. (2005) suggested that due to their relatively long environmental half-life, many PhACs may be accumulated to the measurable levels in aquatic ecosystems. Concentrations of PhACs were found to be less than one ppb, while the combined concentrations beat ppm ranges [2]. These drugs are highly active and interactive with receptors in humans and animals and are toxic in nature towards health threatening organisms such as bacteria, fungi and parasites. Moreover, human and animal health are affected by various types of organisms and also targeted by PhACs. Therefore, PhACs may have some potential effect on the aquatic and terrestrial organisms [3]. They are usually uncovered as waste for a long time. Therefore, many scientists have started to discover the effects of organisms to various PhACs [4]. Some drugs like an analgesic and anti-inflammatory are universal for their applicability in the medical field and in effluents of WWTPs. They are discharge recipient water at concentrations range of μg/L. For an example, the concentration of diclofenac is found in WWTP as 1.4 μg/L [5].

Due to presence of carboxylic moieties (-COOH) and one or two phenolic hydroxyl groups (-OH) most of these types of drugs are acidic in nature. Antibiotics are used generally to prevent bacterial infections and they are used in veterinary applications as food additives at sub-therapeutic doses to treat food efficiency and promote growth [6]. Carballa et al. [7] reported that wide application of antibiotics may lead to bacterial resistances. The occurrence of different drugs in sewage sludge of WWTPs and surface is well reported [8, 9]. Common PhACs present in various industrial effluents is summarized in **Table 1.**

2. Sources of PhACs in water and wastewater

2.1 Agriculture and agriculture industry

Variety of PhACs made from recombinant proteins potentially has greater efficacy and fewer side effects than small organic molecules [10]. Bacteria or yeast commonly produced the recombinant proteins [11]. However, pharming does not require expensive for the production of proteins or their metabolic products. Also, the production capacity can be rapidly climbed up to meet the demand. It is projected that the expense of producing a recombinant protein via pharming will be less than 60–70% of the current cost [12]. Uses of large amount of water and causes extensive pollution are found in agricultural industry. Overflow from agricultural fields often contains fertilizers, eroded soil, pesticides and pharmaceuticals that could able to form a major source of water pollution [13].

2.2 Health care facilities

Varieties of antibiotics have been isolated from urban and hospital wastewater [14]. It has been found that they simply could pass through aquatic environment and be transferred to surface water [15]. Kim and Tanaka [16] suggested that both wastewater treatment processes and the microbial ecology in surface water were disturbed by antibiotics and disinfectants.

Chang et al. [17] found different PhACs including analgesics, beta-blockers, non-steroidal anti-inflammatories, alpha-antidepressants, anti-cancer drugs, anti-fungal agents, opiates, antibiotics, anti-coagulants, diuretics, anti-anginals, anti-diabetics and hypolipidemics are detected by in hospitals effluents. Unregulated disposal of unused and expired medicines is the primary inception of PhACs into the environment from hospitals and health care facilities [17]. Rejection of syringe into the hospital drain off after application on the patient's body also an important source of PhACs is [18].

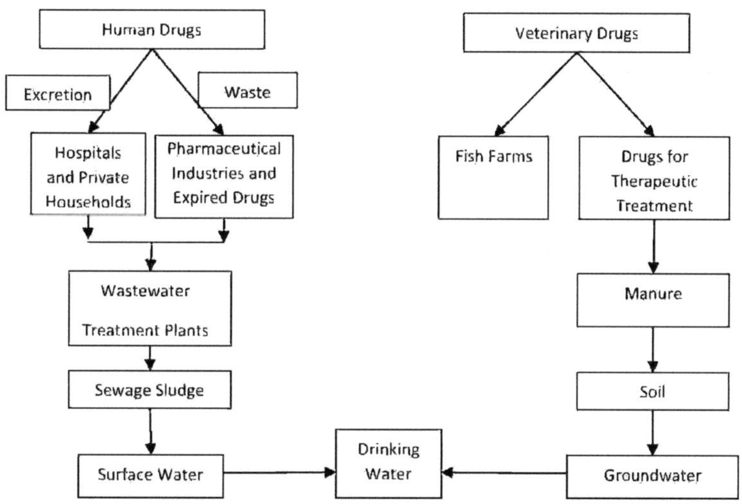

Figure 1.
Pathways for inception of pharmaceuticals and their metabolites in the environment [20].

Parameters	Typical values
Drinking water, µg/L	0.3
Surface water, µg/L	2
Ground water, µg/L	1
Municipal sewage (treated), µg/L	10
Biosolids (treated), µg/kg	10000
Agricultural soils, µg/kg	10

Table 2.
Concentrations of pharmaceuticals in water and solid wastes [2].

2.3 Surface water and ground water

Due to incomplete elimination pharmaceutical products, the residues of these products can enter the aquatic environment [19]. The typical concentration of PhACs in water and solid wastes is summarized in **Table 1**. However, the concentration in untreated industrial wastewater varies from ppb to ppm levels. Different pathways for initiation of pharmaceuticals and their metabolites in the environment are shown in **Figure 1**. The typical values of different parameters of pharmaceutical industry wastewater are shown in **Table 2**.

3. Techniques for treatment of pharmaceutical wastewater

3.1 Adsorption technique

The efficiency of adsorption process is studied by numerous workers for treatment of wastewater containing varieties of drugs. Especially the porosity and surface area of adsorbent shows the extent of adsorption [19]. Dutta et al. [21] reported that both adsorption and desorption efficiency of 6-aminopenicillanic acid (6-APA) in aqueous effluent using activated carbon as an adsorbent was found to be 93% and the process is highly reversible in nature. About greater than 90% of oestrogens is removed from both powdered activated carbon (PAC) (5 mg/L) and granular activated carbon (GAC) can remove [22]. However, dissolved organic compounds (DOC), surfactants and humic acids participate with binding sites to block the pores within activated carbon structures [22]. A filtration step is important to increase removal efficiency before treating micro pollutants using PAC [23, 24].

High molecular weight compounds reduce the blocking of micropores that leads to decrease in carbon demand. Thus, PAC will be suitable for the treatment of pretreated effluent with a low organic loading [23]. Separation of fine carbon particles is the general difficulty with PAC treatment. An additional step of separation is usually needed such as sedimentation, which necessitates the use of precipitants, or via (membrane) filtration.

3.2 Membranes processes

Membrane-based separation methods like MBR (membrane bioreactor), MBR/RO (MBR followed by reverse osmosis) and UF/RO (ultra-filtration followed by RO) are used for the removal of PhACs from wastewater [22]. Maeng et al. [25] suggested that PhACs like ibuprofen, naproxen, caffeine and acetaminophen and can be expressively removed using MBR and the degradation efficiency can be as high as 82%. However, the adaptation of microorganisms to less degradable compounds can occur due to its enhanced sludge retention time (SRT) in MBRs. MBR treatment has a better performance (removal >80%) than the conventional processes for diclofenac, ketoprofen, ranitidine, gemfibrozil, bezafibrate, pravastatin and ofloxacin. Chang et al. [17] obtained about 95% COD and 99% BOD reduction from a 10 m^3 per day capacity MBR operated at a pharmaceutical facility. Nano filtration (NF) and RO membranes are more efficient in eliminating PhACs having different physico-chemical properties. The removal using NF is mostly over 85%, except for gemfibrozil (50.2%), bezafibrate (71.8%), atenolol (66.6%), mefenamic acid (30.2%) and acetaminophen (43%) [26]. Short circuiting of membrane or failure of membrane support is responsible for the reduction of permeate quality. However, the retentate must be treated further to degrade the more concentrated form of PhACs.

3.3 Biological treatment

These processes use to remove contaminants by assimilating them and it has long been a support of wastewater treatment in chemical industries using bacteria and other microorganisms. In any biological system, the main factor is the supply of an adequate oxygen as cells need not only organic materials as food but also oxygen to breathe. A wide range of natural and xenobiotic chemicals in pharmaceutical wastewater are recalcitrant and non-biodegradable in nature. Anaerobic processes are not always effective in removing such substances [23]. Conventional activated sludge treatment (AST) with a long hydraulic retention time (HRT) generally is the choice for pharmaceutical industry wastewater [27]. It needs a lower capital cost than advanced treatment methods and a limited operational requirement. However, it suffers from the production of large amounts of sludge [22]. Removal efficiencies are decreased due to development of more resistant microorganisms towards many PhACs [28]. Ibuprofen, naproxen, bezafibrate and estrogens (estrone, estradiol and ethinylestradiol) showed a high degree of removal while sulfamethoxazole, carbamezapine and diclofenac displayed limited removal efficiency [29]. A few studies are carried out using sequence batch reactors (SBRs) and MBRs to improve the efficiency of AST [29]. Ileri et al. [30] achieved removal efficiency of 82% biochemical oxygen demand (BOD), 88% chemical oxygen demand (COD), 96% NH_3 and 98% suspended solids (SS) from domestic and pharmaceutical wastewater in a SBR operated for 4 h aeration followed by 60 min sedimentation. In another study, slightly lower COD removal efficiencies between 63 and 69% are reported [31]. MBRs are known to be effective for the removal of bulk organics and can replace traditional methods when operated in combination with a conventional AST [32]. The main advantage of MBRs over AST is that they require less space and can also treat variable wastewater compositions [17]. Biologically active filters are also used for pharmaceutical wastewater treatment and can remove PhACs [33].

3.4 Advanced oxidation processes (AOPs)

Advanced Oxidation Processes (AOPs) those are generating the very reactive radicals, such as hydroxyl radicals ($HO^•$) which are able to react with most of the organic compounds. The pollutants and by-products are degraded through a series of complex reactions. In the first step, $HO^•$ radicals react with organic compounds through electron transfer leading to formation of organic intermediates and after that species react with dissolved oxygen to form peroxyl ($ROO^•$) radicals which undergo rapid decomposition. The overall process leads to partial or total mineralization of pollutants [34].

3.4.1 Fenton processes (FP)

Fenton's reagent, a mixture of Fe^{2+} (catalyst) and hydrogen peroxide (H_2O_2) which produces $HO^•$ radical, a strong oxidizing agent (E^0 = 2.8 vs. NHS). The mechanism of FP is studied by several workers [17, 35]. The main reactions occurring in Fenton oxidation of organics are appended bellow (Eqs. 1–4):

$$Fe^{2+} + H_2O_2 \rightarrow Fe^{3+} + OH^- + HO^• \quad (1)$$

$$Fe^{2+} + HO^• \rightarrow Fe^{3+} + OH^- \quad (2)$$

$$HO^• + RH \rightarrow H_2O + R^• \quad (3)$$

$$R^{\bullet} + Fe^{3+} \rightarrow R^{+} + Fe^{2+} \quad (4)$$

where, $R^{\bullet}$ is alkyl free radical.

The major parameters like solution pH, amount of ferrous ion, concentration of H_2O_2, initial concentration of pollutants/ PhACs and presence of other background ions [36] that are affecting FP. The optimum pH for FP generally ranges from 2 to 4. At pH > 4, Fe^{2+} ions are unstable, and they are easily transformed to Fe^{3+} forming complexes with hydroxyl ion. Moreover, under alkaline conditions H_2O_2 loses its oxidative power as it breakdowns to water [17]. An effluent pH was Adjusted usually before addition of Fenton reagent. Increase of Fe^{2+} ions and H_2O_2 concentration boosts up the degradation rate [37]. The use of excess amount of H_2O_2 can deteriorate the overall degradation efficiency of FP coupled with biological treatment due to toxic nature of H_2O_2 to microorganisms [38]. Fenton oxidation of organics/ PhACs can be inhibited by PO_4^{3-}, SO_4^{2-}, F^-, Br^- and Cl^- ions. The inhibition may be due to precipitation of iron, scavenging of $HO^{\bullet}$ radicals or coordination with Fe^{3+} to form a less reactive complex [39].

3.4.2 Photo-Fenton processes (PFP)

Photo-Fenton process ($H_2O_2/Fe^{2+}/UV$) involves formation of $HO^{\bullet}$ radicals through photolysis of hydrogen peroxide (H_2O_2/UV) by UV-irradiation along with the Fenton reaction (H_2O_2/Fe^{2+}). In presence of UV irradiation, ferric ions (Fe^{3+}) are also photo-catalytically converted to ferrous ions (Fe^{2+}) with formation of additional $HO^{\bullet}$ radicals (Eq. 5) [40].

$$Fe(OH)_2^{+} + h\nu \rightarrow Fe^{2+} + HO^{\bullet} \quad (5)$$

Likewise, PFP gives faster rates and higher degree of mineralization compared to conventional FP [39]. The reaction can be driven by low energy photons and it also can be achieved using solar irradiation [39]. The employment of solar light significantly reduces the operational cost. Another important advantage of PFP is that iron-organic complexes formed during Fenton oxidation can be broken under the illumination of UV light [41].

3.4.3 UV/H_2O_2 photolysis (UVP)

UVP includes H_2O_2 injection with continuous mixing in a reactor equipped with UV irradiation system (wavelength 200 to 280 nm). UV light is used to cleave O-O bond of H_2O_2 forming $HO^{\bullet}$ radicals. The reactions describing UVP are presented below (Eqs. 6–11) [42]:

$$H_2O_2 + h\nu \rightarrow 2HO^{\bullet} \quad (6)$$

$$H_2O_2 + HO^{\bullet} \rightarrow HO_2^{\bullet} + H_2O \quad (7)$$

$$H_2O_2 + HO_2^{\bullet} \rightarrow HO^{\bullet} + H_2O + H_2 \quad (8)$$

$$2HO^{\bullet} \rightarrow H_2O_2 \quad (9)$$

$$2HO_2^{\bullet} \rightarrow H_2O_2 + O_2 \quad (10)$$

$$HO^{\bullet} + HO_2^{\bullet} \rightarrow H_2O + O_2 \quad (11)$$

Reaction 6 is the rate limiting because the rates of other reactions are much higher. In UVP, a higher initial H_2O_2 concentration produces higher $HO^{\bullet}$ radical concentration (Eq. 6), which decomposes the target compounds. However, an optimal H_2O_2 concentration exists because overdosing of H_2O_2 leads to reaction with $HO^{\bullet}$ radicals leaving off $HO_2^{\bullet}$ (Eq. 7). UVP is quite efficient in mineralizing PhACs [42]. A disadvantage of UVP is that it cannot utilize solar light as the source of UV illumination. The required UV irradiation for the photolysis of H_2O_2 is not available in the solar spectrum [43]. H_2O_2 has poor UV absorption characteristics and input irradiation to the reactor is wasted if the water matrix absorbs UV light.

3.4.4 UV/TiO$_2$ photo catalysis (UVPC)

Photocatalysis is the acceleration of a photoreaction using a catalyst in presence of light/photon. It is a well-recognized approach where light energy is employed to excite the semiconductor material producing electron (e^-_{cb})/hole (h^+_{vb}) pair (Eq. 12) which eventually involves in the detoxification of pollutants (in water or air). e^-_{cb} from the valence band (VB) is promoted to the conduction band (CB) of the semiconductor and a h^+_{vb} is created in the VB. The photo generated e^- migrates to the surface without recombination can reduce and oxidize the contaminants adsorbed on the surface of the semiconductor [44]. e^-_{cb} react with surface adsorbed molecular oxygen to yield superoxide radical anions (Eq. 13), while h^+_{vb} react with water to form $HO^{\bullet}_{ad}$ radicals on the surface of the catalyst (Eq. 14) [45].

$$TiO_2 + h\nu \rightarrow e^-_{cb} + h^+_{vb} \quad (12)$$

$$e^-_{cb} + O_2 \rightarrow O_2^{-\bullet} \quad (13)$$

$$h^+_{vb} + H_2O \rightarrow H^+ + HO^{\bullet}_{ad} \quad (14)$$

TiO_2 is widely used as a photocatalyst due to high photo-catalytic activity, low cost, low toxicity, high oxidation power, easy availability and chemical stability under UV light (λ˂380 nm) [46]. TiO_2 has two common crystal structures i.e., rutile and antase. TiO_2 Degussa 25 consisting of 20% rutile and 80% anatase is considered as a standard photocatalyst. Organic compounds can undergo oxidative degradation through reactions with h^+_{vb}, $HO^{\bullet}_{ad}$, and $O_2^{-\bullet}$ radicals as well as through reductive cleavage by e^-_{cb}. The key advantages of UVPC are treatment at ambient conditions, lower mass transfer limitations using nanoparticles and possibility of use of solar irradiation. UVPC is capable for destruction of a wide range of organic chemicals into harmless compounds such as CO_2 and H_2O [47]. The major factors affecting UVPC are initial pollutant load, amount of catalyst, reactor design, irradiation time, temperature, solution pH, light intensity and presence of ionic species. The use of excess catalyst may reduce the amount of photon transfer into the medium due to opacity offered by the catalyst particles [36]. The design of reactor should assure uniform irradiation of the catalyst [48].

3.5 Advantages and limitations of AOPs

AOPs using H_2O_2 and Fe^{2+} suffer from the requirement of acidic conditions, interference by inorganic ions, iron-organic complexation and formation of iron sludge. Some of the above limitations can be overcome when heterogeneous photocatalytic treatments like UVPC is used. However, uniform illumination of UV light and separation of catalyst particles could limit the application. Application of artificial UV light increases the cost of treatment and also poses health hazard to the working personnel.

The typical advantages of iron based AOPs are:

i. The process is capable to destroy a wide variety of organic compounds even without formation of toxic intermediates.

ii. It offers a cost-effective source of $HO^{\bullet}$ radicals using easy-to-handle reagents.

iii. In FP and PFP, both oxidation and coagulation take place simultaneously.

iv. Effective in destruction of refractory PhACs to improve biodegradability and produce an effluent that can be treated biologically as a finishing step.

4. Conclusions

AOPs undergo through different reacting systems such as homogeneous or heterogeneous phases and in light or dark. It causes consecutive unselective degradation of organic materials. Complete mineralization occurs even at very low concentration and the byproducts formed may be environmentally non-hazardous. Biological treatment is recognized as the cheapest available technology to remove and degrade organic contaminants. However, advanced separation technology gives very inefficient degradation of PhACs because they are usually resistant to biodegradation and characterized by low BOD/COD ratio. Partial Fenton oxidation yields more biodegradable products together with the destruction of inhibitory effect towards microorganisms in the downstream biological treatment. It also increases the overall treatment efficiencies compared to the efficiency of individual process. AOPs can be employed for the detoxification of PhACs until the biodegradability is improved to a level amicable for subsequent biological treatment.

Acknowledgements

We gratefully thank the Indian Institute of Guwahati (India), for providing the necessary research facilities to the Department of Chemical Engineering and Central Instruments Facility (CIF).

Author details

Ardhendu Sekhar Giri
Department of Chemical Engineering, Indian Institute of Science Education and Research Bhopal, Bhopal, India

*Address all correspondence to: agiri@iiserb.ac.in

IntechOpen

© 2020 The Author(s). Licensee IntechOpen. This chapter is distributed under the terms of the Creative Commons Attribution License (http://creativecommons.org/licenses/by/3.0), which permits unrestricted use, distribution, and reproduction in any medium, provided the original work is properly cited.

References

[1] Murphy RJ, Jones DE, Stessel RI. Relationship of microbial mass and activity in biodegradation of solid waste. Waste Manage. Res. 2005;**13**:485-497

[2] Kolpin, D. W., Furlong, E. T., Meyer, M. T., Thurman, E. M., Zaugg. and Buxton, H. T., "Pharmaceuticals, hormones and other organic wastewater contaminants in U.S. streams, 1999-2000: A national reconnaissance", Environ. Sci. Technol., **36,** 1202-1211 (2002).

[3] Adams C, Wang Y, Loftin K, Meyer M. Removal of antibiotics from surface and distilled water in conventional water treatment processes. J. Environ. Eng. 2002;**128**:253-260

[4] Ahmed A, Daschner FD, Kummerer K. Biodegradability of cefotiam, ciprofloxacin, meropenem, penicillin G, and sulfamethoxazole and inhibition of waste water bacteria. Arch. Environ. Contam. Toxicol. 1999;**37**:158-163

[5] Ternes TA, Stuber J, Herrmann N, McDowell D, Ried A, Kampmann M, et al. Ozonation: A tool for removal of pharmaceuticals, contrast media and musk fragrances from wastewater. Water Res. 2003;**37**:1976-1982

[6] Ellis J. Pharmaceutical and personal care products (PPCPs) in urban receiving waters. Environ. Pollut. 2006;**144**:184-189

[7] Carballa M, Omil F, Lema JM. Removal of cosmetic ingredients and pharmaceuticals in sewage primary treatment. Water Res. 2005;**39**:4790-4796

[8] Gulkowska, A, Leung, H. W., So, M. K., Taniyasu, S., Yamashita, N. and Yeung, L. W. Y., "Removal of antibiotics from wastewater by sewage treatment facilities in Hong Kong and Shenzhen, China", Water Res., **42,** 395-403 (2008).

[9] Li, W., Shi Y., Lihong, G., Liu, J. and Y Cai., "Occurrence, distribution and potential affecting factors of antibiotics in sewage sludge of wastewater treatment plants in China", Sci. Total Environ., **446**, 306-313 (2013).

[10] Kulakovskaya TV, Vladimir M, Kulaev S. Inorganic polyphosphate in industry, agriculture and medicine: Modern state and outlook. Process Biochem. 2012;**47**:1-10

[11] Conesa C, Calvo M, Sanchez L. Recombinant human lactoferrin: A valuable protein for pharmaceutical products and functional foods. Biol. Adv. 2010;**28**:831-838

[12] Hartmann T, Kummerer K, Hartmann A. Biological degradation of cyclophosphamide and its occurrence in sewage water. Ecotoxic. Environ. Safe. 1997;**36**:174-179

[13] Giri R, Ozaki H, Takayanagi Y, Taniguchi S, Takanami R. Efficacy of ultraviolet radiation and hydrogen peroxide oxidation to eliminate large number of pharmaceutical compounds in mixed solution. Int. J. Environ. Sci. Tech. 2011;**8(1)**:19-30

[14] Nie XP, Liu BY, Yu HJ, Liu WQ, Yang YF. Toxic effects of erythromycin, ciprofloxacin and sulfamethoxazole exposure to the antioxidant system in Pseudokirchneriella subcapitata. Environ. Pollut. 2013;**172**:23-32

[15] Filiz A, Fikret K. Advanced oxidation of amoxicillin by Fenton's reagent treatment. J. Hazard. Mater. 2010;**179**:622-627

[16] Kim I, Tanaka H. Use of ozone-based processes for the removal

of pharmaceuticals detected in a wastewater treatment plant. Water Environ. Res. 2010;**82**(**4**):294-301

[17] Chang CY, Hsieh YH, Cheng KY, Hsieh LL, Cheng TC, Yao KS. Effect of pH on Fenton process using estimation of hydroxyl radical with salicylic acid as trapping reagent. Water Sci. Technol. 2008;23:34-39

[18] Huseyin T, Okan B, Selale S, Tolga H. Use of Fenton oxidation to improve the biodegradability of a pharmaceutical wastewater. J. Hazard. Mater. 2006;**136**:258-265

[19] Gautama AK, Sabumona PC. Preliminary study of physico-chemical treatment options for hospital wastewater. J. Environ. Manage. 2007;**83**:298-306

[20] Heberer T. Occurrence, fate, and removal of pharmaceutical residues in the aquatic environment. A review of recent research data. Toxicol. Lett. 2002;**131**:5-17

[21] Dutta M, Baruah R, Dutta N. Adsorption of 6-aminopenicillanic acid on activated carbon. Sep. Purif. Tech. 1997;**12**(**2**):99-108

[22] Snyder S, Adham S, Redding A, Cannon F, Carolis J. Role of membranes and activated carbon in the removal of endocrine disruptors and pharmaceuticals. Desalination. 2007;**202**:156-181

[23] Deegan AM, Shaik B, Nolan K, Urell K, Oelgemoller M, Tobin J, et al. Treatment options for wastewater effluents from pharmaceutical companies. Int. J. Environ. Sci. Tech. 2011;**8**(**3**):649-666

[24] Hartig C, Ernst M, Jekel M. Membrane filtration of two sulphonamides in tertiary effluents and subsequent adsorption on activated carbon. Water Res. 2001;**35**(**16**):3998-4003

[25] Maeng SK, Choi BG, Lee KT, Song KG. Influences of solid retention time, nitrification and microbial activity on the attenuation of pharmaceuticals and estrogens in membrane bioreactors. Water Res. 2013;**47**:3151-3162

[26] Castiglioni S, Bagnati R, Fanelli R, Pomati F, Calamari D, Zuccato E. Removal of pharmaceuticals in sewage treatment plants in Italy. Environ. Sci. Technol. 2006;**40**:357-363

[27] Alaton I, Balcioglu IA. Biodegradability assessment of ozonated raw and biotreated pharmaceutical wastewater. Arch. Environ. Contam. Toxicol. 2002;**43**:425-431

[28] Khetan S, Collins T. Human pharmaceuticals in the aquatic environment: A challenge to green chemistry. Chem. Rev. 2007;**107**(**6**):2319-2364

[29] Radjenovic J, Petrovic M, Barcelo D. Analysis of pharmaceuticals in wastewater and removal using a membrane bioreactor. Anal. Bioanal. Chem. 2009;**387**(**4**):1365-1377

[30] Ileri R, Sengil I, Kulac S, Damar Y. Treatment of mixed pharmaceutical industry and domestic wastewater by sequencing batch reactor. J. Environ. Sci. Heal. A. 2003;**38**(**10**):2101-2111

[31] Aguado D, Montoya T, Borras L, Seco A, Ferrer J. Using SOM and PCA for analysing and interpreting data from a pharmaceutical removal from a P-removal SBR. Eng. Appl. Artif. Intel. 2008;**21**(**6**):919-930

[32] Noble J. MBR technology for pharmaceutical wastewater treatment. Membr. Technol. 2006;**9**:7-9

[33] Aziz JA, Tebbutt THY. Significance of COD, BOD and TOC correlations in kinetic models of biological oxidation. Water Res. 1980;**14**:319-322

[34] Oppenlander T. Photochemical purification of water and air. Membr. Tech. 2003;**11**:17-29

[35] Chamarro E, Marco A, Esplugas S. Use of Fenton reagent to improve organic chemical biodegradability. Water Res. 2001;**35**(**4**):1047-1051

[36] Gogate PR, Pandit AB. A review of imperative technologies for wastewater treatment I: Oxidation technologies at ambient conditions. Adv. Environ. Res. 2004a;**8**:501-551

[37] Li W, Nanaboina V, Zhou Q, Korshin GV. Effects of Fenton treatment on the properties of effluent organic matter and their relationships with the degradation of pharmaceuticals and personal care products. Water Res. 2012;**46**(**2**):403-412

[38] Gogate PR, Pandit AB. A review of imperative technologies for wastewater treatment II: Hybrid methods. Adv. Environ. Res. 2004b;**8**:553-597

[39] Pignatello JJ, Oliveros E, Mackay A. Advanced oxidation processes for organic contaminant destruction based on the Fenton reaction and related chemistry. Crit. Rev. Environ. Sci. Technol. 2006;**36**:1-84

[40] Moraes JEF, Quina FH, Nascimento CAO, Silva DN, Chiavone-Filho O. Treatment of saline wastewater contaminated with hydrocarbons by the photo-Fenton process. Environ. Sci. Technol. 2004;**38**:1183-1187

[41] Miralles-Cuevas S, Oller I, Sanchez Perez JA, Malato S. Removal of pharmaceuticals from MWTP effluent by nanofiltration and solar photo-Fenton using two different iron complexes at neutral pH. Water Res. 2014;**64**:23-31

[42] Boxall ABA.The environmental side effects of medication. EMBO reports. 2003;**5**:1110-1116

[43] Haddad T, Kummerer K. Characterization of photo-transformation products of the antibiotic drug ciprofloxacin with liquid chromatography–tandem mass spectrometry in combination with accurate mass determination using an LTQ-Orbitrap. Chemosphere. 2014 http://dx.doi.org/10.1016/j.chemosphere.2014.02.013

[44] Chen X, Mao SS. Titanium dioxide nanomaterials: Synthesis, properties, modifications, and applications. Chem. Rev. 2007;**107**:2891-2959

[45] Gurkan YY, Turkten N, Hatipoglu A, Cinar Z. Photocatalytic degradation of cefazolin over Ndoped TiO_2 under UV and sunlight irradiation: Prediction of the reaction paths via conceptual DFT. Chem. Eng. J. 2012;**184**:113-124

[46] Leonidas A, Perez-Estrada SM, Aguera A, Fernandez-Alba AR. Degradation of dipyrone and its main intermediates by solar AOPs identification of intermediate products and toxicity assessment. Catal. Today. 2007;**129**:207-214

[47] Chatterjee D, Dasgupta S. Visible light induced photocatalytic degradation of organic pollutants. J. Photochem. Photobiol. 2005;**6**:186-205

[48] Ray AK. Design, modeling and experimentation of a new large-scale photocatalytic reactor for water treatment. Chem. Eng. Sci. 1999;**54**:3113-3125

Chapter 22

Human Health Consequences of Endocrine-Disrupting Chemicals

Hassan M. Heshmati

Abstract

Daily use of chemicals is an essential part of modern life. Endocrine-disrupting chemicals (EDCs) are a heterogeneous group of exogenous chemicals or chemical mixtures that interfere with the action of hormones and consequently cause adverse effects to humans and wildlife. The number of EDCs has markedly increased over the past 60 years. Humans are constantly exposed to hundreds of EDCs mainly through air, water, and food. Exposure to EDCs (*in utero* or lifetime) may be a significant component of the environmental origin of several medical conditions. The developing fetus and neonate are more sensitive than adults to perturbation by EDCs. The prenatal damage can cause adverse consequences later in life (developmental origins of adult disease). In many cases, the damage is irreversible. There is also a possibility of transgenerational effects. By interfering with hormonal functions, EDCs can contribute to a variety of dysfunctions and diseases including obesity, diabetes, reproductive disorders, and cancers. Information on long-term effects of chronic, low-dose exposure to EDCs is relatively limited. EDCs represent a global threat for human health and cause a high cost for the society. Promoting public knowledge and initiating preventive measures will help minimizing the health and economic consequences of EDCs for future generations.

Keywords: environmental contaminants, endocrine-disrupting chemicals, human health, preventive strategies

1. Introduction

Daily use of chemicals is an essential part of modern life. EDCs are a heterogeneous group of exogenous chemicals or chemical mixtures that interfere with the action of hormones and consequently cause adverse effects to humans and wildlife. They represent an emerging research field. The number of EDCs has markedly increased over the past 60 years. Humans are constantly exposed to hundreds of EDCs mainly through air, water, and food [1–9].

Exposure to EDCs (*in utero* or lifetime) may be a significant component of the environmental origin of several medical conditions. There is also a possibility of transgenerational effects. By interfering with hormonal functions, EDCs can contribute to a variety of dysfunctions and diseases including obesity, diabetes, reproductive disorders, and cancers [1–4, 10–46].

EDCs represent a global threat for human health and cause a high cost for the society [47]. Promoting public knowledge and initiating preventive measures will help minimizing the health and economic consequences of EDCs for future generations.

2. General characteristics of EDCs

2.1 Definition and identification of EDCs

In 2002, the International Programme on Chemical Safety belonging to the World Health Organization conducted a comprehensive evaluation of EDCs and proposed the following definition: "An endocrine disruptor is an exogenous substance or mixture that alters function(s) of the endocrine system and consequently causes adverse health effects in an intact organism, or its progeny, or (sub)populations."

EDCs are chemicals, mainly man-made, but also naturally occurring substances that can be found in plants or fungi, that interfere with hormonal signaling pathways. The EDCs are active at very low doses, impact health, and can have persistent effects [1–5, 10, 11, 13, 16, 48].

The first scientific statement of the Endocrine Society in 2009 provided a wake-up call to the scientific community on the risks of EDCs for human health. The second statement of the Endocrine Society in 2015 provided a global update on EDCs based on the available data in the literature [10].

The experimental screening process of the EDCs using animal data is time-consuming and costly. Computer-based (*in silico*) methods have been developed to predict the effect of the EDCs on the endocrine receptor [5, 49]. One popular method is the molecular docking approach.

2.2 Origin of EDCs

There are over 140,000 man-made chemicals. In 2015, the total production of chemicals in the European Union (EU) was 323 million metric tons, 205 million metric tons of which were considered hazardous to health. The Endocrine Disruption Exchange lists approximately 1,000 agents that have been characterized as EDCs (**Figure 1**).

Figure 1.
EDCs are mainly man-made chemicals.

EDCs originate from several sources including phytoestrogens (e.g., genistein), industrial (e.g., dioxins and perchlorates), agricultural (e.g., organochlorines, organophosphates, and carbamates), residential (e.g., bisphenol A and phthalates), medical devices (e.g., bisphenol A and phthalates), and pharmaceutical (e.g., diethylstilbestrol and parabens) [1–8, 10, 11–13, 15–25, 31, 33, 44].

The EDCs can be found in our everyday lives in a variety of products including dust, soil, water, food, cosmetics, soaps, shampoos, toothpastes, plastic containers, toys, nicotine, and fertilizers. The United States (US) Environmental Protection Agency (EPA) estimates children ingest 60–100 mg of dust per day from indoor environment. Among multiple EDCs present in food, it is notable to mention monosodium glutamate (used as a flavor enhancer), genistein (found in soy-based foods), and high-fructose corn syrup (used as a sweetener). The use of plastic packaging is on the rise. The worldwide plastics production reached 380 million metric tons in 2015, with approximately 40% used for packaging. Around 60% of all plastic packaging is used for beverages and food.

2.3 Routes of exposure to EDCs

The exposure to EDCs is mainly unintentional. EDCs remain intact in the environment and become widely distributed geographically. They are able to travel very long distances in the air. EDCs can accumulate in the food chain and be ingested by humans. Exposure to EDCs begins before birth, and even before conception. There are several routes of exposure including air, water, food, skin, vein, breast milk, and placenta [2–8, 10–13, 15, 16, 18–21, 23, 25, 31, 39, 41]. Humans can be exposed simultaneously to several EDCs and this is a challenge for the interpretation of the epidemiological studies [14]. Professional workers (e.g., workers using pesticides) are at higher risk of exposure to EDCs.

2.4 Metabolism of EDCs

EDCs accumulate in adipose tissue or binds to proteins. Most EDCs are highly lipophilic and are stored in adipose tissue. Non-lipophilic EDCs are bound to albumin. EDCs may have long half-lives (months or years, e.g., organochlorines) or short half-lives (minutes, hours, or days, e.g., bisphenol A) [10, 12, 14, 36]. The liver is responsible for metabolizing EDCs and may also act as a storage site for lipophilic EDCs. Lipophilic EDCs are more resistant to degradation. Detectable levels of numerous EDCs exist in human body fluids (e.g., blood and urine) and tissues (e.g., adipose tissue and liver).

2.5 Mechanisms of action of EDCs

EDCs interfere with the action of hormones (**Figure 2**). They may interact with or activate hormone receptors (membrane and nuclear receptors), antagonize hormone receptors, alter hormone receptor expression, alter signal transduction in hormone-responsive cells, induce epigenetic modifications in hormone-producing or hormone-responsive cells (e.g., DNA methylation and histone modifications), alter hormone synthesis, alter hormone transport across cell membranes, alter hormone distribution or circulating hormone levels, alter hormone metabolism or clearance, and alter fate of hormone-producing or hormone-responsive cells [1, 3, 4, 9, 10, 12–21, 24, 27, 28, 33, 35].

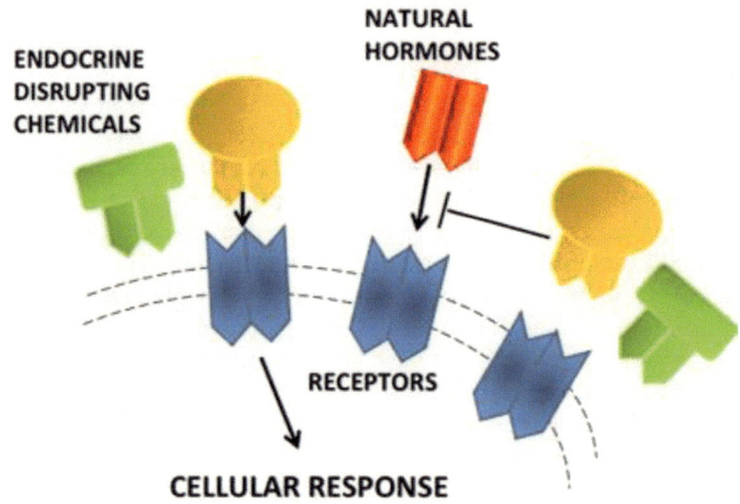

Figure 2.
EDCs interfere with the action of hormones.

3. Consequences of exposure to EDCs

The endocrine system is a complex network of glands (or tissues), hormones, and receptors controlling different functions and insuring the homeostasis of the organism.

EDCs pose a threat to humans. They alter the homeostatic systems through environmental or developmental exposures. By interfering with hormonal functions, EDCs can contribute to a variety of dysfunctions and diseases. Every endocrine axis may be the target of EDCs. Exposure to EDCs (*in utero* or lifetime) may be a significant component of the environmental origin of several medical conditions including obesity, diabetes, reproductive disorders, and cancers (**Figure 3**) [1–4, 10–46]. A specific EDC may be innocuous by itself but when associated with other EDCs may cause hazardous effects (cocktail effects). The EDC mixtures are the most complicated situations to investigate.

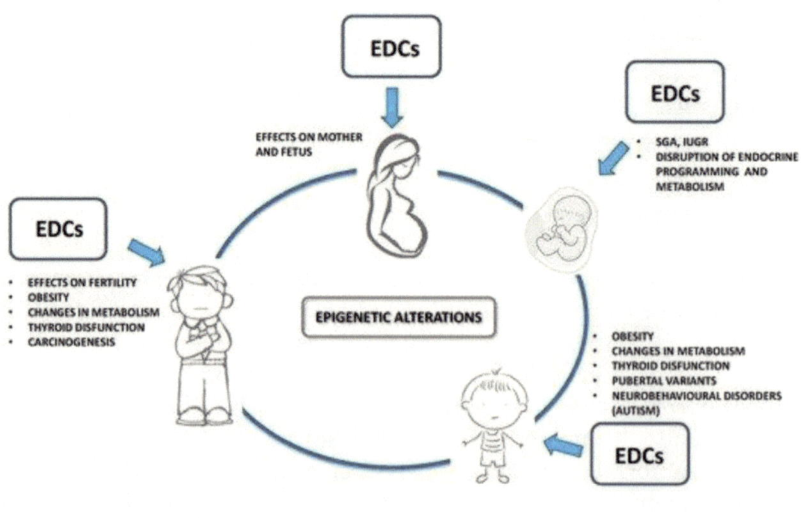

Figure 3.
EDCs can contribute to a variety of dysfunctions and diseases.

The susceptibility to EDCs and the resulting deleterious effects may be further enhanced by the current climate change.

3.1 Obesity

Obesity is a worldwide pandemic associated with increased morbidity/mortality and high cost for the society [50–52]. Although alterations in food intake and/or decrease in exercise are important contributing factors to obesity, they cannot fully explain the current obesity pandemic. Obesity pandemic coincides with the marked increase of the chemicals in the environment over the past 60 years.

Some EDCs can impair regulation of adipose tissue and food intake, reduce basal metabolic rate, and predispose to weight gain and obesity despite normal diet and exercise. They can also cause resistance to weight loss if subjects are on anti-obesity diet and/or drug. These EDCs are called obesogens (or metabolism-disrupting chemicals) [2, 4, 10, 12, 15–20, 26–33, 36]. The list of obesogens is continuously growing. Approximately 50 chemicals have been implicated. They include monosodium glutamate, nicotine, bisphenol A, phthalates, parabens, and tributyltin (non-exhaustive list).

Obesogens have several target tissues including adipose tissue, brain, liver, stomach, and pancreas. At the level of adipose tissue, obesogens promote obesity by inducing an increase in the number of adipocytes (by activating nuclear receptor signaling pathways critical for adipogenesis) and storage of fat (**Figure 4**) [17].

Perinatal exposure to obesogens is associated with overweight and obesity in children. Some obesogens (e.g., bisphenol A and tributyltin) are able to induce heritable changes that are propagated through multiple generations without any new exposure (transgenerational inheritance) [17].

White adipose tissue is an important reservoir of lipophilic obesogens (many obesogens are lipophilic chemicals). Rapid weight loss increases plasma levels of lipophilic obesogens and may contribute to weight cycling (yo-yo effect).

The dramatic increase in the prevalence of obesity, especially among children, shows that intervention actions are needed urgently. Exposure to obesogens should be reduced or avoided especially in fetus and neonate.

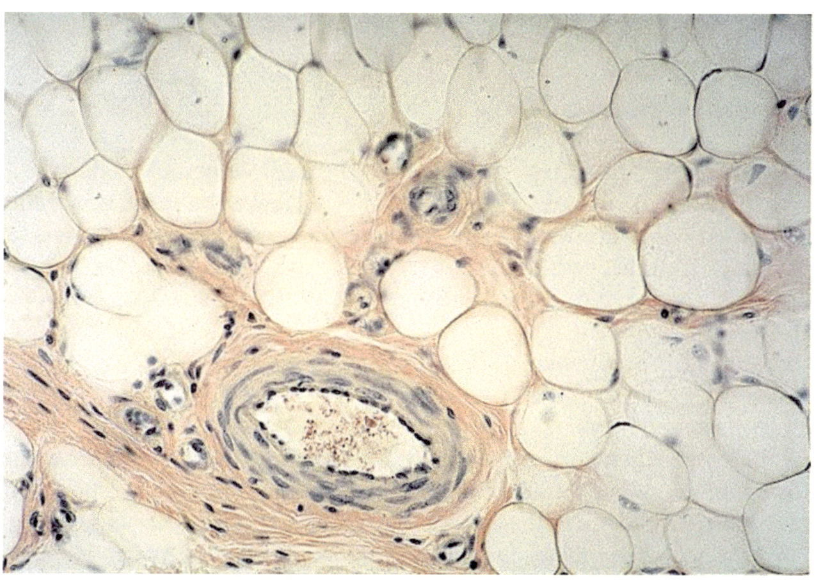

Figure 4.
Obesogens alter lipid homeostasis to promote adipogenesis and lipid accumulation.

3.2 Diabetes

Diabetes (type 1 and type 2) is a complex metabolic disease resulting from deficiency of insulin secretion and/or action [35, 53]. The incidence of diabetes has risen significantly over the last several decades [35, 54]. The role of several EDCs in the development of diabetes has been extensively investigated. However, prospective studies are still needed to support the current findings (**Figure 5**) [3, 4, 10, 15, 16, 34–37].

Prenatal and early-life exposures to EDCs can play a role in the development of type 1 diabetes by increasing the risk of autoimmunity and affecting β-cell development and function [37]. EDCs with androgenic activity (e.g., bisphenol A) may interfere with β-cell function, impair insulin secretion by accelerating insulitis, and cause type 1 diabetes [35].

Several EDCs (obesogens) may promote the development of type 2 diabetes through weight gain and the resulting insulin resistance. Exposure to bisphenol A leads to insulin resistance and type 2 diabetes [35].

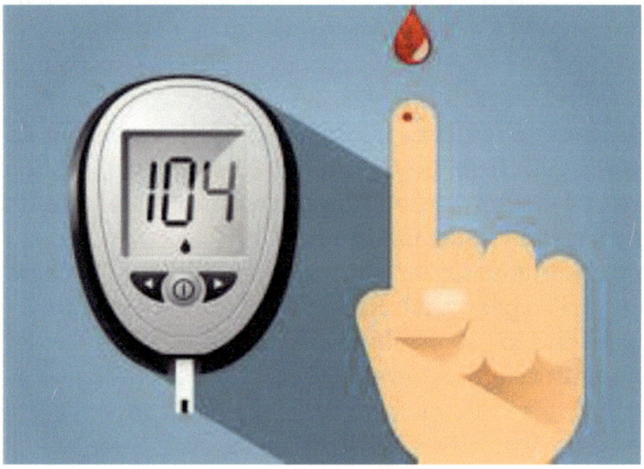

Figure 5.
Exposure to EDCs can cause diabetes through multiple mechanisms.

3.3 Reproductive disorders

The hypothalamic–pituitary-gonadal axis is the most vulnerable endocrine axis to EDCs action. Several disorders have been reported including intersex variation (ambiguous genitalia), cryptorchidism (undescended testicles), hypospadias (abnormal opening of urethra), precocious puberty, infertility, polycystic ovarian disease, endometriosis, uterine fibroids, and cancers [1–4, 10, 12, 13, 21–23, 25, 38–40].

3.3.1 Male reproductive disorders

Over the past several years, male reproductive health has been on the decline with the increase incidence of congenital malformations and poor semen quality [23, 40]. Experimental and epidemiological studies support the hypothesis that prenatal exposure to EDCs with estrogenic and/or antiandrogenic activity (e.g., diethylstilbestrol, bisphenol A, and phthalates) may disrupt the secretion and/or action of two Leydig cell hormones (testosterone and insulin-like peptide 3) regulating testicular descent, leading to cryptorchidism in newborn (**Figure 6**) [40].

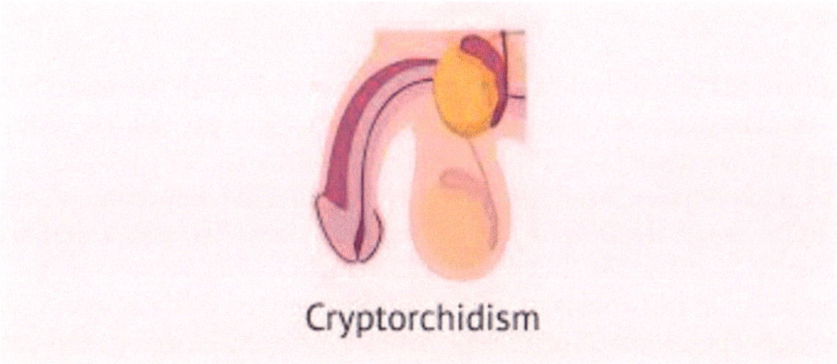

Figure 6.
Maternal exposure to EDCs may predispose to cryptorchidism in newborn.

3.3.2 Female reproductive disorders

The first clinical warning with EDCs came from diethylstilbestrol, a potent estrogen mimic, given to millions of women 50–80 years ago to prevent miscarriage. A large number of children exposed *in utero* to this chemical developed genital malformations and cancers (e.g., vaginal adenocarcinoma) while the exposed mothers had an increased risk for developing breast cancer [3, 38].

Exposure during pregnancy to several EDCs (e.g., bisphenol A and phthalates) is associated with inflammatory cytokine levels in maternal and neonatal circulation and increased risk of low birth weight [25, 41].

3.4 Cancers

Exposure to some EDCs (e.g., dioxins, organochlorines, arsenic, and cadmium) may promote the occurrence of different cancers including thyroid cancer, testicular cancer, prostate cancer, uterine cancer, breast cancer, skin cancer, and lymphoma (**Figure 7**) [2–4, 10, 12, 13, 18, 21, 22, 38, 44, 45].

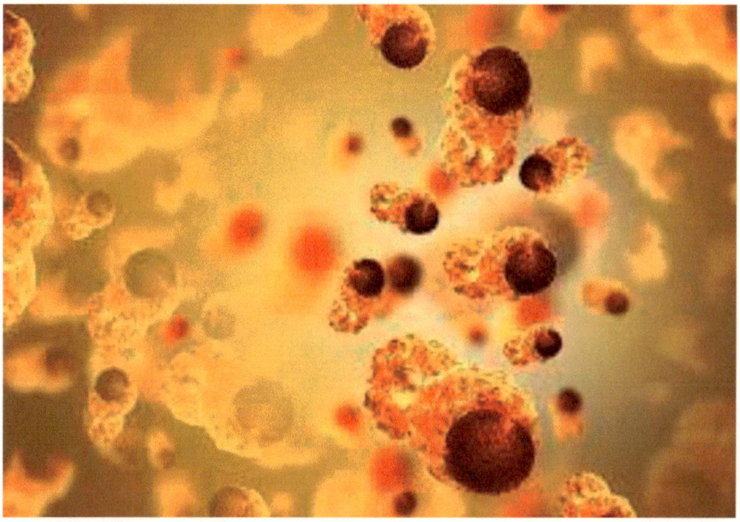

Figure 7.
EDCs can promote the occurrence of different types of cancer.

3.5 Others

Exposure to EDCs has been reported to be associated with increased incidence of cardiovascular, respiratory, liver, kidney, neurological/psychiatric, skin, and immunological disorders [2–4, 10, 13, 16, 24, 42–44].

Skin is a body barrier providing protection from environmental physical and chemical harm. Several EDCs (e.g., dioxins, phthalates, parabens, and arsenic) can act directly on different skin cells (e.g., keratinocytes, sebocytes, melanocytes, stem cells, and fibroblasts) and cause a variety of skin disorders such as chloracne, hyperpigmentation, allergic contact dermatitis, aging, and cancer (**Figure 8**) [44].

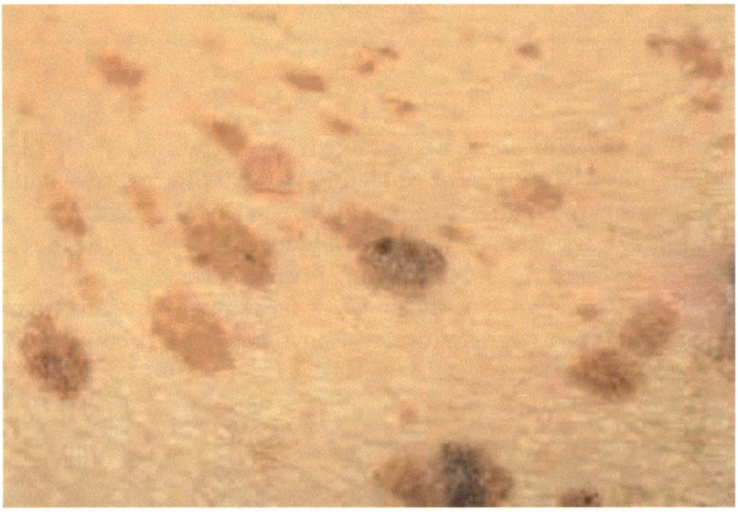

Figure 8.
EDCs can cause a variety of skin disorders.

3.6 Timing of exposure to EDCs

The timing of exposure to EDCs plays an important role for the health consequences of EDCs.

Pregnancy is a sensitive window for EDCs exposure. Pregnant women are exposed to numerous EDCs (e.g., bisphenol A, phthalates, parabens, and flame retardants) which can cross the placenta and affect the fetus. The developing fetus and neonate are more sensitive than adults to perturbation by EDCs (**Figure 9**) [3, 4, 9, 10, 14, 16, 17, 19, 25–28, 37–39, 41, 43, 46]. There is a higher sensitivity in fetus and neonate due to rapid cell division and differentiation, lack of protective mechanisms (e.g., DNA repair), competent immune system, or mature blood/brain barrier, and increased metabolic rates. During fetal development, different organ systems begin to develop at different time periods. Therefore, the susceptibility to EDC exposure and health consequences depends on the critical period for a given target organ system. The prenatal damage can cause adverse consequences later in life (developmental origins of adult disease). Effects on early development are of special concern as these effects are often irreversible. Oxidative stress caused by EDCs can be the mediator of several adverse health outcomes (e.g., obesity, diabetes, and cardiovascular disease in adulthood) [16, 19, 46]. With EDCs, there is also a possibility of damage to future generations (transgenerational inheritance) [10, 16, 17, 27, 28].

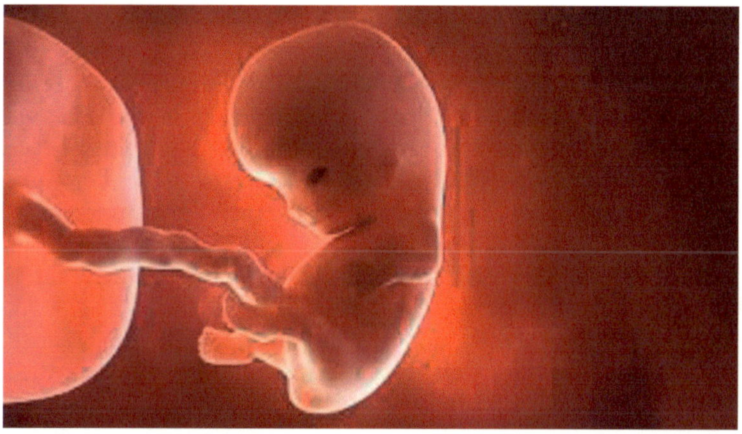

Figure 9.
EDCs can severely impact the developing fetus.

3.7 Dose and duration of exposure to EDCs

The intensity of exposure to EDCs varies between the United States of America (USA) and the EU because of differences in regulations. For example, EDC exposure is much higher for organophosphate pesticides in the EU and for polybrominated diphenyl ethers in the USA [47].

Humans are at the top of food chain. They may store large doses of multiple EDCs according to the process of bioaccumulation and bioamplification, generating effects with unknown consequences [12]. No safe dose of EDC exposure can be established. Information on chronic low-dose exposure to EDCs is relatively limited.

3.8 Gender effect of exposure to EDCs

Based on epidemiological studies, gender may play a role on the impact of EDCs (**Figure 10**) [12, 16, 42]. EDCs exert sexually dimorphic effects in metabolism regulation through interactions with sex hormone receptors. Bisphenol A appears to have specific effects on behavior of both sexes (increase in externalizing behavior in girls versus increase in internalizing behavior in boys).

Figure 10.
Gender may influence the health consequences of EDCs.

4. Preventive strategies to reduce exposure to EDCs

EDCs represent a global threat for human health and cause a high cost for the society [47]. Promoting public knowledge and initiating preventive measures will help minimizing the health and economic consequences of EDCs for future generations.

Policymakers are caught between competing interests, those of organizations acting to protect health, and companies working to increase commercial profits. EDCs challenge regulators on how to translate science into policy. It is important to establish and agree on the criteria defining and identifying the EDCs and the level of risk to human health.

Several agencies (e.g., US EPA and European Food Safety Agency) are regulating the EDCs. Legislation and regulation have been implemented over the last few years to control the exposure to EDCs. There are differences in regulations between countries, including between the USA and the EU. For example, countries with significant heavy chemicals industry are less open to changes towards greener chemicals production [3, 11, 48, 55].

Exposure to EDCs cannot be entirely avoided. However, it is possible to minimize the exposure to EDCs [3, 4]. The following recommendations should be considered (non-exhaustive list):

- Take the shoes off before walking into the house.
- Wash hands before preparing or eating food.
- Use filtered water to minimize phthalates intake (install a filter on the faucet).
- Consume low-fat low-meat fresh food (instead of processed and canned food) and organic produce to reduce the ingestion of EDCs (especially pesticides).
- Avoid beverages and foods stored in plastic containers. Replace plastics used in food preparation (for storage and heating in microwave) with glass, ceramic, stainless steel, and bisphenol A-free products to decrease the consumption of bisphenol A and phthalates. Keep water bottles cool to reduce bisphenol A leaching. Minimize the use of nonstick cookware. Throw away any scratched nonstick pans.
- Increase the recycling rates of packaging plastics.
- Use organic, natural cosmetics. Prioritize makeup and perfume products that are free of phthalates, parabens, and triclosan. For sunscreens, mineral-based products containing zinc oxide or titanium dioxide as active ingredients should be preferred.
- Minimize the use of bleached paper products containing dioxins (e.g., paper towels and disposable diapers).
- Prefer ecological household cleaning products.
- Avoid flame retardant-treated clothing and furniture.
- Use alternatives to plastic toys.

- Do not burn conventional candles. Avoid air fresheners (try a vase of dried lavender instead).

- Perform regular ventilation of the indoor environment. Open windows to allow clean air in when possible.

- Avoid touching receipts to minimize exposure to carbonless/thermal paper.

Some of the above recommendations are difficult to implement for practical and/or financial reasons.

5. Cost of EDCs

EDCs are costing society hundreds of billions of dollars each year. Due to regulatory divergence and according to a relatively recent report, the disease costs in the USA were around 2.3% of the gross domestic product, higher than in the EU (around 1.3%) [47].

Regulatory actions to limit the most prevalent and hazardous EDCs could have substantial economic benefits. The costs of regulatory actions should be compared with the costs of inaction.

6. Conclusions

EDCs are a heterogeneous group of exogenous chemicals or chemical mixtures that interfere with the action of hormones and consequently cause adverse effects to humans and wildlife. Humans are constantly exposed to hundreds of EDCs mainly through air, water, and food.

EDCs pose a threat to humans and the environment. Exposure to EDCs (*in utero* or lifetime) may be a significant component of the environmental origin of several dysfunctions and diseases including obesity, diabetes, reproductive disorders, and cancers.

Promoting public knowledge and initiating preventive measures will help minimizing the exposure to EDCs and the resulting health and economic consequences for future generations.

Conflict of interest

The author declares no conflict of interest.

Author details

Hassan M. Heshmati
Endocrinology Metabolism Consulting, LLC, Anthem, AZ, USA

*Address all correspondence to: hassanheshmati@yahoo.com

IntechOpen

© 2020 The Author(s). Licensee IntechOpen. This chapter is distributed under the terms of the Creative Commons Attribution License (http://creativecommons.org/licenses/by/3.0), which permits unrestricted use, distribution, and reproduction in any medium, provided the original work is properly cited.

References

[1] Wuttke W, Jarry H, Seidlova-Wuttke D. Definition, classification and mechanism of action of endocrine disrupting chemicals. Hormones. 2010;**9**:9-15

[2] Preda C, Ungureanu MC, Vulpoi C. Endocrine disruptors in the environment and their impact on human health. Environmental Engineering and Management Journal. 2012;**11**:1697-1706

[3] Encarnacão T, Pais AACC, Campos MG, Burrows HD. Endocrine disrupting chemicals: Impact on human health, wildlife and the environment. Science Progress. 2019;**102**:3-42. DOI: 10.1177/0036850419826802

[4] Hall JM, Greco CW. Perturbation of nuclear hormone receptors by endocrine disrupting chemicals: Mechanisms and pathological consequences of exposure. Cells. 2020;**9**:13. DOI: 10.3390/cells9010013

[5] Schneider M, Pons JL, Labesse G, Bourguet W. *In silico* predictions of endocrine disruptors properties. Endocrinology. 2019;**160**:2709-2716. DOI: 10.1210/en.2019-00382

[6] Bang DY, Kyung M, Kim MJ, et al. Human risk assessment of endocrine-disrupting chemicals derived from plastic food containers. Comprehensive Reviews in Food Science and Food Safety. 2012;**11**:453-470. DOI: 10.1111/j.1541-4337.2012.00197.x

[7] Groh KJ, Backhaus T, Carney-Almroth B, et al. Overview of known plastic packaging-associated chemicals and their hazards. Science of the Total Environment. 2019;**651**:3253-3268. DOI: 10.1016/j.scitotenv.2018.10.015

[8] Wong HL, Garthwaite DG, Ramwell CT, Brown CD. Assessment of occupational exposure to pesticide mixtures with endocrine-disrupting activity. Environmental Science and Pollution Research. 2019;**26**:1642-1653. DOI: 10.1007/s11356-018-3676-5

[9] Alavian-Ghavanini A, Rüegg J. Understanding epigenetic effects of endocrine disrupting chemicals: From mechanisms to novel test methods. Basic & Clinical Pharmacology & Toxicology. 2018;**122**:38-45. DOI: 1111/bcpt.12878

[10] Gore AC, Chappell VA, Fenton SE, et al. EDC-2: The Endocrine Society's second scientific statement on Endocrine-disrupting chemicals. Endocrine Reviews. 2015;**36**:E1-E150. DOI: 10.1210/er.2015-1010

[11] Linnecar A. Endocrine disrupting chemicals and the battle to ban them. World Nutrition. 2017;**8**:95-108

[12] Lauretta R, Sansone A, Sansone M, Romanelli F, Appetecchia M. Endocrine disrupting chemicals: Effects on endocrine glands. Frontiers in Endocrinology. 2019;**10**:178. DOI: 10.3389/fendo.2019.00178

[13] La Merrill MA, Vandenberg LN, Smith MT, et al. Consensus on the key characteristics of endocrine-disrupting chemicals as a basis for hazard identification. Nature Reviews Endocrinology. 2020;**16**:45-57. DOI: 10.1038/s41574-019-0273-8

[14] Lee DH, Jacobs Jr DR. Methodological issues in human studies of endocrine disrupting chemicals. Reviews in Endocrine and Metabolic Disorders. 2015;**16**:289-297. DOI: 10.1007/s11154-016-9340-9

[15] Le Magueresse-Battistoni B, Labaronne E, Vidal H, Naville D. Endocrine disrupting chemicals in mixture and obesity, diabetes and related metabolic disorders. World Journal of Biological Chemistry.

2017;**8**:108-119. DOI: 10.4331/wjbc.v8.i2.108

[16] Papalou O, Kandaraki EA, Papadakis G, Diamanti-Kandarakis E. Endocrine disrupting chemicals: An occult mediator of metabolic disease. Frontiers in Endocrinology. 2019;**10**:112. DOI: 10.3389/fendo.2019.00112

[17] Lee MK, Blumberg B. Transgenerational effects of obesogens. Basic & Clinical Pharmacology & Toxicology. 2019;**125**(Suppl 3):44-57. DOI: 10.1111/bcpt.13214

[18] Yang O, Kim HL, Weon JI, Seo YR. Endocrine-disrupting chemicals: Review of toxicological mechanisms using molecular pathway analysis. Journal of Cancer Prevention. 2015;**20**:12-24. DOI: 10.15430/JCP.2015.20.1.12

[19] Yang C, Lee HK, Kong APS, Lim LL, Cai Z, Chung ACK. Early-life exposure to endocrine disrupting chemicals associates with childhood obesity. Annals of Pediatric Endocrinology & Metabolism. 2018;**23**:182-195. DOI: 10.6065/apem.2018.23.4.182

[20] Kassotis CD, Stapleton HM. Endocrine-mediated mechanisms of metabolic disruption and new approaches to examine the public health threat. Frontiers in Endocrinology. 2019;**10**:39. DOI: 10.3389/fendo.2019.00039

[21] Jeng HA. Exposure to endocrine disrupting chemicals and male reproductive health. Frontiers in Public Health. 2014;**2**:55. DOI: 10.3389/fpubh.2014.00055

[22] Bonde JP, Flachs EM, Rimborg S, et al. The epidemiologic evidence linking prenatal and postnatal exposure to endocrine disrupting chemicals with male reproductive disorders: A systematic review and meta-analysis. Human Reproduction Update. 2017;**23**:104-125. DOI: 10.1093/humupd/dmw036

[23] Rehman S, Usman Z, Rehman S, et al. Endocrine disrupting chemicals and impact on male reproductive health. Translational Andrology and Urology. 2018;**7**:490-503. DOI: 10.21037/tau.2018.05.17

[24] Nowak K, Jabłońska E, Ratajczak-Wrona W. Immunomodulatory effects of synthetic endocrine disrupting chemicals on the development and functions of human immune cells. Environment International. 2019;**125**:350-364. DOI: 10.1016/j.envint.2019.01.078

[25] Birks L, Casas M, Garcia AM, et al. Occupational exposure to endocrine-disrupting chemicals and birth weight and length of gestation: A European meta-analysis. Environmental Health Perspectives. 2016;**124**:1785-1793. DOI: 10.1289/EHP208

[26] Agay-Shay K, Martinez D, Valvi D, et al. Exposure to endocrine-disrupting chemicals during pregnancy and weight at 7 years of age: A multi-pollutant approach. Environmental Health Perspectives. 2015;**123**:1030-1037. DOI: 10.1289/ehp.1409049

[27] Chamorro-Garcia R, Blumberg B. Current research approaches and challenges in the obesogen field. Frontiers in Endocrinology. 2019;**10**:167. DOI: 10.3389/fendo.2019.00167

[28] Egusquiza RJ, Blumberg B. Environmental obesogens and their impact on susceptibility to obesity: New mechanisms and chemicals. Endocrinology. 2020;**161**:1-14. DOI: 10.1210/endocr/bqaa024

[29] Marraudino M, Bonaldo B, Farinetti A, Panzica GC, Ponti G, Gotti S. Metabolism disrupting chemicals and alteration of

neuroendocrine circuits controlling food intake and energy metabolism. Frontiers in Endocrinology. 2019;**9**:766. DOI: 10.3389/fendo.2018.00766

[30] Heindel JJ. History of the obesogen field: Looking back to look forward. Frontiers in Endocrinology. 2019;**10**:14. DOI: 10.3389/fendo.2019.00014

[31] van der Meer TP, van Faassen M, van Beek AP, et al. Exposure to endocrine disrupting chemicals in the Dutch general population is associated with adiposity-related traits. Scientific Reports. 2020;**10**:9311. DOI: 10.1038/s41598-020-66284-3

[32] Ribeiro CM, Beserra BTS, Silva NG, et al. Exposure to endocrine-disrupting chemicals and anthropometric measures of obesity: A systematic review and meta-analysis. BMJ Open. 2020;**10**:e033509. DOI: 10.1136/bmjopen-2019-033509

[33] Griffin MD, Pereira SR, DeBari MK, Abbott RD. Mechanisms of action, chemical characteristics, and model systems of obesogens. BMC Biomedical Engineering. 2020;**2**:6. DOI: 10.1186/s42490-020-00040-6

[34] Mimoto MS, Nadal A, Sargis RM. Polluted pathways: Mechanisms of metabolic disruption by endocrine disrupting chemicals. Current Environmental Health Report. 2017;**4**:208-222. DOI: 10.1007/s40572-017-0137-0

[35] Sakkiah S, Wang T, Zou W, et al. Endocrine disrupting chemicals mediated through binding androgen receptor are associated with diabetes mellitus. International Journal of Environmental Research and Public Health. 2018;**15**:25. DOI: 10.3390/ijerph15010025

[36] Lind PM, Lind L. Endocrine-disrupting chemicals and risk of diabetes: An evidence-based review. Diabetologia. 2018;**61**:1495-1502. DOI: 10.1007/s00125-018-4621-3

[37] Howard SG. Developmental exposure to endocrine disrupting chemicals and type 1 diabetes mellitus. Frontiers in Endocrinology. 2018;**9**:513. DOI: 10.3389/fendo.2018.00513

[38] Reed CE, Fenton SE. Exposure to diethylstilbestrol during sensitive life stages: A legacy of heritable health effects. Birth Defects Research Part C - Embryo Today: Reviews. 2013;**99**:134-146. DOI: 10.1002/bdrc.21035

[39] Rich AL, Phipps LM, Tiwari S, Rudraraju H, Dokpesi PO. The increasing prevalence in intersex variation from toxicological dysregulation in fetal reproductive tissue differentiation and development by endocrine-disrupting chemicals. Environmental Health Insights. 2016;**10**:163-171. DOI: 10.4137/EHI.S39825

[40] Fénichel P, Chevalier N, Lahlou N, et al. Endocrine disrupting chemicals interfere with Leydig cell hormone pathways during testicular descent in idiopathic cryptorchidism. Frontiers in Endocrinology. 2019;**9**:786. DOI: 10.3389/fendo.2018.00786

[41] Kelley AS, Banker M, Goodrich JM, et al. Early pregnancy exposure to endocrine disrupting chemical mixtures are associated with inflammatory changes in maternal and neonatal circulation. Scientific Reports. 2019;**9**:5422. DOI: 10.1038/s41598-019-41134-z

[42] Deierlein AL, Rock S, Park S. Persistent endocrine-disrupting chemicals and fatty liver disease. Current Environmental Health Report. 2017;**4**:439-449. DOI: 10.1007/s40572-017-0166-8

[43] Toft G, Høyer BB. Prenatal exposure to endocrine-disrupting

chemicals and child behavior. Current Opinion in Endocrine and Metabolic Research. 2019;7:43-48. DOI: 10.1016/j.coemr.2019.06.008

[44] Ju Q, Zouboulis CC. Endocrine-disrupting chemicals and skin manifestations. Reviews in Endocrine and Metabolic Disorders. 2016;**17**:449-457. DOI: 10.1007/s11154-016-9371-2

[45] Costas L, Infante-Rivard C, Zock JP, et al. Occupational exposure to endocrine disruptors and lymphoma risk in a multi-centric European study. British Journal of Cancer. 2015;**112**:1251-1256. DOI: 10.1038/bjc.2015.83

[46] Neier K, Marchlewicz EH, Dolinoy DC, Padmanabhan V. Assessing human health risk to endocrine disrupting chemicals: A focus on prenatal exposures and oxidative stress. Endocrine Disruptors. 2015;**3**:e1069916. DOI: 10.1080/23273747.2015.1069916

[47] Attina TM, Hauser R, Sathyanarayana S, et al. Exposure to endocrine-disrupting chemicals in the USA: A population-based disease burden and cost analysis. The Lancet Diabetes & Endocrinology. 2016;**4**:996-1003. DOI: 10.1016/S2213-8587(16)30275-3

[48] Slama R, Bourguignon JP, Demeneix B, et al. Scientific issues relevant to setting regulatory criteria to identify endocrine-disrupting substances in the European Union. Environmental Health Perspectives. 2016;**124**:1497-1503. DOI: 10.1289/EHP217

[49] Satpathy R. Application of molecular docking methods on endocrine disrupting chemicals: A review. Journal of Applied Biotechnology Reports. 2020;7:74-80. DOI: 30491/JABR.2020.108287

[50] GBD 2015 Obesity Collaborators, Afshin A, Forouzanfar MH, Reitsma MB, et al. Health effects of overweight and obesity in 195 countries over 25 years. The New England Journal of Medicine. 2017;**377**:13-27. DOI: 10.1056/NEJMoa1614362

[51] Gadde KM, Martin CK, Berthoud HR, Heymsfield SB. Obesity. Pathophysiology and management. Journal of the American College of Cardiology. 2018;**71**:69-84. DOI: 10.1016/j.jacc.2017.11.011

[52] Shephard RJ. On determining how much obesity is costing society. The Health & Fitness Journal of Canada. 2019;**12**:80-116. DOI: 10.14288/hfjc.v12i1.276

[53] Punthakee Z, Goldenberg R, Katz P. Definition, classification and diagnosis of diabetes, prediabetes and metabolic syndrome. Canadian Journal of Diabetes. 2018;**42**:S10-S15. DOI: 10.1016/j.jcjd.2017.10.003

[54] NCD Risk Factor Collaboration. Worldwide trends in diabetes since 1980: A pooled analysis of 751 population-based studies with 4.4 million participants. Lancet. 2016;**387**:1513-1530. DOI: 10.1016/S0140-6736(16)00618-8

[55] Michel C. How to regulate endocrine disrupting chemicals? Feedback and future development. Current Opinion in Endocrine and Metabolic Research. 2019;7:21-25. DOI: 10.1016/j.coemr.2019.04.009